Life is a Piece of Cake

Life is a Piece of Cake

A Whisper from the Silent Generation

Captain Don Wright

WingSpan Press
Livermore, California

Published by WingSpan Press, Livermore, California

www.wingspanpress.com

Printed in the United States of America

ISBN 978-1-59594-293-7

Cover design by Michael Manoogian
Illustrations by Babe Sargent
Edited by Susan Owens

Publisher's Cataloging-in-Publication Data

Wright, Don
Life is a piece of cake : a whisper from the silent generation / Captain Don Wright.
p. cm.
Includes bibliographical references.
ISBN-13: 978-1-59594-293-7
1. Air pilots— Biography. 2. U-2 (Reconnaissance aircraft). 3. Airlines— United States—Biography.
TL540.W74 2009
629.13`092—dc22   2009922296

For Maude and Millard Hudson
the keepers of my childhood

and for my grandchildren
Austin, Holly, Jillian, Bobby, Jack, Patrick, Allison, and Teige

Previous page: Aerial view of Maude and Millard Hudson's farm, Centerline Road, Wales Hollow, New York, ca. 1950.

Table of Contents

Foreword

2008

Don Wright, one of the relatively few pilots to have flown the spectacular U-2, is a high-altitude aviation pioneer. But Don's view of life extends beyond the lofty cockpit vision of the Earth from above 70,000 feet. His experiences embody the American spirit of adventure, spun here in an entertaining tale I found hard to put down.

The U-2 was the first of America's high-altitude reconnaissance aircraft. It was conceived in secrecy during the height of the Cold War and built by a hand-picked team led by famous aircraft designer Kelly Johnson. For more than 50 years this sleek, aerodynamic marvel, often dubbed the Dragon Lady or the Deuce, has continued to play a role in our country's military preparedness, yet there have been just over 1,000 pilots who have actually flown her. Don Wright, U-2 pilot 192, is one of them.

In the years Don served as an elite member of the early U-2 pilot team, high-altitude flying was literally being invented with every takeoff. The partial-pressure suit keeping him alive was basic, uncomfortable, and archaic compared with current technology, and almost nothing was known about the short- and long-term effects of high-altitude exposure. Each mission was a test flight, and mistakes often meant accidents, loss of life, and the attention of the President of the United States.

The U-2 continues its reign in the twenty-first century as the most challenging aircraft to pilot in the U.S. inventory. It unapologetically taps into the deepest skill-reserves of any pilot daring enough to strap it on, and it is unforgiving of any shortness of skill, fortitude, or confidence. Today's U-2 is equipped with a sophisticated GPS (global positioning system), as opposed to the crude sextant/drift sight arrangement of early models, and the engine is more reliable. The plane also has been enlarged a bit, resulting in some improvement in aerodynamic stability (but not much), and the pilot now wears a full-pressure suit, the design of which has been directly influenced by those 50-plus years of lessons learned. Still, I find piloting the U-2 to be the most challenging, the most scary, and the most satisfying experience I have ever known. When talking about flying the Deuce, a common saying around the squadron bar is "You're ten seconds away from disaster at any given moment." The view alone is worth it.

Lt. Colonel Jeff Olesen, USAF

U-2 pilot Lt. Colonel Olesen is a recipient of the 2002 Kolligian Trophy for a remarkable aircraft save over Iraq in 2001. This trophy, established in 1958 and named after a young lieutenant whose aircraft disappeared off the coast of California in 1955, is awarded each year by the air force chief of staff in recognition of outstanding feats of airmanship. Lt. Colonel Olesen is only the second U-2 pilot to receive it.

Preface

2008

From the time I was a kid, one of the things I've enjoyed most has been the opportunity to experience new places and to meet and talk with people from a wide variety of backgrounds. When I retired in 1994 after 11 years in the military followed by 28 years as a pilot with American Airlines, I soon found a new spot to use my unflagging curiosity and gift of gab: Toastmasters International. Toastmasters is a nonprofit organization whose members work together to improve their communication and leadership skills, and I felt at home in my local chapter almost immediately.

In the speeches I gave at chapter meetings, I drew upon many of the stories from my early life. I was born in the middle of the Depression to a mother who was educated, charming, and attractive—a world traveler and an adventurer. She was also smart enough to leave my father two months before my birth. This was a woman who could and did have it all. Except for the difference in their financial status, she might have been the model for the flamboyant *Auntie Mame*. Best of all, I was her full partner.

I grew up during the Second World War and spent my teenage years in spots around the world with my mother and stepfather. At the age of 21 I joined the U.S. Air Force, realized my boyhood dream of becoming a pilot, and eventually flew the legendary spy plane, the U-2.

I knew that some of my life experiences were out of the ordinary, but it had never occurred to me to write a book about them. Yet as I told these stories in speeches at Toastmaster events, my new friends encouraged me to connect the dots in writing. And so I began.

Using deathbed reminiscences from my mother, coupled with my own memories and buoyed by scraps of saved documents and memorabilia, I've attempted to tell my story in a way that will help the reader understand not just my experiences but also something of the times in which they occurred. This has been an extended effort, taking more than seven years, and although I've tried to be as accurate as possible, the tales recounted here happened long ago. Some of the names have slipped from memory, and some of my recollections have needed imaginative support, but the story that unfolds here is as true a yarn as the circumstances allow.

Those who read this book today may recognize people, places, or events that have played a role in their own lives. To those who read it many years from now, specifically my great- or great-great grandchildren not yet born, I hope I've provided a way for you to know, at least a little, what life was like in the days of your Grandpa Don.

Prologue: 70,000 Feet and Descending!!!

1965

The view was magnificent—a panorama of crystal clarity and brilliant hues. I could just see the curvature of the Earth on the horizon, and the land below appeared as a single dimension, a bird's-eye view from one of the highest-flying aircraft in the world. My body was encased in a partial-pressure suit and space helmet, standard gear for a flight into the stratosphere. The plane was a single-engine, single-seat air force reconnaissance aircraft, designated the U-2. The flight was one of my last in a training program I'd begun more than two months before, a "howgozit" ride to see if I could hack the mission in this out-of-this-world environment.

Just a short hour earlier, I'd slipped above 60,000 feet, received clearance from air traffic control for VFR (visual flight rules), and clicked off the radio. As I climbed above 70,000 feet, I could almost count the revolutions of the Pratt & Whitney jet engine as it ticked over. Otherwise, the silence was absolute. I was as alone as I'd ever been, though it occurred to me that at that moment I was probably physically closer to God than any human on the planet.

Now it was time to go home.

The requirements of the mission were limited, but the most important was the descent. The long, thin wings of this aerodynamic marvel supported the machine with minimum drag, but the U-2 flew close to the coffin corner. Deviating from the proscribed speed by even a few knots could be deadly, a reality that required vigilant concentration and precision flying. To prevent a flameout in this oxygen-starved environment, I could throttle the engine back only slightly. Instead, I extended the gear and speed brakes to create an aerodynamic drag and allow the aircraft to descend.

During the ground flight briefing, my instructor had spelled out in great detail what was to happen next. "Stopcock the engine, Don. You need the real-life experience of flying in a controlled situation with your pressure suit fully inflated."[1]

---

[1] Stopcocking the engine shuts it down.

1

"You gotta be kidding," I'd exclaimed, but the instructor had just nodded and smiled.

I reestablished radio contact with air traffic control and began a wide downward spiral over Davis-Monthan Air Force Base outside Tucson, Arizona. I had plenty of time to run the required checklists and retest the suit with an override button that inflated it temporarily. Everything worked perfectly.[2]

Okay, I thought, *it's now or never.* With a slight hesitation and a quick upward thought, I stopcocked the engine. The partial-pressure suit worked as advertised. Compressed air filled the enmeshed capstans, pulling the suit tighter and tighter until my entire body was encased in a gigantic bear hug and I lost about 90 percent of my mobility. Gradually, my breathing reversed as oxygen was forced into my lungs, which had been trying to breathe out against the pressure. I'd experienced similar conditions in the practice chamber on the ground, so the feelings were not totally unfamiliar. But this time it was real, claustrophobic, and fearsome.

Surviving was only part of the equation. I also had to think and fly the aircraft, and in order to relight the engine, I had to glide to a much lower altitude, to a place where there was enough oxygen for restarting. That powerless glide took at least 15 minutes.

Adrenaline pumped through my system, clearing my brain and clarifying my thoughts. I almost reveled in the discomfort, an accomplishment of mind over matter that produced a sense of euphoria and caused me to laugh out loud. I was enjoying this strange new adventure.

At 35,000 feet, I followed the ten steps outlined in the checklist for relighting the engine. Soon the comforting growl of the Pratt & Whitney filled the cockpit, the pressure suit deflated, and I took a long, deep breath.

The ride home was a short one, but the road I'd taken to get there had been long and winding, a journey of many miles, many years, and a million lessons.

"How'd it go, Captain?" my instructor asked after I landed.

"Piece of cake, Sir. Piece of cake."

---

[2] Dedicated by Charles Lindbergh in 1927 as the then-largest municipal airport in the U.S., Davis-Monthan became a military base in 1940 and has served in that capacity ever since.

Part I: 1914–1947

Previous page: Reproduction of the cover from a scrapbook
given to me in 1947. The identity of the artist is unknown.

Chapter 1 – The Final Journey

It was a cool spring evening in 1988, a little after nine o'clock, when my wife Polly picked up the phone in our apartment in Toulouse, France. "It's for you, Don," she said, and I could tell from the look on her face that this was the call we'd been anticipating for months.

The voice on the other end was firm but solemn. "It's time to come home, Don" said my stepfather, George Kenna. "Your mother has run out of time. The doctor said this morning she has only a few days left, a week at most."

Polly and I were spending a year in Toulouse, where I was serving as the liaison between my employer, American Airlines, and Airbus Industries. As an airline captain and a check airman (a pilot who instructs and maintains airline standards), my job was to train pilots on the company's newly purchased Airbus 300/600. By this time, Polly and I had been in Toulouse for some months, and everything was going well. The job was interesting and challenging, and because Polly was fluent in French, we were able to fit into the neighborhood and enjoy some of the local spots that those who spoke only English might have missed.

After decades of travel to foreign lands during George's career as an army officer, he and my mother, Elizabeth (Betty) McNerney Wright Kenna, were retired and living in Nokomis, Florida, a small town on the west coast near Sarasota.

Betty, as I'd called my mother since childhood, suffered from a blood disease called aplastic anemia. When it was first diagnosed, she'd been given only months to live, but through a combination of modern medicine and her incredible will to survive, she'd beat the odds for more than a dozen years. Now her system could take no more. A few days before, she'd received the last of the life-sustaining blood transfusions that provided the cells her body couldn't produce on its own.

Betty was in the hospital, George said, and she was in no pain, but she was looking forward to seeing us as quickly as possible. "We'll be there," I said, "just as soon as we can." When I hung up, Polly and I held each other for a moment, gathering our strength for the days ahead. Then I made some calls to arrange for time off and book our flights, and she went into the bedroom to pack. It was going to be a long ride home.

We left early the next morning, flying first to Paris, then to Miami, and finally on to Tampa, the closest major airport to Nokomis. On the flight we reminisced about the character of this amazing woman who, despite her total enjoyment of where she was now, would soon be on her way to a better place. Nobody had taken greater advantage of what life had to offer than my mother. She was an opportunist, born into a feisty home and smart and popular in school. She married in secret when she was barely 19, incurring the wrath of her family when the marriage was revealed and separating from my father before I was born a year later. They divorced when I was about two, but adversity didn't slow her down. She continued her education, took advantage of employment opportunities during and after World War II, and traveled the world. Best of all, I'd been a full partner in her adventures. When I saw the movie *Auntie Mame* I thought, *That's my mom, not as rich but just as funny.*

Betty married George in 1948 when I was 13. A charming hostess and skilled bridge player, she became the quintessential officer's wife. The two of them complemented each other perfectly.

Our flight was uneventful. Due to the six-hour time difference, we arrived in mid-afternoon, emerging from the Jetway into a bevy of fellow travelers, mostly vacationers eager to claim their spot on the beach. George met us at the airport, a serious guy of average height dressed in freshly pressed khakis and a crisp, light blue sports shirt. He'd been retired from the army for nearly a dozen years, but he was still military in bearing, graying well, and in excellent health. It was impossible, however, not to see the worry in his eyes. On the drive to the hospital, he explained the situation. Because Betty's body could not accept more blood, when the effects of her most recent transfusion ran out, she would die. "In the meantime," he said, "she's eagerly awaiting your arrival."

When we reached the hospital, George dropped us off at the front door while he went to park the car. The day was bright and sunny, a typical Florida afternoon, and the hospital lobby was decorated in soft, inviting tones. As we walked the brightly lit corridors to her room, however, I was filled with a sense of dread. I pictured my mom the last time I'd seen her, just before we left for France. At five feet two inches tall, she'd still been trim and attractive, her rich brown hair barely touched with gray, and she'd exuded a vitality that belied her 73 years. What would she be like now?

At the door to her room, Polly knocked softly. "Come on in!" Betty's voice rang out clearly. Startled, I pushed the door open and there she was—

the same chipper, cheerful woman I'd known all my life. Dressed in light-gray slacks, a soft, coral-colored shell, and open-toed sandals, she was sitting on the edge of the tall hospital bed with her legs dangling over the edge. She immediately jumped to the floor and gave us a huge hug.

"Let's go home," she said.

"Whoa, what's going on here?" I replied. "You're supposed to be sick."

"Well, of course, I am," Betty said matter-of-factly. "I'm sure George has told you I've received my last pint of blood. But I still have about a week or so, and I want to spend it in my own home."

As it turned out she had exactly eight days, but that afternoon life was pretty much business as usual. George arrived from the parking garage, a nurse settled Betty into the requisite wheelchair, and the five of us formed a caravan through the hospital's corridors to the main lobby and then out into the Florida sunshine.

It was no more than a few miles from the hospital to Betty and George's house in a charming mobile home park in Nokomis. "It's a good thing you removed the trailer hitch," I teased them. "Otherwise, we might get hauled away tonight." This was a long-standing joke between us, and everybody laughed. In reality, their home had all the charm of a traditional dwelling. Colorful flowers grew in pots on either side of the front door, and the sweet smell of oleander wafted from a bush under their bedroom window. It was cool inside, the blinds pulled against the afternoon sun, but as soon as we came in, Betty asked George to open them.

"I love the sunshine," she said. "One of the best things about living in Florida is that for much of the year, the inside and the outside can almost blend into one."

Betty sat down in her favorite chair while George and I unloaded the car and Polly made iced tea. After a few minutes, we all settled in the living room. "You look wonderful," I said, which seemed an almost ridiculous thing to say to a dying woman, but it was the truth.

"Why, thank you, Sir," Betty replied. "I feel pretty good, too, though I tucker out easily. In fact, I think I'd probably better lie down for an hour or so before dinner. That way I can enjoy the evening with the both of you. Gosh, it's great to see you."

I reached out and squeezed her hand. "It's great to see you, too," I said, and then I had an idea. I don't know why it hadn't occurred to me before—maybe because I expected to find my mother in much worse condition than she appeared—but all of a sudden it seemed like one of the best ideas I'd ever had. "Say, Betty," I started, watching her carefully to gauge her reaction. "Since you have all this excess energy—we all laughed—how would you like to talk about some of the good old days for posterity? I could pick up a tape recorder and over the next few days, I could run it while we reminisced. What do you say?"

Betty was silent for a moment. Then she smiled. "I'd like that, I think. Yes, I would. Tell you what. I'll take a short rest, you go out and get what you need, and we'll start right after dinner."

"It's a deal," I said, and within the hour Polly and I were scouring the mall for a cassette recorder and tapes. That night, after a delicious meal of baked chicken, tossed salad, and fresh green beans, we gathered in the living room and I set up my gear. Betty watched with interest. I could almost hear the wheels turning inside her head. What would she choose to talk about?

As it turned out, she didn't need much prompting. "Where did it all begin?" I asked, and Betty took the opening and ran with it. Her voice was as strong as I'd ever heard it.

Chapter 2 – Betty Remembers

My mother, your grandmother," Betty began, "was Alice Besse. She was born in 1891 in the small town of Springville, a farming community on the railroad line south of Buffalo, New York. She grew up in the same house, graduated from the local high school, and was active in the Presbyterian Church and her community. She was a pretty girl, just a little over five feet tall, but she was somewhat headstrong.

"My father, Paul McNerney, was the 13th child in a first-generation family from Kilkee, County Claire, Ireland. At the age of 12 he started work as a butcher, and he gave every penny he earned to his family. In spite of his job, however, he also found time to go to school. He graduated from Hutchinson High School in Buffalo with a good enough academic record that he was accepted at West Point, but for reasons that were never quite clear, he didn't enroll. Perhaps his old-world upbringing and sense of family responsibility prevented him from taking that big of a step away from the familiar. Instead, he got a job with the Pennsylvania Railroad, the source of a glamorous and sought-after career in those days, and he rose steadily within the organization.

Alice Besse, ca. 1907.   Paul McNerney, 1909.

"Like most small towns of the day, Springville often held dances, and on one of those dancing nights, Alice and Paul met and hit it off: he a dapper, handsome Irishman, she a vivacious and available maiden who loved to dance the night away.

"The rest is history. Like so many couples, they married too soon, without really knowing each other, and lived in misery ever after. Their first and most important battle was over religion. Mother pledged that any children they had would be brought up as Catholics, but she never let the shadow of the Catholic Church touch her body. The marriage quickly deteriorated, no doubt aided by generous helpings of 'I told you so' from family and friends.

"I was their second child," Betty continued, "born September 22, 1914. My brother Robert was four years older and my brother Dan five years younger. My sister Carolyn was born when I was ten. My parents filled the times in between these births with anger and fighting, followed by periods of separation. Despite the upheaval, however, my childhood was fairly normal, at least until the accident when I was five.

McNerney family, ca. 1925.
L. to r.: Paul, Carolyn, Betty, Dan, Alice, and Robert.

"In those days, even fairly small kids played outdoors with little supervision, and I was crossing the street one day when a large touring car hit me. I had a fractured skull, and for days afterward I was at death's door. I can remember drifting in and out of consciousness, and each time I came to, it seemed the same priest was hovering over me, giving me the last rites. Even though I eventually recovered, remembering that scene has given me nightmares my entire life.

"Even though we moved in and around Buffalo every year or so because of my dad's job, I did well in school and was popular with the other kids. When I was in my teens, Daddy was promoted to yardmaster."

Betty paused, tucked her legs up under her in her chair, and resumed her story. "I started high school at South Park High in Buffalo. The principal was Robert Bapst, though for some reason we nicknamed him 'Unc Gates.' Unc was of the old school—tall, dignified, and strict. Under his rules, boys and girls even used different stairways and sat on opposite sides of the classroom. New York schools were leading the country in those days, and at South Park they stressed academics above everything. Each quarter the names of the students and their academic standings were read aloud in assembly. Those with highest distinction earned between 95 and 100, with distinction between 85 and 95. I usually got between 85 and 87. I was very competitive, but my social life did take its toll.

"When we weren't mastering the three Rs, we had other diversions, such as learning Italian operas that we performed at assemblies. I can still remember some of that music today." With that, my mother broke into an aria, filling the room with a voice as clear as the teenager who'd sung the same music so many years before. After it was over, she sat back and giggled like a schoolgirl.

"I was feeling my independence in a lot of areas back then," she went on, "and one of them was religion. I just wasn't happy with Catholicism, and for some time I'd been secretly attending the South Buffalo Presbyterian Church, which was across the street from the church where we belonged. Eventually, I joined South Buffalo Presbyterian with a friend, and this caused a ruckus in the family. When my mother and siblings decided to join, too, it was the rest of the family against my dad, and the ruckus became a rift that never healed."

Betty was silent for a moment, and we could almost see her mentally turning back the clock to her girlhood. "I had two especially good friends growing up," she said, "Doris Robertson and Jean McIntyre. Jean came from a family of eight kids. Her Scottish father had a store at the end of the trolley line that also included a branch of the post office and a luncheonette. We could buy penny candy there, and sometimes Jean and I bought an ice cream soda for five cents and split it.

"Then in 1929, just as I was starting my junior year of high school, Daddy was promoted to assistant trainmaster in Mingo Junction, Ohio. For the first semester I stayed in Buffalo and boarded with Doris' family, but at the beginning of the second semester I moved to Ohio and started at Mingo High. Boy, was that a different way of life. Mingo Junction was a tiny mill town. The people talked differently, and in school, the boys and girls mingled freely. They even passed each other love notes on yellow paper. I had a wonderful time at that school. I was on the student council, and being the new girl, I got my share of those love notes.[3]

"One of the things I remember most about Mingo Junction is my mother learning to drive. Back then you didn't need a license to drive in Ohio; you just had to get someone to show you what to do. Well, Mother bought an old Model T Ford and somebody showed her how to drive it, but at the beginning she was horrible. On one occasion I was in the car with her when she went up a hill, forgot to shift or put on the brake, and went right back down again. People had been killed in that spot, but when I complained she said, 'If you don't like it, get out.' I got out. She eventually became a good driver, though she never stopped believing she was always right.

Betty McNerney, 1931.

"In 1931," Betty continued, "I graduated from high school and Daddy was promoted to trainmaster in Wheeling, West Virginia. We moved into a company house in a part of the city called Elm Grove. It was a big house, with an attic and a nice lot next to a park with a playground. Daddy was making good money, and although the Depression was taking its toll in this coal and steel town, I can honestly say we didn't feel it. Mother bought us nice clothes in Pittsburgh, and one year I remember having two or three spring coats, including one of black silk.

"Jobs, however, were not plentiful, especially for young people, so my older brother Robert and I enrolled at Triadelphia High School for postgraduate courses. I also took tap dancing lessons. The teacher charged 50 cents a lesson, and once I won a dance contest. My partner and I performed to the tune of *Wedding of the Painted Doll*. I was the painted doll.

"I made a lot of friends in Wheeling and we were always doing something—dancing, climbing mountains, or hiking. Sometimes we went on

---

[3] Mingo High closed in 1993 after 100 years in operation. Students in Mingo Junction now attend Indian Creek High School in Wintersville, OH.

day trips to a little shack in the mountains where we'd cook food over an open fire. The quickest way to get there was to swing out over a ravine on 'monkey ropes' made of weeds. After we'd eaten and sung songs around the campfire, it was too dark to return via the ropes, so we walked down the mountain and through a couple of cemeteries. I don't know that any of us would have taken this route alone, but faced with a bunch of laughing, singing teenagers, any ghosts lurking about would have probably headed the other way.

"One of the fellows I dated in Wheeling was Howard, the student major at Linsly. We went dancing and to the movies, and we sang. Howard was a good-looking guy, with light-blond hair and a charming smile, but he was very egotistical. I don't think he ever even kissed me, but I do remember the feel of his arms as we danced to "Stardust" by Hoagy Carmichael. It was my favorite tune.[4]

"As the Depression grew deeper, the railroads were affected more and more, and after a while Daddy was bumped from trainmaster to yardmaster and transferred back to Buffalo. I missed my friends in Mingo Junction and Wheeling, but we were happy that Daddy was still employed, since so many were not. Once we got settled, I got a job as a secretary and started taking courses at Buffalo State Teachers' College, just across the street from Albright Art Gallery near Delaware Park. I hated that school." Betty paused, her expression a grimace. "All they taught was how to be a teacher, and I didn't want to be a teacher. What I really wanted was to study drama at Carnegie Tech, now Carnegie Mellon, in Pittsburgh, but there was no money. The state teachers' college was my only option.

"To make some extra money, I babysat for a woman named Helen who had two little girls. I'd worked for her before we moved to Mingo Junction and she was glad to have me back. Helen was both rich and unconventional. The rich part was due to a thriving business she'd inherited from her father. The unconventional part came from the fact that she didn't live with her husband and she had a string of steady boyfriends. Although Helen was some years older than I, she was a fascinating person and we got to be good friends.

"One Saturday in the summer of 1932, just a couple of months before I turned 18, Helen and her current boyfriend asked me to join them for a picnic on a double date with a fellow named Ken Wright. Helen's boyfriend was an undertaker, and he was pretty dull company, but Ken and I hit it off right away. He was good looking, about six feet two, and had curly blond hair and spectacular blue eyes. He also had a fancy Packard car.

"Not long after that picnic," Betty continued, "I learned that Ken had been in trouble with the law and had a generally bad reputation, but somehow

---

[4] Linsly Military Institute was a well-known private school in the area.

13

none of that mattered when I thought about those gorgeous blue eyes. Of course, once my mother and father heard the details, they were appalled. They ordered me not to date him, which was exactly the wrong challenge to offer my almost-18, headstrong self. We dated anyway, and after chafing for more than a year at the restrictions placed upon us, we decided to marry in secret in the fall of 1933. I had just turned 19, but in order to get a license I had to say I was 21. Of course we didn't want an announcement in the Buffalo papers, so we drove into the country with a couple of good friends in search of someone to marry us. We found a little white church in West Falls, where the minister lived across the street. That day the organist just happened to be at the church practicing, so we had a cute little wedding. Then we went home and pretended nothing had happened.

"About this time, my mother, not knowing what to do with her obstinate daughter, went to see Unc Gates at South High for advice. His recommendation: 'Let her go out with Ken now and then, but set the hours.' And so we struck a deal. I was allowed to go out with Ken as long as I had a date with Richard for every date I had with him."

"Wait a minute," I said. "Who was Richard?"

Betty laughed. "Richard was an old boyfriend I'd had since about the age of 14, and I considered him just a friend, but he was someone my parents approved of. Richard knew that Ken and I were also dating, though not, of course, that we were married, but I don't think he thought much of Ken, since he referred to him as the 'pickle and potato man.' Ken loved farming, and one year he'd planted cucumbers and potatoes in great quantity. Unfortunately, that summer it rained and rained, and there was no harvest.

"After about three months, we finally told our parents the truth. Afterward, we moved in with Ken's family, who lived on a small hobby farm on Quaker Road in East Aurora. His folks were older than mine, in their 50s when we married. His father, Tom, was a successful carpenter and a good guy. His mother, Lorinda, was originally from England, and I guess we were just two different people. I thought of her as a fussy little old lady, and the chemistry between us just didn't work. To complicate matters, by this time I was pregnant. When the tension became too much, Ken sold his Packard and used the money to rent a small apartment for us, but the only work he had was a series of odd jobs, and we were always on the edge of poverty. Since there was a lot of resentment and anger over our marriage, neither set of parents did much to help.

"My father did come over at one point to offer Ken a job with the railroad. Instead of being grateful, his response was, 'I'm not going to work in any goddamn office. I like to be outside.' I was more than seven months' pregnant and we had nothing, but he wasn't willing to take the job. That was the last straw. When he wouldn't budge, I left and went back to live with my folks. A couple of days later, Ken came to the door, saying he had been promised a job in Florida and asking me to come with him. He still didn't have any money, and I just couldn't do it. He left the next day."

What a story! It had taken Betty a couple of hours to get through this tale, and although it was obvious she'd enjoyed herself, it was more than time to call it a night. Polly and I were tired, too. We were still operating on Toulouse time, and although we'd dozed on the plane, our bodies were crying out for a good night's sleep.

Betty stood up and stretched while Polly and George gathered up the coffee cups we'd brought in from dinner and took them to the kitchen. I gave my mother a hug. "Thanks for doing this, Betty," I said. "What a walk down memory lane."

"No," she replied, "thank you. I'm having a ball, and I can't wait to continue tomorrow."

Chapter 3 – Betty Continues

1934

The next morning, I awoke refreshed and intrigued. What tales would my mother regale us with today? It was almost ten o'clock when I wandered into the kitchen in search of coffee, only to find Betty and George reading the paper with coffee in hand. Polly was at the fridge, extracting the makings of a bacon-and-egg breakfast.

"You look great this morning," I said to my mother, and indeed she had a peaceful glow about her that was hard to miss. "Are you feeling okay?"

"Other than being a little tired," she replied, "I'm feeling just fine, and I'm definitely looking forward to those scrambled eggs."

It was another beautiful day, with puddles of sunshine spilling over the kitchen and everyone in it. While Polly cooked, I poured myself a cup of coffee, filled tall glasses with freshly squeezed orange juice from the local farmers' market, and set the table. It was a morning like so many others I'd spent with my mother over the years—good food, good conversation, and an easy camaraderie that we'd had since my childhood. This morning was particularly special, since I knew it would be one of our last.

After breakfast Polly and I quickly did the dishes while Betty kibitzed from her spot at the table. Then we all adjourned to the living room and I started the tape running. "What happened on the day I was born?" I asked.

"Well," Betty answered, "Ken was still gone and I was living with my folks on Gary Street, just off Seneca in South Buffalo. My doctor, Robert Irwin, lived about 20 miles away out near Kenmore, but on the morning of August 14, he came over to the house to check me out.

"After the exam, Dr. Irwin said everything was fine and I had at least four or five weeks to go. You must not have been listening, however, because the doctor wasn't gone long before I started to feel pretty bad, and by three in the afternoon I was having strong contractions and asked Mother to call his office. They agreed to send a nurse over, but by the time she got there, it was

16

nearly seven in the evening. I was upstairs in the bedroom alone; the family was downstairs finishing dinner.

"As soon as she examined me, she said, 'Oh my God, the head,' and called the doctor. In the meantime, to keep you from being born before he got there, she made me pant like a dog. Believe me, it made an impression. I couldn't look at a panting dog for years.

"Finally Dr. Irwin arrived, having left a Clark Gable movie at the Shea Theater. 'Let go,' he said, and out you came. It was a good thing he was there. You were enclosed in a veil, and if that wasn't enough, the cord was wrapped around your neck. Fortunately Dr. Irwin knew just what to do; otherwise, you might not have made it."

Betty paused, remembering the events of that night. "Obviously, you can't remember," she laughed, "but believe me, it was quite something." She looked relieved, even now, that the doctor had arrived in time.

Of course, she was right. I couldn't remember, but I could just imagine: *My first flight: delayed takeoff, and then, just after launch, enclosed in a veil and with the cord wrapped around my neck—several times. I was in trouble already. Mayday! Thank heavens the good doctor was skilled with his hands. In no time I could breathe freely and uttered a lusty yell. Thanks, Doc. I guess I should have waited before doing aerobatics.*

"The doctor left after he knew we were both okay," Betty continued, "and your grandfather buried the placenta in the backyard. I was not quite 20 years old, but it was the beginning of a new time for both of us. You added a lot of warmth to that household. Everyone was so excited to have a baby around, and it's a good thing. As it turned out, you were the only grandchild for ten years."

Chapter 4 – The Dad I Never Had

1934–1938

Itook a deep breath, trying to imagine Betty as a new mother at the age of 19. "What happened next?" I asked.

Betty smiled. "Well," she said, "the entire family moved almost immediately

Betty and me, 1935.

to a larger house on Cushing Road, still in South Buffalo. You were one happy baby. You shared a room with your Uncle Dan, and people fought over taking care of you. You also spent many a mile touring around town in a large English pram we bought for you. Initially, your Aunt Carolyn was a bit jealous. After all, she was only ten and up until then, she'd been the baby of the family herself. She soon came around, however. Even she could see that having a baby in the house seemed to help smooth the troubled waters of the McNerney clan. And you were a bright kid. You walked and talked early and were the center of your grandparents' lives. They seemed able to love you as they couldn't love each other. In fact, you were a neutral and healing influence, sometimes even more so than their own children.

"Times were still difficult. We had very little money and no financial support from Ken, so I couldn't go to school full-time. Instead, I got a job working in a department store. When I got my paycheck, I gave my mother all of it except for carfare, and one winter almost the only thing I had to wear was a knitted two-piece dress. I wore that dress everywhere.

"One thing I did do was to take some evening Adult Ed classes in a school that had been set up on the site of an old grocery store. The rooms were heated with individual little stoves so we were always cold, but the school offered a lot of interesting courses and I was glad to be there. One of the things they taught was typing, but since I'd already had some typing, they asked if I'd like to come into the office and type some things for the school—on a purely voluntary basis, of course. Well, I did, and what I ended up typing were lessons for the contract bridge classes. That's how I got interested in the game."

"Did you *ever* get any child support from Ken?" I asked.

"No, I didn't. In fact, I never heard a word from him until the winter of 1936, when you were about 18 months old. I was still friends with Doris Robertson and Jean McIntyre, and one day Jean told me they'd both heard from Ken. He was back in town, he had a good job, and he wanted to get in touch with me. Well, we started to write, although I didn't mention this to anyone at home. After we'd written for a few months, we met several times and eventually decided to get back together. When I told my mother, I saw her truly grieve for the first time. She literally got down on her knees and begged me not to do it, but when she couldn't convince me, she said, 'Okay, but if you go, that's it.' And it wasn't only me she was angry at. When Jean came to help me move and Mother found out her role in the business, she was furious. In fact, she didn't speak to Jean for years.

"Not surprisingly, our reunion was short-lived. We lived in a sort of bungalow, and I was making less than $2 a day at the department store. Ken had lost the job he had when we first got back together, and after a while he was drinking and not working at all. One night he came home drunk and drove his car over all the lawns near our apartment. Then he came in and told me to get out. Since I was on the outs with my own family, I had no place else to go, so I called his parents and they came and got me. As time passed, I got another job and Mother and Daddy began to come around. At first I think they were willing to see me because they wanted to see you, but after a time I was asked to dinner and eventually invited to move back in.

"The following year, 1937, I agreed to go out with Ken on New Year's Eve, but as luck would have it, I developed a bronchial infection that caused me to cough so hard I broke a couple of ribs. At first I didn't want to admit I was too sick to go, but eventually I had to tell him, and he was so angry that I knew this time it was really over. Some time later, I was walking home from the movies with a friend when Ken and a friend of his came along in a car and tried to talk with me. I was near Jean's folks' store, so I ducked in to get away from him and called my mother to come and get me. She came in her new

19

Oldsmobile, a replacement for the trusty Model T, but when we got home, Ken was already there. He came out from behind some bushes and kicked in the driver's-side window of Mother's car.

"Before we arrived, he'd thrown rocks at the house and broken some windows. Someone called the cops, and when Ken saw them coming, he took off over a fence. The police issued a warrant for his arrest for 'malicious mischief,' and he had to appear before the assistant district attorney, a woman named Winifred Stanley who later served in Congress. The DA ordered him to pay for damages and when he didn't, the court kept increasing the amount, which eventually amounted to more than $1,000.

"In the meantime, I wanted a divorce, but in New York State the only grounds were adultery, and you had to prove it. So I made Ken a deal: I would sign papers releasing him from his debt if he would provide me with the evidence I needed to secure a divorce. He agreed and the divorce was final in 1938. This time he was ordered to provide child support, but he never paid a cent."

As I listened to her story, I thought of my mother as a young woman, in the height of the Depression, with a low-paying job, a toddler to support, and a deadbeat ex-husband. But I never heard her complain, not then and not now. I was glad to be getting her story on tape; it was something I looked forward to sharing with my own children.

Betty was ready for a break. While she rested I thought about all that happened in the first couple years of my life. Of course, I couldn't remember most of it, but she told me that during the time she and Ken were trying to get back together, I became cranky and rebellious. I must have been glad when it was over. In fact, one of the first things I do remember was the move back to my grandparents' house. "Donald," Betty had said, "we're moving to a better place, a place where you'll have new opportunities and new friends to meet." Throughout my childhood I heard variations of those words again and again, and each time they proved to be true. The places I saw, the friends I met, and the opportunities I had as a result of our vagabond existence have much to do with the man I became.

"Life is good, Donnie," she would say, "and getting better every day." And so when Ken was finally out of the picture, he became a sort of Jekyll-and-Hyde character, treated more with humor than with bitterness. In some ways, I owe him. If he hadn't left, if he'd remained involved in our lives, it would have been violent and terrible, and I never would have lived the adventures I have.

Chapter 5 – The Early Years

I loved living with my grandparents. Betty came and went—to college and to work—taking advantage of the challenges and opportunities available to a young, attractive woman of her day. Occasionally she moved to an apartment, and sometimes we lived in an apartment together, but life was tough, and both jobs and money were scarce. I became quite independent, content in my role as a member of the extended McNerney clan, and I was a happy, friendly kid.

I wondered how much my mother remembered about those times, but I didn't have to wait long to find out. By the following day, she was eager to continue our journey into the past. "Let's get started, Don," she said after breakfast. "Do you have enough tapes for all of this?"

"You bet," I said. "And I know you have enough stories."

Betty laughed. "Let's take this carafe of coffee into the living room. I think it's going to be a long morning."

As Betty settled into her chair and poured coffee for both of us, I thought back to some of my earliest memories as a kid.

"Do you remember Bobby Bumpus?" I asked.

"I sure do," Betty said, laughing, "particularly the day that you and Bobby and a girl from the neighborhood were having a pissing contest around the tree in our backyard, and the girl won, from a standing position no less. Your grandmother and I were watching from the window, and we thought it was all very funny."

"You know," I said, "I don't think it surprised me that she won, even at the time. Nothing a woman can do ever surprises me. Perhaps I was in on the beginning of the Women's Movement. Do you think that little girl might have been Gloria?[5]

---

[5] The Gloria referenced here is Gloria Steinem. Born in 1934, Ms. Steinem is a journalist, activist, and one of the leaders of the Women's Movement that began in the 1960s. In 1971 she founded *Ms. Magazine* and later established the Ms. Foundation for Women, an organization dedicated to helping underprivileged women.

Betty laughed. "Could be," she said, "could be."

"Bobby had something to do with my conduct at the South Buffalo Presbyterian Church, too, didn't he?" I asked. "I liked that church; we had great treats after Sunday school."

"As I recall," Betty said, "you liked church quite a bit, especially the day you took the opportunity to entertain all assembled with some new words you'd learned from Bobby. While the congregation was deep in prayer, you took your three-year-old self out of the Sunday school classroom and into the sanctuary, where you shouted 'you're a bunch of piss pots' from the front of the church. I didn't know whether to laugh or cry."

"I'm not sure I remember my actual performance. I do remember being propelled home that day for the first spanking of my life, an event that made a definite impression. After that, I never said another bad word in South Buffalo Presbyterian or any other church, so I figure God forgave me. The Presbyterians forgave me, too, I think, since they gave me a Bible later on. In fact, I still have it."

Betty smiled. "Your adventures weren't limited to the church, you know. There was also that time we went to visit some friends who lived in the country, and it turned out they had an outhouse. They also had a cat, which you captured and tossed down the outhouse—one of your less-than-perfect moments.

"Most of the time, though, you were a pretty responsible kid. You started kindergarten in September of 1938, when you were only four. That's when we were living above Metzger's Bar and Grill, where I worked as a secretary for the princely sum of $21 a week. This was double what I made working in the department store a couple of years earlier, but money was still tight. You did chores for the pennies you received, and in the evenings I went to college."

"I remember those times," I said, "going to P.S. 22 and coming home to our flat above the bar. I had milk and cookies and went out to play, and you came to check on me on your breaks. I know you've said it was a pretty rough section of South Buffalo, but back then all cityscapes looked the same to me.

"Of course," I continued, "what stands out most about Metzger's for me was the day I almost got hit by the car. I must have been five. I was walking home from school and had just about reached the stairwell to our flat when a car came straight toward the sidewalk, its brakes screeching. Missing me by no more than a few feet, it crashed into the front wall of the building. The air smelled of gasoline, and the sidewalk was littered with bags of groceries that had flown out the car windows. There was an old man in the driver's seat, and he and his wife just sat there, blood flowing down their faces. I guess they were in shock. I remember going over to talk to them, and then you came running out of your office and sent me up to the flat to wait while you went for help."

Betty shook her head. "That was one terrifying afternoon. A few feet one way or the other and that car would have hit you. We had to find a better place to live."

"I figured as much, because it wasn't long before I heard those magic words: 'Donald,' you said, 'we're moving to a place where you'll have new opportunities and new friends to meet,' and away we went to the Kenmore Apartments, a building with an elevator and an incinerator for refuse. And I did get to meet new people. In fact, I was beginning to believe I might get to meet almost everybody in South Buffalo."

Betty was quiet, perhaps thinking about some of the close calls of those days, and I was remembering another close call of my own.

The Candy Thief

Because of the times, or perhaps because I lived in a world with so many adults, I had more freedom than most kids and was trusted to a great degree. Maybe that's why I've always felt bad about the following incident.

When we lived at the Kenmore, Betty was seeing a lawyer named Hymie Davidoff who treated her, and me, very well. They dated often and talked nightly. One night while they were on the phone, I slipped out of the apartment and went down to the local store. I cased the candy section, found what I was looking for, and snitched a bar, but the owner had spied me. When I tried to slip out of the store he shouted at me to stop, and I dropped the ill-gained loot and ran like the wind. He chased me for a while, but I outfoxed him. By the time I got home, I was exhausted and panting. Fortunately, my mother was still talking with Hymie and didn't seem to notice.

That night I did a lot of thinking. In my imagination, I was visited by my guardian angel. In spite of entertaining the congregation with salty language at age three, I must have learned a few theological precepts at South Buffalo Presbyterian, one of them being the concept of such a heavenly creature looking out for me. I also knew, however, that she—a female angel, with just the right mix of wisdom and wit, seemed to fit the bill—was not going to tolerate dishonesty. We decided I wanted to be a good person, and I resolved then and there to lead an honest life.

Nothing was ever said about my foray into crime, but very soon afterward I was back with my grandmother. I often wondered.

Chapter 6 – Life with Grandmother (and Grandpa, Too)

1939–1941

Grandmother's presence was commanding. She had an enormous sense of self-importance and determination, and she took no nonsense from anyone. Her homes were always immaculate, and there was no task that she wouldn't tackle. To this day, I've never enjoyed food prepared by a better or more capable cook, both in terms of variety and efficient preparation.

When she was busy, Grandmother was chipper and happy, especially while doing her housekeeping, but to hang around her kitchen, each person had to contribute. For ten years, I was her only grandchild, and under her critical eye I learned everything from how to peel potatoes to how to dry a dish. Even the thought of picking at food rather than enjoying it would invite her caustic remarks, and as a result, cooking is as natural to me as household duty and food is one of my greatest pleasures.

I enjoyed being around adults, because in conversations they treated me as one of them, laughing at and with me as I tried to fathom life. When I was very young, I was especially gregarious, unafraid of any social situation, and adults seemed to enjoy my company. Unlike many children who look at the floor and shuffle their feet when spoken to, I looked at the speaker, asked and answered questions, and made comments. I was a child who was curious about everything—life, the world, the church. In some ways, I was more comfortable with adults than with my peers. We moved so often that I was always the new kid on the block. This meant I was never part of the in crowd, but I was rarely the goat of the group, either.

Money was used wisely during the Depression by almost everyone. Even if one was employed, the national feeling of poverty and despair was all-encompassing, and waste by rich or poor was a sacrilege. Although we thought of ourselves as poor financially, as did most of our friends and relatives, we actually were better off than most. In any event, being poor carried no shame, and we were rich in other ways. We had independence, we were well-read, and for entertainment, we listened to the radio and played cards and board games.

Around the dinner table each evening, and sometimes later in the sitting room, we discussed the day's activities and world events. I was always interested and included in these exchanges, where profanity and sexual innuendo were unheard of, or if used, were far more sophisticated than my young ears could comprehend. After a while, I became quite knowledgeable about some of the things going on in the world, but the family was careful never to expose me to adult burdens.

I was also the proud and privileged owner of a library card, and if somebody went to the library, I always tagged along. An evening at home often found everyone reading, the room quiet except for the occasional guffaw or sharing of a witty passage. For outside entertainment, Grandpa often took me to a Saturday matinee at the movies, where the program included a Walt Disney cartoon, a Movietone newsreel, and a feature film with cowboy heroes such as Hopalong Cassidy or Roy Rogers and his horse Trigger. Twenty-five cents covered admission and a cherry Coke.[6]

Grandpa was small in stature, walked like a Banty rooster, and was as cocky as Grandmother was confident. When he came home from a day's work on the railroad, it was a grand event for me. He always wore a suit and tie, but at day's end his hands, face, and clothes were covered with dust from the coal that made those wonderful engines shake the ground with thunder and heat. I would stand in the lavatory as he covered his face, arms, and hands with soap and scrubbed the dirt away. He then stropped the blade of his straight-edged razor to a sharp edge, foamed his cup of shaving cream with a soft brush, and dabbed a spot of the rich lather on my nose before starting to shave.

After his ablutions, we discussed his work and occasionally played a bit of ball. Then he retired to his overstuffed chair in the woodshed for a cigar and the newspaper. These sojourns in the woodshed were sacred to him, and during them he was best left alone.

A whiff of cigar smoke is nostalgic to me to this day, but as you might guess, Grandmother was a pioneer in the crusade against smoking. Even though Grandpa was restricted to the woodshed, she often complained of his "cigar odor," and no cigar was ever smoked in her house. In fact, if she'd had her way, cigarettes would have been forbidden as well. As soon as one butt rested in an ashtray, she clucked away at the errant smoker.

---

[6] The Fox Film Corporation, which eventually became 20th Century Fox, produced Movietone News from 1928 until 1963. In the days before television, these newsreels, which were shown in theaters before the main feature, provided moviegoers with visual information about world events.

Cars were as important then as they are now. Grandmother had learned to drive a Model T Ford back in 1929 or '30 when the family lived in Mingo Junction, West Virginia. At the time, she may have been one of the first women drivers in the state. She was as aggressive behind the wheel as she was in the rest of her life, and tales of her adventures on the road are legendary. She could also twist a wrench or change a tire without hesitation.

In 1935, Grandmother traded in the Model T on a brand new 1936 Oldsmobile sedan. A couple of years later, Gramps purchased a 1938 Buick Roadmaster, a huge machine that he kept immaculate and stored in a heated garage. They both enjoyed driving, and being in the car was one of our greatest sources of entertainment. How often I heard the words, "Let's go for a drive." Away we went, enjoying the verdant countryside south of Buffalo, a glorious area of well-kept, fertile farms. Grandmother was quite fussy about what she used in her kitchen, and we often picked up milk or eggs at our favorite farms. When fresh fruits and vegetables were in season, it was an especially wonderful excursion. And always before coming home, we stopped for a double-scoop nickel ice cream cone of maple walnut, my favorite flavor except when strawberries were in season.

At least once a year, Gramps took me to Crystal Beach, a resort on the Canadian shores of Lake Erie. To reach this popular destination, we boarded a boat at the docks in Buffalo. Passengers had the run of the vessel, and we often split our time among observing the giant pistons that drove the boat, watching the sea, and enjoying the holiday mood of the other tourists. In true Canadian fashion, the amusement park and adjoining beach were well-maintained, litter-free, and landscaped with beautiful flowers. The park offered the usual delights: hotdogs and cotton candy, plus the most incredible cinnamon candies. Gramps enjoyed these outings as much as I did, and they helped form a special bond between us.[7]

Life with the McNerneys may sound like a paradise of peace and contentment, but there was another side to it. Although my grandparents doted on me, they hated each other, and it had been a long war. The fact that Grandpa was a Catholic and Grandmother a Presbyterian had rendered their so-called mixed marriage a recipe for disaster. The Catholic Church did not allow divorce, so these two feisty people lived and fought for years in a union that never should have happened. Fortunately, by the time I came along, they had forged an uneasy truce.

I loved them both dearly, but when they were together, or even talking about each other, it was painful. As far back as I can remember, I resolved that

---

[7] The Crystal Beach amusement park closed in 1989 due to financial problems, but the cottage community of Crystal Beach maintains its charm into the 21st century.

if I had to resort to that sort of bickering to stay in a relationship, it would be far better to depart the scene.

My grandmother's ultimate goal in life was to migrate from South Buffalo to the suburban town of East Aurora, so we moved frequently, each time to a slightly better neighborhood as Grandpa's salary permitted. As we trekked through towns and hamlets southeastward toward Grandmother's Mecca, I often heard variations of the mantra, "Donald, we're moving to a better place. You'll have new opportunities and get to meet new friends." And indeed I did. Sometimes I felt as well-known as the pope. *Who's the guy in the beanie? I don't know, but the kid next to him is Donald Wright.*

And so the years went by: 1939, 1940, 1941. These were stress-filled times for the adults, but for me the days were mostly happy. And then our attention was riveted on the radio. It was December 8, 1941, the day after Pearl Harbor. President Roosevelt spoke of "a date which will live in infamy" and America plunged into World War II.

Chapter 7 – America Goes to War

1941–1942

Once we entered the war, everything changed. There was very little unemployment, and it wasn't long before the Depression was over and prosperity returned. Everyone had a mission, and they took that mission very seriously. You couldn't go anyplace without seeing people in uniform, and since most of the men were overseas, women made up the main workforce in America. At school, kids sold war bond stamps for a nickel apiece. And it seemed as if every boy had a little red wagon to collect newspapers and cans for recycling into material for the war. In fact, I can't remember *not* having a job and my own money. Everyone pulled together in a common cause; it was a no-work, no-eat policy.

Many things were rationed, including sugar and meat, so we ate differently, too. Grandmother fixed lots of new dishes, including macaroni and cheese and one of my favorites, liver and onions. We also grew some of our own food in a victory garden in the backyard.[8]

Not everything was work, however. For example, Betty either learned or invented a type of pig Latin where the word "egg" was placed before each vowel in a word, and she taught it to many of her female friends and relatives. Thus, Betty became "Beggety" and Donald became "Deggoneggald." Imagine the mental agility required to insert the

---

[8] From 1942 until 1946, many foodstuffs in the U.S., as well as clothing, gasoline, and other commodities, were rationed as a way to cope with shortages due to World War II. Although never faced with the deprivations experienced by most of Europe and Asia, families were issued coupons entitling them to buy specified quantities of rationed goods. Having these coupons, however, was no guarantee that the goods would be available, and during WWII, as in WWI, every available patch of ground in many communities across the country was turned into garden plots to reduce pressure on the public food supply. Victory gardens turned up in such unlikely spots as apartment complex rooftops in New York City and parts of Golden Gate Park in San Francisco. At one point during the Second World War, it is estimated that victory gardens produced up to 40 percent of the nation's produce.

appropriate number of "eggs" into a given word and still maintain the pace and fluency of normal speech. Grandmother, Aunt Carolyn, my mother, and their friends would use this crazy language when traveling by bus or streetcar, confusing and stunning the other passengers with the ebb and flow of their conversation. Sometimes I could follow their patter, though I was never able to speak it, but I always worried that someone would accuse them of being Nazi spies as they giggled and chattered away.

Shortly after the war broke out, Betty got a job as a riveter at the Curtiss-Wright aircraft plant, one of the six million women who kept American industry going while the men were at war. Personified by Rosie the Riveter, these women not only produced munitions and matériel, they also heralded the beginning of women's growing economic power.[9]

Betty wasn't the only one of the McNerney clan to serve the cause at Curtiss-Wright; soon Grandmother was working as a riveter, and Aunt Carolyn, after a short, unsuccessful try at college, also went to work there. Uncle Dan, Betty's younger brother, enlisted in the army and worked his way up the ranks, following General Douglas MacArthur through the Pacific.[10]

Just before shipping out for the first time, he married Mary Hoit, an attractive young WAVE from Goffstown, New Hampshire. Mary and Dan met at a USO dance. Her father had been unable to serve in the armed forces during the First World War and when the need arose again, Mary served for both her family and the nation.[11, 12]

---

[9] Rosie was a cultural icon symbolizing the efforts of American women who went to work to help win the war. One of these women was Rose Will Monroe. Originally from Pulaski County, KY, Rose worked in the Willow Run Aircraft Factory in Ypsilanti, MI. Because she was featured in a film and on posters about women working to support the war effort, it was her face that came to represent Rosie the Riveter.

[10] General Douglas MacArthur (1880–1964) was born in Little Rock, AR, and graduated from the U.S. Military Academy at West Point in 1903. He was a career officer who served in various capacities, including Supreme Allied Commander in the Pacific during World War II. From 1945 to 1950 he oversaw the occupation of Japan and is credited with implementing far-reaching democratic reforms in that country. In 1950 he left Japan to fight the Koreans. Although initially successful in Korea, he was relieved of command by President Truman in 1951 for his public criticism of the U.S. government's Korean War policy. In retirement he served as chairman of the board of Remington Rand Corporation.

[11] Started in 1942, the WAVES (Women Accepted for Volunteer Emergency Service) was a World War II-era division of the U.S. Navy. With passage of the Women's Armed Services Integration Act in 1948, women gained permanent status in the armed services and the WAVES officially ceased to exist.

[12] The USO is a private, non-profit organization incorporated in 1941 to serve the

| Aunt Mary & Uncle Dan McNerney, ca. 1942. | Aunt Carolyn & Uncle Walt Shed, ca. 1943. |

(Courtesy of Mary Ann Shed Haney.)

Later, Aunt Carolyn married Walt Shed, a bombardier on a B-25. A sharp, easy-going guy, Walt had been one of the first to enlist when war was declared, and I idolized him. When he was home on leave, he regaled me with war stories and encouraged my dream of becoming a fighter pilot. I can still hear his infectious chuckle as he told his tales, puffing on his pipe, beer bottle balanced on his knee. A bombardier's job was to control the aircraft in the final moments of the attack, and Walt described how tough it was being based on the Caribbean island of Aruba and hunting the German wolf pack.[13]

"How many subs did you get, Uncle Walt?" I asked.

"One," he replied, with a twinkle. "Our plane was flying low, looking for a periscope or a submerging sub, when we saw it dive, leaving ripples in the water. The skipper reversed course, practically jerking the wings off the plane in pursuit, then turned the controls over to me. I had the target in my sights,

---

on-leave recreation needs of the U.S. Armed Forces. The agencies coordinating their efforts to form the USO were National Catholic Community Services, National Jewish Welfare Board, National Travelers Aid Association, Salvation Army, YMCA, and YWCA. By 1944, there were more than 3,000 USO Clubs where servicemen and women could dance, watch a movie, get free coffee and doughnuts, or find a quiet spot to read a book, write a letter, or seek religious counsel. Closed down briefly after World War II, the organization was reactivated at the time of the Korean conflict. Since its inception, the USO has also sponsored Camp Shows at which famous personalities lend their time and talent to entertain U.S. troops around the world. In 2008 and, as its motto says, *Until Every One Comes Home*, the USO continues to serve U.S. service personnel at home and abroad.

[13] German U-boats (submarines) who converged on convoys of merchant vessels in the Atlantic were known as "wolf packs."

but I took my time, making minute adjustments before firing. Bombs away! Afterward, we reversed course again to make sure we got him. If he surfaced, we could always use our .50 caliber machine guns to finish him off."

"Did you get him?"

Walt roared with laughter. "We got him all right—dead on. Problem was, the Caribbean was a sea of red. Our enemy sub turned out to be a whale."

Dan and Walt weren't the only ones having adventures. Not too long after Betty started at Curtiss-Wright, her career, too, took an unexpected turn, and I knew this was one of her favorite memories.

* * *

Betty Becomes an Engineer

"Tell me about Curtiss-Wright," I said. "Just how was it that you ended up going to school on the company?"

"Well," Betty replied, "I was in the lunchroom one day when one of the girls asked me how much college I had. When I told her, she said it sounded like I might meet the education-equivalency requirements for the company to send me to school for further training. You can bet I checked it out right away, and it was true. I was sent to the Curtiss-Wright Engineering and Management Institute at the University of Buffalo for two years, though the courses we took were actually provided by Cornell University. At the end of my schooling, I came out as an engineer with the equivalent of an associate degree, and after graduation, I went back to Curtiss-Wright and worked in the loft on the P-40 fighter.

"Do you remember," she continued, "how interested you were in my wooden kit with its different drafting tools and metal scribes? You wanted to know what I did with all those devices, and I showed you what I was learning, step-by-step. I used a set of blueprints from a practice project to demonstrate how I transcribed and interpolated information from the blueprints onto aluminum sheets. Later on, when I did this at work, we sent the finished sheets to the machine shop, where highly skilled metalworkers cut the transcribed work into jigs. These could then be recopied thousands of times, which meant that each piece that was riveted or bolted onto an airplane was exactly the same."

As I watched her tell this story, remembering her place in the war machine that squashed the Axis, I could see that she still glowed with the pride of accomplishment.

Pitching Pennies for Change

I was seven years old and in the second grade when Pearl Harbor was bombed, and soon everyone in the family was supporting the war in one way or another: Grandpa at the rail yard; Betty learning to be an engineer; and Grandmother and Aunt Carolyn at Curtiss-Wright. Uncle Dan, Aunt Mary, and Uncle Walt were in the service, and Uncle Robert, Betty's older brother, worked for the phone company. He and his wife Erma lived an hour away. Although the adults tried to arrange their schedules around me, they weren't always successful, and I spent many an hour alone. I was actually quite trustworthy. After my adventure as the candy bar thief, I was too scared and too guilty to return to a life of crime, but there were times I scared the dickens out of my mother. One of these was "the penny incident."

"Betty," I asked, "Do you remember when you came home one day and found me standing on the windowsill?"

"Do I ever. It was one of those times when I just didn't know what to do. I'd done pretty well at arranging my schedule to be there when you left for school in the morning and shortly after you got off the bus in the afternoon, but then you came down with the chicken pox. Well, there were just no babysitters available, so we had long talks about you being a good boy and so forth, and I thought all was well until the day I came home to find you standing on the sill of an open third-floor window. Obviously on the mend, you were tossing pennies to the neighborhood kids below. You could have fallen and killed yourself. I knew then that something had to change."

And change it did, but first summer came again. In our gypsy-like migration toward East Aurora, I'd attended eleven different schools over a four-year period, including one year in kindergarten, two years in first grade (maybe it hadn't been such a good idea to go to kindergarten at age four, after all), and one year in second grade. In June of 1942, I was almost eight years old, back on track, and looking forward to long, lazy summer days. Then I heard those famous words: "Donald, we have a wonderful opportunity for you, and you'll get to meet lots of new people." I loved those words. In the past they'd meant different schools and interesting places, but this time the change was on a grand scale.

Chapter 8 – A Country Ride to a New Home

1942

Betty's eyes were still twinkling from recounting my day as a penny pitcher, and I could tell she was eager to tell the rest of the story.

"It was shortly after that that I went to the farm, wasn't it?" I asked.

"It sure was," she replied. "I was concerned about you being alone and eager to find a solution, but once your grandmother took on the project of figuring out what was best to do with you, she moved ahead like a steamroller."

I thought back to that long-ago summer of 1942. "Of course," I said, "I wasn't privy to what happened behind the scenes, but I remember how it all started. 'Donnie,' you said, 'we're working so much that we don't have time to be at home with you, and we find this very worrying. So we've decided the best thing is for you to live with a family in the country.' And I said, 'Great. Whose family?' And you said, 'Well, that's just the thing. We're going on an adventure to find out.'"

Betty laughed. "That's about it. That weekend, off we went in the Olds, your grandmother and I in front and you in back with your carpetbag of clothes and trinkets. We headed south towards Wales Township, where we used to get eggs and vegetables, but beyond that, we couldn't tell you where we were going because we didn't have a clue. All we knew was that living on the streets of Buffalo was not safe, and we felt that farm life would be good for you."

"You must have been really worried," I said, "but honestly, I didn't notice. To me, the whole scheme sounded exciting."

"I'm glad to hear that," Betty replied, "because I was worried enough for both of us, though it certainly turned out okay."

With that, Betty took a sip of coffee and I leaned back in my chair, transported in memory to my eight-year-old self in the backseat of my grandmother's 1936 Oldsmobile sedan.

A Home Away from Home

The first place we stopped was at a farm where Grandmother had bought eggs. She marched to the door through the usual pack of barking dogs, drew herself up to her full five feet one inch, and knocked. A pleasant farm wife with a bevy of kids hanging onto her housedress answered the door.

"Hello, my name is Alice McNerney, and this is my daughter Betty Wright and her son Donald. We work at the war plant and need to board Donald. Of course we're willing to pay, and we felt that your wonderful farm would be just the place."

The woman looked at me, looked at them like they'd come from another planet, and then shook her head. "No," she said, without further explanation. Undaunted, Grandmother thanked her and away we went to the next farm, this one where we'd stopped for vegetables.

"Hello, my name is Alice McNerney," Grandmother began again, going through the same routine and getting the same reaction. After repeating this scenario at several more farms and hearing a refusal at each, we returned home, unsuccessful but not discouraged. When next Grandmother and Betty had a day off, we tried again. In fact, we tried on several trips, though after a while things were beginning to look hopeless. Finally, at what must have been a point of despair for the ladies, we came to a large, well-kept farm near Wales Hollow, a small hamlet just a few miles from Grandmother's house. A family named Hudson owned this farm and the landscape looked promising, but here, too, we were refused. There were already too many kids to feed and too many chores to do.[14]

Grandmother bought some eggs anyway. Just as we were ready to drive off, Mrs. Hudson looked down at her feet, looked up at me, and held out her hand. "Wait a minute," she said. "I have an idea. My cousins Maude and Millard have a farm off the Centerline Road, just a mile or so from here. They're older and don't have any children; maybe they'd be willing to take the boy in."

We lost no time following up the lead. I remember it was lunchtime, and as we walked onto the porch, a black and white terrier wagged his tail in welcome. "Yes?" said the woman with the wonderful, kind face who greeted us at the door. Maude Hudson, she said her name was, and with that Grandmother was off and running.

---

[14] Wales Hollow, now called Wales Village, is located in Erie County, NY, on the western edge of the town of Wales, approximately six miles east of East Aurora. It was originally called Woods Hollow after James Wood, one of the first settlers in the area in the early 1800s.

"My name is Alice McNerney, and this is my daughter Betty Wright and her son Donald. We work at the war plant and would like to board Donald. Your cousin on Route 20 recommended you, and we hope that you can help us out. We are willing to pay for his keep." Attracted by the commotion, Maude's husband Millard and their hired hand Judd came out of the kitchen. If Maude was the quintessential farm woman, Millard was certainly her counterpoint: a slender man with a pleasant demeanor, slightly bent over, probably in his 50s but seeming mighty old to me. His skin was bronzed to a shining umber and his ears were *huge*.

While the adults chatted on the porch and Grandmother and Betty admired the beauty of the rolling hills and orderly fields, I played with the dog. Things seemed to be progressing, when all of a sudden Maude surprised us by making the usual excuses as to why I couldn't stay. We had no choice but to leave. Grandmother thanked her for her time and complimented her once again on the beauty of the farm; then we all got back into the Olds. I could tell Betty and Grandmother were disappointed, and by this time, so was I. For a moment I'd thought this was going to be the place. Grandmother put the car in gear and turned it around. Maude hadn't moved. As we started down the drive, I remember looking at her face, and she was looking right back at me. Just then, she raised her hand. Grandmother stepped on the brakes.

"Leave the boy," she said quietly. "We'll give it a try." I could feel the atmosphere inside the car lighten up, and within minutes, a tear was sliding down Betty's cheek and both women were giving me hugs goodbye. As the Olds disappeared in a cloud of dust, I stood in the driveway with Maude, Millard, and my carpetbag. My greatest adventure so far was about to begin, and it lasted nearly two years.[15]

A Day on the Farm

Maude spoke first: "Better get up to the house, wash up, and eat some dinner before the men go back to the fields." We walked up the hill and into

---

[15] In the context of 2008, when parents are often afraid to let their children play alone in their own yards, choosing to board one's child with strangers may appear to be extraordinary behavior. However, in the early 1940s, when daycare was virtually unavailable and nearly every able-bodied adult was contributing directly or indirectly to the war effort, families had to find creative ways to keep their children out of harm's way. Londoners sent their offspring to live with families in the country to protect them from bombs. Many American families also made difficult choices. My family chose Maude and Millard Hudson, or perhaps they chose us. In any event, the time I spent on the farm was far from a hardship; in fact, it was one of the most rewarding periods of my life.

a kitchen filled with light, warmth, and wonderful smells. Dinner was still on the table, and a raspberry pie was cooling on the windowsill. Maude showed me the single water tap and pan, and I washed my hands. Then I sat down to a heaping plate of chuck roast; potatoes, peas, carrots, and green beans from the garden; homemade relishes; and a tall glass of fresh milk. For dessert, there was that raspberry pie. I knew I was home.

While I finished my meal, Judd took a walk and Millard stayed in the kitchen, sitting on a straight-back chair, picking at his teeth with a toothpick. He was quiet, looking through the open window at the fields and rolling purple hills beyond, while Maude chattered away to me as she cleaned up. It was a setting of peace and tranquility, one that I would experience many times on the farm and one that taught me much about their relationship. I don't remember Maude and Millard ever so much as touching each other, but the ambiance of good feeling, trust, and mutual comfort in that kitchen spoke volumes about the love between them.

Millard and Maude Hudson on their 50th wedding anniversary, ca. 1960.
(*Image extracted from group photo provided by Nancy Hauber Holmes.*)

At one o'clock sharp, the men returned to the fields, and Maude invited me to look around the house while she did her chores. This was a classic New York farmhouse. An open side porch (enclosed during winter, I learned later) led to the kitchen door, which was the main entry. The kitchen was large and airy, with a wooden table surrounded by spool and caned straight-back chairs, and the smell of the thousands of meals prepared there permeated the very walls. The focal point of the room was a woodstove of cast iron and chrome, which was almost always burning. Fuel for this behemoth came from stick wood that Maude split with a hatchet on an old stump just outside the back door and stored in a woodshed off the kitchen. On the other side of the room was the pantry, its shelves lined with row after row of Ball jars containing delicious relish, tomatoes, beans, and other vegetables. There were also jars of canned meat, pale sentinels among the more colorful vegetables, since the Hudsons didn't have a refrigerator or freezer.[16]

Although I was soon to discover that the house had no indoor plumbing in the traditional sense, Millard was quite proud of his innovative way of furnishing the kitchen with running water for washing and cleaning, though not for drinking. In the rafters above the woodshed, he'd mounted a giant cistern. This device collected water from the roof, which then ran through the stove to a tank. Among other things, that tank was to warm my "hinder" on many a winter day to come.

Next to the kitchen was a combination dining/sitting room. Maude later explained that they rarely ate a meal in this room but used it instead for relaxing in the evenings. The room had comfortable chairs with reading lights, and the table was stacked with farm records, with space to play cards at one end. The walls were lined with bookshelves, and one corner contained a quaint, curved-glass case with shelves of memorabilia, including a Kodak box camera and pictures, bits and pieces of pottery, and a set of china. One shelf held a collection that particularly stirred my imagination—Indian artifacts and pottery that Maude had found on the farm. At the entrance to the room was a huge floor grate. In winter, it supplied heat from the wood-burning furnace in the cellar. An old rug on the floor had the indescribable smell of farm: a mixture of hay, food, manure, and animal sweat. To this day, that particular aroma is as sweet to me as pollen to a bee.

Straight ahead of the dining/sitting room was the front porch. To the right was the parlor, which also had a slightly musty farm smell, and Maude's bedroom, a small, tidy room with lace curtains and bedspread. Upstairs were two more bedrooms, Judd's on the left and Millard's down the hall to the right. A comfortable cot and a bureau were just outside Millard's door, and on

---

[16] The Ball Brothers Glass Manufacturing Company of Buffalo, NY, introduced a line of glass jars for home canning in 1884. By the early 1900s, Ball was a household name. In the 21st century, the company serves the international market with a diverse line of metal and plastic containers, still used primarily for food, but they no longer manufacture glass jars.

this cot I found my carpetbag. My city clothes had been stacked in the bureau drawers.

When I got back to the kitchen, Maude and I went outside. Standing under one of the magnificent sugar maples that graced the lawn, she gestured with a sweep of her arm as she described the layout of the Hudsons' 100-acre farm. The house and barn sat on the highest ground, surrounded by outbuildings and fields. At the back of the property was a large creek, and a small brook flowed in season through about 40 acres of woods. Millard leased an additional 50-acre parcel across Centerline Road.

When Maude encouraged me to explore, I didn't need a second invitation. I excused myself and took off for the barn on a dead run. When I rolled back the door, the sweet barn smell of the nearly empty structure was almost overpowering. A couple of pigs grunted from their pen, and I met Harold the bull, standing securely in his stanchion with a ring in his nose. I went out through the back door and stood in the barnyard, taking in the giant white building with its gambrel roofline and two silos. From there I went 'round to the front of the barn, which was at a higher level, and slid back another giant door. From here I could see the hayloft as well as the grain bin filled with oats, wheat, and milled grain. I climbed a ladder and jumped into the sweet-smelling hay. Then I slid down the hay chute to the barn floor. What a place—like a giant amusement park, only better.

Next stop was the milk house, an insulated stone room with several 20-gallon milk cans cooled by water drawn from deep in the earth and circulated by an electric pump. That night at supper I learned that this was the first year Maude and Millard had electricity, and they were darn proud of it.

After climbing the short, steep hill back toward the house and veering to the right, I came to a toolshed full of farming machinery. Behind it was the two-holer, a traditional outhouse with a half-moon carved in the door and the Sears, Roebuck catalogue inside for entertainment and other uses. Just beyond, at the edge of a huge produce garden, were rows and rows of flowers and the chicken house.

Now I was in Maude's domain. She was working in the garden, where her early zinnias, interspersed with gladiolas, were a forest of flaming color. She pulled up a couple of young scallions, peeled down the top skin, pinched off the root, and handed me one. As we munched away, she began teaching me the ins and outs of growing good things, like the tiny carrots with their fern-like tops and the tomatoes that were just beginning to form. She was a lively and delightful conversationalist, with the unmistakable intonation of the country farmer. After a while she said, "Okay, Don. You'd better head down toward the fields where the men are working."

Just below the house, along Centerline Road, was a prime piece of land planted in corn, which was now about knee-high. Other fields were planted in wheat, oats, and potatoes, and a myriad of fenced cow trails separated field from pasture. Starting down one of these trails, I spotted Millard cultivating a potato field on the other side of the brook. He was perched on the metal spring seat of the cultivator, a machine powered by Prince and Polly, a team of sweating workhorses. When he saw me, he waved me over a wooden bridge, sat me on his lap, and handed me the reins. As Millard clicked the horses down the windrows, I held on tight, marveling at the size and strength of beasts that could shake the earth with their powerful hooves. I was also fascinated by the communication between man and beast. "Ha! Ha! Baaaak," Millard said, sometimes in a voice almost pleading, as if the horses would do his bidding based on emotion alone.

Climb on up, son. The view's fine!
(*Illustration by Babe Sargent.*)

All too soon we headed back to begin the evening chores, and I watched Millard and Judd milk the cows and clean the barn. Maude was in the kitchen preparing supper. In the country, the main meal was dinner, which was almost always served at midday. Supper was usually leftovers, warmed up from the noontime meal. That night and many a night thereafter we had hash, a creation

Maude concocted by adding onions, peppers, cold meat and whatever to the leftover dinner potatoes. Along with the hash, I had another glass of cold milk and some fruit pie, and before the light faded in the west, I was fast asleep in my cot. I may have been only a few miles from home, but the city boy had become a country boy in a single day, and I couldn't wait for the adventure to continue.

Chapter 9 – Learning the Lessons of Farm Life

1942

As I soon learned, farming in the summer is dawn-to-dark work and the days start early. By the time I woke up the next morning, Millard and Judd had done the milking and Maude had prepared a huge breakfast of bacon, eggs, potatoes, toasted homemade bread, coffee, and milk. Judd, a young bachelor, was one of the many farm workers who were deferred from the military. These deferments, which had little to do with desire, were based on the need for muscle in the workplace. He was a nice-looking, powerful man—friendly, but often quiet.

While we ate, Maude chattered away, discussing the weather, her egg business, and the beauty of her gladiolas. Millard, or Mill as most people called him, didn't talk much, but he listened carefully, and they both included me in the conversation as if I had lived with them for years. Judd said nothing at all.

That day I investigated the far reaches of the farm, returning to the house only for dinner. By day's end, I'd splashed in the creek, eaten wild strawberries and raspberries until I thought I would burst, and reveled in my good fortune at landing in such a paradise with such fine folks.

On my way home in the late afternoon, I saw Mill coming in from the woods, herding the cows for milking. I eagerly joined in to help, clicking the stanchions closed as each cow went into her respective place and observing the milking operation with great interest, but I sure was getting hungry. Finally, the last cows were milked and let out to pasture, and I headed for the door.

Judd stepped in front of me. "Where're you going?"

"Supper."

He laughed. "Not so fast. We do the chores before supper." Millard was sweeping at the far end of the barn. Judd handed me a shovel. "You scrape the cow plops into the gutter, while I grain Harold, Prince, Polly, and the pigs."

Huh? I shook my head, leaned the shovel against the wall, and started for the house. This city slicker wasn't about to shovel manure. Judd grabbed

41

me firmly by the arm. "Everybody's got to pitch in, son," he said, and gently handed me the shovel again. I threw it down, kicked him in the shin, squirmed away, and sprinted out of the barn.

I was quick and shifty, and as he chased me through a gully near the back of the house, he fell on his side. The resulting scrape left a huge, bloody abrasion. The chase was over, and I slunk sheepishly into the house. It was a very quiet supper—even Maude was subdued. After the dishes were cleared away, she went to the phone and turned the crank.[17]

"Hello, Gert" she said to the operator. "I hear it might rain tomorrow."

"Could be," Gert replied. "How's your corn doing?"

The conversation went on that way for a bit until Maude said, "Gert, would you ring Sheridan 0530?"

Oh, good God, I thought, *that's my mother's number in Buffalo*. I held my breath as the phone rang and rang, but no one answered. Maude thanked Gertrude for trying, and without further comment, we all went to bed. That night I prayed for two things: that they would forgive me, and that I would have the good sense not to test the limits in the future. Where *was* that guardian angel when I needed her? Had she been on vacation?

After a still-quiet breakfast the next morning, Judd asked if I'd like to help him work the potatoes on the back 15. I replied with enthusiasm and a genuine sense of relief. After my boorish behavior of the day before, I was determined to learn all I could and to pull my weight while doing so.

We went out to the toolshed where Millard kept his 1937 John Deere tractor. Standing near the flywheel of this green monster, Judd checked the oil, greased some fittings, and primed the two-cylinder engine, explaining why and what he was doing as he went along. When he was finished, he placed his huge hands on the flywheel, rocked it back and forth until it gained momentum, and then, with a twist of his muscular body, pulled through the stroke. The engine turned over but didn't catch: SSSSSSSSSSSS-HA--HA---HA, and the flywheel came to rest with the sound of a panting dog.

---

[17] Prior to World War II, many U.S. residences with telephone service, particularly those in rural areas, had "party lines." Two or more households shared the same line and each had a distinctive ring (for example, three longs and one short). In some areas, subscribers could dial local calls directly; in others, all calls went through a central operator. This operator often became a focal point for the community: part answering service, part weatherman, part purveyor of local gossip. Since those on a party line could listen to each other's conversations, phone service was often looked on as a community resource rather than as a means of exchanging private information. The vast majority of party lines were phased out by the 1970s.

After making some minor adjustments, he spun it again, and this time: POP----POP—POP-POPPOPPOPPOP, that wonderful sound so familiar to John Deere fans everywhere.[18]

Judd climbed up on the iron seat, and I was right behind him. Off we went to cultivate those potatoes, and from my position on his lap, he let me drive and work the controls. This time I was determined not to mess up, and I gave my full concentration to keeping the V-front wheels positioned so as not to damage the crop. We worked half the morning, with only a brief break for water and a chat. I probably didn't apologize because I didn't know how, but I think Judd could tell I was contrite, and he forgave me without speech. By dinnertime, everything seemed back to normal. I had dodged a bullet, learned a lesson, and was reminded, once again, that refusing to cooperate on the farm was like saying bad words in church: Once the mistake was made, it was too late to take it back, but a smart person didn't do it again.

My first week with Mill and Maude sped by, every day a new adventure. Looking back, I may have learned more that week than during any other single week in my life: facts about machines, animals, milking, and doing chores. My chores were easy: feed the pigs, hay and grain Harold the bull, change the filters in the milk cans, and help clean up at night. By week's end, I was proud of myself and of my contributions to life on the farm. How did they ever cope before I arrived?

Sunday was a light day, only four or five hours of work milking and feeding the herd, but there was other activity afoot. Grandmother, Betty, and Aunt Carolyn were bringing my red wagon and my bike—it looked like I'd passed muster—and coming for Sunday dinner. Millard and I found the main course in the henhouse, a nice-looking rooster that we carried by the legs to the chopping block near the back door. After a couple of practice swings, I chopped off his head and delivered the dead carcass to Maude. She showed me how to help clean and pluck it, and I watched her start the chicken stew.

Once dinner was simmering on the cast-iron stove, I waited with some apprehension for my kin, and it wasn't long before the Olds showed up in the

---

[18] John Deere began the company that bears his name in 1838 by building and selling a polished-steel plow that let pioneer farmers cut clean furrows through the Midwest prairie soil. As the company grew it began to manufacture other farm implements, and in 1918 it purchased a tractor manufacturer. The first tractor with the Deere name, the two-cylinder Model D, was introduced in 1923, and the John Deere tractor, along with the Farmall brand manufactured by International Harvester, became a mainstay of U.S. farmers. As of 2008, John Deere is a major conglomerate, producing commercial and consumer products, including tractors, for the U.S. and international markets.

drive. Before we sat down to eat, Millard gave them a short tour of the barn, and Maude showed them the henhouse and her beautiful garden.

Dinner was festive but somewhat awkward. Grandmother was a lady with superior airs, and I could tell she didn't entirely approve of Maude's cooking. I think she felt it lacked the finesse of her more citified ways, but I thought it was delicious. Toward the end of the meal, I was beginning to relax when my mother asked Maude if she had called Tuesday evening. "I was visiting the neighbors," Betty said, "and I ran back to the apartment just as the phone stopped."

"No," Maude said slowly, "I don't recall doing that." Whew. Sometimes you make the train and sometimes you don't. Perhaps that day my angel was fooling with me a bit, but just in case, I was careful to add nothing to the conversation. After dessert, I excused myself, explaining that I had a dam in progress in the woods.

"Nice to see you; so long," and I was out the door. When I returned later in the day, they had gone, apparently satisfied that all was well.

Although it could have been otherwise, the transition from my living with my family in the city to living with Maude and Millard on the farm was relatively painless for all of us. Grandmother and Betty could see that I was happy, which probably helped to alleviate any guilty feelings they might have had. And I was now a farmer with chores, responsibilities, and endless fun. In some ways I thought of them as city folk from another life.

As time went on, my mother and grandmother visited less often, but Grandpa was a frequent sight, purring up the drive in his immaculate '38 Buick Roadmaster. Both Maude and Mill liked him and he them, even though their backgrounds were worlds apart. I, too, was glad to see him, as he and I were very close. His own children had chosen sides, and as often happens in a conflict when the woman has a powerful personality, they had chosen their mother. Thus, it was up to the next generation (me) to interact with the warring factions, and this I was only too happy to do.

The Farmer and His Wife

As days on the farm rolled into weeks and then months, I had ample opportunity to observe Mill and Maude amid the rhythms of everyday life. Millard had only an eighth-grade education, yet he kept up with the news and was well informed. He didn't talk a lot, so I never found out much about his background. Instead, he was that rare individual who listened attentively, never interrupted, and responded when necessary with grunts: yep, nope, or the guttural German *da*.

Grandpa comes for Sunday dinner on the farm.
L. to r.: Millard, Maude, and Grandpa with Spot.

He was so homely he was spectacular, with huge ears, sparkling blue eyes, and a continually bemused expression. He was also brown as a berry, and when he rolled up his sleeves to wash for dinner, his skin showed the stark contrast between brown and white. His gnarled hands, scarred from a

45

series of minor mishaps, were as strong and as rough as coarse sandpaper, and although he wore a truss to keep his many ruptures in place, he could lift like a young buck.

In every aspect of life, Millard was methodical, working hard at an orderly pace and rarely hurrying. He lived life by routine: up by 5 a.m., then down to the barn to milk and feed the animals. Hitch Prince or Polly to the sledge, load it with 20-gallon milk containers, and drag it to the stand by the road, where the milk truck showed up at the same time day after day, regardless of the weather.

After the truck left, Mill returned to the barn and rubbed down the horse before returning to the house for breakfast and a short break. Then off he'd go to the fields until dinner, sometimes working with Judd and sometimes alone. Dinner was an hour-long event: wash up, sit by the window and read the *Buffalo Courier-Express* for 15 minutes, eat, sit and meditate for another 15 minutes, and return to the fields.

Mill with Polly and Prince.

On hot summer days, the cows stayed in the woods until Mill and I fetched them for milking. Mill walked with a rolling gait, using a staff to guide the cows and steady himself, so of course I had to have a staff as well. I peppered him with questions and comments on these walks, and Mill seemed to enjoy what I had to say. Usually we found the cows in the coolest part of the woods by the brook, and more often than not, they'd ruined the dam I'd built the day before. "COOOOOM, BOSSS, COOOOOM," Millard's deep voice bellowed, and I followed his steady, patient stride as we led the cows out of the coolness and back to the barn.

When the milking was finished, we cleaned the gutters with a shovel and wheelbarrow, a chore you can bet I now did without question or complaint. We then grained the livestock and, depending on the season, turned them out to pasture or gave them hay. The last chore of the day was sweeping the barn between the rows of stanchions. I can still see Millard, head down, legs bowed in his rubber boots, and wielding a straw broom: sweep, sweep, steady, steady—the rhythmic, methodical motion by which he lived his life.

After supper and a final check on the livestock, Mill spent time reading, doing the books, or playing a game or two of rummy with me. No man was ever more even-tempered or content with his lot in life, and during my time on the farm, I was almost always by his side, helping and keeping him company. Again I thought, *How did he ever get along before I got here?*

Maude, who was as outgoing as Millard was taciturn, was a woman of great inner strength and a full partner on the farm. She was short and somewhat stout, with thin skin, a strong body, and hair that was always rumpled, no matter what she did to it. In addition to cooking, washing, and doing the housework, she mowed the large lawn and maintained a huge vegetable and flower garden. This was a woman with a true green thumb: Plants just grew for her, and she often sold cut flowers along with the extra produce.

She also took advantage of the farm's many berries, both cultivated and wild. Starting with spring strawberries from the garden and the sweetest, smallest wild strawberries from the fields, she spent hours picking, making shortcakes, and putting by endless jars of jam to add to the rows in the pantry. The saga was repeated with raspberries and blackberries, and there wasn't a day without a fresh fruit pie cooling in the window, just waiting for our enjoyment after a day in the fields.

Sometimes I went along on these berry-picking expeditions, my favorite being elderberries. A huge hedgerow of them grew by the back 20, and I stripped them off by the handful, gobbling them down little stems and all. Before long, my hands and face were purple with the juice, and there's no doubt I ate as many as I contributed to the berry pail.

No matter what she was doing, Maude was always delightfully cheerful, and I loved being with her, listening to her stories of the earth and the farm. In the evening when her chores were done, she often came down to the barn. After Mill removed the milking machine, she helped strip the cows of their remaining milk and then cleaned the machine while Millard finished his chores.

Just inside the barn door, a sign on the wall read, "If I only had one cow and she only had one teat, I would still use my Surge milker." All cows, however, were not in agreement with this sentiment. Milking machines create noise as well as pressure on the teats, and sometimes one of Mill's young cows just coming into milk was terrified by this mechanical process. In that case, Maude conditioned the cow for the machine by milking it by hand.

I watched how carefully she stripped the cows. She balanced on a three-

Hey! It looked easy when Maude did it.
(*Illustration by Babe Sargent.*)

legged stool, placing the pail between her legs, or in some cases on the floor, to extract that final bit of milk. The cows were mellow and plump. Their bags varied in size, as did their teats, and they knew Maude and trusted her as she went about her work. The first time I tried to emulate her technique, I sat on the stool and buried my forehead in the cow's belly, placing the bucket on the floor as I couldn't get it to stay between my legs. I grabbed a teat and squeezed. The cow twisted in the stanchion with a distrustful, wild look in her eye, kicked over the pail, stepped on my foot, switched her shit-covered tail in my face, and knocked me on my butt. Despite this inauspicious beginning, eventually I developed the strength and dexterity to do the job well, which meant that Maude was relieved of a chore and I was proudly earning my keep.

In addition to her other tasks, Maude maintained the chicken coops, and after a while one of my chores was to collect the eggs. Although it took practice to learn how to slide my hand under a sitting hen without getting pecked or cracking the eggs, in this area, too, I soon felt my presence to be indispensable.

In the evenings when Mill worked on the books or played rummy with me, Maude checked the day's eggs for deformities or blood spots by looking at each one through the light of a candle. Those that passed muster were packed for sale in her popular egg business. Today's eggs are checked for imperfections using electricity, but the process is still called "candling."

Like Millard, Maude had only completed the eighth grade, but she read magazines and the daily newspaper, listened to the radio, and helped with the books. She was a keen observer of life and knew how and when to extend kindness to those around her. For example, one of the neighbors who lived down the road was a loud, stout woman named Edna. Edna laughed like a hyena, and both the trailer she lived in and the ground surrounding it looked like a war zone. If that weren't enough, her two sons were in the state prison for one crime or another, and she swore like a trooper. I'd never been around profane people, and her language fascinated me. "She's just low class and doesn't know any better," Maude said by way of explanation, "but she has a good heart."[19]

Maude often bought eggs from Edna, claiming that her own eggs were spoken for, and Edna's car rarely left our drive without some produce or a chunk of meat that was "just going to waste." "Why do you buy eggs from her," I asked. Maude explained that Edna needed the money, and looking back, I can see that this arrangement worked for both of them. Maude was able to offer help with compassion, and Edna was able to accept that help with dignity.

Mill and Maude were a well-matched team, and I never heard a cross

---

[19] The educational standards of the late 19th and early 20th centuries were such that students finished the eighth grade with a working knowledge of language, math, and history unknown to many of today's high school graduates. For example, "Give rules for [the] principal marks of punctuation" and "A wagon box is 2 feet deep, 10 feet long, and 3 feet wide. How many bushels of wheat will it hold?" were questions from an 1895 eighth-grade examination on file at the Smoky Valley Genealogical Society and Library in Salina, Kansas. Maude and Millard would have been in the eighth grade between 1900 and 1903.

word between them. They married later than most and may have been distant cousins, as Maude's maiden name was also Hudson, and the area contained many members of the extended Hudson family. Although they slept in separate bedrooms and I never witnessed any loving, physical contact between them, at least for once there was no bickering. *What a relief*, I thought. *This is the way it must be for a couple to be happy.*

Maude and Mill were childless and knew little about raising children. As a result, I was left unsupervised far more than I might have been in another family, and I don't remember this ever causing a problem. In general, I abided by the few rules that existed, did my chores, helped out when I could, and loved the increasing responsibility I was given; in fact, I sought it.

Clothes Make the Man (or Woman)

People that I knew dressed for themselves rather than for others; they had pride in their appearance no matter what their class or financial position. Rich or poor, heavy or slender, how you looked was a reflection of who you were and how you felt about yourself. In my case, I may have been passed around like a hot coal in a foundry, but I was always dressed properly, and farm life had its proprieties, too.

Maude worked in a housedress, but she changed to a newer, neater dress each evening. Inside that unrefined exterior was a lady who loved to dress up for get-togethers. Millard always wore a blue work shirt and one of his three pairs of bib overalls: a working pair, an after-supper-and-chores pair, and a dress-up pair that were starched and creased. I can think of only one or two occasions when I saw him in a suit. When he laughed, his huge Adam's apple bobbed above his shirt collar.

Now that I was a farmer, I wanted to dress like one, too, and so the first chance we got, Millard took me to the nearby town of Strykersville in his 1937 blue Plymouth sedan. Being an Oldsmobile man, myself, I teased him about his car and its velour seats, but I was thrilled when we went to the feed and general dry goods store and he bought me some bib overalls just like his. All summer long, I lived in those overalls or in shorts, minus a shirt except for dinner, with underwear and shoes dispensed with as well. When we entered the house, the men left their shoes or boots by the door. Maude left me a bucket of water for my bare feet.

Monday was washday, and Maude scrubbed our clothes on a washboard and turned them through a hand wringer. We washed ourselves at the pump before eating and, for more extensive ablutions, bathed in the brook. When the weather got cooler, we occasionally filled the galvanized tub in the kitchen and took turns bathing, each person using the same water.

At Grandmother's, cleanliness had truly been next to godliness, and admittedly things were not as clean on the farm, but for farmers we were cleaner than most. And we must have done something right, as we rarely suffered from colds or sickness of any kind.

Solving the Mystery of Harold

One of my chores was feeding Harold the bull. Although Harold was huge, sleek, and well-muscled, he didn't seem to do much, and I couldn't quite figure out his function on the farm. One day, Millard asked if I wanted to go with him when he took Harold to the Ulrichs. One of our closest neighbors, the Ulrichs had a farm down Centerline Road about a quarter mile away. "Sure," said I, noticing that Harold seemed quite docile as Mill placed a clip stick in his nose ring and started off.

Harold woos his lady fair.
(*Illustration by Babe Sargent.*)

"Why are we taking Harold to the Ulrichs?" I asked. Mill, sparing even more words than usual, muttered something about visiting Molly, and I let it drop.

When we reached the farm, the Ulrich boys were waiting for us, and we all marched into the barn. Molly was in her stanchion, her demeanor one of romance and anticipation. As Harold mounted her, the Ulrich boys laughed. "Brace yourself, Molly!" Then (good golly, where did *that* come from) Harold penetrated her, and they both seemed to enjoy the experience. Afterward, Harold was a bit reluctant to leave, but with his nose ring we soon had him home and in his stanchion, and Mill asked me to give him a double ration of grain.

Okay, I got it. Harold had an enjoyable job, didn't have to work too often, received double rations when he performed, and was grumpy when not employed. Did this have something to do with why the boys tried to lure the girls into the woods? If so, I wasn't entirely sure why the girls resisted—after all, Molly had seemed to enjoy herself—but I figured it would get clearer in time. Plus, I now had a start on the language of love: Brace yourself, girls!

Chapter 10 – Old Family and New Friends

1942

Soon after I arrived at the farm, Maude and I took a walk down the road to the Darbees. A smaller and less tidy operation, this farm was owned by wizened old Grandpa Darbee and his wife and occupied by three generations. Two of the Darbee grandsons, Nathaniel and Bruce, were just about my age, and we hit it off immediately. Soon we were inseparable, spending time after chores having earthy horse ball fights or jumping in fresh cow plops and trying to spatter each other with the gooey mess, which oozed through our toes. We built lean-tos in the woods, gorged ourselves on the fruit of the season, and played in the brook, though we did stay away from the deep-running creek at the back edge of the farm. We also used the brook to create an elaborate dam system, complete with rapids through which we raced leaf boats. Boys from surrounding farms would often join us, and though we sometimes tried to get the girls into the woods, we never had any luck. *Just as well*, I thought. *What would we do with them? They didn't even enjoy jumping in cow plops.*

By the height of the growing season, we had our own hideaway, a labyrinth of trails through cornstalks that, rich with summer sun and rain, towered over small boys. At the crossroads of the trails we beat down some of the stalks to create a "house" with walls, and we even had our own outhouse. We spent many a happy hour in this pint-sized preserve, and at harvest, Millard never complained about the lost corn.

On Sundays, I often went to church with the Darbees. I had always enjoyed church, but Maude and Mill didn't attend often. The Darbees belonged to the Tabernacle Church, an evangelical congregation that met at the Roycroft Inn in East Aurora. I enjoyed the experience. To be a Christian was natural and easy for me, no matter how it was presented.

Occasionally Grandmother and Betty came to visit. I was glad to see them, but I really didn't have much time. I was busy with my chores and adventures in the woods with my friends, and, besides, I could tell that my grandmother was uncomfortable. Although she lacked advanced education, Grandmother had risen above her background, and she prided herself on being "proper." She was well-read and well-spoken, and she dressed carefully and with class. In contrast, when she looked at me, she saw a farm boy in bib overalls with unruly hair (cut by Maude with sheep sheers) and bare feet that looked as if I'd stomped in a cow plop. If she only knew. In addition, my vocabulary now emulated many of the farmers. Sentences peppered with "yep" and "nope" and phrases such as "I ain't et yet" had replaced the more sophisticated speech patterns of my citified past.

Unlike Grandmother, Betty saw some humor in the situation, and she would come with her friend, Hymie Davidoff, to share Sunday dinner. And of course, Grandpa was always welcome, entertaining one and all with his yarns of the rail yard.

The only times Maude and Millard became tense or angry with my relatives was when my father came to see me. As a young child in Buffalo, I saw my father rarely. When I lived on the farm, I saw him only twice. The first time he came in his convertible with a new girlfriend and wanted to take me out for the day. Maude had an instinctive distrust of Ken, but when he said, "How about the races?" and I responded with glee, she went along with the plan. I had a great time that day amid the speed, noise, and commotion, but when we returned to the farm late in the evening, Maude was angry and worried.

The second time Ken showed up with a different woman—a wife, this time, as well as I can remember—and again, Maude reluctantly let me go. But the new wife was rude and threatened to lock me in the trunk, and when I was really scared, my father didn't rally to my side. Later I told Maude what had happened, and she must have confronted him, because I never saw my father again. Bravo, Maude. Nobody messed with "her boy."[20]

A Boy Needs a Dog

Skip, the black and white terrier that greeted me on my first day at the farm, was old and crippled. His days of being able to keep up with an active youngster were long gone. Soon he had to be put down, and when the Hauber family up the road had a litter of fox terrier mutts, Maude let me choose one just for me. We had always had a family dog and cat at Grandmother's, but this was going to be *my* dog, and I chose carefully: a black and white male. I named him Spot.

[20] When I was 18, I talked with Ken on the phone, but after that day at the farm, I never again laid eyes on him. To the best of my knowledge, he passed away in the early 1970s.

On Spot's first night home, Maude helped me arrange a cardboard box in the kitchen that was big enough for both of us, and we bedded down together. Oops, what's that? At three in the morning, I woke up to find my nightshirt covered with wet spots, after which I promptly retreated to my cot. Spot now had a nickname, and he kept it forever: Spotty Stinker.

In spite of this rocky beginning, Spot was smart and easily trained, and we were now a quintet: Maude, Millard, Judd, Spot, and me. Each member of the team had his or her responsibilities on the farm. Spot did his part by proudly depositing a dead woodchuck on the doorstop each day. It seemed he was determined to single-handedly eliminate the species from western New York.

Country Get-Togethers

Saturday evening was usually reserved for visiting. Maude changed to a fresh dress and Mill to his starched and pressed bib overalls and a clean blue work shirt. In eager anticipation, I donned my bib overalls, washed my hands and feet, and away we went in the Plymouth. Maude sat in the backseat, as prim and proper as a queen, while I sat in the front and harassed Mill about his fancy car with its velvety seats, as opposed, of course, to the finer qualities of the Oldsmobile.

At the hosting farm, the menfolk sat on the front porch and complained about farm prices (way too low), the rain (way too much or way too little), and the war (worry over their boys in combat). Unwinding after a week of hard work, they drank beer, smoked cigars, and used profanity. Occasionally, even Millard said something funny that was off-color, but since he wasn't given to using such language, he usually sounded like an amateur actor flubbing his lines.

The women gathered in the kitchen, gossiping and giggling. Sometimes a Gold Star Mother was present and received comfort from her friends.[21]

Among both the men and the women, I was known as Mill and Maude's boy. I'm not sure if anybody knew my name. "How's the boy doing, Millard?"

---

[21] American Gold Star Mothers was established in 1928 to offer solace to mothers who had lost a son in the First World War. It was later expanded to include mothers of fallen servicemen and women from World War II and subsequent conflicts. According to its charter, the organization is committed to "perpetuate the memory of those whose lives were sacrificed in our wars." During World War II, approximately 300 gold stars were awarded each day. As of 2008, the ranks of Gold Star Mothers continue to grow as sons and daughters give their lives in service to their country.

"Good. What'd you pay for chicken feed last week?"

Kids at these gatherings were plentiful, and I made instant friends. We played joyously, with little or no conflict, and there were no bullies. Sometimes we organized a pickup softball game or shot a few baskets, but mostly we did farm stuff: jumping and falling into the hay while walking a beam in the barn, playing hide and go seek, climbing trees or ropes, or playing tag.

I enjoyed these activities, but when everyone headed to the creek for a swim, I rarely joined in. For one thing, polio had ravished many youngsters of my generation, and swimming and water were associated with that feared and dreadful disease. For another, I was afraid of drowning. Water was great to drink, to wash with if forced, or to dam the brook, but I had never learned to swim and I stayed out of deep water. I still do.[22]

On most of these excursions, boys and girls played together, but the farm girls rarely got caught in the grain bin or haymow, usually slipping through the net with giggles and laughter. They, too, knew about Harold and had helped many a calf being pulled out of a cow's body. As for me, I still didn't fully understand the game, let alone the rules, but it sure looked promising.

---

[22] Polio (poliomyelitis) was a paralyzing disease that terrified many in the first half of the 20th century. It struck its victims, mostly children, without warning, though its most famous victim may have been Franklin Delano Roosevelt, who contracted the disease as an adult in 1921. In the early 1950s, Jonas Salk developed a polio vaccine, and by 1955, thousands of children were being vaccinated. In 1962, the Sabin oral vaccine replaced the Salk injection, and by the year 2000 the disease was nearly eradicated worldwide.

Chapter 11 – School Days and Other Forms of Learning

1942

My first summer on the farm was nearly over. The corn was tall and beginning to tassel out, and the maple tree in the front yard sported a branch of yellow, gold, and red. Fall was coming—no denying it—and one morning Maude and Mill loaded me into the Plymouth for a trip to the dry goods store in East Aurora. There they bought me some new bib overalls and a blue shirt like Mill's. They also bought me underwear, socks, and sneakers.

"Why, Maude? I don't wear those things."

"That's the rules for school."

"Come on-n-n."

Mill piped in: "A rule's a rule." Since this was the first "rule" I'd heard in the nearly three months I'd lived on the farm, I grudgingly accepted it.

On September 8, 1942, the Tuesday after Labor Day, I started off to school in my new duds, sporting a shiny book bag for my first day in the third grade. The one-room schoolhouse was a mile away, and Nathaniel and Bruce Darbee joined me as we ran up the hill with Spot at our side and pulling my red wagon behind us. The school served grades 1 through 6, and our teacher, Ms. Caroline McConnell, was a pro. She enjoyed children and had dealt with farm kids for years, but she also knew how to clamp down on us like a lid on a boiling pot. We were eager to learn, but we were also restless after our summer of freedom. At the end of the day we burst out of the doors with joyful exuberance. I whipped off my sneakers and socks, jumped in my red wagon, and coasted home down Centerline Road.

Each school day thereafter I set off with Spotty Stinker, either riding my bike or pulling the wagon behind me. When I was in class, Spot hung around the area, occasionally depositing a freshly killed woodchuck at the schoolroom door. I loved this school. For one thing, even though I was officially a third grader, I could take the subjects I loved and at which I excelled—reading, literature, and art—with the sixth graders. I read every book in the schoolhouse, plus more that the teacher would bring in for me. In science I was at a third-grade level, but my math and spelling were poor. At spelling bees, even though I was sometimes placed with first and second grades, I was always the first to sit down.

Our one-room-school classroom in Wales Hollow, 1946. I'd moved on by then, but Bruce and Nathaniel Darbee are in the second row, second and third from the left. (*Courtesy of Nancy Hauber Holmes.*)

School was a self-contained operation so we had chores to do: bringing in wood for the potbellied stove when the weather turned cold, helping with lunch, and cleaning up. We were one happy bunch of kids, and Ms. McConnell was magnificent.

There was only one fly in the ointment. I knew that Grandmother had reservations about me living on the farm, and this worried me. I had found my paradise, and I didn't want to lose it. It wasn't that Grandmother didn't like Maude and Mill. She appreciated them as hard-working and competent, but she felt they were on a lower social plane. She did not approve of her grandson slipping into farm-boy mode, and she would have pulled me off the farm in an instant if she could have found someplace more acceptable.

Sometimes I wondered if Grandmother might have been a queen or princess in a past life.

My concerns about this issue were strongest when the Buffalo entourage came to visit, and one of those visits was scheduled just after school started. Grandmother, Betty, and Aunt Carolyn were coming to dinner. On the day of the event, I was having a séance down in the woods at my favorite hideout, a lean-to I'd built on a cliff above the brook at the edge of the hemlock forest and maple grove. I can still smell the scent of hemlocks stirred by the breeze and see the shafts of light streaming through deep green maples splashed with fall color. Not even Nathaniel and Bruce were aware of this site. This was my place, my connection with earth and space, a mystical spot of contentment and happiness. It was in this place that I made my first mature decision.

I knew that to remain in paradise, Grandmother had to be convinced I was holding my own on the rungs of the social ladder. On this point Betty, Carolyn, and even my grandfather were minor players. Grandmother Alice was the boss; hers was the only decision that counted. So I came up with a tactical, political compromise: When my family was at the farm, I would be what they wanted me to be, a prince fit for Grandmother the queen.

I washed in the brook with soap and water, put my town clothes—now a bit too small but still presentable—and added shoes and socks. Once everyone arrived, I talked properly and as much as possible became Little Lord Fauntleroy. It worked; the visit was a roaring success. Maude and Grandmother raved about the rolling hills and fields ablaze around us and declared this part of America unequaled for year-round beauty, and thereafter Grandmother visited infrequently. Now that she felt I was okay, an occasional call or letter sufficed. Maude never commented on my Sunday-dinner antics, but when Grandpa or my mother and Hymie visited in the future, they were more than welcome. After all, they didn't pose a threat.[23]

---

[23] A classic children's book by Frances Hodgson Burnett, *Little Lord Fauntleroy* was first serialized in an English magazine in 1885 and published in book form in 1886. It tells the story of a poor American boy who inherits a fortune and goes to live in a mansion in England with his cold, unfeeling British grandfather. In 1936 the book was made into a film starring Freddie Bartholomew as Lord Fauntleroy.

Chapter 12 – Fall Rituals and Winter Tales
1942–1943

I still had chores to do on weekends and before and after school, including slopping the pigs, feeding Harold, and caring for Jessie, the goat Maude had bought for me at the county fair. Early in the fall, the corn harvest was in high gear, and I tried to help as often as possible. Mill and Judd ran a horse-drawn cutter to cut and bind the corn, which was then loaded onto the hay wagon and brought to the silo. Back at the barn, a chopper and blower, driven by a belt system from our faithful John Deere, reduced the crop to pieces suitable for silage. In the house, the pantry shelves were bulging with food Maude had put by; the silos served the same purpose for the animals.

Farm life could be repetitious, but even so, I learned something new almost every day. There were very few things I was forbidden to do, but when Millard or Judd asked me to stay back from the farm machinery, I listened. Every piece of gear we hooked up to the tractor or team had moving parts or sharp tines that offered a million ways to maim or kill, and I was smart enough to recognize the need for caution. My next encounter with danger, however, had nothing to do with the farm's mechanical monsters.

Shortly before Thanksgiving, Millard and Judd built a fire under a large tub filled with water. "What's up, Mill?" I asked.

"Time to process the pig," he replied. After the water had been heating for some time and the tub was a steaming cauldron, Millard set up a tripod next to it and Judd led the hog out of the pen with a stick through the ring in its nose. It was the same stick that we used for Harold. Once the hog was positioned properly, Judd dropped a couple of makeshift lassos over it and pulled tight so the critter was hog-tied and could barely move. Then the men passed a line from its rear feet through a pulley system Mill had set up on the tripod, and Judd straddled the animal and slit its throat.

At this point, all hell broke loose. When Mill and Judd tried to snatch the leads through the pulley system, the hog wrenched himself out of the rope sling. He squealed wildly, thrashing around in front of the barn and knocking over the tub of boiling water. He was banging into anything in the area, and we were in the area. The three of us scrambled to the top of the milk house, the first and only time I saw Millard abandon his methodical, steady demeanor.

The pig soon expired, and we somewhat shamefully set up the tub again. When the water was ready, we gutted out the carcass, dunked it into the boiling cauldron, and shaved the coarse hair from its pink hide. Meanwhile, Maude was standing over the stove, rendering lard from the fat covering the guts. It was my job to supply the guts, and I ran back and forth to the kitchen toting buckets overflowing with steaming entrails. After the pig had been sufficiently processed, the carcass was quartered and left to hang in the barn. The next day, Maude canned certain cuts for us to enjoy in the summer when no refrigeration was available. Millard took the hams and bacon to the smokehouse, a small building that had been on the farm since day one and was used every year for just this purpose. The smoking process took awhile. In the meantime, we enjoyed fresh pork kept from spoiling by the cool temperatures of fall.

Processing the pig.
(*Illustration by Babe Sargent.*)

Winter in the Country

Winter comes hard and early in western New York, but I was accustomed to the snow and I liked it. For the mile trek uphill to school in the morning, I wore bear-claw snowshoes, dragging my Flexible Flyer behind me. There was hardly any traffic on Centerline Road, so at night I could belly-flop on the sled for a quick and exciting ride home.[24]

The harsh weather did make it harder to visit friends who lived a distance away, but I never minded the isolation. In fact, I really liked hanging around with Mill and Maude. They were kind and interesting companions, and they never seemed to tire of my company. Every day since arriving at the farm, I'd sat on Mill's lap beside the double-hung window in the kitchen and tried to get him to say "uncle" by bending back his gnarled finger. Usually I was the one who laughingly cried "uncle."

The farm work to be done outdoors in winter was greatly reduced, though we still had to milk morning and night, feed the animals, and clean the barn. Most of the time, the snow was too deep to move the manure wagon, so we piled manure in the barnyard, one wheelbarrow at a time, to be loaded into the spreader come spring.

After morning milking, even in the coldest weather, Millard hitched either Prince or Polly to the sledge and took the milk to the pickup point on the side of the road. Tamping down the snow with the sledge, rather than plowing, is what kept the drive open. I'll never know how Mill managed to lift those milk cans, given his several hernias, but I never heard him complain. He returned to the barn to rub down and feed the horse after the milk truck came, working at the same slow, steady pace regardless of the outside temperature. When I wasn't in school, I was by his side.

After morning chores we read the *Courier-Express* and chatted about the events of the day. One of my favorite sections was the comics, especially *Terry and the Pirates*. My imagination was fertile, and reading about the exploits of Terry and his fellow aviators in the Far East made me feel a part of the war. The planes they flew were the same P-40s that Betty and Grandmother were building.[25]

---

[24] The Flexible Flyer, one of the first steerable sleds, was invented in 1889 by Samuel Leeds Allen, a farm-equipment manufacturer with a love of sledding and a need to keep his factory workers at the S. L. Allen Co. busy during the winter months. The company was sold in 1968, but the sleds, which are known for their sturdy wood construction and bright-red eagle logo, are still manufactured in 2008.

[25] Created by cartoonist Milton Caniff, *Terry and the Pirates* was a syndicated, action-adventure comic strip that ran from 1934 until 1973. After America's entry into World War II, Terry joined the U.S. Air Force, and the strip became focused on the war. One

I was also stirred up by reading fine books—lots of them. That winter, Jack London was my favorite author.[26]

Millard and Judd took advantage of the reduced winter workload to oil, grease, and repair tools and machinery during the day. After supper, hardly a night went by without a hard-fought rummy game, even though my small hands were barely able to hold all the cards. And the checkerboard was always set up, a continuous game in progress between chores.

With less to do in the fields, winter generated a greater social life in our farming community, including church suppers, bingo, and whist, one of Maude's favorites. And as for news of the wider world, the radio in the barn was always on, and sometimes the one in the house as well. Maude had an old, dog-eared atlas from which she tracked war events as they unfolded, so the war was always with us, but much of our time and energy was focused on planning for the planting and rotation of crops.

Maude and Mill may not have been formally educated, but they were well-read and had a lifetime of experience with proper farming methods. As I was learning to appreciate more and more, farming was an amazingly complex business, and to be successful took careful planning. Decisions like which crops were to be planted in which fields were very important, and in this planning process, I was treated like a full partner. My opinion was solicited, and Mill and Maude shared almost every decision with me. Best of all, they included some of my suggestions in their plans.

We got huge amounts of snow that winter, often accompanied by blizzards that racked the house and barn, but inside we were warm and safe. The wood-burning furnace, fed by huge tree butts that Mill had sledged the previous winter, filled the dirt-floor cellar. Any residual morning chill was cured by Maude's cookstove, from which breakfast smells of home-smoked bacon and biscuits wafted into every corner of the house. In the evenings when Millard and I played rummy, Maude would often kibitz while standing over the large floor grate between the kitchen and sitting room. The heat from this grate warmed the entire downstairs, and Maude's housedress would billow out like a parachute from the warm air below.

---

episode in which Terry's trainer gives a speech about the responsibilities of a fighter pilot was read aloud in Congress to become part of the Congressional Record.

[26] Jack London (1876–1916) was one of America's most prolific writers. During his short life, London worked as a laborer, factory worker, oyster pirate on San Francisco Bay, member of the California Fish Patrol, journalist, rancher, sailor, railroad hobo, and gold prospector. He was a master at portraying the people of his life and times, as well as man's never-ending struggle against nature. His more than 50 books, plus numerous short stories, articles, and letters, continue to enthrall readers to this day.

Near the Christmas holidays, Millard and I took Prince into the woods to get a Christmas tree. We settled on a beautiful spruce. Prince dragged it back through the snow, the bells on his harness tinkling in the winter stillness, and Millard and Judd set it up in the parlor. That Sunday, Maude invited Grandmother and Betty for dinner. The table was laden with the many delights Maude had put up during the growing season, plus the usual chicken, which I had dispatched and cleaned. After the meal, Maude brought out a box of antique ornaments and put a record of Christmas carols on the windup Victrola. Grandmother and Betty stayed to help decorate. We hung the ornaments on the tree and festooned the old farmhouse with hemlock and pine boughs. It felt, looked, and smelled like Christmas, and I was as happy as a boy could be.[27]

As the day wound down, Betty asked if I'd finished packing what I needed to spend Christmas vacation in the city. I squirmed around. *My place was here. Christmas was here,* but I didn't know how to say it. Betty looked at my face. "Would you rather stay on the farm?" she asked.

"Oh, yes," I said, probably with far more enthusiasm than called for. "Maude and Mill depend on me to help with the chores. I have to feed Harold, I have to gather the eggs, and my goat Jessie needs me."

After a short powwow, Grandmother and Betty conceded that since they were each away for many hours of the day—Grandmother at the war plant, my mother at her engineering classes at the University of Buffalo— maybe I *would* be better off on the farm. They started to get ready for the drive back to East Aurora, but before they left, I showed them the picture of my favorite Daisy BB gun, the most popular brand of a young boy's right-of-passage. I had torn that picture out of the Sears, Roebuck catalogue and carried it with me for weeks, showing it to anyone I thought might be of influence. I even prayed about it. Usually my nightly prayers were non-specific, but in this case I described the gun in great detail, just in case God wasn't looking at the picture. And to keep the cost down, I was always sure to mention that it was the single-shot version I coveted. Grandmother and Betty were noncommittal.

---

[27] Introduced in 1901 by the Victor Talking Machine Company (later RCA-Victor), the Victrola was a windup phonograph used in the days before electricity was widely available. Original models of the machine were equipped with a huge horn through which sound was projected. In later models, the horn was internal. Although other firms produced these types of phonographs, people often used the term "Victrola" as a generic name for the device. By the 1920s, electric units had captured a large share of the phonograph market, although windup machines continued to be used into the 1950s, particularly in rural areas.

A Boy and His Gun

On Christmas morning 1942 we awoke to a driving snowstorm—a perfect, glorious day. The hills were covered in snow like frosting on a cake, but farm chores must be done regardless of weather, even on Christmas. After milking, haying, and graining the cows, we came in to a bountiful breakfast, then cranked up the Victrola and sat down to exchange gifts. My heart was filled with anticipation, but though I'd been scouting under the tree for days, I saw nothing long and slim. Perhaps they'd hidden it.

"You go first, Don," said Maude, and I opened the smallest package. Hand-knit mittens. Nice. I handed Millard the gift I'd wrapped for him.

"Thank you, Don." He tore open the wrapping paper: a package of red bandana handkerchiefs. With a big smile, Mill reached under the tree and handed Maude her present from him. Maude took it and handed me another. It was a pair of hand-knit wool socks. I knew they'd come in handy, but I was starting to get worried. There was only one present left with my name on it. It was in a big box. Could it be that the gun was in there?

"Is it okay if I open this last present?" I heard myself saying.

"Sure, go ahead, Don," said Maude. I gingerly tore at the wrapping paper, but as each piece came away, my confidence sank. The box was filled with playing cards and a checkerboard. I let out a sigh. Great. Would I ever feel like playing again?

I felt deserted. Everyone had let me down, even my guardian angel. Maude seemed to notice my disappointment. "Don, you must be tired from the excitement of the day. Why don't you go upstairs and lie down?"

"Yep, I think I will." I'd had so much hope. I had prayed; I had asked; I had done everything I could possibly think of to bring this treasure to my side. My head was heavy and my trigger finger itched. As I clumped slowly up the stairs, each footfall sounded like a broken drum. This was the worst Christmas ever.

When I reached my cot, I turned around and flung myself onto it backward, but something was in the way—something big, and long. It made a crackling sound. I jumped up and pulled back the covers. Could it possibly be? I ripped off the wrapping paper and there it was: my brand new, single-shot, Daisy BB gun.

Clutching this treasure in front of me, I ran down the stairs, screeching with joy, while Maude and Mill convulsed in laughter at my amazing discovery. My prayers had been answered. My guardian angel had not failed me. This was the best Christmas ever.

From that moment on, the gun and I were one. I carried it to school each day, even though we weren't allowed to fire around the schoolhouse and I had to leave it by the coat rack. Several other boys received guns as well, and some models even had pump action, but I didn't envy anyone. I got exactly what I asked for.

Shortly after vacation, I was on my way to school one morning, trudging up Centerline Road with my pack and my gun strapped to the Flexible Flyer. Spot was by my side, on alert for any intruders, when suddenly he stopped, pointing with a quiet yelp to the snowdrifts by the fence. Sure enough, hiding in the eagerness of my imagination, deep in the snow-covered shadow of the sugar bush, were two soldiers: a Jap and a Jerry. With Spot at my heels, we sneaked up on them, crawling as close as possible until I snapped a twig. Crack! The intruders bolted for the woods, but not before I was able to snap off a quick shot. Unfortunately, reloading took some time. I had to remove my mitten, find a BB in my pocket, cock the gun, and continue the pursuit. Just as they disappeared over the hill toward Canada, I was able to fire again.[28]

I stumbled back onto the road and ran to school, my snowsuit wet and my cheeks ablaze with exposure and excitement.

"I suppose you have a good excuse for being late, Donald?" said Ms. McConnell.

"Yes Ma'am, could I speak to you in private?" She led me to the foyer where I explained my encounter with the two Axis soldiers. She listened with rapt attention, mused a second, and then thanked me for saving America from the first-known attack on the homeland. "However," she said, "I suggest we keep the story between us so as not to panic the population."

I didn't have any more confrontations with the enemy that winter, but I did pit my expertise against the wild beasts of our woods. Earlier I'd found a bunch of leghold traps in the shed. Mill showed me how to use them and helped me set a trapline for skunk and muskrat. After that, it took me one or two hours a day, depending on the weather, to hike or snowshoe into the woods, check and reset the line, and return. Every weekend I skinned any skunk or muskrat I caught and placed the skins on a stretcher. At the feed store in Strykersville, I could sell skunk skins for a dollar and muskrat skins for five dollars. This was a great business, feeding both my pocket and my imagination. I wasn't exactly sure what the buyers were doing with all those pelts, but Maude had a suspicion that my hard-won catch was being trimmed, dyed, and stitched into "rabbit-fur" coats.

---

[28] A Jerry is a nickname for a German, particularly a German soldier. There is no clear agreement as to how this name came to be, though the Merriam-Webster dictionary notes that the word originated in 1915, indicating it was a term probably used as early as the First World War.

Spot and I loved the adventure and the challenge of maintaining the trapline, but there was one drawback. Dealing with skunk skins meant that I always had a slight aroma about me. Because of the smell, Maude insisted I leave my trapline clothes in the shed, and when I came in, my skin was scrubbed to a fare-thee-well. Maude didn't have many rules, but this was one of them.

Tales of famous French trappers who braved the American West had always captivated me, and living on the farm often brought their adventures to life. As soon as the barn faded behind me on my way to check the line, I shed my common being and become "LeBarge, ze famous French trappeur." Alone with my imagination in the heart of the Alaska wilds, I was ever on the alert for danger.

Wait. What's that sound? Spot stopped, looking at me with the signal we both understood, and I dropped to my knees and crawled silently over the crusty snowdrift by the hedgerow. Peeking over the edge through a gnarled tree, I spotted a giant wolf standing over a freshly killed moose. His yellow eyes sparkled with the excitement of the hunt. Spot and I were safe, hidden from his view, and besides, his attention was on the beast moving toward him: a massive grizzly bear, awakened from hibernation. The bear was ten feet tall and hungry. The wolf bristled and bared his fangs with a snarl.

Whoosh. The crusty snow gave way beneath me. The wolf and grizzly turned to attack. I stood and calmly snapped off a shot, scoring a direct hit in the yellow eye of the attacking wolf. Even though he was severely wounded, he bounded towards us. Then, with a final lunge, he uttered a long, bloodthirsty yowl and collapsed inches from my feet, dying in the snow. While I reloaded my trusty gun, a process made easier by the slot Grandmother had knitted between the thumb and forefinger of my mitten, Spot held off the grizzly. I fired again and again, but to no avail. I didn't have the firepower, and the grizzly was about to devour my faithful companion, who had fastened himself to the bear's snout. There was no time to reload. I grabbed the hot barrel in my hands and began clubbing the giant bear until he dropped dead next to the wolf.

Spot and I were spent, but we still had to complete our mission: checking the trapline before dark.

Home at last, we burst through the kitchen door, happy, wet, and a bit odiferous from the skunk we'd pulled from the trap and left in the skinning shed.

"Any kills today, Don?"

"Yep, got a couple of skunks and had a heck of a battle."

Life is a Piece of Cake

"How's that?" asked Millard. I told him about the wild animals that had almost finished us.

"Whew. Sure am glad you got 'em," said Mill with a twinkle in his eye. "Next thing you know they'll be after the cattle."

Late in the winter, I was walking toward the barn when I saw Freddy the Fox up by the henhouse, looking for a way in for dinner. He froze in his tracks, hoping I hadn't seen him, but by then I was far too experienced a hunter to be faked out by a mere fox. I began to cut a serpentine path towards him. He ran. I fired off a quick shot. Darn, I missed. He loped toward the pasture a short distance away, then stopped. Tossing a look over his shoulder with his sly, laughing face, he pretended to challenge me. I sneaked toward him. He sauntered a few feet farther, keeping just out of range. I snapped off another shot and watched as the BB dug a furrow through the snow several feet away. We continued this game. When he'd had enough, he turned and trotted toward the woods, his bushy red tail waving a victory salute.

Chapter 13 – Spring Thaws and Summer Harvests

1943

H ey, Spot. How about a trip to the woods?" Spot wagged his way to the door.

"Would you like me to pack you a lunch?" Maude asked.

"You bet." Maude ripped off a chunk of homemade bread and sliced a goodly piece of yesterday's roast. To this she added a container of half milk and half cream, mixed with a dollop of Hershey's chocolate syrup, and loaded it all into a backpack with a few kitchen matches.

The minute I was out the door, a blast of winter morning bit into my face. Wow, maybe this wasn't such a good idea, but Spot was already dashing downhill on the crust of the fresh snow. With hands beginning to feel the cold, I strapped on my bear-claw snowshoes, put on the backpack, and picked up my gun. *I might run into Freddie the Fox,* I thought, *and I've got a score to settle with him.* Spot was far ahead, yelping with joy at the prospect of finding yet another woodchuck. Warmed by the heat of the physical exercise, I settled down to a fast walk.

We soon reached my favorite spot deep in the woods, where the hemlocks and maples created a windbreak above the now-frozen creek. "Hot dog, it's still here," I cried out to Spot as we found the lean-to we'd built just before winter settled in. "Let's gather some twigs and get the fire going to warm the hot chocolate." I began to look for twigs, and Spot hunkered down on the moss inside the lean-to to watch, lifting a curious eyebrow at all this human activity.

On the trek down I'd worked up a sweat, but now I was beginning to get cold again. I took off my mittens and struck a match. Soon the hot chocolate was simmering over a fine fire, and I laid out the bread and meat and reached for the warm drink. Whoops. My head hit the roof of the lean-to, knocking a curl of snow into the fire. The fire went out, the sweat I'd generated earlier clung to me like an ice sheath, and suddenly I was freezing.

Spot moved out of the shelter and watched from a snowdrift a few yards away.

"Come here, Spot." I called. "We'd better head back." With stiff fingers, I strapped the snowshoes onto my feet and picked up the gun and empty backpack. I left the food and drink in the lean-to; I was just too cold to mess with it. The dogtrot back to Maude's welcoming kitchen soon warmed me again, but I was mighty glad when we arrived.

"You're back early," Maude said.

"Yep." I told her of my foiled adventure, and she served me a cup of foaming hot chocolate, with the promise that dinner would be out soon. Warm and toasty once again, I curled up on the well-worn couch with my latest Jack London adventure. It was London at his best in *To Build a Fire*, a story about a man, his dog, and the inability to light a fire. It's a dramatic tale—suspenseful, realistic, and fatal. I looked down at Spot and caught his eye. He lifted his head and yawned, licked his chops, and went back to sleep. You rascal, Spot.

Finally it was March. The snow was beginning to rot and evaporate, and Millard was getting into the fields. "Where's Mill?" I said one day as I flew in the door after school.

"Over in the 50 across the road," answered Maude.

"What's he doing?"

"Spreading manure."

I took off, running as fast as I could down the road and across the field. I could see Millard in the distance, standing in the bed of the wagon and driving the team, when—*pow*—something grabbed me by the face and threw me on my back into the slushy snow. The pain was tremendous. I stood up, dizzy and with a mouth full of blood. What had hit me? Then I saw it: I'd run full speed into a barbed wire fence. I started back to the house, fighting tears of pain and using my dirty, wet mitten to stop the blood flowing from my torn lip.

Maude took one look at me, cleaned me up as best she could, and dressed my upper lip, but the scar showed for years. Thank heavens Grandmother didn't visit that day, or my farming career would have come to a screeching halt. When she finally did see the wound, which by that time was healed, she grumbled that it should have been stitched. Was my Hollywood career over before it began?

Fortunately, small boys bounce back quickly, and it wasn't long until I was experiencing my next adventure—maple sugar season. We didn't have a sugar bush, but the Ulrichs, the farmers just above us where Harold found romance, were glad for help with their sugaring operation. Like most farmers, Mill enjoyed sugaring, and he would often help out in exchange for a gallon or two of the rich, golden syrup. As usual, I was by his side to watch the team drag a large tub on a sled through the bush and the men fill it with sweet maple sap. The evaporation process through which sap is turned into syrup usually occurred over a weekend, 24 hours a day until the batch was used. It took 40 gallons of sap to make a gallon of syrup.

The magic of a full moon and a hardwood fire gently burning under the trays of sap, the sweet smell, and the quiet, friendly camaraderie—this was a man's night out. Every now and again, we tasted the brew or threw a small dipperful into the snow and gorged on the cold, sweet sugar, but the night sky and the bubbling sap led to subdued conversation and a lot of silent staring into the fire. Most nights I was the only kid at the sugarhouse, but the other farmers made me feel welcome. Partly this was because I could carry on a conversation, and many of them weren't used to interacting with a kid in this way. Partly it was because I was Millard's boy. People liked Mill, and they knew that I was as good for him as he was for me.

Mill, Spot, and me.

Soon the last of the snow was gone, and the well-rested farmers prepared for another season. Mill and Judd plowed the fields as soon as the land was dry enough to use, and we retrieved the seed potatoes that had been stored in the cellar, cutting two or three eyes out of each in preparation for planting.

Within weeks the first crops of the season—potatoes, oats, and corn—were in the ground.

About the same time, the winter wheat came in, giving the farmers an opportunity to use the new combine they had purchased collectively. This machine was huge, cutting the wheat and separating the chaff from the straw in a single operation. The farmers went with it from farm to farm and field to field, working as a team from dawn to dark. Each man took time out in turn to do his own chores, and the women and girls brought feasts of food to the fields. We ate in shifts; the combine never stopped. When the week or so of intense work was finished, the granaries were bursting with fresh wheat, and the co-owners of the combine threw a huge party to celebrate, complete with music, games, and more mounds of delicious food.

School had just let out, and we were as delighted as kids anywhere. Third grade had been satisfactory, if a bit uneven. Art and reading were great. Everything else, although marginal, was good enough, especially since I had begun to develop a begging technique to help pass most subjects. I was promoted to the fourth grade.

After shedding my shoes along with my schoolbooks, I was looking forward to continuing my summertime pursuits of the year before. My feet were beginning to toughen up, and I'd already been working on repairing and improving the dam system in the brook. I was eager to help on the farm, and this year I was older, wiser, and bigger.

Making Hay in the Sunshine

The transformation of a field of waving, colorful grass into mature, golden hay is one of the most satisfying events of farm life, but it is also one of the most labor-intensive. In fact, the original reason school calendars included a "summer vacation" was to enable the students, many of whom came from farming families, to help with the hay harvest. To harvest the hay on our farm we used two sidebar cutters, one connected to the tractor and the other hitched behind Prince and Polly. Each winter, Millard sharpened the cutters' triangular blades to a razor's edge in his usual, meticulous way, so when the hay was ready, so was the machinery. A day or so after cutting, depending on the weather, we ran the tedder, a machine that fluffed and spread out the cut grass in order to hasten drying. Subsequently, we used the siderake, a contraption with several rows of teeth mounted on a wheel, to gather and pile neat furrows of fresh hay up and down the field.

The real fun began once the hay was ready to be brought in. Each farmer had his favorite hay-collection system. Millard used one that involved a series of slings, and of course, since Millard used it, I knew this was the best approach. First he placed a sling on the bed of the hay wagon that was hitched to Prince and Polly. Then, to the back of the wagon he hooked a loading device that tined up the furrows of hay and tossed them into the sling. Once a sling contained a foot or so of hay, he would place a new sling on top of it and begin again, until four or five were full.

When we were cutting, I ran back and forth from the tractor to the horse-drawn cutter, hitching a ride when my legs grew tired. With Spot at my heels, I also served as gopher to bring ice water from the house or parts from the toolshed.

When we were loading, I drove the team while Mill and Judd placed the slings and guided the hay with pitchforks. Spot did his part by running along behind us, chasing unsuspecting rodents. Without even looking at the hay, I could tell when the wagon was full by watching Prince and Polly. If the powerful muscles on their hindquarters were bulging, it was time to go. Mill jumped onto the seat beside me and carefully backed up the team. "Baaaackkk," he pleaded and clicked, and in my shrill, boyish voice, I tried to emulate him as he moved the wagon into the correct position. Mill or Judd then unhooked the loader and we headed for the barn.

Safely navigating the treacherous, rutted farm roads and the wooden bridge spanning the brook with a full load of hay was one of the trickiest parts of the operation, and when team and wagon were safely in the barn, I heaved a sigh of relief. We used a block and tackle track system to lift the hay-filled slings to the rafters, 50 feet or so above the barn floor. Then, using a trigger system and rope pull, we moved the sling into position, tripped the trigger, and let the hay tumble into the loft. As the depth of the loft increased, I would often crawl into a sling, ride it across the barn, and drop with gales of laughter into the sweet-smelling haymow.

Haying was an intricate dance involving man, machine, and weather, a dance often choreographed by forces beyond our control. Breakdowns could be time-consuming and a thunderstorm could blow up at any time, causing a delay of several days. As a result, I was totally focused on the task at hand, so wonderfully tired by nightfall that I had no time or energy left to manage my secret hideouts in the woods or check on my complex dam system in the brook. I was a farmer. My help was needed and recognized, and that feeling of usefulness contributed to the building of my character.

The Best Potatoes Ever

One evening, Mill and I were walking through the fields when he reached down and pulled out a clump of potatoes. "Don, take a look at this. These are the finest potatoes we've ever grown. Let's take a load to the farmers' market in Buffalo and sell them. Anything this fine, we should share with the world." This was the longest speech I'd ever heard Millard make, and shortly thereafter, spurning the mechanical picker in favor of hand-selection, Millard, Maude, Judd, and I took to the field with spades. We harvested four or five hundred pounds of the most beautiful, well-shaped potatoes ever grown and packed them into the Plymouth until it was sagging on its overloaded springs.

The next day, after doing the morning chores a bit early, Millard and I headed for the big city. Although most of my life had been spent in Buffalo, this was my first trip to the city since moving to the farm. We were both looking forward to a day of adventure, exploring, and profit. I had a 50-cent piece in my grubby paw, anticipating all the wonderful treats I could consume. As we took in the sights on the road into town, Mill and I teased each other about cars and tractors.

We purchased a booth where Mill could back in the Plymouth and set up shop. He sat like a storefront Indian by the piles of potatoes, while I ran around exploring and observing the other stands. There was no doubt about it. We had the finest produce at the market. Every now and again, with hands sticky from cinnamon candy or ice cream to share with Mill, I would run back to our stand. As the morning wore on, one-by-one the other farmers sold out and departed, until we were one of the few booths still occupied. In the early afternoon, we finally left. We had not sold a single potato. The ride home was deathly quiet, containing none of the exuberance of our morning excursion.

Finally, I choked out the agonizing question. "Why, Mill? Why didn't they want our potatoes? They're perfect! World-class. Not a blemish. Hand-picked."

In his stoic way, Millard wordlessly shrugged his shoulders without explanation.

We arrived home in time to help with the chores, unload the potatoes into the potato bin, eat a cold supper, and go to bed.

I almost never cried. But that night, I cried myself to sleep.

The summer raced by, and in September 1943, I started the fourth grade. My family still called or visited occasionally, and they came to love the beauty of the farm and to appreciate Maude and Millard. Even Grandmother was grudgingly accepting. My goat Jessie gave birth to twins, and after some debate, I honored my mother and my aunt by naming the goats after them. Betty was delighted. Carolyn never forgave me.

Chapter 14 – Airplanes and War

1943

A lthough the rhythm of farm life went on much as it always had, as a
nation we were deep into World War II, a war that in 1943 we had
no guarantee of winning. The flag flew everywhere, and Americans
worked for their country with vigor and dedication in any way that they could.
In our case, the world's people needed food, and we were producing it. Most
homes had a banner of stars in the window that indicated a family member at
war; some displayed the gold star of a fallen warrior.

Even before America entered the war in 1941, President Franklin D.
Roosevelt had advised each city to organize its own civil defense system to
plan and prepare for future dangers. To oversee and assist communities with
this daunting task, the President created the Office of Civilian Defense. By
the fall of 1943, the civil defense network in western New York State was
fully established. At last farmers had a chance to participate directly in the
defense of their country. One weekend, on a hilltop close to our place, the
local farmers built a tower to spot enemy aircraft. The tower was equipped
with a crank phone connected directly to the command center. This event was
inspirational and fun and the women-folk laid out a spread befitting a king's
table. There is nothing better than a bunch of farmwives in a cook-off.

In order to do our jobs, we occasionally went to the schoolhouse in the
evening after chores, where a civil defense representative briefed us on the
silhouettes and profiles of various aircraft—friend and foe. Although there
were certainly female "spotters" during the war, in our community this was
a task taken on primarily by men. Perhaps the women had more than enough
to do with all of their other responsibilities. Kids usually didn't participate
either, but Mill took me along every time. I knew and loved airplanes, and
even though I was only nine years old, I was probably the best in the room at
this identification exercise. After all, most of the men in my family were at
war, and the women were working in war factories building some of the very
planes we were learning about.

Already I could build models, which I did with some regularity with help from Millard, but studying the silhouettes of the many aircraft was only a beginning for me. I had to know as much as possible about them. Heck, if the war would only last another ten years, maybe I'd even be flying them. My favorite was the P-40 Warhawk, with its shark-tooth nose and blazing machine guns. Both Betty and Grandmother were helping to build this beauty, and they'd told me many tales of its successes.

One of the earliest of American-built fighters, the P-40 was flown by Allied aviators all over the world, including General Claire L. Chennault's Flying Tigers, who blazed their way into American hearts during the China campaign. With sharks' teeth painted on the noses of their planes, they had a spectacular kill record. Even though the plane was heavy and underpowered, it was a rugged fighter, and thousands of them held the line until more efficient models were designed.[29]

The C-46 was another aircraft built by the Curtiss-Wright plant in Buffalo where my mother and grandmother worked. Primarily a graceful, high-flying cargo aircraft, it flew the "hump" over the Himalayas from Burma, supplying the brave citizens of beleaguered China.

There was also the P-38 Lightning, a do-it-all fighter: reconnaissance, light bomber, interceptor. If the P-40 was the most romantic of our aircraft, the P-38 fork-tailed devil was one of the most dangerous. Built by Lockheed and designed by Kelly Johnson, the ultimate can-do aircraft designer, it was a climb-fast, go-fast killer and one of the most exciting planes used in the Pacific. You can bet I whiled away a few hours in class drawing pictures of that beauty.[30]

Most of the balsa models I built were of a British fighter called the Hawker Hurricane. This famous aircraft was immortalized through its part in the Battle of Britain in 1939 and 1940. Although I was too young to remember those events clearly, they were already part of the folklore of the

---

[29] The Flying Tigers (also called the American Volunteer Group or A.V.G.), was an all-volunteer, American civilian force that fought Japan under the auspices of the Chinese prior to and after the start of World War II. Started by retired Army Air Corps officer Claire L. Chennault, the A.V.G. was established in mid-1941 and officially disbanded on July 4, 1942. General Chennault returned to active duty in the spring of 1942, four months after Pearl Harbor.

[30] Clarence L. "Kelly" Johnson (1910–1990) joined Lockheed in 1933 as a tool designer and retired in 1975 as a senior vice president. Over the course of his career, he played a role in the design of over 40 world-renowned aircraft. Nearly half of these were his original design, including the F-80 and the high-altitude U-2. In 1964, he was awarded the Medal of Freedom by President Lyndon B. Johnson for his contributions to the nation's security.

war. The Hurricane, along with the British Supermarine Spitfire, was one of the European Theatre's best war machines. Both planes had eight blazing machine guns to fight the Nazis. Would they keep Hitler from taking England? I was counting on it.

The P-39 Airacobra, designed by Bell Aircraft and built in the Buffalo area, was another favorite. With its engine mounted behind the pilot, the plane was equipped with a cannon designed to fire through the propeller shaft. Though tough to fly, this plane was an excellent aircraft in the hands of a skilled aviator, but a real pilot-killer for a rookie. Most of these models were sent to Russia.

The North American P-51 Mustang was as beautiful as it was fast, as graceful as it was deadly. A marriage of American and British technology, it was crowned with the Merlin engine and one of the finest aircraft built in the U.S.A. It was used as a long-range fighter to protect the monster bomber formations over Germany.

The North American B-25 Mitchell was a light bomber. These planes were best known for their use during Lt. Colonel Jimmy Doolittle's 1942 raid on Tokyo, the first blow of the war against the Japanese islands. Colonel Doolittle's pilots and crews, who flew off the tiny deck of the aircraft carrier Hornet, gave America its first ray of hope in the Pacific.[31]

On the offensive, we had the heavy bombers: the Boeing B-17 Flying Fortress and the Consolidated Aircraft B-24 Liberator. Their missions were fraught with danger. At the beginning of the bombing campaign, the life expectancy of a bomber crew was seven missions. I figured this was another good reason to fly fighters.

In addition to learning about our own aircraft, we also studied German planes. After all, if the country came under attack, we had to be able to identify enemy aircraft.

The German fighter that everyone worried most about was the dive-bombing Stuka, its screeching whine imprinted on my memory by Movietone News. The Messerschmitt 109, Germany's front-line fighter, was first and foremost in their inventory, followed by the Focke Wulf 190. The Germans had set the world standard for aircraft, but, once awakened, the Brits and the Yanks were giving them a run for their money. Of course, we were

---

[31] James Harold Doolittle (1896–1993) won the Medal of Honor for his role in leading the raid over Japan. Afterward he was promoted to brigadier general and served as commander of various operations in Africa, the Mediterranean, and England during the remainder of World War II. After the war he returned to civilian life as an executive with Shell Oil but continued to serve the air force as a civilian advisor for many years.

primarily watching for bombers, although the capabilities of the Axis powers were limited. Could the Germans bring the Junkers 88 or the Heinkel to our shores?

The most famous Japanese plane was the Mitsubishi Zero and the Mitsubishi "Betty bomber," also known as the death tube of Admiral Yamamoto. Along with my fellow students, I learned about these and other aircraft on the silhouette charts. It was a propaganda ploy, and it worked, because it pulled all of us into the war. If there was to be fighting on our own shores, as a nation we were prepared for the worst.

The tower was manned 24 hours a day. When Millard was on duty, I went with him, even if I had to skip school to do so. I felt that my future was in aviation, and I wondered when I would be closer to my dream.

Chapter 15 – One Skunk Too Many

1943–1944

The school year passed quickly as the rhythm of the farm continued for a second season. With the spring thaws, I started gathering my traps to store them for the summer. I'd had a successful run the year before and had used some of the profits to purchase more traps, so my trapline was now more extensive.

On this day, Spot and I were mushing along with my sled, picking up traps and collecting a couple of skunks. I was carrying my "bonking stick," a 12-foot-long rod with a weight on one end that Millard had made for me. I used it to bonk the skunk before it got me. All went well until I got careless, marching within six feet of the final trap without spotting the very alive and very angry skunk. The next thing I saw was a yellow pyramid of spray.

He got Spot and me both, full face and body. Afterward, my eyes burned as if I'd been hit by a flamethrower, and Spot burrowed through the snow like a mole on a mission. Trying to rub the hurt from my eyes, I dove into a rotting snowbank. The half-frozen water helped the sting, if not the smell, and after a bit I pulled myself together. I bonked the skunk, retrieved the trap, and trudged home dragging the sled. Spot was whimpering behind me.

Maude took one sniff and shooed us off to the shed. "We'll probably have to burn your clothes," she said, which was fine with me, since I couldn't get out of them quickly enough. She brought us a bucket of hot soapy water, and I started on the way back to olfactory acceptability. This was my darkest hour, and to make matters worse, I could have sworn I heard something. Yes, there it was, the unmistakable rumble of Grandmother's Olds. My goose was cooked for sure.

Within minutes, both women were scrubbing me down, clucking like two old hens. Once they were satisfied that I might pass muster in polite company, Grandmother took a long look at my still-irritated eyeballs. "Maude," she said. "Donald's eyes look like two green emeralds lying in a bed of rubies. I think I'd better have Dr. Pierce in East Aurora take a look at him." Maude agreed, and while I dressed in clean clothes, she started to tackle Spot, who in addition to smelling terrible was quickly beginning to resemble a drowned rat.

I bid Maude and Spot goodbye, climbed into the Olds, and set off with Grandmother for town. "Whatcha doin' visiting today?" I asked, using my imperfect farm talk.

"It's Saturday, and I wanted to show you our new house," Grandmother replied. A chill went down my spine. After years of trying, Grandmother had finally bought her dream house at 30 Park Place in East Aurora, and it was obvious she was ecstatic. Would this change in status affect me?

After a visit to Dr. Pierce, who gave me both a clean bill of health and the suggestion that I change my profession, we drove to the new place. No question about it. This was Grandmother's nicest home so far, and she'd had at least ten of them in my lifetime alone. She started to give me the tour: her bedroom, Grandpa's, Betty's, Carolyn's, and then—uh-oh—mine, a small room toward the back of the house overlooking a perfect garden. The room was furnished with a rock maple twin bed and a chair and table to match, purchased just for me.

Was there more to Grandmother's visit than her desire to show off her new house? That evening, as we all gathered around her table devouring a scrumptious meal, I learned the rest of the story.

"Donald," said my mother, and my ears perked up. I knew that when I heard that word, either something very good or something very bad was soon to happen. "Now that we're in this wonderful new house," she continued, "we're all going to be together again. You can finish the fourth grade here in East Aurora, join the Boys Club, and enjoy this wonderful town."[32]

My eyes misted over, and it wasn't just skunk residue. "B-b-but," I stammered, "Maude and Mill need me! Spot and the animals need me!"

"I know," Betty said, "but we've talked it over with Maude and Mill, and they think they can manage if you come out weekends and holidays and help with the chores. Look at it this way. You haven't lost anything; you've actually gained. You'll be living in a new home, and you'll be with your family again. Plus, you'll get to meet new people and experience new opportunities."

There they were, those magic words again. I mulled over this "new opportunity" while gorging on one of Grandmother's delicious apple pies. After

[32] The Boys Clubs of America had their beginning in 1860 when a group of women in Hartford, CT, felt that boys who roamed the streets should have a place to go. In 1906, several clubs joined together to start a nationwide movement. In 1990, the name was changed to Boys & Girls Clubs of America, and in the 21st century, boys and girls are nearly equally represented. Clubs are open every day after school and on weekends, providing a place where kids can learn the skills they need to succeed in life.

I finished, the family led me to the garage. Sitting next to Grandpa's Buick Roadmaster was a brand new Schwinn Roadmaster, a bike just for me.

Grandmother's dream house at 30 Park Place,
East Aurora, New York, photo ca. 1970s.

My mother was right; I did double my fun. I not only made new friends in the neighborhood, I also knew the farm was always there, and I went out every chance I got. When the weather was nice, I rode the six miles from East Aurora on my trusty Schwinn. If the weather was bad, someone drove me. Maude, Mill, and Spot were always glad to see me, and because of the predictability of farm life, little changed between visits. Prince and Polly, the great workhorses, still carried the main load of the heavy hauling, and Harold stood ready for duty. My goat Jessie ran the barnyard, teasing the unwary with a butt on the hinder, as the plowing and planting, harvesting and putting by, marked the rhythm of the seasons.

I had been more than happy on the farm. In fact, living there might have been the most important experience of my life. If my guardian angel had been responsible for some divine intervention that enabled Maude and Millard to foster me in that perfect environment, I was surely grateful.

Maude and Mill were not regular church-goers, but they reflected the values found in Galatians 5:22: "The fruit of the Spirit is love, joy, peace, patience, kindness, goodness, fidelity, gentleness, self-control. Against such things there is no law." As a result, on the farm I learned everything I needed to know to thrive: the need for work and for play, an appreciation of beauty, the power of love and compassion, the value of organization, the principles of sound business management, the importance of morals, and perhaps above all, an appreciation for the sure, steady approach so necessary in life. I left my country speech and bib overalls behind, but I took those survival skills with me to my fourth-grade class in East Aurora Elementary.

Chapter 16 – East Aurora: Home, Sweet Home
1944

As I looked up from my reverie, I saw that Betty had dozed off, but she opened her eyes when my wife Polly came into the room.

"You know, Betty," I said, "I loved those years on the farm."

"I know you did," she replied. "I missed you a lot, but I think you were just about as happy as a boy could be."

"I was, but it was also exciting to come home. And speaking of home," I said as I gathered up the tapes and recorder, "how about some home-cooked lunch?"

"That's just what I was coming to tell you," said Polly. "Lunch will be ready in five minutes."

After we ate, Betty went to lie down for a nap and Polly and I took a walk around the neighborhood. The warm, sunny afternoon, the soft breezes, and the shadows cast by the trees along our route took me back to the next phase of my childhood.

A Country Boy in the City

At that time, East Aurora schools were as good as public schools get. The classes were well-planned and divided by ability. Because of my remarkable reading skill, I was placed in the A class, and because my last name started with W, I was seated in the last row—a combination of factors that bore all the makings of disaster. I just wasn't A-class material. Yes, I could read and draw, but my proficiency in spelling and math was marginal, and at the back of the room, far from the teacher's watchful eye, it was easy to slip into dreamland. As soon as the pace of learning or the subject became boring, my mind raced off to the woods or the war, flying fighters, killing the Krauts or the Japs, and making the world safe for democracy.

Outside the classroom, my ability to play softball and basketball was average, but in gym sports—climbing ropes and such—I was superior.

The upper body strength and coordination I'd developed helping Mill and Judd were paying off. My social skills, especially in comparison with the more-sophisticated town kids, were another matter. I was careless in dress and talked like a farmer, and for the first time I was the butt of jokes and sarcastic comments. Although the other boys accepted me a little, probably because some of the farm still clung proudly to my being, the girls ignored me completely. Most of the time this was pretty much okay. I wasn't entirely sure what girls were good for, but I enjoyed watching them nevertheless.

One incident in particular sealed my fate in my new school. In hindsight, I had a ripe head cold the day it happened, and I should have stayed home. Instead, I sat in the back of the classroom, bathed in the warm sun shining through the window, snuffling away. Naturally I didn't have a handkerchief; that's what sleeves were for. All of a sudden, a sneeze erupted from the depths of my being. It was a powerful sound, echoing through the classroom, shaking the building to its very foundation. Before I had time to get my hands to my face, gleaming globules of crystal projected through the air, shining in the sunlight like Christmas ornaments and landing on the desktop and seat in front of me.

The sneeze: East Aurora Elementary, 1944
(*Illustration by Babe Sargent.*)

Time stopped! The girls recoiled in horror and covered their noses; the boys laughed and cheered. The teacher sprang at me like a lioness, grabbed me by the earlobe (the only dry spot available), and pulled me out of the room. "You nasty, filthy, stupid farm boy," she shouted, dragging me to the nurse's office. The nurse was more understanding, but she still sent me home, along with instructions to stay there until I recovered.

Normally I went to the Boys Club after school, a wonderful place to play or work on hobbies, but that day it was too early and I was too sick, so I walked home and shivered on the screened porch for a couple of hours until Grandmother returned from her job at Curtiss-Wright. I was cold and miserable, but I was even more embarrassed. *Wouldn't it be nice*, I thought, *if my mother came home that night and said, 'Donald, we have some wonderful news; we are moving to _____, where you will meet new friends and have new adventures'?* Alas, it didn't happen, and after a couple of days I returned to school and slunk into my seat in the rear of the classroom.

As if on cue, the boys pulled out hankies and blew their noses, while the girls wrinkled theirs in disgust. For days afterward, if a girl accidentally brushed against me, she would run to the girl's room and wash and gargle. Eventually, the incident "blew" over, but not before I acquired a new nickname: "farmer Don, the snot-nosed kid," a moniker that pretty much squashed any chances I might have had of inviting one of the girls to the grain bin to explain the function of Harold or try out my sophisticated talk of love.

At year's end, I was promoted to the fifth grade. My grades covered the usual range: A's in reading and art down to D's in math and spelling. Even worse, I'm pretty sure some of those grades were more a result of my growing skill at begging for special consideration than a measure of my academic prowess. Or perhaps the teacher was afraid that if she failed me, she'd get me back the following year, a fate she no doubt considered distinctly unhealthy. One way or the other, my lack of understanding in certain academic areas followed me for years to come.

Summer of '44

I got my first city job that summer, a *Courier-Express* paper route. I enjoyed getting up early, especially since Gramps and I had breakfast together—Nabisco shredded wheat and three-minute boiled eggs. After I delivered my papers, I boarded a bus to the Boys Club day camp, located in the woods close to the farm. Here we played capture-the-flag, ran races on the huge green, and played volleyball and softball. There was no ugly competition here. We picked new teams daily. When it rained we worked on crafts under canvas canopies, building hammered-copper ashtrays and spoon holders, carved boat models and ceramic gadgets. We also started out swimming twice a day, but after one kid ended up in an iron lung from polio, the counselors shut down the swimming hole. I felt bad for the kid, but since I couldn't swim and was happiest avoiding water altogether, I wasn't sorry to see this change in schedule.

Each day I scanned the paper for news of victories and defeats. America was winning the war, and I felt pretty sure it wouldn't last long enough for me to fly a P-51, but I could still hope. Around the dinner table each evening, we discussed the war first and jobs second, and as a young businessman, I contributed experiences I'd had with some of my paper route clients. No matter what I did, there were people who just wouldn't pay, but if I stopped delivering the paper, the company threatened to fire me. Sometimes life just ain't fair. Once I complained to Grandmother about a client, and she descended on him like a tornado. After that I kept quiet. For one thing, I thought I should handle these problems myself. For another, I felt that even the most deadbeat clients didn't deserve the abuse Grandmother was likely to heap upon them.

In addition to my paper route, I had responsibilities at home, helping in the garden and mowing the lawn with a push mower. I was also expected to keep my room tidy, though not overly so, and I ran errands on my bike, usually down to Hill's, the corner store/drop-off point for the papers I delivered. This was a task I particularly enjoyed, because Hill's had a vast assortment of magazines that they didn't mind me browsing. Most weekends I spent with Maude and Millard, getting my friends who were also carriers to cover my route in exchange for returning the favor during the week.

Overall things were going pretty well, though when I walked into a room, I often interrupted what seemed like huddled conversations about my welfare. Obviously people were concerned about me, but I was far more worried about the prospect of returning to East Aurora Elementary. On August 14th, my tenth birthday, Betty and Grandmother threw a party with all the relatives who weren't overseas. Maude and Mill were invited as well. It was a huge success, with plenty of presents, fun, and laughter. The grand finale came just before people went home, when my mother announced, "Donald, as a special present we're giving you the opportunity to meet new friends and have new challenges."

"Where now?" I asked. Maybe I wouldn't have to go back to East Aurora after all.

"We're sending you to Linsly Military Institute, a superior school in Wheeling, West Virginia." At this point, all the kin gushed on about Linsly being one of the finest preparatory schools in the country and how they were sure I'd be happy there, especially since I loved all things military. It seemed that everybody was in on this "wonderful" surprise except Maude, Millard, and me.

Okay, I thought. *Anything will be better than returning to East Aurora Elementary.* Little did I know. Farm kid to military student. Alpha to omega. Freedom to Gestapo![33]

---

[33] Attorney Noah Linsly founded the school in 1814 as an academy for boys and girls. From 1861 to 1988, only boys were admitted, and between 1877 and 1978 Linsly was a military school. As of 2008, The Linsly School continues to thrive, engaging over 400 boys and girls in grades 5 through 12, three-quarters of them day students, in its challenging curriculum.

Chapter 17 – An Introduction to Linsly

1944

As I thought about my time at Linsly, I realized that I'd never asked why my mother and grandmother had selected that particular school. "Why Linsly?" I asked Betty the next morning, when we were once again settled in the living room with cups of hot coffee and my trusty recorder. "Did you know somebody there?"

"No," she replied, "but when we were living in West Virginia after I graduated from high school, I'd dated that fellow Howard who went there, and he thought the place was great. And from going to dances on campus with him, I knew it was a beautiful facility. We were really at our wits' end. With everyone working, we just couldn't provide the supervision you needed at home, but you also had to be in a place where you could get a first-rate education. At the time, Linsly seemed just the ticket, especially since they had recently changed the rules to admit boys your age."

"I remember you said the teachers were well-educated, but the best news for me was that they were all men. My last teacher at East Aurora was the one who'd dragged me out of class by the earlobe, making an ugly situation worse. She was meaner than a half-dead skunk in a leghold trap and I was more than happy to leave women teachers behind."

Betty chuckled. "I can understand that," she said. Then she paused. "You know, speaking of teachers, I think your Linsly yearbook is somewhere in that box of mementoes in the closet."

I was just curious enough to search, and lo and behold, I soon had my hands on a record of events that had taken place over 40 years before. In addition to documenting the achievements of individual students, it was obvious that the yearbook was intended as a promotional tool. The introduction described Linsly as the oldest preparatory school west of the Alleghenies, sitting on 20 secluded acres in the West Virginia countryside. It also said they were looking for boys with character. Well, there was no doubt I'd had character. Just ask anyone at East Aurora Elementary.

"Linsly enrolls only high-type boys," I quoted to Betty. "Linsly is not a school for problem boys, boys-rich, boys-poor, but boys who are above the average in ability and aspiration. This makes an atmosphere in which a boy is apt to stretch to his best." Obviously, they hadn't known about my checkered past. I wondered if the East Aurora school authorities had conspired to hide my reputation from the admissions office so that they wouldn't have to deal with me again.

I continued. "Unique: Linsly is for boys only. The program is designed for boys. Boys like Linsly." I really appreciated this aspect of the place. After the sneeze incident, girls were not at the top of my list.

And finally, "Freedom: Linsly is free to adjust the teaching methods to the very latest and best in pedagogy. Textbooks are changed frequently to keep ever abreast of the times."

"Sounds impressive, doesn't it," Betty said.

"It does, and back then I was excited about going. I knew it would be more regimented than the farm, but I figured anything would be better than East Aurora."

"Well, they were certainly regimented about what you could and couldn't bring," Betty said. "Not only that, everything you did bring had to be labeled. I can still see Grandmother sewing 'Donald Wright' tags into pillowcases, blankets, and clothes—even into socks and underwear."

Betty was looking out the window, but she wasn't seeing palm trees and hibiscus. Instead, she was focused on the green of a late summer morning in 1944. "I took some vacation time to take you down there," she recalled. "We rode the Pennsylvania Railroad to Wheeling."

I smiled at the memory of that train ride, the sense of adventure, of travel to exotic places. It wasn't quite *Terry and the Pirates*, but it wasn't East Aurora Elementary, either.

"Other than riding in the switching engines with Grandpa at the rail yard," I said to Betty, "it was the first time I'd been on a train, and I was thrilled. Since I'd be traveling alone when I came home for vacations, I remember that you took great care to show me how to board, where to sit, and where to stow my gear."

"That was a fun trip," my mother said. "We were so close to where I went to high school that we got to visit with many of my friends, and they wanted to hear all about my job at Curtiss-Wright. I was pretty proud of that job, and they were quite impressed that I'd just been asked to christen a new C-46 airplane called *Bonds A-hoy* for being the top war bonds salesperson in the entire plant. They were impressed with you, too. You were always so good at carrying on a conversation with adults, and my friends enjoyed talking with you.[34]

"And they were so nice at the school when we arrived," she concluded. "After touring the place and meeting some of the staff, I knew you were in good hands."

"I thought so, too. Some of the other kids were having trouble saying goodbye, but by that time my life had been so varied this was just one more adventure. I've got to tell you, though, once the parents left things changed radically."

Betty looked pensive. "Other than talking about your friends and the food, you never said much about Linsly back then, Don. Were you unhappy there?"

Now it was my turn to gaze out the window. The Florida landscape morphed into a crowd of boys standing in the sunshine on a warm afternoon. Some were confident, some lost, and a few had tears in their eyes. For a moment, all was still. And then the x!@$# hit the fan.

Another Kind of Education

"Ten-shun!" blared Major Lockhart, the school president. Could he have escaped from the Reich and be hiding out on campus? What followed was bedlam—hollering, shouting, and posting against the wall by our tormentors, the high school upperclassmen. We were marched from area to area to get uniforms and gear, then taken to our quarters in a beautiful old mansion. It had been converted into a dormitory, with an apartment in the middle for the housemaster and his wife. The housemaster was fearsome-looking. His wife, also employed by the school, was a pleasant-looking woman who turned out to be as kind and loving as she appeared.

As we moved into our dorm, the upperclassmen harassed us to the point of exhaustion. There were four boys to a room, with adequate space to stow the belongings we'd brought and the gear we'd been issued. Everything had to be folded or rolled and placed in the drawers just so. The bed was to be

---

[34] War bonds were Series E U.S. savings bonds specially labeled as "defense bonds," "war bonds," and for those who felt they could not invest in war for reasons of conscience, "civilian bonds." To help children and those of limited income save for a bond, war stamps were also available, starting at ten cents a piece. From 1941 to 1946, over $185 billion dollars of securities were sold, and over 85 million Americans invested in this effort. Bonds paid a 2.9 percent return after a 10-year maturity. Series E bonds, although no longer labeled "war bonds," were for sale until 1980, when they were replaced by Series EE bonds.

made in military fashion, with 45-degree corners and the blanket pulled tight enough to bounce a dime on it. *Yes, Sir. No, Sir. Three bags full, Sir.*

The harassment continued in the days to come, and although I was a quick learner, I wasn't quick enough. I acted like a wise guy, was rebellious, and didn't learn from experience. I hated what was happening, and I would let anyone know who asked. Not only did I flip my mouth, I just could not do what was expected of me, no matter how hard I tried.

So far, the only good thing I could see about the place was the chow. I loved to eat, and the food was scrumptious and plentiful. They obviously hadn't heard of rationing at Linsly. We had meat at every meal. I was developing a keen eye for what was put before me, and when some of the other kids didn't like the food, that was fine with me. I would scarf down theirs as well.

Many of my housemates were living away from home for the first time, and they acted like a bunch of sniveling babies. They couldn't sleep, and every time someone hollered at them, they started crying. Once I saw this, I was determined that during my time at Linsly I would not cry for anyone or anything, and I never did.

Once classes began, I discovered that the classroom instruction was superior, and although I was a far cry from the top, I certainly wasn't at the bottom. No doubt my performance was aided by the fact that studying was required and distractions in class were not tolerated. If my sneeze had occurred here, it would have been handled quickly and with ceremony: a firing squad at dawn and full military honors at burial.

We were issued real rifles, but they were spiked so as not to shoot, a precaution that saved more than one life. We also learned the manual of arms and how to march. I liked marching. I couldn't roll my socks properly, but on the drill field I was hot stuff.

Life with the Good Captain

Each of our activities, inside and outside the classroom, had rules. If we broke the rules, we were issued demerits. Demerits accumulated throughout the week and were tallied after class on Fridays. If we received over a certain number (and my demerit box was always full to overflowing), we had to do "tours" in the evenings and during our time off. A tour consisted of marching on the parade ground in a box pattern, wearing a Class A uniform, with weapon shouldered. Every half-hour of marching, which included a five-minute break to rest, was counted as one tour. By the end of the first month, I'd been assigned enough tours to last ten years.

Life is a Piece of Cake

Every Friday night the housemaster, whom we called "the good captain," invited certain discipline cases to his quarters for special punishment. Since I always had been insubordinate during the previous week—I just couldn't help myself—this was a party I never missed. Also, much as I tried, I couldn't seem to fold my socks and underwear satisfactorily. I was beginning to realize how much had been done for me in the civilian world: folding and storing my clothes, laying them out for me, making my bed, and so forth. And speaking of beds, since mine so rarely passed inspection, some upperclassmen had quit giving me demerits out of pity, but I never asked for mercy.

"Drop your pants, reach over, and grab your ankles," said the housemaster. Off came the good captain's fat belt. Whop. Whop. Whop. Normally, he would continue until the boy would cry, and most boys cried immediately. I was too stubborn to cry, and the good captain's eyes narrowed every time he looked at me. His goal was to break me, but I never gave in. I never told anybody at home about it, either.

The housemaster's wife was especially kind to me. Perhaps she felt sorry for the whippings. Often she would take some of the boys to church or to town for shopping or a stroll. On one of these walks, a bum staggered toward us with his pecker hanging out. One of the boys asked, "What's with him?" She replied that he was a crazy drunk. Never without a wisecrack, I pointed out that he was going to have a hard time getting a job as a service bull on a farm. She stifled a laugh.

In class I coped well, and I enjoyed sports more than ever before or since. At Linsly everyone was allowed to play, not just the hotshots. The precision and skill of the drill field was also exhilarating, especially since I could tell left from right (something not everybody could do), and while others were being harassed, I escaped to dreamland. Gradually the upperclassmen became friendlier, and although I never fit in completely, the continuous harassment abated. The beatings did not.

"This hurts me more than it hurts you, Mr. Wright."

Sure, Captain, I thought. *Just pound away so that I can go about my business.*

* * *

As I came out of my reverie, I looked over at Betty. She was watching me intently, still waiting for an answer to her question. I'd never told her about the beatings. Too proud, I guess, but if she wanted to know now—the good and the bad—it was okay by me.

"It was a long time ago," I began, "and it's water over the dam, but there were parts that were pretty rough." Betty put her hand on my arm.

"The housemaster beat some kids every Friday night, and I was usually one of those who got a whipping," I explained. "Sure, there were plenty of times I was out of line, but usually I hadn't done much of anything. I think it was enough provocation for him—we called him the good captain—that I wouldn't give in."

"Good Lord, Don, why didn't you tell us?" Betty asked, her face a mask of shock.

"I don't really know. I knew everyone at home had their hands full, and there were a lot of things about the place that I liked. Maybe I thought if I just hung in long enough, he'd stop. I must have been under a heck of a lot of stress, though, because I bit my fingernails more than I ever had before, and for a while I wet the bed. Of course, I never told anyone that, either. I slept on a towel, and after lights-out I went to the bathroom and rinsed out the evidence."

"Oh, Don, you *were* under stress. Were you still wetting the bed when you came home for Christmas vacation?"

"No, by that time I'd stopped, thank heavens."

* * *

Ready for action in my Class A uniform at Linsly Military Institute, 1944.

Thank heavens, indeed. If the good captain had found out, he probably would have died of a heart attack from the stress of beating the crap out of me, and I would have been drawn, quartered, and buried in a pauper's grave for causing the extra exertion.

Fortunately, there was a respite nearby. The Manions, a family my mother knew from our days in the Kenmore Apartments in South Buffalo, now lived in Wheeling, and on occasion I was allowed to spend a weekend with them. Their daughter Charlene was my age, and on one of these visits I escorted her to the movies to see Judy Garland in *Meet Me in St. Louis*. Since this was my very first "date," I was on my best behavior, carefully avoiding discussions of Harold or my vast knowledge of reproduction.

December 1944: time for Christmas break. I boarded the train for home dressed in my Class A uniform. It wasn't that I loved being at Linsly, but I was proud of that uniform. Wearing it somehow made me feel closer to the men and women fighting the big war. They say clothes make the man, and there was no doubt my military demeanor and ability to communicate with adults impressed the other passengers. But I just couldn't pull off being mistaken for a fighting man.

At home, everybody was glad to see me, but when I complained at dinner about the breaded pork chops at school, I got little sympathy. Rationing was in full force and most families, including mine, had no pork chops at all.

Christmas was festive. The war was going well, and everybody in our family was still alive, although Uncle Dan spent most of his day at the front or close to it. I spent some time with Mill and Maude on the farm, and while they were suitably impressed by my uniform, I was soon back in bib overalls helping in the barn. At the end of vacation, I boarded the train back to Wheeling well-rested, filled with Christmas cheer, and having missed at least three Friday whippings.

It was good to be back. I had made several good friends, and we all had settled into our own way of coping. And for the first time in my school life, my grades were satisfactory across the board; I was succeeding without begging. Much of this was due to the fact that the teachers took the time to do their job. I learned at Linsly that there is no such thing as a learning disability; there are only teaching disabilities. Of course, it helped that if we stepped out of line, the firing squad was waiting.

Chapter 18 – Making the Grade

1945

Both as a part of gym class and as an extracurricular activity, boxing was an important sport at Linsly. Students were classified from mite weight to heavyweight. I was in the mite weight class, and I took the training very seriously. Never in my life had I been particularly successful in any sport, but here I aimed to win. Boxing took precedence over walking tours, and I still had a lot of tours to walk.

I fought three bouts at Linsly (three rounds to a bout) and discovered a lifetime of lessons in each of them. First, be in good shape; second, have patience; third, be smart; fourth, pace yourself; fifth, be able to function in pain. Looking back, it's easy to see how I applied those lessons in later life.

Before the first bout, my hands were buried in giant gloves and my stomach was buried in butterflies. The coach offered last-minute instructions; the referee briefed us on the rules. Prancing on my toes like Joe Louis, I waited for the bell. *Attack!*[35]

Everything I'd learned was gone in a flash, and my opponent fared no better. Two skinny boys, face-to-face, flailing our arms like windmills, we were fatigued much too soon. After what seemed like an eternity, the bell rang. Back to the corner, bathed in sweat; two rounds to go. Advice from the coach: "Slow down. Remember what you've learned." *Bell.*

I dropped into a fighter's stance, not because I remembered to do so, but because it was easier to hold up my arms. My opponent did the same, and while we each had the occasional windmill, this time we got in some jabs. Then *pow*—a punch to the nose that made my eyes water. I pressed on. *Bell.*

More advice: "You're doing good. Hold your arms higher. Jab. Watch your footwork." *Bell.* One round to go, and I was as tired as I'd ever been. This time there was no windmilling; in fact, there was very little of anything.

---

[35] Joe Louis (1914–1981) began his professional boxing career in 1934 and was undefeated in his first 27 fights. He became heavyweight champion of the world in 1937, a title he held until his retirement in 1949.

We were both exhausted, drained physically and mentally and barely able to lift our two-ton arms. *BELL.*

The ref called us to the center of the ring, held up my hand, and announced the victor: *me*. For a moment, euphoria. Then I remembered I had to do it all over again the following day. Even so, victory felt great, and that night at dinner all of the winners were smiling smugly. By the next day, I was ready to go, and this time I used better pacing and launched fewer windmilling attacks. The fatigue was intense, but at the end I still had something left and I won handily.

I'd made it to the finals, and I wanted this win more than I'd ever wanted anything in my young life. It was almost as if victory would somehow eliminate my fingernail biting, my pissing in the bed, and even the good captain's whippings. Normally I was a peaceful guy, but in this case, I'd worked up a fierceness that surprised me.

Now what was it the coach said to do?
(*Illustration by Babe Sargent.*)

My opponent was Ed Stumpp, a friend and the best student in class. We were about equally matched, and on fight day we faced off in the center of the ring, received our instructions, and retreated to our respective corners. The bell rang, and once again I forgot everything I knew. I was as aggressive as possible, attacking like a crazy animal and windmilling away. Ed backed off, retreated, and fought a fine tactical battle. *Bell.*

I'd won the round, but I'd also violated three of my five boxing rules: patience, being smart, and pacing. Back in the corner, the coach was in my face. "What's the matter with you? You're doing everything wrong. Slow down, fight smart, be patient, pace yourself," but it was too late. I was punched out and ready to quit. *Bell.*

I heaved myself to my feet for round two, hardly able to hold up my hands. Initially, Ed didn't realize what bad shape I was in, but as we waltzed around, his punching became more accurate and it hurt. I staggered through the rest of the round. *Bell.* That one was Ed's.

Once again, the coach gave the usual advice, but to no avail. This time, Ed could smell blood, and in the final round he attacked with a vengeance. He knew he only had to pace himself for two more minutes, and because he hadn't used his reserve, he was able to fight hard. To me, those two minutes lasted forever, and when it was over, the ref called us to the center of the ring to announce the forgone conclusion: Ed Stumpp was the mite weight champion of Linsly Military Institute.

The coach had taught us that in boxing, as in life, the first round is carried by hype, and the second round is survived by conditioning, but the third round requires pure guts. It was obvious I needed to work on that third round. I wasn't sure if Millard would understand or approve of boxing, but that day I learned once again how necessary a steady, methodical approach is to success. I also learned that it's hard to be steady when you've just been poked in the nose and your eyes are stinging like crazy.

The Grand Finale

The rest of the year roared by. I'd shaped up, received more demerits than almost any other kid, and become a minor legend for absorbing a steady diet of Friday-night whippings. Then it was V-E Day: Tuesday, May 8, 1945. Nazi Germany had surrendered unconditionally to the Allied forces, and that Friday the good captain gave me a reprieve. Perhaps he was feeling a soft spot for the future protectors of America, or maybe he was just wearing out. I'll never know, but from that day on the spankings were far less frequent and I began to feel more comfortable.

One day toward the end of the term, some of the seniors invited me to join them behind the shed by the brook. *Wow, I am fitting in*, I thought. When I got there, three or four guys were puffing on corncob pipes, the absolute forbidden fruit. One of them lit a pipe for me, and as I sat on a stump, happily puffing away, they said, "Wait here. We have another surprise," and ran off to get it. Soon the good captain rounded the shed, and I didn't have to wait 'til Friday evening. He whipped me on the spot, so hard that even the bigger boys winced. My hinder was throbbing and I was mad as hell at the setup, but my major concern was "Please don't tell my mother."

I finished the year with a draw: grades okay, deportment zip. "See ya next year," I said to my roommates, and off I went to East Aurora on the Pennsylvania Railroad. It had been quite an adventure. I'd enjoyed the orderliness, proper discipline, and cadence of military life and I made new friends. I also learned a million lessons. And I never again had to worry about being a fat ass—it had been pounded to the bone.

Chapter 19 – Homecomings

1945

B ack in Florida in 1988, we'd finished dinner and were once again ensconced in the living room. Betty had changed into a soft pink robe and matching slippers. This was our fourth day in Nokomis, and Betty was growing tired. She walked more slowly, and each afternoon she took a long nap, but her voice was strong and clear as she talked about the summer I came home from Linsly in 1945.

"I'll never forget the day you got off the train," my mother recalled. "The war in Europe had been won the month before, and Curtiss-Wright had nearly stopped making P-40s. They'd also cut production drastically on the C-46, and your grandmother's job at the plant was over. She'd worked hard and done a great job, but she was thrilled to be resuming her position as matriarch of the clan. And everybody was glad you were coming home."

"What I remember," I said, "was asking if you were sending me back to Linsly the next year. When you said no, because now Grandmother would be home during the day, it made my homecoming that much sweeter. I guess if I had been returning, I'd probably have told you more about what actually went on there. As it was, everything at home was happening so fast it just didn't seem as important anymore. I sure do thank you, though, for not sending me back."

Betty laughed. "You're welcome, but since we're playing 'true confessions,' you might want to know that there was a letter included with your grades suggesting that it would be best for all concerned if you didn't re-enroll. Maybe you just wore the good captain out."

"And you're right about things happening in East Aurora," she continued. "I knew my job at Curtiss-Wright wouldn't last much longer, and a friend told me that the Foreign Service in Washington was hiring people to help with the reconstruction in Europe. That sounded like a grand adventure, so I wrote to the State Department for more information and soon after sent in my application."

While Betty was starting to plan for a new career overseas, I resumed my entrepreneurial efforts at home by becoming a substitute paperboy for the *Buffalo Evening News*. The lad whose route it was wanted the summer off, and that was fine with me. I traveled the route on my trusty Schwinn, and I could hit the keyhole of a front door from 30 feet away, with only an occasional rooftop landing.

During the day, I went to the Boys Club day camp, and once again swimming was part of the curriculum. We had a good swimming hole and a competent instructor, but I just couldn't get it. "Just lie on your back and you can float all day." Sure. I did as he said, and within seconds my feet sunk to the bottom and I was gasping for air.

Every now and again, I rode out to the farm with one or two of my pals and camped out in the woods of my 150-acre playground. Maude provided the chow: a few eggs or a chunk of dinner roast and bread, along with generous portions of her delicious pies. Now that I was older, my buddies and I found additional hideouts and developed an even more sophisticated dam system.

Ever since the war began, it had been front and center in the minds of most Americans, including the children. Instead of following the baseball standings, as many kids do today, we'd followed the war, talking of Anzio and Normandy, D-Day and the Bulge, and daydreaming of fighters and bombers, tanks and armor. Now that the war in Europe was won, its true horrors were beginning to be shown in the newsreels and newspapers, and the devastation was almost unbelievable.

The troops were coming home but not to stay. The Japanese were still very much in the mix. Clever opponents, they fought to the death with a fanaticism that Western civilization couldn't fathom. No one had any illusions about the final cost of victory.

Franklin Roosevelt was dead. Harry Truman had been sworn is as President. And although the family was split politically and there was great debate around the dinner table about what should happen next, we all agreed that our great generals would soon be victorious.[36]

August 6, 1945: *Hiroshima*. August 9, 1945: *Nagasaki*. A terrible weapon ended a terrible war. And for a time, the world was at peace.

Finally: Peace

"You know, Betty, the thing I remember best about that summer was my birthday. It was a Tuesday, and the family was holding a party for me. We had hotdogs and potato salad, and everyone was excited because we knew the war would end soon. Afterward, I blew out the 11 candles on my cake. It was angel food, my favorite. Just as Grandmother began to slice it, the fire whistles started

---

[36] Franklin Delano Roosevelt, after four terms as President of the U.S., died at Warm Springs, GA, of a cerebral hemorrhage on April 12, 1945.

screaming. We could hear car horns and people shouting and then all the church bells started to ring at once. It was one heck of a birthday celebration."

August 14, 1945: V-J Day. The Japanese surrendered and World War II was over. After years of courage and sacrifice, the United States and its Allies had made the world safe for democracy, and our boys were coming home. Everyone was glued to the radio and newspapers and magazines flew off the racks. We couldn't consume enough information. Smiles were everywhere. This was the happiest Americans had been since before the crash of 1929, and their future was now.[37]

"You're right," Betty said. "It was an incredible celebration. I'm not sure I ever saw anything like it, before or since. Of course, once the war was over, the military no longer needed our planes, and Curtiss-Wright soon closed down. I hadn't heard anything about my Foreign Service application, so in the meantime I decided to go back to school to brush up on my typing and shorthand.

"Each day I took the bus from East Aurora into Buffalo, attended morning classes, and took the bus home. One day shortly after the term started, I was waiting for the one o'clock bus in front of the school when someone ran out to say there was an important telephone call for me. I was so frightened; I thought something had happened to you or to Mother or Daddy. I didn't know what to do. If I went back in to take the call, I'd miss the bus, and there wasn't another for two or three hours. So I told the school to say I was on my way, got on the bus, and sat on the edge of my seat all the way home.

"When I got there," Betty continued, "my mother took one look at my face and burst out laughing. It seems there hadn't been a disaster after all. She'd just called to tell me that a man from the State Department had been at the house investigating my background. He'd gone through everything, even looking in my bedroom drawers. Well, I guess my drawers must have passed muster, because he left word that he wanted to interview me at the Buffalo Hotel where he was staying. Later that afternoon, Mother drove me in to see him, and it wasn't long after that I was hired as a Foreign Service agent. I would be working for the Office of Political Affairs in Berlin, but first I had to go to Washington for training."

"I remember how excited I was, how excited we all were, about your new job," I said. "Of course, I missed you when you left for Washington and later when you were overseas, but living with Grandmother was a treat, especially since nobody prepared a better meal. I particularly looked forward to Friday nights. Since rationing was still in effect, we didn't have meat all that often, but every Friday night we had lamb or pork chops.

---

[37] On October 24, 1929, prices on the New York Stock Exchange, the largest stock market in the world, collapsed. Known as Black Thursday, many people mark this day as the beginning of the Great Depression.

"'Here's a nice pork chop, Donald,' Grandmother would say, but she never gave one to Grandpa. She served *him* macaroni and cheese, scooping it onto his plate like a misfired cow plop. Finally I got up the courage to ask why Grandpa got macaroni when the rest of us got chops. Grandmother said it was because he was Catholic and Catholics couldn't eat meat on Fridays. I can tell you, it sure made me glad to be a Presbyterian."

Betty laughed out loud. "Good thing that was before Vatican II," she said, "or you'd have been sharing that pork chop."[38]

Back at East Aurora

September 1945, and I was back at East Aurora Elementary, the scene of my greatest humiliation. On this, the first day of sixth grade, I walked into school with some dread, but I needn't have worried. The guys were friendly—we'd been in camp together all summer—and if the girls remembered "the sneeze," they didn't bring it up. Maybe I was going to be in the inner circle after all. I hoped so, because I was starting to notice girls in a new way, particularly one of the prettiest in the class. It seemed something was happening to her 11-year-old body. I still felt too shy to talk to her, but maybe I should reconsider. Otherwise, how could I share my vast knowledge about Harold and words of love in the grain bin? Did she have a bike? Could she ride that far? Slow down, big boy. My mind never stopped.

My grades in military school had been quite good, so once again I was in the A group. But East Aurora was not Linsly. Unhampered by thoughts of the good captain and spared from scrutiny in my usual spot at the back of the room, I spent a lot of time daydreaming. My interest in what the teacher was saying soon started to slide, and my grades weren't far behind. I was following my own study guide, pondering the mysteries of life sparked by the blaze of golden maples in the crisp fall air or the sight of one of the girls looking my way. In fact, after devoting significant amounts of daydreaming to the effort, I came to the conclusion that three things were really important to me. The first was career (that was settled—I was going to be a fighter pilot), the second was food (I loved everything), and the third? Well, I wasn't so sure about the third, but I knew it revolved around women.

---

[38] The Second Ecumenical Council of the Vatican, or Vatican II, was convened by Pope John XXIII in 1962 and closed by Pope Paul VI in 1965. Often credited with modernizing the Catholic Church, the council relaxed various rules and regulations, among them the prohibition against eating meat on Fridays. Since Vatican II, church members must refrain from eating meat only on Fridays during Lent.

Chapter 20 – Endings and Beginnings

1945–1947

My educational performance at East Aurora was less than stellar. Although I no doubt contributed to this state of affairs by daydreaming, our teacher, once again a female, was particularly strict with the boys. The girls, it seemed, could do no wrong. In spite of the teacher, however, I loved art. I found it a wonderful way to express myself, and although I was optimistic by nature, working on an art project made me even happier.

Shortly before Christmas, the school scheduled an open house for parents and friends. I'd done a painting of the farm that was my best yet, and I couldn't wait to show it off. Even better, Betty was home on a final leave from Washington before being posted to Germany, so she could attend.

On open house night, I brought my mother and grandmother into the classroom where art projects were displayed, but my painting wasn't there. In fact, the only pictures on display were those done by girls. "Where is my grandson's painting?" Grandmother asked. Begrudgingly, the teacher dug through a stack of artwork on her desk, pulled out my picture, and stood it up for their appraisal. Betty sparkled with pride, Grandmother nodded appreciatively, and I felt like a star, but as we walked out of the room, the teacher dismissively stuffed the painting back into the pile. My mother noticed this insult (thank heavens Grandmother didn't, or the teacher would have been dead meat), and later we discussed it.

"Life isn't always fair, so get on with life," my mother said. It was a hard lesson— sometimes we don't get credit when credit is due—and it was one that would prove useful again and again. Sadly, however, from that time forward my creative work in art stopped being a priority.

Christmas 1945 was wonderful. Everybody was home from the war alive, including Uncle Dan and Uncle Walt, Aunt Carolyn's husband. Dan had probably been the most at risk. He'd island-hopped with MacArthur's forces and had the best perspective of the war I'd ever heard. His uniform was ablaze with campaign ribbons and medals, and although he spoke with little emotion, he never tired of entertaining me with stories of his many adventures and descriptions of the places he'd been. He told of the jungle rot that ravaged his body as he slogged through New Guinea. He showed me a bloody Japanese flag and a tattered uniform stripped off a dead enemy soldier, but I never heard him express hate, only a quiet resolve. Dan was a career officer, so instead of being discharged he was on his way to Frankfurt, Germany, to join the occupation forces. Mary had been discharged from the Navy and was going with him.

As children and teenagers, the majority of young adults in America had felt the pinch of the Depression, and many had gone from high school directly into the military or into civilian jobs supporting the war effort. When it was finally over, those who survived had a renewed enthusiasm for education, family, and work. More than anything, they wanted to get on with their lives and the lives of their children. Cars, homes, consumer goods, and education were all available; optimism reigned; and it soon seemed that every married woman in America was pregnant.

Typical of this group was Uncle Walt. Like thousands of returning servicemen and women, Walt came home to a loving spouse and a new child every year and a half. He also took advantage of the GI Bill and was soon enrolled in engineering school at the University of Buffalo. To support his family until he graduated, he delivered milk from dawn until school started and sacked groceries on the weekends, but he still had time to laugh, hike, and be a dad.[39]

My mother left for Germany on February 26, 1946. The devastation was appalling, she wrote, but her life was busy and enjoyable, and she was doing and seeing things most people only read about in books. One of her letters contained a vague promise that I would join her sometime. I liked that idea, but in the meantime I kept busy with school, delivering the *Courier-Express* (I'd gotten my old route back the previous fall), and Boy Scouts. As a Scout, I'd advanced through the ranks to second class, but since I had never learned to swim, further promotion was out of the question.

I also continued my love affair with books. For its day, East Aurora had a phenomenal library. I spent many hours there, and the books I didn't finish, I brought home. Jack London was still my favorite author, and as I mushed through the snow delivering my papers, I took on the persona of his characters, just as Mark Twain's Tom Sawyer and Huck Finn were my summertime companions.[40]

---

[39] The GI Bill, often considered to be the last piece of legislation of Franklin Roosevelt's New Deal, provided educational benefits and low-interest, zero-down-payment home loans to those who had served in the war. Although benefits have changed over the years, servicemen and women in the 21st century, whether serving in peacetime or wartime, can still take advantage of the GI Bill.

[40] Samuel Clemens, known to millions as Mark Twain, created Huckleberry Finn for

Playing Ball

Winter melted into spring, and baseball season renewed my interest in becoming the new Ted Williams, great Boston Red Sox hitter and Marine Corps pilot. At Linsly, I'd played sports under controlled conditions and done okay. This experience, plus the used catcher's mitt Grandpa had bought for me, made me feel fairly confident.

In East Aurora, however, there were no adults involved. We simply ran to the park and chose up teams. One hotshot tossed a bat to another and they went hand-over-hand until the last to hold the knob of the bat picked first. The waiting boys were chosen one by one until just a single boy remained. Then the verbal struggle began—you take him; no, you take him, it's your turn—until finally one of the captains gave in. "All right, I'll take him today, but you have to take him tomorrow. Got it?" The loser then turned to me.

"Here's the deal, Wright. You play the fourth right fielder, and if the ball comes your way, you stand clear so the first right fielder can catch it. Oh, and unless we're 20 runs ahead, you can't bat. Deal?"

"Deal." I made the team. It was better than not playing, and maybe the other right fielders would trip and fall and I would make the impossible catch. As the ball started over the wall, I'd save the day in front of a Red Sox scout who just happened to be in town. Then the Sox would bring me to Boston for special training. What the heck. What's life if you can't dream big? And besides, I could always look forward to that 20th run.

One day I showed up at the park early, at the same time as Harvey Stinger, one of the nicer hotshots. Harvey was a good guy and a great athlete, but earlier that spring a car had knocked him off his bike and fractured his skull, and this was his first day back. "Let's play catch," he said, and I was thrilled. We started tossing the ball back and forth, and my confidence grew. *I'm not really a bad player,* I thought. *I just need a chance.* At that, I went into my very best imitation of Bob Feller's windup and let the ball fly. Good golly, it was beautiful.[41]

In the meantime, Harvey turned around to talk to one of his friends.

"Harvey!" I screamed in panic. He whipped back, ducked, and caught the prefect strike in the mouth. Blood was everywhere, and I felt as if someone

---

his 1876 novel, *The Adventures of Tom Sawyer.* In 1884, Twain wrote *The Adventures of Huckleberry Finn,* the story of Huck and his friend Jim, a runaway slave, as they made their way down the Mississippi River on a raft.

[41] Bob Feller, born in 1918 in Van Meter, IA, was a major league baseball player for the Cleveland Indians from 1936 to 1956. With a career record of 266–162, he was inducted into the National Baseball Hall of Fame in Cooperstown, NY, in 1962.

had plunged a cold knife into my chest. Dirty rotten farmer. Snot-blowing, nail-biting, pants-pissing kid. And now a killer! Harvey lived near the park, so his mom was there in a flash to rush him to the doctor, and I took my catcher's glove and trudged home. Later that morning, she showed up at our door, gave me a hug, told me that it wasn't my fault, and said that Harvey was going to be okay. He was, and there were no hard feelings, but the incident pretty much finished my baseball career. Maybe checkers was safer.

Our East Aurora baseball team, 1946. I'm in back, third from the right. Harvey is sitting, in the light-colored sweater.

Life in Transition

Despite my difficulties in school, I finished sixth grade with acceptable marks, which I achieved with minimal begging. Summer was filled with fun and adventure, a repeat of the previous year. Plus, I began to talk to the girls. I wasn't yet ready to invite them to the grain bin, but at least I could carry on a normal conversation.

Betty wrote that she was having a great time. She was dating a man named George Kenna, an army officer well respected by his peers. He'd joined the Army National Guard in 1938 while still in high school and had soon become a sergeant. In his time off, he'd worked toward a bachelor's degree by taking night and correspondence courses. When the war broke out, the army sent him to OCS (Officer Candidate School) and he was now a major. She said a lot about George. What she didn't say was anything about me joining her in Germany, but that was okay by me. For the time being, I was satisfied with my life at home.

In September 1946, I entered the seventh grade at East Aurora Junior

High, and this time I was placed with my intellectual peers. My reading and comprehension skills served me well, but being in the C group of an A–E system was just right for me. I also had a couple of real dates with a nice girl named Twyla Cotton. We went to the Boys Club for a movie that was run backwards while we laughed uproariously, and we went to a dance. We liked each other, but we were painfully shy. Growing up isn't easy.

By the beginning of 1947, snow was everywhere, and I was getting tired of my paper route, especially of the jerks who hid behind their doors when I showed up with a dripping nose and my receipt book. One day, just as I'd started to conjure up a new bunch of daydreams, a letter came from Betty.

> *Donald dear,*
>
> *I have wonderful news and a great opportunity for you to meet new friends and see new places. You're going to join me in Berlin ASAP.*
>
> > *Love, Betty*
>
> *P.S. George has asked me to marry him and I've accepted. I'm sure you'll like him, but unfortunately he's been reassigned to the Canal Zone in Panama and we won't marry 'til next year.*

What great news. I was more than ready for another new beginning, and frankly, I thought being married would be good for my mother, as well as save a lot of explanation from me. In those days, divorce was rare and unacceptable, but I'd never wished it otherwise. If Betty had stuck with my father, life would have been far different, and I was grateful for the courage she'd shown in recognizing her mistake and moving on.

Part II: 1947–1950

Previous page: The *S.S. Ernie Pyle.*

Chapter 21 – Twelve Years Old and Bound for Berlin

1947

Back in Nokomis, Florida, in the spring of 1988, it was morning once again, and my mother was noticeably weaker, so I decided to set up the recorder in her bedroom. Betty sat up in bed, supported by several pillows and wearing a soft yellow dressing gown that set off the sparkle in her eyes. It had been a little cooler the night before, but this morning the sun was streaming through the windows, creating a patchwork pattern on the pale green bedspread.

As I fiddled with the wires and placement of the mic, Betty and George were talking about when they met. "Thinking about those times after the war brings back so many memories," Betty said. "We had a grand time in Berlin before you left for Panama, didn't we?"

"Yes we did," George replied, squeezing her hand.

"I had a grand time, too," I said, "though I'm sorry I didn't get there until after you'd left, George. In fact, it was one terrific adventure, starting when I got Betty's letter. After that, it didn't take long to work out the details: passport, military orders, deciding what to bring. Pretty soon I was ready to go. I was thrilled, and Grandmother was thrilled for me. I guess she figured I'd managed to get myself from Wheeling to Buffalo by myself at the age of ten. Why not the North Atlantic?

"I was scheduled to sail from Brooklyn Navy Yard on Monday, February 24, 1947, on the Merchant Marine cargo vessel, the *S.S. Ernie Pyle*. The fare was $230. A couple days before I was to depart, Grandmother and I boarded the Pennsylvania Railroad for New York City. We traveled by Pullman car, no doubt due to Gramps pulling some strings, so when we arrived at dawn we were rested and raring to go. What a sight! The day was cool and clear and the skyline was magnificent.[42]

---

[42] In 1862, George Pullman started a company that manufactured and operated railroad sleeper cars. At its heyday in the 1920s, the company owned and operated

We checked into the Hotel Piccadilly, and for the next two days we were happy tourists. We rode the subway, ate at the Automat, and saw *The Yearling* starring Gregory Peck. We even took in the Rockettes at Radio City Music Hall. Before we knew it, it was time for me to go and we hailed a cab for Brooklyn." [43, 44]

* * *

Sitting with my mother in 1988, sharing the details of my transatlantic adventure, I could almost smell the stale cigarette smoke and feel the well-worn upholstery of that New York City cab ride so many years before. At the Navy Yard, the terminal was no more than a niche in the largest building I'd ever seen. Millard's barn could have fit in it a hundred times. Everywhere I looked there was a frenzy of activity: people milling about, forklifts toting cargo, and tugs hauling freight wagons. The noise was deafening.

Grandmother and I checked in with a sour-looking clerk. "Who's going to look after this boy?" he asked with a challenge in his voice.

"He's perfectly capable of looking out for himself," she replied sharply, and although we could tell he didn't like it, he took my stack of military orders and ripped off his copy. In the meantime, six young ladies had joined the line behind us.

"You're going to Germany alone?" the prettiest one asked.

"Sure. How about you?" I had no trouble talking with older women; it was the nubile ones my own age that made me tongue-tied.

"We're going overseas as well, on the *S.S. Ernie Pyle*," she replied. [45]

---

up to 9,800 cars. In the 1940s, an antitrust settlement forced the firm to separate its operations and manufacturing activities. The operations arm, known as The Pullman Company, continued managing sleeper cars on the nation's railroads until 1969.

[43] In 1912, entrepreneurs Joseph Horn and Frank Hardart opened the first Automat in New York City at 1557 Broadway. Food was dispensed through small, coin-operated windows and replenished as needed by workers in an on-site kitchen. Unlike modern vending machines that offer food wrapped in plastic or paper, Automat food was served with real china and glassware. By 1939, there were 40 Automats in the city, but as other fast food options became popular, the concept died out. The last Horn and Hardart Automat closed its doors in 1991.

[44] Started in 1925 by Russell Markert in St. Louis, MO, the Rockettes were originally known as the Missouri Rockets. They made their New York City debut at Radio City Music Hall on December 27, 1932, where they have made their home ever since.

[45] In August 1945, the name Ernie Pyle was assigned to a C-4 cargo ship by the United States Maritime Commission. Pyle, who was born in 1900, worked as

"Well, then, I guess we'll be shipmates."

"How old are you?" she asked.

"Almost 13." Okay, so I stretched it a bit.

After the ladies checked in, they started an animated conversation with Grandmother. As it turned out, none of them had ever been overseas either, and they were even more excited than I was. They were also somewhat uneasy. After we chatted in the terminal for a bit, one of the gals said to Grandmother, "If you'd like, I can keep an eye on Donald." *Great,* I thought, *that's just what I need, six silly women watching over me, a kid who's ridden the rails to Wheeling and back alone.*

Grandmother accepted with heartfelt gratitude.

The clerk told us to board. I walked onto the pier with my six girlfriends and looked up at the sheer sides of the largest ship I'd ever seen. Of course, it was the only ship I'd ever seen, but this did not in any way detract from the majesty of the occasion. I gave Grandmother a hug, shouldered my well-traveled Linsly duffel bag, and followed the girls.

A seaman met us at the top of the ramp. He looked over my girlfriends for what seemed like a very long minute and then told us to follow him. The deck looked like a garbage scow: Orange rinds, apple cores, and such were everywhere. Much like her namesake, the *Ernie Pyle* was a working ship, not necessarily pretty and clean, but efficient, good at its job, and, above all, proud.

We followed the seaman down a ladder to the hold, an area that had been divided into small, open rooms filled with tiers of bunks. The gals were given a semi-room, a spot that could be at least partially closed off, and I had a room alone. It was cleaner below decks than above, but it was a far cry from what the Navy deemed shipshape. The air smelled faintly of unwashed bodies and vomit.

As soon as I found my room, I dumped my duffel bag on the bunk and joined the gals on deck to watch the ship cast off. There were only seven passengers and precious little cargo, so we were riding high in the ocean. Soon we heard the thunderous ship's horn and watched the dockhands throwing off the mooring lines. On the ocean side, a tug was easing us away from the dock.

Waving us away with a white handkerchief and growing smaller every

---

a roving correspondent for the Scripps Howard newspaper chain and became a war correspondent during World War II. His pieces were famous for capturing the perspective of the common soldier, and in 1944, he won the Pulitzer Prize for journalism. In April 1945, he was killed by Japanese fire on a small island in the South Pacific.

minute, Grandmother stood outside the terminal in her trench coat and scarf. I waved back, watching until she faded into the mist. The gals had disappeared, no doubt eager to get out of the cold and wet. A seaman asked if I would follow him to the bridge, where the ship's master, Captain Thompson, met me with a warm smile and a handshake. "Later, one of my seamen will give you the grand tour," he said, "and after that, you're free to roam the ship at will." Was I lucky, or what? First a 150-acre farm, now an entire ship.

I spent the next couple of hours on the bridge, watching the captain maneuver through New York Harbor. There was a lot of water traffic coming and going, and the men on the bridge were all work. Then we passed the Statue of Liberty and the tug was gone. I hadn't shed a tear during my entire stay at Linsly, but the sight of that Lady really choked me up. Soon after, we left the safety of the harbor and, as it turned out, the last smooth water we were to see for weeks as we thrashed our way to Le Havre, France, and then to Bremerhaven, Germany.

It didn't take long before I understood why the ship had rails everywhere. This small vessel, with its miniscule cargo, bounced like a cork going over Niagara Falls. I was on a never-ending roller coaster.

By chow time, we were in open sea and I was famished. The food was warm and plentiful, and the metal tray it was served on latched to the table so that it didn't slide to the deck. Everyone—officers, crew, and passengers—ate in the mess hall, and at first I was too hungry to notice that the gals weren't there. Soon somebody asked me to fetch them. They must have missed the chow call.

I scrambled down the ladder and after announcing myself, eased into their room. Good God! Six females lay disheveled on their bunks, surrounded by ropes of multicolored vomit that had splashed onto the deck. Their faces were the color of school paste, and when I tried to communicate with them, more specs of vomit flew as they gagged with the dry heaves. I didn't know what to do. "I guess you girls aren't feeling so good," I managed to squeak out, but before they could offer much of a reply, I escaped to fresh air. The smells and sounds coming from that room were enough to gag a maggot.

Back on the bridge, the captain asked how the gals were doing. "Not real well, Sir," I replied, remembering my military jargon from Linsly. Taking my shoulders in both of his hands, Captain Thompson looked me square in the eye.

"Son, they're all yours," he said. "Your job on this ship is to nurse those women across the North Atlantic."

Oh, man, how gross, I thought, but I quickly answered, "Yes, Sir." Then, holding my breath, I found a mop and rags and started cleaning up. The ladies were still dry-heaving, but the sounds began to diminish as each fell into a tortured sleep. Later, a sailor handed me some medicine to give to them when they woke up.

And they were going to look out for me?
(*Illustration by Babe Sargent.*)

That afternoon I got the tour. The gregarious sailor who showed me around explained that the *Ernie Pyle* was neither a Liberty nor a Victory ship but a "C-4," so designated in 1941 when the United States Maritime Commission took over the plans from American-Hawaiian Lines, for which the ships were originally designed. In all, 75 C-4s had been built. Some were used for cargo and others for troop transport.

The beauty of the ship, he said, was its speed. It could cruise at 17 knots, something no U-boat could match. It was 522 feet long, had a 72-foot beam, and displaced just over 14,000 tons. With a cruising radius of more than 12,000 miles, it was perfect for its tasks during the war, and now that peace was here, it was beginning to attract commercial interest.

The sailor went on to explain the ship's somewhat disheveled condition. It seemed that one of the post-war tasks of the *Ernie Pyle* had been to bring displaced persons from Europe to America. These folks, who had been cast about the Continent during the war, were both helpless and homeless. Ironically, my mother's job was to identify these very individuals—deserving souls with relatives in America—and separate them from former Nazis and their ilk. *No wonder the air smells foul below deck,* I thought. *When the ship was filled to overflowing with these desperate survivors, many of them ill, a mess must have been inevitable. After all, look at the trouble I have on my hands with only six sick women.*

Our final stop on the tour was the engine room, where I got a cheery greeting from all on hand. I loved this spot immediately. The smell of the oil, the sounds of the machinery thumping away, and the almost-tropical heat were a pleasant relief from the chill on deck. The engine room crew let me know I was welcome anytime, and I took them up on the offer almost daily.

After the tour I returned to my female charges, bringing them the seasick medicine along with hot tea and crackers, but it was several days before anything worked. Occasionally, I escorted one or another of them above deck, but most of the time the North Sea kept the ship awash and the gals in their bunks.

"I wish this were two years ago," one gal said as she clung desperately to the rail on one of these excursions. "Then with luck, maybe a Nazi sub would torpedo us and this misery would be over."

I couldn't imagine these women ever getting on another ship. Maybe they'd be lucky enough to find European husbands.

The foul weather continued, and even some crew members occasionally looked green around the gills, but the heaving of the ship never affected me. In fact, I couldn't have been happier: free to roam at will and surrounded by tales of war. The war fascinated me—every aspect of it, and these seamen had sailed in great convoys that supplied the troops in Europe and Russia. They told of the routes that placed their ships in some of the worst weather in the world, the constant sniping from German subs, and the harrowing rescues after being torpedoed, as many of them had been. Even when they survived the initial explosion, they explained that the chance of rescue from the wild, oily seas had been slim, especially since a ship that slowed down or broke formation in order to aid a colleague was often picked off by the Germans. One fellow claimed that the Merchant Marine had suffered the second highest death toll of any service during the war. When the seamen talked of their many lost friends, I asked "Why did you still do it?" but they just shrugged their shoulders.

Even more intriguing than the sailors' tales was the ship itself, and I explored it from stem to stern. Nobody worried about me. The sailors trusted my good judgment; and my so-called protectors were locked in their quarters, too busy praying and barfing their way across the Atlantic to be concerned about my welfare.

My favorite spot was the bridge. Day and night I watched, spellbound, as the navigator worked to get a shot through the storm-filled skies. He tried to train me to do the math, but it was beyond my skill level. Too bad I hadn't encountered him sooner. Perhaps if I'd known how useful math would turn out to be, I'd have paid more attention in the back row of my numerous classrooms.

For recreation, I played cards with anyone who had time and usually held my own, but much of my time was spent alone, observing life at sea. Since every day was stormy, we were operating at low speed to keep from shaking apart, and the seas broke over the ship almost constantly. Outfitted in heavy clothes and a yellow slicker, with the sting of sea spray on my exposed face, I loved to be above deck. The wind shrieked through the masts and rigging, and the ship's plates sounded like a steel-drum orchestra as the seas pounded the hull. I was in hog heaven.

I was neither fearful nor sickly, but I learned to respect the sea and to be careful around the machinery that moved the ship, much as I'd learned to respect the machinery on the farm. I also realized very quickly that I never wanted to be a sailor. I still couldn't swim, and the North Atlantic was both hostile and *cold.*

At last, after nearly two weeks at sea, we saw the coast of France through the low-lying clouds. As we eased by the breakwater into the port of Le Havre, the waves abated and we could see destroyed hulks lying by the sides of the harbor. We were very close to where the Allied armies had landed on D-Day, and everyone on board was conscious of the tremendous effort put forth here and throughout Europe to defeat the enemy.[46]

I, of course, was on the bridge to help dock the ship. Who was going to help on the way back?

Ashore on Foreign Soil

After all was secure, Captain Thompson asked if I'd like to go ashore. You bet. I wanted to view the destruction firsthand, but the French official, a small man with thin lips and a pencil-thin mustache, wouldn't let me off the ship. The epitome of the petty bureaucrat, he stood with open palms, showing how helpless he was to alter the facts. "I'm sorry, Monsieur," he said, "but your passport does not have ze French visa, and zat is ze rule."

"Is that so," said the skipper, who, seeing the look on my face, took me to

---

[46] D-Day, June 6, 1944, was the day the Allies invaded northwestern Europe. Nearly 3 million troops crossed the Channel from England to Normandy, France, in the largest sea invasion in history.

his stateroom, pulled out a seaman's card, and wrote "Cabin Boy" on it. Once again we started to disembark, this time waltzing by the official. Although he pursed his thin lips in frustration, the man had no choice but to let us pass. After all, it was "ze rule."

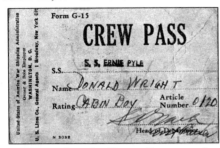

My entrée to Le Havre, France, and the realities of post-war Europe, March 1947.

To my disappointment, once ashore we saw little evidence of destruction. A few buildings were down, but most of the area had been cleaned up, and the citizens were going about their daily lives. We hadn't walked far when the captain and one of the mates slipped into a bar. The mate ordered three beers, setting one of them down in front of me. "Boy, you deserve this," he said with a laugh. "In our family, when a quart of beer was cracked, I always got a fruit juice glass full, and it never hurt me. So drink up." And I did.

By the time we got back to the ship, cargo was being winched aboard and the girls were lined up at the rail, watching soberly. They knew we still had to navigate the English Channel, which was nearly always turbulent. The usual blasting of the horn signaled our return to the sea, and we entered the Channel to Bremerhaven. Fortunately, this part of the trip was fairly smooth; even the girls didn't get sick.

My mother in her Foreign Service uniform, Berlin, 1947.

March 10, 1947. Bremerhaven was a far cry from Le Havre. Piles of rubble surrounded the few buildings left standing, and there was a smell in the air that I came to associate with the whole nation—the stench of death and despair. As the rain continued its steady beat, everything was a depressing shade of gray, brown, or black. In this town of sadness, even the skies cried.

Just as the mood of the place was beginning to get to me, I saw my mother standing on the dock under an umbrella. Dressed in the olive green, military-style uniform required by the State Department and smiling from ear to ear, she added a splash of color to the otherwise dismal landscape. It was a joyous reunion. Grandmother had cabled my time of arrival, along with the assurance that I was being carefully attended to by six State Department girls. My mother never got a chance to thank them, however, since even as we spoke they were running away from the ship and the sea forever. I did, however, get to introduce her to Captain Thompson and many of the crew, and she thanked them profusely for bringing me safely to Germany.

Chapter 22 – Stranger in a Strange Land

1947

It was now more than half a lifetime since the day I stepped off the ship in Bremerhaven, but my mother remembered as though it were yesterday. "You must have thoroughly enjoyed that voyage," Betty recalled, smiling. "If nothing else, you may have been the only one on the ship who survived with his stomach untouched. I'll never forget your face when you got your first look at Bremerhaven, though. I guess I'd grown accustomed to the extent of the damage, but now I was seeing it through your eyes."

"I was shocked, that's for sure," I said. "Everywhere I looked there were piles of rubble, and the terminal looked like a skeleton. Nothing held the roof together but a few girders, and I remember that the rain kept drizzling on us as we waited for clearance. When they called my name, I went into a small anteroom and handing over my passport and visa to the German and GI officers there. After my experience at Le Havre, I was prepared for the third degree, but they hardly glanced at my documents. 'Welcome to Germany,' they said, and waved me through.

"And then," I continued, "as soon as we went outside, you pulled out a pack of cigarettes and flashed them at the first vehicle that passed. That's when I learned the value of cigarettes."

Betty laughed. "They were certainly better than money," she said. "Back then, either we didn't realize how bad they were for us, or maybe, in light of the damage all around us, the risk seemed pretty minor. All I know is that if you wanted to get anything done in post-war Germany, cigarettes were essential."

* * *

At Betty's offer of smokes, a U.S. military truck with a German driver squealed to a halt, and she asked him, in her fractured German, for a ride to the railroad station. We climbed into the truck, and after a short ride during which the driver literally drove over, through, and around mounds of rubble, we pulled up in front of another ruin of a building, this one with the roof blown off and the rain pouring in.

"How much?" Betty asked.

"*Vier.*"

"*Nein,*" said Betty. "*Zwei.*"

They settled on *drei*, and she handed over three cigarettes, the currency of a defeated nation. As we waited for the Berlin Express, I was awestruck by the sights, sounds, and smells. Most passengers were women, clothed in dirty-looking broadcloth wraps. The only men about were cripples, also dirty and usually wearing one or more parts of a German uniform. A few of them followed us with their hands out.

We sat on a bench under a piece of roof that still clung to the rafters, shivering and waiting for the train. Betty lit a cigarette, which immediately drew a crowd. After smoking half of it, she handed the remainder to a desperate-looking man who bowed and nodded, "*Danke, danke, danke.*" The single drag he took must have pushed the smoke into his toes, because it never exited his body. He then snuffed out the butt, placed it in his pouch like a treasure, offered another bow and *danke*, and disappeared. Betty said nothing. She didn't have to: The scene before us captured everything that needed to be said.

Eventually, the train backed into the terminal. I'd seen this train a million times, captured through the eyes of Republic's P-47 Thunderbolt gun cameras and shown on Movietone News.[47]

On this day, however, most of the coach windows were covered in plywood and the engine wore patches where .50-caliber bullets had penetrated. I'd been brought up on the glories of war, but this was the reality. There was damn little glory here.

Before long, this rickety excuse for transportation pulled out of the station into the moonscape of a once-beautiful city, rumbling into the night at about 20 miles per hour. Once we reached the countryside, the neat fields gave an appearance of normalcy, but the skeletal remains of each station along the way jerked me back to reality. It took 18 long hours to reach Berlin, much of it sitting on sidings waiting for other trains to pass on the single remaining track.

Our car was noticeably nicer than the others, staffed by a German attendant and equipped with a pot-bellied stove, a snack station, and hot

---

[47] The Thunderbolt, also known as the Jug, was one of the main fighters of the U.S. Army Air Force in World War II. It was equipped with eight .50 caliber machine guns.

drinks. Its worn-down benches had long since abandoned any pretense of comfort (no Pullman sleepers here), but except for an occasional piece of paper or other trash, the car was clean and the ashtrays were always empty. In fact, during the entire year I was in Germany, I never saw a cigarette butt. The minute they were relinquished by the original smoker, they were in somebody else's pouch.

My mother had lived in Germany a little more than a year by the time I arrived, so she was able to brief me on what to expect. German marks were the official currency, but they were so devalued there weren't enough to purchase even the basic necessities. Thus the popularity of other forms of compensation: cigarettes, coffee, and chocolate bars, all of which were officially illegal and totally ignored by the authorities. Greenbacks were also treasured, but they were somewhat controlled, and people could be arrested if they used them without caution.[48]

The official American money used in the PX, commissary, and clubs was called scrip. Because it was easy to counterfeit, it was changed often and without warning, and one could exchange only that which could be explained.[49, 50]

As a rule, Betty went on to explain, Germans were not dangerous. To the contrary, almost everyone was on the edge of starvation, clothing was scarce,

---

[48] The German mark, or Reichsmark, was the official currency of Germany from 1924 until June 1948, when it was replaced in the Federal Republic of Germany (West Germany) by the Deutsche mark. When East and West Germany were unified in 1990, the Deutsche mark remained the official currency of the country until replaced by the Euro, which was introduced as electronic currency in 1999 and became legal tender on January 1, 2002. The term "greenback," slang for U.S. dollars, was first applied to paper money printed by the U.S. government during the Civil War. The ink used on the back of these bills was green.

[49] With a rich history dating back to 1880, PX (post exchange) and BX (base exchange, the air force version of the PX) facilities offer goods and services to U.S. military personnel at home and around the world. Maintained and administered by the Army and Air Force Exchange Service (a joint military endeavor), PX and BX facilities (including an online presence) are available for use by all active-duty military personnel, retirees, and reservists, as well as by U.S. State Department officials serving in foreign countries. As of 2008, there were more than 3,100 such facilities in the U.S. and abroad.

[50] Military Payment Certificates (MPCs), also known as scrip or Mickey Mouse dollars, were introduced in 1946 to avoid flooding the market in post-war Germany with U.S. dollars, which were devaluing the local currency. The government determined, however, that in order to be effective, scrip would have to be used by all U.S. military personnel serving overseas, and it remained in use, in one form or another, until 1973.

and during the winter, though everything that could be scavenged was burned, people still froze or starved to death. On the other side of the coin, the U.S. government did all it could to see that the occupying Americans wanted for nothing. Although mostly dried or canned, food was plentiful, and milk and cheese were flown in daily from Denmark. I had already observed that almost everybody smoked, and I was soon to discover that booze flowed like water.

When I asked my mother about the Nazis, she laughed. It was a miracle, she said, but she had never met one. It seems the entire German population hated Hitler and had been secretly rooting for the Americans to win the war.

On the other hand, the Germans also despised the Russians, strongly disliked the French, and barely tolerated the English. The Russians had devoured the city and its people as they swept through Berlin, much as the Germans had done on the Russian front. The more one knew about the war, the easier it was to see that each nation had more than enough reason to hate the others. Human dignity, kindness, and tolerance had been ground into the mud of Europe, and it would take a long time for them to be resurrected.

My New Home

Along with her friend, Polly Frederick, Betty had been issued a house at Am Fischtal 70C in the Zehlendorf district, close to Onkel Tom Kino subway station, which was named after the main character in Harriet Beecher Stowe's *Uncle Tom's Cabin*. As we made our way to Berlin, she told me the place was spacious and welcoming. It was under repair because the roof had been nearly blown off in the Battle for Berlin, but the workmen were almost finished. Plus, it came equipped with two maids, a gardener, and a fireman for the furnace. I couldn't wait to see it.[51]

* * *

"We rolled into Berlin about dawn," I prompted, watching as Betty rearranged herself among the pillows and sipped a cup of tea. I could tell she was tiring, but there was no question she wanted to continue. "The skies were steely gray, and once again, I couldn't believe the level of destruction. I remember that the driver gave us a tour on the way home, and the rubble looked to me like rolling hills, with spectacular ruins protruding from them."

---

[51] Fought between the Soviets and the Germans, the Battle for Berlin was one of the final battles of the European Theatre during World War II. It began on April 6, 1945, and by May 2, the Germans had surrendered and the Soviet flag flew over the Reichstag, the former German Parliament building.

Ruins of Kaiser Wilhelm Church, Berlin, 1947.

Betty took up the story. "We drove down the Kurfürstendamm, Berlin's main boulevard," she said, "past the ruins of Kaiser Wilhelm Memorial Church and the bombed-out Chancellery of the Third Reich. When the driver pointed out the Chancellery balcony, where Hitler had given many of his speeches, we stopped and I took your picture, complete with Hitler salute. You were one tired kid that morning, but you took in everything, and when we finally got to the house, you couldn't decide whether to explore or talk with the maids."

"Frau Steinkopf and Frau Strohm. I can still see their faces," I said. "Wasn't Frau Steinkopf an aristocrat or something? I know that in post-war Germany, jobs were almost non-existent, and those who were fortunate enough to have them sometimes turned up in the strangest places."

"She was," Betty confirmed. "Frau Strohm was just an ordinary German, but Frau Steinkopf was from the upper class. Her father had been in the foreign service, and she'd been married to a general, one of the many German officers who never came home from the Russian front."

"That's right. I remember now. Didn't you see her again in the 1970s?"

"I did. When George and I were in Berlin in 1975, we went to visit her. She was living in the home she'd had before the war. It was a mansion, really, with tall ceilings and the most gorgeous grandfather's clock I've ever seen. And this time, her servants waited on both of us. Back in 1947, however, she was no better off than anyone else, and she was terrified of the Russians. After the Battle for Berlin, she told me that her daughters climbed trees to avoid being raped."

"Later on," I said, "I really came to appreciate her and Frau Strohm as well, but that first day I was so tired when I finally hit my room on the third floor that all I could think about was sleep."

"And sleep you did," Betty confirmed. "In fact, I don't think you woke up until Polly got home from work that evening."

Chapter 23 – *Ich bin Berliner*

1947–1948

My mother met Polly Frederick soon after she arrived in Berlin, and they remained friends for the rest of their lives. Originally from Sewickley, Pennsylvania, a small town near Pittsburgh, Polly had spent the war working for the Foreign Service in London. She was a clever mimic of the sound of V-2 rockets and buzz bombs, and she even claimed to have been somewhat of a fatalist, occasionally sleeping through the attacks. When the Germans surrendered, she was one of the first noncombatants to enter Berlin, and she'd been there ever since.

Polly Frederick, Berlin, ca. 1946.

Other than my mother, Polly was the first American I met in Germany, and we hit it off immediately. That night after dinner, she and Betty took me to meet the neighbors, eight State Department girls who shared the house catty-cornered from us with Astro, their boxer dog. These women bore no resemblance to the timid travelers I'd encountered on the ship. In fact, they were destined to become some of my dearest friends.

The next morning, Betty issued me a pack of cigarettes for cash, and I boarded the bus on my way to seventh grade at the army school. The bus was a 2½ -ton truck, outfitted with a canvas top and stairs. It was staffed with the usual female German monitor, one of the many make-work jobs created to help ease the problem of massive unemployment. Military brats rarely stand on ceremony, so by the time we arrived at the school, I'd already met most of the kids on the bus. "Where're you from?" and "What's your name?" were all it took to generate instant friendship.

The school was spectacular, as most army schools are. The teachers were adventurous and knowledgeable, and discipline was never a problem. The reason was simple. One warning warranted a call to your sponsor, the head of household responsible for the conduct of his or her dependents. One more and the entire family was sent back to the States, or for all we knew, before a firing squad. As a result, nobody ever raised a voice. We loved where we were and what we were doing, and we tried to make life good for all. Of course, this was before children had civil rights, but everybody benefited, even the occasional bad kid, who was treated in kind.

The war had been over for nearly two years, yet from the looks of the city, it could have ended the day before. The downtown area was a pile of rubble, with Kaiser Wilhelm Church and a battered Brandenburg Gate protruding from its center.[52]

No matter where you went, every German had his or her tale of woe. Thousands of men had gone to war and never come back—most of them killed on the Eastern Front—and I rarely saw a whole man the entire time I was in the country. Those who were not broken in body—missing an arm or a leg—were broken in spirit. The women, left behind when their men went off to war, were now dressed in rags or dirty-looking wraps, with sniveling, confused children clinging to their sides.

One of the most prevalent make-work jobs for these women was chipping cement from the bricks of destroyed buildings and piling them neatly for later reconstruction. A common joke of the day involved a diplomat who visited the military governor in Berlin. "How did you sleep?" the governor asked the diplomat over breakfast the next morning.

"Quite well, thank you, considering that the trains ran all night."

"Trains?" the governor said. "There's no railroad in this area."

The following day, the governor asked the same question and received the same answer. That night, the two gentlemen agreed to sit together to see what the noise was all about. Sure enough, it wasn't long before the diplomat's room was filled with the unmistakable sound of a continuous train. The men donned their coats and went to investigate. Not far from the hotel, they came across a line of hundreds of women, rhythmically passing freshly chipped bricks, one to another: *Danke-schön, Bitte-schön; Danke-schön, Bitte-schön*—the rhythm of the rails.

---

[52] The Brandenburg Gate, which is 65 feet high and 213 feet wide, was built in the late 1700s. Once the western gate to the city, the Nazis used it during World War II to symbolize their power. After the war, it was restored by the East and West German governments but was closed in 1961 when the Berlin Wall was erected. In 1989, the Wall fell and the gate reopened, symbolizing the unification of the city and the country.

Adjoining our backyard was Am Fischtal Park, one of the sites of the Battle for Berlin. The park and its surrounds formed an eerie landscape of twisted armor, destroyed tanks, and graves. One day after school, I came home to find canvas curtains set up in our backyard. Behind them, German laborers were digging up shallow graves, bagging the remains of their warriors and carrying them to a waiting truck in the street.

To our parents' chagrin, we boys took full advantage of this playground of war, though we did use caution in case we came across an unexploded mine. Occasionally we would find a rusting rifle, bayonet, or other artifact, but I never heard of anyone setting off a mine. Perhaps the battle happened so quickly that mines weren't used.

Axis meets Allies: with my friend Dietrich in Berlin, 1947.

And I found a Nazi! Dietrich, my best and only German friend, was a proud and handsome lad about 14 years old. He was weaned in the Hitler Youth, fought the hated Russians in the Battle for Berlin, and bragged that he had personally killed many of them. He had a picture of himself at age 11 beside a rifle twice his size. He spoke English well and liked Americans, but he was unapologetic about his role as a soldier or his participation in the Hitler Youth.[53]

Before I went to Germany, I had looked upon the war almost as a romance novel, filled with victory and heroism and the exploits of my beloved fighter pilots, but I had little appreciation for the sacrifice and misery of the combatants on both sides. Like most Americans, I had despised all Germans, not understanding that the many paid dearly for the ambitions of the few. Walking the streets of Berlin in 1947 washed away these preconceptions. Even though I was well-fed and well-clothed, it was impossible not to feel the universal deprivations of war.

---

[53] The Hitler Youth was a paramilitary organization of the Nazi Party that existed from 1922 until 1945, when it was disbanded by the Allies. From 1936 onward, membership in the organization was compulsory for all German young men. In 1923, there were about 1,000 members. By 1940, membership had grown to 8 million.

To the Victor, the Spoils

The German people were often depressed and nearly always destitute, but many of the roadblocks to alleviating their deprivations lay with the victors: Russians versus Americans, British, and French. The French, especially, were out for revenge, and the Brits, in their highbrow way, became a bit feisty as well. On the other hand, the Americans, without a doubt some of the kindest and least-prejudiced people in the world, often treated the Germans as erring but forgiven children. Many GIs shared freely of what they had with German individuals or entire families.

In a point of legality, much of this sharing would not have passed the military governor's black market test, but then again, the black market was often the only market there was. Everything was for sale: Meissen porcelain, paintings, antiques. The starving survivors couldn't eat that sort of stuff, so life was a complex system of barter, with cigarettes being the main currency. Grandmother sent boxes filled with cartons of Camels and Lucky Strikes, and Betty, who had wonderful taste, used them wisely to barter for art and furnishings for her anticipated new home with George. Every now and again she attempted to ship some of her purchases home, but many never made it. "From each according to his ability to each according to his needs," preached Karl Marx, and this maxim was employed again and again as my mother's boxes passed through the Russian Zone.

Household possessions were not the only area in which the Russians took what they wanted. When they overran the city in the Battle for Berlin, they ravished every female they could find, "just as the Germans did to our women," a Russian colonel told me at a party.

Strangely enough, at one time Russians and Germans had liked and respected each other. Thanks to the brutalities of despots Stalin and Hitler, however, any Germans who fell under the Red Star paid and paid and paid. There are no written records or accurate accounts of the countless Germans who disappeared or of what happened to them, but as the Russian colonel said, they did to the Germans "just as the Germans would do to us."

Once the occupying forces included American, French, and British armies as well as the Russians, wholesale rape was no longer tolerated. However, those interested in sex found more than enough women who were willing to accommodate their needs for a price. From the women's point of view, the choices were few: chip cement or haul ashes, and hauling ashes was easier.

Two cigarettes were good for a quickie with a so-so gal, and a pack bought a night with a beauty queen.[54]

Every man seemed to have a blond on his arm, and my time in Germany, despite my previous knowledge of Harold and his ladies, provided a sex education second to none. Venereal disease was so prevalent that barracks' films depicted horror stories of scabbed peckers falling off bodies, testicles being carted away in wheelbarrows, and every other disgusting thing that can happen to a man's favorite possessions. Boxes of rubbers and pro kits, designed for after-the-act disease control, could be found in every barracks, Club, bathroom, or hangout; and "Beware of Veronica *Danke-schön*" echoed a cautionary note on Allied radio. Even the newspapers had facts and ads to help control STDs. All these warnings may have helped some, but the fact remained: Two cigarettes for a blond was a mighty tempting proposition.

To everyone's delight, rubbers also provided entertainment for the younger set, who would blow them up and fill them with water. More than one German was knocked off his or her bike by a water-filled "rubber" balloon from a passing school bus, as the harried monitor tried to gain some control. Of course, neither my friends nor I even thought of such perverted behavior.

Despite the physical and psychological ravages of war and the many depravities of peace, there was still a great deal of culture to be enjoyed in post-war Germany, and Betty made certain I was exposed to as much of it as possible.

My mother knew everybody who was anybody. Almost every Sunday after church, we went to brunch at Truman Hall, where the military governor, General Lucius Clay, would pay his respects to my attractive and vivacious mother.[55]

Betty also hired the concertmaster from the Berlin Symphony to teach me to play the piano. The price of a lesson was a pound of coffee, but despite the man's best efforts, any musical talent I might have had remained latent. Eventually he told my mother, "Keep your coffee; you're going to need it more than I." Next she turned to the school, which offered lessons in various instruments. I chose the clarinet, and although some kids got instruments that

---

[54] Hauling ashes is a euphemism for sex that comes from the early days of blues lyrics, a venue in which the double entendre is common.

[55] Constructed in 1946 of reclaimed rubble from buildings destroyed by Allied bombings, Truman Hall, with seating for a couple hundred troops, was the main dining hall for U.S. military and government personnel stationed in the area. Starting in 1950, facilities such as shops and a PX began to be added, and the area became known as Truman Plaza. When Germany was unified in 1990, soldiers from the Western Allies began to depart. After the last of them left in 1994, the entire area was torn down.

worked, mine was among the lot furnished by some greedy war profiteer. All it did was shriek.

If the Germans and Russians had any common ground, it was in their love of music and dance. The world-famous Theater des Westens, which opened in 1912 and was rebuilt in 1922 after a fire, was in the Russian Zone. Although the theater had suffered damage to its roof during the war, repairs were nearly complete, and those who attended dressed in their finest. The Russians had resplendent uniforms adorned with decoration, with fine ladies at their sides, though I suspect the ladies were not Russian. The Americans and other Allies wore their more modest uniforms, and the Germans, though often tattered, carried themselves with pride.

Every Saturday night, Betty and a covey of her friends went to the opera, ballet, or symphony. I was always invited, and I was delighted to go, since by this time the only farm boy left in me consisted of wonderful memories of that era of my life. The performances featured the finest stars of European opera and ballet, and my mother knew them all. As self-appointed social director for our State Department neighbors, she'd discovered that coffee and cigarettes could often entice these veteran artists to perform for private parties, and she took full advantage of the situation.

Five of the eight State Department girls in Berlin. Laverne, Judy, Pearl—I can no longer recall all of their names, but they were the beginning of my fascination with women.

The gals of the State Department were classy chicks—well-educated, attractive, and dressed to the nines—and we developed a mutual admiration society almost as soon as I arrived in Berlin. My being around seemed to bring them closer to the brothers and friends they'd left behind, and I was thrilled by the attention. It wasn't long before they invited me for dessert nearly every night (I told you I was smooth), and when they rented a 40-foot sailboat on Lake Plötzensee, I was the guest of honor. I, of course, was always available to escort them to dinner at Truman Hall or to the movies, as long as they paid.

After a while, the gals fought so much over being my friend that I started to rate them on a scale of 1 to 5, assigning new ratings each week. One of the best ways to rate high on my list was to invite me to dinner, especially since their cook had been the pastry chef for Hermann Goering, former commander of the Luftwaffe. I was scrupulously fair in my ratings, I thought, but when I shared my system with them, they were very insulted. Obviously, I had a lot more to learn about women.

Since they were so full of adventure, the gals loved to throw lavish parties. At one of these events, a costume party, the guests ranged from political advisor Robert D. Murphy, who later became U.S. Ambassador to Belgium, to a group of Russian officers. The Russians brought a variety of alcoholic beverages enjoyed by all. Some guests enjoyed themselves so much that they climbed into the bathtubs and went to sleep. When they woke up, they were unable to climb out again without help. I don't recall indulging in the alcohol, but I did go to the party dressed as a little girl, which was probably mind-numbing enough. Betty said I looked beautiful.

Acquiring proper attire for other social occasions was easily accomplished, assuming one had the wherewithal. A custom-tailored suit and accompanying shirt could be had for a pound or two of coffee or some chocolate bars and a few smokes. My personal tailor claimed proudly that although he'd never belonged to the Party himself, he'd been very popular with the Nazi upper echelon. There was no way to verify this claim, since as Betty pointed out, Nazis of any ilk were a rare commodity in post-war Berlin. I never met enough of them to fill even a small bus.

On August 14, 1947, the State Department girls gave me a fabulous 13th birthday party, inviting Betty, Polly, and me to their home for dinner. Their chef prepared my favorite meal, rack of lamb and all the fixings, followed by a cake fit for royalty. As a gift they presented me with a beautiful Airedale puppy, complete with a red ribbon around his neck. I named him Jerry, and he became my constant companion.

After the festivities were over and we'd confined Jerry to a puppy-proof corner, this proud 13-year-old *man* escorted his ladies to hear the opera *Hansel and Gretel*, where each of my escorts took turns sitting next to me. At the close of the performance, the stars paid their respects and my ten delightful cohorts and I boarded the subway for home. It was a perfect night.

The Cold War had not yet officially begun, but the Russians loved to tweak the Allies, and since the electrical plants were in the Russian Zone, one of their favorite tricks was to cut the power. Normally, blackouts lasted for no more than 30 minutes, so when the lights went out in the subway, we recognized the drill, turned on our flashlights, and prepared to wait it out. This time, however, the lights stayed out, and after a while, we joined the other passengers on a walk beneath the city. We kept it light and cheerful, but we had our concerns. After all, this was the same subway the Germans had supposedly flooded during the war, drowning thousands of prisoners in the process.[56]

We finally emerged near the Kurfürstendamm into a city teeming with rain and lit only by the occasional headlights of a passing vehicle. Undaunted, we flagged down a truck, hoisted our drenched bodies into its bed, and sang and giggled our way home. What a way to turn 13!

Lessons Learned

Frau Steinkopf was an elegant, proper woman who spoke many languages, had traveled the world, and was accustomed to life's finest pleasures. Now she came to work on a bicycle and attended to my every need. She woke me in the morning and prepared my breakfast, washed and ironed my clothing, and saw that I was properly dressed (if only I'd had her at Linsly). She also attempted to teach me German. I called her Steiney, and although she initially bristled a bit at the informality of this friendly young kid, we got along well.

Steiney and I spent many hours together, and she spoke often of the friends and family she had lost, the hardships she'd endured, and the many hours she'd spent in cellars while the Allies relentlessly bombed her city to smithereens. She focused particularly on the Russians, the atrocities they had bestowed upon her and her countrymen and their ignorance of things we accepted as commonplace. Having no experience with indoor plumbing, she said, many Russian soldiers thought a flushing toilet was a magic sink. Or, unable to figure out how to turn on the simplest of stoves, they broke up furniture to build a fire on the floor in order to prepare a meal. "When the Americans arrived," she said, "it was a huge relief. If you have to lose a war, lose to the Americans."

When we went into the Russian Zone, the differences in culture were obvious even to me. The soldiers were fearsome in their baggy, careless uniforms, and while there were times when everything was calm, there were other times when it was more than a bit frightening. The Russians didn't speak German or English, and they didn't plan to learn. They thought the Americans were soft because we didn't beat up on a people who were already beaten, both physically and spiritually.

Although she was industrious and tried to do a good job, it was obvious

---

[56] The ideological conflict between the United States and the USSR (Union of Soviet Socialist Republics) during the second half of the 20th century is known as the Cold War.

that Steiney had far more experience being done for than doing for others. This became obvious when Frau Strohm was away for some reason and Steiney had to make dinner. On one such occasion the menu included baked potatoes, but when we sat down to eat, we found the potatoes had been peeled before baking. Explaining that baked potatoes were done "with the skin and all," Betty felt she'd cleared up the misunderstanding until the next time, when she came home to find naked potatoes roasting in the oven, a pile of peelings baking alongside them.

In addition to Steiney, I was constantly querying other Germans, as well as Americans and Russians, about their wartime experiences. Based on the answers, I sometimes wondered if we'd been in the same conflict. I particularly asked the Germans about the Jews. "We didn't know," said most, though I sometimes sensed pride and arrogance in their answers and they never looked me in the eye. Some mumbled about the Treaty of Versailles and tried to pin the guilt on leaders of the world. And just as Ike predicted, a few denied the Holocaust had ever happened. There's no question that most Germans were shocked and horrified by Hitler's "final solution," but underneath it all, they knew that they, too, had contributed to the hate and persecution that caused it.[57]

Now that the war was over, there was one thing upon which the entire populace did agree: The German economy was in ruins. This meant that the black market was thriving, and with my private cache of cigarettes, I soon became a big-time operator, junior grade.

One of my most spectacular successes involved a tiny, four-note harmonica I found in one of the semi-destroyed shops. After I took it to school and discovered that everybody wanted one, I went back to the shop and bought the one-armed owner's entire stock for a pack of Camels. (In those days I used cigarettes only for currency. I wasn't yet dumb enough to smoke them myself.) The next day at school, I set up shop in the cafeteria. By the end of the lunch hour, I'd sold every instrument for 50 cents a pop, and the place sounded like a harmonica band. To the delight of the teachers, the fad only lasted for a week, but it was a week from which I profited greatly.

Despite the black market, currency and possessions were insufficient to purchase even the bare necessities of life for many in post-war Berlin.

---

[57] Dwight David Eisenhower, known as Ike, was the nation's 34th President. He was born in 1890 and grew up in Abilene, KS. During World War II, Ike held posts of increasing responsibility until he was appointed Supreme Allied Commander for the invasion of Europe in 1944. After the war, he became president of Columbia University but was called back to active duty in 1950 to command the NATO (North Atlantic Treaty Organization) forces in Europe. He was elected President in 1952 and served two terms. He died in 1969.

This was brought home to us in a new way when the girls lost their beloved boxer Astro to kidnappers. The Germans are fierce dog-lovers, sometimes feeding their animals before themselves during the dark days of the war. So when the MPs found Astro's remains over a fire pit in Am Fischtal Park, we were heartbroken, but we also understood, more than ever before, the absolute desperation of the German people.

We, too, were robbed—on three occasions—though fortunately of inanimate possessions only. On one occasion, deep in the night, we actually heard the intruders but kept quiet out of fear for our lives. After the third break-in, Bill, an agent from the CID (a branch of the military police detective force) started spending nights on our couch in hopes of catching the thieves. Nobody was ever caught, but Bill provided us with entertaining company in exchange for many a great meal, and the robberies stopped. In addition to being an expert shot and having a black belt in karate, Bill was a personable guy who was more than willing to share stories of his war adventures. One day he asked if I wanted to go with him to visit a prison. You bet. Shucks, I'd never even seen a prison, except in the movies.

This former Nazi prison was an ominous structure, its cells dark and cramped. "Why don't you step into one," Bill dared, and when I did, he slammed the door shut, locked it, and started to walk away.

"If you're going to be a black marketeer, you'd better get used to being a jailbird," he said, and my heart hit my toes. Somehow my foray into the harmonica business had gotten back to him, and he was letting me know just how serious it could be. My first time in the jug. When he let me out a short time later, he wasn't nasty, but he wasn't laughing, either.

Black marketeering was a bit more serious than shouting nasty words in church or stealing candy, but the end result was the same. Once caught, I had sense enough not to do it again.

The Residue of War

Material goods were not the only area of shortage in post-war Berlin. Most of the occupying forces, military or civilian, were there alone. Those who were married (almost always male) had left their dependents in the States. Those who were single (the majority female) were looking for someone with whom to spend the rest of their lives. There were also thousands of single German women who had lost their loved ones in the war. As a result, for every German war bride or marriage between Americans serving abroad, there were countless tales of women, both German and American, being left behind when their partners, who had claimed to be single, returned at the end of their tours to a wife and family in the U.S.

These lessons were not lost on my mother and her friends, so when Betty was introduced to a young officer named George Kenna not long after her arrival in Berlin, she went to great lengths to make sure he was single as advertised.

* * *

Looking over at George and Betty now, more than 40 years after their marriage, I smiled as I recalled the story. "Do you remember," I asked my mother, "what a hard time George's friends gave him when you two started to date?"

Betty laughed. "Do I ever. I'd seen so many young women become the victims of soldiers who claimed to be single when they weren't, and I was determined it wasn't going to happen to me. George's fellow officers knew this, and they played it to the hilt. 'Hi George,' they'd say when they saw us together, 'how's the wife and kid? Oops, sorry George.' Poor George had to prove himself again and again."

"Then once we got engaged, George was posted to Panama and we had to postpone our marriage for a year. Of course, in the meantime it was great to have you there. Between my friends and the diversions of working and seeing the country, I had a great time in Berlin, and I loved being able to travel to other places in Europe.

"One of my favorite things to do," Betty continued, "was to take tours on a luxury train called the Dreamliner that had once belonged to Hermann Goering. The train, which could travel at 75 miles per hour and accommodated up to 26 passengers, had been 'requisitioned' by the U.S. government, and one could sign up ahead of time for various trips. I went to Beethoven's home in Bonn, to Cologne, and—one of my favorites—to Rothenburg, a walled city from medieval times. After one of the tours, though, we all became deathly ill. Some people even had to be hospitalized. It seems the restaurant in the city we'd visited had served stuffed eggs that had gone bad, and everyone who had eaten them came down with botulism."

"I remember those trips, too, especially the one where you and Polly went to the death camps. I really wanted to go, too, but you wouldn't allow it."

"We'd heard stories, Don. I thought it was more than any young kid should have to see, and I was right. It was a horrible sight, but I'm glad we went. No one should ever forget what happened there."

"On a happier note," I said, "you and I took that wonderful trip to Frankfurt to visit Uncle Dan and Aunt Mary and their baby Michael. Then we went to Bavaria and Switzerland."

"That was fun," Betty said. "Remember when we stopped in Munich on the way and we got out and walked through the city?"

"I'll never forget it. I thought I was numb to destruction after being in Berlin, but that morning I don't think anything could have prepared us for what we saw. When we walked out of the terminal at dawn, we saw a city so devastated it looked more like a moonscape than a habitat for human beings. There was literally nothing left except jagged hills of rubble. I've often thought since that military historians who scoff at the effectiveness of airpower should have seen what we saw that day. We may not have stopped the German armaments industry, and we didn't break their spirits, but we certainly did break their cities."

"But then there was Bavaria." Betty grinned from ear-to-ear. "It was so beautiful, and the people had happy faces and well-fed bodies. And at Berchtesgaden, I took your picture in the window of Hitler's Eagle's Nest."[58]

"You know, after living in Berlin where everything was perpetually gray, that trip was a tremendous relief, wasn't it?" I said. "Austria was beautiful. I loved touring the salt mines in Salzburg and eating fabulous German meals. I think that was the first time I'd actually eaten traditional German food. Heaven knows the Germans didn't have any in Berlin."

"What I liked the best," Betty said, "was Switzerland. It was like night and day: death and destruction versus peace and beauty. San Moritz, Lake Lugano, Lake Lucerne, the zoo in Basel—I think that trip gave us both the will to go back and keep at it."

"I agree. Living in Berlin where people were depressed, starving, and living on the edge, and then seeing areas that hadn't been destroyed, made me understand in a whole new way how truly horrible the war had been and how important it was to make sure it never happened again."

---

[58] Also known as the Kehlsteinhaus or Hitler's Tea House, the Eagle's Nest is a chalet-style building high in the mountains of Bavaria near the Austrian border. It was built as a 50th birthday present for Adolph Hitler and presented to him in 1939, but he rarely used it. In 2008, the facility is operated as a tourist attraction.

Chapter 24 – On the Road Again

1948

My mother's contract with the State Department was up in February 1948. I was 13 years old, I'd been in Germany for nearly a year, and I'd seen and absorbed a lifetime of education and adventure. Between Steiney and a professor from the University of Berlin, the latter paid for with the usual pound of coffee, I also could speak passable German. At school, my teachers had been excellent, and although my grades were the usual composite of highs and lows, they'd been achieved with a minimum of begging.

We left Germany as we'd arrived—in the rain, surrounded by ubiquitous hues of gray, brown, and black—but when we reached Tempelhof Airport for my very first flight, my adrenaline was pumping. There it was, a Douglas DC-4, gleaming silver with the orange lightning bolt of American Overseas Airlines. Along with 60 or so other passengers, we walked across the tarmac and I bounded up the stairs behind my mother. The pilot, copilot, and navigator were already in the cockpit. As I turned to follow Betty to our seats, a hand attached to an arm with four stripes grabbed me by the shoulder.[59]

"Where're you going, boy?"

"To my seat, Sir." My military school training kicked in immediately.

"Wouldn't you rather ride up here?"

"Sure!" Within minutes, I'd been introduced to the copilot, engineer, and navigator and was sitting in the jump seat, taking it all in. As the crew performed their duties, the captain made me a part of the action, explaining everything that was going on. I loved it: the smells unique to the cockpit, the actions of the crew, and, most especially, the operation of this reciprocating engine aircraft.[60]

---

[59] A subsidiary of American Airlines, American Overseas Airways was later sold to Pan Am (Pan American World Airways).

[60] The reciprocating engine is a type of internal combustion engine used in propeller-type aircraft.

Soon the giant airplane was buttoned up and the sequence of starting the engines began. The captain looked me in the eye. "If you're going to ride up front, son," he said, "you'd better earn your keep. So when I tell you, you pull those fuel levers over there." The windows were open, and as I followed his instructions, I could hear the cough, cough, staggered cough, and then the roar of the engines as they came to life in a cloud of smoke. Once all four engines were cranked, we taxied through blowing, rainy, low-ceiling weather to the number one spot for takeoff, where we were cleared into position. The pilot and crew ran up the engines, checked the magnetos and other operating parameters, and completed a multitude of checklists. The tower cleared us for takeoff and we began to move, slowly gaining momentum as the heavily loaded aircraft trundled off the end of the runway and up into the murk.

This was living. I had almost no clue as to what was going on, but I took in everything. The pilot and copilot were busy flying, talking on the radio, and manipulating the aircraft's many controls. Behind them the engineer was working his panel. After what seemed like no more than seconds, we burst into bright sunshine and a new world opened before me.

In the bubble at the top of the cockpit, the navigator sprang into action, using a sextant to make calculations and marks on the flight plan. We were scheduled for stops in Scotland, Iceland, and Labrador before our arrival in New York. I'd started an atlas in Germany, adding information

Just before leaving Berlin in 1948; a world traveler at age 13.

about countries I'd visited, sights I'd seen, and events I'd experienced. Imagine how much I'd be able to add after this trip. Just the thought of flying over England was a thrill, since so much of the war had been wrapped in the mystique of staging and flying out of Great Britain.

As we flew over the British Isles toward Scotland, the weather began to deteriorate further. We experienced heavy turbulence, and I saw the buildup of ice as the crew inflated the de-icer boots to break it loose from the wings. The crew members chatted with me as we flew, but I could feel the tension in the air. After reaching Glasgow, we spent hours in a holding pattern, waiting for the ceiling to rise enough to land. There were huddled conversations about the closest alternate airport. Finally, the crackling sound in the headset from the Scot in the tower: "You're cleared to land." Using a fairly new radar technique called GCA (ground-controlled approach), the Scot talked to the captain until the ground came into view, or in this case, until we touched down, since I don't remember breaking out of the murk before the wheels thumped onto the runway.

That flight from Berlin to Glasgow was one of the defining moments of my life. I always knew what my fate would be, but sitting in that cockpit, surrounded by the instruments of aviation, the friendliness of the crew, and the excitement of propelling this 60,000-pound monster into the sky, seared the dream into my being forever.

Betty, too, had enjoyed the trip. While I was playing ace pilot, she'd organized a social group among the other passengers.

* * *

I was enjoying our walk down memory lane, but by this time it was past noon and everyone was getting hungry. Betty put on her slippers and walked into the dining room, where Polly had laid out a delicious lunch of chicken salad and fresh fruit. After we finished eating, the four of us sat around the table sipping coffee. "Do you remember our ride home from Germany?" I asked my mother.

"Do I ever," she replied. "When the captain invited you to sit in the cockpit, I was so excited for you. And when you came back to see me after we landed in Glasgow, you were absolutely glowing. You'd often talked about becoming a pilot, but that day I knew you really meant it."

"Me, too," I said, "especially when the captain talked me through the refueling and refilling routine as if I were going to fly the mission. And when he let me help start the engines, I was in dreamland for sure."

"Speaking of dreamland," Betty said, "I think it's time for me to take a nap. I'm looking forward to continuing this evening, but right now your very tired mother needs to get some shut-eye."

Polly and I cleared up the dishes and were soon settled in the guest room for a rest of our own. While Polly read, I climbed into the skin of that 13-year-old flying ace, sitting on a Glasgow runway in 1948, waiting for the weather to creep above the minimum visibility required for takeoff.

* * *

Eventually we were given clearance, and the bird became airborne once again. The drone of the Pratt & Whitney engines was mesmerizing, and the crew began to spell each other for a rest in the small bunks off the cockpit area, a rotation I shared from time to time. Over the North Atlantic en route to Reykjavik, Iceland, we broke into the clear, and when the copilot eased out of the right seat for a break, he waved me into it. I was grinning from ear to ear.

After a short briefing, the captain handed me the controls. I know this sounds dramatic, but the plane was extraordinarily stable. It may have seemed advanced in 1948, but in reality it was an unpressurized, lumbering beast that required very little input from the pilot. When minor correction was necessary, the captain patiently talked me through the maneuvers.

The crew seemed to enjoy having me with them as much as I enjoyed being there. I loved their camaraderie, teasing, and inevitable war stories. The pretty young stewardesses came to the cockpit often, flirted and giggled with the crew, smoked cigarettes, and ruffled my hair. The food was hot and basic, and despite the inevitable grousing from the crew about the fare, I thought it was fine. Of course, then as now, I think almost all food is fine. About the only thing I don't like about eating is being late for meals.

Our trip consisted of approximately 24 hours of airtime, and the captain let me share the controls on several other occasions. Altogether, I probably spent a couple of hours "flying" that plane, but in my mind I was another Lindbergh, making aviation history at the helm of a DC-4.[61]

Flying over the North Atlantic in the winter was a challenge, but we finally received clearance to land in Reykjavik. The ride down was a roller coaster. With winds at the limits permitted for landing, we bounced and thrashed our way to touchdown. Meanwhile, the cockpit was filled with that magic smell, a combination of adrenaline and sweat that permeates cockpits the world over when the going gets tough.

"Piece of cake," the captain said as we taxied in, and everyone grunted in agreement.

It hadn't seemed that easy to me, but as I observed the paperwork and planning for the legs ahead, some of the pieces started to fall into place. Finally, after flying over icebound Greenland, we landed in Labrador at dawn. The captain didn't have a relief crew, so he decided to stop for a six-hour rest break. Everyone left the plane but the flight engineer, who stayed on board to periodically run up the engines. Otherwise, the cold would have shut down the aircraft and we'd have had to wait for a hangar to thaw it out.

The early morning weather was clear and brilliant—light winds and a temperature of minus 35 degrees Fahrenheit. As the sun sent shafts of multicolored rays over the frozen landscape, we were directed by a fur-clad

---

[61] Charles Lindbergh (1902–1974) was the first pilot to fly nonstop across the Atlantic Ocean. His historic flight took place on May 20–21, 1927.

member of the ground crew to a ramp far from the terminal. "Wait 'til you feel this!" said the skipper.

The doors opened, and passengers and crew deplaned into what looked like unheated school buses for the drive to the Operations building. It was beyond cold. The hairs of my nose felt like needles, and the penetrating, frigid air pierced every part of my body. At the end of the ride, we entered a warm, cozy mess hall and grabbed a tray for the trip down the breakfast line. The cheery GIs served up slices of toast topped with a suspicious-looking, greenish-brown substance.

"What's that?" I asked.

"SOS, my boy, and you'll love it," said the GI behind the counter. And so I did. That morning in Labrador, I began a lifetime romance with *the* icon of the military mess. I added a couple of perfectly cooked eggs, some hash browns, bacon, sausage, coffeecake, homemade toast and jam, and several glasses of cold, fresh milk. I love mess hall chow, and this meal was fit for a king.[62]

After breakfast, the passengers rested in a couple of military-style barracks and the crew in individual rooms. In just a few hours we were back on the airplane, which thanks to the efforts of our intrepid flight engineer was, if not actually warm, at least a drastic improvement over the school buses.

Off to New York City, U.S. of A.—the home of the giant PX where the streets are lined with gold. This was the land to which the war-ravaged displaced persons of Europe yearned to come and begin again for the hundredth time, a land of freedom unknown in the rest of the world.

New York, however, was socked in, so we landed in Boston, refueled, and finally reached our destination nearly 36 hours after leaving Berlin. The passengers were disheveled and exhausted, except of course, for me, who had been promoted to honorary crew member, and my mother, who was still her chipper, animated self.

When I left the flight deck, I thanked the captain and the rest of the crew profusely. "When I grow up, I'm going to fly for American," I said. Many years later, I did just that.

---

[62] SOS (shit on a shingle) is a euphemism for the often-served, military-kitchen staple of creamed chipped beef on toast.

Chapter 25 – Betty Goes to Panama—Me, Too
1948

After spending the night in a hotel, Betty and I took a cab to Penn Station and caught the train for Buffalo. Grandmother picked us up and briefed us on the changes at home.

First of all, Grandfather had moved to the Knights of Columbus building on Delaware Avenue. Their constant warfare had finally exhausted them both, and the move didn't surprise me one bit. In fact, I was sure that Gramps was a lot happier in his new digs. The other big news: 30 Park Place was on the market. It hadn't sold yet, but *ouch*. This was Grandmother's dream home, and I had always thought of it as my home, too.[63]

All the kin were gathered to welcome us and to bid adieu to Betty, who was leaving almost immediately for Panama. She and George were to be married there on February 17, 1948, nearly a year to the day after I left New York for Europe on the *Ernie Pyle*, but I wasn't invited. What a heck of a note. After all, how many kids get to go to their mother's wedding? And besides, I couldn't wait to see the jungle. But Betty said she'd send for me later, and so far her word had always been good.

After she left, Aunt Carolyn and Uncle Walt Shed moved in. They were in the process of purchasing a house and needed a place to stay until the deal was complete. Once again I was surrounded by people I loved, but I still had to finish the eighth grade at East Aurora Junior High. Would I be remembered as that snot-nosed, fingernail-biting farmer or welcomed as the suave, international traveler I had become? Alas, it was neither. I was just another kid, stuck in the back row at the top of the bottom third of the

---

[63] Founded in New Haven, CT, in 1882 by Father Michael J. McGivney, the Knights of Columbus is a Roman Catholic men's fraternal organization. As of 2008, it had over 1.7 million members in the U.S. and several foreign countries. The Knights of Columbus building at 506 Delaware is one of Buffalo's architectural landmarks. It was constructed ca. 1868 as a mansion for businessman Chillion Farrar. The Knights purchased and greatly enlarged the building in 1915 and sold it in 1985. However, they retained a 70-year lease to the legendary building cellars, where, as of 2008, a Knights-sponsored health club called the Catholic Club is open to members of all denominations.

class. Oh, man! This was bad news, because if I wanted to continue with my German, I needed to be with the whiz kids in the A class. Through creative begging, and with a little help from Grandmother, I managed the switch, but the results were mixed.

On the one hand, the prettiest girls were in the A class, and although they hadn't quite forgotten my checkered past, I did notice that strange and wonderful things were happening to their bodies. On the other hand, the academics were intimidating. I did well in German, but otherwise, I was drowning in a cauldron of information. The A class was simply too advanced for me, and I started to lose confidence in my abilities. I did, however, learn to play golf. The school offered the sport as part of the curriculum, and the coach was an excellent, patient man. We competed with other schools in the area with great success, and I enjoyed the game without ever once hitting another player in the mouth with the ball.

When I wasn't figuring out how to make it through the school year, I often visited Grandpa at the Buffalo Knights. He had a nice room, he looked and sounded better than ever before, and on Fridays he got fish for dinner instead of the dreaded macaroni and cheese. He also had a new job. Gramps had loved working for the railroad, but when he turned 65, he'd been forced to retire. Undaunted by this temporary setback, he bought a new birth certificate. (Obviously, Berlin was not the only city with a thriving black market.) Now that he was 55 again, he got a job as a chauffeur for the General Foods Company. With a new career to keep him occupied and relieved of the stress of living with Grandmother, he was one happy man.

I also spent many weekends at the farm, visiting with Maude and Mill and helping with chores. They were happy to see me and often commented on how sophisticated I'd become. If they'd known of my attempts to apply some of this newfound worldliness, though, I'm sure they wouldn't have approved.

Some of my fellow students at East Aurora were kids I'd gone to school with in the one-room schoolhouse. After sixth grade, all the farm kids were bused to East Aurora, so I had friends in both city and country. One weekend, six of these farm pals joined me as we celebrated the grain harvest, and at long last, we managed to invite two farm gals into the grain bin. They weren't the brightest girls in the world—after all, they'd agreed to go with us—nor were they particularly pretty. In reality, they were sort of chunky and plain, and one fellow said they looked as if they'd never used a bar of soap. But we'd heard that they visited grain bins and haymows with some regularity. In other words, they were just perfect.

Somebody produced a pack of cards, and we started playing strip poker.

Perhaps cards were a waste of time, but we were sports, and although I was not the instigator of any of this, it sure looked promising. Before long, the boys were in various stages of undress. Lacking the finesse of the more skilled players, the girls were naked. Rings of dirt encircled their necks, arms, and plumpness, and drops of dried sweat clung to those rings like brown pearls. They were looking prettier every minute, and I was sure that some real action was about to commence. Then the barn door rolled open.

"Charlie? Charlie? You in here?"

"Yeah, Dad, I'm here."

"Whatcha doin'?"

"Nothing, Dad, just checking out the crop."

"Well, we've got to start the chores."

"Okay, Dad, I'll be right there."

The love fest was over. Charlie went off with his dad, and the rest of us pulled ourselves together and departed through the rear barnyard, grain streaming from the pockets and seams of our clothes. Just then I caught a glimpse of a white flying object. My guardian angel was back. Damn. Sometimes she protected me too well.

A few days later we were having lunch at school, bemoaning paradise lost, when Charlie commented that those were the dirtiest girls he'd ever seen. Someone else suggested that, in a week or so, the wheat in the grain bin just might start to germinate in the wet spots, and wouldn't that be a sight. Six dirty-minded eighth grade boys laughed themselves back to class.

By the end of the school year, I had a lot less to laugh about. I wanted to be in high school more than anything in my life, but the academic year had been a disaster. My grades were dismal, and I had groveled so much that the knees of my custom-tailored britches were worn out. "Ah, Mrs. Brown, I've been jerked from pillar to post, endured incredible hardships, was frozen and starved in war-torn Germany, suffered through unbearable farm life, and lost my father before I was born, which left my mother penniless and starving on the streets. Please give me a break and change that F to a D."

"But Donald, in order for me to do that I would have to add 20 points to your grade."

"What are a few points, ma'am, when you are the finest teacher in the world? I've tried to be attentive, but sometimes the hunger pangs cause me to lose my concentration."

Some teachers were harder to convince than others, but finally, miracle of miracles, I was promoted. And then came the letter from Betty. "Donald, dear, you have an opportunity to meet new friends and have new adventures." I loved those words.

145

Life is a Piece of Cake

On June 26, 1948, Grandmother drove me to the Buffalo Municipal Airport for my trip to Panama. It was an Eastern Airlines flight, with stops in Washington, D.C., Miami, and Havana, and as soon as I boarded I invited myself up to the cockpit. I was hoping for a repeat of my adventures on the way home from Berlin, but it wasn't to be. The captain politely but firmly directed me to the passenger section.

After a couple of hours' layover in torrid Miami, plus a brief introduction to Havana—as different from Berlin as night from day—we landed in Panama. When I got off the plane, it felt like a steam room. Betty was there to meet me, pretty as a picture in a tropical summer dress and on the arm of her new husband, George Kenna. Since George had left Berlin before I arrived, we had never met, and I wondered if he had a doubt or two. I shouldn't have worried. He was an army major with a military bearing, but I had my own military bearing from that formative year at Linsly. Besides, he was in great spirits, having just won a few thousand bucks in the Panama National Lottery. We got along well.

The airport was on the Pacific side of the isthmus, near Fort Clayton where George worked. We lived at Fort Sherman on the Atlantic side. Once a vital artillery defense post for the Canal, Fort Sherman was now used exclusively for military housing. The ride home took about an hour, the verdant jungle on one side of the highway and the Canal on the other. It was just getting dark when we arrived, but I could see that the house was large and airy and located next to a seawall about thirty yards from the ocean. To my surprise, there wasn't a window in it, just screens with Venetian-blind-like shutters. Even more surprising, it stood on stilts, ten feet in the air.

A cheerful black woman named Carrie, who I learned was our full-time servant, greeted us at the door, and soon afterward I hit the sack. It had been a long trip. The next morning I awoke to the sound of a waterfall surrounding the house. The rain pounded on the metal roof with a violence I'd never experienced. It was so intense it seemed anyone caught in it would surely drown—there was simply no room for air. I was sure we'd be washed away.

With some anxiety I went looking for Betty and George, only to find them enjoying their morning coffee as though nothing was amiss. George took one look at my face and quickly assured me that the storm was common and occurred several times a day during the rainy season. Whew. What a relief.

Carrie was serving breakfast, and now that I was confident the house would stand until the end of the meal, I dug in with gusto. Fruits I hadn't tasted before accompanied the usual fare of bacon, eggs, and rolls. Everything was delicious, the rain soon dwindled to a patter, and the sky was bright blue and peppered with giant white thunderheads.

Tarzan, the Coconut Boy

Time to explore. As I ran down the coarse lawn toward the water, I noticed thousands of fearsome-looking land crabs, clacking their claws as they scurried sideways into holes they'd dug in the lawn. It reminded me of a scene from a horror flick.

The bay front was lined with coconut palms swaying out over the water. And the bay itself was teeming with life: schools of tropical fish, menacing barracuda, and huge manta rays that splashed their wings as they broke the surface. Betty and George soon joined me and explained that nobody swam there. I assured them that the thought of swimming had never crossed my mind. Manta rays or not, the only water I was willing to submerge myself in was bathwater.

I felt like Tarzan in my own tropical paradise. "Hey George, Betty, you want a coconut? I'll climb the tree and knock one down."

"Sure, but be careful."

Because of the swayback of the palm, I walked up the first half of the tree. Beyond that, the trunk was rough enough to grip with my feet and provide handholds as well, and soon I was close to the top. Several coconuts beckoned, just inches away. As I paused to rest, I made the mistake of looking down. Yikes! I was way out over the ocean. The fear bug grabbed my groin, but I was determined not to retreat, even though George and Betty were looking mighty nervous.

"Be careful, Donald," my mother cried.

I moved forward just enough to start swatting at a coconut. At least I thought it was a coconut, until it exploded into action. I had hit a wasp nest, and to show how pissed they were, its occupants immediately enveloped my head, stinging away. The pain was intense, but if I let go, I'd fall into the ocean and either drown, since I couldn't swim, or be devoured by a passing barracuda, or possibly both. I loosened my hold just enough to half-slide, half-scramble to the base of the tree, the wasps fighting for a bite every inch of the way. As soon as my feet hit the ground, I dove into the grass, swatting and wiping my face, and in a moment the varmints vanished as quickly as they'd appeared. My face burned with hurt.

Betty and George stared in shock at my red and swelling kisser. Then everyone sprang into action. Betty wrapped my head in a towel soaked in cold water, and George drove us to the army hospital in his '46 Pontiac. The hospital was only about ten minutes away, but the swelling had already started to go down by the time we arrived. Even the pain was abating. There was nothing that the doctors could do, but they asked us to stay for an hour or so, just in case. By the time we left for home, the swelling was totally gone, leaving a blush of red that disappeared in a couple of days. I had suffered at least a hundred bites, and why the effects were so minimal defies explanation to this day. Maybe my tarnished angel felt sorry for me and gave me a break. All I know is, my next coconut came from a fruit stand. It helped the local economy and it was a lot safer.

Exploring Fort Sherman

Fort Sherman had a long and colorful history. Named after General William Tecumseh Sherman of Civil War fame, the fort was constructed beginning in 1912, just two years before completion of the Panama Canal. It served a pivotal role in Canal defense and was used by the U.S. military during both world wars. Now the big 16-inch guns were gone and the jungle had almost swallowed the concrete storage sheds, but the gun emplacements were still there, along with approximately 20 miles of boardwalk that connected them.

Harry, the one other kid on the base, was just my age, and we spent hours exploring those abandoned boardwalks, a pastime that was both fun and dangerous. The network of trails all looked the same. The foliage seemed to grow hourly, so we were often lost, though we never admitted it, plus on occasion we were pitched into the jungle swamp through holes in the rotting wood.

The jungle had a million critters, and from our boardwalk perch we saw them all. Sometimes they were too close for comfort, like the day Harry and I rounded a corner and almost tripped over a snake big enough to swallow both of us and look for more. We ran like the devil and stayed away for a couple of days, but the lure of the unknown soon overcame our fear and we were at it again. Another time we encountered the biggest wildcat I'd ever seen, and it was hard to tell which of us set the record for speed of escape. Maybe the cat was frightened too, but we didn't stick around to find out. After that, we were careful to make enough noise in advance to scare away anything larger or more dangerous than we were.

All of this play was fun, but I was used to earning my keep, and it had been a long time since I'd held a job, or, for that matter, had any responsibility at all. I was still an enterprising entrepreneur, however, and it didn't take long before opportunity presented itself. It seemed that there were only three officers' wives at the fort, Betty and two others. Avid bridge players all, they needed a fourth, and I was a quick study. After a few lessons from Betty, who was an expert player and enjoyed teaching, my job was to play bridge at least three hours a day. What a summer: three lovely ladies with whom to while away the hours, a jungle to explore just outside my door, and ample opportunities in between to restore myself at the Officers' Club pool.

We spent a lot of time at the O Club, eating dinner there often and enjoying the other residents of the fort, mostly young and adventurous war vets who were happy to be alive. George and I also enjoyed each other. He was quiet, studious, and hardworking, and I knew the drill and the relationship of my behavior to his career. He rarely had to speak to me about discipline, and I was never confrontational. After all, life couldn't get much better, but if I decided to test the limits, it could get much worse, and for what?

Sometimes Harry and I went into Colón, the nearest town, where the level of poverty was staggering. The streets were cesspools of filth. The food was suspect, since refrigeration was almost unknown, and most of the markets were breeding places for flies. Nevertheless, the natives seemed happy and carefree.

On the base, the servicemen and their dependents were a close group. Nobody was very well-paid, but the fringe benefits were great. The commissary and PX were very reasonable, competent medical care was available, movies were dirt-cheap and air-conditioned—the only place to enjoy this luxury— and entertainment at the Club was frequent and fun. The nation was grateful for the efforts of its service personnel, and it treated its warriors well.

Before long, summer was drawing to an end and it was time to figure out where and how I would go to school. Then George got new orders. "I have good news, Donald," Betty repeated for the umpteenth time in my young life. "We're being transferred to Fort Bliss in El Paso, Texas, where you will have an opportunity to meet new people and enjoy new challenges."[64]

As it turned out, there were new challenges all around. George went to work in antiaircraft artillery, the soon-to-be home of the Nike missile, and I became a cowboy.

---

[64] In 1849, U.S. Army troops set up a military post on the banks of the Rio Grande. In 1854, the post was named Fort Bliss in honor of Lt. Colonel W. W. S. Bliss, an aide to General Zachary Taylor. The fort was moved five times in the 19th century and flew the Confederate flag during the Civil War. Fort Bliss played a pivotal role in preparing troops for our nation's defense during World War I and World War II. Before the end of the Second World War, it became an antiaircraft artillery center. As of 2008, the facility comprises approximately 1.1 million acres in Texas and New Mexico and is the largest of 16 U.S. Army Training and Doctrine Command (TRADOC) installations.

Chapter 26 – Hot Times in the Southwest

1948–1949

We had driven along the Canal countless times, but because our army ship left from the Pacific side, I was finally able to experience this tremendous feat of engineering from the water. The ship was comfortable, with decent quarters for officers and enlisted personnel alike. There was even room for George's Pontiac.

We spent most of the trip on deck, soaking up the sun or playing bridge. After a few days, we landed in New York City, visited George's kin in Queens, and drove on to East Aurora. Grandmother still lived at 30 Park Place (she must not have been trying very hard to sell), and when we arrived, the family was gathered there to check out Betty's new husband. A quiet man in a family of talkers, poor George was really under the gun, but since we were soon off again, he didn't have to endure the scrutiny for long.

On the way to Texas we took our time, stopping to tour various sights and enjoy the flavor of the countryside. I had never been farther west than West Virginia, so this trip was a real eye-opener. When we arrived, we found a small house off the base and were settled within a couple of days. Hello, Texas.

For the first time in my life, I was living in what could be called a normal family environment. Our house on Hamilton Street was brand-new. A cement-block, stucco-covered structure with a swamp cooler, it was typical of the hot, semiarid climate of El Paso.[65]

In this house my mother became exactly what she was born to be, an officer's wife. She had all of the necessary attributes: style, intelligence, wit, good looks, refined social graces, and a phenomenal ability at the bridge table.

---

[65] A swamp cooler (also known as an evaporative cooler) is used primarily in arid climates. It consists of a large, box-like frame with walls of wet pads, normally made of cedar shavings or cellulose. Inside the box is a fan that blows outside air through the pads, which are continually soaked by a water pump. As the air from the fan evaporates water molecules from the pads, it is cooled about 20°F and then blown through the house and out a vent.

She could play bridge with the best and the worst players and make the game equally enjoyable for all. She was a far more social animal than George, and it worked to both their advantages.

When I arrived in Texas, I weighed 120 pounds and wore size 12A shoes. In typical adolescent fashion, I could trip over a pebble, and the smell of chocolate or a Coke would cause my face to erupt in a mass of pimples. And although I could carry on an intelligent conversation with any adult, with my peers I was often tongue-tied, especially with the fairer sex, who occupied my mind more and more.

It was September 1948 and I was soon enrolled in Austin High School, a well-run operation with nearly 2,000 students, some of whom were other army brats and immediately friendly. I settled in without a problem, determined to study hard, get good grades, behave myself, become a football hero, and eventually fly fighters. The classes were small, the teachers were adequate, and it was a new experience for everyone, a level playing field as we found our place in this adventure called high school.

I had a better than fair chance. Heck, even my previous placement in classes too advanced for me didn't make a significant difference. As usual, however, I was placed in the last row with the other W, X, Y, and Z kids, and between daydreaming and laziness, I started to slip. The teacher was a distant presence in the front of the room, the sun was warm, and my mind wandered to other pursuits, at least until some cute chick walked by. Then my thoughts were abruptly rerouted to places I hadn't yet fully sorted out. In most subjects, I slogged along with a solid D+ to C-. If not for my ability to beg, failure would have been inevitable.

Outside of class, I wasn't doing so well either, since every time I attempted to engage a girl in conversation, my mords got all wixed up. I did, however, try out for the football team, spending two days of hell doing calisthenics and running up and down the stadium steps before being cut. I was fast, but my 120 pounds just weren't enough. Obviously, I'd have to find another way to impress the gals.

Agriculture and Angst

Austin High had a serious agriculture department that offered several courses as electives. I was sincerely interested, but the Ag students had a closed-shop approach, and the price of admission was whipping with a homemade paddle, made by the whippee. Thanks to the good captain at Linsly, I'd been whipped by a pro, so I took the bait without much hesitation and was soon an accepted member of the Ag class. I enjoyed the subjects and worked hard, getting lots of hands-on training and pretty good grades to boot. One of my homework projects was to raise a small flock of chickens, so I took over the garage, ordered thirty Rhode Island Red chicks from Sears, and raised them without losing a single one.

In addition to my Ag pals, I hit it off immediately with another freshman named Bob Stewart. We ran with a group of good guys who played sandlot football, hiked, laughed, and made lewd suggestions about the girls, though they were suggestions none of us had the guts to pursue. The girls, on the other hand, totally ignored us. They were much more interested in the sophomores and juniors. Here we were, young studs ready to show the world our stuff, and nobody cared.

Finally I cut one girl out of the pack. (I was beginning to talk like a Texan.) She was pretty, with glasses and braces, and her name was Gretchen. We went to a couple of movies together and enjoyed each other's company. Was it possible that something more might be in the cards?

About this time, one of the local movie theaters advertised the most up-to-date film on the taboo subject of sex. To gain admission, you had to prove you were sixteen, but Bob and I were determined. Borrowed IDs in hand, we stood in a line that snaked around the block, joining many of our peers who were just as curious, and just as clueless, as we. Inside, the theater was filled with teenage boys trying to act bored, but most of them, including the two of us, were more embarrassed than anything else. We tried not to catch the eye of the few females brazen enough to be there. The production was fuzzy, cheap, and poorly acted, showing a clumsy courtship and a romantic interlude. As the moment of truth approached, the camera flashed to a close-up of the woman's hand, in which she held a perfect rose. Appropriate vocal expression. Pause. Suspense. And then, with a final moan, she crushed the rose.

Armed with this addition to my knowledge of love, I quickly made a date with Gretchen. On her porch after a much tamer movie, I got up the courage to kiss her, a closed-mouth kiss, thank goodness, or her braces might have inflicted bodily harm. This and further kisses seemed to go well, so after a bit I plucked a rose from the bush by her front door and handed it to her. "How sweet and thoughtful of you, Don," she said. Now we were getting somewhere. I embraced her again, but she continued to hold the rose in her hand. After another sweet embrace, I suggested she crush the rose. With some reluctance she did, but she didn't moan. Was she too immature to understand the ways of love? When I talked the situation over with Bob, we concluded that maybe we'd missed something, but the movie was no longer playing in the area. I didn't try the rose trick again

I also struck out in the employment arena. Each afternoon after school and on Saturdays I would go from store to store looking for work, but I couldn't find a job anywhere. The best job available was bagging groceries, but it seemed I was always a day too early or a day too late to snag this prize. It's true that I was long, gangly, and uncoordinated, but I wasn't shy. Even so, I just wasn't having any luck selling myself. It seemed impossible even to obtain a paper route, though occasionally I was able to come up with a replacement job. The best I could do was an occasional lawn-mowing job or helping around the house, so money was scarce.

Fall passed into winter and then into spring, and I was still struggling, treading water at the top of the bottom third of my class. With luck and concentrated begging, perhaps I would pass. My biggest worry was English grammar. You'd think this would have been one of my best subjects. After all, I could speak properly, and I could discern the difference between good and poor writing, but even with extra help, diagramming sentences remained an unsolved mystery. What I needed was a diversion to get my mind off my troubles, and soon one showed up in a brand new Pontiac. Grandmother had come to Texas.

Not long after we moved to El Paso, Grandmother finally sold 30 Park Place and moved in with Uncle Walt and Aunt Carolyn. Things did not go well. The stereotypical mother-in-law, it was her habit to cause a ruckus wherever she went, and after a few months, Uncle Walt had had enough. He gave Grandmother her marching orders, and Betty and George agreed to give her a new, permanent home. My mother and my grandmother got along well, and Grandmother was a fine housekeeper in spite of her faults. Perhaps this new arrangement would work. Personally, I was glad to see her, as she and I had always been close.

South of the Border, Down Mexico Way

The school year had only a few weeks to go, and although it looked as if I might pass (just barely), the summer stretched before me with no job prospects in sight. Then Bob asked if I would be interested in spending the summer at his dad's ranch in the high desert of Mexico. I was incredulous. "Sure," I replied, and immediately started to plan how to present this idea to Betty and George.

During the school year, Bob lived with his mother, who worked at a local department store, and his very attractive sister Helen, who was a senior at Austin High. Another, older sister named Caroline lived in New York City. Bob's mother worked long hours during the day and spent most of her evenings sewing. She was a classy lady, but she seemed perpetually worried, having seen, I surmised, far better times.

Bob's father lived on the family's ranch in Mexico, and it was here that we were to spend the summer. Within the week, I talked with Betty and George, Betty talked with Bob's mother, and Bob and I were on a roll, preparing for what turned out to be one of my most bizarre adventures yet.

Bob's dad was a man of vision. He wanted to make the world a better place, and he took concrete steps to make it happen. In the 1930s he had inherited a large sum of money. He'd used some of it, in conjunction with a Mexican aristocrat, to develop a silver and lead mine in the high desert, about 100 miles south, as the crow flies, of the Big Bend country of Texas. The two men constructed a village for the miners and their families called Santa Elena. The small, adobe homes had metal roofs and real floors, features that the Mexican peasants had rarely seen. The men also built and staffed a school and a small hospital, paid decent wages to their workers, and treated them with respect. Things were going well, and Bob's dad built a fine home outside of town.

Then, in the late '30s, silver and lead prices plummeted. The workers lost their jobs, sold their metal roofs, and fled. Santa Elena became a ghost town, an unfulfilled dream symbolized by an empty school and hospital and a tangle of abandoned huts.

Although he'd lost a good deal of money, Mr. Stewart salvaged enough to keep the house and purchase a large ranch adjacent to it. He approached ranching with the same zeal and forward thinking that he had approached mining, bringing in Brahma bulls from India to upgrade the stock and improve their ability to flourish on the high-desert fodder. Life was hard, but it was still prosperous, and when the world plunged into war, his herds were well-established.

Once World War II was over, however, Texas farmers began to campaign against Mexican beef. Their most successful, and perhaps most legitimate, gripe was the discovery of hoof and mouth disease in the southernmost area of the country, after which importing beef from Mexico was no longer permitted. Bob's dad now had a herd of cattle he couldn't sell and a mine from which he couldn't make a profit. Hoping and praying that life would someday return to normal, Mr. Stewart stayed on the ranch. Mrs. Stewart returned to El Paso to educate the kids and peck out a living. Only in the summers was the family sometimes reunited.

Bob was looking forward to seeing his dad, and I was looking forward to a summer of experiences I could use the following year to impress the girls. Since hunting was the main form of sustenance on the ranch, the first thing

Bob and I did in preparation, much to the dismay of my chickens, was to construct a rifle range in the garage. Practicing with shorts in a single-shot .22 rifle, we became quite accurate. On weekends we went into the desert, honing our skills on tin cans and anything that moved.[66]

There were no stores near Santa Elena, so we needed to bring with us everything we'd need, including Levi jeans, cotton shirts, sneakers, and handcrafted, Tony Lama cowboy boots. The boots fit perfectly.[67]

EL PASO PUBLIC SCHOOLS
SUBJECT REPORT CARD
AUSTIN HIGH SCHOOL.

Pupil _Wright, Don_
(Last)   (First and Initial)

Subject _English_ Section _I_

TERM: Fall Spring   Year _1948-49_

Grade Period	Subject Grade	Deportment Grade	Days Absent	Remarks
1	F+			Entered late
2	D	a	0	
3	F	a		

Term Average __F__   Credit Allowed __no__   Light Solid

Counselor _____

Blackmon H. R. Teacher

Clark Class Teacher

(OVER)

TO THE PARENT

The grade on the reverse side is the grade earned by the pupil in the subject during the grade period indicated. If it is good we commend the pupil; if it is poor, you may find the reason for this poor grade checked below by the class teacher, or given under remarks.

The passing grade is D; "recommendation" grade C; "honor" grade is A. Standards are such that about one-third of the class make above C. This office will be open at any time for a conference with the parent concerning the work of the pupil. We invite you to visit the school.

Yours truly,

W. W. WIMBERLY, *Principal*

REASONS FOR POOR GRADES IN SCHOOL	GRADE PERIODS		
	1st	2nd	3rd
1. Absence and Tardiness			
2. Lack of Study	✓	✓	✓
3. Inattention in class			
4. Poor foundation	✓	✓	✓
5. Too many outside interests			
6. Speaks too little English			
7.			

Signature of Parent

1 _Elizabeth A. Kenna_
2 _Elizabeth A. Kenna_
3 _Elizabeth A. Kenna_

Form 347.   25M.   7-48.   a/c 208A/1.   P. O. 3647A.

Freshman English at Austin High, 1949: The beginning
of my English grammar woes.

---

[66] .22 cartridges have a shorter case length than the standard .22 LR (long rifle) cartridges and are used primarily for practice by the recreational shooter.

[67] Born in 1887, Tony Lama was apprenticed at age 11 to a shoemaker in Syracuse, NY. At the turn of the 20th century, he joined the U.S. Calvary, where he served as a cobbler for the soldiers at Fort Bliss, TX. After completing his tour of duty, he set up shop in El Paso, perfecting his craft and becoming famous for making the best-fitting, most comfortable boot possible. He died in 1974, but the boots that bear his name are still sold more than 30 years later.

Ammunition was very expensive south of the border, and Bob's dad was almost out, so we also needed to bring a supply of shells for the ranch's .22, .30-30, and .30-06 rifles. Bringing ammo into the country was illegal, but we figured we'd fill our pockets with .22 longs and hope for the best. For the larger caliber bullets, we soon found an ally in Grandmother. Turning her considerable domestic skills to the problem at hand, she crafted bandoliers for Bob and me to wear across our bodies, each of which held hundreds of shells.

Bob's dad also asked if I'd bring my chickens. Perhaps he thought those Rhode Island Reds would upgrade the local flock, who were probably descendants of chickens that had arrived with Cortez.

School finally came to an end, and despite my most sophisticated begging, my English teacher, Mrs. Clark, had failed me. I would have to repeat the course the following year. I did better in *Español*. Having lived in Mexico as kids, Bob and his sister Helen were already fluent in Spanish. I had a long way to go, but at least I'd earned an honest C. I was sure going to need it.

Chapter 27 – Becoming a Cowboy

1949

Bob's mother and my grandmother drove us to the railroad station at Juárez. In addition to having several crates of chickens in tow, our pockets were stuffed with .22 shells and our bandoliers filled with 50 pounds of ammunition. Loose clothing covered the evidence, but in order to avoid clanking, we walked as stiffly as possible. No one gave us a second look. After all, people didn't usually smuggle stuff *into* Mexico. An accessory before the fact, Grandmother got quite a kick out of the situation. Perhaps in a former life she'd been a smuggler as well as a queen.

Bob and I had been to Juárez many times before, wandering the dusty streets and watching young women sell their wares from stalls with a blanket serving as a door. For kicks, we'd bargained for wares that we didn't have the money to pay for, gone to a bullfight, and enjoyed tough steak, frijoles with tortillas, and a beer, all for a quarter. Except for the smiling faces and sad, loving music, in many ways Juárez reminded me of a war zone.

The train was comfortable, and we settled in for the trip to Chihuahua, a couple hundred miles south of the border and our first stop on the way to Santa Elena. The fare was incredibly cheap, so we could afford first class tickets, and our fellow passengers were from the upper class, well-dressed and elegant. As the train moved into the interior, we looked out on a scene that had changed little since the 1800s. The roads were dusty and unimproved, with horses and donkeys the main form of transportation, and the villages were composed entirely of adobe buildings. We saw little evidence of electricity, and water came from a pump or spring in the village plaza.

Chihuahua itself was a very large small town, dusty, unkempt, and smelly. We hired a couple of barefoot peasants to transport our chickens to the local train while we clanked along behind, weighted down by our illegal bounty. We were hot and sweaty, but we were careful not to complain. In Mexico, the ammunition strapped to our bodies was worth more than we were.

The local, a conveyance so old Pancho Villa probably took it, chugged along on a narrow-gauge line at a top speed of ten miles per hour. We were traveling east to El Oro, the closest railhead to the ranch, and sometimes the train was so slow that Bob and I jumped out and trotted along beside the open carriage. Heck, even the train from Bremerhaven to Berlin was better than this bucket of bolts.[68]

Every passenger carried produce, and many had a quarter of beef, a goat carcass, or some live chickens tied by the feet. Flies were everywhere, and although we traveled for 100 miles, there seemed to be no regular schedule. The train stopped anytime anyone wanted to get on or off. In between, vendors sold hot tortillas stuffed with something ground, along with sodas, coffee, and beer. Unusual smells permeated the air, and happy laughter came from the children who, although dressed in rags, were as neat as they could muster and played with toys made from bits of cardboard and sticks.

Seeing Americans was an unusual event for adults and children alike, and they were even more surprised to learn than Bob spoke Spanish like a Mexican. Bob was a cheerful, uncomplicated guy, and he was quite friendly with the natives, who had much to say about our chickens. We took care to conceal our bandoliers and bulging pockets, but in a pinch, I'm not so sure what would have gone first, the chickens or the ammo.

We climbed into more mountainous country as the day wore on, and just as it started to get dark, we pulled into El Oro, a town right out of the Old West. Horses were hitched to rails along the dirt street, a few bare bulbs shone from adobe homes and businesses, and a generator thumped in the night. Bob's dad, also named Bob, was there to meet us, along with Luz, the ranch foreman. Mr. Stewart was a slightly portly fellow with a smiling face and balding head, and I liked him immediately. After complimenting me on the chickens, he directed us to the 2½-ton truck that served as transportation when anyone from the ranch came to town. This vehicle had passed its prime years before, but it was perfect for traversing the rough, high-desert country. Bob and I loaded the chickens into the truck bed, and the four of us headed across the plaza to the only restaurant in town.

In the best Spanish tradition, the plaza was a hub of activity. Young, unmarried men and señoritas walked in opposite directions, each taking the other's measure in the dim light. We were happy to sit still, digging into tough steaks, frijoles, and tomatoes with salsa after our many hours on the train. The other patrons ate jalapeños like apples.

Bob's dad spoke Spanish with an American accent so strong that even I

---

[68] Pancho Villa (1878–1923) was a Mexican revolutionary.

noticed, but the Mexicans seemed to have no trouble understanding him. Many people came over to pay their respects, and I could tell that they admired him. They talked up to him, but he never talked down to them.

It had been a long and tiring trip, and since it was still 30 or 40 miles north to the ranch, we stayed overnight in the town's only hotel. Our room had a hard-packed dirt floor swept clean, a window without glass, and several cots, but no sheets or blankets, since patrons brought their own bedrolls. The sounds and smells of the night were delicious, and I was soon mesmerized by the odors of wood fires, frijoles, horses, and manure. Best of all was the music, soft guitars and beautiful men's voices singing of life on the range and lost love. Strangely, I don't remember a single female singer.

Too soon, barking dogs and bright sunlight announced it was morning. Breakfast was *huevos rancheros*, frijoles, tortillas, and coffee, after which we left for the ranch. Luz was in the driver's seat, with Bob's dad riding shotgun. Bob and I were in the bed with the chickens. Luz steered our way over rutted roads and through dry and running streambeds, never once getting out of first gear. Once we used a winch to pull ourselves across a chasm.

That morning was the last time all summer that we were in the "big city," the last time we saw electricity or rode in the truck or enjoyed any of the amenities that we young Americans were used to. When we arrived in Santa Elena, we entered a time warp, and for the next three months we lived in the 19th century. I loved every minute of it.

Home on the Range

The Stewart casita was a traditional Spanish dwelling, built around a patio. The kitchen was in the back, equipped with a woodburning stove for everyday use and a kerosene stove for the times kerosene was available. Off the kitchen was the dining room, bordering on the patio and containing several pieces of ponderous Mexican furniture, along with the treasure of treasures: a Servel brand kerosene refrigerator. This was one survival tool we appreciated daily.

Up a few stairs was a large living area that also bordered on the patio and stretched the length of the house. Here the walls were lined with books, from the classics to detective novels. More heavy, leather-covered furniture was augmented by a few straight-back chairs and a worn rug. The house had three bedrooms, two off the living area and one off the side of the patio, which Bob and I used. The patio itself was furnished with a table and comfortable chairs, and we spent many a lazy hour there.

Maria, the housekeeper, was a stout Mexican woman of indeterminate age who cooked and did some cleaning, but the house was obviously suffering without the tender loving care of Mrs. Stewart.

There was no electricity within 30 miles. For inside light we used kerosene; after dark outdoors, we used carbide lamps. These clever devices depended upon a chemical reaction between calcium carbide and water. The water, which was stored in a separate reservoir, dripped into the carbide chamber. The combination produced acetylene gas that, when ignited, produced a bright, gentle flame. The smell of the burning gas was slightly unpleasant but not unbearably strong unless you breathed directly above the flame.

There was no indoor plumbing, just a two-holer located in the yard near the kitchen door. Water came from a cistern on the roof and was stored in a large galvanized tank. Drinking water seeped through a porous stone container that dripped continuously into a reservoir, which cooled it as well. In the kitchen we washed up with rainwater. For a bath we used a mountain stream or one of the cattle tanks. Better yet, we waited for a thunderstorm to turn the patio into a giant outdoor shower.

Our only connection with the outside world was a shortwave radio, which was powered by a generator mounted in the back of an old four-wheel-drive army truck. The truck had a dead battery and four flat tires, but as a generator platform, it fit the bill perfectly. About once a week the mine truck stopped on its trek to pick up ore to take to the railhead, and we could send mail back with it. That summer, though, not a single letter made it out and only one arrived.

The only methods of transportation on the ranch itself were walking or horseback, so the first thing I had to do was learn to ride a horse. Sure, I'd occasionally ridden Prince or Polly on the farm, but that was at a slow walk with Millard holding the bridle. Luz, a wiry old fellow who could do it all, brought me an off-white gelding called Little Tordilla. Another white gelding was called Big Tordilla, but he was massive, and even after I became comfortable in the saddle, I rode him only rarely. Training was short but thorough: saddle the horse, put in the bit, and mount, after which Bob, Luz, and I took off for an hour's ride. Little Tordilla was a smooth-gaited beauty, stable and calm, and we walked, cantered, and galloped without incident. At the end, one tired, sore hombre crawled off, but it wasn't nearly as bad as an encounter with the good captain, and it was a lot more fun.

After the ride, I watched Luz shoe a horse. He began by carefully running his hand down the horse's front quarters and then replacing a shoe. He repeated the process with the rear quarters, gently pulling the horse's hoof between his legs prior to fitting and nailing the new shoe into place. Wanting to demonstrate what I'd just observed, I marched up to Big Tordilla, picked up his rear leg, and started to inspect his hoof. Offended and surprised, the horse turned to me with a wild glint in his eye.

"Get away, Don! Get away!" Mr. Stewart's panicked voice boomed into the silence. Quickly I placed the horse's hoof back on the ground and backed off. Bob's father was white with fright and covered with beads of sweat. Once I was safely out of harm's way, he explained that nobody touched Big Tordilla. In fact, they had to hog-tie him before he could be shod, and even then, it was a dangerous process. Apparently, I was the first and only person who had touched this horse's hindquarters and lived to talk about it. Thank heavens my angel hadn't been on a break at that moment, but I think even she was shaken.

A few days after we arrived, Bob and I climbed the mountain behind the *casa* to the minehead. The mine that had once been so prosperous was now a shadow of its former self. Instead of the 100 or more workers and their families who had lived in the Santa Elena built by Mr. Stewart and his Mexican partner, 65 or 70 people now lived in a cluster of houses a half mile away. The men, with the exception of a half-dozen Mexican cowhands called vaqueros, worked in the mine. The women worked all the time, cooking frijoles, rolling tortillas, and tending children. This village, too, was called Santa Elena, but there the resemblance stopped. The houses were ramshackle adobe, about the size of a one-car garage, with dirt floors and roofs of scrap iron interwoven with sticks, mud, and grass. For a latrine, the villagers used the desert.

When we reached the village, we distributed the chickens. The villagers all knew Bob and were happy to see him. They were equally happy to see the chickens.

Children came regularly in Santa Elena, one a year, and it wasn't unusual for a woman of thirty to have had a dozen children, with maybe eight still living. The children ran free, happy, and naked until they were three or four, but they had jobs from the day they could walk. If there was a school, I never saw it. Just finding enough firewood to cook was a full-time job in this semidesert, and the women and children ranged for miles, bringing back huge bundles on their backs. Life was exhausting and the people were uneducated and desperately poor, but no one actually starved. Frijoles were plentiful and cheap, and meals were supplemented with rice, produce from the villagers' gardens, and occasional game.

Everybody had a few chickens scratching, and those fortunate enough to own a donkey considered it a prized possession. Most of the men had horses, and since they were the only means of transportation, they were well cared for. In fact, these families had so few possessions that almost everything was treasured. Clothing was very basic, at least in the summer: simple dresses for the women; shirts and homemade pants for the men. Those who wore shoes cut them from old truck tires and added toe straps. Nothing went to waste.

Every place I'd lived so far had offered marvelous food in abundant quantities. Grandmother was a superb cook and Maude a master of farm fare. I could still taste the delicacies prepared by Hermann Goering's pastry chef in Berlin, the tropical fruits in Panama, the Southwest flavors of El Paso. At the ranch, however, our diet differed little from that of the Mexicans. For breakfast we had cornflakes or eggs and frijoles. For lunch more frijoles or tortillas, often filled with a goat cheese resembling feta and topped with a spicy salsa of tomato, onion, and jalapeños. In the evening it was the same: frijoles and tortillas, with water to drink. Rarely did we use knives and forks. For one thing, a tortilla made a great scoop; for another, it made for less to wash.

If we wanted meat we had to shoot it, so we never left the house without a .22 rifle, and usually with a .30-30 as well. My .30-30 was a lever-action Remington made in 1894, with a barrel twice the length of its more modern counterpart. All that practice in El Paso was paying off. Most evenings, Bob and I sat by one of the water tanks, waiting for the doves to come in. With the .22, we'd pick off 20 or 30 birds a night, rip out the breast (the only edible part), and mix it with the frijoles.

It wasn't that the fare wasn't good, but it was monotonous and often sparse, and food was constantly on my mind. We did have a dairy cow that Maria milked, and we drank as much as we could hold, but we never killed one of the herd. The cattle represented wealth, if not today then sometime in the future, and as such they were treated as an asset. In any event, to do so there would have been a great waste, since our Servel refrigerator had limited capacity and there was no other way to preserve the meat.

About every two weeks a distinguished Mexican rancher whose spread was close to ours visited Mr. Stewart. He rode a beautiful stallion with a saddle decorated in silver, and he dressed like a lord in a colored suit with silver trim. I got the impression that he and Bob's dad were in business together in the mine, but no one ever talked about the details. The Mexicans showed enormous respect for this man, doffing their hats and bowing whenever they saw him. Occasionally Mr. Stewart would ride over to his place, but Bob and I were never invited.

The ranch was so isolated that there were few opportunities for entertainment, so Bob and I looked forward to the *baile*, a Mexican folk dance that happened in Santa Elena every Saturday night. Every man worth his salt played the guitar and sang, and the women loved to dance, the young señoritas watched closely by the older señoras. The dance consisted of a march around the perimeter of the dirt arena and was done much like a two-step. The unmarried girls were pretty and flirtatious, so Bob and I loved to join in. Bob's dad teased me about taking one of them to the desert on a moon-filled night, but my Spanish was rudimentary and I was both afraid and shy. Besides, there were no roses in Santa Elena. How could she enjoy the act?

Learning the Ropes

Bob Stewart on the ranch in Mexico, summer 1949.

One morning Bob and I went to the mine to observe the operation, which was so primitive it might have looked much the same in the time of Christ. The entrance was in the side of the mountain, a small staging area that almost immediately began a downward spiral into the bowels of the earth. The narrow shaft had been painstakingly hand-hewn out of the crumbling rock and was accessed via ladders made from wood cut in the higher mountains a few hours away. These ladders, no more than poles with rungs lashed to them with leather thongs, were bending and wobbling as we descended several hundred feet to the vein being worked. The only safety considerations consisted of a helmet with a carbide lamp and another lamp we carried as a backup.

Soon we could hear the clip-clip of the picks as the miners broke the ore away from the walls. The chamber being worked was large, and the sound echoed deep into the earth. These miners were the strongest, most compact men I'd ever seen. With muscles bulging, they took great pride in their job and their strength to do it. Several times a day, they climbed hundreds of feet up those rickety ladders to the minehead with wicker baskets containing 250 pounds of ore strapped to their backs. The way they worked reminded me of living on the farm, a steady motion that separated the ore from the walls of the mine and brought it, with its glint of silver or lead, into the light of day.

Since they had lived in close proximity for years, Bob knew most of the men, and when we arrived the miners stopped work to chat. It was almost like going into a cathedral, and we talked in hushed tones, our voices echoing in the stillness. I could follow a bit of the conversation, but not enough to understand all the laughter.

"What's going on, Bob?"

"They're making bets."

"Why?"

"The two strongest carriers want to race to the surface with a full basket, each carrying one of us on top, a load close to 400 pounds."

"Impossible," said I, but I seemed to be the only one who thought so.

Those ladders with their rawhide lashings just didn't look that strong, but money was on the table, and we climbed aboard. As we rode to the surface, these squat, muscular supermen passed each other several times, without hesitation and without any visible effort. When they delivered us into the bright sunshine they were huffing a bit, but no more than normal. This was their job: chipping the ore and carrying it to the surface, day in and day out, for about 50 cents a day. By American standards the working

Catching rabbits, Mexican style.
(*Illustration by Babe Sargent.*)

conditions were deplorable, but these brave, strong men were grateful to have jobs to support their large families. Even so, nobody lived a long life in Santa Elena. The combination of diet and hard labor wore them out, and a man in his forties looked ancient. The women looked old even sooner, since their bodies never got a rest from childbearing and chores.

Bob and I rarely returned to the mine. Being underground that far, especially traveling up and down the spiral of ladders, was both tiring and unnerving. On the surface, however, we ventured far and wide. Little Tordilla and I were well-matched and I became a good rider. I even got so I could leap into the saddle, Hollywood-style, and take off screaming and yelping, though I never approached the skill of Bob or the vaqueros. Sometimes I shot at cottontails from the saddle, although Little Tordilla didn't like the pop of the .22. When I was successful, I would lean over with a whoop, sweep the rabbit off the ground, squeeze the guts out of it, and hang it off the saddle horn for dinner—just like an "ole time" cowboy. Skinned out and twisting on a spit over the coals of a campfire, rabbit provided a welcome addition to our dinners of frijoles and tortillas.

Navigation was not a problem. The mountains were easily identifiable and the desert trails were numerous. Occasionally we bushwhacked, cutting our way through the undergrowth, but that was hard on the horses and on us, even though we wore chaps to protect our legs from the brush and thorny trees. Everything scratched or poked in the high desert, and our hands looked like cowboy hands, rough and scratched. Because the game was nearly hunted-out close to Santa Elena, we ranged pretty far afield, sometimes alone and sometimes with vaqueros, but the mission was always the same: food.

On the range, we learned to rely on nature for much of our diet. By late summer, the prickly pear cactus, when carefully peeled to shed its fir-like thorn, yielded a delicious fruit. The fruit of another cactus tasted like strawberries, providing sweetness as well as moisture. When we found water, it was often cloudy and suspect, but after boiling it and throwing in a handful of coffee grounds, we had a fine-tasting drink. We also made tea with one of the native plants, a brew with a lemon-like flavor. Under other circumstances I might have wished for different fare, but the isolation of the desert made everything more intense. Even our worst meal was delicious.

Some nights we didn't make it back to the ranch, but Bob's dad understood and didn't worry about us. Our provisions and gear were simple: a saddle blanket for ground cover, ripe with sweat from the horse's back; a blanket for warmth; and a poncho for rain protection, though the last was more hindrance than help. The days were hot, but the nights were comfortable, so we usually slept whenever and wherever the daylight left us. Some nights we slept in rain or a thunderstorm. The next day, the hot, dry desert air, combined with the intensity of the morning sun, didn't take long to dry and warm our bodies, but we always covered our saddles. A wet saddle makes the inner thighs mighty tender.

After one of these storms, the desert came alive with a frantic intensity. Colorful flowers bloomed in patches, and dry streambeds called *arroyos* went from gullies of parched earth one instant to raging, four-foot walls of water the next. By sundown, they were dry again.

Occasionally we rode at night, especially when we worked with the cowhands to move cattle or lead horses from one section of the ranch to another. Night travel had its dangers, but nowhere is the sky bigger or the stars brighter than on the open range.

When there was enough food to last for a couple of days, especially when it was hotter than usual, Bob and I would lie around under the awning on the patio and read. The Stewarts' library was extensive, and we consumed everything from the classics to junk. At lunch we'd talk about what we read, and Bob's dad led many a lively discussion on authors such as Alexander Dumas, Victor Hugo, and Mark Twain. If we tired of reading, we entertained ourselves by shooting flies with our .22s. After a time, we became deadly shots, and Mr. Stewart only stopped us when the bullets started ricocheting off the adobe walls.

About the first of August, Mrs. Stewart and Bob's sister Helen arrived, which made things better for all of us. Meals improved dramatically, desert flowers appeared in vases around the house, and music came from the hand-cranked Victrola. There was no doubt a woman's touch made a dramatic difference, but even nature itself was contributing to our improved diet. Corn planted by vaqueros around the water tanks began to ripen, and there's nothing better than corn roasting in the coals while a pot of dove breast or rabbit and frijoles simmers on the stove top.

Helen was a real rancher and could do anything that a man could do. She was also very attractive, a fact that did not go unnoticed, by me or by the vaqueros. One day while she and Bob and I were out with some of the hands, a huge rattler appeared by a mesquite bush. Helen shot it dead. Rattlesnakes were prevalent on the ranch, I knew, but this was the first one I'd seen, and I wanted the rattlers as a souvenir. I jumped down and used a stick to pull the dead snake out from under the mesquite, then jumped back almost immediately. Another snake, this one very much alive, was wrapped around the dead one. Apparently it had been making whoopee, but it didn't live to love another day.

Testing Our Mettle

On a separate part of the ranch, about six to eight hours away by horseback, were several families who bred and trained horses. This area had better water and was greener than most other spots, and the families who lived there in their adobe casas seemed more prosperous. Along with the ever-present chickens, they raised goats. Since there was no refrigeration, the goats' milk was always boiled and then used to make a delicious white crumbly cheese: *queso de cabra*.

Shortly before returning to the States, Bob and I, along with four cowhands from the main ranch, made a trip to this area to bring back a string of fresh horses to the main ranch. We enjoyed being with these isolated families. The señoritas loved to pamper Bob, and by extension, me, and we were more than willing to be pampered. The horses, however, were full of vim and vigor, and once we got to work, it took almost all day to round them up. Finally, toting frijoles and a cold tortilla filled with goat cheese to eat on the trail, the six of us started off with a string of 20 horses for the long ride home.

Before we'd gone more than a few miles, a couple of the friskier horses bolted, and it took another hour to lasso them back before we could continue. Hour after hour we plodded along, eating dust through the bandanas covering our noses and mouths. Eventually night descended around us. A full moon painted the desert with an eerie glow, thunderclaps boomed, and lightning daggers sliced the sky.

The horses were nervous, but we couldn't stop. If we lost them now, they could easily disappear into some uncharted part of the ranch and we'd never get them back. For the first time in my life, I felt close to exhaustion. Fatigue gripped every inch of my body, and Bob wasn't any better off. The vaqueros, in their tough, stoic way, showed no sign of weariness and offered no complaint.

About two or three in the morning, we saw the storm bearing down on us. Before we had time to pull on our ponchos, it hit with a vengeance, a wall of water from the sky that turned the dry roadway into a turbulent, muddy stream. Thunder shook the ground and lightning painted the landscape, reflecting off the eyeballs of the horses in a strobe-like effect. The calming energy of the vaqueros had so far kept the near-panicked horses from stampeding, but the scene had all the makings of a disaster waiting to happen. And then, with a final burst of wind and one more crack of thunder, the storm was gone.

The horses settled a bit, and we rode close together, laughing nervously and trying to act as brave as our chattering limbs would allow. Men and horses steamed with moisture, and our straw cowboy hats hung around our ears like scarves, but one thing was certain: We were awake. Then, just as dawn broke in the east, the ranch appeared on the horizon. To the Moslem it was Mecca, to the Jew the Wailing Wall; to us it was Home. The vaqueros took care of the horses while we rode to the house, rubbed down our own mounts, and joined the family at breakfast.

"How'd it go?" asked Mr. Stewart.

"No problem," we replied.

Bob's dad smiled but said nothing. He knew we'd been to the mountain.

The Big Adios

Just before we left for the U.S., Helen staged a fiesta in the village of Santa Elena. The fiesta included a 200-yard horse race down the straight, hard-packed road just out of town. Everyone old enough to fork a saddle was there. Helen, who was an excellent horsewoman, rode a beautiful and spirited palomino, a tall, proud horse with speed as well as staying power. I rode Little Tordilla, and Bob was on Big Tordilla. After much mulling around, with the animals rearing and biting each other's eyes like a bunch of Thoroughbreds at the Derby, the contestants formed some semblance of a straight line. Someone fired the starting gun, and everyone made a mad dash for the finish line. Helen won easily, with hardly a speck of dust on her. I got caught in the middle, jostled by horses and riders on either side of me as they yipped and screeched down the track. If anyone had fallen, they'd have been trampled in an instant. There were no mishaps, and soon competitors became compadres at a feast spread out on the edge of the road.

The display of food far exceeded anything I'd experienced on the ranch. Large hunks of beef from a cow that had been sacrificed for the event were rotating on spits over mesquite fires. The señoras had prepared steaming cauldrons of frijoles with various salsas, and stacks of hand-rolled flour and corn tortillas sat ready to be filled. Everyone ate as if it were his or her last meal. Tequila, sotol, and beer were consumed in great quantities, though even in the wilds of Mexico, no one was offering any to 15-year-olds.[69]

Out of nowhere, a mariachi band began playing, and soon everyone was dancing. Helen was the queen of the ball, a heroine in her own Zane Grey adventure. The music played on into the night, and gradually the señoras departed with their young *hijos* in tow, followed by groups of guarded

---

[69] Sotol is an alcoholic beverage made from one of several varieties of tall, woody plants of the same name that are grown in Mexico and in the U.S. Southwest.

señoritas. Soon all we could hear was the sound of a single guitar, caressing the stillness with a tune of farewell.[70]

A few days later, Bob's dad and Luz loaded everyone into the truck and we bumped and banged the several hours back to El Oro. Helen and Mrs. Stewart joined Luz on the worn seats in the front, while Mr. Stewart, Bob, and I hung onto the rickety stays in the empty bed. That night we stayed in the same hotel and ate in the same diner we'd visited on our arrival, and the next day the four of us boarded the antique train for Chihuahua. Bob and I carried almost nothing except our toothbrushes, our worn Levi's, and our ever-present straw hats.

I had left El Paso weighing 135 pounds; I returned 10 pounds lighter and hard as nails. Within days, Bob, Helen, and I went back to school. Mrs. Stewart went back to her job at the department store and her worried, late-night sewing. Mr. Stewart stayed on the ranch, hoping for better days.

* * *

---

[70] Zane Grey (1872–1939) was one of the greatest storytellers of all time. Born in Zanesville, OH, he was thrilled by his ancestors' adventures and eventually wrote fictionalized accounts of their stories and the stories of so many others—ranchers and homesteaders, cowhands and railroad men, housewives and wanderers, the men and women who settled the American West.

Chapter 28 – Misadventures in El Paso

1949–1950

Wait a minute. What time is it? Where am I? I looked around the room, then at the digital alarm on the dresser: nearly 5 p.m. I rubbed my eyes and clicked back into the present, a March afternoon in 1988 in Nokomis, Florida, definitely not Mexico. While I was adrift in memories of the 1940s, Polly had obviously tired of her magazine and gone off to start dinner. Even now, more or less awake, it was hard to realize my adventures had taken place so many years before. Heck, if I listened carefully enough, I could almost hear the strains of that Mexican guitarist in the high-desert night. I couldn't wait to share some of my recollections with the others.

After dinner, Betty was ready for more. As the days went by, it was obvious she was growing weaker, but her mind was as sharp as ever, and she laughed out loud as she told stories about life in Panama and revisited some of my misadventures on the ranch. Then we started to talk about what it was like when I came home from Mexico.

"We were certainly glad to see you," Betty said, "though I couldn't believe how skinny you were, not to mention how much you ate to make up for it. Of course, making sure you got all the foods you'd missed that summer gave Grandmother something to do, and that gave us all a bit of relief."

"She always could cause a ruckus, couldn't she," I said, laughing at some of the situations I remembered growing up.

Betty chuckled, too. "She meant well, but somehow she just couldn't help herself from sniping. She would do things like wait until George left for work and then say, 'Betty, he spilled a crumb on the floor.'"

"And what did you say to that?"

"'It's all right,'" I'd remind her sweetly. "'George is paying the bills.'"

* * *

Thinking back, I imagine this type of logic probably worked fairly well. George was a traditional kind of guy. In his view, the men went to work and the

170

women ran the house, so most of Grandmother's shenanigans were probably lost on him, anyway. He liked his job working with antiaircraft artillery, and that fall he and I landscaped the yard of the Hamilton Street house.

Back at Austin High, I entered my sophomore year with renewed vigor, promising myself that this was the year I would buckle down, pay attention, and achieve academic excellence. Unfortunately, my modus operandi lasted about a week, after which I reverted to my natural, daydreaming state. It didn't help that the class was filled with pretty gals whose every movement, even breathing, pulled the blood from my already wandering head. And on top of everything else, I was back in the second half of freshman English, attempting to diagram sentences once again. What the heck did diagramming have to do with flying fighters?

When we weren't in class, Bob and I tried, without much success, to get the young maidens to pal around with us. Although he didn't look it, Bob was now 16 and had managed to beg enough money from his mom to buy a Doodlebug motor scooter. A far cry from a Harley, this bike was tiny, with a top speed of about 20 miles per hour with one rider and 10 miles per hour with two, and that included walking it up hills. Even at that, we were never on the bike long enough to be dangerous. We spent most of our time fixing it.

I tried out again for the football team but didn't last through the first session. I was disappointed, because in terms of attracting the gals, I didn't have much going for me. I was gangly, suffered from acne, and had very little money. I did chores around the house to earn an allowance, but for the life of me, I couldn't find a job. If it hadn't been for daydreaming, my romantic life would have been suicidal.

Bob and I did join a bowling league, a mixed group where we had at least some contact with the fairer sex. The owner of the lanes taught us the game at no charge, the lines were cheap enough that even I could afford a couple of games, and the girls were cute. In fact, one of them was the cutest girl in our class, and we boys circled around her like bees around a hive. A group of us were walking her home one day when J.C., one of my buddies, offered her a cigarette. "How dare you offer me that filthy thing," she said, her tongue becoming a lash. "If you want to be around me, you'd better clean up your act." I learned a lesson that day: Girls controlled the mood, the morals, and the tempo of life.

Bob had smoked since he was eight years old, Mexican cigarettes called *Faros* that cost four cents for a pack of ten and looked similar to "roll your own." He never smoked a lot, but both his parents smoked heavily. My opinion about smoking hadn't changed, much of it due to Grandmother's influence. It was dumb as dirt, it stank, and one had to be stupid to do it. The fact that it was also unhealthy was a given that only the ignorant could ignore.

Winter eased into spring, and at the end of the first semester, I had a firm hold at the top of the bottom third of the class. Freshman English had been a close call, but with a new teacher and some new and inspired begging, I passed with a solid D. Nevertheless, school was boring. The teachers were fine, but my mind wandered—flying, hunting, and girls, not necessarily in that order. I had already been asked to return to Mexico the following summer, and Bob and I were stockpiling ammo with eager anticipation.

In the meantime (just to keep my hand in, of course), I fabricated a small cannon in shop class from a piece of copper tubing with a fuse hole at one end. Then I built a pistol grip and wrapped it with many strands of fine copper wire until it looked like an authentic miniature cannon. Next I crafted a model that looked like a pistol.

Last names beginning with S and W assured Bob and me seats in the back of the room, where it was easy to feign attention with books propped in front of us. Behind those books, however, we spent hours wrapping the guns we'd created. For ammunition, we peeled the paper away from caps and tamped the freed powder into our gun barrels with a small rod. We fired these missiles, with some degree of accuracy, in the school yard during lunch breaks. The noise was deafening—at least as loud as a .45 pistol—and the other guys loved the action. They begged us for details, but we protected our designs as closely as if they were pending patents.

Right before lunch one day, in the middle of our favorite English class, Bob lost his concentration as he was loading a barrel. Distracted by a young beauty as she twitched her way to the blackboard, he tamped too hard on an extra full load. Bang! Smoke and flames erupted from the muzzle as the ramrod launched skyward. The air was so dense it was hard to see, and it was raining bits of ceiling. Someone opened the windows, and after a bit Bob appeared through the haze, looking for all the world like Al Jolsen made up to sing *Mammy*. His face was blackened, his curly light brown hair was singed across his forehead, and his eyebrows were missing altogether. Above him, the errant ramrod quivered in the plaster.[71]

For what seemed like a minute, time stood still. Then the teacher dropped the book she was holding, the door flew open, and the principal and three other teachers rushed in with fire extinguishers. Before he knew what hit him, Bob was hauled out of class by his ear and Mrs. Stewart had to come from her job

---

[71] Born Asa Yoelson in 1885 to a rabbi and his wife in a small Russian village, Jolson emigrated with his family to the U.S. in 1888. He grew up to be a recording artist and star of stage and screen, and was one of many actors who wore blackface when performing in American minstrels. In 1927, he starred in *The Jazz Singer,* the first full-length "talkie" film in which spoken dialogue was used as part of the dramatic action. Jolson died of a heart attack in San Francisco in 1950.

to free him. He spent the rest of the year in detention, and worse yet, he failed English. I tried to teach him my begging techniques to head off this disaster, but to no avail. His grades were higher than mine to start with, and he just didn't have the talent to present a convincing picture of childhood hardships, although the lack of eyebrows was a good starting point.

After that, the gun business became somewhat of a hindrance. Too bad I hadn't sold the rights before it became a taboo hobby. As for my grades, I was holding my all-too-familiar D+ to C- average. Perhaps with some strategic begging, I'd do better.

Toward the end of the school year, a shock of peroxide hair began to be seen around campus, so naturally, Bob and I went to the drugstore for peroxide and alcohol. With Bob's sister Helen's help, we doused our entire scalp three times and then sat in the sun. The result was the weirdest-looking hair in the state of Texas, an orange-blond mess that afforded us a certain hero status at Austin High but caused one heck of a commotion at home. The operation also burned the dickens out of my scalp, and to this day I've never stopped scratching what's left.

That June, Bob and I finished our sophomore year and Helen graduated. She'd missed some school during the war, when the Stewarts were all living on the ranch, so she was a year or two older than her high school classmates and more than ready to get on with life. Earlier in the year, she'd met a pilot at Biggs Air Force Base, and they were married immediately after graduation. He was a big man and very likeable. He also had the job I yearned for, and I tried to glean as much information from him as possible. "Keep your nose clean and do well in school," he advised, and I vowed to do better the following year. After all, school was three months in the future, and Mexico was just around the corner.[72]

The day after the wedding, Bob and I were on the train to Santa Elena, sans chickens but with copious rounds of .22 ammo in our pockets. Over the previous nine months, I'd reached almost my full height and had grown into my legs and feet. I was still skinny, weighing in at 145 pounds, but I was proportional, and Bob, too, was filling out. We thought we looked pretty good, except, of course, for the orange hair. The Mexicans we met en route had many a laugh over the outlandish color, even though our new cowboy hats hid most of it. When Mr. Stewart and Luz met us in El Oro, they also had a good time at our expense. Thank heavens we hadn't gotten tattoos. At least hair grows.

---

[72] Between 1947 and 1966, Biggs Air Force Base was a Strategic Air Command installation. As of 2008, this location is run by the army as Biggs Army Airfield and is located at Fort Bliss.

Chapter 29 – Survival

1950

The previous summer had been one of the most challenging and enjoyable of my young life, and it was good to be back, even if the locals did insist on calling us *Los Palominos*. We put up with the harassment for a while, after which we got out the horse shears. When we were done, nothing remained but stubble. From that point on, my scalp itched constantly and I developed a receding hairline. Who knows how much hair I'd have today if not for those peroxide adventures? I like to think I'd have been the envy of movie stars.

In the intervening year, everything on the ranch had changed. Maria the housekeeper had moved away, the cow had dried up, and game, for some reason, had become scarce. Around the house, Bob's dad was as useless as teats on a boar hog, and he had been living on canned food and tortillas prepared by a vaquero's wife. Fortunately, thanks to Grandmother at home and Maude on the farm, I could cook with the best of them. I had an instant job.

Every evening we sorted pinto beans from rocks, and there were always plenty of rocks. I then soaked the beans overnight and cooked them for hours the next day on the woodstove. Once they became soft, I mashed and fried them in an iron skillet with a blob of lard. Rolling tortillas was another constant. I learned from an expert, one of the vaqueros' señoras, but I knew that if I lived to be a hundred, I would never make them as well as she did. I preferred flour tortillas, but corn was more common, so I made both, and neither Bob nor his dad ever complained.

The rest of the meal consisted of throwing in any meat we could kill. Rabbits were scarce that year, and the doves hadn't migrated to the ranch, so on many a day meat was just a memory. We always had salsa, since tomatoes, chilis, and onions were available at a tiny store in the village, but we were hard put to do without cow's milk. We were used to milk, both drinking it and putting it on cornflakes, the only available cereal. That summer, we ate our cornflakes with water, and for sweetener we scraped brown sugar from a hard block. This combination eventually became more than we could take, and we resorted to breakfasts of frijoles wrapped in fresh tortillas.

After a couple of weeks of this severely abbreviated diet, my stomach rebelled and I developed a full-blown case of the Mexican two-step, wearing a racetrack path to the outhouse. I was still able to cook and ride out to hunt, but I always felt sick and couldn't keep anything down. As I got weaker, I started to lose weight, and for some reason, the thing I craved the most was candy. When the ore truck came around as usual at the end of the week, I wrote a short note to my mother before it left for town. I'd been a little sick, I said, with an upset stomach, but it was getting better. I didn't want to worry her, I stressed, but the one thing I really missed was candy. An answer, if it came at all, would be many weeks away, but at least I'd made the effort.

The next morning, Bob and I announced to Mr. Stewart that we were going to the Sierras near the back of the ranch to hunt for deer. If we didn't upgrade the quality of our food, I felt I might not survive, and we thought our chances of finding game were better away from civilization. In preparation, I cooked a bunch of frijoles and tortillas and put them in the refrigerator for Mr. Stewart. I sure hoped he'd make it until our return.

Bob and I packed some coffee and a several-day supply of frijoles, tortillas, and onions and headed out with José, one of the vaqueros. This was the first time I'd traveled to the western edge of the ranch, and Bob told me it would be fraught with danger. It was about a half day's ride to our destination, including a stop every 30 minutes so I could squirt the desert floor. My bottom was hurting, and to say I wasn't feeling well was an understatement. Once we reached more mountainous country, however, game began to appear, and Bob managed to kill one or two rabbits.

The mountains were steep, a couple of thousand feet high. Over the centuries, cattle and wild game had notched narrow trails into the sides of the cliffs, and these were the trails we must follow if we wanted our quest to be successful. Hanging on for dear life, I followed Bob and José on passages not much wider than the horses' hooves, with the mountain on one side and a sheer drop on the other. One misstep and we'd be over the edge, plunging hundreds of feet to certain death. I was terrified.

Since Bob and José rode ahead of me, they had no idea how scared I was, but there was no way to turn back. I tried to put my fear behind me, and eventually the grip on my guts diminished. Little Tordilla wasn't any happier about the situation than I was, but he rarely stumbled. When he did, I pulled him up with more vigor than usual. At long last, the trail opened into a valley, an oasis filled with towering pines and a trickling stream. We set up camp, and after a dinner of rabbit roasted on an open fire, I felt better. Squirting was down to once an hour.

That night we lay around the campfire, bellies full and bodies cooled by the mountain breeze. José strummed his guitar and sang, and the sound of soft Mexican music drifted into the night. The smells of sweet pine and crackling campfire surrounded us, and the sky above was a canopy of stars. This was wilderness—wild, treacherous, and beautiful—and it was easy to imagine us as the first human beings to set foot in this place. If only we didn't have to return over the same trails.

We awoke the next morning determined to get some venison or die trying, and after choking down a breakfast tortilla filled with frijoles, we moved out before dawn. My weapon of choice was the lever-action Remington, which, in spite of being over 50 years old and a bit awkward with its long, hexagonal barrel, was quite reliable.

It was hard to navigate in the semidarkness; the mountains were a jumble of shapes. Bob told me that these mountains were the bane of his father's existence, so wild that when cattle escaped and got into the arroyos, even the vaqueros couldn't get them out. To make matters worse, the cattle were pretty wild critters themselves. Half Brahma bull, the remainder a combination of native breed and Hereford, they were feisty by nature, and since the ban on beef, Bob's dad hadn't bothered to castrate most of the males.

Just before dawn, we split up. Soon afterward, I was creeping on foot along the steep mountain trail, trying not to think about getting lost, when I rounded a bend to a sight that took away all thought of venison or anything else. A giant bull, horns huge, head lowered, and totally pissed off, stood no more than ten yards from me. His front hoof pawed at the soil of the narrow trail. I looked for an escape route. To my right was a sheer cliff, hundreds of feet down to the valley below. To my left was the mountain, straight up and impassable.

"Nice cow, nice cow," I whispered soothingly. I stepped back, weapon at the ready, though I figured a .30-30 bullet would probably bounce off his monstrous head. Ever so slowly, I continued creeping backwards round the bend. I prayed. Did I see a flash of white—a mystical, angelic smile? I was shaking, but I was alone. Somehow, my guardian angel must have been protecting me, because the bull was nowhere in sight.

That morning I saw more bulls, but none as close as the first, and I was careful to always give myself time and space to maneuver. When the sun was high, I ate my tortilla and frijoles, drank some water from my canteen, had the usual squirt, and settled into a good hunting perch overlooking a slope a couple of hundred yards away. My back was up against a gnarled old tree, my rifle was cocked on my lap, and before I knew it, I'd dozed off. I awoke with a start, not knowing where I was or how I got there.

Out of the corner of my eye, I caught the flick of a white tail. There, on the opposite slope, three deer were grazing. I raised the Remington, sighted carefully, and squeezed off a shot. Damn, I missed. I needed that meat. I leapt to my feet and started levering shells through the old rifle. Of course, the deer took off, but just as they were disappearing over the ridge, one tumbled down and stayed. With a thrill that only those who have made their first kill can appreciate, I let out a war whoop, reloaded the rifle (just in case I ran into a soft-headed Brahma bull), and ran down the mountain. When I reached the young buck, I tore into his gut with my hunting knife, cleaned him out, and placed the liver into a special bag I'd brought for the purpose. Within minutes, José and Bob ran up to join me.

Couldn't we talk this over?
(*Illustration by Babe Sargent.*)

"How'd you know I had a kill?" I said.

"Well," Bob replied, smiling, "from the sound of things it was either that or World War III had broken out."

We fetched one of the horses, strapped the deer to its back, and started back to camp. As soon as we arrived, I started a fire. When it was ready, I added a blob of lard and some onions to the skillet and placed it in the coals. Soon the onions were sizzling, turning liquid brown in the oil. I threw in the liver, and within minutes we were eating liver and onions, smiles on our faces and juice running down our chins. It was one of the best meals of my life.

After dinner I told the story of the hunt, including my encounter with the bull, though I seem to remember I came out a little braver in the telling. The next morning, my stomach was fine and the trots were history. My behind, however, was another story. Between a couple weeks of the Mexican two-step and constant rubbing in the saddle, it took a long time to heal.

The ride out was as terrifying as the ride in, and even today my groin tingles when I think about those heights and my dependence on the dexterity of Little Tordilla. Once we got home, Bob's dad was most appreciative of the meat, which we cut up and stored in the Servel refrigerator. By the time it was gone, we'd gone back to the mountains and Bob had killed another deer, and later on the doves returned, providing even greater culinary variety. Tomatoes, onions, jalapeños, venison, dove, frijoles, and tortillas. We were living well, and my health had returned, but I was still beanpole skinny.

Fortunately, not all the cattle were as ornery as those who'd escaped to the Sierras, and Bob and I often worked with the vaqueros to round them up and move them from one part of the ranch to another. Such trips could last for several days. On one occasion we'd been out longer than we anticipated. It was at least a day's ride back to the ranch and our food was gone.

Mid-morning, we stopped for a break, dismounting not far from a small group of cattle, including a nursing calf. As we surveyed the scene, Bob and the vaqueros started to chatter in Spanish. I had never learned to speak the language well, lazily relying on Bob as a language crutch, but I understood more than enough to know what was going to happen next. We waited quietly until the calf moved away from its mother. Bam! The calf died instantly, and we were on it the minute it hit the ground, ripping out the backstrap and galloping away. We left the rest for the vultures.[73]

We rode for a few miles, stopped and lit a campfire, and cooked the meat as little as possible before devouring it with gusto.

"Whose calf did we kill, Bob?" I asked between mouthfuls.

"Not ours."

"Isn't that rustling?"

"Yep."

"What happens if we get caught?"

---

[73] Also known as the tenderloin, the backstrap contains an internal muscle of the loin on each side of a cow's spinal column and is usually thought of as the most tender cut of beef.

"Don't ask." For the first time all summer my stomach was full, but I'd heard enough. That night, my dreams were filled with cowboys swinging by their necks in the breeze.

Mr. Stewart never spoke much about his financial status, but my gut told me all was not well, and he was always on the lookout for new opportunities. Somehow he heard that agate rock, a semiprecious stone, would fetch a good price in the States. The ranch was a vast wasteland of agate, and soon we were pacing the semidesert, picking up rocks.

Like the summer before, we settled into a routine, each of us contributing what he did best. Bob and I worked the ranch, moving cattle and horses. Bob and his dad were skilled at finding agate. And I was the cook and kitchen help. Once we found game, food was plentiful except for the lack of milk, and I turned out some pretty delicious meals.

A Mother's Love

Now that we were eating right, I was feeling fine and had almost forgotten about my letter home when the ore truck driver pulled up with a surprise. "*Señor* Don, I have a package for you." Hot diggity dog! It was from Betty. She'd heard my plea for candy.

Wanting to savor the excitement as long as possible, I waited until after the noon meal to tear off the paper. Inside was a large tin box imprinted with the words "Fanny Farmer Candies." Slowly I opened the lid, mouth watering in anticipation of the first delicious piece. The box was filled to the brim with aspirin, Pepto-Bismol, Alka-Seltzer, and every other home remedy known to man. Tucked into one corner was a note: "Donald, I hope this will make you better. Love, Betty."

* * *

Nearly 40 years had passed since that day in Mexico, but looking at the box of candy sitting next to my mother's chair in Nokomis, I still ached with the memory of how much I'd wanted just one piece of chocolate from that Fanny Farmer tin. "Do you remember," I said to Betty, "the second summer I went to Mexico, when I wrote you a letter saying I was sick and that I really craved candy and you sent me a box of stomach remedies?"

"Of course," Betty replied. "I was so worried about you."

"Yeah, well I was worried about me, too, but what I wanted more than anything was something sweet. We were all gathered around the day your package arrived—Bob, his dad, and me, looking at the candy box, and . . ."

"I picked that box especially. I thought it would ship well," Betty interjected.

"Right, but you see, we wanted it to be *candy*. We *needed* it to be candy. And it was *Pepto-Bismol*. Yuk. I'd rarely shed a tear since that summer in 1943 when I lived on the farm and Millard couldn't sell his potatoes, but that day my eyes sure misted over. Bob and his dad were sniffling a bit as well. It took me years to forgive you."

Betty laughed. "I can see that now, but at the time it seemed so *sensible*." She picked up the box beside her and held it out to me. "Here, Don," she offered, "won't you have a piece of candy?"

I had two, both of them creamy, chocolatey, and delicious. Then I gave her a hug. After all, she'd only been trying to do what mothers do best: loving and caring.

* * *

One for the Road

It was the height of thunderstorm season, just about the first of August, and Bob and I needed to pick up a couple of horses from the settlement at the far edge of the ranch. Since we planned to ride the horses back, we made arrangements with the weekly ore truck to get us there. This truck was so decrepit it came with two drivers to winch it over the streams and rough spots, but it would deliver us within four miles of the settlement. From there, we had to hike in, bushwhacking cross-country toting our saddles, guns, and gear.

The morning of the trip arrived, hot and sunny as usual, and the truck was right on time. Throwing our saddles, rifles, and bedrolls up ahead of us, we climbed aboard the heaping load of ore and settled in for a birds-eye view of the surrounding countryside.

The drivers stopped about noon at a factory building in the middle of the desert. I knew we'd ridden by this building before, but until that day I'd never seen any activity.

"What do they make here, Bob?"

"Sotol. It's that stuff that's sort of like tequila, but not as strong."

"Oh yeah, I remember. People were drinking it at the fiesta last summer, but they wouldn't give us any."

As we ate our lunch with the few workers, I took in the operation. The building was made of adobe, like everything else in the desert, though this structure was larger than usual. Smoke and steam belched from makeshift chimneys, and through the unfinished walls I could see silver cauldrons of what looked like moonshine, only much larger. Piles of sotol plants, stripped of their spine-covered shells, stood ready to be processed, and mesquite for the fires was stacked carelessly nearby.

After lunch, the drivers went inside, emerging with fruit-juice-sized glasses of clear liquid.

— ¿*Quiere sotol?* the factory honcho asked with a smile.

"Sure," Bob and I replied. After all, we were 16 now (well, I was *almost* sixteen), and surely, if we could hunt deer, relocate cattle, and fetch horses, we could handle a little native brew.

Tentatively at first, but soon with a bit more confidence, we downed the stuff. It burned a bit, but it went down okay.

— ¿*Mas?*

"*Si.*" Neither of us had ever had more than a few beers before, and we had no idea of the power of the drink.

A few small glasses later, we were assisted to the top of the truck, where we promptly passed out. The truck was swaying, our faces were buried in the ore, and before long we were puking our guts out. After what seemed like an eternity, we reached our destination: a fork in a dusty, little-used road in the middle of nowhere. The drivers stopped, dragged us and our gear off the load and into the nearest arroyo, and took off.

By this time we were wide-awake, but we couldn't move. Stiff from the ride and covered with vomit, we were trapped in a nightmare of disorientation and pain. Hours passed, and we hadn't budged. Eventually daylight turned to dusk and then to dark, and it began to rain. The water felt refreshing; it washed away some of the stink if nothing else. All too soon, however, the rain deteriorated into a violent thunderstorm, and water began to run through the arroyo.

"Bob! We've gotta get out of here."

No answer.

"Bob!" I said again, panic rising in my throat.

"Leave me alone," he groaned. At that point, compared with the effort of crawling out of the arroyo, dying in the water seemed as good an option as any.

Finally, I made it to my hands and knees, and Bob did the same. Dragging our saddles and gear, we crawled out of the streambed and collapsed on the bank. Minutes later, a wall of water several feet high roared down the arroyo.

Dawn. The arroyo that nearly killed us in the night was almost dry, and we could feel the sun warming our sick, aching bodies. Better yet, when we drank water, it stayed down. Perhaps life was an option after all. Slowly but surely, we made our way to the settlement, taking until noon to cover the four miles. The señoras were too polite to ask what happened, but they fed us huevos rancheros with all the fixings, hot goat's milk, and cheese. By evening, we had nearly recovered, but by unspoken agreement, we never discussed the sotol factory with anyone.

From Mexico to Massachusetts

One day in late August, we ran into a band of riders who told us the United States had gone back to war. This sounded bogus to us, but we rode back to the ranch and told Mr. Stewart. I could almost read his mind: If the U.S. was at war, perhaps the ban on Mexican cattle would be lifted and he could make a living once again. Later that day the ore truck came in, and we used it to jump-start the old army truck with the generator in its bed. Now we could use the battery to power the shortwave radio. After fiddling with it for a bit, we heard the news: In Korea, the North had attacked the South. Not only were we at war, we were in serious trouble, and it had been going on since June.

It would soon be time for Bob and me to leave, and I was worried about Mr. Stewart. I had tried to bring him along in the kitchen, and sometimes he could light the stove and boil water, but there was no doubt I'd learned more about the classics and life from him than he had learned about basic survival from me.

Even though the ranch was isolated from most vestiges of civilization and reaching it by train was a convoluted process, as the crow flew it was only 100 miles or so from the border. The plan was for us to take this shorter route, returning to the States with the ore truck, which had been loaded to the brim with the agate we'd collected over the summer.

The day we left, Bob and I perched on blankets on top of the load, trying to make ourselves as comfortable as possible. We said our thanks and goodbyes and planned to return the following summer in what we hoped would be a better and more prosperous world. Three Mexicans rode in the cab and took turns driving. The truck—an ancient Ford relic—bucked and ground the long, torturous journey through the wilds of Mexico. For three days we helped winch and repair our way over roads that may never before have seen motorized traffic, eating up the miles and rarely getting out of first gear.

Just before dark on the third day, we stopped at a spot several miles from the Rio Grande, just below Presidio, Texas. From there, the Mexicans walked to a high point to "recon" the crossing. It might have been because of my limited knowledge of Spanish, but it wasn't until that moment that I realized we intended to smuggle this load of rock into the States. (Bob's dad was an intelligent, educated, and humorous man who taught me a lot about life, but he held his cards close to his vest.)

The Mexicans, once satisfied with the situation, drove within a mile of the river and we bedded down for the night. Two hours before dawn, we climbed back on top of the truck and splashed our way across the Rio Grande, at that point just a muddy pond separating one country, and one world, from another. Bob and I jumped down once we reached the highway outside of Presidio. We thanked the drivers and started walking toward town. The Mexicans and their rambling wreck disappeared over the horizon, destination unknown.

Pretty soon, a pickup stopped and gave us a ride. We told the driver we'd been camping in the Big Bend and were going back to school. He dropped us in town, where the first thing we did was locate the nearest drugstore with a soda fountain and order the largest banana split they made. Nothing ever tasted better. After that we bought a couple of candy bars, found the bus station, and caught the next bus to El Paso.

The Greyhound pulled into El Paso early in the afternoon. Bob headed for home and I caught a city bus to Hamilton Street. In my worn Levis, washed-out Western shirt, and beat-up straw hat, I looked like a ranch hand. I was almost six feet tall, had the beginnings of a shaggy beard, and was railroad thin. The trots had trimmed me down; the hard life had kept me there.

I'd learned a lot on the ranch. I was mentally and physically tough, having survived experiences that tested my reserve and my resolve. I had known fear and conquered it, and I could survive eating almost nothing without complaint. It's true that when the going got tough, I could have jumped on a train and gone home, but, honestly, the thought never crossed my mind. For the first time in my life, I'd been homesick, not for people but for the amenities I had previously taken for granted. Overall, I felt I'd run into as many obstacles that summer as I could expect in a lifetime, and the pride of survival and success filled my soul.

I ran to the door and turned the handle, but it didn't open. *That's strange,* I thought. *We never lock the house.* I knocked impatiently, the returning warrior, and before long a strange woman answered the door.

"You must be Donald," she said.

Uh-oh. "Donald" was a word that had always meant change.

"Your father was shipped out to Fort Devens, Massachusetts," she continued. "Here's a note from your mother."

"Donald dear," it began. "The war in Korea has the troops moving and we have been reassigned to Fort Devens. It's in a beautiful area of Massachusetts, just out of Boston near the town of Ayer. You'll love it here, a wonderful

opportunity to meet new friends and another fine school for you to enjoy."
Enclosed was a plane ticket to Boston.[74]

That night I stayed with the Stewarts. The next morning, August 28, 1950, I flew out in the same clothes I'd worn from Mexico, the only ones I had. I was back on American Airlines, its familiar orange lightning bolt pointing the way to my next adventure. The flight stopped in Dallas and New York. At LaGuardia, Bob's older sister Caroline met me to chat.

I stepped off the plane in Boston with nothing but a toothbrush, a box camera, and a couple rolls of film, but I was more than ready for the rest of my life. Bring it on!

---

[74] After serving as the U.S. Army's New England headquarters for nearly 80 years, Fort Devens was closed in 1996. Through a public/private partnership, the site was redeveloped as a planned community, including business and industry, retail establishments, recreational facilities, and residential neighborhoods.

Part III: 1950–1956

Previous page: The tide vies with romance. Romance loses.
(*Illustration by Babe Sargent.*)

Chapter 30 – Welcome to the Great Northeast
1950–1951

It may seem strange that my mother and George left El Paso with no more than a note for me, but Betty knew I'd be okay. She always assumed I would land on my feet; it was one of the things I most appreciated about her. Even so, I couldn't resist kidding her a bit about it now.

"You know, Betty, it was a bit of a shock when I came home from Mexico that summer and found someone else living in our house in El Paso."

"I know, but George's orders came through very quickly, and since I had no way to notify you before we left, I figured leaving a note with the new owners was probably best. But I have to tell you, when you got off that plane in Boston I couldn't believe how much you'd changed."

"I must have looked different. Heck, you and George didn't even recognize me, even when I came right up to you."

"Well, you were so tall, and skinny, and then with your cowboy clothes and a beard, no less."

I laughed. "Oh yeah, I could see right away from the look on George's face that Boston wasn't Mexico. As soon as we got back to the base, he handed me a razor along with the suggestion that I lose the beard and put on some proper clothes. Since I'd been in the same duds for several days, I was more than happy to comply, and dressed in chinos and a sport shirt, I thought I cut a pretty nifty figure. Of course, the chinos didn't fit right, but that was to be expected. Since I'd last worn them, I'd lost ten pounds and grown four inches. It sure was good to be home, though, even if home was in Boston. I loved the fact that you and Grandmother clucked over me like two hens. I guess you were determined to fill out my skinny ribs."

"We were," Betty said. "Besides, George was such a food picker."

"I was *not*," said George.

"You were, dear," Betty laughed, "but Don ate everything we put in front of him and came back for more. He was definitely fun to have around."

"Hey," I said, "after having to cook everything I ate all summer, and most of the time having to shoot it first, you can bet I was appreciative. All I could think was *keep it coming; just keep it coming.*"

We all chuckled over my prodigious appetite, which hadn't lessened much over the years, and then Betty said goodnight. George helped her into bed and Polly and I adjourned to our own room, where I drifted off to sleep thinking of my high school days in New England.

* * *

Fall in Massachusetts is spectacular, and the contrast with the hot Mexican desert made it even more so. Days were warm, nights were cool, and the maples and oaks sported fiery, isolated branches to mark the changing seasons. We lived in base housing, and the constant exposure to bugle calls and marching men stirred my imagination. It was, indeed, good to be home.

The following Monday morning, I boarded the school bus for Ayer High School. It was just like old home week, since I either knew or was recognized by many of the kids. The school itself was a traditional brick building, with small classes and friendly teachers. It couldn't have been more different than Austin High.

September 1950: my junior year and the beginning of another "new opportunity." By this time I was beginning to understand that most folks were average and that getting ahead had a lot more to do with ambition and effort than with being a genius. If I wanted to fly, being stuck at the top of the bottom third of the class wasn't going to cut it, and I was filled with resolve to do better.

Chicks compete for food on the farm by pecking each other. The most aggressive get more than their share; the weakest starve. Some are pecked to death. Human beings have their own pecking order, and though it's less brutal than that of the chicks, I could see that success, or the lack thereof, had a lot to do with one's place in that order. That fall I tried harder than I ever had before. I was rewarded with some success, but unless the teacher was very good and the subject interesting, I still drifted off easily.

It could have been my Texas drawl, but I also found myself being sought out more as a friend and companion, something that was unusual for me. Even better, the girls went out of their way to talk to or brush against me. Maybe *I* was the older guy now; in any case, shy as I was around the fairer sex, I dated on a regular basis and really enjoyed it.

Again, I tried out for the football team, and this time I made it. Of course, only 18 guys tried out, which may have had something to do with the coach's choices, but nevertheless I reveled in my good fortune. I still hadn't put on any weight, and 130 pounds didn't move many bodies, but I was fast.

Just before the first game, the coach called me over to the training room and sat me down. "Whatcha doing, coach?"

"Taping you up."

"I'm not good enough to get in, am I?"

"Sure you are."

The game began with all the fanfare of small-town New England, and the butterflies were thrashing in my stomach. What a chance. I could see the headlines: "Fast Texan intercepts pass to win opening game." By the fourth quarter, we were losing by four touchdowns, with 45 seconds to go.

"Wright, get in there and play right end," yelled the coach. I jumped to my feet and sprinted onto the field, only to fall flat on my face on the way to the huddle. With as much dignity as I could muster, I picked myself up in time to participate in the one play there was time for, but it went the other way and the other team won. I never played in another game. In fact, even though I was at every practice and every game, ready to save the day, I was never even taped up. Despite my lack of participation, that year the school set a record: zero and nine, the first no-win season in the history of Ayer High.

It would have been great to be part of a winning team, but it was by no means a wasted experience. I took some hits in practice and I learned a lot. Nobody bugged me about not playing, and I was as popular with the girls as the football heroes. Apparently, suiting up was enough; who needed to get his brains knocked out?

Just before the end of the season, I came home to hear those familiar words: "Donald dear, George has been transferred to Camp Edwards on Cape Cod. You'll get a chance to meet new people and have new adventures." Before the week was out, we were gone.[75]

George and Betty bought a house on Nickerson Lane in Cotuit, Massachusetts. One of seven villages in the town of Barnstable on the south shore of Cape Cod, Cotuit was about five miles from the base. We moved in on a Tuesday. By Friday, George had received new orders and was gone, transferred to Japan to support the conflict in Korea. For the first time since Berlin, I was the man of the house.

Our first day in the house happened to be Halloween, which in New

---

[75] Established in the 1930s to train Massachusetts National Guard troops, Camp Edwards was leased by the army in 1940. Tens of thousands of troops were trained there in preparation for World War II. The base was deactivated in 1946 and reactivated in 1950 for troop training support during the Korean conflict. As of 2008, the facility continues to flourish as an Army National Guard training site.

England is a big deal. As we unpacked boxes and prepared for that evening's trick-or-treaters, a nice-looking man in his forties came to the door.

"Hi, I'm Tom Pardue," he said, "the preacher at Cotuit Federated Church." Tom explained that the church, established in 1846, was a federation of the Methodists and United Church of Christ (formerly Congregationalists), but that afternoon his visit was distinctly non-ministerial. It seemed that the house's previous owner had left a pistol in one of the kitchen drawers and had sent the good pastor to retrieve it.

After sharing a laugh, we sent Tom on his way, mission accomplished, just as two very cute girls came up the walk. Tom introduced us to our first trick-or-treaters: red-headed Betty (Liz) Hayden and dark-haired Sonja Perry. From that time on we were friends. Sonja was one of the high school loves of my life, and Liz and I are buddies to this day.

High-schoolers from Cotuit attended Barnstable High in Hyannis, another of the town's seven villages. A large, three-story building with ivy-covered, red brick walls, this was the best school I'd attended so far, an assessment I felt eminently qualified to make considering my varied educational experiences. Even so, things did not go well. For one thing, I was at a disadvantage by entering two months after school started. For another, I was placed in class with the college-bound fast learners. *Been here before and didn't do well,* I thought, remembering East Aurora.

English was a particular fiasco. Our teacher, Mrs. Corinne Hurst, was famous in the community. The first woman member of the Cape Cod Association, Mrs. Hurst (Ma Hurst to us) was an excellent instructor, tough and uncompromising. Her classroom was next to the boys' restroom, from which she was known to pull the smokers out by their ears, saving them from expulsion but not from a good tongue-lashing. The first semester was grammar, and Ma Hurst loved to diagram sentences. I failed again. The second semester was Dickens' *A Tale of Two Cities*, which I aced.[76]

Chemistry, another subject that had seemed easy at Ayer High, was a total disaster at Barnstable. The teacher was Mr. Raymond Person, one of the most professional instructors I ever had. He looked and acted like a professor, and although he was strict, he was also patient, especially with me. We both tried hard, but my math background was weak at best, and the formulas just didn't work for me. After about a month, I transferred to general science, a subject I'm sure the professor thought more than adequate for my future life of pumping gas.

---

[76] The Cape Cod Association has been awarding scholarships to students across the Cape and Islands since 1877. Corinne (Weber) Hurst, who received scholarships from the association in 1916–20, was voted the first woman member in 1927.

Eventually, all my subjects were from the general curriculum. I never did well in math—the combination of multiple schools and poor study habits had done me in. However, subjects that entailed reading and understanding, such as English literature, history, and Spanish, were a snap. And in the social skills department, I was doing well. The girls seemed to enjoy my company, and I enjoyed playing the field.

At the age of 16, lust was always on my mind, and with my knowledge of Harold and the words of love, I felt it was only a matter of time before one of these lovely maidens would be disarmed by passion. The ladies, however, were more than smart enough to hold me in check, though neither side ever tired of the game. Sometimes I would go steady, which would last for a week or two, and sometimes we ran in a pack. Either way it was a blast. The interesting thing about the gals was the similarity of their bodies: they all had hourglass figures. Why was that?

Even though I hadn't done much to earn it, I liked being a sports hero at Ayer. Barnstable, however, was just large enough that I failed to make the cut of every team I tried out for. I came closest in basketball but ended up playing in the farm league, which was fun but definitely not varsity. In baseball, I didn't have a chance—just not enough experience. That left track, which turned out to be my sport. It didn't require a lot of skill, and I was fast enough to start the relay and run second or third in the 220 and 440.[77]

Lightning fast and a Texan, too!

History and the Haydens

In the summer, Cotuit was a seaside resort for the wealthy. Once the weather turned cold, it was quiet as death, and most entertainment was

---

[77] In his 1950 portrayal of me as a transplanted Texas runner, fellow student Brooks Kelly captured the essence of my brief track career. Sadly, my participation in the sport was fleeting (and the significance of "The Rhubarb Kid" has long faded from memory), but Brooks went on to launch a career as an award-winning New England artist.

home-based. That winter I spent many hours around the huge dining room table at the home of my friend Liz Hayden.

Liz had a younger brother and three younger sisters, ranging in age from toddler to teen. Cindy, the youngest, was tough as a nail and always busy, her raspy voice echoing through the house. Bobby, a smiling, dimpled redhead, was forever constructing something, his red wagon in tow. Cathy, in her horsy boots with whip in hand, was happiest when riding real horses or, when that wasn't possible, galloping through the living room in her imagination. Jayne, next to the oldest, was quick, witty, and sharp as a tack. Each child was an individual, and the household was in constant motion.

Libby Hayden, Liz's mom, was a deacon at Federated Church and played a strong role in town events. She kept her table laden with New England delicacies for the family and the stream of guests who always seemed to show up at mealtime. A crock of Ma Hayden's baked beans, surrounded by quahogs, oysters, steamers, and a baked bluefish or bass, filled the lazy Susan in the middle of the table. A nearby sideboard often held a ham or even a few lobsters.

Bob Hayden, Liz's dad, ran the Robert Hayden Building Moving Company. Mr. Hayden was a working man, with rough hands, a face lined with creases, and a Pall Mall cigarette dangling perpetually from his mouth. He wore plaid shirts with mismatched ties, rumpled wool britches, and thick, wire-framed glasses held together with ragged bits of electrical tape. He was a trustee at the Cotuit Federated Church, where he served as auctioneer for the church's annual fundraiser; a 32nd Degree Mason; and a member of the town planning board.

Above all else, Mr. Hayden was a raconteur, a man with expertise in many areas and the ability to successfully orchestrate discussions on a wide range of topics. One of the most interesting of those topics was his own life.

"So Fergie," said Liz, calling her dad by his pet name, a shortened version of his middle name, "Donnie can't believe that you were really a rich kid."

"Well, it's true," said Mr. Hayden with a hearty laugh and that raspy rumble that comes from too many cigarettes. "Our family traces its beginnings to long before the American Revolution. During the Civil War, my great grandfather, Jefferson Kimball Cole, was the scribe at Appomattox, officially recording the end of the war. Cole then migrated to New Orleans, where he continued to prosper as the years went by. By the time Gertrude, my mother, came along, the family had amassed enough money to be considered comfortable, and when my mother was a girl, her folks returned to the North. Mother grew up in a home of servants, parties, bridge, and proper afternoon teas. After graduating from Wellesley College, she married

Robert Ferguson Hayden, a dentist and a graduate of Tufts College. The young couple lived in the Cole family home in Newton, Massachusetts, near Boston, where I was born in 1910 and named after my father. I was educated in private schools and studied music—mostly brass. Cornet was my favorite.

"Our family summered in Cotuit at the Lilacs, a beautiful house my mother still owns. In my leisure time, I enjoyed sailboat racing, hockey, and swimming. I had the best of instruction in all of these pursuits, and I was very competitive. The only negative in my life was that I suffered from chronic bronchitis."

Mr. Hayden was quiet for a minute, lost in memories of a lifestyle I could barely imagine.

"When I was a kid," he continued, "my dad was an ardent sportsman. One December afternoon, he sniffed the air, looked at the sky, and said to some of his sporting friends, 'Hey fellas, let's go duck hunting tomorrow morning.' The next day dawned cold, rainy, and rotten—in other words, a perfect day to hunt ducks. Before dawn, the men were hunkered down in the blind, and before noon, they'd filled their bag.

"Stomping home, they were chilled and soaked through, but Agnes, our number one servant, fixed them up with a steaming lunch of chowder and hot chocolate. Even though I hadn't been out in the wet, the weather was truly miserable, and my bronchitis kicked in before the day was over. Father wasn't feeling much better, and we both took to our beds. What a heck of a note: Christmas less than a week away and both of us sick as dogs.

"I felt better in a couple of days, but Father developed a nasty cold he couldn't seem to shake off, and the house was filled with his wheezing and coughing. The doctor came and went, eventually sending a nurse to attend his worsening patient, and Mother began to look extremely worried. After a while, the coughing stopped. Father had died of pneumonia." Even after all these years, Mr. Hayden choked out this story with heartfelt emotion.

"After my father died, Mother's life went on much as before. The family's money was securely invested, so our home and the servants were safe, and she still traveled, played bridge, and went to afternoon tea, seeing the same people, wearing the proper hat and gloves.

"My life, on the other hand, changed radically. I began having discipline problems in a series of private schools—a murky time." He shrugged it off with a smile, but the pain was obvious.

"Then, just a few months before I graduated from high school, the stock market crashed, and like so many other families, our fortune disappeared almost overnight. Mother was able to keep the house in Newton and the

Lilacs, our summer house in Cotuit, but she could afford only one servant. She chose her favorite, Agnes.

"In my mind's eye, I can still see her, Gertrude Cole Hayden, eating breakfast in our elegant dining room, the table set with linen and silver, and Agnes in attendance. After finishing her meal, she changed into a housedress and went into the kitchen, where she helped Agnes make Parker House rolls, chutney, and the other delicacies later sold to her many friends. At noon, she reverted to the lady of the house once again, seated in the dining room, eating her lunch and being served by Agnes. She adapted to her circumstances and she worked hard, but she never missed her Wednesday teas or her Thursday bridge game. Like Americans in every station of life, my mother survived the Depression with courage, grit, and tenacity.

"After barely staggering out of high school, I was accepted at Bowdoin College. Of course, there was no money to pay for college, so I worked nights and weekends to support myself and pay tuition. I even formed a jazz group, the Polar Bear Five, where we rubbed elbows with some of the greats, including Louie Armstrong."[78, 79]

"You haven't said anything about courting Mrs. Hayden," I commented.

"Oh, yes. Well, I was working in construction in Boston, and Libby was going to art school in Boston, and we dated for quite a while. Like me, she was having a hard time financially, so we talked of marriage, half believing the old adage that two could live as cheaply as one. Of course, with the Depression still in full swing, there were no jobs in Boston, so I headed for the Cape, a place of wonderful childhood memories. Once I got here, I somehow managed to buy a chicken farm—25 acres of land and a pond at the end of a lonely dirt road. The farmhouse had no plumbing or electricity, but Libby and I married and moved there anyway.

"Soon this was the first real roadblock in our marriage," Mr. Hayden explained, and Mrs. Hayden nodded her head vigorously in agreement. "When Libby became pregnant with Liz, she was quick to point out that she had no objection to becoming a chicken farmer, but by golly, she was not going to do so without indoor plumbing. You can believe I installed the required fixtures without delay.

---

[78] Established in 1794, Bowdoin is a non-sectarian, liberal arts institution located in Brunswick, ME. Famous graduates include Nathaniel Hawthorne and Henry Wadsworth Longfellow.

[79] Louis Armstrong, nicknamed "Satchmo," was one of the world's greatest jazz musicians. He was born in New Orleans in 1901. From humble beginnings, he became internationally famous, touring with his own and other orchestras and bands and performing in more than 40 films and TV movies, including *Hello Dolly* and *High Society*. He died in New York City in 1971.

"Soon we were selling eggs and chickens and I started taking small construction jobs. A neighbor wanted his house moved to a better location, so I hired some hands and finagled a few relic tractors, trucks, beams, and jacks. Finding help was no problem. There were few jobs to be had and plenty of people willing to take them. The job came out okay, and soon word got around that we did good work.

"In 1937, we won the contract to demolish a 30-room *cottage* in Buzzards Bay to make room for the Massachusetts Maritime Academy. That was our first big break. As long as we cleared the land, no one cared what we did with the building or its contents. It was a shame, because many of the architectural elements, not to mention the paintings and so forth, were pretty terrific stuff.

"Then it occurred to me. If I thought this stuff was worth saving, other people might, too. Like everything else, land was cheap back then, so I bought 100 acres out on Route 28 by Marstons Mills, and the Robert Hayden Building Moving Company was born. We dismantled the mansion, salvaged the interior furnishings along with pieces and parts like fireplaces, stairways, and moldings, and offered them for resale through Treasure Highland, the newly established retail arm of the business. Other jobs followed, along with more treasures, and before long, if you couldn't find what you needed at our place, it couldn't be found.

The Haydens in 1976. *L. to r.*: Libby, Bob, Bobby, Liz, Bobby's wife Mary Ellen, Jayne Hayden Uyenoyama, and Catharine. Children are Jessica Hayden and Dennis Uyenoyama. Missing from picture: Cindy.
(*Courtesy of Jayne Uyenoyama.*)

195

"Business was good, but life on the farm was hardly gracious living, so in 1945 we moved to the Lilacs, my mother's house in town. It's on the main street, overlooking the harbor, and except for occasional visits from Mother, it was used rarely. We built this house in 1950, and I expect we'll remain here for quite a while."

Nowhere was Mr. Hayden's talent for reclaiming the bones of history more evident than in his current home. Most of the materials in this almost-new residence, from the ancient tile roof to the wide plank floors planed from virgin forest, were salvage from buildings Mr. Hayden had moved or demolished. The house welcomed all to its treasure, but it was a jumble of treasure. Mrs. Hayden said it best: "We never do throw much away."

Mr. Hayden's salvage jobs often yielded treasures beyond house parts, so it wasn't unusual to find a sailboat or two or three in the Treasure Highland yard. Each spring, a couple of these gems could be found swinging from a mooring in the harbor, and in the spring of 1951, Liz taught me to sail. (My sailing experiences on Lake Plötzensee in Germany didn't count, since back then I was strictly a passenger.) Liz and I spent many leisurely days that spring and summer sailing around Cotuit Bay or picnicking with friends on Sampson's Island.

Sometimes I sailed with Liz's dad, and on one occasion we joined a race in a Cotuit skiff, a 14-foot, gaff-rigged sloop that had found its way to the yard. Mr. Hayden the skipper was a very different man than the affable fellow I experienced around the dining room table. This man was aggressive, tenacious, and operating on the edge, revealing the competitive streak he developed early in life and that no doubt served him well in his business.

It was the last leg of the race and we were running second at low tide when Mr. Hayden made a tack toward the sandbar in the middle of the bay. "Watch this maneuver, Don," he bragged. "If it works, we'll win."

It didn't.

We hit the bar with a wallop, which snapped off the centerboard and turned the boat over. Stranded on a sandbar far out in the Bay, with the ever-present—albeit a big soggy—Pall Mall dangling from his mouth, Liz's dad used some words I'd rarely heard before.

Eventually the committee boat dragged us back in. Liz was at the dock to meet us. "So Fergie," she grinned, "how was the race?"

Entrepreneur at Work

Mr. Hayden may have been super competitive on the water, but in business he often made contracts on a handshake, contracts that were, on occasion, "forgotten" by his clients. Sometimes he was just too trusting.

He also wasn't one to keep good records, even after an audit revealed that a longtime employee had embezzled considerable funds. Although it was an embarrassing and traumatic discovery, he forgave the employee and allowed him to work on to retirement. Mr. Hayden practiced his Christian values, forgiveness being one of them.

One evening I listened as a couple of his cronies sat around Mrs. Hayden's table reminiscing about the bad old days. "Times were tough back then," said one. "We only made 25 cents an hour, but it was a heck of a lot better than no money at all. And when there wasn't enough work, Bob kept us busy pulling nails for resale."

"Bob gave us a paycheck every Friday," said the other, "but he might ask us to hold it until he gave the word. Sometimes we'd have several checks in our pocket, and when a payment came in, he'd tell us which ones to cash. Of course, along with those Friday checks, he always included a chicken or two."

"That's right," said the first fellow. "No matter how bad things got, nobody ever went hungry."

Bob behind the wheel of a Hayden company classic.
(*Courtesy of Jayne Uyenoyama.*)

The Depression was long and desperate.

I looked upon the Hayden household as my second home, but in my own home, being the man of the house wasn't all it was cracked up to be. For one thing, the house needed attention, and it wasn't long before I'd painted all the trim. My mother, painfully aware of my less-than-stellar academic record, looked upon this newfound skill as a good sign. "My, my, what a good painter you are," she said, "and there's definitely a future in it. Housepainters are in demand."

"Sure," I said, "when I finish my flying career."

Next it was wallpaper. I papered the bedrooms and baths. "My, my," said Betty, "look how every seam matches. I hear there's quite a demand for expert paperhangers."

"Yep," I repeated, "as soon as my flying career is over." I put on a brave front for my mother, but there were times when I was beginning to worry. Once again, I'd failed the grammar half of English, and I hadn't even tried to beg. Ma Hurst would have laughed me off my knees.

That summer I had a job at the First National Grocery, stacking cans, sweeping floors, and bagging groceries. I was saving for my first car, so at a buck an hour, the money was welcome, but it also brought home the need to do better in school. No question about it, the thought of a lifetime stacking cans was more depressing than my young and active mind could take, yet my fellow workers were just as smart as I. How did they end up with such dull jobs?

Chapter 31 – Wheeling and Dealing

1951

By midsummer, I'd saved enough to buy a 1932 Chevy coupe from a neighbor for $25. The engine didn't work and the insurance cost more than the car, but heck, I didn't have a driver's license anyway. Besides, the rest of the car was fine. The first thing I did to the car was to paint it, and a fine job it was: red, white, and blue, with a checkerboard design on the hood. The engine took a bit longer. After I spent many hours under the hood, it roared into life, but the knock in the rods was so loud you couldn't hear yourself think.

Soon after, I traded the slicked-up coupe for a neighbor's 1929 Model A with four different wheel sizes and the roof and floorboards rotted through. As far as I could tell, however, the engine ran fine.

In August, Polly Frederick, Betty's friend and our housemate in Berlin, came to visit. Polly had settled in Washington, D.C., after returning to the States from Germany, and she and Betty tried to get together at least once a year. Betty said there was no way she was going to be seen in my Model A, so Polly agreed to go with me to get my driver's license. The examiner was a little wary, since finding a place to put his feet where they didn't drag on the ground was a challenge, but I passed without a problem. Maybe he figured I was in better shape than the car, or maybe he was willing to do whatever it took not to endanger his life again.

Now that I had wheels, I had higher hopes for my love life, although money continued to be a problem. Yes, I had a job, but I also had to save for school, and the Model A needed gas and continual "routine" maintenance. I never had enough cash to fill the tank, but I discovered that by asking for 20 cents worth, many times the attendant would feel sorry for me and give me 30 or 35 cents worth. Tires were another matter. Some lasted as little as a week. It was a good thing replacements could be found at the junkyard for a buck.

There was also the problem of no roof and no floor, something my paltry wage at the grocery couldn't begin to address. My mother, a serious businesswoman, offered help. She'd sell me a piece of plywood for $20, but I had to sign an IOU, which she explained that she'd keep in her cookbook until I paid off every red cent, with interest. I took her up on the offer, but I had a tough decision: floorboards or roof. Roof won. Then I discovered that one of the cylinders had been blocked off, so even the engine wasn't that great. There was nothing to do but resign myself to frequent breakdowns, but hey, the neighbor didn't get such a good deal either.

My best friend in Cotuit, Bob Frazier, and I solved many of the world's problems as we rode to school in that fine car, but we made sure we took the same route as the school bus in case we needed a backup ride.

Bob was a serious guy with his sights set on being a musician and a teacher, but he had a jokester's sense of humor. When it came to dating, he was fearless, which meant he often ended up with the cream of the class, but in another area he was much more cautious. Like me, he'd never learned to swim and was generally wary around water. One night Liz and I, ever the conspirators, decided to pull his chain by inviting him for a moonlight sail.

It may have been Bob's first sail ever, and when the wind started to come up, we could feel his tension. "I'm a little worried about that wind," I said to Liz with as much of a straight face as I could muster.

"Me, too," she replied soberly, just as another gust captured the sail and we heeled over until the water lapped at the gunnels. At this point our passenger was looking a little green, so I let go of the sheet (the line that holds the sail) and the boat flopped back to an even keel. Bob, thinking I'd accidentally dropped the sheet, grabbed it with such force that he almost tipped the boat over. What started as a prank could have left us swamped far from shore. We righted the boat without incident, chastised ourselves for our foolhardiness, and apologized to Bob, but he never sailed with us again.

Bob Frazier, 1952.

I fared better on land. The gals liked my car, and sometimes I'd have four or five of them hooting and hollering as I sped downhill at speeds of up to 30 miles per hour. Finally, I had the means to move my love life to the next level. Up 'til then, the gals I'd dated were ready for the nunnery, but this time I wanted one with a racy reputation. It wasn't long before I found Suzy Q., a cute chick of some notoriety and a perfect candidate for my initiation to the ways of the world. She even smoked, which we all knew was the first step to a life of sin and decay.

This dude was ready. I knew about Harold, the words of love, and the crushing of roses. I'd listened to the older guys, and I had a hot date and a fine car. Finally, the crucial evening arrived. After some preliminary action at the drive-in, I drove to the beach in Hyannis. The night was clear and starlit, moonbeams shimmered on the sea, and the waves lapped quietly beside us. I couldn't think of a more romantic setting.[80]

After making out for a while, I pulled Suzy Q. over to my side of the car. She giggled as she slid over the gearshift knob. *A good sign*, I thought. When she whispered in my ear, with some urgency, that she was getting wet, I was greatly encouraged. Even at my level of knowledge, I knew this was a positive development.

"That's good," I whispered huskily.

"Not that way, you damn fool. My feet are wet."

"Feet?"

"Yeah, feet."

Sure enough, I'd parked too close to the water, and the tide was washing over where the floorboards should have been. What to do? Should I lose the moment to save the car? Maybe if I was quick enough, I could move away from the water and continue my quest, but when I turned the key, nothing happened. Still hopeful, I ran down the beach to the nearest car and asked if they would tow me to higher ground. I was rudely turned down—something about being busy and "let it wash out to sea, you jerk."

All thoughts of love driven from my mind by the rising tide, I was now in rescue mode. I plunged into the water with crank in hand, and after several exhausting turns, the engine sputtered to life. Suzy Q. sat quietly during this operation, temper steaming, and the atmosphere didn't improve much on the way home. Despite my profuse apologies and the promise of borrowing my mother's new Pontiac on our next date, she refused to see me again. I was back to the virgin nuns, whose motto was "You ain't gonna get none."

---

[80] Drive-in theaters project a movie onto a large outdoor screen at the front of a parking area equipped with individual car speakers and landscaped to give each vehicle a clear view. The first U.S. drive-in opened in Camden, NJ, in 1933. By the late 1950s, there were 5,000 such theaters across the country. Catering primarily to families with children, theater owners added amenities such as playgrounds and concession stands to boost revenue. The increase in the number of homes with TVs, plus the advent of cable and video recorders, nearly killed the industry by the end of the 1980s, but in the 1990s, some theaters reopened and others were built, rekindling interest in this entertainment venue.

My '29 Ford, captured for posterity by
Barnstable High classmate Bill Childs.

Needless to say, good girls were far preferable to no girls, so after the beach fiasco, I took the plywood off the roof and made floorboards. When it rained, I covered the roof with a makeshift canvas tarp, and I tried to get my dates to look at the situation philosophically. "It's kind of like riding on the ranch," I explained, playing up my exploits of the previous summer. "The rain's warm, and when it stops, we'll dry out." This philosophy generated mixed results.

My job at First National kept me in gas money, but it never got less boring. One thing I did discover was that employees who smoked got more breaks, probably because the boss smoked, too. So like a damn fool, I took up the habit. I hated the fact that my mother smoked, and she'd warned me against it, but once I started, she accepted it without much of a fuss. I suppose she figured that telling me it would shorten my life was an exercise in futility. At first, it tasted like cow plop and inhaling hurt my throat, but soon I was burning holes in my clothes and smelling foul like all the other smokers. I was also eating up my hard-earned cash. A pack of cigarettes cost about the same as a gallon of gas.

Before I knew it, school had started. I was a senior, but if I didn't pass sophomore English grammar, graduation was by no means a sure thing. I also needed two years of college before I could qualify to enter the air force as a cadet in the pilot training program. If I wanted a chance at that higher education, I'd better get busy. Trying to head off all possibilities of failure, I selected only enough courses to fulfill—barely—the requirements for graduation. Sophomore English grammar was scheduled for second semester.

Once I settled the academics, I had another big decision: Should I try to become a football hero or continue to work at First National and keep my Model A alive. The team was shaping up as one of the best ever, and although I now weighed 145, I was a long way from football-player physique. I was, however, fast as lightning, and I had a good work ethic.

What to do? Go for the gas money and cigarette money or improve my chances for female companionship? The dilemma was settled by a chance meeting with a land surveyor. He offered me work for better pay than I would ever see at the grocery, and I took a job slashing underbrush so the surveyors could run their transit lines. It was back-breaking, manual labor, but the money was good and I learned a lot about another profession I didn't want to pursue.

That fall, I sat on the sidelines as the team played its way to the second undefeated football season in Barnstable's history. Many times I regretted not being on that team, but considering my 45 seconds of football greatness at Ayer the year before, perhaps it was just as well. I was, however, a dedicated team booster. I escorted as many young ladies to the games and after-game entertainment as possible, and when the boys vowed to let their sideburns grow until the season was over, mine were the longest.

Another, more serious factor influencing my job-versus-football decision was that smoking had sapped my endurance, and I wasn't ready to quit. In fact, during the many times and in the many places I couldn't smoke, smoking was all I could think of. Bob Frazier, my buddy and frequent passenger on the way to school, was smart enough not to have taken up the habit, but he never complained when I'd pull over each morning for a last couple of puffs before class. I always made sure we were close to the school in case the Model A's temperamental engine decided not to start again, but one morning I got a little too close.

Barnstable had a rule that students couldn't smoke within two blocks of the school building. From a practical standpoint, the rule was rarely enforced, but the one day I parked just within the two-block zone, who should walk by but Mr. Connor, the assistant principal. He knocked on the window and asked me to stop by his office first thing. I wasn't worried; his son BK (Briah Kerr Connor, Jr.) was in our class, and I was sure I'd get away with a verbal warning. Wrong! Not only did he give me the next week off with no chance to make up my grades, I still had to do the work. "Sorry, son," he said, "but a rule's a rule." This turn of events did nothing to help my tenuous academic standing, but I knew how to take it and I did. Fortunately, Bob was not punished for guilt by association.

In between concentrating on academics, work, smoking, and the fairer sex, I was starting to think seriously about the future. Aptitude tests in my junior year had pointed toward mechanics, and with this in mind, I set my sights on Wentworth Institute of Technology. Arioch Wentworth was a Boston entrepreneur who made his money in soapstone, marble, and real estate. When he died in 1903, he left the bulk of his estate to "found a school to furnish education in the mechanical arts," along with the names of seven directors he wished to implement his bequest. In 1904, these men chartered the institution bearing his name, and in 1911, the school opened its doors.

By the 1950s, Wentworth was known worldwide for being able to interpret the intentions of the engineer and communicate them to everyone from the craftsman to the laborer in the field. With the school's two-year course in Aviation Technology, I could fulfill my college requirement for the Air Force Aviation Cadet Program and enjoy my studies at the same time. Besides, rumor had it that even someone with my record could be admitted. Now, if I could only pass sophomore English grammar.

Chapter 32 – Saved by the War

1951–1952

The political situation in America was disturbing. Although it seemed necessary, the war in Korea was costing many lives and an unaccustomed division in a nation that usually spoke with one voice about world affairs. At the same time, the world was in disarray. The USSR and its allies were pushing on all frontiers, atomic power was shared with at least four nations, and many U.S. citizens feared a fifth column from within. [81, 82]

Reports of the Rosenberg spy trial and alleged communist connections in Hollywood and the academic community, combined with news of the war, were alarming. Everyone knew young men who had been killed in Korea, and within the next year many of my friends would enlist or be drafted. I even debated whether I should join the marines for a tour and then fly. [83]

Closer to home, my friends and I were convinced that communist infiltrators in the undergarment industry had conspired with the fathers of America to drain the brains of the country's young men. The collusion worked like this: The dads encouraged their daughters to wear rubberized girdles. The girdles, the reason for those uniform hourglass figures, also protected the

---

[81] Declared the Union of Soviet Socialist Republics in 1922, the USSR (also known as the Soviet Union) expanded its western borders during and immediately after World War II to include the Baltic States of Latvia, Estonia, and Lithuania as well as other territory. It also exercised strong influence over the Eastern Bloc, which consisted of the post-war communist governments of the German Democratic Republic (East Germany), Poland, Hungary, Czechoslovakia, Bulgaria, Romania, and Albania. East and West Germany became one nation in 1990. In 1991, the USSR fell and dissolved into separate nations.

[82] Referring in this context to communist spies, the term "fifth column" is credited to Emilio Mola Vidal, a nationalist general during the Spanish Civil War. It refers to any clandestine group that attempts to undermine a nation's solidarity.

[83] Julius and Ethel Rosenberg were convicted of passing U.S. atomic secrets to the Russians and sentenced to death in April of 1951. After numerous appeals failed, they were executed in June of 1953.

young maidens' bodies from their dates. By the time the boys discovered the mechanism for removing these devices, we'd either forgotten why we were doing so or curfew had arrived, either of which resulted in grievous harm to our physical and mental well-being.

The nubile, young females, their bodies arranged into luscious curves, caused males to lose their powers of concentration. The plot was insidious: blood rushing to other parts of the body left faces pale, eyes glazed, and eyelids drooping. The girls, knowing what their breathing and walking did to the male brain, pursued this teasing with vigor. In the classroom, this prevented the boys from gaining a proper academic education. Women began to take over the universities, while lust-filled men were sent to war. These communists had to be stopped.

Just before Halloween, I got another chance with Suzy Q. It was a warm October night, rare for the Cape, and I knew she was ready. Why else would she go out with me? This time, I picked a dry, grassy knoll, as far away from the water as possible, and after some preliminary kissing and giggling, her breathing became fast and demanding. I pulled her toward me over the gearshift with manly force, but she resisted. Could I have misinterpreted her desire? I pulled again, but the harder I tugged, the more she resisted. Finally she snapped out of my arms and out of the car like an arrow, landing on the grass in the missionary position. Her girdle, caught on the gearshift lever, had functioned as a giant slingshot.

For a moment, neither of us moved. Then a sound came from the dark, followed by the face of a uniformed townie cop shining his 14-battery flashlight on the situation. "I'll rescue you," he said to Suzy Q., never asking if rescue was what she had in mind.

"Donald," he said to me, much more sternly. "I'm shocked at your conduct here tonight. If it weren't for the fact that your father is fighting off the Korean hordes, I'd run you in."

I said nothing.

After that, I thought about becoming a priest. However, I figured Grandmother would kill me, so my love life went back to good girls and good times. Sonja Perry and I went steady for quite a while, and with one exception, my grades were the best they'd ever been—a solid C average. Second semester had started, and along with it the dreaded sophomore English. Ma Hurst, true to form, was tormenting me with grammar and diagramming sentences.

If I passed English, I'd graduate, but by the end of February, things were looking grim. I was clearly failing, and no amount of begging was going to pull me out of this mess. I turned to my guardian angel. Surely she couldn't abandon me now. She knew how much I wanted to fly, and another year in high school would be unacceptable to both of us.

Her answer came out of the mouth of my mother. "Donald," Betty said one day after school, "George has been assigned to remain in Japan, and he has sent for us to come right away. I know this upsets you, but look at the bright side; you'll get to meet new friends and see new sights."

I tried to look at least a little subdued, but I could almost feel that angel dancing on my shoulders. Much as I didn't want to leave Sonja, she knew I had a much better chance of passing sophomore English almost anywhere other than Barnstable High, and she gave me her blessing. Grandmother went off to stay with some of her other children, and Betty and I shut down the house.

We departed within the week. Before we left, I sold the Model A for a rowboat and a twisted-steel shotgun. Neither was functional, but it was better than abandoning my beloved car to the junkyard, and I knew I could always work on my new acquisitions sometime in the future. (Japan might be the adventure of the moment, but Nickerson Lane was to remain our legal address. Cotuit was home.)

Living on the Cape had been a blast. I'd had good times, made good friends, and managed, despite my best attempts, to maintain my virtue. I'd miss my pals, and I was pretty sure they'd miss me, but there's no doubt that Ma Hurst was relieved to see me go.

We were scheduled to travel to Yokohama, Japan, but first we had to get from Cape Cod to Seattle. After closing down the house and saying goodbye to friends and family, we set off on a cross-country trek.

* * *

By Land and By Sea

It was our sixth day in Nokomis, another beautiful Florida morning, and each day Betty grew visibly weaker. She was now spending much of her time in bed, and it was apparent that there wasn't a lot of time left. Still, when Polly brought in her breakfast tray and I appeared in the doorway with a cup of coffee, she greeted us as always.

"Good morning, you two," she chirped. "I'm a little tired this morning, but if we don't spend too long, Don, I'd like to talk some more. Are you up for that?"

"You bet," I said. These were truly precious hours we were spending together, and I was grateful already that I was capturing my mother's voice on tape. Betty ate some breakfast while I set up the recorder. After Polly had taken away the tray and she was settled with her coffee, she indicated she was ready to continue.

Betty and I had had a blast driving from Cotuit to Seattle, and I knew the trip would be fun for her to recall. "Do you remember when George sent for us from Japan and we drove across the country?" I asked.

"Do I ever," she replied. "Your grandmother was less than happy about having to give up her home with us on Cape Cod, but she got a chance to stay with other family for a while, and you and I got to have another adventure. At first I was a little worried about making the trip in the dead of winter, but you were enjoying yourself so much you ended up doing the lion's share of the driving. I just sat back and enjoyed the view."

"The driving was easy," I recalled. "We didn't encounter much bad weather on the southerly route, and, of course, having the 1950 Pontiac didn't hurt, either."

"Oh, yes," Betty said with a smile, "my trusty Pontiac and good old Route 66. We did about 500 miles a day, as I recall, ending up in Los Angeles before heading north. And we stopped at such interesting places along the way."

"One of my favorites," I said, "was Pasadena. I think we arrived there on the most perfect day the world has ever seen. We ate outside in that terrific restaurant and talked about how nice it would be if we didn't have to leave. And in San Francisco we had lunch at the Top of the Mark on Nob Hill, where the view was magnificent. Then we drove through the redwoods—I'll never forget my first sight of them—and up the northern coast. We had some good times, didn't we?"

"We sure did," Betty said as she lay back against the pillows. "It's such fun to think about those days, but now I'd better take a short nap." As her eyes closed, George propped more pillows around her and tiptoed out of the room. I leaned back in my chair. Before long, I was 17 again, steering my mother's Pontiac up the foggy Pacific coast in the winter of 1952.

* * *

We were in Seattle for two weeks before our transport, the reconfigured cruise ship *U.S.S. LaGuardia*, arrived. Meanwhile, we lived at Fort Lawton in a barracks-type arrangement called Hostess House. The fog was constant, soaking mind and body just walking across the street, but the camaraderie of the army community, where everybody knew somebody and friendships began instantly, more than made up for it. Military families are a tough lot.

They know that world events can affect their lives directly, sometimes in a heartbeat, and as a result they have a certain level of discipline, combined with an unbridled zest for life. Live now, the theory goes, for tomorrow you may be dead or alone.

Once our troop ship arrived, the Pontiac was stowed in the hold and Betty and I were given spacious quarters commensurate with George's rank as a lieutenant colonel. (Nowhere is the concept of RHIP [rank has its privileges] more clearly defined than in the military. If you want better perks, you attain a higher rank by staying longer and working harder, or you depart. The same structure exists, to one degree or another, in all parts of society, but in the military the choices are clear-cut.)

Packed into the lower decks were draftees and volunteers, the cannon fodder of war. These young bucks, 17 or 18 years old and fresh from high school, were eager, worried, and, fortunately, fairly well-trained. Training had improved a lot since the Korean "police action" began in 1950, but in many ways Korea was still the most difficult conflict we'd ever been in. Although supposedly a United Nations effort, it was, in fact, a regional conflict, controlled by the major powers, fought primarily by the U.S., and understood by neither the citizenry nor some of the participants. The enemy massed by the thousands, a throwback to World War I or even to the American Civil War. By the sheer weight of their numbers, they used their bodies as weapons, and when we mowed them down, the same number or more appeared the following day.

Mistakes had been made since the war began, lessons learned, and tactics changed, but by this time a familiar stalemate existed on the battlefield. Still, the battle waged in winter and summer, in some of the harshest terrain and fiercest weather Americans had ever faced. The long negotiations for peace had begun, but the process was frustrated by the combination of Asian patience and communist delay, pitted against the American interest in immediate results. Navigating this minefield of divergent cultures and ideologies was the first real test of our resolve.

When I thought about the soldiers on the decks below us, I could feel their plight. In three short months, with a bit of luck (okay, a lot of luck), I would be a high school graduate, and unless the war ended soon, I might end up volunteering or becoming draft bait myself.[84]

In addition to the soldiers, there must have been 60 dependents and

---

[84] An armistice ending the conflict in Korea was signed on July 27, 1953, at Panmunjom, a village on the border between North and South Korea in what was established as the Demilitarized Zone. As of 2008, a formal peace treaty has never been signed.

children on the ship, including about 20 teenagers. All of us had traveled by sea before, and we teens were in our element. Not even the winter storms could deter us from having a good time, and we partied en masse—dancing, singing, playing cards, and just hanging out. Many times we talked with the troops from the fantail of the ship. After all, we were nearly interchangeable in years and desires, and they especially liked to yak with the gals.

As the trip neared its end, we sometimes paired off, and once again I was ready to flaunt my vast experience with the opposite sex. Alas, I had forgotten that these gals had been around the block a time or two. To a woman, they were more than prepared to deal with the likes of randy young men, and besides, body armor was still in vogue. It seems that even military fathers were in on the plot to foil our lustful intentions.

Lessons of the East

George met us in Yokohama with a bouquet of flowers and a huge smile. He had secured quarters in Area II, close to where we docked. The quarters were pleasant and well laid out, and we had two servants to take care of our every need.

Japan was a stubborn and tenacious nation, but MacArthur had done a remarkable job of reconstruction, and by 1952 the country was well on its way to democracy and self-rule. On their part, the Japanese were polite, hard-working, and amazed at the evenhandedness of the GI. This is not to say that our troops were choirboys. The war in Korea continued to be an unpopular conflict where the climatic conditions were extreme, the enemy endless, and peace evermore elusive. So when the troops came to Japan for R&R (rest and recreation), they played hard, usually in districts set aside for such play. Nevertheless, both our fighting men from Korea and our troops stationed in Japan were almost always law-abiding and well-behaved. Military justice can be harsh and unforgiving.

In Berlin, I observed the ethical treatment of the Germans by the U.S. Starting with the human spirit, our able leaders tried their level best to repair and restore the country. In Japan I saw the same thing, although because of differences in culture, it was sometimes a harder sell. Even when critics tried to deny our motives, we persevered with the kindness and humility inbred into our young nation, and the reconstruction of our enemies' territory was unequaled in the world's history (a fact often glossed over by cynics and pundits).

I was proud of my country and felt it the fairest and finest nation the world had ever seen. I believed that Europe under the Marshall Plan, Japan under the all-seeing eyes of MacArthur, the United States under Truman, and the European Theatre under the command of Eisenhower had all been in the right place at the right time. Unfortunately, many of our Allies, bogged down in socialism, were finding it much more difficult to recover from World War II.

In the midst of this world drama, my personal drama centered on graduating from high school. I knew that my new school would be spectacular, and it was. One of the very few buildings that had survived the war in this land of wood and paper structures, it had previously been a school for girls. The teachers were outstanding and the students self-disciplined and motivated, particularly as graduation grew nearer.

For the third time, I walked into the second half of sophomore English, slithered to my seat, and tried to become invisible. The teacher, Mr. Robert Chard, was a fresh-faced, crew-cut guy who taught English and world history. He turned out to be a terrific teacher, able to make any subject dynamic and interesting, but all I could see that first day were the chains of English grammar getting ready to weigh me down.

Mr. Chard welcomed me to class, came over to shake my hand, and gave me a copy of *A Tale of Two Cities*. Our homework assignment was to read a couple of pages and write a short essay. The next day my paper was returned with an A.

I couldn't believe my good fortune. At Yokohama High, the grammar portion of the year had occurred during the *first* semester, and I was back with Dickens' classic, a book I'd read three times already. After I received an A on the next few assignments, Mr. Chard called me aside to ask why my record showed two previous failures. I stammered a reply about the teacher having it in for me or some such gorp, and he let it drop.

The rest of the year was a pleasure. I finished with a strong A in English and higher-than-normal grades in my other subjects. I also confirmed what I'd suspected for some time: There is a direct relationship between effort and success.

As army brats, we were more mature than our high school counterparts in the States. We'd seen and observed far more than the average kid and we handled it well, but we also knew how to have a good time. Headquarters was the bowling alley, where games and hamburgers were a dime each and Coke was a nickel. We also had the availability of our parents' cars, and we dated almost every night. Often we'd go to the cliffs overlooking the ocean and sing old-time songs 'til we were hoarse.

Booze was readily available, with beer our drink of choice. We were all 17 or 18, the war was being fought with 18-year-olds, and we figured that if we were almost old enough to serve and die, we were old enough to have a beer. Besides, drinking on the economy was well within our budgets. Beer was a penny and a mixed drink a nickel (heck, a whole meal cost only a quarter), yet rarely did alcohol become a problem. To err meant your father was gored. The army held to the age-old belief that responsibility begins with the individual, and that thought was never far from our minds.

We did find young ladies to go steady with, but often, just as things looked promising, they returned to the States. This was always a sad and sometimes tearful event. At the dock, guys and gals, some staying and some going, held opposite ends of colored paper streamers. With longing and promises in their eyes, they listened as the Army Band marched back and forth playing "California, Here I Come" and "The St. Louis Blues." Then, with a mighty blast of the ship's horn, the longshoremen cast off the giant lines, the props of the tugs beat the waters to froth, and the ship slid away from the dock. Eyes glistened as streamers broke and friends and lovers faded away, in most instances never to see each other again. Those left behind reminisced about friends lost.

Each time I participated in one of these sendoffs, I inevitably discovered some cute young thing in need of solace. Being a kind and generous person, I usually invited her for a line or two of bowling, followed by dinner and dancing at the Officers' Club 'til the sweet parting of the night.

Better to Have Loved and Lost

One of my romances that year turned quite serious. The attractive young lass lived in Tokyo, so I spent many days and nights riding the subway. These rides were a lesson in meat-packing, as the gentle Japanese turned into animals trying to squeeze as many bodies as possible into the cars.

The Suzy Q. of Tokyo and I became an item. Her father was a high-ranking officer, but he had neglected his duty, since his daughter often ventured forth without her body armor. Perhaps due to the possibilities presented by this lapse, she also had earned a somewhat racy reputation. To me, however, she was the picture of innocence. Normally Betty offered compliments about the women in my life, but about this girl she said nothing. This was my mother's way—when she felt something was negative she was noncommittal—but even her silence could not deter me from pursuing my new love. I was truly smitten.

Once in a while, George allowed me to drive the Pontiac, and on one such occasion I took Suzy Q. to the cliffs above the ocean. The only gratification that occurred that night, however, was when she backed down on the gearshift lever with a salacious bit of laughter. I returned her to her palatial home in Tokyo, but I had high hopes for better luck in the future.

After many more dates, none of which resulted in grand passion but all of which were fun, we spent an evening at the Club. After dinner we rented a boat to float in the moat surrounding Emperor Hirohito's palace. The breeze was soft, the moon was full, and the water glistened with reflected moonbeams. Soon we were locked in an embrace. Whispering sweet words of love, I found myself professing my feelings and asked her to tie the knot. Suzy, with some passion in her voice, accepted.

The next evening, the maid's night off, Betty and I were drying the dinner dishes when I told her and George of my proposal and exclaimed how happy Suzy and I would be. With an even tone in her voice, Betty said, "That's nice; pass me the platter." Gosh, I was expecting more of a reaction than that.

A couple of weeks and a few dates later, Suzy and I were once again ensconced in George's Pontiac, looking down on the crashing waves of the Pacific. Suddenly, she pushed back from my advances and whispered the words that no teen, particularly a future aviation cadet, wants to hear: "I'm pregnant."

"Pregnant?" Good golly, innocence and lack of knowledge can get a guy in a lot of trouble. Unless I was hallucinating, we had never become intimate enough to cause this problem. What would Harold think? She hadn't even crushed the rose!

"How?" My voice was quivering.

"Peter."

"Peter? Of course it was a peter." I exhaled. I knew I was innocent of the deed.

"No, no, no," she said, "not what you're thinking. Peter Smith."

"You mean Peter Smith, the tackle on the football team. You mean the guy whose hair melds into his eyebrows and who failed basketmaking?"

"Yep."

I was torn between feeling sorry for her and a profound sense of relief. "Didn't he leave on the last ship?" I asked.

"Yep, and I'm on the next one, without my parents."

All well and good, but what if the baby looked like a Pontiac? Fifty years later, a good lawyer might sue General Motors and get millions in a paternity suit.

Why was my mother so smart? And had my guardian angel been having a bit of fun with me? After all, she knew that to be a cadet one had to be single.

Chapter 33 – Pomp, Circumstance, and Full Employment

1952–1953

D onald," my mother said, "could you help me this morning. I have a busy day at the Wives' Club running the bridge tournament."

"Sure," I replied, always the helpful lad. "What's up?"

"I need you to go to the docks and meet the *Hari Maru*. It's a freighter."

Hmmm, I thought our black market days were behind us, but perhaps one more foray into crime would be interesting.

"What exotic trinket shall I pick up?"

"Grandmother," Betty replied, laughing.

It seems that Grandmother McNerney had booked passage on a tramp freighter in New York and sailed the seas for 50 days to join us in Japan. I imagine her arrival generated a grimace from George, but for me it was fine. I was the only man in her life that she really liked, we were good company for each other, and she never treated me like Grandpa or I wouldn't have hung around. To me she was a chipper, fun woman who indulged me with homemade bread and fruit pies, and I loved her for it.

Grandmother soon rearranged our home the way she thought it should be, which was fine with Betty and George. George's life was the army; home was just where you hung your hat. Betty was in social heaven, where the women played cards, entertained, and did good works for the needy. Grandmother became commander-in-chief on the home front. She never asked the servants to do anything that she wouldn't do herself and they respected her, even when she taught them the ways of the American cook. The kitchen was her domain, and nowhere was she happier.

The graduation ceremony at Yo High, on June 5, 1952, was much the same as anywhere else (except, perhaps, for the fact that the students wore clothes handmade by Japanese tailors), but graduating from any high school, anywhere, was an enormous milestone for me. The sounds of *Pomp and Circumstance* still make my eyes water. Could this be because I fell to my knees and kissed the feet of the principal as he handed me my diploma?

Yo High graduation. I made it
(*back row, second from the right*)!

During the banquet that followed, Betty made several spurious comments about how miracles do happen, but at least she didn't bring up the possibility of me becoming a housepainter, paperboy (man), tree trimmer for surveyors, car mechanic, grocery clerk, snow shoveler, or landscape worker. I said I was going to be a fighter pilot, and I was almost ready.

My mother left me with no illusions about where she stood on this subject. "Donald, I know that you want to be a fighter pilot, and I applaud your ambition. However, your academic performance so far has been deplorable, and although it's not all your fault, much of the responsibility falls on your shoulders. I know that you need two years of college to become a pilot, but I'm not sure there is a college that will take you, even if you do have an advanced degree in negotiation (she was too proud to say begging). You should also know that in the event that you find such a college, I will not contribute a single penny of my hard-earned money until you have successfully completed one year."

"What you're saying, cruel mother of mine, is '*get a job*'"?

"You broke the code, flyboy. It's your nickel or no nickel."

Well, at least I wasn't alone. Nearly all the graduates of Yo High's class of 1952 stayed in Japan to work. The vitality of the military and the occupation of the country were energizing to all, and I had the added plus of living at home, with two doting women and two servants to take care of me.

Since jobs were plentiful, I had many choices of employment, and I was soon working for the post office as a supervisor in the Totsuka Mail Order Department. Based on the concept pioneered by mail-order giants like Sears, Roebuck, Totsuka sent trucks filled with Noritake china, embroidered silk jackets, china dolls, and the like to Korea, where representatives set up shop near the front lines. GIs could fill out order blanks and pay for their merchandise right then and there. Back in Japan, we filled the orders from our warehouses and sent the merchandise directly to America.

Totsuka employed about 50 people, both American and Japanese, and my job was to supervise 20 hard-working Japanese laborers, most of them ex-army. Nisei (first-generation Japanese Americans) were employed as translators and secretaries, but most of the time the workers and I relied on a combination of smiles, grunts, and Pidgin English. I learned a few words of Japanese during that time, but I never developed any skill with the language. I did, however, learn something about leadership. Taking my cue from Grandmother, I never asked anyone to do something I wouldn't do myself, and the workers seemed to respect my attitude, even though it was not the typical Japanese way. (From what I'd observed of Japanese society, the higher up the chain of command, the harsher and more demanding a leader became.)

Don Wright, 1952—high school graduate and gainfully employed.

This was the first job I'd had that I truly enjoyed. It was physical, it provided social contact, and it gave me the opportunity to make important decisions almost hourly. Some orders were rumpled and streaked from mud; others had addresses that were so poorly written we weren't sure the gifts would arrive. Nevertheless, most packages got through. Sometimes we received feedback from the recipients. When we got complaints of breakage, we sent a replacement. A few letters were melancholy and appreciative, explaining that our package was the last gift the writer received before the dreaded telegram. These were the types of letters that made me feel closest to the troops. They were also a reminder that, very soon, my number could come up. I thought a lot about the challenge.

In addition to being both enjoyable and useful, the job paid well, especially in a country where a nickel went so far. A good portion of my paycheck went into a savings account; some went to my mother for rent. With the remainder, I played hard. Japan, like any nation devastated by war and a wartime economy, was wide open and exciting. The rule was that there were no rules, although common sense prevailed. We dressed to the nines; drank, smoked, and chased women. Occasionally we went to formal dances at one of the many Officers' Clubs. And, since a haircut was a dime and a massage a quarter, we looked and felt our best while doing so.

Sometimes one or more roving congressmen would be shocked and dismayed at the "easy" life of the military in Japan. However, when they were invited to the front lines, where our soldiers were being shot at and freezing their balls off as they dragged the dead and wounded bodies of their buddies to a collection point, these same Congress critters would decline the invitation. Or, they would eat SOS and dried eggs close enough to hear the rumble of the big guns and then brag to their constituents about their courage and sacrifice. The way I looked at it, the job I was doing was important, and I enjoyed the perks of the country without guilt. I figured my day in the barrel was coming soon enough.

My three best pals, Rob, Bill, and Gary, were in the same boat. We all had interesting jobs with a great deal of responsibility, lived at home with minimal expense, and had the use of our families' new cars: a Chevy, an Olds 88, a Jaguar, and our Pontiac. A fabulous foursome, we enjoyed the high life and attacked it with vigor. We also relished the low life, enjoying the food and entertainment in various hot spots in Honmoku, home of the city's famous red-light district. Our unofficial headquarters was a nightclub in the Pacific Hotel. There was much for sale there and in the clubs and whorehouses nearby, but we didn't have to sample the wares to soak up the atmosphere. Instead, we enjoyed the shows and drank Nippon beer (though not to excess, since working with a hangover was more than uncomfortable).

We also hung out with our warriors from Korea on R&R. These gregarious GIs enjoyed every moment of life, resting little and recreating a lot. They knew that tomorrow they could die. Naturally, I gravitated to the aviators, whose flying hands were part and parcel of every conversation. They used their hands and arms to simulate various formations, twisted their bodies in strange attitudes to complete the picture, and sometimes even heisted a foot onto the table to represent a bad guy on the attack. Humor and laughter were part of the game, and they took a ton of friendly harassment from their supposed listeners.

One Friday night, Rob, Bill, Gary, and I went to an Italian restaurant in Honmoku, where we planned to have a fine dinner before gravitating to the O Club for bingo and dancing. As usual, we were in high spirits and dressed to kill. We were shown to a table in the center of the noisy restaurant, where we ordered large glasses of Nippon beer and started to share our war stories of the week. Before long we were shouting and using hand gestures to make ourselves understood over the din. In my exuberance, I accidentally knocked over my beer and the bubbling brew landed square in Rob's lap. Normally such a mishap would have been a cause for laughter, but that night Rob had a short fuse, and he picked up his beer and flung it in my face. My fuse blew in return, and within seconds I was across the table, punching him in the schnoz.

The restaurant was packed with troops on R&R who needed little provocation to let off steam. The place exploded into a barroom brawl worthy of a John Wayne Western. The troops laughed and fought like a bunch of madmen, smashing tables and throwing bottles. When we heard the police sirens we ran into the restroom, kicked out the window, and fled—bleeding and laughing—into the alley. None of us suffered more than a few bruises and a scratch or two, and we made peace with our apologies as we went into the night.[85]

Transitions

I had put off selecting a college as long as possible. I wasn't ready to go back to school under any circumstances, but unless I got two years under my belt, I'd either be painting houses, stacking cans, or toting a rifle through the mud of Korea.

My pal Rob solved my problem. After having taken a year off after high school to join his military dad in Yokohama for the experience and to earn some money, he was going to San José State in California. His description of the place sounded idyllic: the playground of America, with big trees for the football players to swing from on their way to class and women with bottomless bank accounts who outnumbered the men and were always on the prowl. "Nobody has ever failed to graduate," Rob assured me. "In fact, you don't even need to go to class very often. Just pay a pittance and hang on." He handed me an application. "Fill this out. No one has ever been turned down for admittance."

The place sounded like just what I needed, especially after Rob assured me that no one there had ever heard of diagramming sentences. I sent the application by airmail and settled down to dream of scantily clad gals chasing me through the treetops. Maybe I could even play football. I was up to 150 pounds and I could always quit smoking.

---

[85] John Wayne (1907–1979) was a major film star of the 20th century. Born Marion Robert Morrison in Winterset, IA, he originally turned to films to help pay his college tuition. The result was a career spanning five decades. Wayne made more than 175 movies and played the leading role in 142 of them. Although he acted in a number of film genres, he is best known for his roles in American Westerns.

Within two weeks I received an answer. Stuffing the unopened envelope into my pocket, I called my cronies for a night of celebration at the O, with dinner and drinks on me. After we'd been seated and were sipping our beer, I slit open the envelope with great ceremony and extracted the contents. It was my original application, with the word REJECTED stamped across the front in large red letters. Not even *try again next year*, just REJECTED. For about 20 minutes, I went into a funk. Then I started to feel bad for those California girls and the members of the San José State football team. Both groups would be deprived of my talents, and besides, Peter Smith might be a member of that team. We could have compared notes.

While I was preparing to step off the threshold into adulthood, my mother was pregnant with my soon-to-be brother. She was older than the norm and her pregnancy was difficult, the last three months of it spent in bed. Even these were good times, however. I spent a lot of time keeping her company, and we both read every book we could find. My favorite was *The Caine Mutiny,* by Herman Wouk. We also had great discussions about books, the meaning of life, recent wars, and the sanctuary of our country. Betty was an exuberant patriot. She had seen more of the world than I, yet we both marveled at how forgiving and generous America was. It was not just the government, but religious institutions and individuals as well.

In March of 1953, my brother Christopher was born and George's tour was complete. However, in order to maintain the baby's welfare, we couldn't travel Stateside for six weeks. Leaving was difficult because of the many fine friends I'd made, but having done it so many times before, we were all experts at coming and going. *Goodbye* was not a word; *see ya later* was our motto. The chance of running into my army friends in the future was unlikely, but we were ready to leave, all of us going into the world like a pod of seeds, eager to spring forth in our own right. Even Betty's Pontiac was getting a new lease on life. Since American cars were sought-after in Japan at that time, we sold it for much more than it was worth and bid it a fond farewell.

After my experiences in Japan, every aspect of my life seemed better and brighter. I had learned by reading and observation, I had met wonderful people, and I had earned and saved enough for at least my first year of school—maybe enough for all of it. This was a good thing, because dealing with Betty the businesswoman was a challenge. Don't they have usury laws for parents?

Our ship back to the States was the *Sultan*, another converted luxury liner. It was filled with cheering, combat-hardened men, with the walking wounded, and with dependents, all of whom were eager to return to America, the land of the big PX. This time I was one of those laughing and crying passengers holding a paper ribbon tied to someone on shore. The Army Band struck up "California, Here I Come," followed by the "St. Louis Blues"; the ship's horn issued its deep bellow; and with the help of tugs churning the bay, we began to move. One by one the streamers broke and we bid Japan adieu. We stood at the rail until only ant-like figures were visible in the distance, then headed for our cabins to unpack.

"June," I exclaimed as I bumped into an attractive gal with a cry of recognition and a big hug. The lady of my life on the way over, June had come down from the north of Japan to be my date for graduation from Yo High, and it was good to see her again. Off we went together to the snack bar.

The first day out of Yokohama, we encountered a typhoon. We shimmied and shuddered as the props pulled out of the water and the waves broke over the ship. For the first few days, the storm kept many of the passengers below decks, reminding me of March 1947 when I nursed the State Department girls across the North Atlantic on my way to Germany. This time, June and I stood on the upper decks and felt the flying spray, returning wet and laughing to the salon and her mother's worried expression. Betty never even looked up. I think she knew that my angel was very protective.

Once the storm eased off a bit, the teenagers had a blast, singing, dancing, snacking, and reminiscing about good times and bad. Each of us knew somebody, and soon everybody knew everybody. At best, life as an army brat is glorious. In any case, it's never dull.

Grandmother, George, and Betty never got seasick either—too many sea miles under their belts, I guess. My brother Chris, on the other hand, couldn't keep anything down, and we took turns holding or walking him almost every minute of the long trip to Buffalo, but he was still miserable. Poor Chris.

By the morning we reached California, the seas had calmed and the rising sun outlined the Golden Gate Bridge against the sky. A symbol as touching as Lady Liberty on our eastern shore, sailing under the Golden Gate Bridge, particularly on a return voyage from overseas, is an amazing thrill. The troops shouted and hollered so loud I thought they could be heard everywhere in the good ole USA, and there wasn't a dry eye on deck.

After a short stay in San Francisco, we boarded an American Airlines flight to Buffalo with a stopover at Chicago's Midway Airport. Back on home turf, we had a huge family reunion, including Uncle Robert and Aunt Erma; Uncle Dan and Aunt Mary, in town between army assignments; and Aunt Carolyn and Uncle Walt. Walt had been called back to the air force and was flying Boeing B-29s loaded with A-bombs from Barksdale Air Force Base in Louisiana, but he had taken leave for the occasion. Add to the mix the scads of children, and this was a truly happy time in our family's history.[86]

Grandfather was not invited to these events, but I spent lots of time with him. He still lived at the Knights of Columbus in downtown Buffalo and was enjoying life like never before. We reminisced about my years on the farm and the things we'd done together during my childhood, especially our trips to Crystal Beach, one of the highlights of my summers. I also watched him work out in the gym. He jumped rope with the skill of a boxer, and on the light bag he was quick and his footwork coordinated. He showed me some amazing feats on that bag.

After visiting family, the first place I went was to the farm. Maude and Mill were excited to see me, though Mill was just about out of the farming business. He had so many internal injuries from the occupational hazards that bedevil farmers that he was almost too crippled to work. They had a new form of entertainment, though—a television set—and we watched a program about the war and Truman's firing of MacArthur a couple of years before. At the time, all three of us had been angry at Truman, yet after the macho nonsense cleared, his decision not to attack China seemed sound. Of course, the Chinese were in North Korea, but the world preferred to treat them as stealth fighters, almost pretending they weren't there. Along with thousands of others, Maude, Millard, and I agreed: The war in Korea was so filled with double-talk and distortion, it's a wonder the world was surviving as well as it was.

I spent a month on the farm. Afterward, I joined Betty and George at our house on Cape Cod. My gals there had all found others, but we remained friends, sailing and playing the rest of the summer away. I didn't even have to work; my bankroll from Japan was sufficient for my needs.

---

[86] Established in 1933 in northwestern Louisiana, Barksdale Field was named after Lt. Eugene Hoy Barksdale, U.S. Army Air Corps, who was killed during a test flight in 1926. The field was dedicated in 1933 and renamed Barksdale Air Force Base in 1948. As of 2008, this 22,000-acre facility continues to serve the country in support of U.S. efforts in Afghanistan and Iraq.

Chapter 34 – Plotting a Course for the Future
1953

On the ship home from Japan I'd begun worrying about how I was going to get into college. I'd completed an application to Wentworth Institute of Technology, my original school of choice, but with my dismal record and after my experience with San José State, I knew it would take more than a postage stamp to get my foot in the door. June, my shipboard companion, offered a solution. "Hand-carry your application," she suggested. "Be as personable as possible and negotiate your way in."

I'd decided to take her advice, and today was negotiating day. I drove into Boston in bright summer sunshine and located the school on Huntington Avenue. It was an imposing structure, built at the turn of the century and dedicated to the trades and excellence. I was imposing, too, I thought, dressed in a tailor-made silk sport coat with a snazzy-but-tasteful shirt and coordinating tie. After all, first impressions happen only once, and I didn't want to blow my chances by not looking the part.

I walked into the admissions office, offered my application, and requested an audience with the man in charge. The secretary told me to put the application in a basket on her desk and the powers that be would review it and let me know. This would never do. My negotiating skills kicked into high gear as I begged my way to a face-to-face encounter with the man.

The registrar, George Pierce, was a friendly but busy fellow. He listened patiently to my reasons for wanting to attend his fine institution, and he let me babble on about my sad life of despair: fatherless; bouncing around the world from school to school; surviving the deprivations of war-torn Europe; suffering hunger in the wilds of Mexico; and being dragged kicking and screaming to Japan, where, technically, a war was still being waged. I refrained from mentioning that I also stole candy bars, rustled cattle, and smuggled semiprecious stones across the border.

When I finished, he shook my hand and nodded noncommittally.

"Leave your application in the basket in the secretary's office," he said, "and we'll let you know." I'd hoped for more—perhaps an offer of acceptance on the spot—but the day was not wasted. I took a tour of the school and found it much to my liking. The emphasis was on mechanical arts, a term I could appreciate, and as promised in the literature, the curriculum was both structured and hands-on. When we stopped at the AME (Aircraft Mechanical Engineering) Department, I spoke with Ozzie Elwell, the department head. A most impressive man, Ozzie was also a good salesman; his description of the coursework made it sound not only interesting but fun. I came away with a good feeling all around. Who knew what the future might hold, but even if it turned out I couldn't fly airplanes, with an education from Wentworth I could at least work on them.

Back on the Cape, I waited for a decision, sailing and dating to keep my mind off the future. Liz had a Cotuit skiff in the harbor, and many were the days we spent dashing from island to island, picnicking or digging for cohogs and steamers. Often the cherrystone clams never even made it into the skiff. We husked and devoured them on the spot. Cotuit oysters, famous worldwide, endured the same fate—scarfed down raw and delicious under the hot summer sun. Evenings we spent at the drive-in movie, followed by stops for ice cream, frappés, hotdogs, and fries. That summer, the world *was* my oyster. The future was soon, but not right now, and I enjoyed a carefree interlude before stepping with both feet into the adult world.

About the middle of August, I still hadn't heard anything, but I just knew something positive would turn up. In any case, I still had at least two weeks before panic set in. Then my mother's friend Marion Odence—character, entertainer, and Cotuit socialite—invited us to a lawn party. Mrs. Odence's events were not to be missed, and this one proved no exception. The people were interesting, the food was incredible, and the night was clear and calm, a star-studded canopy over the evening's festivities.

I hovered around the snack table, munching my way through the raw bar and sea delicacies, through the vegetables and dip, and finally through the hot hors d'oeuvres. Once I'd had my fill, I began scanning the crowd for a lonely young beauty who might need company. In the meantime, a middle-aged gentleman who heard I'd recently returned from the Far East asked about my travels. He introduced himself as Mr. Smith, and when I learned he was well-traveled himself, I regaled him with a few of my war stories. One thing led to another, and soon we were discussing current books, all of which I'd read that summer.

"Where are you going to school?" he asked, after we'd been talking for quite a while.

"I hope to go to Wentworth," I replied.

"Wentworth is an excellent school, but wouldn't you be better off in a four-year college where you could obtain a degree?"

"Yeah, I suppose, but there are four factors involved," I said. "The first is that my goal is to become a fighter pilot, and in order to do that I only need two years to enlist in the air force and join the Aviation Cadet Program."

He nodded in acknowledgment. "What are the other three?"

Second, I explained, my high school record, due in no small measure to having attended 20 different schools since kindergarten, was deplorable. Third, I had earned enough money for maybe two years, and my mother, pretty and wonderful as she was, wasn't going to back an intellectual loser, especially one who could paint houses among other, even less-appealing jobs. Fourth, almost all schools in the East required entrance examinations, and the chances of me passing said exams were nil to none.

Laughing, he agreed that my goal of flying was a good and noble one, but with some authority, he also explained that I was more likely to excel in my chosen field with a four-year degree, earned at a school that offered ROTC (Reserve Officer Training Corps). I'd have an easier time in pilot training as a lieutenant. An attractive prospect, I agreed, but for all the reasons I'd just listed, it wasn't possible.

"Sure, it's possible," he replied. "In fact, you're already accepted."

"Where?"

"At Brandeis College."

"How do you figure that?"

"It so happens," Mr. Smith replied, "that I am the registrar of students at the college, and you have the kind of knowledge and ambition we very much want to attract. If you accept my offer, you can take the entrance exams after your first year, and perhaps some scholarship money could become available, although that is a definite maybe." He went on to explain that Brandeis was a very new school, named after the first Jewish U.S. Supreme Court justice, and that it was well-endowed and had outstanding credentials.[87]

"The school is looking for diversity in its student makeup," he continued.

[87] C. Ruggles Smith was the son of John Hall Smith, founder of the Middlesex College of Medicine and Surgery, which later became Middlesex University. When the elder Smith died in 1944, Middlesex was suffering from financial difficulties and C. Ruggles gave up his law practice to assume the presidency. In 1946, the trustees transferred the charter of the university and its campus at Waltham, MA, to a new board who established Brandeis University. In 1948, Smith became the first director of the Brandeis Office of Admissions, which until 1955 included the functions of the registrar's office.

"Currently, most of the students are Jewish, and we want to appeal to all creeds and colors, all ethnic and religious backgrounds." He also remarked that my varied background was an advantage that would work in my best interests as well as those of the school.

I was flabbergasted. I thanked him for the offer and said I'd like to talk it over with my mother. Could I call him?

He agreed and we exchanged numbers and parted.

This had been an amazing evening. First of all, I love cocktail parties with excellent food. Second, my angel had surely arranged this chance meeting. When I told Betty about my conversation with the gentleman from Brandeis, she was very enthusiastic. Not once did she mention my mechanical skills or what a fine housepainter I was. She was particularly impressed by the mention of a scholarship, an idea she had never before heard associated with my name.

The following morning, there was a letter for me in the mailbox. "Congratulations, Donald," it said, on official, imprinted stationery. "You have been accepted to Wentworth Institute of Technology, in the Aircraft Maintenance Engineering course for the class of 1955, starting September 1953."

I accepted immediately.

Later that day I called Mr. Smith, thanked him again, and turned him down. It was an outstanding offer, and my choosing not to accept it was not as cavalier as it sounds. My goal was to fly. It was a goal founded on years of dreams, and after two years of higher education, I would be one step closer to achieving it. My preparation for college, particularly for the coursework of a traditional curriculum, was checkered at best. Wentworth's more hands-on approach was one I felt I could understand. Despite my mother's sometimes misdirected comments about my abilities, I *was* mechanical. I was also blessed.

It was one of my best decisions of my life.

Chapter 35 – What's an Institute of Technology?

1953–1955

It was time to buckle down. I knew absolutely where I was headed, but I also knew that in order to get there, I had to focus as I never had before. Life was more than dreaming.

Even if I got through Wentworth, I had never really flown. Did I have the talent? How about health? Nothing indicated that I couldn't pass a rigorous physical. Eyes? Okay. Hearing? Okay as well, but still, there was no guarantee I had what it took to get to the cockpit. All I could do was work as hard as I could and hope for the best, at the same time preparing for a fall-off position.

Thanks to my mother's refusal to provide me with every possession I desired, my need to work for a living was always on my mind. I'd already had enough menial jobs, and while working at Totsuka Mail Order in Japan had been a good job, it wasn't something I'd have wanted to do for the rest of my life. If work was going to take up the majority of my waking hours, I was determined to make certain the jobs I had were interesting. And besides, it was *my* hard-earned money that was paying the tuition.

In early September, the class gathered for introductions. At that time Wentworth was an all-male institution, and our class consisted of about 20 guys of varying backgrounds and ages. Many were vets from the war in Korea, where an armistice had been signed just a little over a month before. These were highly motivated, serious students. One of them, Jim Miller (not a vet but motivated all the same), became my roommate for the next two years. Jim was bright and very steady, and we hit it off at once. My high school experiences left huge gaps in what I should have known, and it took help from a dedicated staff and good friends such as Jim to develop my pattern for study and success.[88]

Unlike high school, we were there because we wanted to be, and the

---

[88] Women were admitted for the first time in 1972.

school had the quaint idea that the teacher's job was to teach and the student's to learn. Classes were small and the instructors, as a rule, good to excellent. If an instructor wasn't up to snuff, he was let go. Conversely, if a student was having trouble, he was counseled and encouraged, but if he still couldn't cut the mustard, he, too, was gone.

The president of the school, Dr. H. Russell Beatty, was a benevolent dictator who knew better than to treat us as adults, a mistake made by many of the other schools in the area. A controversial leader who expected the best from everyone, Dr. Beatty brooked no compromise in his search for excellence. We were at Wentworth to get an education, and should we ever forget it, he was there with a stern and meaningful reminder. He preached morals and honesty, and along with his wife, he exposed us to culture and cultural activities. At school assemblies, much to our chagrin, we were even expected to sing.

The outside of the Wentworth building may have been classic architecture, but inside it was equipped with the latest in machines and technology. In the program of Aviation Technology, the government dictated much of the curriculum, which was divided about equally between classroom and shop. The goal of the program was to qualify for an A&P (Airframe and Powerplant) Mechanic's license, which is issued by the FAA (Federal Aviation Administration). Technicians who work on aircraft must either have this license, which actually takes more time and effort to obtain than training to be a pilot, or work under the supervision of someone who does. Welding, foundry, machining, woodworking, blueprint making, mechanical drawing, and sheet metal working, as well as more conventional courses in physics, mathematics, and even English were included in the program of study.

The shop courses were my favorite, and it was in these I received my highest grades. I loved working with my hands and felt that success was mine, but I also did better in pure classroom subjects than at any other time in my life. Physics made sense; the projects were interesting and I received the second A of my academic career. (The first had been in Japan during my third go-round with *A Tales of Two Cities* and was thus not particularly noteworthy.) Math, on the other hand, continued to bedevil me. Poor preparation plus my propensity to drift off created a nightmare. As the classes got more difficult, I continued to fall behind until, in the end, I barely survived the subject.

The school didn't provide dorms in those days, so Jim and I lived in a variety of apartments throughout the Back Bay area, including one stint in a fraternity house on Commonwealth Avenue. Two other friends and fellow students, Jack Carlin and Ken Nylen, usually lived close by. Our rents were cheap but never cheap enough, so money was a continual problem.

To save pennies, we either ate in the school cafeteria, where the food was both plentiful and cheap, or we ate at home, where I was the primary cook. Grandmother had taught me well, and I could make a mean stew from chicken wings and necks, or combine scraps of beef with rice or spuds for a satisfying meal. Jack, who'd worked for a dairy before coming to school and whose parents lived in farm country, kept us supplied with milk and cheese from his hometown. He also made an occasional culinary contribution of hot dogs stuffed with cheese and wrapped in bacon.

Along with most everybody else, I still smoked, so money for cigarettes was another issue. Jim and I saved our butts, shredding them into a sack for rolling our own at the end of each month's money cycle. What a nasty habit.

On weekends we partied. Boston is the Mecca of youth, packed with schools teaching everything imaginable, and our parties, though occasionally rowdy, were never dull. Thanks to my receding hairline, caused in part by my generous application of peroxide in El Paso, I could easily pass for 21. Thus I became the procurer of beer.

I was also having good luck with women. My main flame was an attractive Italian gal from Boston. Dorothy was fun, loved life, and partied genteelly. Although we never went steady, we were never far apart. One evening after a date, we were smooching a bit when she became very serious. "Don, I need to talk to you."

Uh-oh, I thought, *she's serious and I'm not.* Marriage was far from my mind, and pregnancy was not a factor.

"What's up?" I asked.

"I'm going away tomorrow, and I won't be back for a long time. When I return, I won't be the same person."

This sounded like pretty tough punishment for having an occasional beer under 21, so I waited for more.

"I'm entering a convent to become a nun."

Silence. This was a helluva note. Could I have driven this pretty lady to a nunnery? Grandmother would have a fit. Grandpa might nominate me for the Knights of Columbus "Man of the Year" award—going beyond the call of duty to supply the Church with its needs. I didn't understand, then or now, but I wished her well.

I soon had other lady friends, but I tried to steer away from those Catholics. In case I had anything to do with it, I didn't want the bishop sending notes of thanks to my mother.

Speaking of my mother, she, George, and my brother Chris, joined once again by Grandmother, were back in Germany. But I was not alone. Jim Miller's folks, wonderful and generous people from the town of Harwich Port on the southern coast of Cape Cod, became my surrogate parents. And when we visited Jack Carlin's home in Bernardston, a farming community in the western part of the state, his folks, too, treated me like family.

Initially, we made these trips in Jim's '46 Pontiac coupe with a bum engine. We overhauled the engine, but the car soon collapsed, at which point we pooled our resources and purchased a '47 Lincoln sedan. The Lincoln had a Ford engine and would barely get out of its own way, but it looked good and kept us mobile until after we graduated.

I acquired two other possessions my first year at Wentworth: a dog and a '41 Ford. The dog, named Dawg after much consideration, had been abandoned in the street when he was about six months old. He was a black, short-haired, medium-sized pooch, probably part Lab with a few other varieties thrown in for interest. Dawg was calm, friendly, and adaptable to our crazy schedules. The car was far less cooperative. From the engine to the convertible top, it was a disaster. I took off all the chrome and filled the holes in the body with lead, but the job was never finished and the result looked terrible. On top of everything else, when it rained the top often refused to budge, a sure-fire way to lose all but the most intrepid female companions.

Fortunately, neither Dawg nor the car cost much to maintain, but even with such frugalities, I was spending more than I had planned. Pleading my case to the woman who bore me would have only invited comments on what a good housepainter/wallpaper hanger I could become, and I was way too proud for that. Just in time, help arrived in the form of a part-time job.

The Wentworth Aviation Department had been awarded a contract by MIT. The task was to build radio racks for the Aerobee, a weather rocket used by the government. Because the racks held precision equipment in place, they also had to be built to precise measurements. Roger Swanson, new AME Department head and the project leader, made certain the racks met MIT standards. A few of us worked on the project almost every day for three hours or so after school, and we found Mr. Swanson to be both a fun leader and a hard driver. The work was challenging, and perhaps because we had to work so hard at organizing our time, our grades actually went *up*. Weekends weren't affected, so we still had time to party hearty, and the wages we received were put to good use. Sometimes we even made it through the month without having to roll our own smokes. Eventually we were doing so well that we could fill the gas tank instead of pumping the customary dollar's worth.

On the Ground and in the Air

It felt good to have a few bucks in my pocket, and as summer approached, Jim and I looked for jobs to provide the maximum monetary reward while still allowing time for fun. Before long, we accepted offers to be "line boys" at Hyannis Airport on Cape Cod. The pay: the princely sum of a dollar an hour. Hyannis was only a few miles from Jim's folks' house at Harwich Port, so they invited me to live with them for the season. They even welcomed Dawg, who played his part well as the perfect canine guest.

It was a good summer. Our main job duties consisted of parking and fueling airplanes and carrying bags for the hundreds of passengers who flew to the Cape each week. Our busiest times were Friday nights, when a host of private and corporate planes deposited the rich and famous for a weekend of fun. As soon as they landed, we were there to tote their bags, eager for a chance to rub elbows with the upper echelon but even more eager for a generous tip. Some of the most interesting Fridays involved the arrival of the Kennedy clan, which always meant a mass of action and confusion. Kids were everywhere, running, playing, and having a great time. JFK was just becoming a national figure and locals surrounded the area to observe and enjoy their hero. Jack tipped well; other family members totally ignored the common folk.[89]

Another of our responsibilities was to *prop* small planes. Because many light planes didn't have starters (or if they did, the starters didn't work), we used the propping method to bring an engine to life. The process worked like this: The pilot set the brake, made sure the magnetos were off, and pushed on the plane to verify that the brake was set. Jim or I then moved the prop to the ten o'clock position, placed both hands on it, and with a leg kick for leverage, snapped it around. After a couple of spins, the engine coughed to life.

One day a doctor flying a Beechcraft Bonanza couldn't get his starter to work. "Boy," he shouted to me, "prop my plane." Usually I wouldn't have propped such a large engine, but it was part of the job description. I positioned myself in front of the plane and went through the usual litany.[90]

"Parking brake set?"

"Yes," he replied.

"Magnetos off?"

"Yes."

With a sense of foreboding, I reached down to set the prop in the proper position. Suddenly, the engine fired off. The blade literally parted my hair, leaving a fine red mark on my scalp as I half flung myself, half dove out of the way. The good doctor, who hadn't turned off the magnetos after all, simply

---

[89] John Fitzgerald Kennedy was America's 35th President.

[90] One of the most popular private planes ever manufactured, the Bonanza Model 35 was introduced in 1947. The slightly altered Model 36 is still in production as of 2008.

waved me off and taxied away. Jim saw the event and rushed over, but I was okay. I was somewhat miffed, however, not knowing whether I was lucky to have survived or unlucky that the incident happened at all.

One of the best parts of the job was the opportunity it afforded for social life. During our time off, there were always plenty of things to do and plenty of people to do them with. One thing I wanted to do was learn to fly. I could take lessons in a Piper J-3 Cub from George Parmenter, owner and operator of the Cape & Islands Flight Service.[91]

George was an industrious guy, rugged, determined, and with little time for small talk, though he wasn't unfriendly. A marine fighter pilot who had flown the fierce Vought F-4 Corsair in the Pacific during World War II, he was treated with great respect by the entire aircraft crowd.[92]

Despite my enthusiasm, my meager pay wouldn't buy much flying time, so in exchange for lessons I worked for George in my time off. The mundane part of the job was washing airplanes. The more colorful part happened each Sunday morning, when George and I boarded his ancient, fabric-covered Cessna T-50, lovingly referred to as the Bamboo Bomber. Every week, regardless of weather conditions, we flew to New Bedford and loaded up the Sunday edition of the *Standard-Times.* When the plane was almost full, we'd climb over the papers and sit in the pilot seats, while someone else filled the remaining nooks and crannies, sometimes packing in so many papers that the tail had to be held up until we started the engines. On Martha's Vineyard and Nantucket, we reversed the procedure, except that there someone had to unload a portion of the cargo before we could climb out to help. Looking back, it was a suicide mission—in case of an accident there would have been no way out—but at the time it was an opportunity to be in the air. Even if I wasn't at the controls, it was time well-spent.[93]

Of course, what I really wanted was to be at the controls of the Piper Cub, and my first chance came one Saturday morning when George flew an

---

[91] The Piper J-3 Cub, introduced in 1938, originally had a 40-hp engine and sold for $1,300. During World War II, the army purchased over 6,000 of these planes in a military version designated as L4-A or O-59. Nicknamed the Grasshopper, wartime Cubs were used around the world for artillery fire direction, pilot training, glider pilot instruction, courier service, and frontline liaison. Production of the J-3 Cub ceased in 1947.

[92] The Corsair was produced from 1940 until 1953. During World War II, it was used extensively in the Pacific Theatre and was much feared by the Japanese. It was still used by the air forces in some countries until the 1960s.

[93] The T-50, Cessna's first twin-engine aircraft, was introduced in 1939 and used during World War II by both the U.S. Army Air Corps and the Royal Canadian Air Force as a trainer for bomber and transport pilots.

F-4 Corsair to Hyannis from Weymouth Naval Air Station, where he was a pilot in the Reserves.

He parked the F-4, climbed down, and headed for the Cub. "Let's go, son," he said, and off we went for about an hour. George was a demanding instructor, but he flew like he was part of the airplane and he talked me through the maneuvers with ease. After we landed the Cub and debriefed, he let me climb all over the F-4. Its six machine guns, four-bladed propeller, and R-2800, 2,000-horsepower Pratt & Whitney engine really made my juices flow. Sitting in the hot seat, almost every visual clue was blocked by the long, gleaming nose. I felt like a real pilot, but how in the world did one see to land?

By the end of the summer, I had stowed and unloaded a lot of papers and washed a lot of airplanes, but George was busy and had only been able to spend a small amount of time with me in the J-3. I never got enough hours to solo, but at least I knew I could fly. One more year at Wentworth and I could apply to the air force and become a fighter pilot, a dream that had occupied the back part of my mind for as long as I could remember.

Fit from work and play and sporting a respectable Cape tan, Jim and I loaded up the '41 Ford with our few possessions, the most notable of which was a moth-eaten deer's head with a cigarette dangling from its rotting lips. With this trophy hanging over the rear of the open convertible, we fit the quintessential image of carefree college boys. Once back in Boston, however, we were in the groove: study and work during the week, play on the weekends.

Punching My Tickets

The second year at Wentworth was even more interesting than the first, and I remained engaged mentally most of the time. My grades hovered in the C+ to B- range, better than ever before in my scholarly career, even though I worked after school and was careful not to neglect my social life. My worst moment was the final exam in advanced math. I'd lost my way early in the course and my grade going into the test was marginal at best. When the instructor placed the final in front of me, my lack of knowledge hit like an oncoming train. I was unable to complete a single problem. I took a stab at the multiple-choice answers and turned in the exam. Of course, I failed miserably. This was the only time at Wentworth I had to resort to begging and telling my sad tale of woe. Fortunately, the instructor was sympathetic, and I passed with the minimum mark required to meet Dr. Beatty's stringent grading policy.

Jack Carlin, Sky Lyman, and me in 1955, just before graduation, on our way to a job interview in Sky's Cessna 170. We didn't get the job, but we traveled in style. (*Jim Miller probably took the picture.*)

At the end of the two-year program, the FAA tested the entire class for the A&P Mechanic's license. Every one of us passed with flying colors. I took an additional test and received a Ground Instructor's license, which meant I was authorized to teach the same subjects I had just taken. I wasn't sure I'd ever use that license, but one can never have too many tickets.

Wentworth Institute of Technology is an excellent place to learn a plethora of trades, and it was the perfect school for me. It suited my personality, gave me a first-rate education, and more than prepared me for a variety of employment opportunities. I knew I would be a better pilot because of what I learned there, and if for any unthinkable reason I was unable to fly, I was equipped to pursue a fine profession.

* * *

One Step Closer to the Dream

"Don, are you listening?" Betty's words brought me back to the present with a start.

"Sorry," I replied, "I thought you were still asleep, and I've been off in dreamland myself, musing about Japan and my days at Wentworth."

"Oh, Don," Betty replied. "You've talked so often about Wentworth. It's a shame George and I were in Germany for the better part of your time there, but at least we were back for graduation."

"Boy, do I remember that day," I said. "You and George drove up from Fort Wadsworth on Staten Island. It was great to see you. It was also great to be graduating, and I felt on top of the world."[94]

---

[94] Known as "Guardian of the Narrows," Fort Wadsworth was a military post from the

"It was a lovely occasion," Betty agreed. "The weather was perfect that day, warm and sunny, and we enjoyed the drive so much. And then, of course, it was wonderful to watch you walk across that stage."

"I'd worked so hard," I said, "and was so excited to be finished, that when I got to that stage filled with dignitaries and received my certificate from Dr. Beatty, I almost fell to my knees to kiss his feet. Fortunately, I managed to maintain my dignity."

Betty laughed. "Never mind. Despite what you have to admit was a somewhat spotty academic career, you earned every bit of that certificate. Afterward, we ate at the Toll House Restaurant, remember?"

"Ah, yes, the home of the toll house cookie."[95]

"That's right, it was," said Betty, "and as I recall the rest of the food was delicious as well. Hey, speaking of food, I think it's about time for dinner."

Polly had cooked a leg of lamb, one of Betty's favorite dishes, and that evening we had a meal fit for royalty: piping hot, succulent lamb, mashed potatoes, peas, and salad. We assumed that Betty would want hers on a tray, but she surprised us by coming to the table. Despite the circumstances, it was a festive occasion, but it was the last time she left her bedroom.

The next morning, Polly and I sat by my mother's bedside as she dozed on and off, smiling every once in a while at some memory she was reliving in her mind's eye. Towards noon, she gathered her strength long enough for one last talk. We reminisced about the many places she and George had lived, about some of her triumphs in bridge, about Grandmother and other family members. We also talked about my life in the military and beyond, as I related some of the funny incidents I'd been involved with over the years. By the time we wound down, it was mid-afternoon.

"You know, Don," she said, "I've always been so proud of you. It's true there were days when I thought you had a better chance of becoming a housepainter than a pilot, but you've proven me wrong again and again, and I've enjoyed every minute of your success."

"Thanks," I said quietly, as I watched my mother drift into sleep. "I couldn't have done it without you."

17th century until it closed in 1994. It is now part of the Gateway National Recreation Area.

[95] In 1930, Ruth and Kenneth Wakefield opened the Toll House Inn in Whitman, MA, in a building that had served travelers since 1709. While baking for her guests, Ruth accidentally created a new dessert that became so popular she made it again and again. Soon her recipe for "toll house cookies" was published locally and later acquired by Nestlé, who continues to print it on bags of chocolate morsels to this day. The Wakefields sold the inn in the 1960s and it burned down in 1984, but the toll house cookie has become an American institution.

Less than 48 hours later, Betty McNerney Wright Kenna passed away. She was 6 months short of her 74th birthday.

* * *

My mother was an extraordinary woman who met life head-on and enjoyed each day she was given. I will always miss her, but the lessons and values she left behind live on in me, in my children and grandchildren, and in the promise of generations stretching far into the future. In the months following her death, I thought a lot about those values, about her life and mine, and about the path I followed after graduating from Wentworth in the summer of 1955.

Lt. Colonel George Kenna and Betty
McNerney Wright Kenna, ca. 1960.

Chapter 36 – Join the Marines?

At last! After a lifetime of dreaming I could press on, and the sooner the better. Ever since Betty worked at Curtiss-Wright during the Second World War, I had wanted to fly. In the intervening years, reading books filled with pictures of proud airmen and their flying machines and watching air shows of the Curtiss P-40s and C-46s had continued to feed my imagination. The war had been a big part of my youth, so the army and the navy also played a role. But army life was messy and since I couldn't swim, the navy was definitely out. Besides, after my trip across the North Atlantic on the *S.S. Ernie Pyle*, I knew there was darn little romance on the open seas.

More to the point, most of the real-life military folk I knew were air force, and my mind was filled to overflowing with facts and figures about the planes they flew—the P-40, the North American P-51 Mustang, and especially the Lockheed P-38 Lightning. How fast were they, how high could they fly, how much did they weigh, how big were the engines? Some kids recited baseball facts; I knew airplanes. No wonder my grades in school were so low. My destiny was to be an air force fighter pilot, and I had room in my brain for important things only.

When I worked for George Parmenter in the summer of 1954, I hung around him as much as I could to get him to talk about his experiences in combat. Our conversations were brief, but they always came back to flying for the U.S. Marine Corps. Eventually George gave me a small compliment— he said I had good hands—and he brought me a brochure on naval aviation.

I'd thought a lot about what he said since then. The smell and feel of the F-4 Corsair had won my heart, and the requirements for marine pilots were very similar to those of the air force for aviation cadets. No problem. I'd been working a lifetime to fill the required squares and I'd just checked off the last of them, the two-year college requirement. I did some research and found that the navy's NavCad (Naval/Cadet) tests were easier than the Air Force

Officers' Qualification Tests, commonly known as the stanines. In fact, to quote a marine I questioned, the NavCads were a "piece of cake." In the test-taking department, this assessment was music to my ears, and I made up my mind. Goodbye, air force! Hello, marines![96]

Jim, too, was excited by the prospect of being a fighter pilot, so a few weeks before, I'd signed up both of us to take the NavCads. The tests were scheduled for the day after graduation at Weymouth Naval Air Station, about ten miles from Boston. But first things first.

It was graduation night, and after saying goodbye to our folks we had some celebrating to do. In deference to our commitment the next morning, we limited ourselves to a few beers with some pals and our current girls, but when the alarm went off in the morning, my mind was still fuzzy. I propped open one eye and looked around. The ashtrays were full, the bottles more numerous than I remembered, and my mouth tasted like the entire Russian army had marched through. Thank goodness for the rescuers: cigarettes, coffee, and aspirin.

On the way to the test we met our buddy Jack Carlin. From the looks of him, Jack had obviously spent the previous evening in less physically debilitating pursuits.

"You guys look like hell," he said. "Where're ya going so early?"

"To Weymouth to take the NavCad tests," I replied.

"Hey, let me go with you."

"Naw, Jack, we're going to be marine fighter pilots."

"I'd like to do that, too."

"Jack, you can't be a marine. You don't drink or smoke, although I do admit you chase some mighty fine women." Jim pulled me aside and pointed out that it might be good to have Jack along, since his '52 Ford actually ran. Otherwise, we'd be relying on the '47 Lincoln, with its old, flat-head V8 Ford engine.

Jack drove.

And so it was that we arrived in style, with plenty of time to yak with the other 20 or so candidates. We even ran into George Parmenter, on base for his Reserves weekend.

"What are you boys doing here?"

---

[96] Navy and marine pilots are both trained by the navy. They may serve together, on a carrier or on land, each group under its own command. Stanine (standard nine) is a statistical method of scoring tests based on a nine-point scaling algorithm. First used by the USAF during World War II, stanines were employed in the military, the private sector, and educational institutions for many years. In 2008, stanines are used primarily for educational assessment.

"Taking the NavCads, Sir."

"How long do they take?" George asked.

"All day, with an hour off for lunch," I replied.

"Meet me at the Officers' Club," he said, "and I'll treat you all to lunch."

We started testing in a training building at nine o'clock sharp. The tests were timed, a series of multiple-choice questions administered by an old navy chief. I'd never tested well, but I'd always managed to get by. The fine education I'd received at Wentworth was still fresh in my mind, I had two FAA licenses in my pocket, and I'd completed about six hours of Piper J-3 Cub time. Plus, I had a vast interest in aeronautical information. Of course, my brain did feel a bit dull (maybe we should have put off last night's celebration), but I wasn't worried. This was supposed to be easy—a piece of cake.

The tests were broad, with a lot of emphasis on math, my nemesis. At the breaks, everyone worried aloud about various sections, and as I am naturally competitive, I started to feel better as the morning wore on.

At noon, George met the three of us at the O Club just across the street and treated us to lunch. The Club was bustling with activity, with men in flight suits doing the pilot hand-talk. Laughter and excitement electrified the atmosphere, and I couldn't think of anywhere else I'd rather be. Hello, marines, I'm on my way.

Back at the testing site, the chief had posted two lists on the door, just about splitting the group in two. Each list was assigned to a different room. I suspected that the other group was going to be sent home. Jack was in that group. Gosh, I hoped he'd wait for us.

Jim and I strutted (already I had developed what I thought would be a marine fighter pilot walk) and waited for the chief to deal with the other candidates. When the chief arrived, he told us without further ado that we had failed to meet the testing standards of the United States Navy. However, we were acceptable to join up as enlisted men. I was dumbfounded. Surely he'd made a mistake, but of course he hadn't. I could hardly breathe. My eyes were stinging and my mind was roaring a dozen different tunes, all discordant. Up until that day, if I couldn't think of a perfect word to describe an event or occasion, I'd just invent a new one. That afternoon, I could neither remember nor coin a word to express my torture.

I was so distressed I couldn't even act cool. Jim said he'd wait for Jack, but I ran off the base and hitchhiked home. So much for my young mind to absorb in such a short time. When I got back to the gloomy dump we lived in, I took Dawg, who still liked me despite my performance, for a romp in the Fens. By the time I got back, I was already moving from despair toward sad and getting better. When the Good Lord put me together, he gave me an extra charge of optimism and the good sense to learn from my mistakes, and this occasion was no exception. After all, I still had another option: the air force.[97]

Jack passed the NavCads and went on to earn his wings of gold as a navy pilot. I was forever proud of him, but I had learned a huge lesson: A piece of cake did not mean success without effort. What it meant was tough, but doable.

The next day, Jim, Jack, and I happened to hook up with a navy pilot who had just gone through training. As much as it hurt, I listened to him regale us with tales of his cadet experiences. One of his most descriptive tales involved the Dilbert Dunker. Prior to flight training, the cadet, wearing full parachute and survival gear, is strapped into this device, which is then rolled on a track into a huge pool and flipped upside down. The cadet had to un-strap, swim out from under the device, inflate his life vest, and swim to shore. Prior to this trick, he had to demonstrate swimming skills and survival techniques that would daunt an Olympic medalist.

About this time I broke in with the obvious: "What happens if you can't swim?" He laughed and replied that the navy provided extra instruction in swimming and survival.

"What if you still can't hack it," I asked.

"Wash out or transfer to the ranks," he replied. Or maybe an honorable discharge? Considering my total lack of swimming skills, had I passed the NavCads, I would have been in a world of hurt. A surge of good feeling ran through my body. Whew, a close call and a lucky failure. My guardian angel let me dangle a bit, but it was a great life lesson. And to top it off, Jack said the chief told him Jim and I had missed the cut by only one question.

When we got back to our apartment, I took my picture of the F-4 Corsair off the wall and replaced it with my shot of North American's F-86 Sabre, 15,000 pounds (loaded) of sleek air force beauty. Goodbye, marines! Hello, air force![98]

---

[97] The Fens is an urban wild area and park in the Back Bay area of Boston, designed by architect Frederick Law Olmsted in the early part of the 20th century. Olmsted is the same architect who designed Central Park in New York City.

[98] The F-86 fighter jet was first produced in the late 1940s by North American and was used extensively during the Korean conflict. Production of this plane ceased in 1956.

Chapter 37 – Marking Time and Moving Ahead
1955

The Monday after the NavCads, Jim and I each received a letter inviting us to join the workforce at Sikorsky Aviation in Bridgeport, Connecticut—ASAP. A couple of duffel bags and 20 minutes later, we loaded Dawg into the Lincoln and rolled into a sunny June day, seeking our fortunes. We were hired on the spot, assigned to work at the final assembly operation at the airport in Stratford, just a few miles down the road from company headquarters.

Jim worked the night shift as a technical rigger on the S-58 helicopter. I also worked on the S-58, but on the day shift, where my job was to install a Wright 1820 radial engine in 50 hours. To make certain the job could get done within a week, two hours of overtime were mandatory each day. The problem was, the engine could be installed in six hours.

Under the government contract, we had an open union shop, so I didn't have to join the union, but the fact that I didn't do so caused some consternation among my fellow workers. The foremen were competent and forceful, but they demanded that everyone look busy at all times, and I hated the job with a passion. Each morning I punched in (I can still hear the che-chung of the time clock), and ten hours later, bored and weary, I punched out.

We were making a good buck so we rented a house in Stratford, and soon Jim bought a real car. I kept the tired old Lincoln, the idiosyncrasies of which corresponded perfectly to my level of frustration. I was a fast, competent worker, and I loved the challenge of a job well done. Slowing my pace to match what was obviously a deliberate mismatch between time required and time expended was making me miserable.

I learned to cope with the boredom by sleeping little at night. I'd arrive each morning tired, wrap my body around the engine in the engine bay with a ratchet wrench on a nut, and hunker down to snooze. Relatively safe from discovery, I awoke instantly to the thumping of someone boarding the helicopter, thus becoming a master of deception. Sometimes I affixed a pocket book out of sight of the casual observer and lost myself in another world. Certainly I took a million smoke breaks. It was a helluva way to be an employee, but between the combination of union and company work rules and the incidents of outright fraud, it was impossible to work as I knew it.

In my time off, I hung around bars and dance halls or went to ball games. We lived about an hour from Yankee Stadium, and although I'd been a lifelong Red Sox fan, I was thrilled to watch players like Mickey Mantle and Yogi Berra. The Yanks always seemed to find a way to win, and many a game was decided in the ninth inning. Another great lesson: Never give up.

Sometimes, however, being off from work brought little relief. My friends were on their way to work when I was coming home, and it seemed the crowds I found to run with were either drunks or saints. I wasn't a good fit in either camp. I wasn't even clicking with the chicks.

The night of my 21st birthday, August 14, 1955, I had no one to celebrate with. All my friends worked the night shift, so I went to a bar, bought my first legal drink, and went home to bed. I was bored silly, and my future felt nonexistent. A couple weeks later, even the Lincoln died. Jim helped me tow it to a wrecking yard, and under cover of night I left it at the gate. I was afraid that if I showed up in the daytime, they'd make me *pay* them to take it. I didn't buy another the car, even though I could have swung it financially. Subconsciously, I must have known a change was coming.

There was one bright spot during those months of misery. A fixed-base operator at the Bridgeport Airport near Stamford was offering flying lessons in the Piper J-3 Cub. I was making enough money to afford lessons, and at the end of my sixth flight, the instructor said, "Pull over here, Don, and I'll jump out." What sweet words. With the instructor gone, the Cub leapt into the sky. The little yellow plane and I danced in the traffic pattern, shooting landings, bouncing in the wake of a giant TWA Super Connie, oblivious to any danger. I laughed and sang at the top of my voice. I can do it! I can do it! One more square filled in.[99]

As much as I loved flying, however, time spent in the air didn't make the work at Sikorsky any more palatable, especially after a foreman caught me reading and started timing my breaks. Life was going from bad to worse, and my brain was getting as rusty as my old car in the junkyard.

One day I saw an air force recruiting poster in the window of the

---

[99] A fixed-base operator is anyone who operates an aviation business at an airport facility. Most airports house such a business, which usually operates and sells airplanes and offers flying lessons. The Lockheed Super Constellation, a propeller plane designed for TWA, was in production from 1943–1958, first as a military plane dubbed the C-69 and then as a commercial aircraft.

Bridgeport post office, complete with the silver wings of a jet pilot. The armed services placed recruiters in post offices in those days, and it just so happened that a recruiting sergeant was on duty. "I want to join the air force," I said, and the sergeant was more than happy to oblige. After I finished the paperwork, however, I noticed that my reporting date was four months down the road. "Whoa," I said, "I need to go immediately."

"Sorry," the recruiter replied, "but the air force is cutting back, and all the schools for basic training are full."

I had one more card to play. "Sergeant," I said, "I have two years of college and an A&P license. My plans are to join the aviation cadets as soon as I'm prepared. I need to join up *now!*"

The sergeant looked at me intently, then got on the phone and stated my case to a major in Hartford. "Young man," he said when he hung up, "it's time to put your affairs in order. The day after tomorrow, you'll be on a bus to Sampson Air Force Base on Seneca Lake near Geneva, New York." The next morning I turned in my resignation at Sikorsky, ending what felt like the longest employment of my life: 4 months, 1 day, 2 hours, and 20 seconds.[100]

Stepping Out of Dreamland

It was Saturday, October 15, 1955, a brisk fall day that was perfect for new beginnings. I'd trashed my few possessions and left Dawg with my pals, and I arrived at the bus station with nothing but a shaving kit and the clothes on my back. I was one happy volunteer.

I'd been close to the military for several years now—the often rough-hewn, lesser educated enlisted men, as well as the more sophisticated officers who had the privilege of higher learning. Both sorts had come from the farms and towns of America to save the world from tyrants, and I had an unabashed admiration for them. The air force, like every branch of the service, offered opportunities for leadership, responsibility, and technical training that would take decades to present themselves in many civilian fields. They were also more interested in my potential than in my academic achievement. Sure, there were risks and hardships involved, and it was no way to get rich quick, but it was exactly what I wanted. After all, the air force had jets and needed a few good men to fly them. I intended to be one of those few.

---

[100] Used by the Navy as a naval training station from 1942–1945, this property was transferred to the air force in 1950 and officially designated Sampson Air Force Base in 1951. The base closed in 1956 and is now owned primarily by the state of New York and operated by the Finger Lakes Park District as Sampson State Park.

The chartered bus left at 1800, packed with a bunch of scruffy guys who spent the next ten hours foregoing sleep in order to get to know one another. It was a choice we would come to regret.[101]

About 0400, we pulled into the receiving center at Sampson. Despite the hour, the scene was one of mass confusion. Multiple buses were coming and going, and what seemed like thousands of recruits were milling around. When the doors opened on our bus, 40 disheveled, lost souls stepped off into 90 days of the most intense reformation of our young lives.

"Where did they dig up this bunch of worthless humanity? This is the worst bunch of potential airmen I've ever seen," shouted the sharpest noncom I'd ever encountered. Amid these and continuing insults, we learned that the slender, handsome African American (or Negro, race being more traditionally defined back then) standing before us was Airman 1st Class Sandy M. Bryant, a three-striper and our military training instructor (TI). Airman Bryant wore a dignified military bearing more typical of a marine, and he let us know—in no uncertain terms—that for the next 90 days we were his.[102]

The night was pitch-black, illuminated solely by the beams of flashlights as TIs herded their charges into ragged formations. The murmurs of tired, scared recruits and the shouts of wide-awake TIs were matched by the steady plip-plop of a cold drizzle, a perfect beginning for what would turn out to be 24 hours of hell. Our first march was to the clothing line. Like deer in the headlights, our eyeballs reflected a thousand emotions—fear, confusion, dismay. "Follow me," barked Airman Bryant as we marched into the night, and we did just that. In fact, for the next three months, we were rarely out of his sight.

At the clothing building, which was bathed in surreal, fluorescent light, we were given fatigues, socks and underwear, shoes (which, of course, didn't fit), shaving gear and toothbrush—and a large duffel bag to stow it in. Civilian clothes, cookies baked by distraught mothers, and other artifacts of our previous lives were to be packed up and shipped home. This was okay by me. I had nothing to mail and no particular place to send it, anyway.

Next came several lines of barbers who buzzed us down to the scalp,

---

[101]   Military time is measured by the 24-hour clock. Thus, 1800 is 6 p.m.

[102]   Also known as a noncommissioned officer or NCO, the noncom is an enlisted member of the armed forces who has been given authority by a commissioned officer. Noncoms serve as administrative or training personnel and as advisors to the officer corps. They provide a vital link between the common soldier and the commissioned officer. An Airman 1st Class is equivalent to a sergeant today. Training instructors (TIs) in the air force are roughly the equivalent of DIs (drill instructors) in the marines or chief petty officers in the navy.

followed by a march to our new home, a two-story barracks straight out of a World War II movie. On the first floor near the entry, Airman Bryant had a small, neat room. The rest of us lived in the remainder: open bays with 20 single beds lined up on each side, a total of 40 men per floor. At the end of each bay were the latrines. Each of us was assigned a bed and a footlocker, but there were no chairs. There was no time to sit down.

One of the many barracks at Sampson, my home away from home.
(*Photo ca. 1950, courtesy of Geneva Historical Society.*)

There were countless rows of these barracks and thousands of airmen being trained at the same time. The camp was organized into divisions called flights. The 80 men in our barracks were in the 4734th Flight, which, along with other flights, made up the 3655th Training Squadron. The 3655th was part of the 3650th Military Training Wing.[103]

None of this came as a surprise to me, since everything I'd known in my life so far had been in some way connected to the military. I'd heard all the stories of basic training. I'd also heard stories of war and of horrendous POW experiences, so I knew how important it was to prepare. Besides, anything was better than working at Sikorsky and dealing with its labor union. Or was it? By now it was about 0900 and we were exhausted, but after a five-minute break, it was back outside for a half-hour of calisthenics. As the rain seeped

---

[103] The air force hierarchy consists of flights, squadrons, groups or wings, and numbered air force. Flights make up a squadron, squadrons make up a group or wing, and wings make up a unit of the numbered air force. The exact makeup of each of these categories varies, but here's an example. A flight has anywhere between 10 and 80 men and women in it. Three flights might be assigned to each of four squadrons, two squadrons to each of two wings, with the wings under the command of, say, the 15th Air Force. These same types of divisions exist in the army, but with different names: squad, company, battalion, regiment, army.

under my collar, I wondered why I hadn't waited for the draft, or at least until next week, or next year, or the next decade.

Finally, we were marched to the mess hall, our first food since snacks on the bus, and I realized I was more hungry than tired. I'd been a fan of the military mess all my life, so another line with a metal tray and the most wonderful smells and sounds in the world was more than fine with me. I wasn't disappointed. I heaped my plate with SOS covered with three or four fried eggs, strips of crisp bacon, and a dollop of Tabasco sauce. Yum. The bread was freshly baked, with jam on the side, and there was an endless supply of milk, coffee, and juice. We probably chowed down 6,000 calories at that meal, but I knew we'd burn them and then some.

So far, this was the best breakfast of my young life, but not everybody felt that way. Even though we were starving, some guys pushed their food around like society babes at a food kitchen. These were the mama's boys, easy to spot even at this stage. I, on the other hand, was loving it. I had found a home.

If we could have gone to bed right after breakfast, the day would have been redeemable, but it was not to be. First we marched to the parade field to work on formations, the drizzle our constant companion. "Hup, two, left right," barked Airman Bryant, followed by shouting and insults to match our ever-growing fatigue and made worse by the perennial 10 percent who can't tell left from right. When would it end? Finally, cold, wet, and miserable, we returned to the barracks, but the day was still not over. Next came lessons on how to make a proper bed—square corners with the blanket tucked tight enough to bounce a dime—and how to roll our clothes. There was a place for everything, and survival depended on following the rules.

Within what seemed like minutes, we were ordered to change and form up outside for the march to lunch. Once again, fatigue took a backseat to hunger in the presence of delicious smells and sounds. Eat all you can, man. This is living.

It was back to the drill field after lunch and then to a classroom, where our seasoned TI began the task of drilling military subjects into our heads. The classroom was warm, and my neck just couldn't support my head. "Heads up, mister," I heard through the fog, and the rest of the afternoon passed in a jumble of dozing, standing 'til sleepiness passed, additional harassment, and more mind games.

Fighting our collective mental haze, we finished the afternoon by marching to the mess hall for dinner, another warm, tasty meal. It was dark by the time we got back to the barracks, and my body was on autopilot.

"On your knees, airmen," barked our tormentor, "and scrub that floor with Clorox until it gleams an unearthly white." Airman Bryant's flight competed with other flights, and it seemed that clean floors were a major consideration in the contest.

Taps: the most beautiful sound in the world. I dove for the sack in total exhaustion, mulling over the day, thinking about . . .

"Hit the floor, Airmen!" Airman Bryant's voice shattered any pretense of sleep.

"Whaaaa?" We'd only been in the sack for a minute, five minutes to be exact. What was wrong? In a voice that only TIs can use, Airman Bryant explained that somebody had made a black mark on the bleached floor. "I am being personally graded by my superiors," he said, "and I am *not* going to allow a bunch of worthless, inferior, substandard recruits to destroy my record."

We hit the floor in our skivvies, and since it was past lights-out, used flashlights to guide our progress. When I managed to sneak a peek at the barracks next door, I saw beams of light dancing around it as well. The point of the day was to corral our resistance, and fatigue was the best and easiest way to accomplish the task. This TI was doing his job well.

At about 2200, we were finally allowed to sleep. Never in my life have I slept better, at least until 0400, when "Reveille" wrenched us back to reality. Where was I? How did I get there? Everyone was still tired, but it wasn't long before life flowed through our young bodies. I made it through the first day, I thought, and I'll make it through the remaining 89.[104]

---

[104] Derived from the French word for wake up, "Reveille" is a bugle call used chiefly to wake military personnel.

Chapter 38 – A Broader Perspective

1955–1956

About half of the men in our flight were from the Bridgeport area, mostly lower middle class white guys. The rest were from the Bronx, mostly blacks with a few Jews thrown in for good measure. At an average age of 18, these were tough, uneducated fellows. Only about 20 of them had graduated from high school. To use a term popular today, we were a diverse bunch. If there was any racial strife, however, I never saw it. Despite what I thought was a low educational level for the most sophisticated branch of the service, we were soon forced into a team. Airman Bryant was the most impressive, efficient, and toughest noncom I'd ever seen, and he knew that bickering about our differences would do nothing but waste valuable time. He may have been black and proud of it, but he looked at and treated us as one color only: marine green.[105]

Each day started the same: a scratchy bugle call over a WWII speaker system at 0400, then 20 minutes to find an empty toilet, shower, shave, and make our beds. (With the exception of having to shave, I went through the same drill at Linsly Military Institute back when I was ten years old.) Standing at attention at the foot of our beds, we waited for Airman Bryant to inspect our handiwork. Beds that didn't pass inspection, usually most of them, were torn up by the TI as he barked his orders: "This time, do it right." The offenders, frustrated with suppressed anger, complied. Afterward, we formed up outside for the morning routine, calisthenics—jumping jacks and pushups—and running in formation. Then we marched to chow, the highlight of my day.

If other flights marched single-time, we double-timed it. Competition was the rule of the day, and this led to a flicker of pride. We're getting better more quickly than the other flights, we thought, or at least that's what we

---

[105] Marine green, a term used by all branches of the service, means that personnel are judged by their performance, not by the color of their skin, their ethnic background, or their religious affiliation.

were led to believe. "We're number one," we chanted. It made the torture easier to bear.

Maybe because I was older and more widely traveled than my mates, I soon discovered I could quell the occasional sob or quiet a disagreement with a smile or pat on the back. Up until then, I'd never thought of myself as a leader, and heaven knows I hadn't been much of a student. At Sampson, however, I learned quickly and found time to help others; when we had a task to do, I led the way. The better the task was accomplished, the easier life became, a fact one didn't need a formal education to appreciate.

At the end of our first week, Airman Bryant called me in and pinned a sleeve over my left arm that read "Student TI." From then on, my job was to form the troops, march them to chow, and bring them back, along with other assorted tasks. One of these duties, my most important and enjoyable job, was to go to the mess hall almost every night and prepare sandwiches for the TIs and their helpers.

The food supplied by the air force was first-rate, and I knew how to make a superb sandwich. Soon the mess hall cooks got to know me and my important mission, and I was given free rein in the kitchen. The bakers supplied hot bread and rolls, upon which I would heap slices of salami, baloney, sliced roast beef, leftover steak and gravy, and anything else I could find or invent. I garnished these creations with fresh lettuce and tomatoes, then added mustard, mayo, pickles, onions, and horseradish. Sandwich duty was a great responsibility, so of course I felt honor-bound to test these concoctions before feeding them to the TIs. I was on a feeding frenzy, but the work was such that I never gained a pound.

Our days were a balance of exercise, chow, marching drill, and academics. Our platform instructors, often airmen or sergeants without a great deal of formal education, were excellent. Skilled, focused, and determined, these men were dedicated to providing the information we needed to succeed. It was, of course, a carrot-and-stick approach. If you failed, there was always something more difficult and less appealing, like permanent KP. At the end of most courses, students would rate the instructor on a scale of 1–10. If he failed to measure up, KP was an option for him as well. The system obviously worked, because within a month we could do every task asked of us. From a disparate bunch of ragtag recruits, we'd become a team, and a proud team at that.[106]

Yes, there were some casualties. A farm boy who was unable to tell left

[106] KP, or kitchen police, is duty associated with food preparation or cleanup and often used as punishment for failure to meet standards or for minor infractions of the rules.

from right and who refused to shower (though a midnight GI bath with scrub brushes and lye soap helped the latter) was eventually discharged, as were a few of the big-city boys who just couldn't conform. With discipline and education, however, the rest measured up and blossomed, due in no small measure to the efforts of our superior TI.

Airman 1st Class Bryant was dedicated to his job and to his recruits, and we learned to be tough because he was tougher. On the shores of Seneca Lake, January is one of the coldest and windiest places on earth. Since the system failed to provide us with parkas, we faced this weather in nothing but light field jackets, and we were always cold, particularly on the drill field. Airman Bryant led those drills with no jacket at all, ramrod straight in his immaculate fatigues, acting as if it were summer. I was impressed.

Testing has never been my forte, and I knew that over the course of the program we would be formally tested a total of three times, once after every four weeks. Failure was always a fear; if you didn't pass, corrective action up to and including discharge would and did occur.

The week of our first test, almost everyone in the barracks was filled with apprehension. I tried to remain calm, but I couldn't help reliving my disastrous experience with the NavCads. The day of the exam, I marched the troops to the testing center. We had four hours to complete fifty questions, with no interruptions or help. The testing sergeant came in to brief us: "All questions are multiple-choice with four possible answers," he began. "Use a black pencil to fill in the circle beside the right answer."

I got out my pencil along with all my excuses. I'm tired, I thought. Of course, we were all tired, not that it mattered as the sergeant counted down the time: 10 seconds, 5 seconds, begin. It was 1300 sharp.

Question number one: The color of a stoplight is:

○ *Red* ○ *Black* ○ *Green* ○ *Yellow*

Question number two: If a tower is ten feet tall, how many inches tall is it?

○ *120* ○ *200* ○ *1400* ○ *1600*

Was this some kind of joke? I answered the remaining 48 questions, of similar ilk, in less than 15 minutes, then looked around at my comrades. Many were obviously in distress and straining their minds to the limit. A few looked as relieved as I. I put my head down, and for the next 3 hours and 35 minutes, I slept. It was the best, most uninterrupted sleep of my short air force career. I couldn't wait for the next test.

As the weeks went by, our flight won almost every competition in which we were involved, from sports to clean floors. The envy of the base, we marched through basic farther, faster, and with more pride than anyone else. At least, that was our story, and we were sticking to it. Even so, it wasn't all roses. One night, for example, a Jewish guy and a black guy really got into it, and I ended up in the middle as peacemaker. We were all a bit scratched and bruised the next day, but Airman Bryant never asked about it, and there were no recriminations.

Toward the end of training, we were given a barrage of tests assessing our aptitude for everything from heating specialist (coal shoveler) to advanced electronics. With the knowledge I'd gained at Wentworth, I easily passed a technical school bypass test, which meant I would be assigned directly to the field. This dude was schooled out.

We were also asked to complete an assignment preference request. I listed Germany, Japan, or Asia, but when the assignments came out, I had been posted to the 551st Periodic Maintenance Squadron at Otis Air Force Base on Cape Cod, six miles from our house in Cotuit. So much for travel to exotic lands. Maybe somebody thought they were doing me a favor.

On a cold day in the middle of January 1956, we were promoted from lowly recruits to airmen 3rd class. Our flight had earned best flight award, and I had completed what turned out to be one of the most rewarding experiences of my life. The leadership, diplomacy, and decision-making skills I learned in basic training were invaluable. Even when supervising the bleaching of floors, I was establishing my capability as a leader (though, on occasion, I did have to demonstrate the proper technique for slow learners).

As I checked out, Airman Bryant shook my hand.

"You're the best student I've ever had," he said.

"Why's that, Airman?"

"Because," he said with a twinkle in his eye, "you make the best damn sandwiches in the U.S. Air Force!"

The military offers the opportunity to improve in every facet of life, sometimes through coercion, but mostly through competitiveness and pride. It is an organization in which I was proud to serve. To this day, even in old clothes, my gig line—shirt line, belt buckle, and zipper—is always straight.

Part IV: 1956–1959

Previous page: Walking tours at Spence Air Base, 1960.
(Courtesy of Ray Sack, Class 60-E, and the Spence Air Base history Web site.)

Chapter 39 – On My Way

1956

I had a ten-day leave and travel time before reporting to Otis Air Force Base, so I hitched a ride to Staten Island. Grandmother was living elsewhere, but my folks were still stationed at Fort Wadsworth. I couldn't wait to show off my neatly pressed uniform with its single stripe.

I also needed a car loan. Cars were an important part of my life. A car-less winter on the Cape would be like serving an isolated tour at the North Pole, but my starting salary at Otis was a meager $92 a month. My mother was an understanding banker. She floated me a loan of $200 at 4 percent interest on a 2-year note and I bought a 1950 Olds 88.

Jim Miller, my buddy from Wentworth, was still working for Sikorsky and living in Stratford, though in a different house than the one we'd rented together. He'd also met Peggy, the gal of his dreams. "Stop by for a day or two on your way to Otis," he said when I phoned. "You can meet Peggy and we'll throw a party for you."

I showed up for the party at Jim's house in uniform. For one thing, I was proud of my status; for another, I didn't own any civvies. Jim had corralled a good-looking blond for me named Loretta, and we hit it off immediately. Loretta was full of giggles and fun, and before long the booze was flowing. We were all a bit tipsy, and after 3 months of being locked up with 80 guys, I was as horny as a three-peckered billy goat. As soon as I could, I maneuvered her back to the study where I turned down the lights, put on some quiet Louie, and prepared to make up for lost time.

After a smooch or two, Loretta whispered breathlessly in my ear. "Don, did you forget to shave?"

Damn. I knew I'd forgotten something. "Stay right there," I said. "Don't move."

I headed for the bathroom, saw it was occupied, and ran back to the study to make sure she was still there. She was, batting her eyes at me and blowing kisses. "I'll be back ASAP," I said, in what I hoped was a tone of sophisticated anticipation.

At last the bathroom was free. I lathered the area around my mouth—no time for more—and whipped out my trusty Gillette. It hurt a bit as I was slashing away, but I was totally focused on the picture in my mind—blue-eyed blond awaits. When I finished, I checked the mirror and let out a hair-raising shriek: A mixture of blood and shaving cream was running down my face like a faucet. My face stung like crazy, and my freshly pressed air force shirt had become a soggy mosaic of red, white, and blue.

In my tipsy state, I hadn't closed the razor before using it, and my face was a map of little slashes. My shrieks attracted most of the other partygoers, who burst into laughter at my predicament. Liberal applications of towel, ice cubes, and styptic pencil staunched the flow, but every time I smiled or talked, a few spots of blood spurted to the surface.

The romantic interlude was over, but Loretta was kind enough to invite me to Sunday dinner (anything for the boys in blue). That weekend, her mother put on a great Polish feast, and her little brother, who was fascinated with my slashed face, kept making me laugh so that little beads of blood would erupt on my cheeks. I didn't stay long, and Loretta didn't offer to exchange addresses. Methinks she was not a true patriot.

At Home at Otis

Otis Air Force Base/Camp Edwards. George had been stationed at Camp Edwards just before shipping out to Japan in 1950, so I'd visited the place a hundred times. The base had a rich and varied history. As early as 1936, it had been used by the Massachusetts National Guard. In 1938, it was dedicated as Camp Edwards and its airfield named for Frank Otis, a prominent Boston surgeon and pilot killed in 1937 on a cross-country training flight. During World War II the facility was used extensively by the army. The air force became a separate military branch in 1947, and in 1948 it took control of an expanded Otis Field and renamed it Otis Air Force Base.[107]

Now I was to be a part of that history. As a member of the 551st, I was assigned to Master Sergeant Burndt, a grizzled vet from before World War II who was knowledgeable and easy to work for. Our squadron operated several RC-121 aircraft. RC stands for radar cargo. The ships, Lockheed Super Connies, were outfitted with huge radar domes and a crew of a dozen or so

---

[107] In 1977, the base was redistributed into three parts: the Otis Air National Guard Base, Camp Edwards, and the U.S. Coast Guard Air Station. Together, they are known as the MMR or Massachusetts Military Reservation.

radar operators. Nicknamed picket air ships, these planes would sit on-station off the North Atlantic coast, like a picket line, for up to 15 hours at a time, ready to call fighters to protect our shores. The Cold War was heating up and we had a mission to accomplish. I'm not sure how history will rate that mission, but we executed it to the best of our abilities.

As a ground mechanic, I was assigned to a specific RC-121. When it was flying, I was off; when it was on the ground, I was there. The aircraft had four 28-cylinder Wright R-3350 engines, each of which was equipped with three power recovery turbines or PRTs. These devices used the exhaust to deliver more power to the engines, but they also increased the need for maintenance. So after each mission, we not only had to refuel, which took the better part of an hour, we also had to change about 20 spark plugs and at least two PRTs. My hands were always cold, cut, and bleeding; it went with the territory.

All of this was hard, physical work, and both the officers and the noncoms treated us with respect. After a while, the job became routine, but it was always challenging, and it wasn't long before I was promoted to crew chief.

Social life at Otis was lively, which meant I had plenty of gals to date. One of them was a transplant from San José, California, an attractive brunette named Barbara who worked as a secretary on the base and lived with her sister and brother-in-law, a fellow airman. She was interesting and fun to be with, and we spent many hours together.

I also met a couple of guys who became great pals. One was Lou Silva, who came from the Portuguese community near New Bedford. Hardworking and dependable, Lou had a cheerful disposition and didn't envy the officers or the more sophisticated, educated people of the world. He was a highly skilled mechanic, and like the typical airman, he did his job and then some. He and I, along with another pal, William (Robbie) Robinson, had fun chasing the gals, tinkering with cars, and hanging around a couple of beer gardens drinking brew and playing pool. Ninety-two bucks a month kept us close to the bone, however, so we also took on extra jobs pumping gas and picking cranberries.

Picking cranberries has to be the most backbreaking work in the world—walking the bogs on your knees with a multi-tined, handheld rake, rocking back and forth to strip the berries from the vines. I figured the financial rewards were worth it, at least on the first day when I was able to harvest several crates. My production slowed to a trickle on the second day, and the next few days were so painful I could hardly move. The cheerful migrant laborers I worked with could harvest incredible amounts with a minimum of discomfort, and they encouraged me to keep at it. With their help, I managed to persevere through the pain, but this type of labor is enough to keep even the most unambitious student in school and trying hard.

Unintended Stowaway

One day, after picking cranberries in the morning followed by a six-hour shift at the Texaco station, I met my RC-121 after its mission. Another aircraft had broken down and mine needed to be turned around ASAP. I changed a few plugs and called in the specialists to change out some black boxes. Refueling took about an hour—7,000 gallons in several tanks. I was just short of exhausted, but I still had two hours to go before the crew reported for the mission. I mulled over my options. Back to the barracks for a quick rest? Not enough time. Midnight mess? Naw, I was just too tired.

Aha. The plane had crew bunks in the back. Maybe I'd just crawl into one, curl up on the parachutes stored there, pull the drapes, and rest my eyes. Just for a few moments, just until the flight engineer arrived.

I was immersed in a kaleidoscope of sounds, colors, smells, and confusion—migrants, cranberries, gas, cars, girls, tools, food, noise, airplanes, reciprocating engines. Throbbing, throbbing, throbbing. No, no. I want jets. Fighters, not props. Twisting and turning, I sat up.

Whap! My head hit the bunk above me and I fell back against the parachutes, sweating and breathing hard. Where in the world was I? Peering through a crack in the drapes, I saw an alien bathed in the greenish glow of a flickering screen. Had I been captured by little green people who were taking me in a flying saucer to a distant planet? How bad could it get?

Slowly my confused mind sorted things out. It was much worse than bad.

Suffering from cranberry-induced exhaustion, I'd fallen asleep and was now well into a 15-hour mission—the ultimate taboo. Some months ago I'd tried to do this legally, angling for an observation flight. The idea had been firmly vetoed by my commander. I could see the headlines now: airman thrown into brig for disobeying orders. Worse yet, since nobody knew I was there, I was AWOL. Goodbye, cadets. Hello, chain gang.

Wait a minute. The fact that nobody knew I was there just might be my saving grace. Who saw the mission off? Was I already in trouble?

First things first. My head hurt were I'd mashed it into the bunk, and I had assorted discomfort in places where the metal fastenings of my parachute mattress had dug into my back. I was also hungry and thirsty, and I had to take a leak. Again I peaked through the drapes at the rows of airmen sitting in front of radar screens. Wait! I knew one of them, and he was walking toward me. He stuck his foot onto my bunk and hoisted himself into the bunk above.

"Charlie," I whispered.

Nothing.

Again, a bit louder. "Charlie!"

"Who's that," he whispered back, "God?"

"Not hardly," I replied. "It's good ole Don Wright."

"What the hell are you doing here?"

I gave him a quiet, quick rundown of my situation.

Charlie tried to suppress a guffaw. "Wait a minute. I'll be right back."

He quickly returned with a crew meal, some water, and an empty bottle. I scoffed down the feast, drank the water, and used the empty bottle for relief. Then I rearranged the parachutes for greater comfort, rolled over, and went back to sleep. When I woke up, the tires were screeching on the runway.

The plane taxied to the ramp and stopped. When I heard the door open, I waited for a bit, then slipped out of my tomb and made my way to the cockpit, where the aircraft commander was filling out forms.

"Good afternoon, Airman Wright. You're certainly Johnny-on-the-spot today."

"Yes, Sir. I take my job seriously."

About that time, Lou stuck his head through the cockpit door. "Airman Wright, I've chocked the aircraft and directed the ground support folks—just like you asked."[108]

"Thanks, Airman Silva, I'll be down to finish the job as soon as the major debriefs the aircraft."

Lou had covered for me, both at the beginning of the flight and at the end: a good friend, a bit of good luck, and a *very* good angel.

Growing Pains

Lou and I had something else in common: We both loved cars. After a few months at Otis, I sold the Olds and bought a shiny red 1953 MGTD. It was a smiling car and a magnet for gals. It also was very delicate. At high rpms, the engine sounded so-o-o-o good it became unglued several times, a feature that managed to keep me in the poorhouse.[109]

Lou's love was a brand new Pontiac convertible, bright yellow with a Continental tire kit. To capture his dream, he went down to the recruitment office and reenlisted, using his reenlistment bonus as a down payment. The

---

[108] Chocking means placing blocks under the wheels of an aircraft to keep it from moving.

[109] The MG was a sports car produced in England from the 1930s through 1980, except during World War II when production facilities were redirected to the war effort. The TD model was produced from 1949 through 1953.

huge monthly payments that followed, however, meant at least one extra job, and sometimes two.

Some months later, I introduced Lou to a cute chick at the Texaco station where we both worked. She loved the Pontiac, she soon loved Lou, and it wasn't long before they were married. Unfortunately, theirs was not a story with a happy ending. Lou lost the car to a repossession agency, and his wife left soon after. Robbie, who was more savvy with his money, married a lady in Falmouth just off base and did fine.

Chapter 40 – Setting Sail

1956–1957

O tis was only six miles from Cotuit and Barnstable High, but when I went back in my air force uniform with its shiny single stripe, it felt as if I were in a time warp. My first stop was the Kettle-Ho Diner, where I'd whiled away many an hour drinking frappés and yakking with my friends. And even though the draft was in place, most of the guys I knew back in 1951 were still there. World tensions were down, and military service could be easily avoided. As for college, a lot of these guys lacked the funds, the initiative, and/or the academic credentials to swing it. In many ways they were suffering from what I called the *mom conspiracy*—keep them home, safe from war and the world, even if it did mean they'd likely be stacking cans and sweeping streets. Aim them toward an early marriage and having kids—a safe but mundane life.

My mother had never coddled me, and I'd had a remarkable amount of freedom growing up. Even so, until I joined the air force I'd been a boy. In my three months of basic training, I'd been motivated more than ever before. I'd also been given more leadership opportunities than at any time during the first 21 years of my life. The program worked. I was now a man.

As I watched my old pals, stagnant, perched on swivel stools at the Kettle-Ho or "standing on the corner, watching all the girls go by," the irony hit me. Even though they'd never left home, these lads were in greater danger than I. Without ambition or discipline, they were far more likely to engage in the only condoned form of murder in the USA: drinking and driving. This sport was one the military simply did not allow. In fact, the surest way to join one's pals back on the street corner was to exhibit such behavior.[110]

The guys at the diner were dreaming of living. I was living my dream, and the air force was giving me the discipline and the training to make it happen.

---

[110] This is a quote from the lyrics of "Standing on the Corner," a popular song by Frank Loesser from the 1956 musical, *The Most Happy Fella*.

Home at the Haydens

The best part of my trips to Cotuit was visiting Bob and Libby Hayden. In high school I'd considered the Haydens' place my second home, and I still loved visiting them, particularly on Saturday nights when Mrs. Hayden filled the lazy Susan in the middle of the dining room table with Boston baked beans, codfish cakes, hot dogs, steamers, and Cotuit's world-famous oysters. Of course, I delighted in regaling my pals with tales of this culinary paradise, so one Saturday in early spring, Lou, Robbie and I dropped in conveniently around dinnertime. It turned out that my friend Liz, the Haydens' oldest daughter, was also home from Simmons College that weekend, accompanied by three of her friends. Dinner table conversation was lively, eclectic, and nonstop.

"How's the boat coming?" Liz asked.

"Terrific," I replied. The boat was a Snipe, a small wooden sailboat I'd found months before weathering away in the back lot of Treasure Highland, the retail arm of the Haydens' building-moving and salvage business. Thanks to Mr. Hayden, the price was so low it was practically a gift, and over the winter, when I wasn't working or studying for my cadet tests (I was still determined to become a fighter pilot), I'd rebuilt it to a fare-thee-well. To set it apart from the average Cape Cod craft, I'd even driven to the New Bedford textile mills and found a snazzy plaid remnant, which now covered the deck under several coats of clear marine varnish. So in answer to Liz's question, I described in great detail how beautiful and graceful the boat was now, along with how much time and effort it had taken to rebuild it.[111]

"So what's her name, and when do we get to try her out?" asked several people at once.

"How about in the morning," I replied. "I haven't christened her yet, so after the sail, why don't you gals help with the name?" The gals thought this was a fine idea. Unfortunately, Lou and Robbie had to work, so I was left with entertaining these four beauties all by myself. It was a daunting task, but I was pretty sure I could do it.

The next morning, I launched and rigged the Snipe, then pushed her off the beach for a shakedown cruise. When racing, the boat was designed to hold two people, but for more casual pursuits—like taking four beautiful gals on a picnic—it could accommodate a few extra passengers.

It was a beautiful day, warm with mostly steady winds, clear except for a few cloud puffs. The boat had a couple of minor leaks, but with a tweak on the rigging, the nimble craft seemed to plane through the bay. When I

---

[111] The Snipe, designed by William Crosby in 1931, is a 15½-foot, one-design racing dinghy with two sails: a mainsail and a jib.

looked back, four pretty gals stood on the dock with their cooler of drinks and lunch.

I decided to put on a show. Speeding toward the dock, I executed a couple of well-timed and coordinated tacks through the wind, a neat, controlled maneuver. The sails were crisp and full, the colorful masthead pennant snapped in the wind, and as I headed for the dock, the gals watched appreciatively. The breeze had picked up a bit and I was enjoying showing off my skill for such a willing audience, so at the last minute I decided to jibe. When planned, a jibe is an effective, fast-turning technique. Unplanned, it is foolhardy at best and dangerous at worst, since it sweeps the boom across the deck with great force.[112]

Uh-oh. Either my timing was off or a gust of wind had hit at the most inopportune time, but one way or the other, I'd jibed too late. My poor, unnamed beauty roared under the dock and through the pilings, ripping mast, boom, sails, and stays out of the deck and rendering a giant hole in the sinking hull. From under all of this, I emerged unhurt but very embarrassed.

As soon as Liz saw I was alive and well, she began to tease me unmercifully. "If you ever do get to fly fighters," she said, "I hope your landings are better than this. Oh, and by the way, the four of us talked it over, and we think *Submarine* might be a great name for your boat."

As we ate lunch on the dock, I took another boatload of kidding, but afterward the gals did help me drag the dead hull back onto its trailer. "Look on the bright side," one of them said as I drove off, "with any luck, maybe Mr. Hayden can resell it as a planter."

Choices and Chances

In October 1956, after being a member of the air force for a year, I received a good conduct ribbon; in November, I received orders for a second stripe (airman Second Class) from my squadron commander, Major Joe Riley. These honors were fairly automatic assuming one kept one's nose clean, but considering the near-brush with discovery during my 15-hour sojourn on the RC-121, I wore them with more-than-usual appreciation.

Major Riley knew of my dream to become a fighter pilot, and he was very encouraging, but I had more to do to get ready. I took night courses in math and studied as much as I could for the dreaded stanine tests. I even quit

---

[112] When jibing, one turns the stern of the boat so that the opposite side of the boat ends up facing the wind. The opposite of this maneuver is tacking, which means turning the bow of the boat so that the opposite side faces the wind. The boom is a long spar that extends from the mast to hold or extend the foot of a sail.

smoking, which I'd done before when I needed extra brainpower. Still, I was afraid to apply. When I failed the NavCads in 1955, the day after I graduated from Wentworth, I knew the air force cadet program remained an option. This time, there would be no second chance. I needed a nudge.

The nudge came on a cold day in December. I was wrapped in my regulation parka, its fur-edged hood hugging my face so that only my eyeballs showed, and I was frozen stiff. I had just finished refueling the RC-121's seven fuel tanks and was straddled around the last of them, a torpedo-shaped tip tank on the edge of a wing, when a Lockheed F-94 Starfire fighter interceptor taxied by. The canopy was down, and the pilot looked up and waved his gloved hand at me. *He* looked warm and toasty. He also looked happy, and *he had my job*!

"Sgt. Burndt, I want out of this outfit. I'm going to go for cadets, and I need time off now."

The sarge was a good guy, and he'd long been aware of my ambitions. "You got it, Wright," he said, "and good luck." The next day, 15 airmen showed up for the preliminary test. Those who passed would be sent to Westover Air Force Base in Chicopee, Massachusetts, near Springfield, to take the stanines and a physical.[113]

I passed. In fact, I was the only one who passed. Victory was sweet.

At Westover the following week, the stanines took place over two grueling days and covered nine separate subjects. This time, ten guys, civilians and airmen, took the tests. When they were over, we hung around in a gloomy circle, complaining and whining to each other. It had been impossible, we agreed. No one could pass. By the time we broke up, I was already trying to invent a better word for despair. We were to report back for the results at 0800. That night I slipped into a dreamless sleep, too exhausted even for worry.

By morning, I had regained my normal surge of optimism. The gloom of the preceding day had passed, and I showered, shaved, and reported to the testing center.

At 0800 sharp, the officer in charge read off nine names. "Gentlemen," he said, "you are excused," and nine guys left the room. Again, I was the only one who'd passed.

Shortly thereafter, I made it through a long and difficult physical. Yes, victory is *very* sweet and life is good, but I'm sure my guardian angel was right by my side. Wasn't she?

---

[113] Constructed as an army air base in preparation for U.S. involvement in World War II, Westover has been operational since 1940. After the war, it gained fame as the launching point for the heroic Berlin airlift, which operated for more than 300 days in 1948 and 1949 during the Russian blockade of surface traffic to West Berlin. As of 2008, Westover is the largest Air Force Reserve base in the U.S.

Chapter 41 – Back in the Heart of Texas

1957

It wasn't long before I received my orders: Report to Class 59-Echo, Lackland Air Force Base, Texas, on October 16, 1957. That left me six months to go at Otis, during which time I was both a conscientious crew chief and a saint. I didn't smoke, drank a beer only occasionally, drove within the speed limit, and dated rarely. I was as prepared as I could be, and I was determined that nothing would go wrong.[114]

The 15-month cadet/officer flying program was broken down into three phases: preflight training for three months, primary flight training for six months, and basic flight training for six months. Those who made it through the program received the wings of a jet pilot. Those like me who were not already commissioned officers also received their commissions as second lieutenants. Then came advanced training and transfer to an Operations squadron. All told, I was in for two years of damn hard but immensely enjoyable work, and I couldn't wait. In the interim, I interrogated every pilot officer who'd take the time to talk with me. Their answers were always the same: When they were going through it, the program was a tiger—intense and tough, but in retrospect, it was a piece of cake. By this time, I knew about that phrase. What it boiled down to was 4 years of West Point discipline crammed into 15 months, with flying thrown in.

When I left Otis, the air force gave me a one-way ticket from Buffalo, New York, to San Antonio, Texas, and my gal Barbara gave me heartfelt goodbye kisses along with the promise to write faithfully during my months in training. As well as anybody could remember, I was the first airman from our squadron to be accepted into the cadet program, and I think Master Sergeant

---

[114] Prior to World War I, Kelly Field was established near San Antonio, TX, to provide aviation training for a fledgling U.S. Air Service. In 1942, a portion of Kelly was designated as a separate facility and called the San Antonio Aviation Cadet Center (or SAACC). In 1947, SAACC was renamed Lackland Air Force Base in honor of Brigadier General Frank D. Lackland. Kelly Air Force Base closed in 2001, with much of its real estate and many of its functions being absorbed by Lackland.

Burndt was as proud of me as I was of myself. In fact, the day I left, I could swear there was a misty eye in that tough, grizzled face. I just had to succeed: for the nation, for my friends and family, and for the old sarge. After all, he expected it.

The drive from the Cape was beautiful—brisk fall weather, colors at their peak, and a smiling red sports car to enjoy it in. My Uncle Walt and Aunt Carolyn still lived near Buffalo in East Aurora, home of much of my childhood, and they were letting me store my MGTD and civvies at their house. Walt had been my mentor for years, one of the many supermen who'd served our country during World War II and Korea, and it was great to see them again.

After a brief visit and a stop to see Gramps at the Knights of Columbus, I boarded the plane in uniform, my two stripes and good conduct ribbon firmly in place. I was 23 years old and finding it very tough to be humble. "Look at me," I wanted to shout, "I'm going to be a fighter pilot." Instead, I rode quietly, studying some of the military litanies I'd been assigned to memorize.

When I arrived at Lackland, the sky was cloudless, the breeze soft, the temperature moderate—in other words, a perfect first day for the rest of my life. I didn't have to ask where the cadet area was. The occasional sports car and the influx of young, college-age dudes were dead giveaways, but I didn't report in right away. I wanted to absorb the day, relish the glorious surges of pleasure, and tamp down the occasional bursts of apprehension before settling in. I stood at a distance with my light duffel bag (everything else I needed would be supplied by the base) and watched a formation of cadets march by, their heels thundering against the street. It was more than impressive; I was in awe, and I couldn't think of a better word to invent for the occasion.

Becoming a Cadet

I looked myself over. Sharp creases in my pants and shirt: check. Shoes shined so they could blind your eyes: check. I took a deep breath and said a prayer. Nobody can really challenge life alone, and I wanted to make sure my guardian angel was right there beside me.

I walked into the reception center, where I was approached by two guys with ramrod-straight military bearing, sporting the black shoulder boards and white stripes of cadet rank. With a welcoming smile and a handshake, they introduced themselves: McCullough and Pope.

"Airman Wright, great to see you," said McCullough, and Mr. Pope gave me a hearty slap on the back.

"How was your trip?"

"Get enough to eat?"

"Great," I replied, beginning to relax a little. Maybe this tiger training had been tamed a bit since the guys I'd talked to had gone through it.

"How about a Coke?" asked Mr. McCullough.

"Yeah, that would be great. Thanks."

Mr. Pope popped the top of an ice-cold Coke and handed it to me. I took a long, grateful drink. "Come on over here, Airman Wright, and sign in," he said with a smile.

By signing my name, I became an official member of Class 59-Echo. Assuming I successfully completed the program, I had just committed myself to five more years in the air force. For the next six weeks, I had committed myself to a sojourn in hell.[115]

"*Hit the wall, mister,*" shouted McCullough.

Shocked, my back hit the wall.

"Suck in your gut, bury that chin in your chest, and get your heels together." Six inches from my startled face, the two men bombarded me with verbal abuse, a film of sprayed saliva mixing with the line of sweat on my lip and brow. "Your shirt is smudged. Your pants aren't pressed. Did you shine your shoes with a Hershey bar? Answer me, *Mister* Wright."

"No, I didn't," I said with indignation.

"No, I didn't, Sir," screamed Mr. Pope, his pale blue eyes reminding me of a Nazi interrogator. "From now on, all I want from you is 'Yes, Sir,' 'No, Sir,' or 'No excuse, Sir.' Do you understand?"

"Yes, Sir."

"Louder, Mister Wright."

"*Yes, Sir, Sir!*"

Mr. McCullough approached me with a razor. "Do you want those stripes, mister?"

"No, Sir," I said as he cut them off. They were soon replaced with black shoulder boards and one colored stripe, indicating my status as a cadet. Mr. Pope continued the verbal abuse. The treatment was brutal, but neither man uttered a single word of profanity.

I hated them. How dare they shout at a future fighter pilot? Even so, I was wise enough to limit my response to "yes, Sir" and "no, Sir."

There are some things in life for which it is impossible to fully prepare. I knew this was going to happen, yet it still took me by surprise. After what

---

[115] It costs millions of dollars to train a pilot, and those receiving this training are usually committed to serve for some period after they complete the program. The length of this commitment depends upon the needs of the air force at any given time. In 2007, it was eight years.

seemed an eternity, I was marched into a holding room of shocked, scared troops. Pope and McCullough departed to shanghai more newcomers, leaving the rest of us to share our dismay and anticipation.

The first guy I talked to was Bill Williams, a lanky fellow about six feet tall and just short of handsome. Originally from Detroit, Bill was already an airman and had flying status as a crew member. We were the same age, had the same desperate desire to succeed, and hit it off immediately.

Half the class turned out to be commissioned officers—college grads who'd gone through ROTC or the military academies—plus a few OCS grads, almost all of them upgraded noncoms. Most of the other half had completed at least two years of college and passed the stanine tests. This latter group included some men from the enlisted ranks, but the majority came from the streets of America, civilians experiencing military life for the first time. The remaining 5 percent or so were already commissioned officers, trainees from friendly nations such as Denmark, Germany, Iran, Iraq, and Cuba.[116]

Once McCullough and Pope had gathered the remaining victims, the members of Class 59-Delta, ahead of us by six weeks, gathered us into formation. Forward, march to the barber, the uniform line, and finally the barracks. The guys with a military background helped the civilians, and instant friendships were formed. I thought back to the day I arrived at Sampson for basic training, another October morning almost exactly two years before. There were many similarities, but this time I knew what to expect. I was ready, physically and mentally, and I couldn't wait to get started.

The upperclassmen, many of whom had just received their cadet rank, surrounded and harassed us like a pack of wild dogs. The cadet structure, borrowed from the system at West Point, was an air force within an air force. After the first six weeks of training, white stripes were awarded to top performers: six stripes for cadet colonel (the big kahuna), five for cadet lieutenant colonel, four for cadet captain; three for cadet lieutenant, and two for cadet sergeant. The remainder of the class, called blackboards, retained a single colored stripe. The stripe color changed every six weeks to show progress through the program.

Regardless of rank, these guys were sharp and proud, tough and dedicated, and it was their job to teach us the many facets of the military. Some of us, and some of them, wouldn't be able to hack the program, but those able to withstand the physical and mental challenges would join the ranks of an elite flying corps. I intended to be one of them.

[116] The definition of "friendly nation" is obviously subject to change over time.

Yes Sir, No Sir!

It was obvious that the age-old precept of keeping them tired, well-fed, and pressured still worked. Officers—God-like, silver-winged creatures we tried to avoid—were all around us. The days were a blur of exercise, marching double-step and going to class. Some of the guys were having a hard time, especially the civilians who hadn't been through the drill before, but I was thriving.

Classes covering military tradition and a myriad of subjects related to flying were held daily. On the first day, one lecture was about discipline and how we were to be graded. It was okay to be sleepy in class, but you'd better stand up, wiggle your knees, and not pass out. I might as well have stayed in bed; I was walking the line.

For an infraction of the rules we received one or more demerits, and the list of potential infractions seemed endless. Gig line not straight: demerit. Shoes not properly shined: demerit. We were even required to carry a gig pad on which an upperclassman or officer could record an infraction for posting.

We also had daily room inspections and a white-glove inspection on Saturday. Bed not made properly (a dime didn't bounce high enough): demerit. Dust or dirt: demerit. Any one of a thousand other real or imagined inadequacies: *demerit*. Minor infractions normally earned a single demerit. More serious problems such as insubordination, returning late, or being off-limits (somewhere on the base you were forbidden to go) received a combination of demerits and tours. I'd learned about tours way back at Linsly in the fifth grade, and the principle was pretty much the same—one-hour marches in a circle or square while in full uniform. A *6 and 12* (6 demerits and 12 tours) was often accompanied by restriction to barracks and base. More serious infractions merited a *12 and 24* (12 demerits and 24 tours), and the most drastically challenged (though this rarely happened) received a *72-gun salute* (26 demerits and 72 tours). Those who survived the latter became legends.

Each airman was allowed 50 demerits for each segment of the program: preflight, primary flight, and basic flight training. Assuming one did not exceed this magic number by the end of a segment, the counter was reset to zero for the following segment, though unsatisfied tours still had to be worked off. Anyone who did exceed 50 demerits had to appear before an FEB (flying evaluation board), which usually resulted in dismissal. Fortunately, this did not happen often.

To an outsider, the treatment may appear cruel and meaningless, but every mind game had a purpose. For example, prior to crossing a street we had to stand at attention and look left, right, up, and down. That's what we'd be expected to do in an airplane. Failure to remember could cause collision and death.

Much of the training was designed to help us control our emotions under pressure. In the mess hall, cadets sat at tables of ten with an upperclassman at the head. We ate at attention with every arm movement to our mouths a square. Called a square meal, this was just another way to turn on the heat. Asking for anything like salt opened up an opportunity for harassment by the table leader, and if he saw you put too much food in your mouth, he would ask you to recite from memory something like Article IV of the *Code of Conduct*. Put fork down square with edge of table; snap to sitting attention, arms straight down; chew, chew, swallow, swallow, and recite. Not complying fast enough or reciting incorrectly only added to one's troubles, and I learned to eat only mashed or soft foods.[117]

Another favorite dinnertime trick was the pet roadrunner. After a long dissertation on his love and affection for his pet roadrunner, the upperclassman extracted an imaginary beast from his tunic and placed it on the table for its evening exercise. The roadrunner would start around the table, and as he passed in front of each cadet, the cadet was required to lift his plate and say "beep-beep" so the roadrunner was not injured. Faster and faster the bird ran, until one of the cadets would get out of sync and the roadrunner crashed into his plate. The upperclassman would lament the death of his one and only, specially bred roadrunner. The poor cadet whose plate was the murder weapon had to bury the bird in his mashed potatoes while one of our resident blitherers played "Taps" through pursed lips. The rest of us worked hard to keep a straight face.[118]

Since the whole point of these exercises was control, the worst thing one could be was a blitherer, a person who could not contain his laughter. Our flight had two of them: Eugene (Tiger) Taylor and Dick Wade. In some ways, this was good for the flight, since the upperclassmen worked on Tiger and Wade with such passion they almost forgot about the rest of us. Tiger, who wore his heart on his sleeve, was the antithesis of a tiger. The more they attacked him, the harder he laughed. Wade was a good ole boy from the hills of Virginia. He didn't drink, smoke, or swear, and he loved the world. He

---

[117] The *Code of Conduct for the Armed Forces of the United States*, consisting of six articles of personal conduct adhered to by all branches of the service, was developed after the Korean conflict and approved by President Eisenhower in 1955.

[118] "Taps" was adapted from another bugle call during the Civil War. By the late 1800s it had spread throughout the armed forces and was considered a standard at military funeral services.

could have been the model for Gomer Pyle, except for the fact that when he tried to enlist in the air force, he aced every test he took. When they gave him the stanines, he scored nine for nine (a top score of nine on each of the nine tests), an almost-unheard-of performance. At the age of 19, he was chosen for pilot training, but he was still an incurable blitherer.

Because Wade talked like a hick, the upperclassmen thought he was stupid, and they descended on him like a pack of wolves on a wounded deer. The trouble was, he could answer their questions forward or backward, and if asked, probably could have recited the Constitution or quoted Einstein's theory of relativity. By the time the upperclassmen realized they'd been had, weeks had gone by. Wade was still smiling.

Chapter 42 – Turning Dreams into Nightmares

1957–1958

Within the first month or so, 10 percent of the class was gone. We were tested often, and some couldn't cut the mustard. Others chose SIE (self-initiated elimination). "SIE and you'll be free," we sang as we marched, but it was true. If you didn't want to fly with all your heart, it was best to quit, and there were no repercussions. Those who had been civilians were given an honorable discharge and returned to civilian life. Those who were already in the military returned to their previous rank and usually to their previous jobs.

The course was tough, but doable. A few men were incensed by the mental hazing, which admittedly increased the pressure dramatically. Thinking under pressure, however, is vital when flying jets, and this, too, was part of the training.

After a while, the harassment began to ease up, and we looked like we were born in the military. Despite the differences in our backgrounds and experience, the men of 59-Echo were a team. We helped each other when needed, formed intense friendships, and lived by the honor code. I never saw anyone lie, cheat, or steal; even to quibble was a major offense.

Bill Williams and I became close friends. Both of us had had unusual childhoods and learned many of life's lessons as a result. Bill was skilled at word games and crossword puzzles. He was also a wonderful artist; the fact that he drew mostly nudes was fine with me. I know we weren't supposed to be enjoying ourselves, but to me, life was a bowl of cherries, and soon I'd be flying as well.

Of course, my good spirits were also helped by my gal Barbara, who, true to her word, wrote regularly. These letters were my romantic connection to the real world, providing a soft side to the intensity and toughness of my everyday existence.

After we'd been there about five weeks, the 59-Delta class departed for primary flight training, and that Wednesday, six men from 59-Echo were called into the major's office. A Citadel graduate was made cadet colonel (wing commander), another sharp guy was made cadet lieutenant colonel (his executive officer), and Bill and I were made cadet captains (flight commanders). These were the jobs we'd wanted and hoped for, and we were proud as we could be of the four white stripes on our black shoulder boards.

Class 59-Foxtrot was scheduled to report for duty on Saturday, so over the next three days we worked with the cadet wing commander and his lieutenant to consolidate our commands. This time *we* would be the harassers.

That Friday night—November 22, 1957—we went to the Cadet Club a few blocks away to relax, reflect, and live it up a bit. We played bingo and listened to some of the guys do comedy. The laughter and kidding around were lighthearted and wonderful, and Bill and I, though a bit tipsy on 3.2 beer, were at the top of our game.

"All we need to make life perfect," I said, "is a beautiful woman."

"She doesn't have to be beautiful," Bill came back, which drew a laugh from the crowd. "In fact, you know that WAF (Women in the Air Force) area next to ours?"

"Yeah," I said, "but it's off-limits."

And it was, but a light mist was falling, it was darker than a well digger's hinder, and we agreed that we could sneak into the WAF dayroom without being seen. Besides, we rationalized, the women had been locked up, too; they probably needed us as much as we needed them. Obviously, the beer was doing the talking.

In our slightly inebriated condition, Bill and I snuck out of the Club. Keeping close to the shadows, we maneuvered our way outside the WAF dayroom and rapped on the glass. A couple gals looked out. "Get lost," they told us, laughing. Suddenly, the reality of what we were doing sunk in. Here we were, the third highest officers in the class, standing in an off-limits area in our uniforms with nametags in prominent display. "Let's get the hell out of here," I said, and we started back to our barracks.

It seemed like just a few steps when "Halt" boomed out at us from the night.

"Cover your nametag, Bill," I yelled, as the Air Police Airman 2nd Class stepped out of the shadows. We pushed by him and he let us go, but we both knew we were in deep trouble.

Back at the barracks, we went to bed, sick at heart. "If only you give me this one chance, God," I prayed, "I promise I'll walk the walk." Where was that guardian angel when I really needed her, anyway?

Visions of a grotesque painting filled my dreams—orange and white streaks of discord accompanied by a cacophony of equally disturbing noise.

"Get up and get dressed, Wright," barked the air police sergeant who was shining a flashlight into my eyes.

Bill got the same treatment. Sobered and shaken, we were led to an air police van and driven to the brig. Once there, they booked us, took away our belts, and put us in a cell with a can in the corner. Adjacent cells were occupied by drunks and other troublemakers. I stood clutching the high window bars, looking out into the cold, rainy night. In just a few short hours, I'd gone from being at the top of the heap to being crushed by my own foolishness. This was the lowest I'd ever sunk, and it was no one's fault but mine. "I had shit in my mess kit," as the military saying goes, and that night the symbolism fit perfectly.

About 0600, a major arrived to read our rap sheets, which included just about everything but murder.

Off-limits.

Restricted area.

Insubordination.

Drunk and disorderly. And on and on. The final, most serious charge was peeping into the WAF barracks.

The major, who wasn't happy about any of it, inquired about the last charge with some disgust. "We weren't peeping, Sir," I blurted out in our defense. "We were begging to come in out of the rain." Did I detect a small smile? Maybe not, but at least he bailed us out. Restricted to a room by ourselves for the remainder of the weekend, our food brought to us like two guys on death row, we had plenty of time for reflection, self-hate, and guilt.

At first formation on Monday, December 2, we were marched in front of the entire wing, where our esteemed cadet wing commander, the Citadel Puke, spit out the charges against us. In ramrod-straight, marionette stance, he squared off in front of each of us and cut the four-day-old white stripes off our boards, after which we were marched back to our holding room. The whole scene was reminiscent of Dreyfus being stripped of his rank in the French army.[119]

We weren't sure what would happen next, but it didn't take long to find out. "Dress in Class A khakis and report to Captain Bruland's office," we were told. "The FEB will convene at 1500."

The flying evaluation board consisted of the captain and two lieutenants,

[119] In 1894, Alfred Dreyfus (1859–1935) was an officer in the French military when he was wrongfully convicted of treason and sent to Devil's Island. Years later, he was pardoned by the French president and finally fully exonerated by a military commission. The events surrounding this miscarriage of justice are known as The Dreyfus Affair.

Jack Godwin and John Weedon. We knew these lieutenants; they were two of the guys who had lobbied for us to be cadet flight commanders, but we had created an impossible situation.

I went in first. I had never looked more military, even wearing my good-conduct ribbon. I also had never been more scared. The captain's office was arranged like a courtroom. A sergeant, the equivalent of a court reporter, sat to one side, while Captain Bruland, flanked by his lieutenants, sat behind the bench. There was no jury—my fate rested in the hands of these three men. I saluted and snapped to attention.

"At ease, Mr. Wright," said the captain. "Start at the beginning and explain the situation." I told the story as it happened. I didn't add or subtract, lie, quibble, or whine. After asking a few questions, he told me I was excused. I snapped to attention, saluted, and returned to the reception area. Bill went in next. When he returned, we sat staring at the floor, awaiting our fate. We didn't exchange a word. After about a half hour, the sergeant came out and asked us to return.

From the expressions on the faces of our inquisitors, it was impossible to guess the verdict until the captain began to speak. He began by saying a lot of things about our character that I'd rather forget. Then he got to the bottom line. "If it were up to me," he said, "I'd not only wash you out of the cadets, I'd wash you out of the air force. Lieutenants Godwin and Weedon, however, want to give you another chance, and since the FEB is a democratic process, we've come to a compromise. You will each receive a 72-gun salute. Keep in mind, this not only means you'll walk 72 tours and be restricted to barracks; it also adds 26 demerits to those you already have. Wright, that brings your total to 42 and yours, Williams, to 43. If you get to 52, you'll be washed out without another FEB, and *I am going to make it my personal business to see that you both reach that number.*"

The lieutenants were silent, though I thought I detected a twinkle in their eyes. Bill and I had nothing more to say.

"*Dismissed,*" barked the captain, and two very sober but very relieved cadets left the room. We did our first four tours the next Thursday—Thanksgiving Day—followed by an additional four tours each that Friday, Saturday, and Sunday. Around and around we walked, passing on each rotation within 20 yards of the WAF barracks. The WAFs, those cruel and sadistic creatures, loved it, and they'd wait until just the right moment to flash their bare boobs or bums at us as we passed by. Of course, we were shocked at their crass behavior, but we somehow managed to maintain our military bearing and dignity. As befitted the occasion, we were truly thankful.

We had escaped—at least for now. For the next six weeks, our fellow cadets kept us in the middle of groups to protect us, and we led a subdued, monk-like life. Lieutenants Godwin and Weedon protected us, too, steering us out of the way of other officers, and we slid through the remainder of our time with high grades and a low profile. Our biggest challenge was "the shadow," a notorious tactical officer dreaded by every cadet who had ever served at Lackland. Overly tall and skinny, he was a cunning and merciless lieutenant who merged with the night shadows to lay a gig on the unsuspecting or careless. I was up to the challenge. Back on the farm at the age of eight, I'd learned from Freddie the fox how to duck out of sight, blend into the crevasses, and become invisible.

Bill and I both pulled through—by the skin of our teeth. I finished with 50 demerits and a post to Spence Air Base near the town of Moultrie in southern Georgia. Bill's total came in at 51. He was posted to Graham Air Base in Marianna, Florida.[120]

My guardian angel had made me toe a close line, but it was a lesson I never forgot. I was one sober young man when I received my preflight graduation certificate, and after the ceremony, I slithered out of the rear gate of Lackland like a fox leaving the henhouse.

[120] Named after World War I hero Lieutenant Thomas Lewis Spence, Spence Air Base opened in 1941 and trained nearly 6,000 World War II pilots before closing in late 1945. It opened again in 1951 during the Korean conflict and trained another 6,000+ pilots before closing in 1961. The property later became the home of the Sunbelt Agricultural Exposition, but from late 2004 until late 2006, the air force once again used the field for flight training missions, scheduling exercises around Exposition events. Graham Air Base started out as the Marianna Army Airfield, an active training base for Army Air Force pilots from 1942 until it closed in 1946. When it reopened to provide primary flight training for air force pilots in 1951, it was named after civilian William R. Graham, head of the Contract Primary-Flying Training school at this site.

Chapter 43 – Primary Flight Training:
One Down, Two to Go

1958

I flew into Moultrie on a Southern Airlines DC-3 on a mild January day in 1958. My cab driver was a good ole boy, and as we headed southeast toward Spence, he gave me the rundown on Moultrie, the area, and the air base. "You're one of them flyboys, aren't ya?" he said. "Well I've got to tell ya, y'all sure are welcome. The natives love havin' the base here. Some of our folks have jobs out there; the boys come into town and spend their money; and our young gals don't mind seein' all them pretty faces, either. 'Course, that don't mean anythin' goes on that shouldn't, if you know what I mean. In fact, from what I've heard, all the boys out there are real gentlemen and a credit to their country."

When we got to the base, he insisted on showing me around: the flight line with its gleaming, prop-driven Beechcraft T-34 Mentors and North American T-28A Trojans (the planes I'd be learning to fly), plus the Officers' Club and the Cadet Club.[121]

Like most Southerners I encountered, the cabbie was generous, hospitable, and patriotic, and he had a great respect for rank and title. At that time, almost everybody in the South had a relative who'd fought in the Civil War. It was a war as fresh in their minds as last week's football game, and many of them still hated Yankees. But they loved Yanks. After the tour, he dropped me at the reception center and absolutely refused a fare. He sure started one of the best times of my life on a happy note.

I was assigned to the 3302nd Pilot Training Squadron. When I checked in I reported to Captain Marcus Dickman, a tactical officer and one of the

---

[121] The T-34 was a propeller-driven, single-engine plane first delivered to the air force as a trainer in 1953. In the 1970s, the navy purchased a variation of the T-34 with upgraded turbine power. T-34s have been used for training by many countries around the world, and in the U.S. some retired T-34s were used by the Civil Air Patrol. Another single-engine, propeller-driven aircraft, the first T-28As were delivered to the air force in 1950.

few military representatives on base. A calm, friendly guy, Captain Dickman read every word in my file with interest. "Tell me about it," he said, and I did. He smiled. "Mr. Wright, you start here with a clean slate—zero demerits—but the rules are the same. Even though you'll be here for 6 months instead of 3, you still can have only 52 demerits before you get an FEB. And in your case, the remainder of those tours and restrictions from Lackland still apply."

"That's fine with me, Sir. My name might as well be Mr. Clean." We both laughed, knowing that discipline would not be a problem. It wasn't.[122]

For the majority of the next six months, I walked off tours and was restricted to my room, which I shared with three other guys. Considering the alternative, it was a piece of cake. Bill, the lucky dog, fared even better. In the first letter I had from him, he reported that when he checked in at Graham, his tactical officer read his file, roared with laughter, and ripped it up. He never walked a single tour, or at least not one carried over from Lackland.

Four separate classes were in training at Spence at any given time. When we arrived, our class, 59-Echo, was at the bottom of the totem pole, with classes 59-D, 59-C, and 59-B ahead of us. The pecking order was still in place, but here each class had only six months to master primary training and learn to fly, and I remember very little harassment.

McCullough and Pope, my chief tormentors at Lackland, were also at Spence, and Dave McCullough and I soon developed what turned out to be a lifelong friendship. Dan Pope was also a terrific guy, but I never got to know him well. One day during a workout I saw him playing basketball. He obviously had not participated much in sports, and his coordination was a bit off. Flying is sport, and coordination is paramount. Soon afterward he was in the washing machine and before we knew it he was gone.[123]

Spence was typical of many World War II bases reactivated for use after the war: permanently temporary but comfortable, with barracks, mess halls, clubs for officers and cadets, and classrooms. Like more than 50 other such facilities throughout the country, Spence was known as a Contract Primary-Flying Training Base. Here training was provided by civilian contractors who supplied flight, maintenance, and support staff and monitored by a small team of military officers and enlisted personnel.

---

[122] The bald, genie-like character portrayed on several household cleaning products manufactured by Proctor & Gamble.

[123] When a pilot in training was "in the washing machine," it meant he was in big trouble, in danger of being dropped from the program due to deportment- or skill-related issues. Most cadets who ended up in the washing machine did not achieve pilot status, though some remained in aviation to become navigators or systems operators.

The contractor at Spence was the Hawthorne School of Aeronautics, owned by Beverly "Bevo" Howard. An outstanding aviator, in the 1930s Bevo had been the youngest commercial pilot in the country, and he had a long string of aerobatic flying awards to his credit. He was a fine example of the dignity of flying, dedicated to his craft and always accessible to his students.

Spence was a happy place, but it was definitely a military facility. Except for the top class, we marched everywhere in quickstep cadence, though there was definitely a cockiness and sense of freedom in the air. The men of 59-B, just six weeks from graduation and ready for basic flight training in the vaunted Lockheed T-33 or the North American B-25, were exempt from this requirement and could walk at will. They had earned the privilege, and the rest of us treated them with great respect.[124]

We spent our first week almost entirely in the classroom, which was located across the street from our barracks. The following Monday, we were divided into groups of four and assigned to our instructor pilots (IPs), all of whom were either World War II or Korean veterans or ex-airline pilots. Mr. John Kitchens, the IP for our group, put us at ease immediately. "We're going to be spending a lot of time together, men," he said, "so I think I'd better tell you a bit about myself. I flew during the war, and later I joined Pan Am, but airline flying is a tough racket: 24 to 26 days around the world, poor pay, lousy hotels, cheap expenses, and furloughs galore. If you're a captain, at least the pay is good, but even so, commercial flying is anything but easy. So when I heard about this job, I jumped at the chance. It pays well, I like to teach, and I'm home with my family every night."

Getting Down to Business

Flying is a very humbling experience, and if a pilot can't or won't listen to criticism, progress stops and tempers often rip. Thus the most important person in a student pilot's life is not his wife or his priest, it's his IP. Mr.

---

[124] A derivative of the Lockheed F-80 Shooting Star, the T-33 is the most widely used aircraft trainer ever produced. It made its first flight in 1948, was manufactured until 1959, and has been used by over 30 nations. The air forces of some small countries still use the plane in the 21st century, and a small number have found their way into private hands. The B-25 Mitchell, the only military aircraft named after a person, was named after aviation pioneer Billy Mitchell (1879–1936). Nearly 7,000 B-25s were produced between late 1939 and 1945, and in 1942, Jimmy Doolittle bombed Tokyo with these planes. In 1945 a B-25 crashed into the Empire State Building in the fog. This incident prompted architects of the World Trade Center to design the twin towers to withstand the impact of a 707-type aircraft.

Kitchens turned out to be a fantastic IP. Soft-spoken, he was a master at demonstrating the proper technique, then getting out of the way to let the student do the job. He knew how to offer constructive critique, but he had little patience with those who violated regulations. In short, he loved flying, he loved his job, and we loved having him as an instructor.

Unless we were assigned to night flights, which came as our skill level increased, the day started at 0500. The cadet officer of the day played "Reveille" with the scratchiest record in the world, and my eyes snapped open. Roll out of the sack, shower and shave, make the bed, and fall in for formation. Double-time to chow, eat our fill, and return to barracks for a 15-minute break. Five hours in the classroom learning about weather, astronomy, navigational instruments, and the like, then chow, five hours on the flight line, chow, study, lights out.

I had never worked or tried so hard before, and as usual, I made sure I never missed a meal. Food at the mess hall was supplied by Mrs. Beulah Kilgore, the Director of Food Services. Momma K, we called her, and Lord, could that woman cook. "I love my boys and like to see them eat their food and enjoy it," she said more than once, and we were happy to oblige. Chicken, spuds or rice Vichy (an alternative to potatoes and one of Momma's southern specialties), steak, roast, vegetables, cornbread, fresh-made biscuits, and rich desserts, all of it washed down with gallons of milk, coffee, or iced tea. We were served family style—all we could eat—and there were no shenanigans from upperclassmen. I doubt if Momma K would have put up with it.

The mess fed more than our bellies, however. Almost every night after dinner, the clapping would begin. This was the time for any cadet who had had a flying incident or who had soloed that day to jump up on a chair, flap his arms like wings, and relate his adventure to the laughter and congratulations of all.

Unfortunately, not all flights had happy endings. One day as we were marching to the flight line, I saw something out of the corner of my eye. It was the flash of a T-28 going almost straight down, followed within seconds by a mushroom cloud. That night, there was no clapping.

Military flying is intense and unforgiving. The job of a good instructor is to give each candidate a fair opportunity for success, but the job is not for everyone, and occasionally familiar faces would disappear. Most who washed out knew it was time to go; others turned in their wings voluntarily, since no one in the military is forced to fly. Those who remained, no matter how skilled, knew that military flying was risky business. On a certain level we accepted this, and when there were more deaths later on, we were reminded of that acceptance. Nevertheless, deep inside most of us felt bulletproof.

During my checkered academic past, many things had been difficult for me, but flying was my game, my love, and my vocation. Finally I could do one thing very well, but the game was still fickle. Every flight was graded, and check flights came often and sometimes without notice. The training was divided into phases: transition (learning the basic controls of flight), instruments (learning to fly "blind"), and performing aerobatic maneuvers. Each phase was a new challenge. Some students could fly and land well, but when it came time to do aerobatics, they couldn't hack it. Others had difficulty with night flying and navigation. We never knew what might unnerve us until we tried it, and because of this, we worried constantly about the next day, the next test, the next phase. Even a bad break—drifting out of an assigned area due to unusual winds or weather—could be the start of a trip to the washing machine.

In addition to classroom and flight time, we worked out every day. Soon we could run miles or do 114 sit-ups and many, many push-ups with few breaks. We also played a lot of flag football. This time I was the quarterback—a little late for high school glory but fun nevertheless—and every other Saturday we had a track meet, a tug of war, or some other manly pursuit. I had always been competitive and I was having a blast, but our antics were more than fun. Physical performance was part of our final grade, so all those workouts contributed, directly or indirectly, to when and where we would fly. Boy was I glad I'd kicked the smoking habit back in Massachusetts before taking the stanine tests for cadet training.

In every aspect of our training, I was doing the thing I most wanted to do in the company of a group of guys who were, for the most part, equally thrilled to be there. Two of these characters were my "roommates Fred." One of them, Fred Gregor, was from the Northwest. He was in love with a beautiful gal back home, and her picture held a place of honor in the room. We knew Fred's girl was special, and everybody in the barracks paid homage to the maharani.

The other Fred, Fred DeJong, had emigrated from the Netherlands after World War II. As a boy, he'd watched American fighters in the skies over his homeland and was determined to follow in their footsteps. Fred was a tall, good-looking dude who spoke half a dozen languages and was one of the smartest guys in our class. He also loved to harass me every chance he got.

I always needed more sleep than most, so given a 20-minute break, my favorite pastime was to zonk out for 19 minutes and 40 seconds of it. Fred looked upon these breaks as perfect opportunities for harassment; he just couldn't leave me alone. One day he pushed too far, and in my half-asleep state, I threw a punch at the old schnozzola. Fortunately I missed, but from that point on my sleep was not interrupted.

In the classroom, Fred was all business. Math had never been my strong point, and while I hovered midway in the rankings, DeJong probably set every record for academic achievement. It was more than frustrating to slave away on a navigational problem, twirling my E6B calculator and taking the total time allotted, only to watch him finish in a flash with his answers always perfect. And yes, he did help me—when I begged. Thanks, pal.[125]

Creative Solutions to an Age-Old Problem

Despite the intense pace and worries about performance, I was happier than I had ever been, with one exception. My life was almost totally devoid of women. On Saturdays, Sundays, and holidays I walked tours, and even if I'd had any free time, I was restricted to barracks. I did get frequent letters from my gal Barbara back at Otis, and the hint of her perfume made me pine even more for contact with the fairer sex.

My pals suffered no such deprivations. As a requirement of the program, all cadets were single, and the local gals were particularly fond of us. They saw us as romantic (try restricted and horny), adventurous, and on the government's payroll. Second lieutenants in the making, we'd soon be earning the enormous sum (including flight pay) of $222 per month. Every Friday night, busloads of gals were shipped to the Cadet Club, but I never saw them. I was honor-bound to myself not to challenge the rules again. Of course, the guys delighted in treating me to wild tales of their conquests, and even though most of it was pure bull, I was a great audience.

Eventually, I found a legal way to preserve my honor while simultaneously gaining access to an almost unlimited source of femmes fatales. Each Friday night, I volunteered as cadet officer of the day, which meant I had to inspect the barracks, the mess hall, the reception center, and the Cadet Club for unauthorized activity. It was a job I took seriously, particularly the part about protecting southern womanhood from the ravages of a bunch of uncivilized Yankee bastards.

Each Friday I would dress in my Class A tailored uniform, don an armband identifying me as cadet officer of the day, and think of myself as Rhett Butler incarnate. I was *shocked* to find such womanizing going on at the Club. Many an evening I felt it my duty to separate a beautiful Georgia

---

[125] The E6B Flight Computer is a form of circular slide rule used primarily in aviation to calculate such things as fuel burn, wind correction, and time en route. Developed by U.S. Navy Lieutenant Philip Dalton in the late 1930s, the device takes its name from its original part number under the U.S Army Air Corps in World War II.

belle from some Yankee dog, after which I would take the lady aside to write a long, slow deposition.[126]

"Are you all right, Miss," I'd ask with concern, and even though the answer was almost always in the affirmative, it was important to be sure. Sometimes I'd have to touch body parts to see if an injury had occurred. After all, lips were delicate, and peach-like skin could be easily bruised. Of course, as an officer candidate I could be fully trusted, and they smelled sooooo good.

---

[126] Rhett Butler was a character in the 1936 novel *Gone with the Wind,* by Margaret Mitchell, an epic story of the Civil War, or the War Between the States as it was known in the South. In 1939 Metro-Goldwyn-Mayer released a movie version, with Clark Gable playing the dashing, pragmatic Butler and Vivien Leigh the equally pragmatic southern belle, Scarlett O'Hara. The film, an overnight success, won eight Oscars, including Best Picture. Rhett is probably best remembered for his classic line to Scarlett: "Frankly, my dear, I don't give a damn."

Chapter 44 – Learning My Craft

1958

Under Mr. Kitchens' guidance, I became more skilled and more confident with every flight. Eventually, I heard him say the magic words: "Pull over here, Mr. Wright, and I'll get out. Go shoot a few landings solo; you're ready and you're doing just fine."

It was true I'd soloed in the Piper J-3 Cub, but the T-34 was a totally different animal. This was an aircraft with flaps, retractable landing gear, and an array of switches that would put the Cub to shame. Alone in the cockpit, I felt the unique exhilaration of knowing my survival depended upon doing my job, and flying this baby was the thrill of my young life.

After a couple of solo flights, I was flying with Mr. Kitchens again to learn more advanced maneuvers. Solo or dual, the T-34, a takeoff on the Beechcraft Model 35 Bonanza, was a fun and easy plane to fly. After six weeks, I had my first check flight with one of the chiefs. Even though I was nervous, I aced it. It felt great!

Moving Up

The weeks had flown by, and Class 59-B was ready to graduate and move on to basic flight training. At the graduation ceremony, Bevo Howard treated all to a demonstration flight in his antique Buecker Jungmeister biplane, including flying upside down along the runway, inches from the concrete, and snagging a banner.[127]

After he finished, a flight of F-86s from nearby Moody Air Force Base put on a show of their own. *Someday*, I thought, *I'll be up there*. In the meantime, our class had moved up a notch and was eligible to fly the T-28A Trojan.[128]

---

[127] Bevo Howard was killed in 1971 when his Buecker crashed. In a tribute to their boss, employees of Hawthorne spent more than 3,500 hours rebuilding the plane, presenting it to the Smithsonian in 1973.

[128] Located about ten miles northeast of Valdosta, GA, Moody (named in memory

The North American T-28A Trojan.
(*National Museum of the USAF.*)

A fighter often used by emerging nations, the North American T-28A Trojan looked a bit like the Republic P-47 Jug of World War II fame, except that it used tricycle gear. The models we flew were underpowered, with an 800-horsepower engine that sounded like a John Deere tractor, but to me the plane had neck-snapping performance. We even wore helmets, making me feel like a real fighter pilot.

Could I master such a complex machine? You bet I could. I did more than fly that airplane; I strapped it to my backside and we became one. The continuous roar of the T-28s on the flight line, mixed with the smooth, higher-pitched sounds of the T-34s, was like a balm, and the smell of oil, that Castrol-like odor common at racetracks, was even sweeter. When the mechanics ran up the engines late at night, we could almost feel the plane beneath us. In the silence that followed, we waited for the new day to begin.

As we became more skilled, cross-country day and night flights were not uncommon. However, a body could get mighty hungry on these treks, which often lasted for up to two hours. Duane Jewell, a pal and fellow cadet from Columbus, Ohio, had an instructor who anticipated this problem. One night he shouted to Duane through the noise, "Hey, Bucko. Want an apple?" Of course, Duane has been called nothing but Bucko ever since.

Our time was packed with academics, flying, and physical training. Before we knew it, Class 59-E was head of the pack, our six months of

---

of Major George Putnam Moody) was opened in 1941 to train Army Air Corps pilots during World War II. It closed in 1947 but was reopened in 1951 to support the Korean conflict. In 2008 it is still an active air force facility.

primary training nearly complete. Now it was time for another worry. The final phase of the program, basic flight training, was divided into two groups. Those who were going to be fighter pilots moved on to the Lockheed T-33, the famous T-Bird. The rest, destined for bombers or duty as cargo pilots, were assigned to the B-25. I was in the top third of my class, and I wanted that T-33 assignment with every fiber of my being.

At long last, I walked enough tours to complete my 72-gun salute. I had dodged the bullet and paid the price, and that Saturday I left the base for the first time. Riding through the Georgia countryside, I felt like a lifer with a presidential pardon, but I was back on base in time for one of the frequent Saturday night dances.

Relieved of protecting the virtue of defenseless southern womanhood, I particularly sought out one of the gals I'd admired from afar. She was wearing a low-cut summer dress, with just enough cleavage to show off her peach-like skin. With her auburn hair glistening softly in the low lights, she was a magnet for those Yankee vultures, and several circled around her. Cutting through this rabble, I offered her my arm, and even though I was dressed in civvies for the first time in months, she recognized me as her dashing protector. Dancing to the tune of *Moonlight in Vermont*, I maneuvered her to the farthest and darkest part of the floor and pulled her close. I breathed in her fragrance and felt her breasts caress my body. In that moment before she pushed me away, I'm pretty sure she felt something, too.

"You, suh," she said with feigned indignation, "are supposed to be an officer and a gentleman, but Ah believe you have lust in your heart."

I stepped back and bowed. "Forgive me, dear lady. Passion has gotten the best of me." She smiled and pulled me close. It was a wonderful night.

The next weekend was a holiday. Armed with a three-day pass, a fellow cadet named Chuck and I set off for Florida in his decrepit, ten-year-old Chevy. We stopped to pick up Bill Williams and a pal of his in Marianna, then headed east toward Tallahassee. Bill directed us to the student union at Florida State, left us in the car for a few moments while he went in, and emerged trailed by four beautiful women dressed in shorts and halter tops. Defying the laws of physics, all eight of us piled into the car. "To the beach," said Linda, the gal sitting on my lap. "My Uncle Bob has an empty cabin there."

Chuck turned the car in the direction indicated, and each time we accelerated or stopped, Linda's perfectly formed body parts caressed mine. Oh, what delicious, sensual feelings. After stopping for beer and snacks, Linda directed us down a deserted road where we stopped beside a cabin at the edge of a beautiful white sand beach. Linda put her key in the door. It didn't work. Had that rascal Uncle Bob changed the lock? Sure enough, it looked new.

"Never mind," said Linda, who ran to the back of the cabin, pushed open a window, and started to crawl through.

"Stop," said I, with my manly Rhett Butler smile. Maidens shouldn't be climbing through windows. I had no choice but to do it myself. Once inside, we set out the chips, loaded some 78s on the record changer, popped a few cans of cold beer, and hunkered down. Let the action begin.[129]

Screeeeeeech! What was that? By the time I stepped out the door, the car had stopped and two enormous guys were charging toward me. "What the f---- are you doing here?" bellowed one of them. I held up my hand as calmly as I could. "It's okay, Uncle Bob, your niece Linda invited us."

"I don't have a niece, and I'm not your Uncle Bob. You sons of bitches are trespassing again, and I'm going to call the police and throw your collective asses in jail for breaking and entering."

Okay, I'm not the brightest light in the sky, but I figured this situation out pretty quickly. We were all in deep doo-doo, but at the moment I was alone with these extraordinarily pissed off rednecks, and I was a terrible liar. I had, however, quite a bit of experience at begging.

"Look here, fellas," I said in my most convincing tone, "we're a bunch of fighter pilots—*okay, I was bit premature*—who are defending our skies from marauding Russians, and these lying, lecherous women deceived us big time."

Never have I negotiated harder or with more at stake. Yes, it turned out, their cabin had been broken into more than once. Yes, the lock was new, and yes, they had screwed up by not locking the window, though I soft-pedaled this last point in the interests of achieving some sort of détente. By this time, the rest of the group had joined me outside and were inching toward the car. I went back into the cabin with "Uncle Bob" and friend. We looked the place over thoroughly; no damage had been done. "We really had no idea what we were getting into," I stressed once again, "but in light of the

---

[129] Music of this era was recorded on flat discs called records. Usually black in color, records are played on devices known as phonographs or record players. Some players allow stacking of multiple records, which are then released one by one to play automatically. The records themselves are identified by their rotation speed: 78s (usually ten inches in diameter) play at 78 rpm. Other common speeds are 33 rpm and 45 rpm. The last 78 was issued about 1960. With the advent of compact discs and other, more modern media, nearly all record production ceased in the 1980s, though some specialty records are still released in the 21st century.

situation, perhaps you gentlemen would be kind enough to take these cold beers and snacks off our hands."

While they contemplated this offer, I made a hasty retreat, jumped into the car with the rest of the gang, and got the hell out of there. We'd definitely been set up, but we'd also fallen for it hook, line, and sinker. Despite some mighty strong provocation to do otherwise, we actually returned those blinketty-blink gals to campus, but not without a few words. Back in Marianna, we spent a pleasant evening at the base, dancing with the locals and reminiscing. That night I had a heart-to-heart talk with my angel. Did she have a weird sense of humor? There wasn't a direct answer, but I got the impression I needed to look a bit closer before I leaped.

Making the Cut

My last six weeks of primary training were uneventful, but the flying continued to be beyond belief, including cross-country flights in the daytime and at night, as well as solo, aerobatic, and instrument flying. Occasionally, Mr. Kitchens would send us up with another instructor, and although most of them were good, they couldn't hold a candle to our superior IP. One of these substitutes took a very different approach. He was a brute of a man, and in the air he bullied and shouted. After we landed, he jumped on the wing and shouted some more. I was worried he might fail me for the flight, but the debriefing was calm. "Good job, Wright," he said as we shook hands. When I compared notes with some of my classmates who had this guy as a regular instructor, they laughed and said that was his normal demeanor. "If you aren't lucky, you shouldn't be a pilot," goes the saying, and I was one lucky guy. Thanks again, Mr. Kitchens.

During my last week at Spence, I had a final check ride with military representative Major Uriel Johnson, a slender man with a fighter pilot mustache and a chest full of ribbons and medals from World War II and Korea. I aced the ride and received a hearty attaboy. His approval meant a lot, and it was one sweet day. Later that week, a formation of four F-86Ls from Moody made a low flyby. Watching their sleek-swept wings gleaming in the sunlight as they flew in perfect symmetry, I was deeply touched. Was this my future?[130]

Our final grade consisted of three parts: academics (classroom training), military (physical training, conduct, military bearing, leadership, inspections,

---

[130] Also known as the Sabre, the F-86 fighter jet was first manufactured in the late 1940s by North American and was used extensively during the Korean conflict. In a succession of improved models (the F-86L being one of them), it became one of the most-produced Western jet fighters during the Cold War.

judgmental aspects of observation), and flying (in-air performance). My academics were not stellar, but they were okay, and I finished in the top 10 percent in military and the top 20 percent in flying. My next assignment: Greenville Air Force Base, Greenville, Mississippi, *flying T-33s*. One more hurdle conquered. Only six months to go 'til the silver wings and maybe—oh, please—fighters.[131]

Graduation was July 16, 1958. Unlike my departure from Lackland, I left Spence through the front gate, duffle bag in hand and head held high. I was feeling on top of the world. Bevo Howard ran a first-class operation, and Mr. Kitchens was the best instructor I ever had anywhere. Captain Dickman and Major Johnson had also been perfect leaders. They treated us with respect and allowed us to develop with a minimum of interference. Primary flight training is the place where young birdmen learn the most, and at the beginning there is so much to learn.

---

[131] This base started life as Greenville Army Airfield, a training facility for pilots during World War II. It was closed for a brief period after the war, then reopened as Greenville Air Force Base. Pilots and other personnel were trained there until 1965. Thereafter the base was closed and the property turned over to the City of Greenville.

Chapter 45 – Practice, Persistence, and Possibility

1958

Ihad a week's leave before reporting to Greenville, and my first order of business was to get some wheels. I took a bus from Moultrie to Robins Air Force Base, about 20 miles south of Macon, Georgia, then hitched a ride north on an air force transport.[132]

The first thing I did was to see Barbara at Otis. It was a short visit. When I left, we were still an item, but it was clear that absence had not made the heart grow fonder. Next I was off to Buffalo, where I picked up my treasured MGTD. Uncle Walt and Aunt Carolyn were glad to see me and I them, but my primary focus was to get to Greenville for basic flight training, and I was eager to head south. John Holody, a Buffalo native and one of my classmates from Spence, had also been assigned to Greenville. Johnny was another one of many young Americans who were given the chance to succeed vis-à-vis the cadet program. The son of a steel mill laborer, he had a keen mind, good hands, and a tremendous sense of fun, and our two-car caravan started off in great spirits on the long trek to Mississippi. In Columbus, Ohio, we picked up Bucko Jewell in the third slot, three guys with our tops down and our spirits high.

We made it to Louisville before my car broke down. Hours later, dirty but unbowed, we pressed on, but eventually I had to drop out of formation. My smiling MG just wasn't hanging together. About 50 miles from Greenville, it died again. By this time, I had a little over 12 hours before having to report

---

[132] Construction of this facility, which was named in honor of Brigadier General Augustine Warner Robins (1882–1940), was started in 1941. During World War II, the base trained tens of thousands of field mechanics and provided maintenance/repair services and supplies. It also played a pivotal role during the conflicts in Korea, Vietnam, and the Persian Gulf. In 2008, Robins is the largest industrial complex in Georgia, with a workforce consisting of more than 25,000 civilian, contractor, and military personnel.

in on July 24th, so I started hitchhiking, knowing I could go back for the car later. A couple picked me up and then drove out of their way to drop me at the base around 2200. These folks were kind, polite, and liked the military, but just to be on the safe side, I talked as little as possible and hoped they wouldn't notice my Yankee twang.

Greenville was yet another permanent, temporary air base, but here our civilian instructors had been replaced by military personnel. A postage-stamp-sized place, it was one of a hundred such bases built during World War II, its buildings almost interchangeable, its function a cog in the mass production that helped America gain a leg up on the world.

There was no Pope or McCullough to greet me here, just the bored young airman of the day. I signed in and he pointed me to my barracks, where I found a bunch of guys sitting around in their skivvies, sweating, laughing, and swapping lies. These fellows, assembled from Spence and other primary training bases, had either chosen or been selected for the T-33. The B-25 boys had gone to Texas, the last class to train on the plane that gave America its victory in Jimmy Doolittle's "thirty seconds over Tokyo."[133]

Buckling Down

It was near the end of July when I started at Greenville, and the heat was constant. The classrooms were air-conditioned; the barracks, where a giant attic fan labored to bring in more hot, humid air than it dispelled, was not. It didn't matter; we were on the final lap, and sitting close by were lines of gleaming Lockheed T-33As.

Greenville Air Force Base, front gate, ca. 1955.
(*Courtesy of Billy Ray Smith, webmaster of the Greenville AFB reunion Web site.*)

---

[133] Doolittle's April 1942 raid on Tokyo was immortalized in the book *Thirty Seconds Over Tokyo*, by Ted W. Lawson, and in the 1944 film of the same name starring Spencer Tracy, Van Johnson, and Robert Mitchum.

A tandem-seat jet, the T-Bird was America's first production jet fighter. The head of Lockheed's design team was Kelly Johnson, primary designer of the F-80, the precursor of the T-33, and of the P-38 forked-tail devil of World War II fame. Any plane designed on his watch was a winner. The T-Bird was a solid, responsive, and forgiving aircraft and the one on which most pilots learned to fly. Originally introduced in the late '40s, its engine was slower to respond than more modern aircraft, but this drawback only helped to teach the skills of planning and anticipation to the burgeoning pilots of the world.

The next morning we formed up early and headed for the mess. Back at Spence, Momma K might have served the best lunch and dinner in the world, but for me, digging into a basic mess breakfast was like coming home. The line stretched before me: my favorite SOS—rich, creamy, brown, and covered with eggs to order—along with bacon, sausage, pancakes, toast made from freshly baked bread, biscuits, and gallons of milk, juice, and coffee. Bring on the day.

After breakfast, we met our instructors, mostly lieutenants or captains, and had our first academic classroom briefings. Then I joined the rest of my flight (Blue Nine, a unit of the 3506th Pilot Training Squadron) as we headed out to meet our instructor pilots. Once again, for the next six months the IP was going to be the most important person in my life.

Although we rubbed elbows with most of the guys on the base—Greenville wasn't that big a place—the members of each flight formed their own special bond. One way the system built this esprit de corps was by issuing patches. All wings, squadrons, and flights had their own unique patches. Some were officially sanctioned by the air force; others were not. Blue Nine's patch was a rascally blue cat painting himself with orange stripes to look like a tiger.[134]

When we got to the classroom at the flight line, something just didn't feel right. Our flight commander was a reserved, serious man, a retread from Korea and SAC (the Strategic Air Command). SAC had come into its own under the command of General Curtis LeMay, a harsh, cigar-chomping World War II hero who was dedicated to our country's defense and its role in the Cold War. Although General LeMay left in 1957 to assume the role of air force vice chief of staff, his hard-driving legacy was still very much in evidence. The men of SAC served a pivotal and necessary role in our country's defense, and they did their jobs well. Humor, however, was not one of their strong suits. I never wanted to be a member of SAC.[135]

---

[134] Beginning in World War I, airmen painted emblems on their planes. Later, these and other symbols were translated to cloth patches that could be sewn onto flight jackets, flight suits, and so forth.

[135] General Curtis LeMay (1906–1990) was the commander of the Strategic Air

At Spence our instructors had been first-rate, but except for Major Johnson and Captain Dickman, Greenville was my first experience with military flyers. Here we faced a group of officers who looked as if they'd eaten boiled babies for breakfast and were now suffering from indigestion. Only one had a relaxed, human look about him. After being introduced, the IPs descended on the students, who were grouped into fours at tables around the platform. Everyone snapped to attention.

Was my angel smiling at me once again? That one human-looking officer was coming toward our table. "At ease, cadets" said Captain E. C. "Easy" Hall as he waved us to our chairs. Guys at the other tables were still braced at attention.

That night and on many nights thereafter, the 40 members of Blue Nine Flight were a subdued group. During our time at Greenville we did our job and did it well, and after a while things got better, but we never felt the joy we wanted to feel. In contrast, Bill Williams, my partner in crime at Lackland, was also at Greenville, but he'd been assigned to Pink Four. This flight, led by an old fighter pilot named Roy Killian, had a naked blond in a champagne glass on their patch. They got the job done, too, but they had a blast doing it.

The Lockheed T-33A Shooting Star.
(*Pima Air and Space Museum, courtesy of Ben Fisher.*)

The saving grace for me was my IP. Easy Hall was a skilled pilot and a superb instructor with a sense of humor. His flights were as smooth as silk, yet he flew very aggressively. Remembering my first flight with him in the

---

Command from 1949–1957. In 1957 he was named vice chief of staff for the air force and later promoted to chief of staff, a post from which he retired in 1965. In 1968 he served as the running mate of independent U.S. presidential candidate George Wallace.

T-33 still makes me tingle. Following the briefing, we suited up in flight gear, strapped on the seat parachute, and walked to a flat trolley for the ride to the plane, parachute banging softly against the backs of our legs. The flight line was bursting with activity and the day was sweltering. Sixty airplanes were scheduled to take off at the same time, with each flight averaging an hour and a half. Heat bounced off the tarmac and blended with the delicious smell of burning kerosene. There was no place else on earth I'd rather be.

I climbed into the pilot's seat, with Captain Hall in the IP's spot. The T-33 was an old airplane, without many of the simplifying devices available on later models, so starting the engine was a complex process involving multiple switches and levers. It was sweltering in the cockpit but too hot outside to lower the canopy. I could have cared less, as I was totally focused on the litany of flight unfolding before me: the whine of the engine, the salute from the crew chief, taxiing with no steering (most military aircraft have no steering wheel), using differential braking to point the plane in the desired direction, extending the flaps, checking the speed brakes, and executing the checklist. In the flight business, checklists are the lifeblood of safety. Memory can deceive, and deviation can cost lives.

Mobile control flashed a green light for takeoff. Because there was so much activity, radio communications were kept to a minimum, and a click on the mic was often the understood signal. I pushed up the throttle, slowly, so I didn't overheat the engine. I'd never felt such power, and the jet picked up speed at a rate faster than I'd ever experienced.[136]

Liftoff: smooth and clean. Landing gear up, flaps up, and then quiet. Through the headset in my helmet, I could hear Easy Hall breathing through his oxygen mask.

It was a perfect summer day. I was flying as I'd been taught, smooth and easy, with gentle turns. There was almost no need for rudder. After a bit, Captain Hall took the T-Bird and demonstrated a few maneuvers; then we flew on toward the transition area.

The air space around the base was divided into three quadrants: transition, formation, and instrument flying. The transition area was dedicated to basic maneuvers and aerobatics, and we started with relatively easy exercises: lazy eights (like sideways figure eights) and chandelles (steep, climbing turns that roll out after 180 degrees at an exact speed).

---

[136] At most air bases, all traffic is handled by the control tower. Training bases, due to the high volume of traffic making approaches and landings, often used supplemental airstrips located away from the main base. These remote airstrips were usually controlled by off-duty pilots in a miniature tower, often a mobile unit mounted on the back of a truck.

"How about some aerobatics, Mr. Wright?"

"Yes, Sir!"

Aileron rolls, the more difficult barrel roll, then a loop, and I felt the familiar symptoms caused by the gut-grabbing 4 to 5 Gs needed to go over the top. Blood rushed from my head to my lower extremities, which in turn narrowed my field of vision, causing a grayout. As we'd been taught, I locked my jaw, grunted, and tensed my muscles to resist the Gs.[137]

"Time to go back, Mr. Wright."

"We just got here, Sir." But that had been over an hour ago, and it was time to head to the home drome. As we approached the field and reduced speed to 250 knots, we saw the line of jets heading toward the end of the runway, spacing themselves for landing. We came in at 1,500 feet and pitched out: a 180-degree, 3-G turn downwind to kill speed prior to lowering gear and flaps. A final turn reduced airspeed to 140 knots.

One of the world's greatest IPs: Captain E. C. "Easy" Hall, Greenville Air Force Base, 1958.

Manipulate the power, pull back the stick, feel the eeerk-eeerk of the tires hitting the tarmac, roll out, taxi to parking. The ground crew waved us to a stop, wedged in the chocks to keep the wheels from moving, and gave the knife-at-the-neck signal to kill the engine.

"How did it go, Sir?" the duty airman asked when I hit the ground. "Great. Aircraft's okay. A piece of cake!" I was almost too jubilant to talk. My eyes were stinging. My heart was in my throat. At debrief, Captain Hall described a maneuver so clearly that I pictured it and then flew it with precision.

The flight had been magnificent and I was walking on air.

When Life Gives You Lemons . . .

In flying, as in life, success depended upon being able to press on no matter what. When mistakes were made—and training was where it was safest to make them—the idea was to use the experience to become a better

---

[137] A person standing still on the ground is experiencing one G (one times the force of gravity). When an aircraft changes orientation rapidly because of tight turns, loops, etc., the pilot is subject to additional G-forces, either positive (when the aircraft pitches up, the nose pulls upward) or negative (when the aircraft pitches down, the nose goes downward). Grayout is caused by an increase in positive Gs.

pilot. In most cases, this was the way it worked, although on occasion, one could still face some chicken crap.

About my second week at Greenville, 2nd Lieutenant "Moon" Mullins, a brand new instructor and our military officer, met our flight at dawn as we marched to a day of flying adventure. Each flight had such a guy, whose job it was to be the inspector for all things military—in other words, everything that wasn't covered by academics or in-flight training. Most of them were good guys. A few weren't.

"Attention," barked Lieutenant Mullins, opening the flight for inspection and trooping the line as if he were a foreign dignitary. When he got to me, he stood square in front of me, spewing profanity and spittle in my face. "Mr. Wright, the tongues of your boots are not shined," he screamed. [138]

I can take it, I thought, *let it rip.* I continued to stand at attention and he continued to yell. Finally he said, "You are a lemon, Mr. Wright. From this time forward, you are to wear a lemon on your dog tag chain so the entire world will know you're a lemon. Do you understand?"

"Yes, Sir."

"Louder, Mr. Wright."

"Yes, Sir, Sir!"

"Dismissed."

None of us could begin to guess why the attack had happened or why I'd been singled out, but the next day, Major John Barker, our squadron commander, stopped me in the hall. "What the hell is around your neck, Mister?"

"A lemon, Sir."

"I can see that. Why?"

"Lieutenant Mullins said the tongues of my boots needed shining and that I was a lemon and that I should wear the lemon."

"Get that f------ thing off," he ordered, wheeling away angrily. I hope the shaft I jabbed into Mullins' back had the same shine as the shined tongues of my boots. We never talked or faced off again, but oh, to be a fly on Lieutenant Mullins' wall.

Playing the Mating Game

During the week, we were busy with academics, flying, and physical training, all to the constant whine of jet engines in the background. A few pilots got to test their parachutes, and occasionally a pilot would buy the

---

[138] Moon Mullins was a comic-strip character in a syndicated strip that ran from 1923 until 1991. Many guys named Mullins ended up with "Moon" as a nickname.

farm—crash or eject—and Uncle Sam got to purchase the finest and most special cotton that farmer had ever grown.

On weekends, we explored the Mississippi landscape, and it was one fine sight. This state was bachelor heaven, and my happy little MG was repaired, smiling, and ready to go. One of our favorite places to hang out was Fieldings Drive-In at the corner of Main and Edison, where the parking lot was filled with fancy cars, British or German models, Corvettes, and so forth. Just months from becoming second lieutenants, we were a safe bet for Greenville bankers and car dealers, and many of my fellow cadets were more than happy to take advantage of their kind offers.

Fieldings' lot was also filled with beautiful women who lusted after our bodies, or at least after our wheels. My MG was considered cute and the gals all wanted a ride. I tried to accommodate as many as possible (one at a time, of course), but our weekend passes ended at midnight and there were oh, so many of them. Prior to taking them for a ride, I did patiently explain that I was Saint Don, the Virtuous, but my temperamental MG seemed to break down often on the levy overlooking the Mississippi or on the shores of Lake Ferguson. When it did we were stranded, and with the moonbeams racing across the river and after my close escape from the lustful women of Georgia and Florida, it was hard to be celibate. Still, I fended them off to the best of my ability.

One afternoon, Bill and I decided to take a break from the mating dance to go bowling—my first time since living in Japan. And who should be there but Dick Wade, my pal from preflight training at Lackland, with a very classy chick on his arm. Where did ole Wade come up with a chick like this? He, with his constant smile, introduced us. Her name was Polly Horne. She seemed a bit uncomfortable in the surroundings.

Over the next few weeks I danced a tune or two with her and talked to her a few times at the Cadet Club. She was a typical Mississippi beauty who lived next to Fieldings and taught Spanish and French at Greenville High School for the handsome sum of $3,065 a year. (Back then, in some ways Mississippi was a third-world country.) Polly was thrilled when I offered to give her the tour in my shiny red MG, but she did comment that the car had a reputation as unpredictable and prone to break down in inappropriate places. I assured her that all was well, and that day the car was on its best behavior. I, too, was on my best behavior, but we agreed it wouldn't do to let the fickle MG overheat. So just to be on the safe side, we let it cool down on the levy while we watched the sun sink into the horizon.

After being locked up with a bunch of fellow cadets who talked of nothing but flying and careers, it was a welcome diversion to chat with Polly.

We started comparing backgrounds, schooling, and ambitions—a huge area to cover considering we were both at the beginning of life and had bright futures. She was well-read and a graduate of Mississippi State College for Women (MSCW), but although she lived a short three hours from the Gulf, she'd never seen the ocean. In those times, most Americans stuck close to home.[139]

We conversed that evening with ease, yet we were somewhat guarded, and she didn't seem to invite the shenanigans I was used to. At first, our worlds seemed light years away. I'd traveled extensively; she hadn't. I was undereducated; she was a college graduate. She was a classical pianist and sang; I was merely a wannabe. She had majored in languages at college and spoke both French and Spanish fluently, with barely an accent. My stab at mastering German had fizzled years before.

But we also found common ground. Polly was very active in the Presbyterian Church and the Westminster Fellowship, and I, too, had remained a lifelong Presbyterian. For one thing, they forgave me for calling them a bunch of piss pots at the age of three, and for another, it took most of my young life for me to spell Presbyterian, and I wasn't up to another spelling challenge. The unpublished church motto, *decent and in order*, spoke to me as well, and both of us agreed that church was a good and neutral place to be. Polly had been born with unquestioned faith, and I had that concerned and discerning angel who was with me at all times, except, of course, on those distinct occasions when I was sure she'd taken a vacation.

Too soon the darkness surrounded us and it was time to return to reality. Polly enjoyed the camaraderie of the air force scene, and I hoped we'd meet again, but I knew it was best not to get too close.

Not all cadets took the same tack. In an area that had seen a lot of economic hardship, we were about to become wealthy wage earners at $222 a month, and then to fly the world's best aircraft in exotic lands. The local beauties knew a good deal when they saw one, and the guys had been locked up for a long time. It wasn't surprising that many an innocent fellow was led to the altar upon graduation.

---

[139] Chartered in 1884 in Columbus, MS, as the Industrial Institute and College, the school changed its name in 1920 to the Mississippi State College for Women and in 1974 to the Mississippi University for Women. Although the 1974 name remains the same, men have been admitted since 1982.

Chapter 46 – Earning My Wings

1958–1959

Captain Hall was an excellent IP and I was an easy and grateful student. I loved what I was doing and it showed, which made life easy for both of us. Check rides came and went, and although I had my share of butterflies, I continued to be competitive. Formation was a kick, too. Soon we could fly in formation with two, three, or four ships, executing the same precise maneuvers in unison. If the lead pulled 4 Gs as he should, numbers two, three, and four would be pulling 5 and 6 Gs.

Aerobatics were a big part of the program, and in reality, we were almost as good as the Thunderbirds, with the significant exception that they flew at 500 feet or less and we were at 25,000 feet.[140]

One day I was leading a four-ship formation. An instructor-student combo was in slot number four; two other students were solo in slots two and three. We were doing well and enjoying the flight. I cleared the area, saw it was free of other formations, and pulled into a loop. Soon came the familiar grayout and tensing of muscles. Peripheral vision closed down like a cone, and I'm sure if a camera could have caught our faces, they'd have looked like contorted masks, loose skin being pulled off the bone.

Over the top, down the back, all's well. Then wham! Another four-ship formation, going the other way and doing a loop as well, sifted through ours, so close that I recognized Wade in the cockpit. The formations dissolved. No one hit anyone else, but each plane returned to base alone. In the fuel time we had left, it was impossible to identify and rejoin our respective flights. When we landed we were soaked in sweat, our flight suits salt-encrusted, and our oxygen mask lines driven into our faces. Despite the close call, it had been a wonderful workout. Pilots are trained to have their heads on swivel, and we always kept the area clear, but when some planes are upside

---

[140] This U.S. Air Force air demonstration squadron was created in 1953 and is dedicated to exhibiting the capabilities of high-performance aircraft and the skill of the men and women who fly them.

down and others right side up and all are traveling about 500 knots, things happen fast.

Everybody who loved jets loved formation, but like anything we did, some were better at it than others. If a cadet wasn't comfortable racing along on a wing with three or four feet separating him from the next guy, it was a huge challenge. Since we started at Lackland, about 35 percent of the class had left, which was about average attrition. Some had dropped out of their own volition; a few others had departed due to military or deportment problems. Most failures, however, were a result of not learning to fly properly in the time allotted.

Now graduation was near, and about a week before we had received our class standings. Out of a class of 100, I was ranked 30th. Available assignments were posted in the auditorium, and each man was called up, in order of class rank, to make his selection.

The choices looked something like this:

F-86L (8 slots)
F-86F (8 slots)
F-100 (6 slots)
BIS (Basic Instructor School) (2 slots)
B-52 (10 slots)
B-47 (6 slots)
C-124 (4 slots)
C-130 (6 slots)
Helicopter (3 slots). . .

The list went on and on. *Please, Lord, save me a spot with the F-86L.* I thought about my Wentworth days, when the F-86 had been the center of my flying fantasies, and here I was, just moments from knowing whether my dream would become reality. Besides, if I made it to the F-86L, I could move on after six months to the Convair F-102 Delta Dagger, the Lockheed F-104 Starfighter, or the Convair F-106 Delta Dart. To me these were the world's most glamorous fighters.[141]

---

[141] First used by the air force in the mid-1950s, the main purpose of the F-102 Delta Dagger was to intercept Soviet bomber fleets. It was later replaced by other aircraft, including the F-104 Delta Dart. The F-102 was used by the Air National Guard in the 1960s and was phased out in the 1970s. The F-104 was a single-engine, high-performance, supersonic jet aircraft used by the air force for about ten years starting in the late 1950s. These planes were also used by the Air National Guard until the mid-1970s. The F-106 Delta Dart, sometimes called the "ultimate interceptor," was used by the air force from the 1960s until the 1980s.

The first pilot went to the stage, updated the number beside his desired choice (4 slots becoming 3, for example), and took a white slip indicating his preference to the sergeant recorder. The Basic Instructor School (BIS) slots went first. If instruction was your thing, this was the best job in the world: lots of flying time, home every night, and great working conditions. Others ahead of me picked fighters; a couple chose bombers. When my name was called I tried not to swagger: F-86L (3 slots; 2 slots left for Moody Air Force Base). Yes!

Cadet Donald R. Wright, Class 59-E, Greenville
Air Force Base, 1958. Note that I managed to
earn back a couple of stripes.

But I knew it was too early to celebrate. I'd made that mistake before. I had one more check ride to pass: a 60-4 instrument flight check. Named after a section of the air force operating manual that defines its parameters, the 60-4 is the examination a cadet must take to become a pilot and that all air force pilots must take annually to maintain their status. The focus of the test is on instrument flying. The pilot to be tested sits in the backseat and pulls a hood on rope slides under the glass canopy. He then takes off, flies from point

A to point B, and demonstrates his ability to set up several different landing approaches without ever seeing outside the aircraft.[142]

Sure I had butterflies—my life and my career were riding on this flight—but I was confident and comfortable with instrument flying. I'd better be; I'd just signed up for the F-86, an instrument-driven, all-weather interceptor.

Dennis Blackman, a major from headquarters, came down to give me my 60-4 check. I saluted and we sat down and briefed the mission. He was a pleasant guy, thorough and nonthreatening. We went to the parachute room, suited up, grabbed our helmets and oxygen masks, and enjoyed a bit of quiet chatter as we rode to the plane. "I'll do the preflight, Mr. Wright," he said when we arrived, and while he went over the checklist, I strapped in and built a nest with my maps and book of approach plates.[143]

Once we were both settled, the major lowered the canopy, I pulled the hood, and we took off. It was a quiet, cool January day, and I put on a good show. The mission was scheduled for an hour and 45 minutes of flight, and I was having the best check ride I'd ever flown.

After about 45 minutes, I heard a voice through the mic: "Okay, Lieutenant."

Lieutenant? "Did I hear right, Sir?"

"Yes you did. That's as good a ride as I've seen. Get out from under the hood, Lieutenant Wright, and congratulations."

Music and cymbals. Is that the *Boléro* in climax?[144]

"Let's take the rest of the ride and play," said Major Blackman. Off we went to the transition area and practiced all the aerobatics we knew. We rolled; we looped; we did Immelmanns (an advanced maneuver named after World War I ace Max Immelmann). You name it; if it could be done, we did it. He did an exercise, then I did one, a friendly competition on what was becoming the best day of my life so far. We pulled Gs 'til I thought the Bird would bend. The plenum chamber fuel tank light came on to tell us we had only about 20 minutes of fuel left, and the major started back to the home drome. With my arms resting on the canopy rail and as happy as one can be, I started up a friendly conversation.

"When did you start flying, Major?"

---

[142] In 1959, only men were trained as air force pilots. Women began training as pilots in the 1970s and as fighter pilots in the 1990s.

[143] Approach plates, which give the pilot the length of runway direction and electronic frequencies to fly to a landing in all conditions, are different for every airport in the world. They are most important when weather is poor.

[144] *Boléro* is a classical piece written by Maurice Ravel in the 1920s. It was made famous in more recent times in the 1979 movie *10* starring Bo Derek.

"Korea," he replied.

"What did you fly?"

"The F-86."

"Oh, man. Get any kills?"

"Yep, got a couple, but I got shot down. When I tried to eject, the canopy blew off but the seat misfired, so I crawled out of the cockpit, hit the tail, and broke my back."

I was hanging on his every word. "What happened then?"

"The chute opened and I was picked up by a chopper, rushed to a MASH unit, and then sent to a hospital in Tokyo."[145]

"Did you ever go back to combat?"

"Yep, but that's a story in itself. I spent a few weeks in the hospital, and when I recovered I was ordered back to combat in Korea. But first I was given a 72-hour pass. That night, three buddies and I went to an Italian restaurant in the red-light district of Honmoku in Yokohama to celebrate."

A cold chill went down my spine. *Naw*, I thought, *it couldn't be*.

The major continued. "We were having a quiet dinner when these punk teenage SOBs next to us got into a brawl. I ended up in the brig in a world of hurt, and those bastards got away."

Ohmagod! Thank heavens I was hearing this tale through the mic rather than face to face. "That's quite a story, Sir," I said with as much of an even tone as I could muster.

Just about then we entered the pattern, pitched out, made a smooth landing, and taxied in. Major Blackman debriefed the mission, offered his congratulations again, and went on his way. I wanted to shout after him, "I'm really sorry about the fight, Sir," but of course I didn't.

That day taught me just how small the world can be. One careless act can cause damage to those we don't even know, and what happens today can come back to haunt us far into the future. Funny how that angel of mine added just the right touch to keep my conscience alive.

After a lifelong love affair with fighter planes and the pilots who flew them, I'd finally filled in all the squares. I was extremely happy, but rather than the wild exuberance I would have predicted, it was a quiet kind of joy. As we waited for graduation day, I was proud, sober, and reflective. During my journey I had slipped and come close to falling and failing, but thanks to

---

[145] MASH (Mobile Army Surgical Hospital) units, familiar to many because of the long-running television program of the same name, were complete, portable hospitals designed to operate in a combat area. The first MASH units were employed in Korea, and they continued to be used in Vietnam and later conflicts. The last MASH unit was decommissioned in 2006.

hard work, a healthy measure of luck, and the help of that lady in white riding on my shoulder, I'd persevered.

The graduation ceremony on January 28, 1959, was understated, and the general who delivered the commencement address (a navigator) predicted we'd all be out of jobs as technology replaced pilots with guided missiles and drones. Fortunately, even he couldn't kill the moment, and I received the silver wings of a pilot and the gold bar of a second lieutenant with a combination of pride and humility. I WAS A JET PILOT!

Polly came to the ceremony and pinned the wings on both Dick Wade and me. I couldn't help but notice how good she looked. *Maybe we'll write*, I thought. Afterwards, I threw my trusty duffel bag in the MG, along with a bag of new officer uniforms that had set me back nearly $500. Despite my $222 paycheck, after buying uniforms and paying for food (only enlisted personnel received free uniforms and board), I was already in debt. Fortunately, an officer's credit is always good.

Sporting our brand new wings! *L. to r:* Me, Dick Wade, and fellow cadet Tom Zellner on graduation day, January 28, 1959.

Transitions

My commission was under President Eisenhower, a patriot I admired for his performance in World War II, his role in the presidency, and his dedication to the security we now enjoyed. I was proud of my country, its leaders, and myself, and I was ready and well-trained to do what was necessary to protect our nation from its enemies.

We had three weeks until our next assignment, and I really wanted to go north to show off my uniform and brag a bit about my success. But February travel in the MG would have been a disaster, and nobody could afford to fly commercial. So I rented a small house in Greenville with two other guys. One was Bill Williams, who was going off to fly the Boeing KC-97 Stratotanker in Texas.[146]

The other was a guy from Blue Nine Flight named Bill Meyer. Meyer was a cultured, enjoyable fella who introduced Williams and me to hi-fi music and had all the expensive electronic accessories to make it happen.[147]

The three of us worked little, pulling only light duty at the base with some flying, and we ate well, mostly steak and lots of it. We also dated almost nightly, our fancy cars a continuing magnet for Mississippi womenfolk. I still had my red MG and Meyer had a beautiful Porsche that he kept shined like a mirror. All in all, it was a relaxed interlude, one of the most enjoyable times of my life.

At the end of our transition period, I took off for Moody in Georgia and Bill went to Texas and was eventually stationed at Plattsburgh Air Force Base in Plattsburgh, New York. Meyer also headed to his assignment, but on the way something failed in the front end of his Porsche and it flipped over. He was killed instantly.[148]

---

[146] The KC-97 was an aerial refueling tanker that the air force began operating in 1950. These planes continued to be used by the Air National Guard until the late 1970s.

[147] Short for high-fidelity, hi-fi was a method used to produce high quality sound without distortion. It reached its heyday in the 1960s and '70s with the introduction of the LP (long-playing), 33-rpm vinyl record.

[148] Plattsburgh, located east of Lake Champlain and only 20 miles from the Canadian border, was the oldest military post in the U.S. The original land for the facility was purchased by the federal government in 1814. From the mid-1950s on, it was used by the Strategic Air Command (SAC). The base closed in the mid-1990s and was converted to an industrial complex operated by the Plattsburgh Air Base Development Authority.

Chapter 47 – F-86 at Last

1959

On the drive east to Georgia, my wonderful little car performed perfectly, and I stopped at a truck stop before I got to the base to shower and shave. As I put on my uniform, I paused briefly to admire that studly guy in the mirror with his silver wings, gold bar, and good conduct ribbon. It was late February 1959, and as I drove into Moody I saw an F-86 stuck on a pole in front of the headquarters building. Only five years before, I'd been studying at Wentworth and staring at a picture of this baby on the wall of my apartment in Boston. It gave me goose bumps.

I signed in and stowed my gear. I was now an official member of the 3553rd Fighter Training Squadron, Class 60-A. Unmarried second lieutenants were housed in the BOQ (bachelor officers' quarters), two-man apartments with a small kitchen. We didn't need more, since we'd be taking most of our meals in the mess, at the Officers' Club, or on the flight line. My apartment mate was Tiger Taylor. Tiger (along with Dick Wade) was one of the blitherers from Lackland and a great stick. Our first order of business was to sample breakfast at the mess. Being the world's leading authority on SOS, I pronounced this variety fine indeed. It even seemed to glow around the edges.

The drill was the same as at Spence and Greenville: academics half the day, flying the other half. We spent the first six weeks under the hood in the backseat of a T-Bird, earning what I guess you could say was a doctorate in instrument flying. Then we went on to the F-86L, the all-weather interceptor.

The F-86L is a powerful airplane, but compared with the T-Bird, it had one of the shortest fuel ranges in the history of fighters: from 25 minutes to an hour and a half, depending on the use of the afterburner. An afterburner adds an enormous amount of thrust to an aircraft, but to deliver that power it literally pours raw fuel into the tailpipe. Several weeks before I arrived at Moody, the limitations of that range had caused a disaster known ever after as Black Thursday.

North American F-86L Sabre.
(Pima Air and Space Museum, courtesy of Ben Fisher.)

On the day in question, the usual mass of 80 or so airplanes, a mix of T-33s and F-86s, took off. No sooner had they cleared the field than an all-encompassing fog rolled in from the Okefenokee Swamp, a huge area east of the base. Conditions dropped to 0/0 and the tower made an emergency recall. Within seconds, jets converged on the radio markers like bees on a hive. The pilots were highly skilled instrument flyers, but the base was soon overwhelmed. Some of the F-86 pilots punched out (ejected from the aircraft and parachuted down); others landed their planes on roads and highways.[149]

Still others joined up in formation, and several groups landed by following the leader as the tower talked him down on a GCA (ground-controlled approach). Of course, this method took much longer to handle all the aircraft, and some pilots just didn't have enough gas to wait. One of my upperclassmen was on the wing in formation at 500 feet when his fuel-starved engine quit. He punched out. My future instructor actually flew to the marker, pitched out like it was a VFR (visual flight rules) day, and picked up the ILS (instrument landing system), accomplishing in about ten seconds what normally would have taken five minutes or more. He was as good as they get.

Nobody believed it could happen and I'm sure heads rolled, but we weren't privy to the details. Nevertheless, by the time our class started, the powers that be were as shy about flying as a virgin on her wedding night. So if

---

[149] At that time, minimums for landing were 200 and a half (200-foot ceiling/ half-mile visibility). In 2008, electronics automated through the autopilot allow airliners and fighters to land under 0/0 conditions, but in 1959, even autopilots were not a common feature, especially in fighters and trainers.

the weather wasn't clear and ten (no sign of storms; ten miles of visibility), we played bridge. Okay, I exaggerate, but you get the idea. There were no deaths from this disaster, but several aircraft were destroyed (no doubt provoking a parade in the USSR), and many pilots earned their caterpillars.[150]

No Time Off for Good Behavior

Now that we were officers, we had fewer restrictions on our free time. And since most of my friends were bachelors, I was prepared to use my experience to lead these young pilots through the fields of Georgia and Florida women. After all, I had firsthand knowledge of their tricky, dangerous, and lustful ways. So when Johnny Holody showed up with a new bride, I was shocked, and when Rud Wasson, a wonderful friend from northern Minnesota, drove up in a new Triumph TR-3 with a lovely lass from home and wedding bands firmly affixed to their ring fingers, I was totally at a loss.

The shock soon wore off, and it wasn't long before I realized that home cooking had been missing from my life. Rud loved to play bridge, his wife Timmy was a delightful hostess, and we would show up at their doorstep unannounced with steaks, beer, and cards for an evening of food and fun.

Otherwise, life really wasn't much different than it had been as a cadet. Second lieutenants were still lower than the south end of a north-bound skunk. In fact, word had it that a second lieutenant rated with a cup of spit.

Like everywhere else in the military, competition reigned supreme. I was doing fine on the flight line and with the military aspects of training, but in academics I began to lose my way. The instructors were outstanding as usual, so I wasn't quite failing, but I wasn't up to snuff either. Old habits die hard, and I found it tough to relinquish my spot at the stag bar in order to study. After all, the worst assignment I could get out of Moody was a Northrop F-89 Scorpion, and these planes were often being changed out for Lockheed F-104 Starfighters, a dream machine for any pilot.[151]

---

[150] Parachutes have been around in one form or another for hundreds of years, but the first ripcord chute was designed by American Leslie Leroy Irvin. Initially used in 1919, it was soon adopted by the American Air Corps and the British R.A.F. Irvin's friends suggested he start a club for those whose lives were saved in an emergency descent by his invention. The result was the Caterpillar Club, so-named because silk was used in the parachute's construction. The club slogan: *Life depends on a silken thread.* From a membership of two in 1922, the club now boasts tens of thousands of members worldwide. Each member receives a gold caterpillar pin with his or her name and rank on the back. Ironically, despite making over 300 jumps, Irvin was never eligible for the club he started.

[151] A jet-powered, all-weather interceptor, the F-89 was used by the air force for

At the end of our first six weeks, we were split into flights and I ended up with Captain John Matthews, a legendary fighter pilot and flight commander we often called Black Jack, though not to his face. The captain was a former member of the Thunderbirds and a reported wild man. He was also a stickler for "sharp," demanding that we wear clean flight suits with a distinctive orange patch on our shoulders, that we wear an orange dickey, and that we lace our spit-shined boots with orange laces. And to make sure we followed these proscriptions, he pulled inspections galore. Oh, man. The lives of our classmates in the other flight were much looser, and they never failed to yank our chains. My IP, Lieutenant John A. Mellor, was a typical fighter pilot. About my age, he was highly skilled, cocky, and always smiling, and he instructed with an edge of humorous sarcasm. He challenged me to do my very best, and since he was intolerant of anything other than 110 percent, I gave 120.

The F-86L was the last derivative of the most beautiful jet ever produced. The F-86A was built just before Korea and held a huge kill ratio over the vaunted MiG, a statistic due as much to the pilot as to the plane. The L model was being phased out as the industrial might of America built even more sophisticated airplanes and armament, but as a training plane it was perfect. It had radar in the nose and a fierce afterburner. It was slightly supersonic, although it took almost a vertical dive and full afterburner to achieve that speed.[152]

Pilots flying the F-86L were radar-guided to the target from the ground. Using onboard radar, the pilot could then close and make the kill, deploying the 24, 2.75-inch Mitey Mite rockets stored in a retractable bay beneath the plane. The joke was that when the internally unguided rockets were released, 6 went straight, 6 went to the left, 6 went to the right, and 5 turned around and came back like a boomerang. The 24th locked up in the tube, and when it retracted, it blew itself and the F-86L to smithereens. And what would happen if we needed it in combat?

Electronically lock on to the target.

Fire.

Put your head between your legs and kiss your ass goodbye.

All joking aside, the F-86L was an important stepping stone in the development of combat fighter aircraft, and I couldn't wait to fly it!

We spent hours in the classroom studying the engineering components

---

several years, beginning in 1953. It continued to be used by the Air National Guard through 1969.

[152] MiGs were fighter planes produced by the Soviet Union and used by many countries, including North Korea during the Korean conflict.

that made this hotrod tick, including the electronics and radar fire-control system. And since all flights in the single-seater airplane were, of necessity, solo, my IP sat with me on the ground, perched on the rail surrounding the cockpit area to explain the function of every control. This plane had more dials and gadgets than any I'd ever flown, and just prior to my first flight, I was blindfolded and had to identify every one of them by touch.

Flying My Dream

Finally the day arrived for my first flight. Parachute, helmet with the ubiquitous orange stripe, and oxygen mask in place, I was ready to go. I did the preflight check: leading-edge slats, dents, leaks, tailpipe cracks, covers off, pins out, a thorough examination of this sleek, graceful machine.

We could mount the aircraft using kick slots embedded in the fuselage, but this day, as we did most of the time, I used a portable stand. Even so, I felt like a cowboy climbing aboard his trusty steed, though the F-86 was neither docile nor well-broken.

Despite all my study time, the jet felt larger than it looked. The crew chief helped strap me in and connected the oxygen and radio cords. My IP would be flying wing, and he sat in the plane next to me, accomplishing his own preflight chores.

The crew chief departed and I had a few minutes alone before takeoff. Here I was, 25 years old and about to realize a lifelong dream. Never one to miss a good time, surely my angel was with me; heaven knows she'd earned the privilege. On my way to this day, I'd tried to stay focused on the prize, but both my eye and my mind had sometimes wandered. A whiff of perfume, the turn of an ankle, or a beguiling smile from the opposite sex had occasionally rerouted my plans, but thanks to my no-nonsense angel, I'd never been completely derailed. Today there were no ladies out there—just me, my dreams, and the sky.

* * *

I heard the check-in in my headset.

"Nails One, how do you read?"

"Five by, Nails Two."

I see the circle of the finger from the ground crew and start the engine. The wonderful growl of the jet drowns out the higher whine of the gyros.

Pre-taxi check. I look at my wingman: thumbs up.

The chief pulls the chocks and pins. I show him my canopy- and seat-ejection pins and salute. Canopy down; it's a cool day.[153]

Completing our taxi checklists, our flight of two heads toward the runway. The tower clears us into position. As always, my mind focuses on any unusual eventuality. I breathe a short word of thanks to the man above and to my angel—the greater the challenge, the greater the need.

Nails Two is tucked in on my wing.

Head back, throttle up, head snapping forward, brakes off, round the horn. The afterburner kicks in with a boom; I'm thrown back in the seat. What spectacular acceleration!

Airborne and a steep climb. Bring up the gear and flaps, then turn out of traffic.

Head back and afterburner off. Another head snap and a huge loss of power.

Nails Two tucks in as we fly toward the transition area. A quiet excitement and pride surges through me as we begin doing turns, lazy eights, and chandelles. I wave Nails Two to trail position and we do the loop, the Cuban eight, and other aerobatic maneuvers. Holy cow, the fuel is almost gone.

Back to the home drome, fly up initial, pitch out, speed brakes, gear and flaps down.

Touchdown! I pop the drag chute to assist with braking, then taxi and park.

As the engine winds down, I pop in the ejection-seat pin.

I scramble out of the plane, eyes stinging. "How'd it go?" says my IP John, with a handshake.

"Piece of cake, Sir. Piece of cake."

* * *

If my professional life had stopped at that moment, it would have been complete. I had flown the dream, the fighter, the vaunted F-86, *and it was just the beginning!*

---

[153] When an aircraft is on the ground, each landing gear assembly has a pin inserted into it to keep it from collapsing due to human error or mechanical failure. The pins must be pulled before takeoff or the landing gear will not retract.

Chapter 48 – Hitting the Target

1959

A fter a lifetime of hope and years of preparation, I was finally learning to fly the plane of my dreams. Each time I climbed into the F-86 I gave a nod to my angel for letting me get this far, sometimes in spite of myself.

For the first part of our training, we spent a lot of time in a simulator. Because this device was entirely dependent on vacuum tubes—the transistor was invented in 1947 but had not yet made it into simulator technology—the electronics room was as big as a house. The simulator failed often, but it was still the most advanced I'd ever seen, and it was an invaluable training aide.

The next step was to practice our attack skills in the air. While flying the airplane with our right hand on the joystick, we used our left hand to manipulate a small control stick that operated the plane's radar. Classmates in T-Birds towed mock targets called drones, three-foot-long shapes coated with radar-reflective metal. The idea was to locate a drone by positioning a white dot over its location on the radar screen. Once the dot and the drone were aligned, we could push a button to lock in the radar-tracking mechanism. It was a difficult task, requiring practice and coordination.

We got feedback on our performance in two ways. First, our instructor watched us from the air, often on our wing. Second, each plane was equipped with Nadar, an electronic black box that recorded our attacks. After each flight, the instructor played back these recordings in the briefing room. They were a vital learning tool, as we could see and feel our improvement. We were good and getting better.

A couple of missions were full-alert, afterburner attacks. We'd take off to 40,000 feet in minutes, simulate a rocket attack (two, if lucky and the intercept was just right), and be scored electronically. Then we'd dive to the runway, declare a fuel emergency, and land: 25 minutes total time.

Other missions were designed to practice aerobatics. During the grand finale, we pointed the sleek jet straight down with full afterburner and cracked the sound barrier. File another check in the book of life.

A few flights were set aside for good ole dogfighting. On one of these, I went up on the wing of my flight commander, Black Jack Matthews. We did some basic maneuvers pulling Gs, chasing each other, and learning a scissors technique designed to get on our opponent's tail for the kill. For a while, Captain Matthews would let me succeed. Then we'd separate and come back at each other. Closing at more than 1,000 miles an hour, we'd pass, pull up, and start fighting again.

I was feeling pretty confident, holding my own against the pro, when I lost him. Turning frantically, I looked around. Where was he?

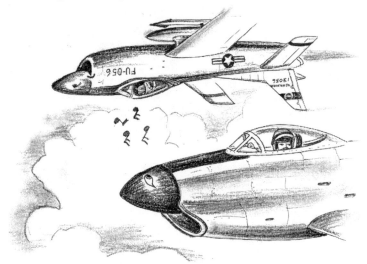

"Off we go, into the wild blue yonder."
(*Illustration by Babe Sargent.*)

Then I heard the whistle in my headset: "Off we go, into the wild blue yonder." I'd found Captain Matthews, upside down, locked firmly in position on my wing. I got the point. We had a great laugh and he complimented me on my burgeoning abilities, but I knew I had much more to learn. The concertmaster versus the student, Mickey Mantle against the college all-star—ours was a profession that required talent, dedication, and practice, practice, practice.[154]

---

[154] Mickey Mantle, named after Baseball Hall of Fame catcher Gordon "Mickey" Cochrane, was born on October 20, 1931. Nearly losing his leg to osteomyelitis when in his teens, Mantle went on to become one of baseball's most valued players, winning numerous awards and setting a record for the longest home run. He retired from baseball in 1969 and died in 1995 at the age of 63.

All that practice kept the adrenaline pumping, but now that we were second lieutenants—as lowly as such status might be in air force parlance—we were exempt from organized physical training. In fact, most of our physical activity consisted of raising elbows at the bar, particularly after flights. Barroom debriefs, unlike their official counterparts at the flight line, were loud, boisterous, and exciting. Hands poised, we demonstrated successful and unsuccessful wing or attack positions. We were totally absorbed in our work. It was more than a job. Flying was our hobby, our lifestyle, and our first love.

On weekends we partied at the Officers' Club, paying homage to bevies of lovely women. We had to be careful, though. The townsfolk, particularly the men, weren't nearly as enamored of us reckless jocks as they'd been at other bases. Could the problem be that we protected the local ladies from these crass rednecks? We never knew for sure, but the police set up camp outside the gate, and heaven help the jock in his fancy car who exceeded the speed limit or was caught DWI.

Despite this less-than-enthusiastic welcome, Georgia food was delicious, the barbeque in particular worthy of the finest in the South. At the S and K Drive-in, situated at the fork in the road to Valdosta, local belles sashayed from car to car, discussing each vehicle's power, speed, color, and rating. Occasionally, a demonstration drive was necessary. The length of the drive was equal to the beauty of the Georgia Peach. With a fancy sports car and a steady paycheck, we were targets of opportunity.

Involuntary Jailbirds

One Saturday, my buddy Jim Mueller asked if I would drive him to Jacksonville, Florida, to pay a rather large traffic fine. Jim was the sharpest guy in our class: Handsome and square-jawed, his shoes were shined to blind. There was never a wrinkle in anything he wore, and I was careful not to stand next to him during inspections; I didn't relish the comparison. Jim's dad had been a P-47 fighter jock in World War II, an ace with over five kills. Sadly, he'd been killed himself on a secret mission just prior to D-Day. Jim was proud of his dad and with good reason, but on this day he was more concerned with his own, ground-based mission. It seemed he'd been pulled over near Jacksonville for speeding and didn't have his driver's license with him. This combination of errors had earned him an exorbitant $80 fine.[155]

---

[155] Pilots with five kills are designated an ace; those with ten kills are a double-ace. Jim's biological father was James Wilkinson. After the war, his mom remarried and Jim was adopted by his stepdad. Later in life, he changed his name back to Wilkinson.

Jim gave the sheriff in Jacksonville a $100 bill, receiving a measly $20 in change. It seems we didn't leave all the predators at the sheriff's office, however. Taking a shortcut home through the swamp in my low-slung, top-down MG, we met up with a large cougar that bounded out of the bushes close enough for us to feel his hot breath. We quickly accelerated out of reach, but I was thankful the MG wasn't in one its cantankerous moods.

Jim had left his own car, an MGA, at the S and K, where he offered to buy lunch. He paid the carhop with the $20 bill he'd gotten that morning and we ate in his car, griping about the unfairness of the local constabulary and soaking up the Georgia sunshine. While we waited for our change, a covey of police cruisers pulled into the parking lot, sirens blaring.

"Wonder what's going on?" Jim mused.

"I dunno."

The next minute, we were surrounded by five cop cars. Seven or eight cops, their Gestapo-like uniforms lending a menacing air, ripped us out of the MGA, threw us in the back of a barred paddy wagon, and drove to the police station in Valdosta. Without so much as a howdy-do, they booked us, took our pictures and fingerprints, and pulled off our belts. Nothing was said about a charge. Finally the sheriff came to our adjoining cells.

"Do you Yankee bastards think y'all can come down here and pass counterfeit $20 bills?

"What are you talking about, Sheriff?" We looked at each other and broke out laughing at the absurdity of the accusation. Then we tried to explain that the twenty came from the Jacksonville, Florida, Sheriff's Department, but our Georgia sheriff was not listening. Finally I broke into his tirade and demanded our right to a phone call.

I wasn't sure who to call, so I asked the switchboard operator at Moody for the base commander. Fortunately he answered.

"Colonel, we're in a tough spot," I said as I explained the situation, and he was there in a flash.

While the colonel looked at the offending twenty, the sheriff stood by, silent but reveling in the importance of his petty authority. In reality, the sheriff was an ordinary-looking guy, but in my mind's eye he was the personification of every stereotypical sheriff I'd ever watched on the big screen: fat gut ballooning over his belt, six-shooter hanging low on his hip, and a cud of tobbaky drooling down the unshaven crease of his weak jaw.

"Let me call a friend, Sheriff," said the colonel, and before long the president of a local bank showed up. The bank president looked at the bill in question. "Well, I'll be darned," he said, "I haven't seen one of these in years."

The sheriff was in his glory. "We're gonna put these boys away for a while," he said with a lopsided grin.

"No, Sheriff, this bill is a 1920s silver certificate, legitimate money and probably worth a bit more than twenty bucks."

Everyone had a good laugh except, of course, the sheriff.

"Let's go," said the colonel.

"Sir," Jim said, "we were booked: pictures, prints, and all."

"Sheriff, let's rip 'em up," said the colonel.

"Can't do that, Colonel; once booked, always booked."

A storm cloud passed over the colonel's face. "Sheriff, if I don't get those booking documents right now, I'm calling the mayor. This town will be off-limits to air force personnel forever."

The sheriff backed down, as bullies usually do, and we got the stuff—but no apology. Maybe he was still punishing us for Sherman's march. All I know is, from that day forward I avoided driving *into* town unless I was driving right back *out* of it on my way to somewhere else.

Chapter 49 – Polly's Story

One night there was a big party at Rud and Timmy Wasson's. When I arrived, I discovered that the Wassons had invited Polly Horne for a visit. Ostensibly, she was in town to see Wade, but I'd been intrigued with this beauty since the time in Greenville we'd talked at the levy until sundown, and I was more than delighted to find her gracing the plains of southern Georgia. I sure hoped she was glad to see me, too.

Polly had adopted our class in Greenville and knew many of us. Wade, the human computer, had often averaged the grades of her high school Spanish and French students in his head. No wonder she was fond of him. But Polly had a dream. She wanted to be a stewardess. She'd always had an ambition to travel, and when she first graduated from college, she'd been hired by Delta Air Lines. Unfortunately, the beginning of the Delta training class coincided with a date to remove a troublesome mark near her eye, and she ended up taking an offer to teach at Greenville High School instead.

Sometime after I left Greenville, she got a second chance and accepted a job with Delta. The requirements were to be comely and attractive and to speak a foreign language; having a degree was a plus. Now she was flying to the Caribbean and Venezuela from her base in New Orleans. The job was a serious responsibility, but it was also a wonderful lark.

I was eager to talk with her again, and we soon found ourselves away from the party, soothed by the harmonic sounds of the marsh and nearby swamp.

"I guess you're just doing a bit of common work before returning to the plantation," I quipped.

Polly laughed, remarking that, actually, her dad was in oil. *Oh boy,* I thought, *this is just what my mother envisioned for me: a rich wife, a plantation, and oil.* After all, it's just as easy to marry someone rich as someone poor. I moved a bit closer and wished I could be more charming.

Polly took all this in, her amusement showing through the sparkle in her eye. "He's in oil, all right," she said. "He's the manager of a Billups gas station, and he's never earned more than $400 a month in his life." I wasn't even disappointed, and I stayed as close as I could as she began talking about her family and its beginnings.[156]

Southerners almost always know where they came from, and their stories are usually filled with pride, humor, and a never-ending cast of characters. Polly came from deep southern roots. Frank Gard and Emma Bryan, her paternal grandmother Nellie's folks, met at a music conservatory in Staunton, Virginia. Her paternal grandfather, Claude Rutledge Horne, hailed from Knoxville, Tennessee, where he'd grown up with his folks, William Asbury Horne and Katherine Kelso Horne, and his siblings William Armstrong, Katherine, and McDonald (Don) Kelso. After Claude and Nellie were married, they moved to Carrollton, Mississippi, a hill-country town above the Delta, where Claude became the prosperous owner of Horne's General Store. All these years later, Polly said, the sign was still there.

Nellie was beautiful and talented, and she and Claude had a prosperous and happy life. Children—Claude Jr., Frank Gard, Emma Louise, Katherine Kelso, Nellie Elizabeth, William Armstrong II (Billy), and Rebecca Charlene (Gardie)—arrived in short and continuous order. But in 1919, when Gardie was only two months old, Nellie, who was suffering from nephritis due to pregnancy, died at the age of 36. She was sitting up in bed and she just stopped breathing. Claude had worshiped his Nellie, and finding it impossible to cope with her death, he abandoned responsibility for their children. Claude's brother, William Armstrong Horne, was a prosperous businessman and cotton trader. He sent some of Claude's kids to a Presbyterian boarding school called French Camp Academy, a kind-but-disciplined school that Polly felt sure was "decent and in order." Uncle Don and Aunt Louise Horne took in young Elizabeth and Billy. Lela Gillespie, an unmarried friend of the family in Carrollton, took in Gardie.[157]

Early in the 1920s, held family folklore, Claude and a local businessman invested in selling gasoline and kerosene. Then they hatched a scheme to sell gas as kerosene and avoid the federal tax. When they were caught, Claude took the fall and spent a short time in jail.

Despite such a rocky beginning, all of the children developed into successful adults. The girls became nurses and Frank a lawyer. Claude Jr.

---

[156] Billups was a southern oil firm with the logo of a hand reaching out and the motto *your friend*.

[157] Located in French Camp, MS, on the Natchez Trace National Parkway, French Camp Academy was established in 1885. In 2008, it still serves as a Christian boarding school, now non-denominational, for children from troubled homes.

was somewhat of a drifter, but he finally settled down in Texas. Billy was the runt of the litter, a child who'd been born sickly. As an infant, he didn't seem to do well on milk or solid food, and although the doctor tried everything he knew, the outlook was grim. Lela Gillespie had suggested that Nellie feed him mashed sweet potato. With nothing to lose, she'd given it a try and Billy had perked up. He was never as vigorous as his siblings, but he grew strong enough to enjoy a normal life.

When an adult, Billy worked "in oil" and become Polly's dad. Like so many folks who have major upsets in their lives, he was an optimistic, cheerful, God-fearing man whose needs were few. He loved the church that gave him so much support, sang in the choir, read voraciously, and was able to squeak in a couple years of college before the crushing Depression forced him to quit school and go to work.

About that time in Polly's yarn, the dinner bell went off and we rejoined the group of young fighter pilots with their wives or gals. Mounds of steak and ribs, spuds, bread, and salad added to the camaraderie of the day.

After dinner Polly and I talked some more. "How about your mother's family?" I asked, and she went on to describe her incredibly beautiful mom, a farm girl from Kilmichael in Montgomery County, Mississippi. Her mother's ancestors had emigrated from the Carolinas sometime in the 1800s, she said. Kilmichael wasn't rich Delta land, but it wasn't hill country either—just decent farmland that grew cotton, watermelons, and lumber. Polly's grandparents, Walter and Lula Allen Hamer, were farmers like their kin before them.

Walter was quiet and overworked, Lula was stern and overworked, and the children arrived early and often: Oscar, Nan, Neal, Pauline, Juanita, Quinby, and Elizabeth. They were not an unhappy family, but like many families of the Depression, they weren't necessarily close.

Their mantra was survival: fun and pleasure were not things they experienced often. They'd inherited the farm and it was paid for. There was no electricity or plumbing, but the place was clean and spacious enough for the large family. The boys were handsome and the girls were southern beauties. But beauty doesn't pay the bills, so everyone worked—before school, after school, on weekends, and in the summers. Tomorrow's crops were the future, and the Hamer kids picked cotton, hauled watermelons, and helped the way farm kids did everywhere.

One morning, hot and tired after several hours in the fields, Walter sat down on the porch, had a stroke, and died. He was 56 years old. At the time, Oscar was in his early 20s and Nan had already left to become a nurse. The others were still at home; Lib was only six.

Relatives in the area offered little assistance and life went on as before:

work, work, and more work. When Lula died the following year at the age of 48, people said she just wore out. The kids tried to hang on, but they couldn't even make the taxes. One enterprising cousin paid the $400 tax bill and took title to the land. The kids got nothing.

Oscar took in Quinby and Elizabeth, and the others scattered. They were undereducated, but they left with a determination that only hardscrabble farming can breed.

Pauline, who was to become Polly's mother, was 17 when Lula died. She recalled with bitterness the day she left the farm. Turning her back on everything she'd known in her young life, she was permitted by her good cousin to leave with the clothes on her back and her new pair of shoes. Like countless others, Polly's mom was a victim of fate and the cruel, worldwide Depression. As a result, she carried a thin current of dissatisfaction that lay just under the surface of her otherwise happy life.

Pauline Hamer and Billy Horne married in 1935. She was 18; he was 24. Ten months later, on February 17, 1936, Polly was born in Winona, Mississippi. When Billy married Pauline, he felt he was the most fortunate man in the state, and he never changed his mind. Polly wasn't sure how her mother felt, but she was a good wife and the marriage seemed to work.

After a couple of insignificant jobs, Billy was hired by Billups Oil as a station manager. By 1942, he was making $50 a week. He worked hard, managed well, and treated everyone, black or white, fairly and with respect. Polly said she never remembered him taking a vacation longer than a three-day weekend, and when she was growing up, he often worked seven days a week.

The family moved several times over the years, mostly into small rentals or apartments. Polly was grown and living on her own before her folks ever owned a home. When they finally did, it was small but well-tended, and it was much appreciated.

At the time I met Polly in 1958, there were many folks in this country who reveled in the misery of Mississippians. The South had fought stubbornly for "separate but equal" in their schools, but what many people in the North didn't realize was that in most aspects of life, the South was already integrated. In some areas, blacks and whites lived back-to-back. True, the majority of whites may have lived in slightly better homes, but poverty was shared by nearly everyone. Whites made up about 20 percent of the population, and the majority of both races respected each other. Blacks referred to whites by the title Mister; whites called blacks by their first names. Although considered demeaning in some circles, this disparity was not intended by most people as an insult, just a centuries-old tradition. The races shared each other's triumphs and tragedies. They laughed and cried together, mourned each other's deaths, and celebrated each other's marriages. In Mississippi during the Depression, there was a dearth of opportunity for all.

Of course, there was a small group of white people who were very rich, and there were poor white trash and rednecks who hated everyone. But the average Mississippian minded his or her own business and tried to put food on the table. He shared with the less fortunate, worshipped God, and prayed for better times. Many, many Mississippi citizens were far better read and more genteel than the glowering press portrayed.

I once asked a good ole boy when the Depression broke down South. "Depression?" he said with a twinkle in his eye. "We was poor before, during, and after; it just didn't make no never mind." In this place of shared heritage, divisions and traditions ran deep, but no stranger ever went hungry.

When Polly left at the end of her visit, I knew we'd see each other again. I would miss our talks and the beauty of this Mississippi maiden who was slowly stealing my heart, but I also couldn't wait to get back to the flight line. In fact, I didn't even ask for her address. At some level I think I knew Polly represented the future, but it was a future for which I wasn't yet ready. My job was becoming more enjoyable every day, and I was having way too much fun living in the present.

Chapter 50 – High-Flying Escapades

1959

The weather at Moody was always a factor. Spring and summer brought thunderstorms that defied description, and the somewhat predictable fog rolled in often.

One morning, just after the tower had launched its usual complement of jets, a huge storm moved rapidly toward the base. When we heard the recall on guard channel, we immediately thought of Black Thursday, the day at Moody in late 1958 when so many airplanes were lost due to dense fog. Was this our turn under fire? En masse, we pointed our F-86 Sabres toward the home drome at maximum speed, trying to beat the storm. By the time we arrived, the giant thunderstorm had already reached the far end of the field.[158]

Four of us joined up in formation; and other pilots did the same. That way, more aircraft could be accommodated at the field. Our formation was the last one airborne, and I was number four. We charged up initial and, just before entering the storm, pitched out on a 180-degree turn to kill speed and lower gear and flaps. Then we dove toward the runway. There were only about 1,000 feet still available for #1, 750 feet for #2, and 500 feet for #3. By the time it was my turn, I could see no more than 200 feet of runway. I smashed down on the concrete, pulled the drag chute, and hit a solid wall of blackness. Wind, rain, noise, and confusion were everywhere. I applied maximum breaking, but I had absolutely no visibility. Stopped! Adrenaline coursing through my body, I sat on the runway in a maelstrom of lightning, thunder, and fear. There was too much noise to radio and nothing to do but wait it out. That's when I noticed a white aberration huddled behind the seat. My angel was back.

I turned and smiled. "Aha, so you're scared too."

The storm blew through as quickly as it began, revealing four perfectly spaced, wet and gleaming F-86s, their drag chutes deflated behind them. Dale Stites was in the lead, a tall dude from Missouri whom I'd met at Greenville;

---

[158] Guard is an emergency channel that is monitored by all pilots and ground controllers.

Jim Mueller was #2; and Richard Wade, still with a smile on his face, was #3. We got an attaboy from headquarters for our performance.

Blame It On the French?

The Officers' Club was the center of our existence. We went to town occasionally—though after my encounter with the sheriff I did my best to avoid the place—but we spent most of our life on base, learning to fly a new mission and a new aircraft. It was a daunting task, and the Officers' Club was an extension of the learning environment.

It was here that we went, still in our sweat-encrusted flying suits, for lively conversation at the stag bar after work. In this watering hole the rank structure was blurred a bit. Even commanders stopped in for a beer or two. Pilots love to swap lies, laugh, and tell jokes, and because of the unspoken code of confidentiality, the Club was a place where they could think out loud about problems and scrapes and how to deal with them. Much of my skill came from the tricks I learned on those evenings.

Bachelors in the BOQ and around the Officers' Club drank steadily, but rarely to excess. In that era, drinking as an officer was not only condoned, it was expected. Those who didn't drink were viewed with suspicion, but as I soon discovered by careful observation, some pilots bought a beer as a ticket to the game and carried it around all night. No wonder the potted palms in the bar looked perpetually drunk.

Up until then my drinking had been limited; as an enlisted man and then a cadet, I didn't have the money, the time, or the interest. And the air force was death on DWI. There was no quicker route to failure or discharge. Nevertheless, a man who could drink prodigious amounts was particularly revered, providing, of course, that he did his job and didn't cause trouble.

Parties at the Club occurred regularly. One of these parties started out much like any other; that is, until somebody made a drink called a French 75. What went into this concoction we had no idea, though we all imbibed liberally. What came out of it, in very short order, was a roomful of drunks who created the loudest, most violent mob scene I'd ever encountered.[159]

Bucko Jewell, a pal since our days together at Spence, jumped on the bar and tore a two-foot-in-diameter decorative watch and chain out of the wall. "I've always wanted a watch and fob," he shouted as he ran out the door.

---

[159] Named after a large artillery gun used by the French in World War I, a French 75 contains a combination of lemon juice, cracked ice, sugar, champagne, and gin, with emphasis on the gin.

Another friend, Festus E. Heanue Jr., whom we called The Earl, sat through the mêlée in his usual spot at the bar. A stocky guy with short arms, a distinctive gait, and a monstrous smile, The Earl was a raconteur par excellence. He hailed from Dorchester near Boston, the Irish capital of the New World, and prior to pilot training, he'd been a navigator/radar operator. The Irish are an amazing race. We drink, laugh, tell stories, and joke around, but we still get the job done. Earl was the embodiment of this temperament. By day he was a dedicated pilot, and on nights and weekends he held court from his reserved seat at the O Club bar, telling Pat and Mike stories to the howls of his appreciative audience.

On the night of the French 75, the craziness finally subsided, but people were left with a stiffness that took time to dissipate (this was one helluva drink). Some guys wove their way to the barracks; others sat dazed in their chairs. Earl was still in his honorary seat, arm poised as if to take a sip. Earl? You okay, Earl? When The Earl was not functioning, something was wrong. Being a little more mobile than most, I guided him from the Club to our barracks a couple of buildings away. He couldn't climb the steps, so I put one of his legs on each side of my body and dragged him up the stairs. The sound of his head hitting each step was not pretty.

Saturday and Sunday were as quiet as a nunnery in Lent. The Earl complained of a headache. Bucko returned the watch and supervised the repair. Since nobody was innocent, there were no recriminations.

Next Step into the Wild Blue Yonder

It was late July 1959, and my six months at Moody were coming to an end. While my flying was still competitive—I was in the top 20 percent—my academics were as low as they could go without washing me out. My military grades weren't great, either. It's not that I was so bad, it's just that others did what was expected of them and did it better. I knew my performance wouldn't warrant a spot with the F-102 and I wasn't proud of myself, but I vowed to do better in the future. And what the heck, the F-89 would do just fine. When the results were tallied for the 30 pilots in the class, I was an embarrassing 29th. Earl was 30th. The difference between top and bottom was numerically small, but the competition was intense and the rewards worth working for.

I love the air force way: Do well and get your choice. We assembled in the briefing room, where a sheet had been hung over the blackboard. After an agonizing wait, the sheet was removed. The board looked something like this:

5 F-106 various bases *(Convair F-106 Delta Dart)*
5 F-104 various bases *(Lockheed F-104 Starfighter)*
15 F-102 various bases *(Convair F-102 Delta Dagger)*
7 F-89 various bases *(Northrop F-89 Scorpion)*
2 T-33 BIS *(Basic Instructor School)* instructors, Greenville, Mississippi

Earl and I looked at each other in shock. Six months ago, when assignments had been passed out after basic flight training, some had considered BIS slots to be a coveted prize. Now that we'd cut our teeth on the F-86, this kind of assignment was at the bottom of the heap. Neither of us wanted to go back to flying T-33s instead of the cutting-edge F-102s, F-104s, or F-106s, but our performance had sealed our fates. Greenville it was.

By that night, my optimism was beginning to return. After all, I'd be away from the trigger-happy sheriff and back in the home of the world's most beautiful and charming women, the land where the "cotton blooms and blows." Yeah. Besides, I was a career officer; my time would come again.

The air force flying corps in 1959 was made up of the Strategic Air Command (SAC), the Tactical Air Command (TAC), the Air Defense Command (ADC), the Military Air Transport Service (MATS), and the Air Training Command (ATC). At Greenville, Earl and I would be part of ATC. Everyone else in our class was assigned to bases under ADC. To tell the truth, I was already looking forward to being a flight instructor, and by golly, I'd be the best there was. I remembered some of my mentors, Mr. Kitchens, Captain E. C. Hall, and others who molded both my personality and my flying abilities, not the least of which was the ability to fly unlimited hours. When teaching is the mission, endurance is critical.[160]

---

[160] SAC was officially disbanded in 1992 at the end of the Cold War. That same year, the new Strategic Command was created. TAC was transferred to Air Combat Command in 1992. Redesignated the Aerospace Defense Command in 1968, ADC was inactivated as a major command in 1979. This organization is not to be confused with NORAD, the North American Aerospace Defense Command, which is a joint operation of the U.S. and Canadian governments that began in the late 1950s and is still in operation in 2008. MATS was deactivated in 1966 and replaced with MAC (Military Airlift Command). In 1992, MAC and the aerial refueling assets of the Strategic Air Command were merged to form the Air Mobility Command. In the early 1990s, ATC merged with Air University to form the Air Education and Training Command (AETC). As of 2008, AETC is headquartered at Randolph Air Force Base in Texas.

Part V: 1959–1964

Chapter 51 – Moving On and Coming Home

1959

I graduated from Moody on August 10, 1959, and headed north. The engine in my MG was becoming more problematic, but I had six weeks of leave coming and figured the car would make it. Barb and I were still writing to each other, though the letters were more and more platonic. Something, or somebody, was up, and it was time to close the book on this relationship. I also wanted to visit my many friends in the 551st at Otis.

The weather was fine, but the closer I got to New England the more the car acted up; I must have changed and cleaned the spark plugs a dozen times. When I finally arrived on the Cape, my first stop was at Barb's, who lived with her sister and brother-in-law.

We jumped into the tired MG and started for the dunes on the north side of the Cape to catch up, but we'd gone only a few miles when the damn car broke down again. I had to call her brother-in-law to come and pick her up. She said she was unavailable for the next few days, so we left it at that. After I got the car running, I drove into Falmouth to pick up parts at the sports car dealership. The owner was a former RC-121 pilot who'd flown at Otis.

A brand new 1959 Austin-Healey 100-6—black, white and smiling—sat on the showroom floor. She captured my heart immediately. The salesman wasn't born yesterday. He saw before him a second lieutenant with good credit, driven by emotion and stupidity. As I left the dealership in my new British beauty, I looked back at the little MG in the parking lot and waved goodbye. Did I detect a tear under her headlight? Perhaps, but love is fickle, and I drove to Otis accompanied by the mellow roar of the Healey's six-cylinder engine and its magical, electric fifth gear.[161]

Many of the troops I'd worked with in the 551st were still there, and I

---

[161] The Austin-Healey was born of a 20-year joint-venture agreement forged in 1952 between Leonard Lord of the Austin division of BMC (British Motor Corporation) and Donald Healey, a renowned automotive engineer and designer. When the agreement expired in 1972, manufacture of the car ceased. The 100-6, in various versions, was produced from 1956 through 1959.

was truly the returning hero. Old pals ran ahead to toss me a salute, and Major Riley gave me a quiet handshake and his congratulations. Sgt. Burndt was as happy as I'd ever seen anyone. Of all the airmen in his long career who'd sought pilot training, he told me, I was the first to succeed. We all went to the midnight mess for chow, which included the world's best SOS. Unfortunately, my pals Lou Silva and Robbie Robinson were no longer there. Robbie had left the service and Lou had been transferred overseas.

That Friday night I had a date with Barb at the Otis Officers' Club. The weather was a bit cool, so I secured the Healey's removable hardtop and slicked up in my Class A blue uniform, complete with gold bar, silver wings, and my good conduct ribbon. *Wait 'til she sees me and the new Healey*, I thought. *What a lucky gal!*

Barb looked as great as always, and that night she was wearing a brand new rabbit-fur coat. As I helped her into the Austin-Healey, the way gallant officers are expected to do, I could tell she was truly impressed. Now for some action, I told myself. I jumped in, lit a smoke, and threw my arm around her for a welcoming kiss. (Yes, I'm sorry to say, I'd taken up the habit again.)

The inside of the car lit up like a Roman candle. The cigarette had swiped across the hardtop and sparks were snapping—all over her coat. There must have been a hundred tiny holes in that fur, and burned rabbit does not smell good. I rubbed the sleeve a bit. "If you don't look too closely," I said, "you can hardly tell." Barb was not impressed.

The remainder of the evening was rather subdued, with dinner accompanied by conversation, and, oh yes, confession. It seems Barb *did* have a new boyfriend, a sergeant radar operator. Saying goodbye was a relief for both of us, but we'd had some great times. Thanks for the memories and the letters, Barb.

Oh, and by the way, the coat cost $150.

Always a gentleman, I wrote her a check, which left me flat broke until payday. Even though gas cost only 22 cents a gallon, the $222 paycheck that had looked so big when I was a cadet still kept me living from month to month. But, hey, it could have been worse; the coat might have been mink.

Joining Red One

Soon enough it was time to head south, and I started off for Greenville in my wonderful new car. A true two-seater with nothing but a ledge behind the seats, it is, to me at least, one of the most beautiful cars ever built. It had wonderful lines, was low to the ground, handled exceptionally well, and ate up the miles. The interior was comfortable, with a heater that worked and roll-up windows. As soon I reach Greenville, I told myself, I'll take off the removable hardtop. Top down and slick as a whistle—what a machine!

On the way I stopped in Marion, Ohio, to visit Uncle Dan and Aunt Mary. A career army officer and one of my favorite mentors, Dan was currently based at the Marion Depot. He was a cheerful, ambitious, determined man who'd been among the first to enlist in World War II. Just before he was sent to New Guinea to fight in the jungle campaign against the Japanese, he'd married Aunt Mary, a Navy WAVE. Later he was selected for OCS, which he attended in Australia while recovering from the ravages of jungle rot. He returned to the U.S. in early 1945 after island-hopping with MacArthur's army throughout the Pacific.

By the end of the war, Mary had resigned from the WAVEs, and when Dan returned home, the couple were reunited and sent for R&R to a facility in Lake Placid, New York. In 1946, he was assigned to Germany as part of the occupation force, where Betty and I visited them in Frankfurt in 1947. Dan passed through America again for a short stay on his way to Alaska, but when conflict erupted in Korea, he was reunited with MacArthur's forces for the Inchon invasion. Aunt Mary was a perfect officer's wife, traveling the world with Dan and volunteering everywhere she went with the USO.

When I started my career in the air force, Dan provided wise counsel and pragmatic advice. "If money's what you're after," he said, "then you should remain a civilian, but if you're a patriot, then the military is the place to be for challenge, excitement, and satisfaction."

They were both pleased to see me, and we spent a pleasant couple of days together. They loved sharing stories of their amazing adventures while traveling the world, and Mary was a skilled hostess. Her table was laden with delicious cuisine and fine wine and their house was filled with music, some of it from Dan who played the saxophone. He also had become a skilled photographer and had both a studio and a darkroom in their home. While I was there, he took some pictures of me in uniform, posed and ready for my next adventure.

I pulled into Greenville Air Force Base on September 30th, dumped my gear at the BOQ, stowed the hardtop for the Healey, and took off for Fieldings Drive-In. It was called Strazi's now, but it was still frequented by Mississippi beauties, and my smiling, sexy convertible was an instant hit. Who says you can't go home again?

After a hamburger served with nostalgia and a Coke, I drove back to the base and reported in. "Welcome back, Lieutenant Wright," said the colonel. "Glad to see you. We need IPs badly, and we'll send you to BIS as soon as we can get a slot.

"I guess you'll want to rejoin the 3506th," he continued. My mind was racing. No way did I want to go back to my old squadron. I'd much rather be in the 3505th, home of Pink Four Flight. In that unit, where my buddy Bill Williams had had a ball, performance went hand-in-hand with a smiling attitude. Of course, I couldn't put it that way to the colonel.

I took a deep breath. "Sir, when I was in the '06th, I was a student. If I joined the '05th I'd be unknown, which I believe would make me a more effective instructor."

"Good point, Lieutenant. Report to Major DesVoigne in the '05th."

"Thank you, Sir," I said with a sharp salute. *Maybe I should consider the diplomatic service*, I thought, trying to suppress a grin.

Major DesVoigne had been at Greenville when I was a cadet, but this was the first time we'd met. I liked him immediately. "You'll be in Red One Flight," he said. "Fly as much as you can. Every hour counts." Flight hours in the air force were hard to come by. Line fighter pilots (the guys assigned to bases under ADC) averaged about 20 hours a month, just barely enough to remain safe. Bomber pilots got a few more hours in the air, plus many long, hard hours in the simulator. Cargo pilots logged more hours than a rear end can stand. As instructor pilots, we could fly as much as we wanted; 75 hours a month was average. It was good duty.

Every weekend, The Earl and I were given the keys to the planes and off we went to San Diego, San Francisco, Las Vegas, Plattsburgh, and sometimes Montreal. You name it; we did it, and all in the name of duty. It was important to build our time in the air for safety, experience, and promotion. Fortunately, we received a per diem allowance for these trips, which meant our hotel and meals were paid for by Uncle Sam.

Even so, money was going to be a problem. After making my car and uniform payments, plus paying for meals, lodging, and smokes, the amount I had left over was less than an airman's pay. And this time I couldn't pump gas or pick cranberries—it just wasn't done in the officers' corps. How much could one make picking cotton? Perish the thought. It just wasn't fair: all these beautiful women and not a rich one among them.

Fortunately, I soon had other things about which to worry. By fall, a few BIS slots had opened up, and at the end of October The Earl and I reported for three months of instructor training to the 3615th Pilot Training Squadron at Craig Air Force Base in Selma, Alabama.[162]

---

[162] Craig Field was built in 1940 by the Army Air Force to provide pilot training (including training for more than 1,300 British pilots) during World War II. It was renamed Craig Air Force Base in 1947 when the air force became a separate branch of the armed services, and it continued to provide training for pilots from the air force and other branches of the service until it was closed in 1977. Portions of the facility operate today as a municipal airport for Selma, AL.

Polly Comes to Visit

Just before leaving for Alabama, I got a call from Polly.

"Hey, where are you?" I asked.

"I'm in Greenville at my Aunt Nan's," she replied. "I had to take care of some business."

My ears perked up right away. *Hmmm, maybe it was a large inheritance.* "How about dinner tonight?"

"Sure."

I picked her up in my shining, impressive Healey and we went to the O Club. No need for funds here, thank heavens; I could charge it.

"How about a drink?"

"No, I don't drink," she said.

Good, I thought. *That'll leave some money in the bank.* "They have great Salisbury steak," I offered.

"That's nice, but I think a filet will do."

Darn. She doesn't drink but she sure likes expensive food. Averages out, I guess. But wow, she looks great. "Dance a bit?" I asked.

"Sure."

"How's Wade doing?"

"I haven't heard," she said. "He went to Richards-Gebaur in Kansas City."[163]

"Probably doesn't know how to write," I quipped, but I was secretly glad. Man, it was nice to see this pretty lady again.

"How about a smoke?" I asked. It was a normal question. Almost everyone in the South smoked, and if you were in the air force and in the South, it was assumed you smoked. Heck, both of Polly's parents smoked. Nevertheless, she didn't like the question one bit, and I got a polite earful about the fact that nobody *she* married was going to be a smoker. She hadn't brought this up when we'd talked at Moody, but I guess this time both of us knew things were different. If we were thinking about the future, she was going to make sure I knew what kind of future she had in mind.

Quiet time. We danced a tune or two, and she shared some interesting Delta Air Lines war stories. Soon I turned the conversation to her youth.

---

[163] This 1,300-acre tract near Belton, KS, built by the city of Kansas City, MO, in 1941, was originally a civilian facility called Grandview Airport. The city deeded the airport at no charge to the air force in 1955, when it was renamed Grandview Air Force Base. In 1957 the name was changed to Richards-Gebaur Air Force Base in honor of Kansas City airmen Francisco Richards II (killed in WWI) and Arthur William Gebaur Jr. (killed in the Korean conflict). The air force deactivated the base in the 1970s and deeded it back to the city as excess property in the mid-'80s.

"It's not very interesting," she claimed, and I countered that everybody's life is interesting. Even at the ripe old age of 25, I'd figured out that everyone had a story to tell.

"You've traveled the world and lived in so many places," she said.

"Okay," I replied, "let's count up your moves," and before long she'd listed 12 moves and 4 schools. The circle was smaller, but many of the joys and problems were the same. She had suffered one sorrow, however, to which I couldn't even begin to relate.

In 1940, four years after she was born, Polly's folks, Billy and Pauline, had another child, William A. Horne III. They called him Little Bill. It was a happy family, Polly recalled, even though looking back she thought both her parents probably had inferiority complexes. There wasn't a lot of money, but by no means did they consider themselves poor. They lived within their means, carried no debt, went to church, and spent time with friends and family on both sides.

One day in the fall of 1942, just around lunchtime, Polly, Little Bill, and Billy were on their way to the post office in their old Plymouth. When they crossed the railroad tracks, the car hit a bump and Little Bill fell to the floor. He started to cry but stopped when Billy comforted him, so Billy finished his errand, stopped for ice cream cones, and went on home. That night a bump formed on Little Bill's head—he must have hit it against the jack on the car floor—and the next morning Billy and Pauline took him to the doctor. The doctor found nothing of concern, but he referred them to another doctor more familiar with head injuries. This doctor also felt it was nothing, but just to be sure, he sent the family to a specialist. At the specialist's office, the small, worried man sat with his beautiful wife and handsome little boy and waited for the verdict. After no more than a cursory glance at Little Bill, the doctor brushed them off. "He'll be okay," he said, and sent them on their way.

Little Bill's condition worsened.

Two weeks later, the specialist called Billy. "I've been meaning to check on your boy, but I've been quite busy. How's he doing?"

"He died, Doctor; *he died!* He had a fractured skull and he died of gangrene."

The tears were flowing as Polly told me this story.

We reflected quietly for quite a while. Why do bad things happen to good and innocent people? That will be my first question when I meet my Maker.

Soon it was time to take Polly back to her Aunt Nan's, and we swapped addresses. As I drove away, the hum of the Healey's engine blended with the sounds of the Mississippi night, and it occurred to me that I might be in training for more than flying jets.

Instructor Training at Craig

Craig was a typical base. The training was intense and the instructors—both IPs and those on the ground—were fantastic. In 1965, Selma would become an icon of the Civil Rights Movement when marchers led by Dr. Martin Luther King Jr. tried to cross the Edmund Pettus Bridge. But in the waning months of 1959 and early 1960, marches for civil rights were just beginning and the city was relatively quiet. We were also exceedingly busy, and we stayed close to base. In our free time, we watched TV in the Officers' Club bar. This was still a treat, as most people I knew didn't own a TV. When we did go out, we enjoyed fine restaurants throughout the city.

Polly came up from New Orleans for a weekend and we drove to Maxwell Air Force Base in Montgomery, Alabama, the home of SOS (no, not the food this time). Maxwell was the home of the Squadron Officer School, one of the best advanced-learning military schools in the world. It also had an incredible Officers' Club. Never had I been in such a distinguished Club with such fine service and dining.[164]

"Wine?" I asked. I was trying to upgrade my act and show my girl a good time, and on this occasion Polly actually had a glass.

My Healey was having a problem, so we'd borrowed The Earl's car for the trip. Earl smoked even more than I did, so of course his ashtray was full and the car stank. Adding to the problem, Polly claimed I smoked a pack on that trip. I said she made me nervous. I could tell that my days as a smoker were just about over. This relationship was getting serious, and if I didn't cut out my habit, it was going to kill me sooner than later.

Polly returned to New Orleans after our fun-filled weekend and I went back to work. I did well at Craig, finishing almost top dog. Earl did well, too. Our Irish gift of gab was an asset here, and I discovered that I really liked instructing.

---

[164] In 1910, the Wright brothers briefly operated a flying school at the site of what would become Maxwell Air Force Base (later renamed Maxwell-Gunter Air Force Base). During World War I, the U.S. government acquired land in the same area to operate an aviation repair depot. Beginning in the 1940s, the site became a pilot training center. Air University, which provides a full spectrum of air force education for enlisted, officer, and civilian personnel, opened at Maxwell in 1946. As of 2008, it remains the main focus of the facility. The Squadron Officer School, which is part of Air University, provides leadership training for Company Grade Officers (CGOs), which include second lieutenants, first lieutenants, and captains.

Chapter 52 – Backseat Driving

1959–1960

Back in Greenville, the greatest test of my young career was about to begin: standardization. There was no question that standards were needed. For example, British tanks used as late as World War II did not have interchangeable parts. If they broke down, parts often had to be manufactured under fire. Fortunately, parts made in America were interchangeable. It was the secret of our industry and one of the reasons for its worldwide success.

SAC was first to apply the concept of standardization to pilots, and it worked. Now the air force wanted to expand it further. No matter the individuals involved, you were to respond to a particular situation in a particular way.

Standardization boards became all-powerful and fearsome. They could make a pilot, a flight, a squadron, or an entire wing fail, and if they failed, heads would roll. The intent was laudable, but as a rigid, all-powerful infrastructure emerged, common sense sometimes fell by the wayside.

Soon ATC took up the standardization cry, and at Greenville, a seasoned senior officer named Captain Jack took the concept to heart. With literally a life-or-death grip on the base, Captain Jack's instructors/interrogators dressed completely in black: black hats, black flight suits, black underwear, black socks, black boots, and black hearts. They'd been around when I was a cadet, but somehow I'd escaped their notice. As an IP, I found myself squarely under their control.

Fear was their weapon of choice and smiling was an unforgivable sin. Before being permitted to fly with students (and every six months thereafter, though sometimes we were called up and tested at random under no schedule at all), each instructor had to pass a standboard. The tester would sit down with a manual and ask questions, page-by-page. We even had to know how many rivets were in the T-33 canopy and its weight—158 pounds, in case it ever comes up. Together with questions about flight operations, this amounted to several hours of interrogation and few, if any, missteps were allowed. Much of the information was insignificant or worthless, but the square had to be filled in. I studied harder than I'd ever done before and I passed, but it took great effort.

Those who got this far then had to demonstrate each phase of flight: transition, formation, and instruments. I did "just okay." I don't think anyone's grade was better than just okay. The pressure was tremendous, and when a man in black randomly picked an instructor or student to be interrogated or to fly, it felt like the Inquisition. Skilled, dedicated pilots failed and were discharged because of these tests. I had never been tested harder or more unfairly, and for no apparent good reason.

My pal Jim Mueller had been caught in this nest of vipers when we were cadets, an event that made our later encounter with the sheriff in Georgia seem like child's play. Jim was one of the top pilots in our cadet class, but when he was grabbed and interrogated for four hours, he failed for one slightly incorrect answer. He was grounded for three days and then interrogated for five additional hours. Jim knew more than the engineers who built the airplane, but the only reason he passed the second time, he felt, was that a lieutenant colonel overheard the proceedings and finally told Captain Jack to stop. It's a sad fact of human nature, but when you give some people a little power, it goes to their heads and they want to take total control.

The good ending to a bad story is that one day during the lunch changeover, Captain Jack and one of his vipers were practicing forced landings—a spiral-down approach simulating engine failure. Prior to landing, the good captain forgot to put down his landing gear and severely damaged the aircraft. Since nobody was hurt, everybody in the line of fire celebrated for days. The tail had been wagging the dog. After that, sanity prevailed and standardization, a good and necessary tool, was used to everyone's advantage.

Despite the specter of Captain Jack, Red One was a relaxed flight. Supervision was fair and welcome, and we did our jobs and did them well. My first students were Bob Blake, a member of the Air Force Academy's first graduating class; Darrell Boyd, a graduate of West Point who switched to the air force; and Curtis Archer. Bob's dad was a graduate of West Point and his brother Jerry a graduate of Annapolis. They may have been the first family to have graduates from each of the academies. Blake, Boyd, and Archer were eager students and fun to fly with, though I'm not sure whether student or teacher absorbed more.

In the T-33, the instructor both flew and demonstrated flight from the backseat of the aircraft. It reminded me of sitting in the marine F-4 Corsair at Hyannis Airport back when I was at Wentworth, the long nose blocking the forward view. I got used to the backseat quickly enough, but there was no question about it: As a new IP, my learning curve was just beginning.

Like most IPs, I wanted my students to succeed and tried to teach them everything I could. A few instructors felt differently, almost bragging about how many they washed out. At the stag bar, these IPs talked about the quality of the guys in the pipeline: They were dumber, less coordinated, less this, less that. After listening to this chatter, you'd think their students were pretty much unteachable.

People learn at different rates, and since, by its very nature, the learning curve for flying allows little room for failure, building confidence is critically important. An alert and well-advised student could request a change of instructor to get the support he needed, but most were reluctant to do so. Pride often got in the way of good judgment, and by the time another IP got involved, the student's confidence was shaken and the washing machine already cranked up. One IP in particular washed out 50 percent of his students and had an inordinate number of aborts, both airborne and on the ground.

Occasionally I flew with some of these questionable IPs. Most of them jerked the aircraft through the skies so abruptly that every turn was a painful experience. My helmet banged off the canopy and my knees turned black and blue from being rapped from side to side by the stick. Smooth is good when flying, but these guys were more at home with the "tiger" school of thought and action. Rather than being aggressive, however, they were just rough. They also tended to make excuses for anything that went wrong. It was always someone else who had a problem, never them. I can just imagine what a great confidence-booster this superior attitude was for their students.

Unfortunately, the same IPs who were poor flyers also tended to be screamers, a fact that ratcheted up the tension to an unbelievable level. We were always short of IPs, however, so their conduct was tolerated. Some students survived this horrendous behavior and went on to earn their wings. Sadly, they often became just like their mentors. Knowing no other way, the bullied became the bully.

Adventures Over the Big Apple

One weekend, a fellow IP named Fred was planning a trip to New York City and looking for a copilot. A girl I used to date lived there, so I agreed to go along.

We were in the infancy of the electronic age, and the T-33 still used tube technology. To fly cross-country, we first had to climb into the electronics bay in the nose of the plane and insert the correct radio crystals for that sector.

In addition, some type of emergency would arise every ten flights of so, and controlling fuel was always a problem. Nevertheless, any trip was an adventure, and I was looking forward to it.

The weather was supposed to be great that weekend in the New York area, so we filed a flight plan for VFR (visual flight rules), meaning it was clear enough to fly, land, or take off without depending on instruments. It was a long way from Greenville to New York, however, and the distance was at the very limit of our fuel capacity.

We were scheduled to land at Floyd Bennett Field, directly across Jamaica Bay from Idlewild Airport. This naval aviation field, however, kept its landing lights turned off except to accommodate the approximate time of arrival posted in a flight plan or in response to a radio-issued landing request.[165]

As we approached New York, the air traffic controller advised us of deteriorating conditions: a huge bank of fog was rolling in. When we tried to reply, the radio failed. This was not an uncommon event, and we continued to descend until we could see the glow of the city. Then the generator failed. Now we *did* have a problem! The generator powered many of the plane's navigation systems; without it we were running emergency systems on battery backup. One indicator so powered was the low-fuel light, and a couple minutes later, on it came. We had 20 minutes of flight left.

Our choices were limited: Bail out or join up on an airliner and land at Idlewild. Just as we passed the shoreline on the lookout for an approaching airliner, the fog cleared as if cut by a cleaver, the runway lights flipped on at Floyd Bennett Field 5,000 feet below in anticipation of a plane that had filed a VHR flight plan filed back in Greenville (yeah, right!), and we swooped in and landed. God bless the navy. In the days when landing without a radio was not uncommon, military bases were rarely surprised when strange aircraft showed up unannounced, and once out of the airplane, we called from the flight line to cancel our VFR flight plan.

We had a relaxed and fun weekend in the Big Apple, but on the way back to Greenville I had to take a leak. This is something that pilots try not to do while flying. At best it's difficult, and at worst it creates a huge opening for horseplay. Fred was flying the plane and I began the process: unstrap the seat belt, loosen the parachute, and unzip the flight suit, all with one hand. The

---

[165] Floyd Bennett Field, located in Brooklyn, was New York City's first municipal airport. In the 1930s the field was also a base for naval aviation reserve squadrons. From 1941 until it closed in 1972, it served as a Naval Air Station. Later it became a unit of the Gateway National Recreation Area, which is still the case as of 2008. Idlewild Airport was built on the site of Idlewild Golf Course in Queens, New York City, and dedicated in 1948. In 1963 it was renamed John F. Kennedy International Airport in honor of the fallen President.

other hand was holding an inverted bullhorn device connected to a tube. To make the process even more difficult, the stick was moving violently, thanks of course to Fred, who was causing as much trouble as possible.

After filling the bullhorn, I pressed the button that's supposed to create a vacuum, thereby sucking the yellow fog out the bottom, through the connected tube, and overboard. The vacuum system failed. There I sat with a horn full of lemonade, struggling with the zipper, parachute straps, and seatbelt, and muttering into the hot microphone, "Damn. What am I going to do now?"

I should never have uttered those words. "Let me help," said Fred, as he promptly rolled the T-Bird on its back, roaring with laughter. At first I had a few comments to make about his ancestry, but soon we were laughing together about the plight of failed equipment, our close call at Floyd Bennett, and our aborted plan to land on the wing of a civilian Boeing 707. Wouldn't our wing commander back in Mississippi have loved to debrief that one? Sometimes I wasn't sure whether my angel was saving me or taunting me.

Changes in the Air

I'd arrived at Greenville in September 1959, and since then I'd been focused almost entirely on becoming the best IP I could be. We all knew things could change overnight, but at the moment world tensions were under control. All of that was about to change.

On Sunday morning, May 8, 1960, I walked into the Officers' Club for the usual long breakfast, perusal of the Sunday paper, and gabfest with my buddies. The place was abuzz with the headlines. Ike had admitted to the world that we were flying a spy plane called the U-2. It had been shot down on May 1 over the USSR and the pilot, Francis Gary Powers, had been captured. "What's a U-2?" we asked. We all thought we had a pretty good handle on the inventory and how we planned to use it, but none of us had ever heard of a U-2.

Excitement permeated the air. Knowledge of the enemy's offensive and defensive capabilities was the best deterrent to war, and the Soviet Union was a dark and sinister area of the world to which almost no one had access. I was impressed and proud of our country for attempting such a dangerous mission and maintaining its secrecy.

With the downing of the U-2, the Cold War escalated a notch and the two superpowers erupted into a volley of propaganda. Military forces were at their highest readiness short of all-out war. Premier Nikita Khrushchev had scored a propaganda coup, and he exploited it to the fullest. On May 16th, Khruschev walked out of preliminary talks taking place just prior to the

Paris peace summit scheduled for U.S., Soviet, English, and French leaders (the big four). The summit dissolved in tatters and the Cold War continued with a vengeance. Khrushchev and Eisenhower faced off and backed off, and although rhetoric trumped retaliation, to the average military pilot this incident only reemphasized our commitment to a very real and dangerous enemy.[166]

Despite the fact that the world seemed relatively peaceful, we had been in danger of war for some time. The USSR had perhaps the largest and most experienced military in the world and no compunction about using it. The armed forces of European nations had been nearly eliminated by the Second World War, and the U.S., for all its military effectiveness, had withdrawn across the sea.

We had geared up temporarily for Korea, but the U.S., like almost all free nations, had disbanded most of its armed forces after World War II. We were committed to a future of peace and prosperity. The USSR was committed to conquering the world.

Fortunately, the United States held a giant trump card: nuclear weapons. We had stopped the slaughter in Japan with them and, if necessary, we could stop an attempted Soviet takeover of Europe. Of course, the Soviets also had nuclear weapons, and strange as it sounds, this nuclear standoff somehow made the world a safer place. Without nukes, we might have plunged once again into world war.

Not long after the U-2 incident, though obviously independent of any cause and effect, we got the word: The powers that be had decided Greenville was outdated and would no longer be used for pilot training after Class 61-B graduated. Moody was going to switch from fighter training to pilot training, and all the Contract Primary-Flying Bases would be terminated. From now on, both primary and basic flight schools would be conducted by military pilots on military bases. Greenville personnel were being split between Moody in Georgia and Williams Air Force Base in Arizona, which was switching from fighter training to pilot training. I wasn't even worried about being sent back to Moody. I knew my angel hated that fat, ugly, tobacco-chewing sheriff as much as I did, and sure enough, my orders came through for Williams.[167]

---

[166] Nikita Khrushchev (1894–1971) was premier of the Soviet Union from 1958 to 1964 and first secretary of the Communist Party from 1953 to 1964. A volatile character, he is often remembered for an incident at the United Nations in October 1960. Flying into a rage over "Western imperialism" while addressing this body, he took off his shoe and banged it on the table to make his point. Part of that rage was no doubt engendered by the U-2 incident.

[167] Named after Arizona native 1st Lieutenant Charles L. Williams, Williams Air Force Base opened in 1942 and closed in 1993. Over 26,000 pilots were trained at this

Many of these changes weren't surprising. For one thing, the Aviation Cadet Program was being terminated forever. Class 61-B was the last one to include cadets; anyone wanting to be an air force pilot in the future would have to have a four-year degree. Also, the air force was cutting back. By the end of 1959, more than half the guys I'd graduated with at Moody had been reassigned to non-flying jobs such as manning radar stations. The needs of the service were paramount, but for guys who'd trained for years for a job they weren't going to get to do, it was a hard pill to swallow. I thought back to my initial disappointment at being sent to Greenville from Moody, realizing now that it had been a lucky break. I might not be flying F-102s, but I was flying.

It took a couple of months after Class 61-B left to shut down operations at the base. During the transition, our assignment was to call in once a week to tell them we were alive and to fly anywhere, any time. Then in late July, I received a promotion and an increase in pay to more than $300 a month. As long as one kept one's nose clean, the promotion was almost automatic. Nevertheless, in exchanging the single gold bar of a second lieutenant for the single silver bar of a first lieutenant, I'd moved up a rung on the ladder, and it felt good.

---

base, more than at any other facility in the country.

Chapter 53 – Kicking the Weed

1960

Polly wrote that she had some vacation time from Delta and was coming to visit family in Greenville in two weeks. She hoped we could get together. *That's great*, I thought, *but she hates smoking.* I knew if I wanted things to work out with her, I had to quit sometime. This seemed as good a time as any, so I stopped cold turkey. Then I started replacing my clothes. I'd burned holes in most of them, and of course they all stank. After about a week my voice worked, and food really *did* taste better.

I'd been smoking on and off for seven years. Each time I quit I vowed it would be the last, but it was so easy to start again—a couple of beers, a few laughs, and there I was, hooked. Even worse, each time I tried to quit it was harder than the time before. This time, I had a great incentive. "I'll never marry a smoker," Polly had said on more than one occasion. "My parents both smoke, and their house smells of smoke. I also worry about my dad; he's not in the best of health, and I know his smoking is one of the main reasons why."

I considered myself a courageous guy. Throw a hand grenade in my path and I'd jump on it with pleasure; show me that machine gun nest and I'd attack it and rip those little men apart with my bare hands. Nevertheless, quitting smoking for good took all the courage and determination I had.

By the time Polly arrived, I'd gotten through the worst of it.

I took her to the Club for dinner and dancing and she looked great. "Notice anything different?" I asked after a while.

"No."

"Are you sure?"

"Yep."

"Well, I guess I'll just have to go out and buy a pack of smokes."

"You're not smoking!" she said excitedly. After that, she sat and danced much closer. Uh-oh, what have I done? I'd better be careful. A handsome young pilot making an exalted salary—I really *was* becoming a target of opportunity. Of course, none of this did a thing to deflate my ego.

After dinner, we resumed our conversation about Polly's family as if we'd left off the day before. "When I was seven," she said, "my youngest brother was born. My folks named him Claude Rutledge Horne III. As a little kid, Rut loved horses. He rode a stick horse everywhere he went, and as soon as he was old enough, he earned the money to buy a horse of his own and board it at a local farm. Every kid needs a hobby, and Rut's probably kept him on the straight and narrow."

I loved hearing these stories, and as we continued to compare notes on our young lives, it was obvious we just seemed to fit. My mother never lectured me about anything that I could remember; she simply expected certain conduct, and for the most part I complied. Why make trouble? Folks did their best and shared what they had, both mentally and materially. I knew that, appreciated the results, and was a happy kid.

Polly's story was about the same. The only thing her father preached was "you're born with a good name. If you lose it, you can't get it back." By example, he demonstrated responsibility, class, and culture. Being rich or poor had little to do with the equation.

Despite his good judgment in many other areas, however, Billy wasn't always a good businessman. "One day," she recalled, "he showed up on the doorstep with a cow he'd traded for work performed. My mom, who knew about such things from her days on the farm, was disgusted. 'That cow's drying up,' she said. And she was right; it never did produce much milk. Another time Daddy bartered for an old player piano. This was a much better deal—I took lessons on that piano for years. I never quite got up to concert standards, but it's a hobby that's given me hours of enjoyment."

The entire Horne family was involved in the Presbyterian Church, participating in the choir, youth groups, and teaching. And although they had little money, Polly dressed well, mostly from the sewing machine of her very skilled mother. She was always given just what she needed and no more, so she embraced the work ethic at an early age. At 16 she landed a part-time job, which gave her some spending money for ice cream, movies, and other extras.

Polly liked school, and in high school she was popular and finished near the top of her class. Finding enough money for college, however, was a close call. Her father and her Great Aunt Louise paid for her first year at MSCW and she managed the rest through careful planning and as much work as time would allow.

In addition to work and study, Polly found time at school for biking, hiking, softball, basketball, and swimming. The swimming was mandatory, but because of a dearth of pools in her childhood and her fear of snakes in the rivers and creeks, it was her least favorite sport. Overall, she did so well that she was elected to Mortar Board, and just to show her I wasn't ignorant, I allowed as how I could mix a mean batch of mortar myself.[168]

The more I listened, the more lovely I found this woman, both inside and out. Maybe she *was* just another conniving southern female looking to hook up with an eligible Yank, but if so it was working. We were falling in love. I could see she was a winner, and the more time I spent with her, the more I felt the pull of attraction.

Polly's dad, Billy Horne, ca. 1949, with his pre-owned 1941 Lincoln, a "great buy" that died two weeks after he brought it home.

Polly's mom, Pauline Hamer Horne, holding Polly, 1936.

---

[168] Mortar Board is a national honor society. Established in 1918, it recognizes college seniors for excellence in scholarship, leadership, and service.

Chapter 54 – The World According to Gib

1960

In my cadet days at Greenville, one of the IPs was a guy named Richard Gibson. When I got back to Greenville after being at Moody, he was still there and we became fast friends. Gib was a down-to-earth guy. He'd been brought up dirt poor, so fancy food wasn't important to him, and he didn't drink. He was also very bright and a continual thorn in the side of the military hierarchy, but his ability to turn out skilled pilots was second to none. His philosophy was simple:

1. Where you are is where you want to be.
2. What you're doing is what you want to do.
3. What you're eating is what you want to eat.
4. (added years later) If your wife buys something, you will like it.

Gib and I took our jobs seriously. The consequences of failure could range from discomfort to—in the extreme—death. Many times we'd sit outside the O Club, yakking against the backdrop of the critters that serenaded the hot Mississippi nights. Our conversations centered on solving problems, finding ways to teach better, and figuring out how best to create pilots who were both safe and aggressive. I guess you could call it teamwork.

We also solved the problems of the world, outlining how we'd handle world affairs. As it turned out, often our solutions were how it happened, or at least, how it should have happened. Sometimes we discussed the circuitous routes that had led each of us to this career we loved so much.

Stretched out, Gibson reached five feet five inches and weighed 150 pounds. He had a sturdy physique, a crisp sense of humor, and the God-given ability to cut to the quick of a problem and solve it with logic. He didn't demand that you like him, just that you respect him, a trait, in the air force and elsewhere, that is often less than appreciated. Gib felt that life is far simpler than most people make it out to be, and his logical

344

solutions and cutting wit did little to make him the base hero, especially among the Jack Armstrong types.[169]

Will Rogers and Gib would have been a team. In fact, they were even related; Will was a distant Cherokee cousin on his mother's side. Rogers was born on a large ranch in the Cherokee Nation near what later would become Oologah, Oklahoma. Gib's ancestors were ranchers who'd been driven out of Kansas during the cattle wars of the late 19th century. Both had a rugged individualism that made them unforgettable characters.[170]

Gib's folks married without a penny or a plan. Just outside Fort Gibson, Oklahoma (no relation), they built a log cabin on a local rancher's land in exchange for looking after his cattle. The cabin had a leaking roof, a dirt floor, outdoor plumbing, and no electricity. James, Gib's dad, wasn't much of a carpenter, and the wind howled through the gaps year 'round. In fact, the logs were so uneven that James hung a swing from one of the protrusions.

James was a product of a frontier mentality combined with the door-slamming effects of the Depression. He eked out a meager existence by vaccinating hogs for fifty cents a day and preserving the fruits of a small garden. Despite its economic woes, however, the Gibson home was a happy one, and with World War II came prosperity. Gib's dad got a job as a supervisor in the local munitions factory, and after the war, the family ended up in Richland, Washington, where James worked at the Hanford site managed by General Electric.

Gib and his siblings were all hard workers, and the money they earned at part-time jobs went into the family pool. It was all for one and one for all in this family, but somehow the money always seemed to be mismanaged and disappear. So Gib sold newspapers at the plant, saved his money, and at age 14 bought 14 acres of arid land on the Yakima River for $1,000.

Eventually the family settled into company housing in town, but for a

---

[169] *Jack Armstrong, the All-American Boy*, was a radio adventure series that aired from 1933 to 1951. The plot revolved around the globe-trotting adventures of the fictional Jack, a high school athlete, his friends Billy Fairfield and Billy's sister Betsy, and their Uncle Jim. Before the series ended, Jack's adventures were also recorded in a book and a series of comics.

[170] American humorist Will Rogers was born in 1879 in what is now Oklahoma and dropped out of high school to become a cowboy. After appearing in Wild West shows, the circus, and two World Fairs, he moved into vaudeville, where he made the transition from rope tricks to humor. He later acted in more than 70 films, wrote 4,000 columns, and authored 6 books. His humor focused on intelligent and honest observations about everyday life, the country, and the government in simple language his audiences loved. He was killed in a plane crash on August 15, 1935, with Wiley Post, the first pilot to fly solo around the world.

time they lived on that land in an old manufactured home, once again with no indoor plumbing. In the meantime, Gib bought a passel of hogs and then contracted with the local army Nike missile site to pick up their garbage. Not only was he paid for his efforts, he had a free source of food for his pigs, which he later sold. Gib's mom showed Great Danes, probably more of a money pit than a moneymaker. Sis was a dancer, and somehow the family found funds to send her to a private dance school. Later, she became a successful showgirl.

Gib might have been brought up poor, but the library was open to poor kids, too, and he was a voracious reader. He was also an excellent student, but in high school his problem-solving ability, combined with his stubbornness, caused him no end of grief. He made A's on his tests, but he refused to do homework, or what he termed "busy work." His grades reflected this losing battle—our Gib was never going to be class valedictorian—and by the time he left high school, he probably held the record for time spent in detention. He went on to Washington State and earned enough credits to graduate in three years, but he stayed four years to earn his commission in the air force. The Air Force ROTC kept him out of the draft; and despite working part-time, being a top shot on the rifle team, and becoming the West Coast wrestling champion, he finished school with a 3.3 average.

With a degree in agriculture and the eventual goal of earning a master's, Gib went off to fulfill his obligation for military service and more-or-less stumbled into pilot training. Here's where our stories differed drastically. I was born to fly; he just happened through the door. My instructors were superb; his were screamers. He could do all that was asked and then some, but perhaps his size or his wit or his ability to simplify caused him continual grief. "If it's a straight line from point A to point D," he'd ask, "then why go from A to D via B and C?"

The unfailing reply: That's the way we've always done it. The military is a wonderful choice of career, but it is steeped in tradition.

After earning his wings, Gib was sent to Korea to join an active fighter squadron, even though his accumulated flight time after training totaled only four hours. By this time, the truce between North and South Korea had been in effect for several years, but the U.S. maintained an active peacekeeping force in the country.

"Your flight log seems to be missing, Gibson," stated his new commander.

"It's all there, Sir."

"But it shows only four hours."

"Yes, Sir, that's all I have."

"Normally," the commander replied caustically, "before being sent to a squadron one attends advanced training."

Knowing Gibson, I'm sure he offered a witty reply, and knowing commanders, I'm sure said reply, especially from a buck lieutenant who looked like he'd run away from high school, was less than welcome.

Nevertheless, orders are orders, so Gibson was told to fly around the local area in the venerable T-33 for 50 hours or so. Afterward and with a minimal amount of sarcastic instruction, he was turned loose in a single-seater F-86F, the instructor screaming at him in a chase plane.

Gib's unit was staffed with a bunch of crusty senior fighter pilots who were unhappy about being in Korea and particularly unhappy about being stuck close to the 38th parallel. After he'd been there about six months, Gib felt sure they were going to give him a Flying Evaluation Board, ground him, and make him the garbage control officer. And then his angel came through.

The practice bombing range needed an officer, immediately. The candidate had to be a rated pilot who had flown the F-86. How much or how often was not specified. Happily for all concerned, Gib departed to a 24' x 24' shack on a mud flat in the Gulf of Korea dubbed Osanman Air Base. Placed in command of three similarly disposed airmen and two Korean guards, Gib commented that few officers so young had risen to command such an international force.

The perfect leper squadron, Gib and his crew settled down to a blissful existence. Many, many miles from Osan, the closest actual air base, and accessible only by helicopter, the range was set up to observe, control, and grade practice bombing attacks.[171]

Accommodations consisted of a hut with four cots and mattresses, sleeping bags, a few chairs, and a diesel generator to run the radios. Food was choppered in every week: cases of cereal, tuna fish, canned meat and vegetables, milk, and eggs. One of the airmen became the cook, which was fortunate. Alone, Gib might have starved to death. Despite his intelligence in other areas, Gib in the kitchen was not a good thing.

The island was hot as hell in the summer, brutally cold in the winter, and nearly devoid of intellectual challenge. One morning Gib woke with a flash of genius. Using duct tape, he marked off a five-foot square and a ten-foot square on the floor of the hut. "Whatcha doin', Lieutenant?" asked the airmen.

"This, gentlemen, is the Officers' Club and that (pointing to the ten-foot

---

[171] Named for the closest town, Osan-Ni, Osan Air Base is one of two major airfields in the Republic of Korea operated by the U.S. Air Force. Construction on the facility started in early 1952; by the end of that year the first combat squadron had arrived. Ever since, the base has played a pivotal role in the defense of South Korea and U.S. interests in Southeast Asia. As of 2008, Osan is still an active base.

square) is the Airmen's Club." He then proceeded to sit in his chair in the Officers' Club and select a book from the many cases of same that had been choppered in. Nothing was too good for our men in blue.

Gib also held English and history lessons, and he played cards and Monopoly endlessly, though after 43 straight losses, the troops mutinied and refused to trade any more property. After grading the bombing runs each day, the men also enjoyed hunting ducks to supplement their diet. When Gib requested more ammo, however, not only was he refused, he was told that the ammo they did have was intended to protect them from an attack. The source of said attack was not specified, though obviously the ducks were not considered a sufficient threat.

2nd Lieutenant Richard Gibson (Gib), keeping the world safe for democracy, ca. 1953.
(*Courtesy of Richard Gibson.*)

Overall, Gib enjoyed the job. He was out of the limelight of the hotshots, and he ran a tight ship. In fact, the commander often radioed to compliment him on the efficiency of his operation; no one before had done it as well. And the best part of all: not one human ever showed up to upset the applecart—that is, until the day the major choppered in. The major, a minion from the inspector general's office, was charged with making random inspections—yep, only in the military.

"Lieutenant, I'm here to inspect your operation, to manage waste and preparedness."

"Just a minute, Sir," said Gib, as he stepped across the room and knocked at the nonexistent door to the Airmen's Club.

"What can I do for you, Sir?" asked an airman.

"I'd like to borrow a table and chair from your Club, Airman."

"Of course, Sir. Let me open the nonexistent door."

"Thank you, Airman. Would you mind also holding the nonexistent door of the Officers' Club?" The airman proceeded to do so.

"Now, Major, please step into my office in the Officers' Club, where I will treat you to lunch." The airmen then proceeded to serve the major and Gib a meal of dehydrated potatoes the consistency of BBs; an unidentifiable canned meat, stringy and whitish in color; and some squishy peas that a greedy war profiteer had passed off to the military as first-rate.

"Lieutenant, what is the purpose of the tape surrounding this table?" asked the major.

"It separates the office of the Officers' Club from the troops, Sir."

About this time, Gibson sensed that the meeting was getting off to a bad start. Could it be that his visitor's sense of humor was somewhat underdeveloped? After his delectable lunch, the major stormed out of the hut. The first thing he saw was a pen. "What is that, Lieutenant?" he asked in his best official manner.

"It's a pig pen, Sir." Sure enough, inside the makeshift enclosure was a 220-pound hog, ready for slaughter. Surrounding the hog were the remains of USAF-issued cereal, eggs, bacon, rice, and whatever else the men had found to fatten him up.

"Why do you have this hog, Lieutenant?"

"Well, Sir, when I was touring the village of one of the guards under my command, I noticed they had the worst-looking porkers I've ever laid eyes on. Since the guard claimed the village raised fine pigs, I thought it only reasonable to demonstrate the proper way to raise a pig, thereby passing on some of my experience to the Koreans.

"We even named him Oscar," continued Gib with that maddening grin, "but the guard was unimpressed. He claimed that our hog ate better than the entire population of his village."

"And what do you plan to do with this hog, Lieutenant?" growled the major in a voice of growing disgust.

"Well, Sir, we had planned to give it to the Koreans, thinking a bit of charity would ease the tensions of war, but then we thought better of it and sold it to the air force for a pig roast."

The major made no comment, but Gib definitely sensed that the inspection was not going well. Turning away from the pen, he asked, "Just how does this range operate, Lieutenant?"

Gib replied. "Sir, bombers and fighter bombers attack the bull's-eye on the mud flats and practice tossing and over-the-shoulder launching of simulated nuclear bombs in the form of 2,000-pound shapes. We grade the drops and call in the scores."

The bull's-eye was located 1,500 feet from the scoring shack, and as the major toured the area, it became apparent to him that some of the bombs had come mighty close to the troops in the shack. One had landed only 75 feet away.

"What instructions have you given to the troops in case of an errant bomb?" asked the major.

"Duck," replied Gib. "At least," he added with a smile, "we don't have to walk far to bury our garbage."

At this point Gib eased off a bit, and the inspection went well until the major checked into the armory of three carbines and one .45 pistol. The weapons were clean and in perfect working order. They just weren't loaded.

"Why, Lieutenant, is there so little ammunition for these arms?"

"We shot it up, Sir, I've been training the troops to be killers, and we're waiting for a new supply."

"Lieutenant Gibson, where is your defense plan?" the major raged. "What would you do if a boatload of North Koreans landed on those mud flats and tried to attack your command?"

"Well, Sir," said Gib, fully aware of how unlikely it would be for North Korean troops to brave the 38th parallel for the purpose of invading his mud flat sanctuary, "I would go into the hut, close the imaginary door to the imaginary Officers' Club and the imaginary door to the imaginary Airmen's Club, grab my toothbrush, gather my troops, and run like hell!"

"Gibson, you should be court marshaled for even thinking such a cowardly thought. Where is your sense of duty?"

Gibson realized immediately that he'd gone too far, and there was no way he wanted to jeopardize his command of this briar patch, which was protecting his sanity. "Actually, Sir, I would like to change my plan," he said, becoming immediately humble and contrite. "The pressure of being at ground zero from the deadly fire of the fighter/bombers and the ever-increasing tension from the threat of attack by the North Koreans, coupled with the fact that we've been at this forward and dangerous position for six months with no R&R, has clouded my deductive and logical thought processes. And so I thank you, Sir, for sharing your experience with this humble lieutenant."

The major waited through this dissertation with growing pride at being able to help this wayward young officer.

With the crooked grin that only he could produce, Gib looked him straight in the eye. "What I'd really do in such a crisis, Sir, would be to go into the hut, close the imaginary Officers' Club and imaginary Airmen's Club doors, pick up my toothbrush, gather my troops, and find you so you could fight those *freaking North Koreans*."

The disgruntled major departed soon after. He didn't even ask about staying for dinner.

Gibson was returned to the main base forthwith. I'm sure his attitude played a large part in that decision, but the major had determined that the bombing range was in fact out-of-limits. In order to meet air force regulations, the scoring shack had to be at least 3,000 feet from the bull's-eye, and there just was not enough room. Thus the Osanman Air Base was closed due to safety concerns, and Gibson lost his command. There was almost an audible sigh of relief from the North Koreans. They knew they'd lost their most fearsome competitor.

As soon as he arrived back at the main base, Gib demanded the week of R&R due him. He was refused and threatened with court matial. A quick visit to the inspector general resolved the issue, and Gib spent a week of debauchery in Japan. When he returned, the powers that be commenced to make the remaining months of his tour as miserable as possible, and his reaction to this treatment kept him one step out of the brig.

Gib was more than disillusioned with military life, but he still had ten months to go on his enlistment. At the end of his tour, hopefully he'd get an honorable discharge and be able to return to school for one or more advanced degrees. He resolved to tough it out.

Then he got a message to report to the personnel officer.

"You sent for me, Sir?"

"Lieutenant," the officer answered, "we've just gotten word of an opening for a skilled young pilot. In order to apply, you must sign for an indefinite extension of three years, but the good news is that after a year at your new base, it's likely you can be discharged into the inactive Reserves."

Gibson cocked his head in suspicion. "What's the catch, Sir? Where is this assignment and what will I be doing?"

"Sorry, but I can't reveal that until you sign up indefinitely," the personnel officer replied.

Oh, man, thought Gib. *Ten more months here may test my sanity, but they could be sending me to Timbuktu. On the other hand, one more year of air force pay and I can save enough for an advanced degree. And I'd be out just in time to start the school year.* "Okay," he told the officer, "I'll sign."

Gib signed the contract and was handed orders to report to Greenville Air Force Base in Greenville, Mississippi.

"By the way, Gibson, you'll love it. The women are beautiful, and you can fly 'til your hinder hurts."

Just before Gib left the country, his Korean judo instructor commented that if Gib stayed for three more years, he could become the judo champ for all of Korea. Gib had an extensive reply to this observation, the most polite version of which was that he wouldn't stay in Korea if they made him king.

Gib reported for duty at Greenville shortly thereafter, his pursuit of further degrees on hold. This time, the air force sent him to advanced training at Basic Instructor's School (BIS). Unbeknownst to him, however, and not explained by the personnel officer at the time (though admittedly, Gib didn't read the fine print), a one- to three-year commitment was added to his contract every time he went to another school or changed airplanes.

By 1960, he'd been a successful instructor for several years. He was hugely popular with his students—aggressive, tough, and humorous—and he brought out the best in each of them. When another instructor gave up on a trainee, the word would come down: Give him to Gibson. And under Gib's tutelage, the student would meet with success. In fact, every pilot Gib ever trained received his wings, a feat possibly unequaled in the U.S. Air Force or in any service worldwide.

Not surprisingly, Gibson's superior officers did not look upon him with the same high regard, although they did respect his abilities as an IP. The air force didn't make a flight suit that fit him; when it accommodated his chest, the legs were too long. The ill-fitting suit, coupled with boots shined the way any decent pig farmer's boots would be, gave him a comical air. Add to this a thinly veiled irreverence, and Gib managed to keep the brass in a constant state of frustration.

Twice a year, students voted for the *instructor of the class*. In Gibson's first class, his four students had finished in the top ten, two of them in the first and third positions, and Gib won the honor hands down. Afterward, his flight commander, a crusty old fighter pilot named Captain Roy Killian, said, "If Gibson's the best we've got, then I'm in a heap of trouble."

In Gib's second class, he achieved similar results and won the honor again, but by this time Captain Killian had changed his mind about this gem of an instructor. The powers that be felt differently, announcing that in the future, the designee would be chosen by a group of selected instructors. Of course, Gib was never again in the running, but those who were always had well-fitting, ironed flight suits and spit-shined jump boots. Some of these men were also good instructors, but such was no longer the main criterion.

When the air force decided it wanted more combat-ready pilots, there was a new emphasis on martial arts, pistol, and rifle training. Gib already had a black belt in judo and karate. Using the skills he'd honed on the rifle team in college, he also became one of the top shots on the All Training Command team, a cadre of the top gunners from multiple air force training bases. And he did all this while maintaining a full training schedule for his students, although he farmed them out occasionally for a lesson or two so he could go to competitions.

Had one of the golden boys accomplished these feats, he'd have been promoted for walking on water. In Gib's case, his flight commander, a passed-over captain, shouted from the squadron leaders' group meeting that he was going to fire Gibson because he was always off competing at one event or another. "Does anyone want him?" he challenged.

From the rear of the room, a quiet, distinguished voice said, "I'll take him."

"What the hell are you going to do with him?" bellowed the frustrated and angry captain.

"I plan to leave him alone. Nobody does the job better," said Schuyler Bissell, a tall, young captain with wisdom beyond his years. Great leaders often have great insight.[172]

---

[172] Schuyler Bissell had a distinguished air force career and retired in 1988 as a major general. After seven years as an IP at Greenville and later as an IP at Williams Air Force Base in Arizona, Gib was assigned to the 22nd Fighter Wing in Bitburg, Germany, where he flew the F-105 and the F-4. By 1968, the U.S. was embroiled in the Vietnam War and Gibson was the Top Gun and air tactics instructor for his unit. Nevertheless, he was passed over for major and RIF'ed (subject to reduction in force). With his wife Peggy, he returned from Germany to attend law school at Arizona State University, finishing first in his class and subsequently forming the law firm of Jerome-Gibson. While still in school, he joined the 161st Air Refueling Group of the Arizona National Guard. In 1983, when he retired from the Guard as a full colonel and Director of Air Operations for the State of Arizona, he was named the outstanding officer for the Group.

Chapter 55 – Boating on the Ole Mississippi

1960

While waiting for my transfer to Williams, I rented a cabin on Lake Ferguson with three other guys. Training was beginning to wind down, and we spent our time ferrying T-33s to other bases—two planes out, one back. In off hours we water-skied, drank beer, ate stockyards full of steak, and generally had a ball. Rumors began to circulate that a pilot's life was steeped in debauchery, drink, and lust. Surely they hadn't heard of Saint Don, the Virtuous.

Polly invited me to New Orleans, where she was living with her folks. "Bring some pals," she said. "I'll line up a couple of Delta stews and we'll go out Friday and Saturday nights." I invited Gib and Don Herrell, the base helicopter pilot, and we decided to make it an adventure. We'd go by boat. The boat was a wooden, 17-foot relic we'd found in the bushes behind the cabin, equipped with an antique, 25-hp Johnson motor contributed by Herrell. We'd been out in this rig on Lake Ferguson a few times, so we knew the boat leaked and the motor had a habit of taking vacations in critical places, but with occasional bailing and a little luck, we figured we'd make it to New Orleans without a hitch. The fact that we had no experience with motorboats, nor had we ever been on the Mississippi, bothered us not a bit.

Barry, one of my roommates from the cabin, planned to meet us in New Orleans with a boat trailer and clothes for our weekend with Polly and her fellow stews. How lucky could these women be? Not only were we pilots, we were Mississippi adventurers.

To say that the trip was not as well planned as it might have been is more than an understatement. We had no operating manual for the motor. We had no charts for the river. We calculated the distance on a wall map in Operations by attaching a string to a pushpin at Greenville and extending it to New Orleans. So many inches of string equaled so many miles, in this case 244 miles. The fact that these were *air miles* passed us by completely.

We knew the river had a few curves, but we figured if we followed it long enough, we'd get to the Big Easy. Huck Finn made it. Or did he? What we didn't know was how fast our craft would go. To figure it out, I drove the boat next to the levee and Gib paced me in a car on the levee bank. At three-quarters throttle, our noble vessel made a respectable 7 mph.[173]

This trip would be a snap. Seven miles per hour divided into the calculated distance looked like an easy three-day trip, but we allowed extra time just in case. In fact, we planned to leave Tuesday morning so we could spend some time fishing. Our first refueling stop was Vicksburg.

Look Out, Huck Finn

Herrell and I were in charge of gas and supplies; Gib was in charge of food and drink. But once we piled 60 gallons of fuel, the food, a small Coleman stove, a cooler, our sleeping bags, and a few clothes into the boat and got in ourselves, the river was lapping over the gunnels. Jettisoning one can of gas gave us about two inches of freeboard, and off we set in high spirits.

We barged down the river like "the little boat that could." Unfortunately, we'd failed to take into account how fast we could go if were fully loaded, which turned out to be about 2 mph. Nevertheless, we were optimistic adventurers; maybe the current would help. The Mississippi near Greenville is contained by giant levees, so we rarely saw a building or another human being, but the weather was beautiful and the winds calm. We stayed close to the center of the river and figured out how to rig up a sun awning. What we hadn't taken into account were the barges.

From the air, they looked small and colorful. Up close and personal, they were the piranhas; we were the goldfish. We had our first encounter under the Greenville Bridge. Propelled by a huge pusher tug, the barge must have been at least 100 yards long. As it bore down on us, I calmly started out of the channel toward the shore.

The damn engine quit.

This was before automatic rewind, and when I threaded the rope-pull, the rope broke. At this point, we grabbed the oars and pulled as if our lives depended on it, which in fact they did. We were so low in the water, I'm sure the barge didn't even know we were there. We just made it to a slightly submerged sandbar when the tug roared by. We were half-swamped by the wake, and there's no question we were scared, but in true pilot fashion, we were too proud to admit defeat.

Once the barge was safely past and I managed to get the motor started, we

---

[173] Mark Twain's Huckleberry Finn and his friend Jim, a runaway slave, made their way down the Mississippi River on a raft.

climbed out of the boat, pushed it off the sandbar, and continued our journey. Around noon we stopped for lunch, tying up to a dead tree protruding from the water.

Gib brought out the food, a case of Coke and 24 hotdogs. No water, no beer, no more grub, just warm Coke and cold, ugly dogs. "Where's the rest of the chow, Gib?"

"That's it," he said with that crooked smile that drove his superiors to the bottle, and at that moment I saw merit in their frustration.

"How about beer and bread and fixings?" I said with some venom. "Surely you're joking."

He wasn't.

Damn. Had I been a provisioning officer, I'd have drummed him out of the service on the spot. As it was, I calmed down and tried to remember the third of Gib's rules for living: *What you're eating is what you want to eat.* I chased down a couple of raw, cold dogs with hot Coke. It was a tough philosophy to swallow.

Gib did mention in a quieter moment that he'd planned to supplement this meager fare with fish and game. However, the only things we managed to catch were a lone catfish, a very angry garfish, and a furious turtle, none of which we ate.

By this time I'd taken over as captain. Neither Gib nor Herrell knew much of anything about mechanics, and I was beginning to question what they knew about food. After lunch, I remanufactured a new rope, fiddled some more with the engine, and cranked it up. It sprang to life with a satisfying purr.

New Orleans, here we come!

Our speed picked up as the fuel burned down until we were going at least 4 mph. I sucked down two more Cokes. Where was Vicksburg? Golly, there were a lot of bends in the river. We followed the channel, although we stayed close to the edge in case we encountered another of those killer barges. Before long we discussed cutting corners; surely a 17-foot, shallow-draft boat, even sitting low, would navigate the straighter course. It worked. We went 100 yards, smiling all the way, before hitting bottom and shearing a prop pin. I made the repairs as Gib and Herrell drank Cokes and kibitzed. Vicksburg had disappeared. Could we have taken the wrong fork? But there wasn't any fork to take.

Night was falling, so we beached the "River Queen" on an island, ate more dogs (still cold—no matches), brushed our teeth with Coke, and hunkered down for the night. When we woke at dawn, there were some strange critter marks in the sand, but whatever night visitors we may have had were gone.

Another dog and Coke for breakfast—what kind of river men didn't drink coffee—and on we went.

The fuel was almost gone, but we were really moving. We must have been going 5 mph. And just where was my angel? There was no way she was going to put up with nothing but dogs, Coke, and danger. Maybe she was on R&R. I didn't share my concerns with my boat mates; they were too crass to understand.

Just as we spotted the Vicksburg Bridge in the distance, the engine turned silent. Out of gas. Two hours later we rowed into town, looking like anything but three of Uncle Sam's finest. The good ole boys at the dock were quite amused. It was pretty obvious they knew we were Yankees, and stupid ones at that. We did our best to maintain a stiff upper lip.

We fueled up and this time, *I* went to the store. I bought bottled water, ice for the cooler, a case of beer, and two lonely Cokes. I'd fix those guys. I checked the rest of my list: snacks, a full complement of groceries, a tin of Maxwell House coffee, and matches. That night I'd give the Coleman stove a workout. We now had good chow and we were fast becoming skilled river pilots.

As we left Vicksburg behind and made our way downriver, the old, ornery engine quit more than once, and I was beginning to dislike barges and river bends. What else could go wrong? We could tell that the day was beginning to close in—Mississippi aviators know the territory—and we kept one eye on the sky while having lunch on a sandbar. It was a lunch to remember. First I laid down a thick slice of rye bread topped by a dollop of Grey Poupon mustard, a spoonful of fresh horseradish, and a slab of red onion. Next I pulled the tab on a can of Maine's finest Port Clyde sardines and lowered them, dripping with oil, onto my masterpiece. Adding a slash of Tabasco ^{sauce} for flavor, I crowned it all with another slice of rye. As my blade came down on this odoriferous delight, dividing it into three parts, Herrell turned away and spat. "I'd drink the Delta before I'd put that in my mouth." Gib laughed and pretended to throw up. I was shocked!

Herrell turned. "Throw me one of those dogs, Gib." To my amazement, they both grabbed a few of those cold, raw hotdogs and wolfed them down. Gib made a growling sound. "What's with all this beer? Where's the Coke?"

"Sorry, chum," I smirked, opening a can with my trusty church key. "Today's the day for a Miller." From the can gushed forth a spray of cool mist, frosting Gib's face.

"You're really pushing it, Don," he hissed. "Now hand me that Coke before I hurl you off this sandbar."

"That makes two of us," said Herrell. "I think we'd better be shoving off. I don't like the look of those clouds coming in from the west."

We pushed off the sandbar, my stomach dancing with joy, and chugged back into the main channel. Two prehistoric-looking garfish jumped out of the muddy water, fighting over a piece of floating garbage before disappearing below the surface. It was cloudy and hot, a typical Mississippi summer day.

The next minute, the sun disappeared. Gib turned to look over my shoulder. "Don't look now, boys, but the sky is about to fall." He'd no sooner spoken than the wind rose up in a fury. Huge, gray-black thunderheads threatened above, and the peaceful river became a wake of angry waves.

Herrell's face said it all. "We're cooked." I didn't even have time to take a breath. The rain hit so hard we couldn't see ten feet from the boat. For all we could tell, we might have been in the middle of the ocean. The wind brought a chill of winter on a downdraft from the stratosphere. The adrenaline rush made it difficult to sit still.

"Got any ideas, Don?" said Gib. Just then our engine began to sputter, and an all-too-familiar sound came out of the fog. The blood froze in our veins.

"Is that what I think it is?" yelled Herrell. "*Is it?*" The sound of the prow wave of an oncoming barge grew louder, just as our engine died.

"*Oh, #%?*^!*," we screamed in unison. With a speed inspired by danger, I desperately re-coiled the rope-pull starter, while Herrell and Gib fought with the oars to pull us towards shore. A black wall of barge erupted just behind us, its wake bubbling over the gunnels and swamping our little boat. We bailed for our lives. Within minutes the barge was past, but the diesel of its pusher tug throbbed way too close for comfort.

The storm left as fast as it had come, leaving us soaked and steaming but alive. The engine started without a problem and I edged our ancient rig toward the side of the channel. With a sigh of relief, we watched the barge that had been a predator moments before disappear peacefully 'round the next bend. We'd come way too close to being propeller food.

Natchez, our next stop, was nowhere in sight, so that night we found another island on which to spend the night. At least this time we had hot chow and cold beer, along with water for my friends.

Our fuel stops on the river seemed perfectly spaced. We ran out of gas exactly five miles short of each of them, but we couldn't carry any more fuel— the boat would sink. By Thursday morning when we rowed into Natchez, we knew we'd never reach New Orleans in time for our rendezvous with Polly and her friends. We called Barry to meet us Friday morning in Baton Rouge with the car and trailer. When we ran out of gas late Thursday, we still had about a two-hour row the next morning to reach our destination. That night we slept on another island.

It was a quiet night. The moon was full, and stray armadillos and snakes pulled themselves out of the water to stroll through our camp. A riverboat, its lights blazing, steamed down the middle of the channel, the music from its calliope drifting into the darkness. We were unshaven, a bit tired, and definitely in need of a shower, but we were more than content. We didn't have a tent or a tarp, so when a storm moved in we just lay there, watching the lightning show and getting bathed by warm, torrential rain. Tomorrow we'd be with those lucky maidens in the French Quarter, regaling them with our stories on the river and in the sky, but tonight we were adventurers, survivors of danger, buccaneers sleeping under the stars. Huck Finn and Jim would have felt right at home.

Cruisin' the Big Easy

The next day Barry met us in Baton Rouge. We loaded the boat on the trailer, shaved, tidied up in the dockside restroom, and headed for the Big Easy. Polly was coming in from a trip later in the day, so when we got to her house, we knew we'd be meeting her folks.

The Mississippi team, cleaned up and ready for fun in the Big Easy.
L. to r.: Gibson, me, and Barry. (*Don Herrell probably took the picture.*)

I walked up to the front door and rang the bell. A beautiful woman opened the door. Wow, this knockout was Polly's mom? When Polly had mentioned that her mom was 43, 43 had seemed like, well, old. But this lady didn't look old; she looked gorgeous.

Then I recalled a bit of advice from my own mother: "Look at the mother of the girl you wish to marry," Betty had cautioned, "because that's what you're going to live with." Was I going to marry Polly? I wasn't sure, but at that moment I felt like one lucky guy.

Polly's dad showed up a little later. "When you meet my dad," Polly had warned, "be sure to claim Cape Cod as home and not New York. Daddy's never been out of the South, and he has some preconceived notions about New York. To him the place is paved over with bad people, the worst sort of damn Yankees."

Polly's folks were kind and polite, and we enjoyed talking with them. Mr. Horne did ask us to move the "River Queen" behind the house—something about degrading the neighborhood.

Polly in her Delta uniform, 1960.

When Polly showed up from her flight, she was beautiful in her stylish stewardess uniform, hat, and heels. The stews of that era looked great, and they loved to strut their stuff. After chatting with her folks some more, we left to pick up the other stews and were soon off to Bourbon Street—four hotshot air force officers and their ladies.

I suggested a diner for dinner, but the ladies weren't having it. Ah well, cotton picking might help, or maybe a round or two of washing dishes to pay for the meal. Never mind: For Polly, it was worth it.

Late Sunday afternoon, after two nights and days of dancing, touring, picnicking, and fun, we drove back to Greenville. We were broke, but we'd had a great time. Besides, the return trip was easy. No barges, no sandbars, no thunderstorms, and no cold hotdogs. Heck, Barry even had enough gas and a map.

Chapter 56 – Heading West to Willie

1960–1961

In August of 1960, I left Greenville for the 3526th Pilot Training Squadron at "Willie," Williams Air Force Base near Chandler, Arizona. It would be tough to be so far away from Polly—I admit it, I was really hooked—but I was looking forward to my new assignment. Willie had started out as another of those permanent, temporary bases, but now it was one of the most popular spots in the air force, and Uncle Sam was putting lots of money into making it a keeper. I guess the brass must have wanted some fun in the sun.

Our base commander, Colonel Richard Abbey, greeted us and explained that since the civilian primary flight schools were closing, Williams would be providing primary flight training in the Cessna T-37 and basic flight training in the Lockheed T-33. When it became available, we'd also be flying the beautiful, supersonic Northrop T-38 Talon. He went on to say that because the IPs from Greenville were so experienced, we were being assigned to primary training, which meant we'd be flying T-37s. The junior, less-experienced pilots would remain with the basic flight school, flying T-33s.[174]

An audible groan went up from the crowd. The T-37A was a small, twin-engine jet with side-by-side seating. Nicknamed the Tweet, its high-pitched, screaming engines could deafen an ant in a nest. *Where art thou, Angel? One more aircraft demotion and I'll being flying models.*

There was one consolation. "When the T-38A arrives," Colonel Abbey concluded, "you gentlemen will be the originating pilots." We managed a weak cheer.

To add insult to injury, before we could train anyone on the T-37s, we had

---

[174] The T-37 was used to teach the fundamentals of aircraft handling, instrumentation, formation, and night flying. The T-37A was first delivered to the air force in 1956; models B and C were introduced in later years. The last T-37C was produced in 1975. Some of these aircraft remain in service as of 2008. The first T-38 supersonic jet trainers were put into service in 1961 and the plane was produced until 1972. As of 2008, the T-38 is still in use.

Cessna T-37B Tweet.
(*Pima Air and Space Museum, courtesy of Ben Fisher.*)

to ferry them to Williams from their former civilian bases in Florida. Chuck Woody, a senior pilot, flew a venerable Douglas C-47 loaded with 20 IPs to several Florida locations. What a blast! Flying over Texas, I led the charge as all 20 of us ran toward the tail of the plane. The old Gooney Bird lurched and staggered close to a stall. We knew Chuck could handle it, though he did offer a few words of pointed advice from the cockpit. After we crawled back into our bucket seats, we behaved ourselves for the rest of the loud, hot flight.[175]

Chuck dropped a bunch of us at Graham Air Base, from which we flew our T-37s back to Arizona in a 12-ship gaggle. The Tweet had a very short range between refuelings, so we traveled in 300-nautical-mile legs, practicing aerobatics and rarely flying more than 500 feet off the ground. It was the most relaxed flying we'd done in a long time. Every month, it seemed, aviation was becoming more regulated and more controlled. Our cross-country odyssey may well have signaled the end of an era.

Settling In

Bachelor quarters at Williams were small apartments located near the Officers' Club. They each had two bedrooms, a shared living area, and a kitchenette. My roommate was Tom Craig, a young married officer whose family had not yet arrived. We were very competitive and flew a lot together

---

[175] During World War II, the C-47 carried personnel and cargo, towed troop-carrying gliders, and dropped paratroopers into enemy territory. After the war, it participated in the Berlin Airlift of 1948–49 and later provided service in Korea and Vietnam. Affectionately known as the Gooney Bird, the plane was nearly 64 feet long and could carry 6,000 lbs. of cargo, a fully assembled Jeep, or 28 soldiers in full combat gear.

to sharpen our skills. We finally resolved the issue as to who was best by agreeing that he did the best Immelmann in the world and I the finest barrel roll. Aerobatics never failed to provide us with a rush, and it took constant practice to maintain and improve our skills.

Tom was smart, perceptive, ambitious, and one of the best-informed men I'd ever known. On subjects ranging from marriage to applied aviation to politics, I learned much from him, and he made no bones about his ambition to become a general officer. There's no doubt he had what it took: He could teach, he could lead, and he was always open to learning more.

Life at Willie Air Patch settled into a routine of work and play. The base was about 30 minutes from Chandler and Mesa, Arizona, a short hour from Phoenix. One of our favorite hangouts was the Baseline Tavern. The steak was fine and the music in the style of Fats Domino.[176]

Among the guys who hung out at the Baseline were three other pilots named Wright. Two of them were immediately dubbed Wilbur and Orville, and I became D.R. (for Donald Robert). The fourth guy, Jerdy Wright, was for some reason spared a nickname.[177]

There were also plenty of women at the Baseline. At the beginning of an era where women were testing the boundaries, girdles were out and birth control was in. Even so, these Arizona beauties were somewhat of a letdown after the belles of Mississippi.

In November 1960, the Democratic candidate, John F. Kennedy, was elected President. Although the dominant political tendency among air force personnel was probably Republican, the service itself was apolitical. Our job was to enforce whatever our politicians needed. On the night of the election, when Kennedy was declared the victor, one sage got up on the O Club bar. "Sharpen those skills, guys," he declared. "We're going to need them." How did he know?

Pilots entering primary flight school, the second phase of their 15-month program, had completed preflight training already. If they didn't wash out, they would go on to basic flight school and the T-33. Our job was to ready them for the task. The plane in which we were to do so was the T-37.

---

[176] Fats (Antoine Dominique) Domino, born on February 26, 1928, is a classic rhythm and blues and pop artist from New Orleans. In 1960, his most popular hit was *Walkin' to New Orleans*. In 1998 he was awarded the National Medal of Arts by President Bill Clinton, but it was lost, along with all his possessions, when his home was severely damaged in August 2005 by Hurricane Katrina. In August 2006, President George W. Bush traveled to New Orleans to present Fats with a replacement medal.

[177] Major Jerdy A. Wright was a superb pilot who was lost in action over North Vietnam in 1966. The North Vietnamese returned his remains to U.S. control in 1988. He is listed on the Vietnam Veterans' Memorial in Washington, D.C., panel 5E, line 129.

Each instructor was given three or four students to train for six months—a moment of truth for student and instructor alike. As it turned out, I enjoyed the job a lot. Taking a student from the freedom and relative irresponsibility of college through the rapid transformation to military pilot was interesting and challenging. I loved instructing and I think it showed, but I never had to inspire anyone: Gung ho was a given.

Since the cadet program was shutting down, the majority of primary flight candidates were either young college graduates from Air Force ROTC or graduates of the Air Force Academy, Annapolis, or West Point. A few were fresh from OCS.

A few students began to trickle in from Southeast Asia, most from countries one needed an atlas to identify. I became involved in training five of them, well-educated young men from the royal family of Cambodia. We were encouraged to show them all courtesies, including them in activities such as hiking and sightseeing, involving them in cultural events, and entertaining them in our homes. Still innocent of the brewing problems in Southeast Asia, we treated them more as an educational challenge than a group of allies.

Most student pilots had never flown before, regardless of where they came from. Some had never been in an airplane. Nevertheless, we started each man in the T-37. Twenty hours later he was solo and safe. Military flying demands complete attention. Inattention and laziness invite the maximum penalty: death. Part of the job was to make certain my students understood this. I treated them with respect, but I allowed no carelessness. A year or two later, prospective pilots put in 35 hours in a Cessna 172 Skyhawk before moving on to the T-37. It probably made for fewer white knuckles, but the pilots we turned out using the direct approach were second to none.[178]

The students I trained at Williams were already officers, but academics, flying, and military deportment were graded the same for all: What you flew in the future depended upon how you performed today. Student officers, however, didn't have to march to chow or class or put up with harassment from those ahead of them. They'd already done that stuff at the academies, at OCS, or in ROTC.

And there was another difference between student officers and cadets: The officers were allowed to marry. I did notice, however, that after some guys took the plunge, both their interest and their work ethic suffered. It couldn't have been the Samson effect; they didn't have much hair to cut. Do you think some other factor became important?

---

[178] Over 40,000 of this four-seater, single-engine plane have been produced since 1956. One of the most popular light planes in history, the Cessna 172 is still being manufactured in 2008.

Another Yank Bites the Dust

Polly and I had seen each other on about ten separate occasions and had written for some time. Since our last visit she'd switched airlines from Delta to Pan Am, the world's preeminent commercial airline.[179]

Polly on my black and white Austin-Healey—the
loves of my life, 1960.

---

[179] From the late 1920s until the early 1990s, Pan Am (Pan American World Airways) was considered by many to be America's premier airline. Initially winning government contracts to carry mail to foreign lands, the airline soon expanded its passenger services and by 1939 had the first weekly service between New York and the U.K. The fare was $375, equivalent to more than $5,000 today. By 1942 the company had a route circumnavigating the globe, and during World War II it was said that Pan Am showed the military the way around the world. The airline continued to provide first-class, innovative service for decades to come. Although the Pan Am brand name has been resurrected on occasion by other airline-related endeavors, the original Pan Am closed its doors in 1991.

I could hear her enthusiasm in the letter she wrote about her decision:

Dear Don,

I'm so excited! I ran into a college friend, Helen Taylor, New Years' Eve in the Hotel Tamanaco in Venezuela. She is flying for Pan Am and is bubbling with enthusiasm about the job, travels, and especially the airline. I've enjoyed flying for Delta; they treat me well, but I so much want to expand my traveling horizons. So—I applied for a job with Pan Am and I've been accepted. I'm off to Miami for training and it looks like I'll be based there, flying primarily to South America. I hated to give up the seniority that I accrued at Delta, but the turnover of stewardesses is rapid; the job is a wonderful lark for young single girls. The letters may be slow for the next six weeks as I'll be in training.

Love, Polly

As a Pan Am stewardess, Polly was living in Miami and flying the new Boeing 707 and Douglas DC-8 from New York to Miami to South America. Her letters sounded like a travelog: Rio, Argentina, Colombia, the Caribbean, Cuba, and Central America. The fact that she spoke fluent Spanish, as well as French, was a distinct asset on this route south of the border. She had layovers in places most folks had only read about, and although they often weren't long enough to recover from her long hours in the air, she still had many opportunities to enjoy the flavor of South American life.[180]

In December I invited her to visit me in Arizona, using some of her complimentary passes. We had a great time dancing, touring, talking, and laughing together. Just before she left I threw myself on bended knee, professed my enduring love, and proposed marriage. She accepted. Look out, southern women: Another Yank bites the dust.

We set the date for Saturday, September 9, 1961, in Greenwood, Mississippi. I would be 27, Polly 25. We'd both traveled a lot, I worldwide and she to the islands and South America. We shared the same values, had much in common, and enjoyed each other's company. We also had a joint vision of our future together. Polly knew she would be wedded to the military as well as to me, and she understood what that would entail.

---

[180] The 707 four-engine jet, introduced in the 1950s, dominated passenger air transport in the 1960s and established Boeing as one of the largest manufacturers of passenger aircraft. The DC-8 made its first commercial flight in 1959, and variants of this model were produced until 1972. In 1961, the DC-8 became the first civilian jet to break the sound barrier.

My mother, grandmother, and brother Chris were living in our family house in Cotuit on Cape Cod while George was on assignment in Korea. I wrote Betty a newsy letter and mentioned, as a P.S., that I'd asked Polly to marry me and she'd accepted.

The news elicited a quick response of the general mom questions. "Who's Polly?" she fired back. "Where is she from? When did you meet her?" Soon Polly and Betty were corresponding and Polly flew to the Cape for a visit. I was happy not to be there, as I knew a verdict on my decision would be soon forthcoming. Fortunately, the three women enjoyed each other immediately and had a rich relationship from that time forward. Whatever may have been said about me on that visit has been lost to history.

Fumes Over Miami

Polly and I only saw each other once more before the wedding.

"Why don't you come on down and visit," she said in one of her letters. "We've a lot of catching up and planning to do."

"Hey, Skip," I hollered across the almost-empty flight line classroom. Skip Coolidge was a fellow instructor and a super baseball player who hailed from Florida. He was usually up for getting extra flight time.

"Yeah, what's up?"

"I'm signing up for a T-33 this weekend to visit my fiancée in Miami. Wanna go?"

"Sure." Then he stopped. "Whoops, I forgot. My wife has reservations for the dinner dance at the O Club. I doubt she'll stand still for a cross-country."

"Come on, Skip, you can eat and dance anytime; cross-countries are hard to come by."

"How long do you figure it'll take?"

"Off the top of my head, I'd say two three-hour legs down and three legs back because of the headwinds, a total of about fifteen hours."

Skip grinned. "That's mighty tempting. Okay, sign me up, but you'll have to help pay for the divorce."

"We can work the morning shift on Friday, leave about noon, and come back Sunday," I proposed. "That'll give us two nights down there. I'll do the flight plan."

"All right," Skip agreed, "but doing it that way we'll sure put some blisters on our butts. Three hours is just about max range for the T-Bird; you'd better plan this trip down to the nitty-gritty."

That Friday, the weather on our way to Barksdale Air Force Base in Louisiana, our half-way point, had been surprisingly good for a late-winter excursion. Tailwinds had taken a bit off the three-hour trip, and after grabbing a sandwich and coffee, we headed out to the freshly fueled bird for the final leg: Barksdale to Homestead Air Force Base, south of Miami. According to the Chamber of Commerce, Miami weather was beautiful, but the Florida peninsula was under an occluded front with low ceilings.[181]

"What do you think, Skip?"

"Looks okay to me," he replied. "If we have to punch out over Florida, it won't matter whether it's clear or cloudy; the alligators will enjoy their meal just the same."

Cleared for takeoff, we cranked the T-Bird and took to the skies. To save fuel, we cruised a little higher than normal—the distance to Homestead was at the absolute edge of our fuel range. Everything counted: altitude and speed, which we calculated on long-range cruise charts; tailwinds; and a bit of luck. Along the way, we carried on a conversation via mics set up through the oxygen masks strapped to our helmets.

"Oh, man, is my butt sore from sitting here," I lamented as I rolled from cheek to cheek. "Whose idea was this, anyway?"

"All yours, old buddy, and by the way, you'd better take a look at the flight plan. We're falling behind. When we crossed that occluded front, the winds fell off completely. We might even have a bit of a headwind."

I did a quick turn on the E6B calculator. "Damn, Skip! It looks like we're gonna run out of fuel about 40 miles short of Homestead. Any 'gators 40 miles north of Miami?"

Skip laughed. "You don't want to know."

"Looks like we'd better drop in at MacDill in Tampa and spend the night," I said. "It's only about 50 more miles.[182]

---

[181] In 1942, the Army Air Corps took over an airstrip in Dade County, FL, originally owned by Pan American Ferries, Inc. They called it Homestead Army Air Field. During the Second World War, many pilots were trained at this facility, including those who flew supplies and personnel over the Hump (the Himalayan Mountains) from India to China. Homestead-trained pilots also took part in the Berlin Airlift of 1948–49. In 1955, the facility was renamed Homestead Air Force Base. On August 24, 1992, the base was devastated by Hurricane Andrew, but despite extensive damage, much of it was rebuilt. Redesignated in 1994 as Homestead Air Reserve Base, as of 2008 it continues to play a key role in our nation's defense.

[182] MacDill was established near a site where, 40 years earlier, troops had rendezvoused for service during the Spanish-American War. Dedicated in 1941 and originally known as Southeast Air Base and then MacDill Field, the facility was renamed MacDill Air Force Base shortly after the air force became a separate branch of the armed services in 1947. During World War II, the base served as a training site for pilots and, in late 1944 and 1945, as a detention facility for German prisoners. The

"Jacksonville Center, this is Air Force 311, flight level 350. We're in a low-fuel state and need to refile to MacDill Air Force Base. Over."

No response.

I repeated the call.

Still no response.

"MacDill approach. This is Air Force 311, flight level 350, 50 miles north, emergency fuel state, unable to contact Jax Center. Over."

Nothing, *nada*. Radio failure again. We were in deep do-do.

Decision time. MacDill was forecast for minimum ceilings; Miami was clear.

"I vote for Miami, Skip. How about you?"

"I second that."

We began a cruise climb, scratching for every bit of fuel economy possible as we staggered toward the operational ceiling of the T-Bird.

"Great news," I quipped. "We're only going to be 20 miles short."

"Wonderful. I suppose you're aware, Wright, that if I had any sense at all, I would now be at the O Club, dancing with my wife and contemplating how I wanted my steak cooked."

"Think of the adventure, Skip. How many guys get to play hide and seek with alligators?"

We had only one ace left in our deck. "Let's shut down the engine," I said, "and glide as far as we can. Then we can aim for a forced landing pattern at Homestead and crank up the engine in the pattern."

"Sounds like a plan," Skip replied.

We arrived over Homestead at about 5,000 feet, flashing our landing lights. We then started a spiral descent, using the predicted winds to choose a runway. On final approach we relit the engine, which rewarded our fuel-preservation measures with a comforting, familiar growl. We wagged our wings and flashed our lights to indicate radio failure, and the tower gave us a green light to land. They also sent a "follow-me" truck to guide us to Operations.

"Any problems?" asked the airman who parked us.

"No, not really," I said. "Just fill her up and send out a radio technician." Skip and I did our best to come off as cool jet pilots, but I think the airman might have noticed our chattering teeth.

We knew better than to share our alligator-bait story with Polly, but we did regale her with other flying tales. Not to be outdone, she had a few of her own. She was bursting with pride at being part of the world's premier airline.

---

base has remained in operation ever since. As of 2008, it continues to serve a vital role in our nation's defense.

From the classy uniforms of the crew to the new, polished jets on which she served, Pan Am knew how to do it right.

"Guys, this airline is the most impressive operation I've ever been around. Just this last trip, I flew with one of the old Clipper flying-boat captains. He shared stories with us about circling the globe and landing in harbors all over the world." In the late 1930s and early '40s, Polly explained, flying was only for well-heeled businessmen or the rich and famous. There were few flights that didn't have celebrities aboard, and the service was equal to the most elegant ocean liners of the era.[183]

Polly continued. "Before the war, Pan Am had a rich history of pioneering international routes. Especially in South America, it had built and manned radio-aid stations, directed the construction of new airfields, and developed the beginnings of air traffic control. When World War II broke out, Pan Am had the worldwide flying experience that the Army Air Force lacked. The company led; coached; and shared radio aids, traffic control, runways, and facilities with the armed forces. It's even rumored that Pan Am agents doubled as operatives in the Office of Strategic Services (OSS), the agency that preceded the CIA.

"Of course," she explained, "all of this clandestine activity is still classified, but if the story can ever be told, it will probably turn out to be one of the more intriguing tales of the war."

All in all, it was a great reunion. Polly and I spent our two days together yakking, laughing, and planning our upcoming wedding. September was just a few months away.

The trip back to Willie was uneventful—two stops for fuel and no close calls. Over the weeks to come, however, Skip did remind me more than once that he'd missed a really great dance.

---

[183] Pan Am's flying boats were named Clippers because of their close relationship with the sailing clipper ships of the 19th century. The Clippers made their first commercial flights across the Pacific in 1936. Later, the name was applied to the company's land-based planes.

Chapter 57 – The Best Class Ever

1961

The class coming up was to be my last before taking leave to get married. On the first day of training, I walked to my table at the flight line to meet my students. They snapped to attention and saluted, remaining so until I invited them to sit down. The military formality and decorum at the beginning of the program was often a shock to the argumentative, college-boy attitude of many students, but it was almost always effective. Flying is based on action-reaction. Debate can mean death.

I could tell that the three guys standing before me were going to do fine: They were chomping at the bit, ready to go.

Tom Westhafer was a tall, handsome dude from Indiana and a graduate of Florida State. His family was in the steel business, and like me, he loved fast cars and good-looking women. Larry Joe (L.J.) Taylor was a farm kid from North Carolina who turned out to be one of the best pilots I ever trained. He caught on more quickly than most students and his enthusiasm was inspiring to all. Charlie Clack was a rangy lad from Oklahoma, a superb baseball player, and an exception to my theory that great athletes don't usually make good pilots. All three were filled with skill, enthusiasm, and a desire to learn.

The flying program is designed to be competitive and challenging. Striving for first place—first to fly, first to solo, first check ride, first military flight—is a mind game, and the combination of desire and enthusiasm figures prominently in success. In the spring and summer of 1961, I felt at the top of my game in both flying skill and the ability to demonstrate a maneuver. Having motivated, enthusiastic students was icing on the cake. It was hard for me to be humble, and my enthusiasm seemed to carry over to them. We didn't just fly airplanes, we flew *jets*. These guys were great: They learned more quickly and flew better than any pilots I'd ever trained, yet we still had a formal military relationship.

Making It Over the Mountain

Both the T-37 and the T-33 at Willie were assigned several specific areas, from ground-level up. Each area was restricted to a particular mission: transition, formation, or instruments. This same arrangement was used at other bases, but in the West the areas were larger and could support more planes.

When flying the morning shift—dawn to noon—the weather was almost always smooth and clear, though Arizona's huge copper mines did smog up certain areas. Afternoon summer thunderstorms, on the other hand, could equal anything I'd ever encountered in the Midwest or South. On some days these storms were so numerous we had to turn constantly to avoid them. We were surrounded by mountains and ground contact was spotty, so navigation could become a problem. All of this was good training, but poking one's nose into a storm is risky business, and sometimes we paid the price, suffering the loss of both aircraft and crew.

One early summer afternoon, Tom Westhafer and I were on a mission in the T-37 over Globe, Arizona, a copper-mining town in our transition area. On this day we were practicing spins, the ability of a pilot to put the aircraft into a position where it is spinning out of control and then to recover from this condition. In the spin maneuver, the pilot starts by pulling the nose up with the power retarded. As the aircraft runs out of speed, it stalls. The pilot then applies full rudder and pulls back on the stick to induce the spin. As the spin tightens up, it accelerates to as many as 50 turns per minute. To recover, the pilot applies the opposite rudder and pops the stick forward.

This maneuver was both confusing and violent, and not all students could cope. Occasionally a student lost control and had to bail out. We probably lost more planes from perfecting spins than from all other causes combined. Even so, we lost relatively few aircraft.

I had picked Globe that day because the continuous belching of smoke from its copper mines gave us the ability to remain oriented over a fixed position on the ground as we practiced this disorienting exercise. Tom and I spun from 20,000 feet down to 10,000, climbed back up, and did it again—as many times as our fuel allowed. Up and down, up and down. Lieutenant Westhafer was good and getting better.

While we were practicing, thunderstorms were building up in all quadrants. Eventually they forced us away from Globe, but I still wasn't concerned. We could always rely on our VOR navigation radio to get us back to base. Soon we were down to the usual 20 minutes of fuel; it was time to head back. "Okay, Lieutenant," I said, "let's go home."[184]

We were flying about 10,000 feet, snaking around the thunderstorms, and all we could see was the desert directly below us. Tom started back with the VOR needle pointed straight ahead as it should be, but I had a very uneasy feeling. Despite the reading, I recognized nothing on the ground.

"Lieutenant Westhafer, do you know where you are?" I said in my most military and imperious voice.

"Yes, Sir."

Good, I thought, *because I don't have a clue*. Fifteen minutes of fuel left.

"Lieutenant, are you *sure* you know where you are?

"I think so, Sir."

"Good." Fuel warning light and ten minutes of fuel left.

"Lieutenant," I said, forcing a tone of impatience. *"Do you know where you are?"*

"No, Sir. Do you?"

"No, damn it. Let me have the bird."

I dove under the storm to the desert floor: nothing but sagebrush.

"Tom," I said, a little less formality seeming appropriate under the circumstances, "check your parachute straps. It looks like we're going to have to punch out."

We were flying on fumes. Tom's eyes were as big as saucers. Suddenly, just above the desert floor, a mountain loomed directly ahead. We roared up and over it, praying our fuel would hold. Much to our surprise, on the other side was a huge air base. B-47s lined the ramp and thousands of old airplanes were parked along the perimeter.[185]

Davis-Monthan Air Force Base, Tucson, Arizona. We declared an emergency on guard channel just as one of the engines flamed out from fuel starvation.[186]

---

[184] Radio navigation uses radio frequencies to determine a position on the Earth. The VOR (Very-high-frequency Omni-directional Range) system is most commonly used over land. The LORAN (LOng Range Aid to Navigation) system is used by ships and planes on the high seas.

[185] The six-engine B-47 was the nation's first swept-wing, multiengine bomber and a mainstay of U.S. strategic defense in the 1950s. Between 1947 and 1956, over 2,000 of these aircraft were built by Boeing, Douglas, and Lockheed. Many were used by the Strategic Air Command. The last B-47s were out of service by the mid-1960s.

[186] Davis-Monthan was named for two military flyers from Tucson who died serving their country. Originally envisioned as a civilian airport, its first runway was dedicated by Charles Lindbergh in 1927, just months after he crossed the Atlantic in the *Spirit*

We set up a spiral flameout pattern, landed, and pulled off the runway. "Shut down your engine and remain in hold position," instructed the tower controller in a no-nonsense tone. We did as we were told. Within minutes, a slew of Air Police surrounded the aircraft, small arms drawn and submachine guns at the ready. Relieved but wary, we climbed out of the plane with two urgent desires: to kiss the ground and to pee. We did neither. Without ceremony, the gendarmes posted us up against the wing. It took quite a bit to convince them we weren't invading marauders, just two lost sheep from the other side of the mountain.

At that time, Davis-Monthan was a SAC base, and it seemed that General Power, in his quest for the security and safety of his nuclear bombers, sometimes pulled stunts like this in an attempt to breach the security of his bases. Pity the commander who didn't respond properly.[187]

Once convinced of our credentials, the powers that be allowed us to crank up our remaining engine and taxi to Operations. The maintenance crew quickly discovered the problem: Our violent spinning had caused the directional gyros in the VOR to process information exactly 180 degrees in the opposite direction. By the grace of God and my guardian angel, Davis-Monthan was exactly 180 degrees in the opposite direction.

I called the squadron at Williams to report our whereabouts. "We're refueling now and will return ASAP."

While maintenance fixed the gyros and fueled the T-37, Tom and I had a cup of coffee. I was not looking forward to my fate at the home drome.

We returned to base and debriefed the mission. Nothing was said by anybody, and I tried to become invisible. Just before we were dismissed for the day, Major Uriel Johnson, one of my mentors from my days at Spence, strode into the classroom. We came to attention.

"At ease, men," said Major Johnson. Then, "Lieutenant Wright, please remain standing."

I was doomed for sure. I stood, red-faced and scared, waiting for the axe to fall.

"Gentlemen, I asked Lieutenant Wright to rise because he saved an aircraft today. As you know, the thunderstorms were horrific and Lieutenant

---

of St. Louis. The facility became a military base in 1940. From 1960 through 1984, ICBMs (intercontinental ballistic missiles) were stored at this site. The missiles are gone now, but as of 2008, the base is still in operation.

[187] General Thomas S. Power (1905–1970) became vice commander of the Strategic Air Command in 1948 under Curtis LeMay. After General LeMay was named vice chief of staff for the air force in 1957, General Power took over as SAC's commander in chief, a post he held until his retirement in 1964.

Wright was trapped away from the base. Rather than penetrate the storms, he chose to fly to Davis-Monthan to refuel and wait them out. Good job, Wright."

If that was the way he perceived the incident, it was fine with me. Thank goodness my angel was along for the ride.

"Please remain at ease," said Major Johnson, and he left.

I sat down, shaking in my boots. Tom Westhafer laid a hand on my arm. "Great job," he said, grinning. "Don, gotcha!"

Chapter 58 – Tying the Knot

1961

It was now early September, almost time for me to depart on a month's leave for my upcoming nuptials. I didn't yet have enough seniority to qualify for base housing. However, using the allowance provided to married personnel, I rented a furnished apartment for us in Chandler—one of several units surrounding a common area. I turned my fine, young pilots over to Tom Craig to finish their course, parked the Austin-Healey in front of our new abode, and hitched a ride on a military transport to Natchez, Mississippi.

Polly's folks now lived in Natchez, where her dad, Billy Horne, was managing another Billups station. Polly had resigned her job at Pan Am—stewardesses weren't permitted to be married at the time—and was waiting for me at her folks' house. The wedding would be in Greenwood, Mississippi, a Leflore County town less than 20 miles from Polly's ancestral family home in Carrollton and close to most of her kin. In Mississippi, everybody is related to everybody, four cousins once-removed.

Under the best of circumstances, marriage is a challenge and a step into the unknown, but a military bride faces a huge transformation. Separations can be quick and long-lasting; in some commands the servicemen spend more time away than at home. On the other hand, instructor pilots assigned to training commands were home for dinner almost every night, and such commands usually lasted four or five years. As an IP, I felt fairly confident that nothing short of structural disintegration could affect me and that at least the first few years of our lives together would be fairly tranquil.

The big day was fast approaching. Betty and George drove down from Fort Monroe, Virginia, where George was now stationed. My grandmother, who was living in a house of her own on Cape Cod, decided she couldn't afford the trip. It was a decision she later came to regret.

George was my best man. Resplendent in his army uniform with colonel's insignia, he cut a fine figure, especially since a full colonel was probably the most revered title in the South. I wore my "mess dress," a formal uniform with medals displayed. Polly wore a stunning white gown and was without a doubt the most beautiful bride ever to have walked down the aisle at the Greenwood First Presbyterian Church.

Polly and me on our wedding day, Greenwood, MS,
September 9, 1961.

It was a wonderful and joyous occasion, from the rehearsal dinner through the modest reception. My mother and Polly were already fast friends, and Betty and George offered the house in Cotuit for a honeymoon. As a treat, Polly's dad leant us his new Plymouth sedan for the trip and off we went: husband and wife.

The Cape is beautiful in September, and we had a wonderful time. We sailed in Cotuit harbor, walked on the beaches, went to shows, visited art galleries, and endured Grandmother's morning coffee visits. She thought we were sleeping our lives away.

There was one advantage of honeymooning on the Cape: Polly had plenty of time to spend with Grandmother in the kitchen. Grandmother may not have been able to come to the wedding, but now that we had come to her, I was hoping she could impart to Polly some of her culinary skills, especially those related to the baking of homemade bread and pies.

Even a brush with Hurricane Esther on September 22 (coincidentally, my mother's 47th birthday) couldn't dampen our enthusiasm. The winds outside, up to 120 miles per hour, howled like a banshee, but inside we snuggled in front of the fire, candles flickering against shadows cast by the storm. It was a leisurely, loving start to our life together,

Too soon it was time to leave. On the way back we stopped in New York City and saw two shows, *Camelot* and *The Sound of Music*, both of which we thoroughly enjoyed. We also stopped in Virginia, where my folks held a reception for us with their army friends. Back in Natchez, we exchanged Billy's car for Polly's Plymouth and the long drive to Willie.

Like most young couples, we didn't yet have a great nest egg. In addition to $500 in savings bonds, we owned Polly's car, which was paid for, and mine, which wasn't. Even so, money was not a factor. At that time, credit cards were almost unheard of, and we were both used to living within our means. A bounced check was a crime in the air force; done more than once, it could result in a shortened career. Like most folks brought up during the Depression and the Second World War, we were very frugal. We didn't do without, but we never committed to more than we could cover in the very near future.

Meeting the Neighbors

Most of the residents in our apartment complex were young marrieds. Our immediate neighbor was student pilot Mike Freney, a recent Annapolis graduate, and his wife Sally. For some reason, Mike had chosen the air force over the navy as a career (maybe he couldn't swim either). The Freneys were typical of the Irish: Mike, gregarious and witty with an extraordinary intelligence; Sally, shy, charming, beautiful, and every bit Mike's intellectual equal. Unabashed lovers, they'd known each other since their teenage years and married the day Mike graduated from the Naval Academy.

The four of us often cooked out and then talked into the night. One evening Mike tried to teach Polly to play poker, a game at which he considered himself an expert.

"Do four of these itty-bitty twos beat your three kings and two queens," she asked innocently in her best southern accent.

Being able to stand only so much humiliation from my bride, Mike turned red and sputtered into his beer. Ever-sweet Polly, however, directed him away from this gross defeat by turning his attention toward his Irish roots. It wasn't long before he began to reminisce.

Mike Freney's Story

Mike was born in Philadelphia, Pennsylvania, in 1938 to John Aloysius Freney and Pauline Paden Freney. He and his younger sisters, Polly and Joan, were each two years apart. Everybody on both sides of the family came from Ireland, mostly from County Galway. However, the only grandparent still alive when Mike was a kid was Pauline's mom, Hilda Paden. Untimely death was a fate more often than not in this family, but Hilda lived to the ripe old age of 96.

Mike's dad graduated from Villanova University and his mom from Rosemont College. Later John became a successful businessman, specializing in real estate, travel, and insurance.

Mike and his sisters were born in Erdenheim, a small suburb of Philadelphia. At a young age they moved to Chestnut Hill. Before John and Pauline purchased the Chestnut Hill house, it had been partially destroyed by fire, but they restored it beautifully. It was a large home, with sweeping porches and spacious grounds. The children had only a five-minute walk to the local Catholic school, to a nearby park, and to a creek for fishing. Mike laughed about the time he spent all day fishing in the creek, to no avail. Feeling sorry for his plight, his sisters bought him a fish at the market to show off at home that night. Unfortunately, it was a saltwater variety, a fish story that provided a good laugh ever after.

The Freney home was filled with happy, sociable people, and the dinner table was the center of life and entertainment. Education and intelligence were a given, and conversations covering a range of topics, mostly religion and politics, lasted into the night. All were asked and expected to participate. On nights when two Jesuits, a diocesan priest, and a Christian Brother were all at the house for dinner, these conversations were particularly memorable. Mike could joust with the best of them, but while we knew him, he avoided any discussion of religion, pro or con.

Discipline in the Freney household was never a problem. The kids grew up knowing what was expected of them—education, debate, and conversation being paramount—and they usually met these expectations without a problem. Mike went to St. Joseph Prep on Girard Avenue, an all-boys Jesuit high school, and although he was selective about those subjects in which he chose to excel, he was a fine student and met with success. He was also a member of the rowing team, a sport I always associated with the determined.

Sisters Polly and Joan both went to Mercy Academy in Gwynedd Valley, where one of their classmates was Sally Murphy. Mike was smitten with this lovely gal, who tended to be a bit rebellious and difficult in this very Catholic school, and their romance flourished. The Murphys were another family of strong opinions, and they, too, were welcomed into the Freneys' extensive social network.

Often during one of the Freney marathon dinner-table sessions, the talk would turn to their Irish roots. There was much to discuss. Mike was named for his grandfather, Michael Aloysius Freaney, who changed the spelling to Freney when he came to the United States. Born at Clonberne County Galway in 1867, Michael grew up to become a successful businessman and a rabble-rouser of the first order. Like so many of his countrymen, he resented and revolted as best he could against the English repression that, for so many years, ground Irish peasant and intellectual alike into the sod. Indeed, there were times that the cattle and horses were treated with greater kindness than the citizens of Ireland.

In 1879, land reformer and socialist agitator Michael Davitt, along with Charles Stewart Parnell, helped to form an organization called the National Land League to fight against the eviction of tenant farmers. Sometime later, Michael Freaney and his two brothers rallied to Davitt's cause under the war cries of "the land for the people" and "Ireland's nation." Soon Michael's capabilities as an orator and organizer became apparent, and he was selected as secretary of the local branch of the Land League.

The Freaneys' hometown in County Galway included a blacksmith shop and a public house. They were a prosperous clan, and their home was famous as a gathering place for the disaffected and a hotspot of insurrection. As a result of the family's activities, two of Michael's brothers were incarcerated, and Michael was on the run, the authorities snapping at his heels, when he showed up in Philadelphia in 1887.

One story claimed that the imprisoned brothers back in Ireland were hanged as horse thieves on trumped-up charges, though this may have been only family folklore. One thing that's certain: After the last of the Freaneys died, the caretaker remained on the property until 1920. The Black and Tans were running wild through the countryside at that time, and after a local resident was executed as a traitor by the IRA, the Tans claimed that the Freaney homestead was the local IRA headquarters. In revenge, they burned it to the ground.[188]

Back in Philadelphia, Michael Freaney (now Freney) dove into the political scene with the same vigor he'd exhibited in Ireland, though perhaps in this case within the law. A self-made man, he became a successful businessman and an officer in the Ancient Order of Hibernians (AOH), striving throughout his life to avenge the wrongs perpetrated on the Irish. He had a brilliant mind, was an outstanding orator, and was faithful to his friends to a fault. He would have been proud of the grandson who was named for him.[189]

Mike's dad John was a mild-mannered, loving man who contracted hepatitis and died in his 40s during Mike's senior year in high school. Afterward, Pauline went to work. Money was tight, but she managed to keep the family together and Mike's sisters Polly and Joan in their private Catholic school.

Mike went on to Villanova University. After a year, he was offered a presidential appointment to the Naval Academy. Each of the Freney children made his or her unique mark on society. Polly became a stockbroker; Joan joined the Sisters of Mercy. After graduating from Annapolis, Mike was becoming a pilot.

Perhaps in part because of his rich family history, Mike was gifted with an enormous intellect and an insatiable curiosity. Although we talked about flying and I was able to offer some suggestions on how to learn better, he wasn't my student or even in my flight, and sometimes conflicting advice can do more harm than good. More often, we talked about the affairs of the world—past, present, and future. Never had I known anyone with such a grasp of world history. He was a voracious reader, a dynamic speaker, and a gifted writer. He had far more to offer Polly and me than we had to offer him, though he did avoid further games of chance with my beautiful bride.

---

[188] The Black and Tans were a paramilitary force employed by the Royal Irish Constabulary (the Irish police force) in the early 1920s to suppress revolution in the country.

[189] The AOH is a fraternal organization whose members must be Roman Catholic and either Irish-born or of Irish descent. Its roots in Ireland are said to go back as far as the 1500s. The American branch of the organization was founded in 1846 and still flourishes in the U.S. as of 2008.

A Fisherman's Tale

Shortly after the infamous night of "teaching" Polly to play poker, Mike found an article in the Sunday paper about fishing in the new resort town of Guaymas, Mexico, about a five-hour drive south of Phoenix. "Let's go fishing," Mike said, and the next Saturday morning, the four of us jumped into Polly's Plymouth for a Mexican holiday.

Guaymas was neither glamorous nor particularly comfortable. It was, however, cheap, and we were determined to enjoy ourselves. Saturday night we got little sleep, mostly due to the cockroaches and other bugs, but on Sunday morning we hired an open boat that provided all the necessary gear we'd need for a day of fishing. The boat's Mexican owner/guide promised to cook any fish we caught. While cruising the short distance to the fishing grounds, Mike regaled us with his prowess in the sport and his vast experience on the banks of Wissahickon Creek near Chestnut Hill. Polly, Sally, and I claimed to have no experience at all, and Mike was patient as he demonstrated proper fishing technique.

Mike Freney, ca. 1980.
(*Courtesy of Shelley Smith.*)

The fish of the day was red snapper, and we were going to catch a mess of them. We stationed ourselves in the four corners of the boat, each sporting a pole with a multihooked line and a bucket of bait. The anchor was out and the sun high. Immediately Sally started pulling in fish—one, two, sometimes three at a time. The boat was filling up with her catch. After a while, she threw her line over with no bait at all, and still they came. Our Mexican guide was amazed at her success.

The rest of us, fishless, simmered in the tropical sun. Mike was beside himself at being beaten by a female once again. But no matter how much he fumed, none of the rest of us caught a single fish. We didn't even get a bite.

Later that night, after a feast of red snapper with a host of spicy accompaniments, Mike managed to regain some of his composure. He was recovering nicely when Sally and Polly allowed—in all innocence, of course—how this had been such a wonderful experience and asked if he had anything else he wanted to teach them. With that, the night came to an unceremonious close.

The next morning all was well and we returned to Willie free-spirited, relaxed, and happy. I'm not sure, however, that red snapper ever tasted quite that good again.

Chapter 59 – Settling In

T he first day back after my marriage leave, Major Uriel Johnson asked me to stop by his office. "Don, you know those Cambodians you helped train?"

"Yes, Sir."

"Well, they're returning to Cambodia and we're sending five pilots who have some fighter experience with them. I've selected you as one of the five."

Married only weeks and still trying to get Polly up to speed on baking bread and pies, a four-month separation did not excite me, and it showed. I begged off.

"I understand completely," said Major Johnson. I'll have no trouble getting somebody else, and don't worry, there will be no recriminations."

Had we not noticed small Vietnamese airmen with fourragère armbands and military honors spread across their chests observing our flight-line operations, the oncoming conflict in Southeast Asia would have been all but invisible. I knew the names of the nations involved and could locate them with the aid of an atlas, but I was absolutely clueless as to how they fit into the scheme of things.

Mike's approach to politics was totally different than that of most people I knew. For one thing, his viewpoints transcended individual parties, left or right. He noticed, studied, and researched the arising situation with vigor, and he believed he had a clear vision of the future. Sadly, most of his predictions, both short- and long-term, proved correct.

I, of course, was the typical gung-ho American: full of myself, our nation, and its ability to spread democracy and good deeds throughout the world. I'd seen this phenomenon in action throughout my young life, and I'd observed few if any setbacks to make me change my mind.

Although Southeast Asia and Vietnam barely made it to the back pages of the nation's newspapers and news magazines, Mike already knew the implications of our potential involvement. He was way ahead of his time, and we would debate the pros and cons of conflict, if it ever came to that, for hours. Yes, something was going to happen; something needed to happen. Mike realized that the Domino Theory was valid at the time and that communist forces were poised for another intrusion into the free world but he worried, even then, about the leadership and abilities of the new administration to cope with such an ominous threat. His viewpoint injected a seed of doubt into my typical military thought processes. That seed germinated as I watched the future unfold.[190]

The five American pilots Major Johnson sent to Cambodia were treated like pariahs, even though their Cambodian counterparts in the States had been treated with kindness and respect. Not one of them survived the war. Maybe it was more than being a newlywed that kept me from taking Major Johnson up on his proposal. Could my angel have been whispering in my ear?

Christmas 1961

This was the first Christmas that Polly and I had spent together. It was also Mike and Sally's first Christmas as a married couple. Never mind that we were in the desert. We were determined to have a real Christmas tree.

The U.S. Forest Service was issuing permits to cut piñon trees at Mogollon Rim in Coconino National Forest, a couple hours north of Phoenix. I obtained two permits and we piled into Mike's pride and joy, a 1941 Cadillac extended-sedan limousine, to get ourselves a tree. But first we stopped in the small town of Payson for a delicious steak dinner. At the Rim we waded through snow to our knees in our fun-in-the-sun Levis and sneakers, cut two fine piñon trees, and dragged them to the car. The trees were far too tall to fit inside the Caddie, huge as it was, so we trimmed them down until we could angle them from the edge of the passenger seat in front to the far left corner of the rear. Polly and I huddled like wet lovebirds in what was left of the backseat, piñon needles pricking our arms and legs. It was going to be a long ride home.

Just as we were leaving, a ranger came up and asked why we'd cut those Douglas-fir trees. "You must be mistaken, Officer," I said. "I'm sure these are piñon trees."

The ranger, who was not impressed, was about to run us in. Quickly, I called upon my former expertise as a negotiator (aka beggar). Mike and I

---

[190] The Domino Theory, put forth by the U.S. government in support of the Truman Doctrine of the late 1940s, held that if a nation fell under communist rule, neighboring nations would soon suffer the same fate.

were soon-to-be fighter pilots, I explained. It wouldn't be long before we'd be laying our lives on the line for God, country, and apple pie.

Fortunately, the officer was swayed by my pleas. Either that or he was convinced a Yankee probably couldn't tell the difference between a piñon and a palm, let alone a Douglas-fir. He gave us a last wave as we drove away, and we roared down the mountain to a joyful Christmas.

Base Housing: Moving Up in the World

Base housing was in short supply and was allocated according to a strict air force policy based on seniority. However, after we'd lived in our Chandler apartment for three or four months, a spot on the base opened up in some old World War II barracks that had been converted into large, furnished apartments, three upstairs and three downstairs. The fact that these living quarters were designated as substandard housing meant that we also got back some of our housing allowance. Amazingly, we paid only $45 a month for more than 2,000 sq. ft. of furnished space.

Our digs may have been substandard to the air force, but to Polly and me and the other mostly newlyweds who occupied them, they were paradise. Kept cool by swamp coolers (those same evaporative-type cooling devices we'd had back in El Paso when I was in high school), the rooms were large and comfortable, and the barracks were close to the commissary, the Base Exchange, and the Officers' Club. One hardly had to leave the base. The young marrieds gathered almost nightly in the warm desert air over barbecue grills, beer, and margaritas. Steak cost 19 cents a pound, and we ate like kings. Sometimes the gatherings split into women comparing notes on household or child-rearing matters and men telling war stories of their flying machines. True pilot wives, however, listened in, learning the lingo and maneuvers well enough to brief a mission.

During the day, the wives often got together for golf, bowling, or tennis. In their off hours, the guys also participated in sports. I joined a softball league, played hard, and learned a lot. Love, life, and flying; it all merged into a fascinating lifestyle.

The weather was perfect almost all the time. In fact, there was so much sunshine we sometimes chased a rainstorm or snowstorm into the mountains, just for a reality check. In summer, we rented cabins on a lake in the Superstition Mountains. In winter, we trekked to the Mogollon Rim to play in the snow, stopping on the way home at a lodge in Payson for dinner by the fire.

There must have been something in the air at Williams. Children were everywhere, and soon Polly was pregnant as well. The hospital was three blocks away and the medical staff was excellent—a combination of career military doctors and young docs fulfilling their service commitment. We had no worries.

On Sundays, we went to church at the base chapel. The military chaplains had adventurous personalities and gave entertaining sermons. They often joined our parties and occasionally flew with us, so they understood the lingo. And of course, it was their job to bring solace to the widow after the occasional crash, an event that brought all of us back to reality.

Polly and I had made a deal soon after we married: If I went to church, she would bake bread. It was a good bargain; Grandmother had taught her well. Polly kneaded the soft dough, let it rise, and then kneaded it again. After several kneadings and risings, the finished product was beyond anything a bakery could produce. When the aroma of baking bread wafted through our open windows in Chandler, it was not unusual to see visitors at the door.

Grandmother McNerney's White Bread Recipe

Measure and stir together in a large mixing bowl:
    1/2 c. warm water
    2 pkgs. dry yeast

Add, stirring frequently:
    1-3/4 c. warm water
    7 to 7-1/4 c. sifted white, all-purpose flour
    3 Tbsp. sugar
    1 Tbsp. salt
    2 Tbsp. oil

Knead dough on bread board for about 5 minutes. Place kneaded dough in a large greased bowl and flip it over twice so that the top of the dough is greased. Cover with a cloth and place in a warm spot to rise. When the dough has risen to double its size, divide in half and knead until all air bubbles are gone.

Shape each half into a loaf and place in a greased bread pan. Put the pans in a warm place and allow the dough to rise until double in size. Bake at 375 degrees for approximately 30 minutes.

Shortly after we moved to base housing, Polly was once again practicing her culinary arts when the doorbell rang. Our visitor was Bill Kluck, a young-looking, fair-haired neighbor we'd met just the day before. A jar of peanut butter in hand, Bill walked into the kitchen of our second-floor apartment. He was obviously after the still-warm loaf sitting on the counter. I lusted after that bread myself, and I was not in the mood to share. Just then, Bill's wife Nancy stepped into the hall.

"Bill, get back in here and let those lovebirds alone."

I liked this woman already; my bread was safe. Then Polly invited them both in for bread and coffee. It was bad enough that Mike Freney had hung around our kitchen in Chandler waiting for bread. And Gib, who also had been transferred from Greenville to Williams, was a frequent consumer of said bread. Now would I have to share with Bill, too? Soon I'd be running a soup kitchen, sans soup.

I tried to be grumpy and inhospitable, but it was impossible. Before long, the four of us were laughing and talking as if we'd known each other for years. Tammy, Bill and Nancy's young daughter, was napping in their apartment, so we'd left our apartment doors open. When Tammy woke up, they excused themselves and left. By this time, the coffee was gone and the bread reduced to crumbs. To top it off, Bill took his peanut butter with him.

More New Friends

Bill was the procurement officer for the entire base. As such, he was responsible for supplying our every need, from aircraft to dishes. It was a huge and demanding task. Some leaders get a job done with vigor, dispatch, and ingenuity; others do the same job with acrimony, resistance, and selfishness. In the case of procurement, how the man in charge does his job affects every operation on base, not to mention the morale of base personnel.

When Bill first arrived at Williams, a major was in charge of the procurement office and Bill, a first lieutenant, was his assistant. The major's tendency to micromanage aggravated everyone from the base commander on down. The primary mission of the base—training pilots—was not compromised by this man, but his negative influence was felt in every other facet of the operation.

The Officers' and Enlisted clubs, the wood and automotive shops for hobbyists, and nearly every recreational event were continually underfunded, a tactic that did nothing to maintain the morale of the underpaid and overworked troops. It was as if the major felt the money for these operations was coming out of his own pocket. Funds had been allocated to improve on-base housing properties and supply the small, efficient homes with necessary upgrades, but the major kept these funds in reserve, also. Progress was at a standstill.

The straw that broke the camel's back, as they say, was television. TV was in its practical infancy; the day had just begun when the common man could afford a set and not call it a luxury. To bring this new technology to the troops, money had been budgeted to install roof antennas on base housing. True to form, the major found a reason why this couldn't be done.

Soon after, the major was gone. Maybe his tour was up; maybe the commander located a "better" slot for him. It's hard to say, but suddenly Bill found himself in the position of acting procurement officer.

Colonel William G. Kluck, ca. 1970.
(Courtesy of Bill Kluck.)

His first act was to send a requisition to his boss, base commander Colonel Richard Abbey, for several bundles of aluminum tubing and several thousand feet of copper wire. Within weeks, antennas began popping up all over the base. "How can this be?" the colonel inquired. "The major didn't authorize the purchase of any antennas before he left."

"Actually, Sir," Bill replied, "you signed the request yourself." A puzzled look came over the colonel's face as Bill explained that the tubing and wire Colonel Abbey had signed for came pre-cut and pre-wired in the form of antennas. With that, the colonel canceled the search for the major's replacement, and Bill found himself in charge of procurement. He was two ranks below grade for the job, but he was a problem-solving, money-saving, can-do guy. He made sure the base got what it needed to run efficiently and effectively, but there were no $100 hammers bought on his watch.

Bill's wife Nancy was a beautiful strawberry blond. She sang like an angel and was the choir director for the Protestant church on base. Like most of the wives, she also ran a loving home and participated in the active social life so necessary to Bill's career. And like Polly, she had a bun in the oven.

Both Bill's and Nancy's parents lived in San Diego and visited often, but they were as different as people could be. Nancy's dad was Commander Hugh Olds, a 1919 graduate of the Naval Academy who had spent much of his life at sea. Just as the Second World War broke out, however, he developed severe medical problems and retired early to a small farm on the outskirts of San Diego, where he raised avocados and roses. Nancy's mom Adele was a quiet, gentle woman and the lead soloist at a large Baptist church in San Diego.

Bill's mother Helen was a *presence*. When Helen stepped into a room, it was as if the famous Bette Davis had entered. She was tiny, imperial, and graceful, but her presence demanded attention.[191]

Bill's dad Chet was six feet five inches tall and a charming raconteur. He was only about 60 years old, but his shoulders were beginning to slump and he seemed much more interested in remembering the past than anticipating the future. Bill's folks were very different people, but they had one thing in common: Bill. They doted on their only child.

---

[191] Bette Davis (1908–1989) was a legendary Hollywood actress who made over 100 films and won two Academy Awards for best actress. She was an independent woman and had the reputation of being difficult to work with, but in 1942 she was the highest paid woman in the United States. During World War II she and John Garfield organized the Hollywood Canteen, a place where servicemen passing through Los Angeles could relax, dance, and hobnob with their favorite screen stars. Although in later years Ms. Davis suffered from health problems, she was still acting as late as 1987.

Chapter 60 – Chet Kluck's Story
(and Bill's, Too)

1962

My flying schedule varied. One week I went to work from 0400 to noon; the next week I started at noon, except when we were teaching night flying, in which case we scheduled special sessions. Polly was busy during the day, so in my off hours I was often home alone. Chet Kluck, Bill's dad, frequently drove up from San Diego to visit his son, usually without Bill's mom, so while Bill was at work during the day, Chet had time to talk. I had time to listen.

"So Chet," I asked him one day, "are you any relation to the General von Kluck of World War I fame"?[192]

"As a matter of fact," he replied, "I believe he was a cousin of my father's. In those days, though, an emigrating family often severed ties with those left behind. I do know my dad's family dropped the 'von' when they came to America."

Chet wasn't sure why his ancestors had left Germany. That's one of the frustrating things about ancestors. Many didn't have the time to record their thoughts, or maybe they thought no one would care, so their descendents are often left with more questions than answers.

The family moved to Minnesota, the land of opportunity for many of the Scandinavians and Germans who came before them. An 1878 booklet published by the Board of Immigration for the State of Minnesota waxed eloquently about the possibilities: "Settlers, what do you want? I promise you health, and, if prudent and economical, wealth and happiness. I promise you a good climate. . . I promise you good lands—there are none better anywhere."

In the 1880s, Chet's dad, William Theodore Kluck, left Minnesota to

---

[192] Alexander Heinrich Rudolph von Kluck (1846–1934) was a German general during World War I. In 1920 he published two separate memoirs of his wartime adventures: *The March on Paris* and *The Battle of the Marne*.

join the Oklahoma Land Rush and settled down on 160 acres of fine land, the deed to which was signed by Teddy Roosevelt. Afterward, he married Maude, a part-Comanche woman, and set about farming. Sometime around the turn of the 20th century, however, the couple packed up and headed west. Chet wasn't sure why, but he suspected farming just didn't suit his dad; he was more inclined toward business.

Somehow Chet's folks ended up in El Centro, California, a hot, dusty farming community not far from the Mexican border. His dad started a general store and the family prospered. Chet was born in El Centro in 1904. He was smart, popular, and a superb athlete. He was also a conscientious worker who clerked part-time in his father's store. When he graduated from high school, he went to the University of California at Berkeley. He had almost earned his law degree when his sister, driving their mother Maude, ran off the road. Maude was killed.

While Chet was a kid in El Centro, his future wife, Helen Girard, was growing up in Boston, where her dad was a contractor with an artisan's touch. Helen loved Boston for its culture and educational opportunities and because it provided an entrée to the elite class she so aspired to join. When Helen was a teenager and her father announced the family was moving to California, her world came crashing down. Her dad owned the local movie theater in El Centro, which made her very popular with the other kids, and she made the best of a bad situation. Even so, she hated every moment of living in what she considered a miserable town.

Helen was popular, beautiful, and talented, and after high school she, too, went to Berkeley. There she and Chet became an item. After Chet earned his bachelor's degree in 1926, he and Helen reluctantly returned to El Centro to help his dad.

The Shell Game

Chet got a job pumping gas at the local Shell station. He may have had a college degree, but he could twist a wrench or change a tire with the best of them. He was a tall, handsome young man with an easy charm and a quick wit, and he remembered the name of every person to whom he'd been introduced. Both an optimist and an opportunist, Chet was an excellent salesman who promoted his product without demeaning the competition. He was proud of what he sold and how he sold it, and his abilities were soon recognized. Shell Oil, the U.S. affiliate of the international giant Royal Dutch Shell, was a world-class organization within which opportunity abounded. Chet took advantage of this opportunity, and with each step up the ladder came more responsibility and greater rewards.

One day in 1928, Chet and Helen left El Centro to party at a speakeasy in Reno, Nevada. It must have been quite a party, because they were married on that same trip in one of Reno's famous wedding chapels.[193]

Helen was the perfect corporate wife: a gracious hostess at ease with people, especially those of the upper-class, with whom she felt a particular kinship. Chet, on the other hand, enjoyed people of all classes, which may have been a contributor to his success.

A series of promotions and accompanying moves, coupled with successful investments, soon brought the couple wealth and security. Chet and Helen were living the life of the up and coming and loving it.

Bill Joins the Team

In 1936 a son was born to this oilman and his classy wife. Little Lord Fauntleroy, more commonly known as William Girard Kluck (and later as my friend Bill), was a much-loved only child brought up in luxury. His parents included him in almost all events, and he was often more relaxed with adults than with his peers. Along the way he met and mixed with people like Chet's friend Jimmy Doolittle, famous World War II ace who later joined Shell Oil as Vice President of Marketing, and Tony Hulman, owner of the Indianapolis Motor Speedway where the Indianapolis 500 race takes place each May.

Living this way could have produced a spoiled, angry child, but instead Bill thrived. Helen, who was quite artistic, spent much time with her young son, and he developed his motor skills early. His attention to detail was honed on projects such as his creation of huge armies of toy soldiers, which were crafted from lead and painted to the perfection demanded by a museum. He also built model race cars and built and flew model airplanes.

Shell Oil's promotion policy reflected the thinking of most big businesses of the era: Expose future leaders to as much variety as possible by tying each promotion to a change in location. This philosophy resulted in countless transfers, and as Chet climbed the ladder, Helen loved every minute of the climb. Bill had gone to as many schools and lived in as many cities as I had, but his schools were always private and exceptional, usually based on the Calvert School model.[194]

---

[193] A speakeasy was a nightclub-type establishment where illegal alcohol was sold. The speakeasy flourished primarily during Prohibition (1920–1933), when the sale or distribution of alcohol was banned in the United States.

[194] The first Calvert School was established in 1897 in Baltimore, MD. By the

As the years went by, Bill continued to learn and grow and Chet continued to achieve. Finally he was Shell's district manager for the Midwest, based in Indianapolis. The family had a fine home staffed with servants and all the corporate privileges accorded a young senior manager on the rise. Chet was totally content. He knew if he turned down the next promotion his career would stop at its current level, but he was ready to stall out and remain in place. Bill, too, loved Indianapolis, and he had been accepted to the Kentucky Military Institute (KMI) in Louisville, Kentucky, the school of his dreams. Bill wanted to be a military man, and this was the place to start.[195]

Helen enjoyed her privileged life in Indianapolis, but to her it was country; New York was the top of the heap. Chet reluctantly accepted the final promotion: Assistant Vice President of Shell Oil, New York City, center of the world.

Chet and Helen moved to the penthouse maintained by the company at the Waldorf and then later to their own penthouse apartment on 181st Street in Manhattan. While his folks traveled in chauffeur-driven limousines and hobnobbed with the rich and famous, Bill went off to KMI. He thrived in military school. It had small, interesting classes and all the extracurricular activities he loved. As a bonus, for four months each winter, the whole school studied in Venice, Florida.

During vacations, Bill got to spend time with his dad. Chet was a pilot and helped teach Bill to fly. Soon he discovered his passion: Flying would be a fine career. Maybe he could be a military pilot, perhaps even an instructor.

By the time Bill graduated from KMI, Chet had been in New York for four years. Then, out of the blue, he was offered a retirement package, a golden parachute. Something unspoken had happened. Did the company think he wanted to retire? Had he crossed swords with someone in a position of greater authority? Was he one of two men being considered for a higher position, and the loser had to leave? Chet never said.

Chet, Helen, and Bill headed for the suburbs of Mexico City. In this land where the cost of living was far lower than in the States, the family's nest egg was large enough to last a lifetime, and they soon resumed their high

1930s, the curriculum was being shipped worldwide for use in private schools and by children being home schooled. In the 1940s, the Department of Defense started to ship Calvert materials overseas to educate the children of U.S. servicemen. As of 2008, over 500,000 children in 90 countries have been educated using Calvert materials.

[195] The Kentucky Military Institute (KMI) was founded in 1845, the third military school in the nation. In 1972, KMI merged with the Kentucky Home School for Girls, the Louisville Country Day School, and Aquinas Preparatory School to become the Kentucky Country Day School.

lifestyle. Within a few months, both Chet and Bill were proficient in Spanish. Bill rode with the Mexican Cavalry in shows and competitions, and Chet became friends with the manager of the MG distributorship. Soon Bill was racing MGs.

Helen was miserable.

She wanted nothing to do with Mexico—its language, its customs, or its people. Her people were in New York and she missed her former lifestyle desperately. Her reaction was understandable and Chet was sympathetic, but to maintain the lifestyle they'd been accustomed to in the U.S. would require an influx of cash.

Chet looked around for a solution. Soon he had an opportunity to invest in commodities, the hands-on transport of perishable goods. It was a well thought-out plan, he thought, and it might have been, had Murphy's Law not kicked in with a vengeance. Everything that could go wrong did: storms, floods, railroad breakdowns, and to top it off, a communications failure. The result was financial disaster. The family left Mexico and returned to the States, but New York was out of the question. They settled in San Diego.

In the meantime, Bill won appointments to both West Point and Annapolis. He gave them both up, however, to join a female friend at San Diego State, silly boy.

The family was no longer rich, but they moved into the lower ranks gently, retaining some residual prosperity. Chet bought a Porsche 550-1500 RS Spyder, and Bill raced it on the amateur circuit. Chet was his crew chief, and the father-and-son team met with great success.[196]

To rebuild the family coffers, both Chet and Helen went to work. Helen ran a bridal store. Her every move was tasteful and attractive, and the store was the epitome of elegance and class. At his age and given his former position, Chet was unemployable at the level his experience should have demanded. So he started over. He went to work as a riveter at Convair, a division of General Dynamics, and worked his way up once again.[197]

The Pilot and His Lady Fair

The year Bill was a sophomore at San Diego State, the college theater

---

[196] The Porsche 550-1500 RS Spyder was designed specifically as a race car and made its debut at the Paris Motor Show in 1953. It was very successful on the racing circuit. A new Porsche racer, also called the 550 RS Spyder, made its debut at the Paris Motor Show in 2006.

[197] After a rich history of serving the country's air and space programs, the Convair plant in San Diego closed in the mid-1990s.

group put on the play *Best Foot Forward.* Bill was lolling around his fraternity
one day when the director of the play sought him out. The male lead had
become ill; would Bill take over? You bet. He'd had some acting experience,
and with his incredible ability to memorize, he stepped quickly into the role.
The female lead was the "Sweetheart of Sigma Chi," a charming, strawberry-
blond songstress named Nancy.[198]

Bill had found his match. He graduated with a degree in marketing and
air science and a second lieutenant's commission earned through the Air Force
ROTC. He was about to fulfill his dream: a military career as an air force
pilot. And best of all, he carried with him his beautiful bride, Nancy Olds.
Bill and Nancy were married in November 1958, just before he accepted his
commission.

Having flown many, many hours with his dad, Bill found primary flight
training to be a breeze. For basic, he was sent to Greenville, Mississippi. My
class was six months ahead of his so we never met, but he also landed in Blue
Nine Flight. Whenever he talked about those days, his eyes narrowed and I
could see the pain in his face. I knew his story almost without hearing it.

* * *

When the IPs from the 3506th lined up in front of Blue Nine Flight, it
was a typical summer morning in Mississippi, hot and muggy. Still suffering
indigestion from their breakfast of boiled babies, they were ready to attack
their future students with vile tongues and an insulting demeanor.

The IP who'd saved me, Captain Easy Hall, was nowhere in sight, and
Bill was assigned to an aggressive midget, the worst of the worst, a wannabe
fighter pilot who thought that jerking the aircraft through the sky was proof
of his manhood. In the Officers' Club bar, the midget bragged not about his
successes, but about his washouts. He needed a stepstool to be seen, but his
foghorn voice could be heard by all.

Bill did fine, not as well as he expected of himself, but under the
circumstances, more than okay. He was a very eager pilot. Close to graduation,
he developed a head cold but flew anyway, part of a four-ship formation.
When it came time to return, he was having problems with his ear and sinuses
in the nearly unpressurized cockpit, so he broke off from the formation and
come down very slowly, even then in great pain. His instructor was furious

---

[198] *Best Foot Forward* first opened on Broadway in 1941. In 1943 it was made into
a movie starring Lucille Ball of later TV show *I Love Lucy* fame. In 1963, the play
opened again as a Broadway revival, this time starring Liza Minnelli in her first
Broadway role.

and made him go to the flight surgeon. The flight surgeon grounded him, claiming Bill had a sinus problem that permanently disqualified him from flying. He was washed out. Later, the flight surgeon at Williams examined him, pronounced the earlier diagnosis hogwash, and tried to get Bill back into flight training, but to no avail. The air force is a well-oiled machine, but like any bureaucracy, there are times when procedure gets in the way of common sense.

Thank heavens the midget and his ilk were a rare breed. The majority of IPs at Greenville and elsewhere were proficient flyers and competent instructors, but each profession has a small percentage of jerks that poison the water.

At Williams, Bill and I flew together on several occasions. He was a dedicated pilot—smooth, alert, and capable.

Chapter 61 – Waltzing with the T-38

1962

We heard the rumblings; the vaunted T-38 was coming. The twin-engine, supersonic, do-all training jet was on its way to our base, and we lusted after it. We also remembered the promise of our base commander, Colonel Abbey, from the year before: "When the T-38s arrive, you gentlemen will be the originating pilots." Now the date of that arrival was within sight.

All T-37 pilots were called to a meeting. We flowed into the briefing room with anticipation. After a few opening remarks, Colonel Abbey dropped the bombshell. "I know you men were promised the first available T-38 slots," he said, "but since then, frankly, you've become too valuable to retrain." He went on to explain that the T-33 boys would be upgraded to the T-38; we'd remain on the T-37s in the primary training school. There was stunned silence. No one erupted during the meeting, but a later slowdown among those affected was the closest to mutiny I'd experienced in any organization.

Military folk are the most up-front people anywhere, and we're used to following orders even if they're distasteful. However, the troops react strongly to deceit, and this was the beginning of a distrustful and suspicious time at our happy base. Eventually, a workable and satisfactory compromise was reached: Both T-33 and T-37 pilots were fed into the T-38 program, and their respective skills worked to everyone's advantage. Generally, people can accept anything, but don't promise and then not deliver.

Training for the T-38 was at Randolph Air Force Base in San Antonio. Polly and I were among the first to go, and we lived in a house just off the base for three months of hard work and play.[199]

---

[199] Known for many years as the "West Point of the Air," Randolph was dedicated in 1930 and has been a flying training base ever since. The base is named for Army Air Corps aviator William Millican Randolph, a native Texan who was killed in 1928 when his plane crashed on takeoff. Ironically, at the time of his death, Captain Randolph was serving on a committee to select a name for the field ultimately named after him.

The T-38 was the finest jet I'd ever flown. My first flight (the so-called "dollar ride") was spectacular: from takeoff to 40,000 feet in about 4 minutes. Somewhere in the high 40s we pulled the airplane vertical with both afterburners on, and the sleek jet stalled and swapped ends like a dart, roaring through Mach to break the sound barrier. The plane could also maintain supersonic speed on the straight and level—quite a fuel-guzzling thrill. It was a short flight because of the hijinks, but I could tell that this airplane was an operational miracle.[200]

I was in my heyday at Randolph. My skills were at their peak and I had plenty of time to fly. To top it off, Polly and I were happy, looking forward to the birth of our first child, and enjoying the air force experience.

The only cloud on the horizon was my IP. For the first time in my career, I had a substandard instructor, a screamer and a real pain in the butt. I actually had more experience and was a much better pilot than he, but he was a major and he was the boss. One of my biggest frustrations was that he rode the stick—I've got it; you've got it. But we both can't have it. He did this so frequently that sometimes I'd remove my hand from the stick and let him fly the airplane. He screamed anyway. On my final flight with this clown, the aircraft must have landed itself; my hands were in my lap the entire time. Fortunately, most of my flying was solo.

Sadly, not all experiences with insensitive or incompetent instructors had a positive ending. One night while Polly and I were still at Randolph, Mike and Sally Freney rushed to the base hospital at Williams. Sally was in labor, but something went horribly wrong. Their full-term baby, the child that this beautiful couple had wanted so much, died at birth.

Mike had already received his flying assignment: C-123s. All he had to do was to fly his final check ride, which was scheduled for the following day. Mike, filled with grief, reported for duty but asked to be released for the day. Not only was he refused, he was forced to fly the check ride, which he failed and then failed again. Quick as a wink he was gone, washed out. His flying career was terminated by this unlucky and fateful turn of events.

There are many cruel people in this world, and this was a violation of human dignity of the highest order. I didn't hear of this tragedy until weeks after the event. When I confronted the officer who'd conducted the check ride, all he could offer was a shrug and a weak explanation of meeting standards or other such tripe.

In 2001, Randolph Air Force Base was designated a National Historic Landmark.

[200] Mach is the numerical representation of how fast an object is traveling relative to the speed of sound. For example, an aircraft traveling at Mach 0.8 is traveling at 80 percent of the speed of sound. A Mach speed above 1.0 is said to have broken the sound barrier.

Flying in Formation

Back at Williams, I was now actively flying three aircraft: the T-33, the T-37, and the T-38. It was difficult to remain current in all three, but it was well worth the effort, and we could fly as many hours as our bodies could stand.

Pair of Northrop T-38 training Talons.
(*Air Force Link: The Official Web Site of the United States Air Force.*)

One of the best experiences in all of these planes, but particularly in the T-38, was flying in formation—two or more planes mimicking each other's every move, wingtips just a couple of feet apart. In addition to being great fun, formation flying taught discipline, skill, and trust.

Students honed their skills in two-ship formations, with both aircraft flying dual (an IP and a student in each plane). At first, the wingman would bounce his ship like a yoyo on a string. As his skill improved, he was cleared to solo. Later on, a lead ship flying dual led a four-ship formation with three solo wingmen. Moving from two ships to four was an exhilarating milestone and a vote of confidence for the airmen involved.

* * *

Taxiing to our position on the runway, we take off in two-ship elements, so close together we communicate with hand signals. With a circular movement of his index finger, the lead slowly runs up the power; with a snap of his head, he releases the brakes. Soon we're airborne. Gear up, flaps up, anticipation high and adrenaline pumping. The lead is smooth; the wingman makes small, continuous corrections with stick and throttle. Another head-snap. Afterburner out, the lead reduces power and the wing plays his position. Beginning a 30-degree banked turn, the lead looks back to find numbers three and four closing in. Like running on a track, if you want to catch the lead, you run onto the infield at a given angle to cut him off. Three and four join in at 180 degrees or less, a delicate maneuver at 350 knots. Once everybody's snuggled in, we turn toward the assigned area. There are airplanes everywhere, like bees leaving a hive.

The lead watches for other aircraft and controls the mission. The eyes of the wingmen are locked on him. When the lead turns, the inside aircraft reduces power and the remaining two increase power. As we become more skilled, it's like a Latin dance: fast-paced, precise movements perfected by repetition. The lead executes multiple maneuvers; the wingmen are locked into the rhythm.

For the grand finale, the four aircraft form a trail, one behind the other, and the aerobatics begin. Starting with a slow roll and a dive for airspeed, we begin to feel the Gs: 4, 5, or 6, depending on position.[201]

The G-suit, a chap-like device, fills with compressed air, squeezing the lower extremities to prevent blood loss from the brain. The higher the G load, the more compressed air fills the chaps; when the Gs are released, the chaps empty. As the pressure builds, we grunt and lock muscles, experiencing the familiar graying and tunnel vision as we look into the twin-engine exhaust pipes of the aircraft in front of us. Too soon the fuel dance begins. We resume normal formation and return to the field. Positioning ourselves for landing, we move to echelon formation—a diagonal, ladder-like arrangement—then fly up initial and pitch out on an 180-degree, 3-G turn to lose speed. We try to pitch out at 4-second intervals. That way we'll have even spacing for landing. Squeaking the sleek jet onto the runway, we turn off and taxi to the ramp.

* * *

Pilots returning from formation were an exhilarated crew: strap marks burned into flight suits by bands of sweat, flushed faces marked with the outline of oxygen masks, the G-suit hose hanging like a phallic symbol. Chattering and laughing, they outlined their maneuvers with a combination of exaggerated adjectives and expressive hand gestures.

During the debrief after a formation flight, an IP rarely had much to say. By this time, students were approaching the end of the program and each pilot had enough skill to assess his own performance.

Every stage of flying required a check ride for the students to advance,

---

[201] A person standing still on the Earth is experiencing one G—one times the force of gravity. When a pilot changes an airplane's orientation rapidly (through tight turns, loops, etc.), the aircraft is subject to additional G-forces, either positive (the aircraft pitches up and the nose pulls upward) or negative (the aircraft pitches down and the nose goes downward). An increase in positive Gs can cause a condition known as grayout.

and in formation flying, the check ride was only as good as the lead was smooth. A bad lead could cost a career, so we always tried to find the smoothest lead possible. My favorites were Gib, my copilot on our boat ride down the Mississippi and the best IP ever; or Chuck Woody, the pilot we'd tried to stall when he flew a bunch of us to Florida in a C-47. These guys were like silk, laying on 4 to 6 smooth Gs during the aerobatics portion so the student could hang in like flypaper.

A few pilots were unsuccessful at formation. Some suffered from an uncontrollable fear of collision, others from lack of smoothness. Fortunately, the vast majority were able to succeed.

Weathering the Dark Side

The military is at the beck and call of Congress, who most often responds to appropriation requests based on world events. When the military is needed, it's respected and treated well; when the world is calm, it's often viewed as a wasted expenditure and treated as a pariah. As we moved further into 1962 and the situation in Southeast Asia began to heat up, the word went out: Train more pilots. The pipeline began to fill, but the number of IPs remained relatively static. It takes time to gear up for increased demand.

The heavy training load meant we were often flying three missions a day instead of two. We loved the job, but flying six hours a day and pulling Gs most of the time was both tiring and tough on the body. We were flying three airplanes on a base manned to fly two, and fallout continued from the broken promise as to who would fly what. All of these factors took a toll on morale. After all, men are merely grown-up boys with expensive toys, and the cure for their ills is often the same as it is for a kid: a pat on the back, a little recognition, and a good night's sleep.

Even more serious, a dark cloud had drifted over Willie: Over a several-month period, there had been a series of crashes, most of them without a logical explanation. Both the pilots and the aircraft involved were tried and true, yet there were few successful bailouts: Almost all of the accidents were fatal.

When the unnatural boom of a crash was heard, fire trucks and official traffic rushed rapidly to the site. The wives sat on their porch stoops with children playing quietly around them, waiting for the blue staff car with the commander and the chaplain to call.

Our wing commander, Colonel Mike McCarthy, was a terrific pilot and a skilled leader. He did his best to hold the show together, but it was a difficult time. Individually, each pilot reflected on his skills and decision-making ability. Collectively, in flights, squadrons, and the wing, we examined each other and ourselves. Inspection teams probed every aspect of flight-related affairs. There were simply no tangible results. No one thing was to blame, but it was apparent that every facet of the base was overworked and understaffed.

Chapter 62 – Flying with Emil

1962

In order to take the load off the main airport, Williams Field, a portable (mobile) tower had been placed at a satellite runway out in the desert. Every couple of weeks, we drew mobile-control duty, two IPs at a time. This wasn't considered great duty, but it did provide a break from the increasing demands of day-in, day-out flying. Activity on mobile control days occurred in cycles; there might be 100 takeoffs in 15 minutes, then a break. A fire crew monitored practice landings. Traffic was supposed to monitor itself, but mobile control was the final authority, checking to make sure gear was down and spacing pilots as they shot multiple touch-and-go landings.

During lulls between flying, we'd plink away at targets in the desert with a .45 Colt pistol or carbine, or just sit and chat. It was a good time for me to relax and explore the backgrounds of my fellow IPs, every one of whom had a story to tell.

One of these aviators was Emil Boado. A fine instructor and a popular pilot, Emil generated sunshine wherever he went. He also played the ukulele and the washtub base. At parties he would accompany himself on these instruments as he sang ditties with lines like "How come my dog don't bark when you come 'round." He made up additional verses as he went along, working each member of the audience into the theme. He had a razor-sharp wit and his songs were always funny, but they were never unkind.

Emil used his musical gifts in the classroom as well. When introducing a new subject to his students, he almost always presented the lesson with a verse, accompanied by a catchy tune on his ukulele. Yes, it was funny and the students loved it, but this unique method of delivery also helped them to retain the information.

"Where're you from, Emil?" I asked during a lull on one of our mobile-control days.

"North Carolina."

"What do your folks do?"

Emil took the ball and ran with it. His dad was a Philippine porter, he said, working for the railroad. His mom was Polish. Watching his expression as he started this story, I had the feeling he'd felt the sting of prejudice but had learned to cover it with his ever-present humor.

In high school, he was a good musician. He was also an outstanding football player—fast and tricky. At 150 pounds, however, he was too light for the college recruiters, so he applied and was accepted to Eastern Carolina State. Air Force ROTC paid his tuition, and when he couldn't afford room and board, he begged a spot to sleep in the boiler room and waited tables for pay. He also tried to join the football team but was rejected because of size; they wouldn't even let him try out. Undaunted, Emil worked out with the team as a stealth player, and because of his humor, the coaches tolerated his presence. He begged for a chance to run with the ball and challenged the team to a kick-off return alone. Finally his challenge was accepted. He scored a touchdown. Shortly thereafter, he became a member of the team and was awarded an athletic scholarship.

Too Close for Comfort

Occasionally we flew with other IPs to refine our skills and share techniques. On one of these practice flights, Emil was my copilot. We taxied out in the sleek T-38 and did every maneuver we could wedge into the hour-and-a-half flight, nitpicking and kidding around as we critiqued each other's technique. All too soon it was time to return to base. I shot up initial, pitched out, lowered the gear and flaps, and turned final.

* * *

Crud, the gear-down warning light must be burned out. It's not possible that the gear isn't down. Northrop, the plane's manufacturer, says the gear *always* comes down.

"Mobile, Nails here, turning final. Fuel low; nose gear light out. Give me a visual, okay?"

Slow flyby. The IP on mobile duty came back: "Main's down; nose is up."

Oh, boy. The IP has alerted the base, the alarm sounds, and we see the fire trucks begin to roll.

We go around two or three more times, trying to recycle the gear. It doesn't work. We dash out of the pattern, leaving the main gear down, and pull 4, 5, 6 Gs. The nose gear's still up.

The wing commander is on the radio. "I suggest you punch out, Lieutenant," Colonel McCarthy says, but he gives us the choice: eject or land. The underside of the T-38 is mostly magnesium. If ignited, it will burn with the intensity of hell.

"Emil, I've never thought of myself as a much of paratrooper," I say, watching the fire crew foam the runway.

"Me, neither."

End of discussion. We're flying on fumes, but I try a "hard" landing on the parallel runway, holding the nose in the air. It doesn't work. Fuel gone, we line up on short final approach and decide to blow the canopy. **Boom!** In case of fire, we'll have an easier egress.

Suddenly, it's like flying in an open-cockpit Stearman. The wind noise is deafening, but my mind is focused completely on the problem at hand: land this plane.[202]

Touchdown! The nose slides on the fire-retardant, slippery foam down the centerline of the runway. It feels like a toboggan ride on crusty ice. As the wounded bird slows to a stop, I shut down the engines and begin to unstrap. "Run, Emil, run," I yell, and we become contenders for the world's fastest 100-yard dash.

There was no fire.

* * *

Both Colonel McCarthy and the base commander, Colonel Richard Abbey, were at the flight line when we landed. Colonel Abbey congratulated us on saving his airplane. "Piece of cake, Sir," I said with a backward glance at the crippled T-38 flat on its belly on the runway. "Maybe this will finally end the curse."

Coincidentally, it did. Many people were involved in correcting Willie's problems, starting at the top, but eventually both working conditions and morale improved. Staffing increased to meet the burgeoning war effort, and pilots started flying one mission (either primary or basic) and one aircraft (the T-37, T-33, or T-38). There also was a defined process for upgrading, and after a while I flew the T-38 exclusively. Most importantly, the string of fatal crashes stopped.

As it so happened, that night there was a dining-in, an event rooted in the ancient military tradition of a commander inviting his officers to dinner. This dining-in was held at the Officers' Club, beginning with a receiving line of all commanding officers and followed by an open bar and formal

---

[202] The Stearman referred to is an open-cockpit biplane originally introduced in the early 1930s. Modifications of this model were used to train army and navy flyers during World War II.

dinner. Colonel Abbey was at the head of the line. Even though hours earlier this man had stood on the flight line watching Emil and me land on the foamed runway and then talking with us afterward, he showed not a hint of recognition. It sort of upset me: Fame is fleeting, but good leadership is based on recognizing those who got you there.

Chapter 63 – Life Lessons

1962–1963

Our son Walt was born in September of 1962. He was, of course, the most handsome of boys and a bundle of energy. Although I could write a volume about what we didn't know about child rearing, most of our friends had children and were willing to offer advice.

One evening Polly and I were playing with Walt when the doorbell rang. A young man and his assistant stood in the doorway. They had a free offer, they said, and somehow assuming they must be legitimate or they wouldn't be on the base, we invited them in. The young man laid out his wares: a beautiful set of the *Collier's Encyclopedia*, a bookcase to hold them, and an upgrade that would give us an annual update volume. Not only were they beautiful, they were free. All we had to do was sign a form saying we would use these extraordinary volumes. There was just a slight charge for processing and the yearly updates: 5 cents a day for the next 6,422 days. "Sign here," the young man said, "and these fine books, these books that will be invaluable when your young son goes to high school and college, will be yours."

It didn't take us long after he left to realize we'd been had, a realization made worse the next day when I heard my students gossiping about one of the goats of the class having been duped into buying an unwanted set of encyclopedias. "Hey, Lieutenant Wright," said one of them, "can you imagine anyone dumb enough to fall for that line?"

As it turned out, we learned a lot from our impulsiveness. Never again did we make a major purchase without analyzing the cost. The books themselves, as it turned out, were as good as advertised, but Walt took an interest in them way before his high school years. Our precocious toddler was taken by the forbidden nature of these expensive tomes, which were lined up in their specially purchased bookcase against one wall of the living room. He delighted in crawling over, pulling out a book, and waiting for our reaction. We tried the "no-no" bit, but Walt, an eager, inquisitive, and above all, persistent child, wouldn't leave the books alone. Finally we gave in and removed the temptation, in the process learning a valuable life lesson: For every problem there are many potential solutions; sometimes it's best to bury one's pride and pick the one that works.

Another of our questionable decisions as new parents was to buy a dog. A beautiful Airedale pup, we named him Tucson—second son. What a huge load to place on Polly. First a precious, precocious child, then an affectionate, frisky pup. Tucson had to be carried up and down the stairs countless times a day as we tried to housebreak him. Fortunately, he learned quickly, Soon after, the two of us went to obedience training, and he quickly became quite a civilized dog.

Now that the base was properly staffed, we were back to a happy, healthy, and busy schedule. My total flying time was about 2,000 hours, and I was still enjoying it and flying well. I was also beginning to feel restless. When an opening in academics as a platform-engineering instructor became available, I went to check it out and then applied. Colonel Charles Proctor, the commander of the ground school, must have liked what he saw, because I was accepted. The job offered a number of plusses: normal working hours in a cool building and the opportunity to meet new and interesting challenges, while still being able to fly with whomever I wished and as much as I could make time for. Naturally, another school was required, this time back at Lackland Air Force Base in San Antonio.

I had no sooner settled into my new office, trying to get acclimated before departing for Texas, when Colonel Proctor came to the door. "The regular instructor is out for some additional training," he said, "so I'd like you to teach the course on navigation." Then he went on leave.

This is what comes of being low man on the totem pole, but navigation? Good God, I could get lost walking to work. Does the world revolve around the sun or vice versa? The next morning, after a hard day and night of studying, I put on a freshly pressed uniform, made sure my gig line was straight, and stepped onto the platform. As I looked at the class of recently graduated Air Force Academy students, with a sprinkling of upgrading navigators, lieutenants, and captains, I could well imagine how Napoleon felt at Waterloo.

Pilot training courses were critiqued by the students, and I'm not sure if I had ever been so ill-prepared in front of so many. At least I looked good. Maybe they would comment on my appearance before unloading on my skills. Through my cotton mouth, I spat out my confession of ignorance and pleaded for help. Then the Irish in me went to work. Using the syllabus and the contents of a few slide trays, combined with a couple of bad jokes, I soon brought the students to my side. I taught what I knew, tried to put myself in their place, and called up various students, mostly the navigators, to teach what they knew. It worked. Within a week or so, we'd learned the prescribed lessons and had a good time doing so. My critique was quite good, Colonel Proctor was happy, and I was off to San Antonio for the ground instructors' course. Another lesson learned: If you're overmatched, ask for help. If you're humble and use self-deprecating humor, the help will be there.

Leaving the Austin-Healey behind, Polly, Walt, Tucson, and I piled into Polly's Plymouth and set off for Texas. There we rented a neat mobile home and I started on one of my most interesting educational endeavors yet. Through lots of hands-on training, I spent three months learning effective presentation skills from top-notch instructors, many of them civilian college professors.

Much like Toastmasters International, this program taught a very specialized communications course in an enjoyable way. We were already instructors in one field or another, but here we could hone our skills. Using our fellow students as guinea pigs, we each were required to present ten lectures, varying in subject and time, over the three-month period.[203]

John McKone's Story

One of my fellow students was Captain John McKone, a SAC select navigator who'd been shot down by the Russians over the Barents Sea in a Boeing RB-47H. Captain McKone used this adventure as a course-long subject. He was a good speaker, and he got better as he fine-tuned his techniques while presenting his story.[204]

The USSR was a vast, secretive, and ominous nation, a nation that the free world knew almost nothing about. In 1956, the U-2 began to gather information about the interior of the country, but that was only part of the puzzle. We also needed information about Soviet air defense radar systems. John McKone's mission was to gather some of that information with electronic eavesdropping devices while flying the coastline of the USSR. The RB-47H flew 50 miles from the coast, well outside the 12-mile limit for territorial

---

[203] Toastmasters International is a non-profit organization that helps people to become more confident and comfortable in front of an audience. It was started by Ralph C. Smedley in a Santa Ana, CA, YMCA in 1924. Initially limited to men, Toastmasters opened membership to women in 1973. As of 2008, the organization has over 200,000 members in more than 90 countries.

[204] Pilots or navigators were designated "select" based on skill and/or seniority. As long as they held this designation, they were often given an additional rank as well (e.g., major instead of captain). The Boeing RB-47H Stratojet was specifically designed for use in electronic reconnaissance. The first RB-47 was completed in 1955. The plane continued in service until it was replaced by the RC-135 in the mid-1960s.

waters. Even so, Russian MiGs would often accompany the plane from a formation position, intercepting almost every mission. Our fighters did the same to Russian intelligence-gathering aircraft on our shores.

During these deep days of the Cold War, several Allied aircraft in this area had been shot down or simply disappeared. On July 1, 1960, just a couple of months after Gary Powers was shot down in the U-2, one of the MiGs opened fire on McKone. With the wing and engine on fire, the sleek RB-47 spiraled into the Barents Sea.

McKone's lectures started with planning for his mission and ended with his release from Lubyanka Prison in Moscow on January 24, 1961. He developed this adventure one bone-chilling episode at a time. After being shot down, he spent many hours floating on the frigid water in a one-man raft before being rescued. Captain McKone and the copilot, Captain Freeman Bruce Olmstead, were the only two of the six-man crew who survived the crash, but neither knew of the other's fate until they were reunited at Lubyanka.

Prior to his capture, McKone had studied the history of the Soviet Union and had a good handle on their paranoia and distrust of the West. After completing the course at Lackland, he was scheduled to lead the escape and evasion survival school at Stead Air Force Base near Reno, Nevada, even though, he noted laughingly, his own escape and evasion had been rather short-lived.[205]

I'm sure our instructors meant for us to focus on presentation technique over content, but the most valuable thing I learned from listening to the tales of Captain John McKone was this: I did not want to get shot down and I did not want to spend a night in enemy waters, or on enemy land, for that matter.

Let's Go Hunting

After returning from San Antonio, we moved back into our converted-barracks apartment and continued our friendship with Bill and Nancy Kluck. With three kids between us (the Klucks now had frisky son Jerry as well as daughter Tammy) we sometimes babysat for each other so each couple could go to the O Club for dinner or to the movies. Our main sources of entertainment, however, were cookouts and games. If a game consisted mostly of luck, we each would win occasionally, but the more that winning depended on skill,

---

[205] Opened as Reno Army Airport in 1942, the facility was renamed Stead Air Force Base in 1951 in honor of Lieutenant Croston Stead, a Reno native who lost his life on a flying mission at the base in 1948. In 1966 the base closed and the property was transferred to the City of Reno. Since then it has operated as the civilian Reno Stead Airport.

the more apparent it became that Bill would triumph. He was a benevolent winner, an unassuming winner, but a winner nonetheless.

Bill's hands never stopped working. He was constantly building toy cars and airplanes, painting clay soldiers, or sculpting. The quality of his every production was superb. The tools he used to create them were the best money could buy. He wasn't rich, but the concept of quality was core to his philosophy of life. His interests were limitless, and he read faster and more often than I thought possible—he was the first proponent of speed reading I'd encountered. Times were never boring when we were with Bill and Nancy.

In addition to couple activities, during hunting season the guys on base often became pioneers, thrashing through desert and mountain to chase deer, elk, javelina, dove, quail, and duck. In fact, at certain times of the year, much if not most of the meat we ate was the result of hunting. It was fun and economical to provide fresh meat for the table.[206]

To add interest to these hunting excursions, I scouted out new and interesting places to explore from the air. One that looked appealing was a cleverly concealed cave in the area of Oak Creek Canyon. After several low-altitude mapping trips, I shared my find with Johnny Holody and Bill Kluck. An old pal from Buffalo, Johnny was the guy who'd driven his car in a caravan with Bucko Jewell and me to basic flight training at Greenville back in 1958. We'd maintained our friendship ever since.

Johnny and Bill could barely contain their excitement, and soon we were planning a weekend adventure. Bill, who owned the only Jeep around, was in charge of supplies. I'd learned the importance of having the right supply guy from my trip down the Mississippi, and no one was more meticulous or thorough than Bill, whether he was supplying an entire base or three guys on an overnight trip.

Finally the day of departure arrived and we were off in high spirits, first on highways, then on back roads, and eventually over paths that were merely indentations in the desert. The tougher the trek, the louder and more insulting the criticism. In fact, both gentlemen, and I use that term judiciously, began to question my ancestry. I tried to ease their minds by explaining that we were about to make a discovery that would put us in the books of great explorers (the *Collier's Encyclopedia Annual*, for one) and cause us to become rich and famous. As darkness approached, however, I realized this quasi-wilderness road was the source of the roughest, most uncomfortable jostling I'd ever experienced, and that included my time on the ranch in Mexico.

---

[206] Javelinas are pig-like mammals found in the deserts of southwestern United States. They normally measure between 3 and 5 feet long and weigh between 35 and 60 pounds.

Bill was not a good sport.

Johnny was no better.

Finally we stopped in the road and began to prepare dinner. Now Bill was in charge, and his idea of roughing it was a table set with silver and fine china—an exquisite meal fit for the king his mother brought him up thinking he was. It was a beautiful moonlit night. Tall mountains surrounded our campsite, and the night sounds were loud and typical—coyotes howling and critters scurrying through the brush. It was so peaceful that my friends even stopped grumbling.

Finally we turned in. John and I threw our bedrolls down in the ruts of the road, like the real cowboys that we were. Bill, with a great deal of fuss and bother, folded up the backseats in the Jeep, inflated his Abercrombie and Fitch air mattress, and covered it with silk sheets (nothing's too good for a king). He then donned his silken pajamas and bid us good night.

We woke with a start in the dead of night, surrounded by thunder, lightning, and the beginnings of torrential rain. Just as Bill tried to lock the doors, John jumped into the front seat of the Jeep and I crawled in back. It was hard to ignore the hiss from Bill's punctured mattress, even over the noise of the storm. The only sound louder was Bill screaming.

Morning broke with the sun shining, and we ate a hurried breakfast before saddling a light pack and rifles. We would hunt our way to the undiscovered cave on foot. After climbing several miles through blind canyons, including a few retreats and reversals, I led them to the mouth of the cave I'd mapped from the air. The taxpayer dollars that made possible my many hours of practice flying had been well-spent. We entered into the unknown with a breath of anticipation. Would we find ancient Indian artifacts, cave drawings, maybe even a skeleton or two? No such luck, unless those Indians had left old cigarette butts, crumpled packs, some yellowed newspapers, and a cold campfire.

"I guess we aren't going to be written up in *Collier's* after all," I commented cheerfully. Bill and John just didn't get it. I swear those guys had no sense of humor. We returned to the Jeep dirty, exhausted, and without any game; we hadn't seen a single creature on the entire trek. Somewhere on the long, quiet trip back to Willie, just to make them happier, I volunteered to recon spots for further adventures. Bill mentioned something about getting me an Article 15 for misusing government equipment. His air mattress was destroyed, his silk sheets torn, his pajamas dirty, and his Jeep badly misused. But I did bring 'em back alive. At least Nancy was grateful.[207]

---

[207] Named after the article so-numbered in the Uniform Code of Military Justice, an Article 15 is a "non-judicial judgment," a punishment a commander can impose for

Teaching from the Platform

On July 28, 1963, I was promoted to captain. Several other guys were promoted at the same time, so we had a large, boisterous party at the Officers' Club to celebrate. I'd filled in a lot of squares to get to that point, and being addressed as Captain Wright, plus receiving the pay increase that went along with the title, felt pretty good. On the platform, however, my new rank wasn't nearly as helpful as my A&P (Airframe and Powerplant) Mechanic's license and my Ground Instructor's federal license. I taught mostly T-38 engineering, plus a smattering of other subjects such as emergency survival. I tried to be accessible to my students, but I knew my limitations. Whenever anyone who looked like a navigator needed help, I remembered the class I'd taught for Colonel Proctor and quietly disappeared.

A few months later our barracks apartments were condemned. Polly and I weren't happy about moving off the base, but we found new quarters at 644 E. Commonwealth back in Chandler, and this, too, led to new friends and adventures. It was a tranquil time in our lives.

Working in academics was a pleasure. Instructors were hand-picked, and the students graded us often and honestly. The syllabus was updated often to keep it as interesting as possible. Student pilots spent half of their day flying and the other half in the classroom, so the group after lunch was sometimes a challenge. Occasionally I slipped a crass and vulgar girlie picture into the slide tray as a wake-up call for those who enjoyed such filth. I never looked myself, of course. Even with such diversions, eyelids became heavy; these guys started their day at 0400.

Testing was fair and the young pilots were interested, interesting, and honest. Any instructor could give a test (always multiple-choice) and leave the room. In my entire air force career, I never saw anyone cheat, even though there was a lot at stake. A pilot's ranking in training determined his next assignment and perhaps his career choice: fighters, bombers, helicopters, or cargo aircraft. Each was vital, but they were very different missions.

My co-instructor in T-38 aircraft engineering was Tom Fincher, a senior captain caught in the promotion freeze. Many majors and captains, some from World War II, had been called up for Korea. Since their civilian careers had been interrupted, many decided to stay in, serve 20 years of active duty, and retire. As a result, rank was so stagnant that often a captain would be 10 or 15 years older than I.

---

an infraction not severe enough for a court-martial. In civilian parlance, an Article 15 would be used to deal with a misdemeanor, while a court-martial would be used in cases of felony.

Tom was an Alabama boy from Auburn University. A short man with a ready smile and a deep rumbling voice, he was the best platform instructor I'd ever experienced anywhere. He could break down a difficult problem or display it in its simplest form and make the most impossible lesson understandable.

Almost without exception, Tom's students gave him the highest ratings possible. Every once in a while, I would be compared to him, which was as good a compliment as I could hope for or expect. We flew often as a pair in formation, with students or cross-country, and we had hours of discussion on topics ranging from kids (he had a bunch) to world affairs.

Chapter 64 – Road Trips

1963

The base had an Aero Club, where several light aircraft were available for anyone to fly, enlisted personnel as well as officers. There was a Piper J-3 Cub; an Aeronca, a similar two-seat slow trainer; a Cessna 140, a tail-dragger; the more advanced Cessna 150, a tricycle-gear aircraft; a four-seat Cessna 172; and a slick, P-51 look-alike called the Navion. What a wonderful opportunity for all who were interested in flying. Even the lowest-paid airman could afford it.[208]

Between our active social life and my job, I hadn't had time to participate in the Club, but I did know they'd had a couple of silly accidents. There were no injuries, but one of the airplanes had been destroyed.

Tom Fincher and I were in our office one day, solving the world's problems, when Colonel Mosier stopped by. Tom and I snapped to, invited him in, and bought him a Coke. The colonel was a good guy, a World War II prisoner of war with a wry sense of humor. At a costume party one time, he showed up in a tattered uniform and shuffled around the show ring as a POW, smoking a half-inch stogie held with a toothpick. He won first prize.

Since our office was off the beaten track and further camouflaged with a sign on the door that read "Broom Closet," we knew this was not an accidental visit.

"Something up, Colonel?" Tom said.

"You boys like flying light aircraft?" asked the colonel.

---

[208] Aeronca Aircraft was founded in 1928 in Cincinnati, OH. It ceased production of light aircraft in 1951. As of 2008, the company is a division of Magellan Aerospace and manufactures engine components and airframe structures. It is located in Middletown, OH. The Navion, originally designed by North American Aviation at the end of World War II, has been built in various configurations by North American, Ryan Aeronautical Company, and Tubular Steel Corporation (TUSCO). One model of this plane, the Rangemaster, was manufactured until 1976. Navions are still in use in the 21st century.

"Not me, Sir, I'm pretty busy with duty," I said in what I hoped was a convincing tone.

"Nor me," echoed Tom.

"Wright, I saw in your records that you have an A&P license."

"Yes, Sir, I do. But I haven't used it much because of the great job I'm doing training Uncle Sam's finest."

"We've had some problems with the Aero Club," the colonel continued.

"Oh?"

"Yep, but we're working on them. Captain Jim Hunley was just elected president." Jim was our most likeable and capable test pilot. He would fly with a crow if he could find a way to fit in. In his former life he'd been an undertaker, and he looked like the happy philosopher. He and his wife Carol must have married in the sixth grade. They had a slew of kids and a zest for life, and Jim had an almost insatiable desire to fly—anything, anytime, anywhere. Fortunately, Carol had remarkable patience with her irrepressible aviator husband.

"Good man, Sir." I said.

"You are elected maintenance officer," said the colonel as he finished his Coke.

I was about to object when my better judgment prevailed. "By the way," said the colonel on his way out the door, "your $15 annual membership fee has been waived."

"Thanks, Sir. That's mighty nice of you."

Well, at least I knew what I'd be doing with my life on weekends. Polly, with her usual cheerfulness, understood. I was a lucky man. A master sergeant who loved to play with light aircraft did most of the maintenance, along with help from some airmen. I inspected the work and signed off on it in the log book.

With his organizational skills, Jim Hunley trimmed down the fleet, and with a bit of rearranging, we soon had a smooth-running Club with never another problem.

Cross Country in the Navion

Willie had twin, 10,000-foot runways, and the Aero Club planes could make ten touch-and-go landings in one pass. This was a different kind of flying and a refreshing change of pace. I was also able to take Polly up with me at times, excursions we both enjoyed.

When the Club's Navion needed a new engine, I helped install it and

Jim and I test-flew it. A large four-seater, more comfortable than most small airplanes and with a sliding canopy, the Navion was easy to fly.

"Hey, Polly, I've got a great idea," I said one night as I came in after work in the summer of 1963. Polly, having heard those words before, got a bit antsy, but I persisted.

"We've a 30-day leave coming. What do you say we take the Navion, tour the East, and visit family?" Polly liked the idea, so we started planning. There were a few problems. For one, the Navion had a radio/navigation system that would have been modern when Lindbergh flew the ocean, a 6-crystal system that—when it worked at all—was limited to about a 30-mile talking range. But hey, why sweat the small stuff? I was a hotshot jet jock. And this wasn't even a jet. It was a stable, safe airplane with lots of range.

It was a beautiful Saturday in September, still desert-hot, so we planned to launch at dawn. The first leg would probably be the toughest, over the Superstition Mountains and on to El Paso. We drove to the flight line and loaded the aircraft while simultaneously chasing Walt and Tucson around the ramp. I parked the car behind the Aero Club building, strapped Walt and Tucson into the roomy backseat, and cranked the engine. I checked on its throaty roar and the magnetos and took off into the cool morning air.

We watched the sun play magic on the Superstition Mountains and Weaver's Needle, a famous desert landmark that plays into the legend of the Lost Dutchman's Gold Mine. We contemplated the history and the gold mine of the legendary Dutchman and the myth of the sun's shadow on the Needle leading to the mine. Walt was quiet and content; Tucson was sightseeing out the window.[209]

After about 45 minutes, Walt fussed a bit; he was hungry.

"I guess it's time to feed him," Polly said. "His bottle's in my purse. Where did you put it?"

"Purse?" I queried. Up to this time in my life, I hadn't been responsible for a purse.

"Well, it was in the trunk," Polly said. "I put it in the trunk, and you unloaded the trunk."

I did a 180-degree turn.

It was a quiet ride back to Willie. Not only did the purse have Walt's

---

[209] Weaver's Needle is a weathered volcanic plug with a summit elevation of 4,553 feet. The persistent story is that a German immigrant named Jacob Waltz, who came to the U.S. in about 1839 and lived in the Arizona Territory from 1863 until his death in 1891, had discovered a large gold mine and left clues to its whereabouts. Fueled by journalistic efforts to the present day, hundreds of people have searched for the Lost Dutchman's gold, but the mine has never been found.

bottle, it also had our money. As soon as we landed and taxied, I ran to the car. Sure enough, there behind the spare tire was the purse.

We refueled and were off again.

This time, the ride over the Superstitions was a bit rougher as the desert heat played with the air currents. Walt slept, using Tucson as a pillow. Polly read. When we passed the same spot where we'd recently turned around, I made some remark to Polly about the Lost Dutchman putting a curse on the Superstitions forever.

At that exact moment, the engine quit. It was deadly silent.

I followed the restart procedure and the engine roared back to life in seconds, though I admit it seemed like minutes. Yikes! I looked over at Polly. She'd pulled her book so close to her nose that the print left a mark, but she kept on reading.

"What was that?" she asked calmly.

"Don't know," I replied, as soon as my heart started beating normally. *Man, she has guts,* I thought. *And beautiful, too. I am one lucky guy.*

When we landed in El Paso, a mechanic and I checked out the engine and shrugged our shoulders. He surmised that a fleck of dirt had passed over one of the carburetor jets, and the explanation seemed logical to me, so we pressed on. The weather was still beautiful and calm; the Navion was comfortable and roomy. We filled the ashtrays with Froot Loops for Walt and Tucson to munch on, and every two or three hours we landed, fueled, and stretched our legs.[210]

That night we stayed in a motel just short of Natchez, Mississippi. The next morning we were treated to a hero's welcome at Polly's folks. At just a year old, Walt was a bundle of energy. He laughed, walked, ran, and even said a few words. Thanks to our obedience-training lessons when he was a pup, Tucson would heel and stay on command. Polly's parents were tickled to see all of us, though Grandpa Billy still didn't know that his grandson was half New Yorker.

After flying to Greenwood to visit more kin, we headed for western New York. We had scheduled a refueling stop in Tennessee at an airport without navigation aids. No problem. We took a radial off the Jacks Creek VOR. VOR signals are like a series of electronic spokes in the sky. Each spoke is similar to a road leading out of a traffic circle on land. To take the appropriate road, you enter the traffic circle, drive around until you come to the right road, and then turn onto it to reach your destination. To use the VOR system, you dial the proper radial into the instrument face

---

[210] Introduced in 1963, Froot Loops is a fruit-flavored, colored cereal manufactured by Kellogg and promoted by a cartoon character named Toucan Sam.

and keep the line centered, using the clock to time the distance out on the desired radial.

We followed this procedure to the Tennessee airport, but below there was nothing but forest. Back to Jacks Creek to try it again. Same result. On the third try, following the same procedure, we saw the airport.

As long as we gave it gas, which, thankfully, was cheap in those days, the Navion flew beautifully. We had no more engine trouble, the weather was great, and although the radio was fairly useless, I navigated as much by highway and railroad as by navigation aids anyway. Walt and Tucson loved the trip; we hardly heard a peep from them. In New York, we landed in Dunkirk. Uncle Walt and Aunt Carolyn picked us up and then threw a big party for us in their lovely, fun-filled home. We even collected Grandpa McNerney from the Knights of Columbus and wheeled him around. Although a stroke had paralyzed half his body, his mind and voice were as good as ever; and he was pleased and proud to inform anyone who would listen about the fine bowel movement he'd had that morning.

Four generations: Grandmother, me, Walt, and Betty at
Hyannis Airport on Cape Cod, 1963.

Next stop was Cape Cod, where we landed at Hyannis Airport, home of my burgeoning aviation dreams. The day we arrived George was at work and my younger brother Chris at school, but Grandmother McNerney and Betty came to the airport and we took a picture of the four generations. Everyone billed and cooed over Walt and enjoyed the dog. The women spent most of their short time together in the kitchen, cooking old-time favorites. At the age of 70, Grandmother was just as feisty and still extraordinarily busy, often taking care of old folks and still driving with the same aggressive style that had made her a legend back in the '30s in her Model T.

Soon we were off again, this time to visit our good friends Mike and Sally Freney in Ann Arbor, Michigan. Mike was in the OSI, the Office of Special Investigations. It was a job for which he was well-suited. Mike had a brilliant, magnetic personality and was an educator of the highest order. Although there was no excuse for the treatment he'd received at Willie that had ended his career as a pilot, he now served our nation in a function that was superior to flying. Many of his opportunities were in the shadow world of counterespionage and investigations, working with information that slipped through the Iron Curtain, and his duty assignments ranged worldwide. From the borders of Korea to the cold concrete walls of Germany, he could be found wherever the Cold War raged. It was here that the communists repressed the common man, while Party members lived like royalty.[211]

No matter where Mike was, his ever-present thirst for knowledge went with him. He was one of those rare individuals who listened as much as he spoke. For him every day was a learning experience, and he sought out those of any persuasion or nationality to learn the pros and cons of their country, profession, or philosophy. This isn't to say that he didn't voice an opinion; he was a wordsmith of the first order, and besides, he was Irish. However, he used his skills to "talk the talk" of an individual or group so they would understand what he was trying to say. His nights and time off were consumed with advanced education, since at the time he was earning a master's degree through correspondence.

Sally traveled the world with him, even to places that "accompanied" travel was frowned upon or, in some cases, forbidden altogether. She was unconventional, too, and in her own way, autonomous. Nobody lived more fully than these two. Mike loved to dine, drink, and philosophize. His personal life was one of delightful excess in almost every aspect, but his professional life was dedicated to the squashing of the communist threat, and no one was more committed to his work.

All too soon it was time to go home. Our trip back to Willie was without incident and Polly had been a marvelous copilot. It had been a wonderful trip, we agreed, but it was good to be home.

---

[211] The political, military, and ideological barrier that separated Soviet-controlled areas from the rest of the world was known as the Iron Curtain. Although the term has its origins in the early 1800s, it was first applied to the Soviet bloc by Sir Winston Churchill, Prime Minister of Britain from 1940–1945 and 1951–1955, in a 1946 speech at Westminster College in Fulton, MO.

Chapter 65 – November 22, 1963

It was lunchtime on Friday. As I started down the hallway, I found the secretaries crying hysterically. John Fitzgerald Kennedy, America's 35th President, has been shot in Dallas and declared dead. As President, JFK had had a hard learning curve in his first 1,000 days, but I really felt he was beginning to get a grip on world affairs. Now the country had lost its leader to a sniper's bullet, the fourth President in U.S. history to die at the hands of an assassin while in office. The events of the next few days were fraught with emotion and disbelief.[212]

With the country in turmoil over civil rights and the escalating conflict in Vietnam, Vice President Lyndon Baines Johnson was sworn in as our 36th President.

Then, as now, few people in the country were as well-read or knowledgeable as military officers. After all, we were the point of the spear; it behooved us to be informed. We also tried to be as apolitical as possible, but LBJ would have been my last choice for anything. He was a legendary southern politician—smart, opportunistic, and selfish. During my numerous stays in Texas, his name had always gotten a chuckle and a wink: "A finger in every pie," they'd say. It remained to be seen how he would perform in the highest office in the land.

---

[212] Other U.S. Presidents who were assassinated were Abraham Lincoln in 1865, James Garfield in 1881, and William McKinley in 1901.

Chapter 66 – Chasing the Future

1964

Polly was pregnant again. And as the months went by, holy moley, was she pregnant! With Walt she hardly lost her lovely figure, but this time she was getting huge. The more she tried to keep her weight down, the bigger she became.

It's hard for a man to really understand this process, but the base doctor was not alarmed. "Got to be at least twins," I said.

"Nope," said the doc. "There's just one of 'em."

Rumblings of War

Although much of our lives went on as usual, the war in Vietnam was becoming a reality, and we were full of ourselves and eager to fight the communist curse. Our leaders were battle-hardened vets from World War II and Korea, victorious and undefeated, but Vietnam was a war we'd eased into without knowing where it began and surely without an idea of where it would end. Ike, among others, had warned about a ground war in Asia.

Armies are thinned out after every war; as a result they can become soft and without direction. It had been ten years since Korea, but our nation's warriors had not followed the usual course. The USSR had sharpened our sword. The air force was trained and sharp, the army was ready to roll across Europe, and the navy had powerful ships and aircraft carriers patrolling the world's oceans. The marines were as prepared as always. We had might, money, and machines. Okay, it was true that the various branches of the armed services didn't talk or compare notes and often fell into meaningless verbal competitions. Nevertheless, our intelligence was as good and as effective as a free society would permit, and we were ready for the Russian Bear.

But this wasn't the Bear.

We were prepared for world war, nuclear war. The conflict in Vietnam was something else altogether. It was a nasty little war, but to us it was good. After all, it was the only war we had.

There were plenty of going-away parties for the familiar faces who were departing, but they were more of a farewell than a celebration. It was a time of fear, reflection, joy, sorrow, and worry; but most of all it was a time of anticipation. After arranging for their families to move back to their homes, pilots began preparing to be sent to Asia. They attended flying schools to learn new aircraft and new missions as they primed themselves to go to war.

I knew that I was fortunate. I was still in the USA, could fly often, and could pick the missions and students that made life fun. My job continued to be demanding and busy. I was approaching 2,200 hours and was flying as well as I ever would. I felt there was no position or attitude that an airplane could be placed in, either accidentally or on purpose, from which I couldn't recover. After all, I'd been tested by a multitude of eager college graduates bent on killing both of us.

I didn't volunteer for anything, but I knew my time was coming. Being a flight instructor is not, and should not be, a lifelong job. After about four years, patience breaks down and one's effectiveness begins to diminish. Teachers in schools and universities have recognized this phenomenon for years, thus the sabbatical. At this time in history, our sabbatical was combat. Pilots approached war in the early days of Vietnam as the next phase of our war games. They flew missions with South Vietnamese pilots to teach them to fend for themselves.

As a military group, we felt a strong sense of patriotism and a zeal for making the world safe for democracy. Most of us considered the war was right, just, and necessary. Propaganda is food for armies, and for the most part we bought the company line. But resistance to the war was beginning to fester throughout America and some troops were returning with stories of mismanagement and confusion. Despite the propaganda, quiet questions were being asked. The blue staff car, with its news of a dead or missing loved one, was becoming a high miler.

Most of our nation's efforts were related to ground support at this juncture of the war; thus all branches of the service were vulnerable to combat. Had I not married when I did, it surely would have been commandos and whatever that led to. Now with a wife and child and another baby on the way, a tour in Vietnam wasn't as appealing. I was ripe for the picking, so I began to explore my options before somebody made a choice for me.

What Next?

Bob Pierini, a gregarious fellow pilot, slipped into our almost-hidden office grinning like the Cheshire Cat. "What are you so pleased about, Bob?"

"I've solved the problem." Like me, Bob was also prime for a transfer.

"So what's it going to be?" I asked.

"TWA," he replied.

"TWA?"

"Yep," Bob said. "Work for the airline and fly with the Air National Guard for fun."

We all had trained with Guard units throughout our careers. Since the beginning of our nation's history, the National Guard had been the backbone of our fighting forces. Their members maintained civilian careers, but when the flag went up, they were often the first called to duty. Air National Guard members from bases across America were our first line of air defense, and they executed their mission with a skill often surpassing that of the regular air force (after all, they usually were older and had been at it longer). In 1964, the primary role of the Guard was to protect our homeland from Russian bombers.

I had to admit Bob's was one solution, but I just couldn't see it. "You've got to be nuts to give up an air force career with almost ten years in already," I exclaimed.

Bob went on about how the jet age had arrived, the airlines were hiring, and the pay, after the first year, was about equal to the air force. He admitted the first year's salary would be a challenge: $500 per month, less than half of what we were making, plus a lot of uninspiring flying, but he figured it would be worth it.

"The unions have finally made working conditions better," he said as he explained the specifics of the deal. I admit he made a compelling argument. Before he left, he threw down an application form and a pamphlet describing the job.

I sat alone for a long time and thought about it. Up until then, I'd never considered commercial flying as an option. I loved the air force—the job, the camaraderie, and the benefits—and I only had 11 years until retirement. It was a disturbing proposition to evaluate: duty, honor, country, God, family, self. If I left, was I bailing out in my country's time of need? Polly and I talked long into the night. As always, she contributed her opinions, but the decision was mine alone. She would stand by me whatever I chose.

I sent in the completed application. When and if they called, I'd check them out at the same time they were looking at me. After all, they might not hire me, and I might not like what they had to offer. Nothing ventured, nothing gained.

Next I went to personnel; there was action in my record. SAC (Strategic Air Command) was making noises about me flying KC-135s, an air-refueling operation. All I had to do was push a bit. With the motto *Peace is our Profession,* SAC was composed of very serious professionals with a very serious mission: delivering nukes when the flag went up. It was hard, dedicated work, with days on alert in bunkers and lots of study and practice.[213]

The humorless commander of Blue Nine Flight when I was in basic flight training at Greenville had come from SAC. It was not a command that had ever interested me, but for a family man, perhaps it was the best option. I'd be home most nights, or at least close by, and families could picnic with the crews on alert. SAC also had the best the air force had to offer in terms of benefits, good housing, good food, superior Officers' Clubs, and excellent gyms and recreational facilities. In terms of amenities, each base was a mecca.

General Thomas Power, the commander in chief of SAC who had replaced General Curtis LeMay, demanded performance and integrity, but he also was generous with rewards. Top crews were given spot promotions to higher ranks, which they kept as long as they performed. SAC was the primary reason there hadn't been a World War III—we held the "big stick." Still I hesitated. *Would I be a round peg in a square hole?* I asked myself and Polly.

Escape, Evasion, and Survival

Regardless of whether I stayed in the air force or left to fly commercial jets and joined the Air National Guard, there was one course I still had to take: survival, escape, and evasion training. In a war, it was expected there would be prisoners, and the goal of the service was that we be prepared for this eventuality.

In the West, prisoners were traditionally treated with respect. There was minimal torture; name, rank, and serial number were usually sufficient. Although some horror stories had come out of the German *stalags*, the actual death rate in the German and Italian camps during the Second World War was about 4 percent.

---

[213] The Boeing KC-135 Stratotanker is the only jet airplane designed specifically for aerial refueling. First flown in 1956, as of 2008 it remains the primary plane used by the U.S. Air Force for aerial refueling. During the Vietnam War, the KC-135 executed over 800,000 refuelings of combat aircraft.

Western armies expected a ratio of four captures to every death. The ratio in the Japanese army was one capture for every 120 deaths. Contrary to the views of apologists who thought the atomic bomb had not been necessary to shock Japan into unconditional surrender, I believe the country would have fought to the last man, woman, and child. The Japanese people have an astonishing tenacity and determination. Not only are they clever and brave, they are also fearless. Rather than surrender during the war, they were expected by their military leaders and their government to die, if not from encounter with the enemy in combat then by their own hand. This was a philosophy for which the West was mentally unprepared.

During World War II, huge armies surrendered—the British at Singapore and the Americans in the Philippines. The Japanese mantra was *to the death*, and their leaders were both overwhelmed and horrified by the lack of fighting resolve in their Western enemies. The Japanese soldier lived by the Bushido warrior code of samurai days, and their treatment of prisoners or "ghost soldiers" as Hampton Sides refers to them in his book of the same name, violated the norms of civilization. The Japanese had signed, but never ratified, the Geneva Convention of 1929; the death rate among their prisoners during World War II was 27 percent.[214]

Being a prisoner of the Japanese was the most intense ordeal that any American fighter had ever faced, but the threat of harm was primarily physical. When the Korean War erupted, our prisoners were again subject to the authoritarian Asian mind and psychology, but this time physical measures were coupled with a new form of mental torture called brainwashing. The sum of this treatment violated everything the Geneva Convention stood for.

In Korea, most servicemen were totally unprepared to cope with capture, and many were destroyed, mentally and physically. I served with and listened to the stories of some of those who survived the Korean camps. Many others never returned; a few went over to the other side. Every now and again, one of these traitors escaped and drifted back to the West, broken and confused. The U.S. had learned from these extraordinary POW experiences and had devised countermeasures to thwart, as best we could, the effects of such treatment.

The goal of the air force was that every air crewman, officer, and enlisted man be as ready as possible to face the possibility of capture. To this end, a survival school had been established at Stead Air Force Base in Reno, Nevada. The program took a month—two weeks in the classroom followed by time in the field and more classwork. It was given year-round.

---

[214] A code developed from the schools of thought of Buddhism, Zen, Confucianism, and Shintoism between the 9th and 12th centuries, Bushido is not unlike the chivalry and codes of European knights of the Middle Ages.

My friend Tom Craig, a Louisiana boy, had attended in the depths of winter, trekking through the mountains on jerry-rigged snowshoes and bedding down in a sleeping bag in the deep snow of the Sierras. His sincere advice to me was to go in the summer, and he noted that August was the best time. When an August slot came available in 1964, I volunteered. Polly was due in September, but I figured I'd be home in plenty of time.

Air force schools were excellent, and this one was superb. It was taught by American and foreign nationals who had been forced down, shot down, or escaped from behind the Iron Curtain. One of the commanders was John McKone, whose harrowing stories I had heard in ground instructors' school. The students were men of all ranks, ages, and commands. Some were in great physical shape; others, regrettably, were not. Nevertheless, failure was not an option. Those who did didn't make it through the first time were retrained, discharged, or grounded.

During the first two weeks we learned about ejection techniques and how to survive in hostile territory and under various topographical situations. A great deal of time was spent on how to survive a POW situation, both as a group and individually.

The next phase simulated a POW situation. We had no illusions about how difficult it was going to be. Nothing, of course, could duplicate the actual experience of becoming a prisoner of war, but we had a feeling this was going to come pretty close.

We reported at 0500, dressed in flying suits and boots. Breakfast was short and simple. Afterward, we were shepherded from class to class, where instructors demonstrated various escape and evasion techniques. Lunch was a sandwich; supper was missing altogether. At dark, already tired and hungry, we were loaded into a truck, given water to carry, and dumped in the desert with a map and goal.

The desert was infiltrated with army patrols whose instructions were to shoot anyone they could catch. If you used the techniques you were taught, they wouldn't "see" you, but take a shortcut and the "enemy" would shoot a clip from a .45 pistol or carbine at you (a clip with blanks, we hoped). A member of the patrol then punched a card that you carried on your person and returned you to the starting point, where you began your escape all over again.

The course was designed like a funnel. It took about ten hours to complete, mostly on hands and knees. To add to the torment, it rained. By the time I was captured, I was exhausted, wet, cut up, and miserable.

Everyone was caught, sometimes with violence. We were pushed and prodded with rifles; some men were knocked down. Each man had his flight suit and boots stripped off and a black bag tied over his head. Buck naked, we were lined up and pushed towards a destination. On the way, our guards occasionally prodded us with gun butts or threw a bucket of ice water over us. Ugh. By now it was dawn, and we'd been in misery for nearly 24 hours.

The sun warmed our naked bodies, but the black sacks over our heads kept us disoriented. We were marched into a cave, where each man was shoved into an individual cell measuring about five feet square and five feet high. It had a dirt floor and a can in the corner to pee. It was totally dark and almost totally silent. We were under orders to keep quiet; not complying resulted in more negative attention and discomfort.

I was exhausted, and for the first time since the ordeal began, I was alone. There was no way to stretch out, but uncomfortable as it was, I collapsed on the floor in a fetal position and was asleep instantly. Within what seemed like minutes, the cell door opened and a heavily accented European threw a bucket of ice water on me. "Why is your hood off?" he yelled. I put the hood back on and he left. I was just about asleep when the door opened again and another foreigner threw a bucket of ice water on me, screaming "Why is your hood on?" Frustration, fatigue, misery, humiliation—it was completely disorientating.

Someone pushed a rice ball and water through a slot in the cell door. I ate and drank as if it were midnight mess. After about 36 hours, pajama-like prisoner-of-war garb was pushed through the opening. A little later, two goons half-dragged, half-pushed me into an interrogation room.

If captured we were encouraged to stick to name, rank, and serial number. However, those in the know realized this might not be enough, so we'd been directed to create a story of how we ventured into "Monrovia."

Someone lifted my hood and I stood blinking under the bright, hot lights in the interrogation room. It felt like I'd endured not hours but possibly weeks, months, or years of imprisonment. A foreign voice from behind the bank of lights began to question me pleasantly, and I answered him with name, rank, and serial number. He was quite persuasive, and I was beginning to feel a sense of warmth and well-being when the door flew open and he was replaced by a Nazi bastard who started the interrogation all over again.

The hood was pulled over my head and I began my story about being lost and straying into "Monrovia." This infuriated my tormentor, and his two goons took me out and dunked me into a pit of ice water. They kept me there until I was numb; then they brought me back to the interrogation room. This time, I was placed on the "green chair," a stick two inches in diameter.

After a second stint in the cave, I was interrogated again. Short of pure torture, our captors used every technique we'd been briefed on in the comfort of the classroom. Time lost all meaning: It could have been two hours, two days, or forever. I did, however, mark for murder six or eight foreigners. They did their work well.

Eventually I was marched to a large holding room, found my flight suit and boots, and was reunited with a hundred or so other prisoners, each of them as miserable as I. After we dressed, we were double-timed to the POW compound. It could have been a movie set, it was so real. We set up a rank structure and were given jobs by the colonel in charge. We were given sacks of chow and had to ration and serve to the troops.

Since escape was both possible and expected, we also set up an escape committee. After a few failures, we managed to get a prisoner out by starting a Hollywood-style brawl on one side of the prison yard while three of our friends rolled under the wire at different locations. Two were recaptured, but the third got away. During the debrief, we got a collective attaboy for that effort.

Those who failed did not go unpunished. One guy who was caught, a lieutenant, was placed in a black box that was adjustable for body size in order to make it as confining as possible. When in it, one would swelter in the sun. This particular guy suffered from claustrophobia, a real factor in making this punishment even *more* effective. If someone really couldn't take it, he'd be grounded, which might wreck havoc with his career, but it was definitely better than the alternative. Everybody in our class got the black box for some period of time.

The combination of being in isolation and living in the POW camp lasted for about a week. Afterward, each man had a private debriefing on the experience. Everybody in our class did fine, but my cover story made me look like a traitor. It's amazing how they could twist my words to mean something totally different than I had intended.

To top it off, my interrogators had taken a Polaroid picture of me "pledging allegiance" to the red-colored Monrovian flag, which showed strongly in the background of the photo. They had chided me as a liar and goaded me to swear that I was telling the truth, and in response, I'd jumped up with my hand in the pledge position. How was I supposed to know that they had a camera and that on the wall behind me was a flag? The result was a photo with the caption "American spy pledges allegiance to Monrovia."

The training events were intensely real, and there were times when I began to believe I was actually a prisoner of war. At the beginning, the fatigue and the constant darkness of solitary confinement were totally disorienting. The POW camp situation was also quite an education. After living through both of these experiences, we probably were better qualified to survive as actual POWs than U.S. servicemen from any previous war.

At the end of this week, we were marched to a hall for a huge buffet, a feast for all to enjoy. Our interrogators joined us. We all had a great laugh and I decided, grudgingly, that I would let them live. For the most part, they were enlisted men originally from European and Iron Curtain countries, and with their accents and harshness, they were as convincing as Hollywood actors.

After a couple of days off to recuperate, we were back in the classroom to rehash the experience. We all agreed that we'd learned huge lessons about ourselves and our ability to survive. Though a marine might scoff at the level and duration of the deprivations we endured, I felt this training was both effective and necessary. I have no doubt that for some who went through it and later became actual POWs, it helped to save their lives.

We had one more adventure to go. For the survival portion of the school, we were split into groups of four or five. Accompanied by an instructor, we were loaded onto a bus and trucked to the Sierra Mountains above Reno. The intent was to simulate a shoot down in enemy territory. For a period of each day, our instructor showed us how to survive in the outback with minimal food and shelter.

Our trainers were outdoorsmen, enlisted airmen or sergeants who loved their jobs and the survival experience. We'd been thoroughly briefed on survival techniques during our two weeks in the classroom. Now we had to apply the theory. We lived in a base camp with a sleeping bag, a change of clothes, and about 600 calories of energy food per person per day. We were also given a single live rabbit to share. We could kill it or let it go. I never heard of a group that let it go.

We had to organize our escape, ration the food, and supplement our diet with whatever we could scrounge in the forest. Remembering my high school summers in Mexico, I knew what to do with that rabbit. After killing and skinning it, I divided up the meat and each guy cooked his piece over the fire at the end of a stick. No barbecued steak ever tasted better. We also discovered a stream freshly stocked with trout, and having fish, rabbit, and edible greens to stave off the aches in our bellies made the process almost human. Each day we followed a map intended to help us escape. Meanwhile, army rangers were hunting us down.

Again, as long as we followed the rules of escape and evasion, the rangers couldn't "see" us. But if one of us walked on a ridgeline or a road or across an open field, he would be shot at and captured, his card punched, and his weary carcass returned to the starting point. Anyone caught twice had the opportunity to do the escape and evasion week again. Not a pleasant thought.

This part of training was toughest on city slickers. For those who'd been Boy Scouts or were outdoorsmen, it was far more tolerable. For me, it felt like another day in Mexico, minus the horse.

The survival school was created, with the best of intentions, in the aftermath of the Korean War, but as it developed it got out of hand. At one point it became such a nightmare that men were actually killed attending. Like the standardization efforts at Greenville under Captain Jack and his black hats, the tail ended up wagging the dog. Fortunately, those in charge learned from their mistakes. By the time I was a student, the instructors at Stead did their jobs harshly, but they did them safely and well.

Being in isolation was the most self-revealing experience of my young life. Could I cope? Yes I could, and some of the mind games I invented when I was in that cramped, dirt-floored box are still with me today. I taught myself to go to a better place. I remember running free on the farm, dissecting a leaf. I can picture the veins of that leaf, then tearing each segment of it and letting it float down the creek, propelled by each eddy and whirlpool to one of the dams I'd constructed. It was an almost Zen-like experience, drawing on my vast collection of mostly happy memories.

The flip side of isolation can be thoughts filled with ugliness. A minor problem can escalate into a nasty, depressing situation that is soon out of control. Negative thoughts can grow like poisonous mushrooms in a dark place, covering every optimistic thought. The yin and yang of the mental process are nearly overpowering, and the ability to push that mushroom aside is a huge challenge. It was a challenge I won: beauty and peace over despair and desperation.

The entire experience—evading capture, surviving in the wild, enduring the deprivations and interrogation of the POW experience—was physically severe and not something I wanted to go through again, but I felt better prepared for having had the training.

At the end of the program, Harrah's, a hotel and casino in Reno, treated us to dinner and $20 worth of chips. This was great fun, but I was eager to get back to Willie. I missed Polly and Walt, and I was about to become a dad once more.

Oh Baby, Is She Pregnant!

Polly's arms and legs were skinny, but her belly was a beach ball. No more Austin-Healey for her; she couldn't ride comfortably as a passenger, let alone fit into the driver's seat. Finally, two weeks before her due date, the doc detected a second heartbeat. We were ecstatic. We were also somewhat relieved, and in celebration Polly ate her favorite treat—a half gallon of ice cream.

At work the guys started a kitty to predict the date of Polly's delivery. For $5, you could estimate the date and time within a six-hour period. The twins obliged by coming out of the hangar, so to speak, at 1600 on their predicted day of arrival in September 1964. Timothy Rutledge Wright was a healthy 6 lb., 15 oz.; Andrew Horne Wright weighed in at 6 lbs., 1 oz.

To top it off, I won the kitty! Our lives were permanently changed for the better, but also for the busier. Three boys in diapers, all at the same time. Friends helped in the daytime and we handled the feedings at night. I've never seen children with as much energy, but Polly and I were a team. We shared everything; when something needed to be done for one of the boys or around the house, whoever had a free hand did it. We'd been married just over three years, and our family of five—six if you counted Tucson, the Airedale—was thriving.

Part VI: 1964–1966

Chapter 67 – Multiple Choices

The enemy in Vietnam was made up of ordinary people—farmers and village folk, men, women, and children, many battle-hardened from a century of fighting the French, the Japanese, and then the French again. We thought globally; they thought locally. They wanted to be free of outside interference, and France had promised that Vietnam would be able to nationalize after the war. Ho Chi Minh, a Vietnamese leader against colonialism, had emigrated from Vietnam to France during World War I. While there he became a socialist and eventually a member of the Communist Party. In 1941 he returned to Vietnam to organize the Viet Minh, a communist organization that opposed the Japanese, the Vichy French who ruled the country during the war, and their Vietnamese allies.

Once the war was over, however, France slowly resumed its power in Vietnam, and the U.S. and other Western nations had so many other problems they basically ignored the situation. Ho Chi Minh and the Viet Minh fought back. Eventually the French were defeated and the country was divided into North and South Vietnam along the 17th parallel. The resulting political climate led inexorably to the war in Vietnam.

By late 1964, many of our early warriors were back from combat in this troubled land, and the troops were already suspicious of the means and methods being used. The "big chiefs" didn't seem to be paying attention to what was really going on in the field. Servicemen and women were losing their lives, politicians were doing all they could to avoid dealing honestly with the problems, and the country was becoming more divided every day.

It was in this climate that I was trying to decide my future. Did I express interest in flying KC-135s to SAC, since I knew they'd been nosing about? Did I pursue a civilian career with TWA, assuming they responded to my recent application? Or did I sit tight and wait to see what else might come down the pike?

In the meantime, I was enjoying a relaxed way of life. Tom Fincher, my co-instructor in T-38 platform engineering, and I had our class notes and organization down pat. When we weren't on the platform, we had our feet up on the desk, engaged in long conversations or reading a good book. Sometimes we even had a nap after lunch.

To make certain we remained undisturbed, we camouflaged the entry to our cubbyhole of an office to look like a broom closet, and we were rarely interrupted. So when a full colonel knocked on our door one day, we were so flustered we knocked over our chairs in jumping to attention. Was this guy lost? Was our cover blown?

"Captain Fincher, would you please excuse Captain Wright and me?" Oh, great. What have they dug up from my past? Did they refigure my 72-gun salute? How will I feed my family?

The colonel dragged over a chair and sat down.

"Relax, Wright," he said with a smile.

He had my personnel file in his hand and was well-informed about Polly, the boys, and me. He'd also talked to my commanders and obviously was content with their answers. Pretty soon I did relax. I could tell this was an interview, but for what?

Finally, he revealed the purpose of his visit. "SAC is looking for pilots to fly the U-2," he said, and he asked if I'd be interested in applying for the mission.

For once in my life I was speechless. "Why me, Sir?" I said when I could get the words out.

The colonel explained. Although the primary role of SAC was to fly nuclear bombers, two other aircraft, the U-2 and the SR-71, were also vital parts of its organization. The U-2 was a difficult aircraft to fly. Lockheed had originally built 55 of these airplanes, but the air force had only 15 or so left. Most had been lost to crashes; a few had been shot out of the sky.[215]

Unlike Gary Powers, most of the U-2 pilots shot down by enemy fire did not survive, though two Taiwanese pilots shot down over the People's Republic of China were captured and imprisoned.[216]

---

[215] The U-2 was put into service in 1956 and, as of 2008, is still in use. The SR-71 was in service from 1964 through the late 1990s. Several SR-71s were lost to accidents; none was ever lost to enemy action.

[216] Following World War II, there was a civil war between the Chinese government and the Chinese communists. The communists won, and the government of the Republic of China retreated to the island of Taiwan. For many years, the United Nations, the U.S., and most countries of the world recognized the Republic of China as the official government of the country, and Taiwan and the U.S. were allies. In 1971, a U.N. resolution admitted mainland China (the People's Republic of China) to the U.N. and gave it Taiwan's seat on the U.N. Security Council. By the 1980s, only a few countries recognized the Republic of China as a separate country. The People's

In 1964, the SR-71, the most advanced airplane in the world, was just coming on line. Dubbed the Blackbird, it was designed by Kelly Johnson, one of the most innovative aircraft designers of all time, and built by Lockheed at a secret aircraft factory in Burbank, California. The SR-71 was a reconnaissance plane capable of flying at Mach 3 (three times the speed of sound).

The first pilots to fly the Blackbird were upgrading from the U-2, and these men were being replaced by some of SAC's top B-52 pilots. The B-52, however, was a huge, complex bomber, and the bombing mission required a team approach—several crewmembers working in close proximity to accomplish a specific and dangerous task. Apparently, the training for this type of mission didn't translate well into the confined cockpit and solo mission of the U-2, and the B-52 jocks weren't working out as well as hoped for. There had been several incidents, including some crashes; SAC was running out of airplanes. Although many of the B-52 pilots were successful, the powers that be had decided it would be quicker to recruit pilots with fighter backgrounds and a high number of flight hours, since these men were more used to a solo role. ATC (Air Training Command) was where such pilots could be found, and I seemed to match the profile.[217]

The colonel made the pitch: the U-2 for four years, the SR-71 for four more. He didn't offer any guarantees—air force requirements are always the governing factor in any assignment—but he didn't ask for a formal contract on my part, either. Except for the automatic one-year extension associated with any move to a new location, I had fulfilled my commitment to the air force and would be free to resign at any time.

At that moment, however, resignation was the last thing on my mind. Talk about drama! Eight years in the cockpit of the world's most interesting aircraft and mission, plus a year to write my memoirs and retire to Hollywood after a 20-year career. I could see myself sitting by my pool in the hills above L.A., sipping mint juleps with my southern belle.

At the end of our conversation, the colonel paused. "Sit straight up in that hard-backed chair, Wright." Strange, but an order is an order. He whipped out a sliding tape measure and proceeded to measure my sitting height. "Perfect," he commented. Then he explained that most pilots who flew the U-2 were shorter than I. "With all the survival gear and the parachute stored under you,"

Republic, which technically claims Taiwan as part of China, released the captured Taiwanese pilots in the early 1980s. As of 2008, Taiwan continues to function independently as the two entities maintain an uneasy peace.

[217] The Boeing B-52 Stratofortress was the country's first long-range, swept-wing heavy bomber. The first B-52s were used by the air force in 1954. As of 2008, the B-52 is still in service.

he said, "there's not a lot of room left for your head." Fortunately, although I'm long-legged, I'm short-waisted. I'd just scaled my first hurdle on the way to flying the U-bird.

I thanked the colonel for his interest. "Sir, let me mull this one over and discuss the offer with my wife."

After he left, I jumped into the Austin-Healey and drove to our home in Chandler. This was big, way too big to wait until the end of the workday. When I arrived, the boys were busily dismantling the house, but Polly, in her usual manner, had the situation well in hand. Before I could say a word, she handed me a letter from TWA. In it was the date for an interview.

Teaching was becoming repetitive and I needed a job change, but I could see my angel was having a ball. Yesterday, it was work as usual. Today, there were three possibilities: the KC-135, TWA, and now the U-2. Such a deal!

Polly and I had a heart-to-heart powwow. The air force was our security blanket. It was the life I'd spent my young years dreaming about, a life of excitement and challenge. It was a life that I loved.

The KC-135 refueling tanker probably made the most sense, but it was so damn ordinary, and I really disliked ordinary. After all, that's why I was in the air force to begin with. If I'd wanted ordinary, I could have always followed my mother's advice and become a housepainter.

The U-2 was an adventure. I could see how this mission could truly make a difference, not only in Southeast Asia but worldwide. TWA was the least likely option, but the comfort of a civilian job was tempting, especially when I thought of my family.

I also felt a patriotic challenge. The war in Vietnam was relatively quiet, a lull engineered by President Johnson for the 1964 election season. (As a campaign issue, war rarely sells.) Senator Barry Goldwater, LBJ's opponent, campaigned on the premise that we should commit ourselves to win or get out, one or the other. Johnson painted him as a war hawk. On Election Day, Johnson won 61 percent of the popular vote and carried 44 states plus the District of Columbia. It was one of the largest vote margins in presidential history.[218]

It was true that the war was becoming suspicious in its execution, but its purpose was noble and it was not yet completely out of control. The United States had a treaty with South Vietnam to protect it from attack; we had similar treaties with many nations. I believed we had a duty to honor that treaty, and

---

[218] Barry Goldwater (1909–1998) was a five-term U.S. Senator from Arizona. Known as "Mr. Conservative," he is often credited for sparking the rebirth of the conservative political movement in America in the 1960s.

that with proper leadership, we could still attain a just result. Unfortunately, our civilian leadership was questionable.

Polly and I talked late into the night. The U-2 won out, no contest.

The next morning I called the colonel and accepted his offer. Within a day or two, I received orders to report the following week to Davis-Monthan Air Force Base for testing and further interviews. Just down the road in Tucson, this was the base where Tom Westhafer and I had paid an unexpected visit three years earlier when the VOR system on our T-37 malfunctioned. It was also the location of the 4080th SRW (Strategic Reconnaissance Wing), home of the U-2. And this time I'd be going in the front door.

During the week before my interviews, I did as much research as possible. The mission was still cloaked in secrecy, but I was able to put together some information that helped to validate my decision.

The Quest for Intelligence

At the end of World War II, the USSR annexed most of the smaller, weaker countries of Eastern Europe, absorbing nation after nation. "From Stettin in the Baltic to Trieste in the Adriatic, an Iron Curtain has descended across the Continent," said Winston Churchill in his famous 1946 speech at Westminster College in Fulton, Missouri. And so it had. Stalin, the arrogant and murderous despot of the USSR, was trying to force communism on the rest of the world, and this well-planned effort had its allies in many other nations.[219]

The basic theories of communism and/or socialism appealed to many, especially to the have-nots. Marshall Dodge and Bob Bryan, storytellers and creators of "Bert and I," a series of humorous Down East stories of the 1950s and 1960s, put it something like this:

> It seems Eben Robay went down to Tremont Temple in Boston one Saturday night to hear Norman Thomas speak about socialism. The next Monday, he was preaching to Enoch Turner over the back fence.
>
> "You know, Enoch," he said, "under socialism, a person shares everything."

---

[219] In 1922, Joseph Stalin (1879–1953) became General Secretary of the Communist Party's Central Committee in the USSR. After he came to power, he initially exiled and later executed old Party leaders and anyone else he suspected of disagreeing with him. In the end, millions lost their lives to his excesses, which ceased only at his death.

> "You mean to say, Eben, that if you had two farms, you'd give me one of them?"
>
> "Yup, if I had two farms, Enoch, I'd give you one of them."
>
> "You mean to say, Eben, if you owned two hayricks, you'd give me one of them?"
>
> "Yup, Enoch. If I had two hayricks, I'd give you one of them."
>
> "Or if you had two hogs, you'd give me one of them?"
>
> "Darn you, Enoch, you know I've got two hogs!"[220]

Stalin was heavy-handed and brutal, and a war of words and ideologies was being waged worldwide. The first post-war showdown was in Berlin, when the Russians cut off all ground transportation into and out of the city from June of 1948 until May of 1949. Through hard work, perseverance, and the brilliant strategy of the Berlin Airlift, the Allies met and won this major ideological battle.

How well I remembered my time in Berlin in 1947. The Russians had control of most of the infrastructure (thus the arbitrary electrical outages, like the one I experienced on my 13th birthday on the way home from the opera), and they clamped down bit by bit. It wasn't long after my mother and I returned to the States that they shut down all entrée except the narrow corridors of flight.

This was only the first of many confrontations. The United States had the A-bomb, but with the help of their spy network and the many scientists captured from the Germans, the USSR soon had an atomic bomb as well. The arms race was on, an expensive Cold War that the world could ill afford but that U.S. and its allies could not abandon. To lose would have meant the end of the free world.

The USSR was ostensibly our ally during World War II, but Stalin's excesses were well known to the intelligence community, and the effort to obtain more information about this dark and secretive regime began almost before the last shot was fired. Because the USSR was a closed society, however, our spy network behind the Iron Curtain was difficult to maintain. When our eyes and ears inside the Curtain were discovered, they were usually disposed of brutally.

The air force stripped down Boeing B-29s and Convair B-36s to

---

[220] Norman Thomas (1884–1968) was born in Marion, OH, and ordained as a Presbyterian minister in 1911. While in the seminary he became a socialist. He was also a pacifist, opposing U.S. involvement in both World War I and World War II. He was the Socialist Party candidate for U.S. President six times.

penetrate the Iron Curtain. However, these aircraft flew neither fast enough nor high enough to achieve the success we needed. Many missions were tried, but most were unsuccessful. The Boeing B-47, one of the first pure jet bombers, made many successful flights around the periphery of the USSR, using side-looking cameras and electronic eavesdropping equipment, but this wasn't enough. The B-47 and the North American B-45 Tornado also made some penetrations, but the political and military ramifications of sending bombers over a nation with which we were not officially at war were enormous. Approximately a dozen aircraft and 80 crewmembers were lost, mostly from shoot downs. Most, if not all, of these aircraft were beyond the technical boundaries of the USSR, but the shoot downs were reported as mechanical or operational losses. Neither side wanted publicity about how overt our attempts actually were.[221]

In the 1950s the Eisenhower administration had tried to sell an "open skies" agreement to the Russians, letting each side fly over the other's territory to check for verification of the treaties in place as well as any treaties that might be signed in the future. The Soviets weren't interested. They already had access to our "open skies" and could take surveillance pictures from commercial airliners and private aircraft. Using our new camera technology, we tried flying balloons over the Soviet Union, but most of them fell into the hands of the Russians; and satellite technology, although on the horizon, wouldn't be available soon enough.

By 1953, the CIA, under director Allen Dulles, and SAC, headed by stogie-chomping General Curtis LeMay, wanted results; and they wanted them yesterday. President Eisenhower was very much a part of these discussions, and his vast military experience made him wary of anything that could cause an accidental war. A committee of six eminent scientists was convened to examine how the U.S. might best avoid a surprise nuclear attack by the Soviet Union. Called the Land Panel and headed by Polaroid's Edwin Land, the panel interviewed many in leadership positions in the nation's military and intelligence communities and was surprised and shocked to discover how little we knew.[222]

The Land Panel, along with the CIA and the air force, explored the

---

[221] The B-45 was the first jet aircraft to be refueled in the air. Although rapidly superseded by the Boeing B-47 Stratojet, SAC used B-45s throughout the 1950s.

[222] Edwin Land (1909–1991) invented the first inexpensive filters for polarizing light, which resulted in Polaroid film. To market this invention, Land and a partner started a company in 1932, which in 1937 was renamed The Polaroid Corporation. During the Second World War, Land worked on military applications. In 1947, he invented the Polaroid instant camera.

possibilities for safe and effective air reconnaissance and concluded that flying over the top was the only way. The scientists believed it was safe to fly at 70,000 feet with impunity, but most aircraft manufacturers didn't think such a design was feasible.

Developing "The Article"

In the meantime, the British firm English Electric had developed the B-57 Canberra, a twin-engine medium bomber. The Glenn L. Martin Company in the U.S. bought rights to produce this aircraft for the air force. Martin adapted some of these jets to have a high-aspect wing, coupled with a more powerful engine that could fly efficiently in the mid-60,000-foot range. Much valuable information was gathered using this fine airplane, but the Soviets countered with advanced MiG fighters and SAM missiles from their advanced rocket program. The Canberra couldn't fly high enough to avoid either of these threats, and besides it was a bomber—at best a public relations risk and at worst the potential spark for another war.[223]

The government had let a contract to Bell Aircraft in Niagara Falls, New York, to design a high-altitude, dedicated reconnaissance aircraft that could fly at 70,000 feet for 3,000 miles without refueling. The result was the X-16. Although no X-16s were ever built, the design for this two-engine jet using the J57 Pratt & Whitney military engine played a significant part in the eventual development of the U-2.

Skeptics continued to feel it was aerodynamically impossible to function at 70,000 feet. Lockheed's famous Kelly Johnson was not one of them. He submitted an unsolicited design to the air force dubbed the CL-282. Basically, it was a lightweight glider created by mating a modified fuselage from Lockheed's XF-104 with high-aspect glider wings. It was powered by a GE-J73 turbojet engine, and Lockheed claimed the plane would fly at 73,000 feet for 7 hours.

General LeMay was underwhelmed. For one thing, he felt the engine was underpowered; for another, he wasn't about to buy into a single-engine aircraft that had no wheels or guns. He was a multiengine man, although in actuality the multiengine theory was flawed. If one of the engines had failed at high altitude, the plane would have had to descend to maintain flight, at which point it would be a sitting duck for the enemy. Carrying the extra weight of a second engine was for naught, but old attitudes die hard.

By 1954, we knew that the USSR had developed and tested a hydrogen

---

[223] The first Canberra prototype flew in 1949. These planes were removed from combat in 1971 but were used by Air National Guard units into the 1980s.

bomb using technology more advanced than ours and in a shorter time span than we thought possible. There were also reports of a new Russian plane called the Bison, a four-engine, swept-wing jet bomber comparable to our B-52. There were serious concerns that the Soviets could launch a surprise attack on the United States. It was imperative that we get the facts, and aerial reconnaissance over the top of the country was the best solution.

The Land Panel began to look with favor upon the rejected Lockheed CL-282 design. They liked its high-altitude capabilities and its single-engine, low-radar profile. However, even if the plane could fly high enough, there wasn't a camera small enough to fit within the restricted confines of the aircraft. James Baker, a young Harvard astronomer and member of the Land Panel, was working on a revolutionary new camera and lenses. At the same time, the Eastman Kodak Company was developing a lightweight film suitable for that camera. Both were optimistic they would succeed.

Another element of the CL-282 design that appealed to the panel was that it provided no place to mount guns or carry a bomb. If shot down, it could never be misidentified as an offensive warplane. And if the CIA, a civilian organization, ran the program, it would be even better. Uniformed military pilots could be considered an act of war, whereas civilian pilots arguably would not be.

In late November 1954, Ike approved the concept that Lockheed had presented and assigned the CIA to manage it. In order to create what was initially referred to only as "the Article," funds had to be provided that would escape the eyes of Congressional oversight committees. The CIA had access to such "black funds," and although many felt that Allen Dulles favored conventional espionage—using agents instead of technology—he appointed Richard M. Bissell Jr., a CIA employee and former administrator of the Marshall Plan in Europe, to spearhead the task.

In an atmosphere of secrecy that probably could never happen again, project Aquatone (the first of many monikers) was launched without as much as a contract. Pratt & Whitney J57 engines, which the government preferred over the GE-J73 engines of the original CL-282 design, were "diverted" from other projects. The air force found itself in the unhappy position of playing second fiddle to the CIA, while at the same time providing the assistance and expertise needed to make the program operational.

The Article was to be built at Kelly Johnson's Skunk Works, a Lockheed factory and secret research center in Burbank, California. This facility was staffed with what many considered the finest aeronautical engineering team in the world. They worked countless hours, literally camping out in the factory. The designers sat no more than 50 feet from the production line, which allowed them to make pencil notations and changes immediately. Johnson was a demanding boss, but morale was extremely high. Everyone involved knew this was probably the most important project of their lives.[224]

Johnson was excused from the usual record of technological specifications dictated by the engineering division at Wright-Patterson Air Force Base. Instead, he was held only to certain performance specifications. The plane was required to be stressed to 2.5 Gs, considerably lower than the requirement for combat aircraft. It was to cruise at 70,000 feet or above, at a respectable 0.8 Mach.[225]

Within weeks, 25 engineers were at work on this top-secret project. And while the airframe was being built, the cameras were being designed.

The Article had an 80-foot wingspan and a fuselage about 50 feet long. Special fuel that wouldn't vaporize at high altitudes was developed for the Pratt & Whitney J57 engine. (This fuel, which used many of the properties of conventional lighter fluid, caused consumers to wonder why there was a mysterious shortage of lighter fluid for the better part of a year.)

In many ways the Article was a conventional aircraft, but the high-aspect ratio and efficiency of the wing made it revolutionary. Altitude was survival, so weight was all-important. Every extra pound meant ten feet of lost elevation. The idea was to fly higher than the enemy, be invisible to radar, and have the maneuverability to dodge missiles.

The Q-bay, a pressurized area built into the aircraft for payloads, allowed a variety of devices to be used, depending on the goals of the mission. To make it easier to load and unload these components, a clever quick-change mechanism was added. It worked much like the three-point hitch on Millard Hudson's John Deere tractor from the farm of my childhood.

---

[224] The term Skunk Works was inspired by the Skonk Works, a backwoods still operated by the character Barnsmell in the 1940s comic strip *Li'l Abner*, by Al Capp.

[225] Wright-Patterson Air Force Base in Dayton, OH, is located partially on land once used by the Wright brothers as a training ground. When World War I broke out, several military installations were established in the Dayton area. In the 1920s, the Patterson family, founders of National Cash Register, helped raise funds to purchase additional land, and a portion of the expanded area was named Wright Field. Later, another portion was redesignated Patterson Field to honor the Pattersons' son, who had been killed on a test flight in 1918. The two fields merged in 1948 to become Wright-Patterson Air Force Base. As of 2008, the base remains one of the air force's most important facilities.

New ways of bracing the structure were also devised. The fuselage was of lightweight aluminum. The tail was bolted on using three high-tension bolts, and the wing, which had to be installed without a through-fuselage spar in order to add room in the Q-bay, was bolted to the fuselage. When needed, an innovative gust-control device would stabilize the aircraft by enlisting the flaps and ailerons to change the aerodynamics.

The cockpit was quite small. The pilot was literally wrapped around a protrusion in the middle, and the parts could have come out of a junkyard. The control wheel was from a much larger plane, the rudder pedals came from the T-33, and various odds and ends could be traced to other aircraft. There wasn't time to make everything new, nor was it necessary. The viewing port contained a drift sight with controllable magnification, as well as a sextant borrowed from the venerable B-29. The port served both functions, with a flapper lever to switch between drift sight and sextant.

In-flight instruments were splashed around the panel like someone had been in a dart-throwing contest, and space was so limited that the radios were stuck here and there, wherever they would fit. Actually, it was better organized than it looked.

No provision had been made for ejection. In case of emergency, the pilot was expected to crawl over the side and jump, though in reality, the possibility of escape was marginal at best. At the altitudes that the U-bird would fly, the pilot needed oxygen to survive, and several pilots who did bail out were lost because of the difficulty of the situation. Later, a lightweight version of the British Martin-Baker ejection seat was devised and, after some initial problems, became standard and safe to use.

Johnson's original CL-282 design had no landing gear. Instead, it took off from a wheeled dolly and landed on its belly with no flaps. Neither the Land Panel nor the air force found this acceptable. The Article had to have landing gear, but how to do so without compromising potential altitude? Eventually, a copy of the B-47 tandem gear was added to the fuselage, and removable landing gear were placed close to the wingtips. Eight months after the project began, the aircraft was ready to fly.

The Bird Takes to the Air

Tony LeVier, the famous Lockheed test pilot, was given the responsibility of finding a secure place to test the airplane. He took off in a Beechcraft Bonanza and located an abandoned lake bed north of Las Vegas. Groom Lake had already been fenced off and restricted by the Atomic Energy Commission. As one of the most "black" or secret of places and almost inaccessible by ground vehicle, it was ideal for the job. Soon the U-2 was disassembled, loaded into giant C-124s, and reassembled on the lake bed.[226]

During the taxi test, the plane accidentally became airborne, an event that caused more than a few nervous moments. The next day, August 4, 1955, LeVier made the first official flight. There were a few oil leaks and some problems with the fuel system, but the plane flew successfully. When he was ready to come down, however, the bird wanted to land headfirst. LeVier solved the problem by landing like a taildragger, almost in full stall, and thus avoiding a porpoise. For an Alaska bush pilot, this wouldn't have been a problem, but to a jet pilot used to tricycle gear, it was a tremendous challenge.[227]

Once the air force saw how successful the Aquatone project was, they ordered 29 of the Article for themselves. In the early days, U-2 pilots, usually former air force personnel, were sometimes civilian employees of the CIA. At other times they were military. It just depended upon the operational and political ramifications of the mission.

The U-2, also known as the Dragon Lady, was on its way. The government had contracted for a total of 49 aircraft (20 for the CIA; 29 for the air force). With one thing and another, Lockheed actually delivered 55—earlier than promised and under projected cost. The entire operation was an extraordinary effort and took the cooperation of many dedicated men and women working under the strictest secrecy. Even in 1964, a complete list of those who worked on the project wasn't available. Despite the lack of bureaucratic oversight, however, rumor had it that Kelly Johnson returned more than a million dollars to the U.S. government—money left over after the planes were completed.

---

[226] The Douglas C-124 Globemaster II could hold more than 200 troops, or it could be used to carry up to 74,000 pounds of cargo, including tanks, field guns, bulldozers and trucks, and, on occasion, the U-2. First produced in 1950, the plane was phased out in 1974.

[227] Like its namesake that hits the water nose-first, during a porpoise the aircraft lands nosewheel first, followed by the small tail wheel, which often slams down with such violence that the aircraft breaks apart. The best way to avoid this problem in the U-2 is to land as close to a stall as possible. Landing a fighter close to a stall, on the other hand, could be fatal.

Chapter 68 – Performance Under Pressure

1965

It was a little over 100 miles from our home in Chandler to Davis-Monthan, and I was in fine spirits the morning I drove there to interview with Colonel John Des Portes, commander of the 4080th SRW. He was friendly, informative, and all business. Prior to the advent of the SR-71, he explained, the organization had had almost no turnover since 1956, when the U-2 came on line in the air force. Now that pilots were being deployed to meet the operational requirements of the SR-71, several new pilots were being recruited as replacements.

The interview process, if one could call it that, was informal. I was guided from section to section, where the leaders checked me out and I took in everything around me. Many of the people I met had been with the program since day one, and they glowed with the pride of accomplishment. These men had a mission, perhaps the most important mission in the military. They were friendly and they laughed and joked around, but beneath the surface their attitude was serious business, and it showed. Their boss, SAC commander General Thomas Power, was the most no-nonsense leader in the air force. The "attitude" started at the top, and buster, you'd better have it or you'd be looking for employment elsewhere.

This elite group was a volunteer organization, so I had no doubt that if I ever wanted out, the door would be open. For now, however, I definitely wanted *in*, and they wanted me. I was sent to Texas for a physical similar to that given to the astronauts. Various tests were involved and my body was subjected to more than the usual indignities, but I made it.

Before I could report to Davis-Monthan, I had to finish up my teaching obligations at Williams as well as learn some advanced, high-altitude survival techniques. I started in an altitude chamber designed to duplicate the problems associated with oxygen deprivation in jet flight. The symptoms of insufficient oxygen are subtle, almost like sleeping sickness, and it's easy to slip into unconsciousness. In the test chamber, these symptoms could be produced under controlled conditions, allowing the airman to recognize the warning signs in time to take appropriate action. Every air crew member had to spend time in this chamber every couple of years. This was not something we wanted to forget.

Crew members entered the chamber in pairs. At different altitudes, one of the two took off his oxygen mask and began to write something. In a remarkably short time, his words were slurred all over the page. His mate put the mask back on, and recovery was almost instantaneous. When I read the slurred mess I generated during my test, it was hard for me to recognize my own handwriting, yet I had no memory of being impaired. It's much like being drunk, without the hangover.

For the better part of the day, I was briefed on the rigors of high-altitude flight. Then several airmen prepared a partial-pressure suit for me. It was made of a girdle-like composition with adjustable laces in strategic places to fit the contours of my body. The David Clark Company had conceived and developed this apparatus, and a representative of the company was there with an air force supervisory sergeant to inspect each step of the operation.

One of the more interesting aspects of the process was the attachment of the collar, a bladder that prevented air leakage into the lower body. "What's your neck size, Captain," asked the technician.

"Sixteen," I replied.

"Hey, Joe," said the technician, "get me a size 14½ bladder." Rubbing my neck to make sure it hadn't shrunk in the last five minutes, I looked at him quizzically.

He laughed. "Captain, if you ain't uncomfortable, we haven't done our job." In order for the seal to work, he explained, the bladder almost had to choke me.

Finally, after a couple of hours of tugging and lacing, I was suited up and ready to go to altitude in a test tank. "How's it feel?" asked the tech rep.

"I feel like a high school girl ready for a first date," I quipped, "except this darn girdle covers everything except my head. Not to mention the choker collar. Am I going to survive in here?"

The rep laughed. "Don't worry," he said. "We know what we're doing. The David Clark Company got its start manufacturing ladies' foundation garments."

After they fastened the helmet to the suit and put on the faceplate, I breathed 100-percent oxygen, a process designed to eliminate the nitrogen from my blood and thus prevent the bends when my body was compressed in the suit. Ironically, both high-altitude flyers and deep-sea divers have to deal with this problem. As I reclined in a semi-resting position on a couch, compressed air was hooked up to the capstan system routed throughout the suit.

"Press the test button," said the sergeant. I did as he asked, and the suit began squeezing my body, almost to the point of pain. It was like a blood pressure cuff at its apex, except that I felt it everywhere. After the crew checked for leaks, I released the button and the suit deflated to its normal, uncomfortable condition.

Attached to a portable oxygen bottle, I clomped along with my entourage to the test tank. The tank resembled a diving bell from deep-sea movie dramas. It was a double-walled chamber with thick glass windows through which the crew could observe the test and rescue me if either the equipment or I failed. They helped me into the seat and transferred the oxygen and other hoses from my suit to the test vehicle. The heavy door clanked shut and I heard them ratchet it down tight. It was like being in a bank vault with windows, except this vault was going to be anything but safe.

"How ya doing, Captain Wright?" asked the sergeant.

"A-okay," I replied. "Couldn't be better."

"Glad to hear it," he said with a chuckle, "'cause this is as far as many candidates get. They become so beset with claustrophobia we have to get them out of there pronto."

Just terrific, I thought, but so far I was feeling fine. As long as they didn't ask me to swim in this thing, I figured I'd make it.

Several airmen were stationed around the tank; they were all business. This could be a dangerous event, and I was the one in danger. It was very quiet; the only sounds were the air being removed from the chamber and my steady breathing. Very gradually, the suit began to expand as the chamber climbed through several thousand feet. The only instrument I could see was an altimeter. I watched the slow rotation: 10,000, 20,000, 30,000, 40,000 feet. The suit began to squeeze my body, and I was beginning to feel some discomfort. The altimeter continued to climb: 50,000, 55,000, 60,000 feet. Gradually my breathing reversed. Relax. The oxygen flowed in. I could breathe, but my body had lost most of its mobility.

My eyes were glued to the altimeter: 65,000 feet, 70,000 feet, *STOP!* The total pressure on my body was just short of unbearable. I was asked to perform minor functions. It took great effort just to raise my arms; I had about 10-percent body control. I could see the airmen monitoring me as I carried on a conversation with the sergeant on the headset.

"How are you doing, Captain?" the sergeant asked.

"Okay," I said, though this time with far less enthusiasm. There was a vial of water in the chamber, and as we approached altitude it had begun to boil. The sergeant commented on it now. "That, Sir, is what your blood would be doing if it weren't for the suit you're wearing."

It's okay to be hot stuff, but this definitely exceeded my desires.

We began a slow descent to sea level. As we lost altitude, the suit relaxed its grip on my body. The test was half over, but there was one more event to go. This, as the sergeant described it, was "the exciting part."

Once again we began the ascent to 70,000 feet. This time, the inner chamber of the double-walled hull was pressurized to 30,000 feet to mimic the interior of the U-2. The suit remained deflated. The outer chamber continued its slow climb. When the outer chamber reached 70,000 feet, the sergeant opened a valve between the two chambers to simulate engine failure, or more realistically, some type of structural failure like an explosion. He began the countdown: 9, 8, 7, 6, 5, 4, 3, 2, 1—*Boom!* The suit filled instantly, cramping down on my body and reversing my breathing. Within seconds I'd lost 90 percent of my mobility, and a cloud of moisture condensed on my faceplate, causing a whiteout. After a moment of controllable panic, I was brought rapidly to sea level. The next thing I heard was the ratcheting of the chamber door as they helped me out and removed the hoses, the faceplate, and eventually the pressure suit.

Everyone was very complimentary regarding my tolerance of the suit and the results of the test. There's no way I could describe the testing process as an enjoyable experience, but I never felt any claustrophobia, and I was satisfied that I could hack that part of the mission. I was glad, however, that this was a square I had to fill only once.

Although I was fortunate to never experience in real life the emergency scenario played out in the testing chamber, I still spent a great deal of time in that partial-pressure suit. Because the suit was designed to allow the pilot to survive at altitude, if necessary, or to descend quickly to a more-survivable lower altitude, it was uncomfortable, unwieldy, and severely restricted movement. But it did the job.

A full pressurization suit that allowed the entire body to live in an artificial environment was being used by the astronauts. This approach was definitely more comfortable, as well as safer for the pilot. Rumor had it that U-2 pilots would be issued full pressurization suits in the near future.[228]

This Was Our War

Williams Air Force Base was beginning to look like the scene of a major

---

[228] In a partial-pressure suit, only the helmet was fully pressurized. Sometime in the late 1960s, these were replaced for U-2 pilots by full pressurization suits.

evacuation. The role of the U.S. as "advisor" was over, and LBJ was plunging ahead into full-scale war. Willie was a treasure trove of skilled aviators with many hours of flying time. We were seriously manning warplanes of every type. Some men had already been to Southeast Asia and were in the pipeline to go again.

Emotion and patriotism were running high; almost to a man we backed the war enthusiastically. We'd learned our skills based on the worldwide communist threat and cut our teeth on World War II and Korea. Some had actually participated in one or both of these conflicts, but for most of us, Vietnam was the first real opportunity to prove ourselves. We were neither diplomats nor intellectuals, but this was our war and we didn't want it to finish too soon. It was our time to shine.

Elsewhere, the rumblings of dissent continued to grow, especially on college campuses. Our elected leaders in Washington were falling into the categories one would expect, though there were occasional warnings from unexpected quarters.

I hardly recognized the new pilots at Williams. The base was involved in a total staff transformation, and many of the replacements had a chest full of ribbons and war stories to go with them. After the usual bravado, however, we began to hear the doubts—not too often and not too many, but they were there. Target selection, the devastating amount of munitions being dropped on an elusive enemy, the combat losses, the reluctance of the ARVN to fight, and the willingness of the Vietcong to die were all topics we hashed out in the bars and ready rooms.[229]

---

[229] The Army of the Republic of South Vietnam (ARVN) was the ground military force of the South Vietnamese government until its collapse in April of 1975.

Chapter 69 – Hurry Up and Wait

1965

Polly and I packed our bags, turned in the keys to our home in Chandler, and set up housekeeping on Kingston Knoll in Tucson, Arizona, a hundred miles and light-years away from Williams. It was March 1965. Walt was not yet three, the twins, Tim and Andy, not yet one; and the three of them were a handful. In fact, they were *several* handsful.

I plunged into work, gung ho, ready to go. Just "fling me in dat briarpatch."[230]

As I soon found out, it wasn't that easy. The normal complement of U-bird pilots was 25. About half of them were at the home drome training and running the business. The other half were flying various types of missions from operating locations around the world. For years this had been a stable group, but with the advent of the SR-71, as soon as a new guy walked in the front door, one of the old hands walked out the back and was on his way to Beale Air Force Base to train on the Blackbird.[231]

The new pilots coming in—about ten of us before the transition was complete—were filled with excitement and eagerness, but the wing wasn't ready to absorb and train that many men in such a short time. As a result, the workload of the qualified pilots doubled, and the training of new pilots lagged from lack of personnel. This was the military way, feast or famine.

In the workings of the SAC bureaucracy, the U-2 was an orphan, a top-secret mission in a command of bombers and tankers. The bomber and tanker crews sat on alert, studying and planning, day in and day out, for the day when the flag went up. Fortunately for the world, it never did.

---

[230] An allusion to the Joel Chandler Harris (Uncle Remus) story, "The Briar Patch." "Don't fling me in dat briar-patch," says Brer Rabbit, convincing his adversary, Brer Fox, that this would be a horrible fate, when, in fact, it is where he most wants to be.

[231] Beale, located about 40 miles south of Sacramento, CA, opened in 1942 as Camp Beale to train army infantry personnel. It was named after Edward Fitzgerald Beale (1822–1893), a 19th-century pioneer. Officially transferred from the army to the air force and renamed Beale Air Force Base in 1948, it is still an active base in 2008.

In contrast, U-2 pilots never flew a mission, other than for training, that wasn't operational. In fact, until the beginning of the disturbance in Southeast Asia, they'd flown the only combat missions in the nation since the cease-fire in Korea.

The pilots of the 4080th were highly decorated, and the wing had proudly received two unit citations, but even as an outsider I detected a tension between them and the more traditional SAC bomber crews.

I was assigned to a flight in the 4028th SRWS (Strategic Reconnaissance Weather Squadron) led by Captain John Wall, an older air force captain and one of the many guys who'd been caught in the peacetime rank structure that was frozen in time. John was a jovial chap who'd flown many different types of aircraft, and as people are prone to do when they're very familiar with something, he sometimes oversimplified the process. Some of his favorite sayings included "no problem Don; it's a piece of cake." I lifted an eyebrow at that one. Or, "same as any airplane, pull back, goes up; push forward, goes down—no sweat."

"That's great, John," said I. "When do we begin?"

"Well, you see, Don, we have a problem. We have a long-term problem and a short-term problem. Long-term, we have too many new guys and not enough old guys to train them. Short-term, before we can check you out in the U-bird, we have to check you out in the T-33. That's the way the operational orders are written."

I heaved a sigh of relief. "John, this is your lucky day. I was born in the T-Bird and I have over 1,000 hours in it. Shoot, I even know how many rivets are in the canopy." All that crazy stuff Captain Jack made us memorize back in Greenville had to be good for something.

Captain John put his arm around my shoulder, "Don, you just don't get it. This is SAC, and we do things differently here. There's the air force way and then there's the SAC way. As far as SAC is concerned, you've never seen a T-Bird."

So I waited in line to learn to fly the T-Bird. While I was waiting for that fine educational experience, I was checked out in the U-3. Better known as the Cessna 310, this was a six-seater, twin-engine prop job that was popular with both civilian and military flyers.[232]

At Davis-Monthan, the U-3 was used to carry people to meetings and to ferry light freight, but its main purpose was to serve as a chase plane for the U-bird. It could fly slow enough to chase and clear the area for the training

---

[232] The Cessna 310 was a twin-engine propeller plane manufactured between 1954 and 1980. It was offered in four-and six-seat models in both military and civilian versions.

aspect of transition in the U-2. It was a hoot to fly and was available almost anytime. More importantly, it was the only thing available for me to fly.

The air force has a policy of allotting fuel and funds to organizations based on how much flying they did in the last quarter. If an organization falls short of that timeline, then the next quarter its funds and fuel (and thus its pilots' airborne hours) are cut back proportionally. Although this accounting scheme doesn't make much sense to the guy on the line, it must work because it's been in effect for as long as I can remember. Many days I would report to work and find my name on the board: U-3, four hours. So I flew around the West, visiting old pals, practicing following orders, and waiting for my number to come up.

Survival Training: One More Time

While I was waiting, I filled another square: a second round of survival training at Stead Air Force Base outside Reno.

Part of U-2 training, in fact the very first part of flying the airplane, is a postgraduate course in survival. The escape and evasion part is skipped entirely; after several days of classroom training, it's straight to solitary confinement.

In preparation, every aspect of the solitary existence is discussed as the instructors explain ways of thwarting interrogation. Things hadn't changed much from my previous spell in solitary. Did I learn anything more? I really couldn't tell. I tried to go into a trance-like existence, and in many ways the harassment was like a dream.

I was in solitary for about a week, and as before, I left with the feeling that, yes, I could hack it. However, I could truly empathize with those poor souls who had spent or were spending months and years as POWs. Training helped, but the main ingredient was guts and determination. Meanwhile, more and more of our pilots were becoming prisoners in Vietnam.

Chapter 70 – A Sobering Look at War's Remains
1965

Soon after I returned from Stead, Colonel Harold Swanson, the squadron commander, had to attend a meeting in Sacramento, California, and he asked me to fly him there in the Cessna. "Glad to, Sir." I said. Anything to get out of the routine was welcome.

The meeting was being held at McClellan Air Force Base. Colonel Swanson said we'd be returning as soon as possible, so after landing and discharging my passenger, I called the tower and received taxi instructions to park. The controller directed me to the other side of the field by the freight docks, where I shut down and pulled out my ever-present paperback book. Every now and then I'd stop reading to get out, stretch, and observe the activity around me. The ramp was filled with C-124s, those huge transports that seemed too big for their wings and were affectionately known as Old Shakey.[233]

Forklifts were zooming in and among the planes like workers in an ant colony. Suddenly, almost as if I were peering through binoculars, the view came sharply into focus. Pallet after pallet of coffins were being unloaded from the C-124s and loaded into smaller aircraft. The task appeared endless.

"What's going on, Sergeant?" I asked the guy who obviously was honchoing the operation.

"It's a load of bodies from Vietnam," he replied matter-of-factly. "We're sorting them and shipping them home."

I was stunned. I have no idea how many bodies were there. Surely there were hundreds. This was the real "body count," not the number of Vietcong killed—the body count McNamara talked about—but our boys, mangled and dead in those simple boxes. The newspapers had started to

---

[233] This base started life as the Pacific Air Depot in the 1930s. Later renamed the Sacramento Air Depot, it officially became McClellan Air Force Base in 1948. The base closed in 2001.

carry accounts of American deaths, but on the printed page it sounded sterile, unemotional.[234]

There was nothing sterile about the rows of coffins stacked in the California sun, filled with men waiting to return to a home they would never see again, to loved ones whose lives would never be the same. I understood the need for war and the call for sacrifice, but nagging doubts were edging into my mind. My doubts were not about whether the war was necessary, but rather, about whether it was being fought to the best of our abilities. I already knew that it wasn't. Servicemen and women at home and abroad were being placed in harm's way on the altar of somebody's ego. The pallets of the dead being wheeled out of C-124s at McClellan were the sacrificial lambs.

The flight back was uneventful and I went back to my usual routine, but the image of what I'd seen was burned into my brain.

Holding Pattern

Every morning, all the officers who weren't operational met in the briefing room. The primary U-2 sites at that time were Cuba and Vietnam, plus several random air sampling sites. As we needed to know, we were made aware of specific routes and locations. The CIA's U-2 operation was totally separate; we were never privy to where or when their planes flew.

After reviewing the operation of the day and resolving any problems, we were briefed by one of the intelligence officers. Operation Rolling Thunder, LBJ's attack on North Vietnam, was killing North Vietnamese troops, water buffalo, and hundreds of $6,000 trucks. We also were losing a lot of multimillion-dollar aircraft and the pilots who flew them. Each day in our briefing we saw the results. I'm sure that some productive targets were destroyed, but far too many others were off-limits.

It didn't take a trained observer to see that we were wasting our pilots, our airplanes, and our honor in this farce. Probably the most distressing things we saw were pictures of the harbor at Haiphong, about 100 miles from Hanoi in the center of the Red River. Here docked the ships of many nations, some flying the flags of our friends and allies, and all providing the North Vietnamese with the supplies of war. The ships and their cargo were off-limits. We had to wait until the goods were concealed by the jungle before we could attack.

After the meeting, each person had his daily chores to do: fly, study, and/or perform one of the million tasks that keep an organization running. At

[234] Robert S. McNamara, born in 1916, was Secretary of Defense under Presidents Kennedy and Johnson from 1961 until 1968.

lunchtime I played handball, and like everywhere else in my life, I was at the top of the bell curve, a C+ or B player.

I loved handball. It used both hands; exercised every part of my body, including my mind; and helped to keep me in the kind of shape I needed to be to fly the U-2. Colonel Swanson loved the game as well, and we would often play together. I remember asking myself: *How can such an old man—jeez, he must be at least 45—play so well?*

Bob "De De" Hickman was another guy I played handball with almost daily. De De was from Alexandria, Louisiana, and had been an all-star halfback in high school. Polly recognized him immediately; it turns out they'd gone to school together.

Finally, after what seemed like an eternity but was in actuality about only four months, the T-Bird training began, a very sedate flying program that truly *was* a piece of cake.

"What mark did you want me to touch on landing?" I'd sometimes ask. "And on which wheel?" The T-Bird was a ball to fly, but that's not what I was there for. Look out, U-2, here I come!

Chapter 71 – Taking the U-Bird to the Sky

1965

Surprisingly, I knew little about the airplane, even though I'd been around for several months. The security of the mission was in its mystery, and the pilots didn't talk much out of school. The phrase "loose lips might sink ships" could have been coined in this outfit.[235]

Compared with the formal training curriculum of ATC, the U-2 training program was rather rudimentary. There was, however, a syllabus, and the training schedule was maintained.

My instructor was my flight commander, Captain John, and although he was a nice guy, it was obvious that training was not his forte. He had a hearty sense of humor, but he overestimated my capacity to learn by osmosis. Each day we reported to a secure area to review the mechanical aspects of the aircraft. The mechanicals—the first step in learning any aircraft—were something that the pilot had to understand thoroughly. At Davis-Monthan, we faced a stiff examination on this stuff by the Standboard, the group at SAC who established the standards of excellence.

At ATC, we'd trained masses of pilots to do a specific task, so we had many training aids. Here, there were only the operating manuals, hard to read and still harder to understand. And with only 55 U-2s built to begin with, and no idea that this would become a career-type airplane, no one had given serious consideration to developing a simulator or a two-seat trainer version.

I can still see Captain J. thumbing through the manuals, pointing out the highlights. Twenty times a day I heard "pull back you go up; push over you go down, unless you pull up too far, then you go down," always followed by a hearty ho-ho. He left me in the tight confines of the room to study, a most difficult task. Reading manuals is the best way I know to bring on daydreams and fatigue.

---

[235] "Loose lips might sink ships" was a phrase created by the U.S. Office of War Information during World War II to remind people not to discuss potentially sensitive information lest it be overheard by enemy spies.

The guys who maintained the U-bird were without a doubt the best in their field, from the airmen, to the sergeants who worked at the various tasks of keeping the system operating, to the civilian tech reps who understood one or more of the specific units or systems that made the mission work. These were the people I learned from. I went from office to shop asking questions, and the guys were happy to share their knowledge with me. Everyone involved worked as a team.

Because of my A&P license, I could really appreciate the construction of the airplane. Many pilots had died learning how to fly it, and each incident yielded more information to share with future pilots. By 1965, the U-2 had become safer to fly, but it was never a plane you could take for granted.

The airplane was built with simplicity in mind. If a cable could do the job, that's what was used. Hydraulic assists, which normally weighed more, were used only when absolutely necessary. Every pound of extra weight meant a loss of ten feet in altitude, and altitude was survival. Gary Powers, when asked how high he was flying when he was shot down over the USSR in May of 1960, famously quipped, "Not high enough."

A list bearing the name of every man who had flown the U-2 was posted in the main Operations room. Every tenth name or so had a star beside it.

"These guys all make general?" said smart-ass Wright.

"Nope, they bought the farm."

Good Lord, I thought, *is there a hole to crawl into*?

By the spring of 1965 there were two operating U-2 types: the U-2A and the U-2C. The Model C was just coming on line with the air force; the CIA had had this version for several years. Although the operational ceiling of the U-2C wasn't much different from its predecessor, it contained many safety and mechanical improvements. It also had a Pratt & Whitney J75 engine, which meant a quantum leap in power. The payload was increased and the time to climb reduced.

Before the advent of the U-2C, SAC was down to about 15 operational aircraft. Most of the others had been lost in the beginning phases of learning to fly the airplane. Plans were in the pipeline to build a two-seat training model, and somewhere scraps of crashed U-2s were being stockpiled to construct such a bird. Everyone felt that the mortality of both pilots and aircraft would improve immeasurably if this unit were brought on line. So far, however, it was just a dream waiting for funds.

The training continued, a combination of my interrogation of men in the know and a daily session with Captain John. After a time, John and I went into the hangar.

I'd spent the greatest part of my life in a love affair with airplanes,

461

most of them fighters. The Curtiss P-40 that my mother worked on during World War II was the hammer of flight innovation. Although it lacked the performance of later designs, with its shark's mouth and blazing guns it was a fearsome machine. And how many hours had I whiled away in class, drawing the Lockheed P-38 Lightning and dreaming of fighting the Germans in this fork-tailed devil? The Republic P-47 Thunderbolt reminded me of flying a tank—deadly, with guns protruding everywhere. The North American P-51 Mustang was everyone's favorite flying machine. And of course, the F-86. From a picture on the wall during my days at Wentworth, this beauty became a reality when I flew her at Moody Air Force Base in Georgia.

Since I was a kid, I'd found it hard not to like every airplane I saw, read about, or flew, but the U-2 sent chill-bumps down my spine. Fifteen feet high and 50 feet long, the 80-foot wingspan of the U-bird was more than twice that of the F-86, even though the plane was only 13 feet longer. In a word, it was *sinister*, yet it had its own kind of beauty. The black coating on the aluminum body gave it a velvet-like appearance, and though it wasn't exactly graceful—the oversized wings seemed awkward at first glance—it had a look of stability and promise, like a young boy whose legs have outgrown his body.

I climbed into the cockpit. John sat outside the plane on the cockpit rail and we reviewed each and every function of the controls. He also briefed me on takeoffs and landings, flight characteristics, and stalls. No book is a substitute for this kind of hangar-flying with an experienced pilot. We rarely discussed navigation or the basic mission. When learning any new aircraft, the transition phase comes first.

The next step was to fly around the pattern in the U-3, locating key points and speeds and, at a higher altitude, practicing stalls. Of course, the stall techniques of the U-2 and the Cessna weren't even remotely similar, but the techniques of entry and exit could be simulated. The rest of the time, I spent hours committing to memory the many emergency items I had to know.

Fortunately, I'd been in the training business a long time. On the parts that were familiar, I pretty much knew what to ask. For the parts that were totally new, however, I didn't know the right questions and John, as good a guy as he was, was not as thorough as he might have been. One thing I *was* sure of: Pull back and you go up; push forward and you go down.

"Wright," said John one morning, "tomorrow you go before the Standboard. You're as ready as you can get, and we fly the first mission the day after."

The Big Green Apple

SAC Standboard was as tough as it got. I was ready, but book learning was never my primary skill and there were literally no mistakes allowed. I knew the major who was the Standboard officer. He was a well-respected, highly skilled aviator, and I knew I was in for a several-hour interrogation and demonstration.

It started in the classroom. He thumbed his way through the operating manual and asked numerous questions. I had the answers—nothing tricky, just the knowledge needed to operate the aircraft. We then took a couple of breaks and moved on to the hangar. Again, I sat in the cockpit and he sat on the rail and we went through the old standby blindfold check: Without looking, point to and describe each instrument and the related procedures involved. Next we covered the emergency checklist and the many items I'd committed to memory. I was hot stuff and doing well. Finally it was over. As we stood by the wing, I began to feel good, that feeling one has when a tough task is over and has gone well.

The major looked me in the eye. "You failed," he said.

Whaaat? "You've got to be joshing me," I blurted out incredulously.

"I said you failed," he countered. "You made one critical mistake."

"What mistake was that?" I asked. I was pissed.

"In a high-altitude emergency bailout where the ejection seat has failed, the first item on the six-point memory checklist is pulling the green apple. You missed that first item."

The green apple released emergency oxygen to sustain the pilot in the 12-mile free fall before his chute opened automatically at 14,000 feet. Colored bright green against the olive drab of the U-2 console, the apple-shaped knob was easy to see and easy to grab.

"Oh man, yes I did, but I started over two steps later and said it right."

"Yes you did, but that's still a failure."

I shut my mouth and calmed down a bit as we continued walking back to Operations. It was nitpicking beyond the norm, but, technically, he was right. We debriefed the rest of the check; that had been the only flaw, but it was a fatal one.

"What happens next?" I asked.

"You will meet with Colonel Martinez, the Operations Officer, tomorrow morning."

Failure in SAC or anywhere else is painful, and it was something that had never happened in my flying career. The major could tell I felt this was cutting the cheese a bit thin, so he went on to tell me a story.

"When the U-2 was based at Laughlin Air Force Base in Del Rio on the Texas border," he said, "Colonel Jack Nole, the commander of the 4028th Squadron, took off on a normal mission. It was a fine, sunny day. Somewhere above 50,000 feet, the aircraft violently pitched over and began to accelerate uncontrollably. The tail broke off and the rest of the airplane began to loop.[236]

"At that time the plane didn't have an ejection seat. Colonel Nole unhooked the several umbilical cords that provided life to the pilot. He pitched out over the side, and after taking a terrible battering, was thrown clear of the airplane, but he couldn't find the green apple to release the emergency oxygen.

"He was beginning to lose consciousness, and with no pressure to keep it filled, his suit was starting to collapse."

As I listened to this story, I knew this was a helluva predicament. If he passed out, his chute would have opened automatically at 14,000 feet, but that would have taken many minutes. And the pressure suit was so tight that if no air came to it from the emergency bottle, then at lower altitudes no oxygen could have entered from without. In other words, Nole would have suffocated when he got to a certain altitude, if he wasn't dead already.

The major continued. "Colonel Nole couldn't find the apple, but he could find the parachute ring. At that altitude, however, and because the true airspeed of the flight was close to 400 knots, the chance of the parachute opening without being torn apart was remote at best. Nevertheless, he had no choice. He pulled the ring, and he must have been at the top of a parabolic curve, because the chute opened gently. Just about this time he found the green apple and pulled it, too. His suit filled, and he was able to breathe and sustain his body despite the enormous pressures.

"From a bailout and open chute at 50,000 feet, it should have taken 33 minutes to drift to the ground. The colonel's oxygen bottle was good for 12 minutes. The chute began oscillating violently. Ironically, every time it changed direction the air would spill, and he descended twice as fast as programmed. When he hit the atmosphere, he was able to open his faceplate and breathe normally. He landed safely, but he was badly shaken.

"And that," said the major in a calm voice, "is why I failed you."

I accepted his explanation wordlessly. Quibbling is a serious violation of an unwritten code, but I still was angry and suspicious. In my mind, I'd done better than good.

---

[236] Laughlin Field, named after Jack T. Laughlin, Del Rio's first casualty of World War II, operated from 1943 until it was closed down after the war. It reopened in the 1950s, and from 1956 until the program moved to Davis-Monthan in the 1960s, it was home to SAC's U-2s, after which it reverted to its primary mission of training air force pilots. As of 2008, it is still an operational base.

I spent a restless and unhappy night. The next morning, the major, Captain John, and I showed up at the colonel's office.

Colonel Martinez was an excellent and articulate officer with years of experience flying the reconnaissance mission. He proceeded to question me about my supposed failure. All I could do was agree that, yes, I had started the procedure improperly. The colonel asked the major if he felt I was prepared to fly. "Yes," he replied. "In fact, the rest of the interrogation went extremely well."

"What's the bailout procedure without the ejection seat, Wright?" the colonel asked.

1. *PULL GREEN APPLE.*
2. *Disconnect seat-pack quick disconnect.*
3. *Jettison canopy.*
4. *Disconnect seat belt and harness.*
5. *Bail out.*
6. *Parachute arming lanyard or ripcord handle-pull.*

The words flowed from my lips like a southern politician at a pig roast.

The colonel walked over and patted me on the back. "Have a great flight tomorrow, Captain Wright," he said.

The Ultimate First Flight

I was as ready as I'd ever been for a first flight. It was even better that it was solo; there would be no one there to pick at me. As an instructor, I'd flown through thousands of takeoffs and landings. There was nothing that could happen to me that I hadn't seen before and survived. I was as excited as the first time I climbed over the rail of the F-86 at Moody six years before.

Captain John and I met three hours before launching and went through the routine for operational flights, with the exception of suiting up in the partial-pressure suit. For this flight I was to wear a normal flight suit and helmet.

At SAC, the pilot was king. In the ready room, a special mess fed us a diet of low-residue food. We had the best steak that money could buy, prepared with eggs and all the trimmings, plus barrels of freshly squeezed orange juice, milk, and coffee. Isn't this the reason I joined the air force to begin with?

After breakfast we stepped into a van for the ride to the plane. There she was—the Article, the Dragon Lady, the Big Black Mother. Airmen were scurrying around doing last-minute chores. Overseeing them, as always, was a qualified pilot sitting on the rail.

John was just finishing the preflight checklist. As he moved away, I mounted the stairs and sat in the ejection seat. Airmen strapped me in, hooked up my oxygen, and then pulled the ramp away. I established communication with the ground sergeant and the tower, then shot a quick message to the man upstairs. Here I am, Lord, about to start my next great adventure, and I do hope that angel of mine's not out partying.

Just before my first U-2 flight, Davis-Monthan Air Force Base, 1965.
The flight was low-altitude, so I wore a regular flight suit.

I wound my finger in a tight turn, indicating that I was starting. Everything was normal—chocks out, taxi clearance. My mind was as sharp and clear as newly fallen snow.

Close by sat the U-3. It would take off first and join up on me later, just prior to landing. The pilot was a major, though fortunately a different major than the one from the green-apple incident. The copilot was John, who was along to help and instruct me as necessary. Just before they taxied, I looked over to find John mouthing the words "pull back to go up."

The pogos at the wingtips created a vibration, and the bird made new sounds as we waddled to the takeoff point. Following was a blue staff station wagon with a huge Chrysler Hemi engine. It was driven by another line pilot and followed by a pickup truck of airmen. After I applied power for takeoff, the airmen would pull the pins, allowing the pogos to separate from the wings on takeoff.[237]

"Nails One, cleared for takeoff," said the tower.

* * *

I nod to the airmen crouched by the wingtips. With no payload, the bird is light; in fact, I think they might have put some deadweight aboard for balance. I push the power up and start to accelerate down the runway. The bird is faster than I would have thought possible; before 1,000 feet of runway go by, I reach the proper speed and the U-2 leaps into the air.

I know that ascent is rapid and that the nose has to be pitched up quickly in order not to exceed the design speed of the wing. I bring up the gear and flaps and reduce power. Normally the climb-out is at a 45-degree angle, but today I want an easy and more controllable climb. I level off at 10,000 feet and begin to fly the profile we briefed on the ground—a few turns, some climbs and descents just to get acquainted, a couple of stalls. It feels good; it's honest and it's different. I've not used a wheel much before, so I'm a bit heavy on the controls, but I also need to remember there's almost no hydraulic help.

I make radio contact with the Cessna 310 chase and we meet. It flies loose formation as I begin the entry into the pattern, something

---

[237] A pogo is a set of removable wheels (one pogo for each wing). About four feet long, the pogo has two non-inflatable tires on one end and a connector on the other end that fits into a housing on the wing. The connector is held in place by a pin. Before the plane taxies, the ground crew removes the pins, causing the pogos to detach automatically once the aircraft leaves the ground.

I've done thousands of times, but not quite like this. I fly up initial and pitch out a slow wide pattern, dropping the gear and setting the flaps, tracking over the ground just as we practiced the day before in the Cessna. Speed set, my eyes search over the long nose. It feels a lot like peering over the nose of that marine F-4 Corsair at Hyannis, back when my flying career was still a dream. Here, visibility is further restricted by a white shield covering the top of the canopy, a thermal protection against UV rays at cruising altitude.

I continue to slow to final approach speed, keeping the nose even higher. She's lined up with the 10,000-foot runway. I'll only need a fraction of it for landing, and I see the blue station wagon about to chase me down. In the past, so many U-birds had crashed at this phase of landing that a pilot in the chase wagon now talks to the pilot in the plane, offering information on height and other help as needed.

I cross the threshold more slowly than I've ever flown in a jet. The car chase begins and the pilot in the blue wagon starts his litany: 10 feet, 5 feet, 4, 3, 2, 1, 6 inches, hold, hold it, HOLD IT BAAAACK, hold it. The bird plops onto the runway. Not bad if I do say so myself.

The chase continues. Hold back the wheel, re-trim, ease up on the power, then silence.

* * *

The tower cleared me for a second launch. Gear and flaps up, I began the turn out of traffic. There, locked onto my wing, was the Cessna 310. John was grinning and had two thumbs up. "Good job, Don," I heard through my headset. He made a few comments and we did it all over again.

I made several touch-and-go landings. On the third one, I didn't hold back enough and the plane landed front-gear first and got into a slight porpoise. However, I went around immediately with no damage done. This was the danger of landing with tandem gear. Once a porpoise began, it could become uncontrollable, eventually causing the aircraft to break up. Pilots had died because of porpoises.

The full-stop landing was perfect, and this time I was briefed to stop on the runway. The airmen in the chase truck rushed to lift the wings and reinstall the pogos. They needed to finish before the fuel ran to the wingtips; otherwise, the job would be ten times harder. While they were working, I had a moment to reflect on the flight. It really wasn't that difficult—different, heavier than a light jet, but if I'd had a few hours in a Cessna 180 taildragger, it would have been routine to begin with.[238]

The airmen finished, the sergeant popped a highball salute, and I taxied to the chocks.

I shut it down, completed the after-parking checklist, and made sure the ejection seat pin was in. The crew popped the canopy and helped me unstrap and crawl down the ladder. John's craggy face was grinning from ear to ear. He was at least as happy as I was that it came off okay. If it hadn't, he'd have been the one left to explain and do the paperwork.

"How'd it go?" he said.

"Super," I replied. "A piece of cake!" My face was flushed and lined from the oxygen mask, and my flight suit was already drying in the desert sun, complete with white sweat lines. Somebody handed me two frosty-cold cans of Coors, a post-flight ritual, and I sucked them dry. Flying required an amazing amount of liquid, especially in the desert.

In the van back to Operations with John and a few of the ground crew, there was a lot of backslapping and much relief. There weren't that many birds left and we collectively worried about them. No reconnaissance platform ever performed better, anywhere or anytime, but other than the U-2Cs just coming on line, as far as we knew there would never be any more.

After I changed, a bunch of us headed to the Officers' Club. The usual gossip, laughter, and bravado ensued. "Hey Wright, I heard you failed the preflight oral. What happened?"

"Yeah, I did," I replied, unable to mask some anger.

"How long did it take?" quipped one of the senior guys.

"Four hours."

"Holy smoke," he replied. "Usually it takes about an hour and the results are almost automatic. Who the hell gave it to you?"

When I replied with the major's name, no one was surprised. He was a known hard-ass, but everyone agreed this was excessive even for him.

A pilot at the end of the bar raised his glass. "I've got it," he said. "SAC's been catching it recently for having almost no standardization failures, so they're grading every function possible on the bell curve."

The bell curve, although a splendid tool for initial evaluation, diminished in relevance the higher up the chain of experience one went. It

---

[238] The Cessna 180 was a four- or six-seat aircraft produced from 1953 to 1981. Many of these airplanes are still in use in 2008. It is a conventional gear (or taildragger) plane, with two weight-bearing wheels forward of the aircraft's center of gravity and the remaining weight supported by a third wheel in the tail.

did, however, dictate a certain percentage of failures. Could all this have been about a quota?

The air force, like many large organizations—civilian or military—lacked flexibility and often common sense. Could this failure affect my future? Perhaps, but I decided to stop stewing about what I considered an injustice. I couldn't do anything about it, and I was determined to focus on my opportunity to fly this amazing airplane.

Chapter 72 – Chaos Theory

1965

At work, standardization ruled. There were checklists for everything, procedures to be followed, predictable situations, scenarios, individuals. At home, with three boys under the age of three, all of them in diapers, the only thing predictable was the lack of any predictability whatsoever. Sometimes I wanted to share a tough day at the office with Polly, but I learned to keep my mouth shut. Our little guys were into everything, and Polly was on the run all day, every day. This was the era of the beehive hairdo, and there were times when Polly's beehive looked like it had been attacked by a wild animal.

This was a busy and active time for both of us. Polly was taking the occasional modeling job, something she did with class and skill, plus it brought in a few bucks. She entered a contest sponsored by the Tucson Models' Guild and almost won, even though most of her rivals were professional models. She was also the oldest contestant, and I bet she was the only one with three active little boys. Had I been the judge, of course, she'd have won hands down. I was proud of her beauty both inside and out, and I admired her zest for life and her competitive spirit.

We still had Tucson the Airedale, who seemed to enjoy living in his "hometown," but we'd sold the Austin-Healey. It needed a lot of work, and we were just too busy to do it. Besides, though we were getting by, money was always tight. Military wives had to be superwomen.

Our social life was as full as time allowed, and the squadron entertained on a regular timetable, mostly at the Officers' Club.

U-2 pilots were an unusual bunch. They drank and partied harder than any group I'd been with, perhaps because the mission was extremely challenging and sometimes downright dangerous. If they'd had a motto, it might have been *live for today, because tomorrow you could be dead.* And live they did, partying, drinking, laughing, and playing. Some pilots also seemed close to God, as reflected in their peaceful demeanor and a wonderful tolerance of their fellow pilots.

Dining-ins were also a riot, the usual delicious meal and good speakers, followed by local talent telling nonclassified war stories. And at SAC these events always included wives. One such dining-in was scheduled for the night after my first mission, but that afternoon the boys had found my shoeshine box and polished the floor, and much of themselves, shiny black. Polly rescued the polish, but in her efforts to get ready for the party she missed the fact that our resident artists had also shined my dress shoes with butter. When I went to put them on, I found globs of the stuff crammed into the toes. We had produced fun-loving little boys, but life was never predictable.

Davis-Monthan Air Force Base, 1965: another calm day at the Wrights. *Clockwise:* Polly, me, Tim, Walt, and Andy.

Chapter 73 – The Mission

1965

T here was no end to the agencies that needed information the U-2 could provide. Information is survival, and incorrect or missing information costs money, time, and sometimes lives. For instance, when Colonel Charles Taylor, the U.S. Air Attaché to the USSR, was watching an air show at Red Air Force Day in Moscow in 1955, he saw more than twice as many Bison bombers as at the May Day parade just months before. It turned out to be a ruse—the Bisons made more than one pass with the same planes—but the ruse worked. The U.S. concluded that the Soviets had a larger strategic force than we did, the military became alarmed at this so-called "bomber gap," and Ike was forced to authorize the purchase of additional bombers to checkmate the USSR.

We'll never know how many battles have been won or lost because of what was known or not known, but this poem, from the book *Deep Black: Space Espionage and National Security* by William E. Burrows, says it better than I can:

> *Who controls reconnaissance watches the enemy;*
> *Who watches the enemy perceives the threat;*
> *Who perceives the threat shapes the alternatives;*
> *Who shapes the alternatives determines the response.*[239]

---

[239] William Burrows is the director and founder of the Science and Environmental Reporting Program at New York University. He is a former reporter for the *New York Times*, the *Washington Post*, and the *Wall Street Journal* and specializes in issues regarding space and national security. Burrows credits Sir Halford Mackinder (1861–1947), a British geographer who wrote about the influence of geography on political events, for the lines that inspired this missive. In the early part of the 20th century, Mackinder developed what he called the Heartland theory: "He who controls the Heartland (the northern and interior parts of the Eurasian continent) controls the World Island (Eurasia and Africa); he who controls the World Island, controls the world."

Within the 4080th, the mission was discussed rarely and never outside the confines of the operational buildings. Even after several months, I still didn't have the big picture, and curiosity was not encouraged. The less we knew about the worldwide mission, the less that could be extracted from us in case of shoot down and capture.

What I did know was that SAC considered itself an active combatant in a worldwide Cold War, and it was easy to understand why. If, heaven forbid, a nuclear war occurred, SAC had the major mission. Everybody from General Power down to the newest grunt went about his business as if this might happen tomorrow. Key players in other branches of the armed services operated with a similar mindset. It was a mindset that most civilians or military personnel from the support side of the operation could never understand.

From the President on down, the people whose hands were close to the trigger had an enormous responsibility, and for the most part they carried it out with single-minded dedication. In the event of world war, each U-2 pilot also had a role to play. It was important that we understood that role well, so I spent much of my spare time in the war room, a top-secret area containing current war plans. Prior to entering the room, we in the U-2 business had to give the guys working there time to cover the detailed charts and operational plans of others' missions.

Our daily briefings, although focused primarily on our missions, were a combined lesson in history and geography, and we frequently saw footage of battles in Southeast Asia. I wasn't a tactician, but it was more and more obvious that we weren't bombing key tactical points. Our fighter-bombers were skilled at devastating the targets at which they were aiming, but were they aiming at the targets that were going to affect the outcome of the war? How about the targets that were obviously more important but off-limits?

Chapter 74 – Flying High

My name was on the schedule more often, and after every flight I was able to fill in more squares on the syllabus. Eventually I became a numbered combat-crew member, the SAC equivalent of a licensed driver. My first few flights were local and dealt with the basic handling of the airplane: takeoffs, landings, and instrument flight. These missions were always flown in the normal flight suit and helmet.

I also spent a great deal of time simulating the flameout patterns so familiar to anyone who flew single-engine airplanes. I spiraled down over the field, calling out several "key" places. Becoming expert at this routine helped to increase the chances of saving the airplane—and the pilot—if the engine failed in real life. On these low-altitude flights, the U-3 would chase me and then clear the area of incursions from other aircraft.

Pull Back to Go Up

Eventually, the morning arrived for my first high flight. I was a bit tense, but for the most part I knew I'd been flying well. I did get the occasional minor porpoise, but it was always controllable. I reported early; it was always easier to fly in the desert before the sunshine filled the sky with unseen bumps.

First, the chow—steak and eggs—then on to the medical unit, where two flight surgeons and several medical technicians were assigned to the wing. Air force flight surgeons are prepared, skilled, and well-respected. Although they could have had easier and better-paying jobs in civilian life, many made the air force a career. They often flew with us in the support planes and, in some cases, they could fly as well as the professional pilots.

Prior to each high or long flight, the pilot received a mini-physical. There were no halfway results; either you were in top shape or you flew another day. For example, a cold could create ear blockages, which could cause severe, possibly fatal, damage. The doc took my pulse and listened to my chest. Like every other member of the U-2 team, he had a no-nonsense approach to this end of the business.

From there I moved on to the physiological area, where a team of dedicated airmen suited me up in the partial-pressure suit. Underneath it I wore the requisite uniform: long johns turned inside out so the seams wouldn't cut into flesh after sitting for hours in the same position. On top I wore an outerwear flight suit to match the climate where the mission was to be flown.

Several airmen worked on me, efficiently and wordlessly. A sergeant inspected the operation each step of the way. These men knew their jobs well and took great pride in their work. If they failed, I would die—simple as that. After all was adjusted, the airmen placed the space helmet on my head, hooked up the portable oxygen, and positioned the faceplate. Just as I did before entering the test chamber, I needed to breathe pure oxygen for a while in order to clear the nitrogen from my blood and avoid the bends.

Captain John says to remind you, Sir: "Pull back
to go up; push forward to go down."

As I was being strapped, adjusted, poked, and prodded, I was not allowed to assist in any way. Earlier in the program, there had been some fatalities that might have been attributed to equipment failure or, in one case, to the faceplate having been removed by the pilot and not properly sealed when it

476

was replaced. These days, the airmen took no chances. Even the gloves they pulled on were veined with compressed air.

The sergeant slapped me on the back and assisted me to my feet, and our entourage clomped to the delivery van. The airmen carried my umbilical cords of oxygen and radio leads.

The Dragon Lady sat on the ramp, surrounded by the usual troops performing preflight chores. She was sleek, black, and beautiful. I climbed into the cockpit, which was covered by a small, white tent being cooled by blowing air. It was hot in that suit, and the idea was to keep the pilot from beginning to sweat, an eventuality that came with its own set of problems. After the airmen hooked me up, a staff sergeant checked me over. Then a master sergeant did the same. Everyone was determined that nothing would go wrong.

This was to be a high, "short" mission, just under three hours. I was to do a maximum climb with a reduced fuel load, execute some preplanned maneuvers, and then, at over 60,000 feet, shut down the engine and spiral toward Earth over Davis-Monthan, this time in a very real flameout pattern.

When I got to 35,000 feet, I was to attempt a light-off (restart) of the engine. When we briefed this mission, my reaction to shutting down an engine that was running perfectly fine was less than enthusiastic. John countered that it was better to experience the partial-pressure suit filling up and restricting my ability to function in a controlled situation. The alternative might be to learn this lesson over hostile territory in a real emergency.

I can't say that this explanation provided any great degree of comfort, but nevertheless, it was part of the package and I was here, ready to go. Everybody cleared away and I established contact with the tower. Soon I was sitting in the number one position, waiting to launch. I received clearance to taxi into position and the airmen pulled the pogo pins.

"Nails One, cleared for takeoff."

I snapped my head forward to signal the airmen holding the wing as I accelerated to full military power. The bird leapt forward, and in less than 1,000 feet I was in the air. I brought the nose up smartly (pull back, you go up) and established a 45-degree climb angle. Four minutes later I was cruising through 40,000 feet. The higher I got, the slower the rate of the climb. Somewhere around 50,000 feet the aircraft was responding as an ordinary plane would at sea level.

After completing several checklists, I turned on the autopilot. Although this was the first plane I'd flown with this feature, the autopilot was critical to the mission. U-birds were designed to fly in the coffin corner, a range of four knots between stall (the bird would fall out of the sky), and Mach (the speed of sound, which would cause the plane to become unglued). It was the autopilot that made this degree of accuracy possible. If for some reason it failed, that was the end of the mission, because the pilot would be totally focused on taking the aircraft to a lower altitude with a wider speed range.

I was heading toward St. Johns VOR, an area in northwestern New Mexico about 150 miles north, northeast from Tucson near the Arizona border town of St. Johns. This area was exclusively ours (not that there was much traffic directly above Davis-Monthan, but it took about 150 miles to climb to altitude and St. Johns was just far enough away to be practical). Everything seemed to be under control as I slipped through 60,000 feet. Above 60,000, my clearance was for VFR (visual flight rules), which meant I was now out-of-sight and out-of-mind. I was able to view the Earth in a totally new way. Gone was the familiar three-dimensional world. The picture before me appeared perfectly flat. Could there be something to the Flat Earth Society? Whoops, guess not. I could just see the slight curvature of the Earth on the horizon.

This was probably the only mission where I'd have time for sightseeing, and I was loving it—one of those supreme moments in life that are truly emotional. My eyes stung a bit, but my hand couldn't reach them because of the faceplate. I wanted to see all I could, but looking up wasn't an option; the view was obscured by the UV cover. I tried to ratchet in the cockpit to look around and down. It didn't help much; the cockpit was built for a midget. Every time I moved, my oversized space helmet hit the canopy. My head stopped about two inches from the top, and my shoulders had about two inches of clearance on each side.

This was the high-altitude version of the dollar ride—a mission with just a few things to do—and the last chance to see if the U-2 was for me. Except for the hum of the engine, I could hear nothing. Since I'd turned off the common frequency, even the radio chatter was gone. If I was going to have claustrophobia, surely this out-of-this-Earth experience would bring it on.

I gradually approached 70,000 feet, turned back toward Davis-Monthan, and began my descent.

Push Forward to Go Down

The bird was so clean and aerodynamic that in order to descend, I had to extend the speed brakes, extend the gear, and set the power just right. If the engine was going too slow, it would flame out. Once everything was set correctly, it took just as long to go down as it did to come up.

As I descended through the high 50s, I made radio contact with the base and reported my position at the pre-established key. "I'm now going to spiral down to a simulated flameout landing," I said in a carefully controlled voice.

"Acknowledged," said the tower, as though this was a perfectly reasonable thing to do.

I shut off the engine. As the gyros wound down, the partial-pressure suit pumped up, clutching my body like a bear hug. Each time I opened my mouth, oxygen flowed in. I had to force it out to exhale. Yes, I'd done it all in the test chamber, *but this was reality.*

The bird was now fully depressurized, the suit had filled with compressed air, and I was almost immobile. Just to move an arm required strength and planning, yet I still had enough mobility to control all aspects of the airplane. Those designers really knew what they were doing.

I wasn't claustrophobic! I did have a moment of something—fear, discomfort, perhaps both—but I had a pretty good idea my angel was along for the ride. I think what convinced me was that flash of light I saw ducking behind the seat when I shut down the engine.

After many, many minutes, the bird approached the re-light altitude—35,000 feet—and I executed the steps on the restart checklist. Sure enough, I heard the growl of the engine coming to life. Pressurization slowly returned to normal and the suit deflated to its original configuration. It felt good, very good, almost comfortable. Now that everything was going to be all right, I caught that flash of white again as she perched on the back of the seat. Even in a cramped cockpit, there's room for an angel.

I continued the flameout pattern, a familiar event in the life of a jet jock, after which I called the base and lined up on final approach. The blue staff car talked me down the final few feet to a smooth landing. The airmen lifted the wingtips, replaced the pogos, and snapped the highball salute.

I taxied back to the ramp, shut down, and waited for the crew to unstrap me and help me down the ladder. In the neck of my fishbowl helmet was what felt like a quart of sweat. When an airman carefully removed the helmet, the sweat splashed onto the ramp. I stood there, both feet firmly on the ground, sucking down the beers that always greeted the returning birdman and feeling a bit emotional. I could hack it. I'd survived two hurdles. The first was to perform at low altitude: Could I fly and land the plane successfully? The second was to take the bird into its element, far above the Earth to a place where danger lurked for the unwary and those who didn't learn well. My next flight would be a profile mission, a long flight that actually accomplished something.

Chapter 75 – The Efficiency Report

I loved being in the air force. Thousands of others were stacking cans or selling men's underwear at Sears—honest work, but dull and routine. Being an Ivy League grad, locked in a cubicle and working one's way to a window overlooking the city, would be just as bad. Here we had a chance to shine without being subjected to prejudice and without having a privileged background. The good old bell curve worked, and for those who were willing to chase their dreams and work to make them happen, the sky was the limit.

At the same time, the armed services constituted a huge bureaucracy with a jillion leaders, all trying to make a place for themselves. The higher you went, the greater your responsibility and the bigger your chance of suffering a career catastrophe, either from your own conduct and ability or from the conduct and/ or abilities of those under your command. It was also no place to get rich. The highest-paid general, the man in charge of thousands of men and billions of dollars of material, was paid a pittance compared with his civilian counterpart.

To be a successful leader in the military took skill and proper schooling, but luck was almost as important. Nothing could sound the death knoll on a military career more quickly than the bad luck associated with a person causing some trouble for which you were ultimately responsible.

The success or failure of an officer's career was recorded in the famous ER or Efficiency Report. Every six months, this report was placed in your file. What was in the report depended on what you had accomplished, or failed to accomplish, within the reporting period. The school or schools you attended, the skill with which you demonstrated your primary duty, and the performance of your sub-duties were all taken into consideration. Perhaps equally vital was the skill of the superior writing the report.

The report was a standard form with columns progressing from left to right—below average to average to superior. The individual completing the report entered a mark for each category being evaluated. A mark on the far left not only meant that the officer couldn't perform, it probably meant even

God had forgotten about him. A mark to the far right, on the other hand, meant that the officer was so superior that God asked him for advice. If you weren't listed in one of the two right columns for every category, you might be smart to apply at Sears.

It was a difficult grading process. Sometimes it worked fairly; at other times, good men failed to progress and poor men did remarkably well. SAC had taken this questionable process to the nth degree.

At the end of pilot training, most graduates, given a choice, elected fighters, and since the system rewarded those who performed at the highest level, SAC sometimes received less-qualified pilots. However, despite the howls of protest from the pilots involved, fighters were being de-emphasized, which meant that at times entire classes were sent to SAC.

Few worked harder or under more pressure than members of the Strategic Air Command. They were called on to perform with skill and expertise above and beyond, plus they spent many hours sitting on alert, waiting for the flag to go up. In underground bunkers, where some crews were minutes away from their armed and cocked B-52s and tankers, alert was pulled often. Others could enjoy a short meal at the Officers' Club with their families.

I'd been in the O Club when the deafening claxon horn went off. The Club emptied in a flash, leaving families to stare in worry and wonder. Blue cars converged on the flight line, sirens blaring and lights flashing, as a procession of giant B-52s took off, one after the other. Watching the planes turn the sky black with exhaust from their eight engines, the earth rumbling and churning beneath them, was a sobering event. We never knew if this was one of the many practice events or the real thing.

By necessity, the selfless men and women who kept this doomsday operation going were never given the credit due them. In fact, most people never knew of the mission at all, let alone the sacrifice of those who made it work. To compensate for this lack of recognition and to reward and inspire their flight crews, SAC gave spot promotions to the next higher rank to crews nominated as "select." This recognition came with a financial reward as well, but the promotions weren't permanent. Instead, they were passed around to deserving people.

Although well-intended, the SAC practice of spot promotions, along with frequent instances of rating pilots as giving advice to God, corrupted the promotion cycle, since other commands were often given the leftovers. Finally somebody at SAC decided that if everyone was rated in the far right column, it was impossible to separate the wheat from the chaff. From that point forward, operational units were instructed to adhere to a new directive: Average was fine; save the right-hand columns for the few individuals who deserved them.

Savvy commanders had heard this garbage before, and they immediately threw the directive into the closest round file. Except at the 4080th. Here the "new" system was adopted, and this organization of 25 hand-selected pilots, the people who'd been bringing home the bacon in intelligence for more than a decade, were rated against each other on the bell curve. In addition, our pilots went into the same promotion pool as the previously overrated SAC guys and the rest of the air force.

Wakeup Call

Behind the main Operations area we had a bar. Stocked with beer and nuts and run on the honor system, the bar was great place to wind down and shoot the breeze without having to watch our words. After one successful flight, I waltzed into this bar area invigorated and full of myself, expecting the usual backslapping and kidding around. Few people were there; those that were could have been at a funeral.

"What the hell's the matter?" I said.

"Promotions have been posted," said a voice from across the room. I wasn't personally up for promotion, but I wandered over to the bulletin board to look at the results of this annual event. Many who were eligible had been passed over, a death knell for a career to say nothing of anticipated income. This was an organization that rarely had a pass-over. The mission was too important; if somebody wasn't good enough to be promoted, he was normally long gone before it became an issue.

I drove home quietly. This was a dark and worrisome day for Polly and me. I was a reserve officer. Without a four-year degree, few made regular-officer status. Normally this wasn't a problem, but if there was a RIF (reduction in force), a reserve officer could find himself unceremoniously reclassified as a staff sergeant with two choices: serve his years until retirement with a sergeant's stripes and a sergeant's pay, but retire based on the pay scale of his highest rank attained; or sever relations with the service and receive a cash stipend.

Up to now life had been a bowl of cherries; even the sky hadn't been the limit. Reality was a cold slap in the face, and going backwards was not something I'd ever contemplated. The current promotion list had no immediate effect on me, but if superior high flyers were being passed over today, what chance did I have in the near or distant future.

Confusion and anger reverberated throughout the wing; calls were made and leaders flew to headquarters. Some of the oversights were rectified, and although the shock faded into the background, the promotion cycles were still displaced.

Shortly thereafter, Polly and I had a visit from Tom Westhafer and his lovely wife, Sue. Laughing, Tom and I reminisced about our infamous flight over Davis-Monthan when we were at Willie. "Do you know where you are, Lieutenant Westhafer," I asked in a mock replay.

"Hell, no, Wright," he replied, "and it's a wonder we didn't run into that damn mountain."

Tom was an experienced pilot who'd flown many missions in Vietnam in a C-130. Like many of his comrades, he'd been let out of the air force early, even though at the same time flight schools were pushing more pilots through to fill the slots the war had created. Tom believed this strategy was part of the phony war of 1964, designed in an election year to assure the voters that everything was under control. Nevertheless, he'd taken full advantage of the situation and was now a pilot with American Airlines.[240]

Tom was enthusiastic about his job and about American as an organization. At the end of a fun evening, he pulled out an application that he'd already signed in the recommendation slot.

"Thanks, Tom, but I'm as happy as a pig in manure. This is a necessary, interesting job, and I'm damn lucky to have it." Tom didn't try to twist my arm (well, not much), but as we talked about the war, he predicted we'd be involved for a long time and suffer a lot of pain.

How often in life a road opens up when another closes down. Polly and I talked more about the airline business, but I just wasn't interested. My heart was with the mission and the air force. I did, however, send in the application, just in case. The promotion snafu had gotten my attention. I was also concerned about the war. After cutting through the bravado, most who had been to Southeast Asia worried about our chances of success. As Tom put it, many of those in the know thought we were "screwing it up royally," and getting our leaders to listen to reality seemed more and more unlikely.

Soon after I mailed the application, I got a call from Bill Williams, a pal since we'd met at preflight training at Lackland back in 1957. Bill had left the air force and was also a pilot for American. "It's a good job, Don," he said, "perhaps not as exciting as the U-2, but have you given any thought to what you're going to do in nine years when you retire?" Ouch. The twins would be 11 by then and Walt 13. *If American calls*, I thought, *maybe I'll talk to them.*

There's no harm in talking.

In the meantime, I continued to fly the T-33, the U-3, and the U-2. I had only to accomplish the high, long mission in the U-2 and I would be combat-ready.

---

[240] Various models of the Lockheed C-130 Hercules, a turboprop, four-engine military transport aircraft, have been in use for more than 50 years.

Chapter 76 – The Third and Final Hurdle

1965

The U-2 navigated by using a sextant, an instrument borrowed from the famous World War II bomber, the B-29. This device was remotely located in the nose, pointing upward and controlled by two verniers in the cockpit. One hand controlled the latitude, the other the longitude. If Captain Cook could have been resurrected, he'd have been at home with this device.

Although flying was never a problem and I was looking forward to my first high, long mission, the idea of navigating with a sextant caused me some concern. I remembered my frequent struggles with the subject of navigation, both as a student and an instructor, but I kept these concerns to myself. Surely some soul would teach me, at least I hoped so.

In addition to the sextant, there was the usual UHF (ultra-high-frequency) radio for takeoff, recovery, and talking to air traffic control when leaving and entering the country. The plane was also equipped with a VOR (Very-high-frequency Omni-directional Range) and an ADF (Automatic Direction Finder). The VOR, a fairly short-range system, was used extensively throughout the world. The ADF was a long-range system that could also be used as a radio— a little in-flight easy listening, anyone? ADF technology had been in service since the 1930s and was somewhat undependable. It also could be easily manipulated. Of course, since most of our flying was over denied territory, these aids were unimportant except during final recovery.

The last and most irritating communications device was the HF (high-frequency) radio. Using the proper bands one could talk around the world by bouncing the signals off the troposphere, that part of the atmosphere that extends from the surface of the Earth to the bottom of the stratosphere. The static-filled frequencies of HF always had an operator yakking in code, providing instructions to every SAC plane that was airborne. The chatter sounded something like this: Corn Boy, Corn Boy, do not answer; break,

break; tree, nail, post. After the operator answered a call sign (e.g., Nails One), any communication had to be authenticated by a complex table, much like a crossword puzzle that changed daily and sometimes hourly. A stop to pick up this table was one of the last things we did before launch.

In December 1965, several days before the final test of my U-2 training, the long profile flight, I was assigned to a squadron navigator to assist with preplanning. First we calculated latitude and longitude, which was predicated on being at a certain place at a certain time.

"Okay," he said, "let's go to the navigation simulator."

I looked up in astonishment. "Simulator? I didn't know we had one."

He cracked a smile and led me to a field out back, where a tug had just pulled up towing a wagon. In the bed of the wagon was the "simulator," a mini-house—actually more like a plywood box. About six feet square and six feet high, it offered little ventilation and no amenities. Thank heavens it was early in the day; otherwise, we'd have roasted. Implanted into the roof was a sextant with two flexible verniers. I sat down on the single seat and dialed the latitude and longitude we'd calculated into the sextant's control.[241]

In the airplane, we flew under the sun or a star at a predetermined time. Today, the mini-house was our airplane. "Here comes the sun, center it," said the navigator, and I looked into the makeshift sextant, waiting for the sun to move over us. It took some time for the demonstration.

"Now read the results and add or subtract them, translated into degrees, from our preplanned course."

Okay, minor math so far, just adding and subtracting. I was breathing a little easier.

The navigator looked over to make sure I understood. "All you'd do now," he said," would be to make a correction to the heading of the airplane. Got it?"

"Yep."

"That's all there is to it, Don. Any questions?"

"Nope."

"Good, let's go to the bar; this exercise has whetted my thirst."

I really didn't know enough to ask any questions, and, surprisingly enough, it turned out to be just that easy.

The day before the mission, the navigator and I spent all day, probably eight hours or so, preplanning the exact course and time of flight. I was going to take off and fly to an initial point (IP) at St. Johns VOR, switch to sextant

---

[241] A tug is a small, heavily powered tractor with many uses in military and civilian life. For example, airport tugs tow luggage-filled carts to and from airplanes on the tarmac.

navigation, and head for St. Louis. Then I'd follow a route that included several preplanned course changes to another IP at the edge of North Dakota. An IP could be a city, a crossroads, a train track, or a river crossing—anything that was easily recognizable from the air.

Once I reached the North Dakota IP, I would switch to drift-sight navigation and fly a very close track, back and forth, until I mapped the state. At this point, I'd be operating much the same as any low-level, cross-country flight using known visual fixes. In the early days of flight, pilots looked over the side of the aircraft and flew by dead reckoning. Looking through the drift sight wasn't much different, except for the fact that our field of vision was more limited. I might be engaged in one of aviation's most sophisticated missions, but the drift-sight techniques would be familiar to pilots who delivered mail in the 1930s.

When I finished mapping North Dakota, I'd pick up a third IP across the state and return to Davis-Monthan using the sextant. On the return trip, I was to fly down the coast of California to Los Angeles and then back to Arizona.

The navigator and pilot, like everyone else involved in the U-2 operation, worked as a team. It was impossible to do any serious calculations in the cramped cockpit, so everything about the mission had to be preplanned before the pilot left the ground. In this regard, the navigator was invaluable, not only for his skill but for his ability to communicate the mission and translate it to a form the pilot could understand.

The navigator used several factors to plan the course, including the location of the IPs, the exact time of the mission, and the true airspeed of the U-2 (seven miles per minute). Using reference books of navigational times, he plotted a course of numerical fixes based on latitude and longitude. Surprisingly, variations in weather were rarely a consideration. At 60,000 to 80,000 feet, winds are very predictable and weather is rarely encountered. On the rare occasions when maverick winds became a factor, the mission was scrubbed because of the inability to navigate effectively.

After he finished his calculations, the navigator completed a *green card* that provided the pilot with all of the navigational data he'd need, as well as information about the various targets to be mapped and instructions for switching the cameras at various times and locations during the flight. The information on this card was essential for meeting the goals of the mission.

The Big Day

On the day of the flight, the alarm went off way before sunrise, and the Operations room was already buzzing when I arrived. Captain John and the navigator joined me for the preflight ritual: steak and eggs, fresh-squeezed orange juice, milk, and coffee. The flight surgeon gave me a real going-over, and I went on to the physiological unit to get suited up. Even though the suit had been custom-made for me, minor adjustments were required prior to every mission. If the suit wasn't fitted properly, the pilot would endure several hours of discomfort beyond the normal miseries of being laced into this girdle-like contraption and climbing into a cockpit designed for a midget.

It took quite a long time to complete the job. Timing was everything, and John was getting a bit nervous. If I missed the IP at St. Johns VOR, the mission would be scrubbed and I'd be up there a long time, burning off enough fuel to land. This was not something I wanted to happen.

Finally I was ready. John had my flight papers, green card, charts, approach plates, and authentication table. We headed for the van and drove to the hangar. We'd hurried for naught; there was still plenty of time.

I climbed into the cockpit and the airmen strapped me in, locking down my faceplate. When their checks were complete, the sergeants rechecked everything; nothing was left to chance. With about ten minutes to go, John sat on the rail for a last-minute briefing.

"It's okay, John," I quipped. "I know the drill: Pull back to go up, push forward to come down. But I do have one question. How the hell do I take a leak?"

He looked at me like the stupid stooge he thought I was, scrambled down the ladder, and came back with three bottles that he stuffed in the seat mechanism behind my left shoulder. He then demonstrated the use of the bottle, which had a funnel and a shutoff to keep it from leaking. I'm sure I'd been briefed on this process at some earlier time, but it had passed me by. I probably hadn't taken a leak in a jet more than five times in my life. The ranges of the planes I'd flown had been short enough that good planning and a young bladder negated the problem.

Today, not only did I need to know about the process in theory, but all of a sudden I needed to put it into practice. In taking the dehydration lecture to heart, I'd apparently had far too much liquid. "John, I've got to piss."

"Not now. Our crank time is in two minutes."

Two minutes later, I was having major regrets that I hadn't taken a preflight leak, but the engine started perfectly. The preflight checklists were complete and, after making a last check of my faceplate, an airman pulled away the ladder and locked the canopy. Technicians removed the protective covers from the Q-bay and the nose. The Q-bay held a giant camera that swung on gimbals and could be mechanically programmed using the green card. In the nose was a camera that allowed flight standards personnel to check the track of the flight.

The sun was coming up in the east like a giant fireball, and takeoff time was in five minutes. The tower cleared me into position and I said my usual quick prayer, hoping my angel was along for the ride.

The voice of the tower crackled in my earphones. "Nails One, cleared for takeoff."

I applied power smoothly and the plane moved down the runway. I then rotated to the familiar 45-degree climb angle and turned toward St. Johns VOR. At 60,000 feet I checked in.

"You're clear VFR above 60," said the controller. "So long and Godspeed." I changed the channel to an exclusive, quiet frequency.

Other than the soothing sound of the engine, there was almost total silence, and never in my life did I have to go as badly. Fortunately, I had a hold of up to 20 minutes before departing—built-in slop time in case of late startup or other unforeseen difficulties—so I'd have a few minutes once I got to St. Johns. Right now, however, I had too much to do. My mind was a jumble, sorting out the holding pattern, calculating the exact time to depart the hold, running a few checklist items. It was all busywork, but it was hugely complicated by the fact that my bladder was about to burst. I approached the VOR still slightly behind the aircraft mentally, but I was catching up fast.

I had 20 minutes to get things right prior to heading out, plenty of time to pee. As I started the process, my knee hit the wheel. It was way out of position, almost pressing down on my thigh. In the U-2, fuel is stored in the wings. Normally, it's drawn from both wings simultaneously, but occasionally the plane burns more fuel from one wing than the other.

I knew that uneven fuel distribution could create a problem. If the wings were out of balance, the autopilot turned the wheel, forcing the ailerons to maintain straight-and-level. When the fuel was in balance, a rudimentary, three-position switch located directly in front of the pilot on the instrument panel was set to off (neutral). If fuel needed to be transferred from one wing to the other, the pilot could flip the switch to the left or the right. This was how we kept the wings level and maintained the trim of the aircraft.

Ironically, that day "pull back to go up" had been John's second-to-last bit of advice. His final words had been "don't let the fuel get out of balance."

"At about 45 degrees of wheel misalignment," he'd said, "the autopilot will disengage, the aircraft will snap over and become unglued in a flash, and you'll be getting your paratroop wings. Ho, ho, ho; don't let that happen."

"Come on John, get serious," I'd replied. "I've been flying jets all my life." Fuel was a problem in every plane—usually not enough of it—but I'd had to deal with balance problems often enough.

Be that as it may, at this very moment the wheel was approaching the magic 45-degree mark. I lunged for the three-position fuel switch in the middle of the panel—left, off, right—and pointed it toward the direction the fuel needed to flow. Just in time, the wheel began its journey back to neutral. The fuel was flowing at a rate of 6 gallons per minute, 36 pounds of change every 60 seconds. I could almost hear it gurgling as it transferred from wing to wing.

Okay, I wasn't going to have to bail out, but the gurgling brought me back to my primary problem. First the container, stored tantalizingly out of reach just behind my left shoulder. I took out my pencil and stabbed at the bottle, my dexterity restricted by the space suit and the layers of clothing.

Finally, bottle in hand, all was ready for relief. Then the real problem began: getting to it. First I unstrapped the seat belt and shoulder harness and released the crotch straps of the tight parachute. Next came a several-minute struggle with a confusing mess of zippers and alignment, made even more difficult by wearing gloves. In the meantime, *Holy cow, the turn; I've got to turn the aircraft and count down the timing in the hold.*

I completed the turn with eight minutes to go and finished the job at hand. A wave of relief washed over my mind and body, and I departed the holding pattern on course and, miraculously, on time.

I'd already set the sextant for the first shot, 15 minutes down course after leaving the hold. Whoops! The wheel was pressing down on my other thigh; the fuel was out of balance again. I flipped the fuel switch the other way and recorded the timing information on the green card. I was beginning to be comfortable with the routine of the mission and was feeling pretty cocky.

Oh, crap. The wheel was now at least 45 degrees over the other way. *I'm going to die*, I thought, as I dove down, flipped the switch, and watched and prayed as the wheel slowly began its journey to the proper position. Carefully taking my first sextant shot, I did the calculations and course correction and made the proper notes on the green card.

Aaghhhhhhhh. The wheel again. I couldn't seem to catch it in the neutral position. I flipped the switch the other way, said a quick prayer, and picked up a pencil. As long as I held the pencil in my hand, it served as a reminder that I needed to balance the fuel. When the fuel was balanced and I was able to flip the switch to the neutral position, I put the pencil down. Later on, I found that this was the accepted technique.

Did I hear female laughter? Was that blankedy-blank angel having some fun at my expense?

It was just about time to preload the sextant and prepare for the next fix when the HF radio began its chatter: "Sky King, Sky King, break, break, do not answer, Alpha, Charlie, Yankee, do not answer." Good Lord, they want me to authenticate a message. Here I am, the wheel flipping from side to side, shooting the sun every 15 minutes and doing calculations for 5 of those minutes, making adjustments for 5 more, and they want to load me up with more work during my 5-minute break?" I tried as best I could to authenticate the code, which was no easy task.

My nose began to itch, but the faceplate kept me from scratching. I tried using my tongue; that didn't work. I rotated my head trying to reach the edge of the shield—nothing. Finally, in a flash of brilliance, I located the bottle of liquid that was on board for drinking; eased the straw from the bottle through the feeding port of the faceplate; and scratched away. Oh, did it feel good."

I began to get into the routine. Every 15 minutes I shot the sun, centering it in the screen using the two verniers hooked into the sextant. I read the results numerically, compared the reading with the green card, computed the difference by adding or subtracting, interpolated the result, and made the necessary course changes. The only correction could be lateral. In the coffin corner, playing with speed wasn't an option; there were only a few precious knots on either side of disaster.

After a while I even found time to sightsee. The slight curvature of the Earth was outlined by a continuous white streak blending into hews of blue, then changing to purple and slipping softly into a smooth, velvet charcoal as my eyes lifted off the horizon. From below, the black aircraft would blend into the dark sky like a leopard blends into the jungle.

"Spying" on North Dakota

I approached the IP at North Dakota, flipped the lever that changed the angle of the mirrors from the sextant to looking down and forward of the aircraft's belly, and began ground-tracking using the drift sight. I'd arrived exactly on time. On the chart there were seven-mile tick marks, each representing a minute; on the green card there were course headings to fly. When over the target area, it was a minute-by-minute flight. I flew back and forth over the state, using a control pad with buttons from A to Z to start and stop photography based on instructions on the green card. Every time I changed the settings, I could feel the thumping of the unit in the Q-bay as the camera swung on a different arc.

The flight progressed smoothly. The work was steady and interesting and before long the mapping was complete. I'd already preloaded the sextant with the latitude and longitude to bring me home, and as I punched more info from the green card into the control pad, the thumping in the Q-bay ceased. I flipped the drift-sight lever and the sextant mirrors reappeared. Then I searched the sky, waiting for the airplane to fly under the sun at the right time, in the right position, so preplanned navigation could resume.

Sure enough, there it was in the center, and after making minor corrections, I proceeded toward the West Coast, flew down the Sierras, over San Francisco, and south to Los Angeles. The green card instructed me to contact a certain radio frequency, which turned out to be an ADC (Air Defense Command) control tower.

"Hello, Nails One. We have some fighters up here who'd like to make some pop-up simulated attacks, okay?"

"Sure, let her rip."

"I need you at angels 60 (altitude); can you climb or descend for me?"

This was a word game. In the days before radar could report altitude, our altitude was our security. It was also our secret.

"I think I'll stay where I'm at, Control."

"Roger, that," said the controller, and I could hear the chuckle in his voice. I heard him giving the vectors to some F-102s.

"Check your two o'clock, Nails."

There they were, streaming along at about 40,000 feet. They pulled up, screaming at my underbelly, for a simulated firing pass. I flipped to drift sight and picked them up. Soon they fluttered and fell. I would have lived to fly another day, and so would they.

"So long, Control."

"So long, Nails. Thanks."

My friend De De Hickman was flying the same type mission over the Northwest when two National Guard F-101s made a pass on him, but in the process one began to tumble. The F-101 was a beautiful, sleek, second-generation fighter, but in certain regimes of flight it was quite unstable. De De watched as the bird tumbled down and down and down. Finally, two ejection seats fired out of the wounded airplane, followed by the comforting sight of two blossoming white silk parachutes.

"You'd better send the chopper," De De told the controller, as a fireball hit the empty plain. Before the next mission, somebody with a dark sense of humor taped a white star on De De's U-bird, indicating a "kill" for the aircraft.

Coming Home

I made the final turn over Los Angeles and headed back toward St. Johns. At the prescribed time, I tuned in my VOR and stowed the green card and assorted logs and papers. For the next half hour, I had relatively little to do.

I began with the descent checklist. Descent was a carefully monitored event. Until the coffin corner opened up, it was a difficult process that couldn't be rushed. After setting the speed brakes out and the gear down to increase drag, I performed a few minor adjustments and settled back for the long ride home. The throttle had three methods of adjustment: the normal stick-like appendage, a large wheel that would reduce the input to the engine as we reached altitude, and a small wheel that could be turned and turned with little apparent effect. Power to the aircraft was controlled by the EPR (engine pressure ratio) gauge, and when using the small wheel, it was almost impossible to see the adjustment. To avoid a flameout, the rate of descent was set according to a chart and controlled in minute increments.

At about 10,000 feet, I popped off the faceplate and rubbed my face all over, scratching every previously inaccessible nook and cranny. I'd been up for 6 hours and 45 minutes, and I was feeling invigorated.

Davis-Monthan VOR was tuned in as I descended over the mountains of northern Arizona. I smiled as I flew over Mt. Lemmon, the peak Tom Westhafer and I had screeched over years before, lost and nearly out of gas. I made contact with the tower and was allowed to make a leisurely approach. Our home was close by, and when I circled the house and looked down, Polly and the boys were waving wildly.

"Look, Mom," I could just imagine the boys saying, "it's Dad in the Big Black Mother."

Soon I was on final and could see the familiar blue staff car and pickup loaded with troops, poised to chase me down the runway. Ten feet, 5, 4, 3, 2, 1, 6 inches, hold it, hold it, HOLD IT, and then the familiar rumble as the tandem gear touched down and I taxied to a stop. The airmen lifted the wings, locked in the pogos, and gave the usual highball salute.

I taxied to the ramp and shut down the bird while the troops scrambled to secure the aircraft. Too exhilarated to be tired, I waited somewhat impatiently to be unhooked from life support systems and assisted down the ladder. But stiff? Oh, man, was I stiff. This must be how it felt to be old. I bent forward while the sergeant pulled off my helmet to the accompanying splash of pooled sweat and an airman handed me the requisite cold Coors.

Captain John stood with a huge grin splashed across his craggy face. "How'd it go?"

"A piece of cake," I replied. To myself, I added *tough, but doable.*

After I had a quick shower, John and I debriefed the mission. "Ah, John, about that bottle bit."

"Yeah, I forgot to warn you about that. The last thing out of the building, it's important to take a leak and get things lined up to get you through the beginning of the mission. Have any trouble with that?"

"No, not much," I lied.

"Have any trouble with the fuel balance?" he asked.

"No," I lied again, "no problem at all."

If this line of questioning keeps up, I thought, *I'll be ready to run for public office.*

"How about scratching your face?"

"A little problem," I answered, "but I solved it with the straw."

"Oh, yeah," he said, "we all carry a stick in our flight suit for that purpose. I guess I forgot to brief you."

"Yeah, I guess you did, John."

"One more thing, Don. Some guys purposefully dehydrate to avoid the stick and bottle trick, but the doc really warns against that."

I guess I'd been had. This must have been an initiation or something, because he hit on every problem that occurred. Nevertheless, I'd made it. I was combat-ready; my training was done; and I was a numbered crew member, ready to go anywhere in the world to do my duty *toward the unknown.*[242]

I was exhilarated and pleased with myself, and home never felt better, but that night I almost got to sleep alone. Those inside-out seams from the long underwear were burned into my body like a brand, and for hours all I could do was scratch.

I was the 192nd pilot to fly the U-2. It is an incredible airplane, designed by Kelly Johnson, the best of the best, and like Millard's 1937 John Deere tractor—both simple and dependable.

I observed only one flaw, an issue that might have sparked a conversation like this one between Kelly Johnson and one of his mechanics at the Skunk Works:

---

[242] *Toward the Unknown* was the motto of the 4028th SRS. Emblazoned on the squadron patch along with a dragon, the motto is said to have been inspired by the 1956 movie of the same name, which was set at Edwards Air Force Base in California.

> *"Mr. Johnson," says the mechanic, "this is one great aircraft. You've thought of almost everything, and I'm sure it will be successful. But I do see one small problem."*
> *"What's that, young man?"*
> *"You forgot to build a place for the pilot!"*
> *"See to that young man, see to that."*

I was now a full-fledged member of the 4028th, but nothing had really changed. I still went to the squadron meeting every morning, did the normal paperwork, played handball, flew one aircraft or the other every third day or so, and drank a beer or two every night. I flew a few long missions in the U-bird and everything went well. I even learned to use the bottle without too much strain, though I still think there must have been a better place to store the empties than over my left shoulder.

Chapter 77 – The U-2 Goes to War

O ne evening after work I was involved in a loud, laughing game of liar's dice in the self-service bar behind Operations. We were playing for beer and quarters and having a ball. Occasionally a player dropped out and was replaced by one of the kibitzers.[243]

"Hey Frank, how goes it?" asked Jim, one of the participants.

"Great" he replied. "Mind if I join in?"

"Sure, just don't whine when we whip you," said Jim with a chuckle.

The game went on, with a lot of whooping and hollering, and soon Frank declared an outrageous hand and upped the ante. We called him and he cleaned our clock, pocketing several quarters and suffering a barrage of harassment. "You're a heck of a lot luckier with dice than flying," somebody popped up with feigned disgust. This opened up a whole lot of good-natured jousting, typical of close-knit groups.

Frank looked familiar, but I just couldn't place him. He obviously was very much at home with the older pilots, those on their way to the SR-71.

"What did you bring in?" someone asked him.

"One of the new U-2Cs from the Skunk Works," he replied. "An upgraded A model with a J75 engine."

Bingo, I thought. Although his old pals called him Frank, this was Francis Gary Powers, the famous Gary Powers who was shot down over the USSR in May of 1960, captured by the Soviets, and imprisoned for nearly two years as an American spy. These days he flew for Lockheed as a test pilot.

He introduced himself to the newer guys. The first impression I had was how normal and unaffected he acted. He fit in like an old glove, one of the typical, easy-going pilots who made up the heart of flying squadrons worldwide. It would be hard to guess that this guy was the lynchpin of perhaps the most significant political firestorm of the decade.

---

[243] Liar's dice is a game played with five specialized dice. Playing well requires the ability to deceive and to detect an opponent's deception.

Kelly Johnson and Gary Powers, with the
Dragon Lady in the background, 1966.
(*National Museum of the USAF.*)

Why Spy?

When President Eisenhower authorized the building of the U-2 in 1955,
he knew that the airplane and its mission could be controversial. CIA head
Allen Dulles and his able assistant, Dick Bissell, were perhaps more optimistic
than Ike, but each man understood the potential of the information the plane
could provide. Flying above 70,000 feet, the U-2 would afford protection for
several years. In 1955, Soviet MiG-15s, -17s, and -19s flew at least 10,000
feet too low to be a realistic threat.

The most worrisome threat to a plane like the U-2 was the development
of surface-to-air missiles (SAMs). The Russians were at least as far advanced
in this effort as the USA, perhaps more so; but at that time, our scientists felt
that no nation had the capability to be effective at high altitude. Although
a missile could potentially get close enough to blow up the U-2 by using
a proximity fuse to shower the sky with shrapnel, the missiles of the day
became unsteerable at very high altitudes. In addition, we believed that the
Soviet Union did not have the radar technology to detect the aircraft at 70,000
feet, at least not in the detail needed to identify it.

That left Murphy's Law—detection and/or capture caused by a
flameout, airframe malfunction, or other unforeseen problem. Those in
charge concluded that the risk was acceptable. The best cover story, Bissell

decided, would be to issue a press release stating that the U.S. had developed an aircraft capable of flying at 55,000 feet to study weather phenomena and turbulence at high altitude. If the plane were shot down or for some other reason failed and the pilot bailed out, there was a very slim chance of his survival. There was also a small, pilot-activated explosive charge that would—theoretically—blow up the spying gear, and nothing on the airplane was supposed to be identified by manufacturer or country of origin. If the enemy got their hands on a U-2, they would know where it came from, but it would be difficult to prove. Of course, a lot of this was wishful thinking, minimizing the possibilities of what really could happen, but it was the information given to the President.

Although Ike's proposed "open skies" treaty had been strongly rebuffed by Premier Khrushchev, the President was very reluctant to authorize overflights of the Soviet Union. He realized that we would be violating international law and, if detected, would incur not only the wrath of the USSR but that of many of our own citizens. "If the USA was on the receiving end," he commented to his advisors, "the reaction would be drastic."

On the other hand, Eisenhower was a military leader as well as a politician. He realized that our live intelligence was insufficient, that we needed strategic information, and that we needed it now. The situation in the world, and our interpretation of it, was spiraling out of control. The Cold War might be an undeclared war, but it was a war nonetheless. Reluctantly, he approved the overflights.

Our first "deep" mission over enemy territory was flown on July 4, 1956; the second flew the next day over several factories and air bases in and near Moscow. In the summer of 1956, I was an airman third class, serving as a mechanic on the RC-121 at Otis Air Force Base. That Independence Day I was watching the fireworks in Hyannis, my dreams filled with thoughts of flying fighters to defend our nation from the Red menace. Never in my wildest imagination did I think we had the technology to achieve what was being accomplished that July 4, let alone that someday I would be associated with the program.

The information obtained by the U-2 was beyond the expectations of even the most optimistic operative. Aside from gathering strategic targeting information, the flights determined that there were far fewer Soviet Bison bombers than we believed. This data, coupled with information obtained from other sources, helped U.S. officials determine that the Bison program was basically a strategic failure.

Everything was going extremely well, except for one small problem. Photographic evidence, as well as pilot visual reports, showed multiple, unsuccessful attacks on the U-2 by Russian fighters. Our supposedly covert missions were being tracked by Russian radar.

The Soviets protested, although privately. They probably didn't wish to acknowledge that we were violating their borders with impunity and they were unable to do anything about it.

Ike temporarily suspended the flights over Russia. Khrushchev was silently furious.

Elsewhere in the world, President Gamal Abdel Nasser of Egypt nationalized the Suez Canal in retaliation for the decision of Western nations not to financially support his project to construct the Aswan Dam. The U-2 was on the scene almost immediately, providing up-to-date, tactical information. Within the month, we provided a strategic and tactical intelligence platform that exceeded all expectations.

Flights over the Soviet Union became sporadic; sometimes as many as 16 months elapsed between missions. Eventually, every flight was personally approved by Ike. Sometimes the President would even change the flight path. He realized, more than anyone, that if a plane went down in the Soviet Union, it would create an unprecedented response, wrecking any chance of a more peaceful world.

In August of 1957, the Soviet news agency TASS announced that the USSR had successfully launched a multi-stage, intercontinental ballistic missile (ICBM), a weapon we weren't even close to achieving. Two months later, the Russians launched Sputnik, the world's first satellite. It was obvious that the Soviets were basing their offense on missiles, not bombers, and the "missile gap" resounded throughout the world.

Loving the attention, Khrushchev boasted not only of Sputnik and his ICBMs, but also of nuclear warheads that could be directed instantly to anywhere in the world. The U.S. Congress screamed for an immediate resolution to the problem.

With great reluctance, Ike approved a few more overflight missions. The intelligence gathered revealed that, yes, the Russians did have large missiles, but they were very localized. Again, coupled with other intelligence, the U-2 images convinced the powers that be that Russian offensive missiles appeared to have huge technical difficulties and did not pose an immediate threat.

Defensive weapons were another matter. The Russian MiG-21 was on line, and Soviet SAMS were accurate enough to bring down a high-flying aircraft. It was true that the missiles took time to prepare and our planes turned often, but Soviet tracking was getting better.

It was obvious that the useful life of the U-2 over the Soviet Union was just about finished, but in April of 1960, the CIA lobbied for just a couple more missions, and while Ike agreed, he was very concerned. A summit meeting of the superpowers was scheduled in Paris on the 16th of May, and nothing was to go wrong. The April 23rd overflight returned successfully, and for the first time, the Soviet Union did not voice an objection. Nevertheless, Khrushchev was still furious—silently furious.

The final mission was scheduled for April 28, 1960.

Chapter 78 – Francis Gary Powers
Tells His Story

1965

It didn't take long for the guys to start talking with Gary about his ordeal. Many of the older hands had been around when Powers got shot down, but they were air force, not CIA, and hadn't been privy to the details. And of course, we young guys were all ears.

"Did you flame out and descend to a lower altitude?" asked one guy.

"I heard a MiG got you," said somebody else.

"I got it from a reliable source that you were barraged with SAMs," a third voice piped up.

"And that the sky was full of parachutes," added a fourth.

About that time, Gary held up his hands with a bemused expression. "Okay, fellows," he said. "I'm going to give it to you from the horse's mouth.[244]

"In January of 1956, a list of pilots in my F-84 squadron was posted on the bulletin board, and my name was on that list. We were to report to a conference room the next day. We knew our squadron was being disbanded soon, so we figured the meeting had something to do with future assignments. What we hadn't counted on was being offered an unspecified, top-secret opportunity by the major conducting the meeting.

"'Why us?' someone asked.

"'You gentlemen,' the major said, 'have the basic qualifications: high single-engine jet time, top secret clearances, and reserve commissions.' That's all that he could tell us, except that if we were interested, we were to report

---

[244] To his air force pals, Francis Gary Powers was known as Frank; however, I have chosen to refer to him as Gary, since this is how he was known to the wider world. As I've related here, I heard Frank's tale that afternoon from beginning to end, but it was a long time ago. In order to make certain I related the facts correctly, I reconstructed the story with help from Powers' book, *Operation Overflight: A Memoir of the U-2 Incident.*

the next day to a local motel room, individually, at a predefined time. In the interim, we were to discuss the situation with no one."

Gary went on to explain that the information at this private meeting was still sketchy. All they really knew was that the mission would be risky, patriotic, and involve long separations overseas, with no dependents allowed. The reason reserve officers were selected was that those in the program would be separated from the air force. However, when their contract was up, they could be reinstated with no loss of promotion. Then came the kicker: If the pilots accepted, their pay would be doubled.

Gary and his wife Barbara had been married only nine months. They discussed the pros and cons: the increase in pay, the challenge of the unknown, and possibly the chance to make an important contribution to the nation, versus the hardship of separation. The decision was mutual and quick: absolutely.

What followed were several months of tests and cloak-and-dagger meetings all over the country, sometimes using false names and identifications. The men were then transferred to Watertown, Nevada, which was called "the Ranch," where they were working for the CIA, which was known as "the Agency." The pilots were "the drivers," the second group to be trained on the U-2. The training was extensive, thorough, and enjoyable. Gary loved flying the bird, especially since these first flyers were really experimental test pilots, helping to redefine pilotage in the vast, unexplored space above 70,000 feet.

Powers joined Detachment 10-10 at Incirlik Air Base in Turkey. Living conditions were fairly basic—small trailers with few amenities—but after a time dependents were permitted, and Barbara elected to join him. Gary flew missions around the periphery of Russia and tactical missions all over the area. He was a civilian Agency pilot flying out of air force bases under shared air force and Agency command.[245]

"What was it like to fly over Russia the first time?" someone asked.

Gary described the day the detachment commander came to him and said "You're it, Powers; you'll fly the first overflight." Although overflights had already occurred from other bases, this was the first one from Incirlik.

After the usual preflight ritual was accomplished and the mission launched, Gary said he felt like a searchlight was shining on his airplane, that his every move was being watched. In reality, this probably didn't happen. Even if it had, the Russians had no way of interfering.

---

[245] Incirlik began life as Adana Air Base, a joint facility of the U.S. and Turkish Air Forces, in 1955. Later it became known as the Incirlik Common Defense Installation and was renamed Incirlik Air Base in 1958. U-2 missions were flown from the base beginning in 1956 and ending when Gary Powers was shot down over the Soviet Union on May 1, 1960. As of 2008, Incirlik is still an active facility of the U.S. Air Force.

It wasn't long, however, before the complexity of the mission overrode any psychological problems. Hours later, he was back at the base, recuperating from the exertions of the long flight, and a fast courier flight was on its way to Washington, delivering information that would help to further our knowledge of the Soviet Union.

In the years to come, Gary flew numerous missions, each time coming back with information to guide our politicians, our military, and the defense industry. When his contract was up, he renewed it and eventually became the high-time driver.

At this point I stopped him. "What preparation did you have in case of being forced down?" I asked.

Powers paused for a moment. "Basically, none," he said quietly. "We had outer flying suits designed for the Arctic, plus maps and money in rubles and gold. We also had a hunting knife, a silenced .22 caliber pistol, and the infamous poisoned pin, though no one ever suggested using it. Beyond these physical preparations, the actual possibility of going down was treated with almost superstitious disregard.

"If the plane were shot down, pretty much everyone believed the pilot would die. In the case of mechanical failure, the options weren't, or couldn't be, discussed, because there weren't any. The Agency could always fall back on the fiction of the U-2 being a high-altitude weather reconnaissance plane (though no one really thought this farce would be believed), but the pilots had nothing. The mission just had to work; the information was worth the risk; and those in the know were on board. We were told that the President was very much in the planning, although information he was given about the survival possibilities of the pilots might have been sugarcoated.

"We pilots didn't discuss it among ourselves, either," he continued. "I guess our gut feeling was why worry about what you have no control over?"

Powers explained that although the Russians couldn't seem to do anything about the overflights, the pilots knew they were being tracked on radar, and everyone involved felt the situation was getting more dangerous. In fact, that's why the flight scheduled for April 28 was to be the final one over Russia. The Big Four were getting ready to meet at a summit in Paris in mid-May, and no one wanted to jeopardize this event.

The mission would take off from Peshawar, Pakistan, and land in Bødo, Norway, nine hours of flight time and 3,800 total miles. The majority of those miles, 2,900 of them, would be over the Soviet Union. It was unusual to take off from Peshawar, and the accommodations on the ground were poor—sleeping on cots in the hangar and eating rations. For security reasons, the aircraft had to be ferried in on the night before the mission. If for some reason the mission was postponed after the plane arrived, it was to be returned to Incirlik and the process repeated as necessary.

Gary spent the Wednesday night of April 27 restless and uncomfortable, trying to get some sleep on his narrow cot. The following morning, the mission was aborted because of weather, a scenario that was repeated on Friday. Each night Powers was more restless; and each night his U-bird, one of the best and most dependable of the fleet, was cycled in and out of Peshawar. The mission planners decided to skip Saturday, the 30th, and try again on Sunday, May 1.

Sunday morning, already fatigued, Gary climbed over the rail of a U-2, but it wasn't his bird of choice. With all the ferrying back and forth from Pakistan, the best bird had run out of time between maintenance checks. The substitute was U-2 #360, a genuine dog and the hangar queen. This plane had crashed on a glider strip in Japan in September of 1959, and the Japanese, with their full regalia of clicking cameras, had advertised it to the world. Afterward, it was returned to the Skunk Works for repair, but it hadn't been right since.

By 0520, Gary was positioned and ready to go. By the launch time of 0600, with the sun beating down on him, sweat soaked his protective long johns as everyone waited for the final okay from the White House. Approval finally came, 20 minutes late, which negated any use of celestial sextant navigation. He'd have to fly using dead reckoning—not an impossible task, but one that was definitely more difficult.

Takeoff and climb-out were normal. When he reached altitude, he gave two clicks on the UHF radio, indicating all was well, and received a single click in reply. He penetrated the border using the preplanned time and headings— not as accurate as the sextant, but still surprisingly precise. The weather below was cloudy, but breaks in the overcast confirmed he was navigating okay. A few miles from Chelyabinsk, the clouds cleared and he began operating the camera, following the instructions on the flight plan.[246]

Darn it. The autopilot clicked off and the nose pitched up—good ole #360 just can't keep it all together. He manually retrimmed the aircraft and reengaged the autopilot.

Damn! The autopilot failed again, this time to a full nose-up position. Gary grabbed the wheel forcefully and hand-flew it back to the proper attitude. Now he had a problem. With the autopilot inoperative, the normal course of action was to abort, but he was well over 1,300 miles into the most important and ambitious U-2 flight so far. He pressed on.

---

[246] Chelyabinsk is a province of Russia located east of the Ural Mountains on the Miass River. In 1957, the Mayak nuclear fuel reprocessing plant located there suffered a serious nuclear accident. Subsequently, the province was closed to all foreigners until 1992.

Just to maintain straight and level when hand-flying the U-2 in the coffin corner is a huge challenge. To continue flying and accomplish the mission—running the cameras, navigating, taking notes, and other details—would take an unbelievably dedicated, disciplined, and well-trained pilot.

Powers was up to the challenge.

About 30 miles southeast of Sverdlovsk, the route called for a 90-degree turn. Rolling out, Gary felt a thump and was thrown forward in his seat. An orange flash lit up the sky, but the engine instruments seemed okay. Then the wing drooped and the nose tucked. Pulling back did no good. The machine was vibrating fiercely. The nose pitched forward, the wings snapped off, and what was left of the fuselage began an inverted spin.

At this point, Gary explained, his mind was in a time warp. Seconds seemed like hours as his suit inflated from the sudden loss of pressurization, severely restricting his mobility. He pulled the green apple, starting the self-contained oxygen.

The violent spinning of the plane continued, thrusting him forward. His hand found the destruct switch, a small explosive charge designed to destroy the sensitive equipment. "Wait, don't flip that yet," he thought; "it will set off the 70-second timer. I'd better wait until I'm sure I can eject." He tried to put his feet into the protective positioning stirrups so his legs wouldn't be cut off when he ejected, but the plane was thrashing too much for him to get in the proper position. He stopped struggling and tried to regroup. Ejection wasn't the only way out.[247]

He found the canopy lever and released it. The canopy sailed away. In the meantime, he'd already fallen to 40,000 feet. He released the seat belt and was immediately thrown half in, half out of the airplane, still connected by the oxygen hoses. No way to activate the destructive device now.

Kicking and squirming, he broke free of the bird and began to float through space. His faceplate had frosted over, so he had no way of judging his altitude. He had no choice but to wait it out, hoping that his parachute would function.

Pow! His parachute opened automatically. This meant he was below 15,000 feet and could safely remove the faceplate. A part of the U-2 sailed past him. Below was verdant farmland, much like the Virginia countryside of his boyhood. A car seemed to be tracking his descent, and two farmers on a tractor sat close to where it looked like he would land. Powers began shredding the charts in his pockets. He also pulled out a silver dollar. Buried in the dollar was the poison pin, a device furnished to each pilot with no instructions for use other than its availability in case of unbearable torture.

---

[247] If the pilot was still in the plane when the charge went off, it would have killed him.

He removed the pin and put it in his pocket, tossing the dollar to the wind. Would a Russian mob tear him apart in anger? Probably not—the average citizen was unlikely to be prepared for an American dropping out of the sky—but just in case. . .

Capture

He hit the plowed field with a crunch; the farmers collapsed his chute and helped him up. Powers spoke no Russian, the farmers no English. After a bit of sign language, one of the farmers held up two fingers and pointed toward the sky. Gary's eyes followed and saw another parachute descending in the distance. He shook his head as the car drove up with two official-looking chaps on board. In the meantime, schoolchildren and adults from the nearby village surrounded him. They didn't seem angry, just puzzled. He was taken to the village and allowed to strip off the pressure suit and put his outer flight suit back on. The officials in the car had already taken his .22 caliber pistol and searched the rest of his pack, but they'd missed the poison pin in his pocket. He had no intention of using it, however, and wasn't sure why he'd carried it in the first place. On previous missions, he'd declined to carry the suicide device. Meanwhile, people had been scouring the fields and were arriving in the village carrying bits of the aircraft. One bit he noticed, with some chagrin, was a roll of 70 mm film.

The officials drove him to KGB headquarters in nearby Sverdlovsk. The town was ablaze with banners and flags like the 4th of July. For a moment Gary thought *holy smoke, are they celebrating my capture*? Then the parade and colors came into focus. Of course, this was May 1st, May Day, the communist holy day.

While a woman doctor checked him over, his thoughts were racing. *The Americans still don't know I'm missing. What cover story should I use? What cover story can I use? They have the aircraft or at least parts of it—maybe the cameras and the film, for sure. Will they put me in front of a firing squad immediately? Hopefully not.*

In Powers' four years of flying the mission, nobody from on high had ever mentioned a cover story. A couple of years before, he'd broached the subject to an intelligence officer. After some thought, the officer replied, "You may as well tell them everything, because they're going to get it out of you anyway." Chilling advice, at best.

Gary began to formulate a plan.

Claiming to be lost was only going to make his life more difficult. "I'll tell the story but muck up some of the facts and events," he thought. "Maybe it will work."

It had to work.

Khrushchev was watching the glorious Moscow May Day Parade, probably wondering when his bombers, fighters, and missiles would bring down his nemesis, when a man approached and whispered something in his ear.

Khrushchev smiled. This was the best May Day ever. He had bagged the Holy Grail of his capitalist enemy.

Chapter 79 – Francis Gary Powers – Part 2

1965

We'd been listening to Gary's story for almost half an hour, during which time no one had moved. It was time to stretch. As soon as we got up and started milling around, the guys bombarded Gary with questions. "So did a missile get you?" someone asked. The Soviet Su-9 had come on line in 1959, and it was reported that this plane was capable of reaching the U-bird's altitude.[248]

"Were you barraged?" asked someone else. "And if so, how come we heard that you flamed out and were descended to 36,000 feet?"

"How about those reports of MiGs?"

"Other parachutes were reported. Is that true?"

Somebody laughingly interjected, "I can hear it now:

> *'Captain Igor, you must take off immediately; the intruder is coming.'*
>
> *'Nyet, I don't have a pressure suit and I've been partying all night.'*
>
> *'Take off immediately; that's an order.' And off he goes, supersonic and climbing.*
>
> *'Captain, the intruder is at twelve o'clock. Comrade General orders you to get him.'*
>
> *'Nyet, I have no missiles.'*
>
> *'Ram him. Ram him. That's an order. Your mother will receive the Order of the Red Banner.'[249]*
>
> *'My mother is dead.'"*

---

[248] The Su-9 was a single-engine, all-weather, missile-armed interceptor aircraft developed by the Soviet Union. It was put into use in 1959 and retired during the 1970s.

[249] First established in 1918 during the Russian Civil War, the Order of the Red Banner was a military honor of the USSR earned by almost all high-ranking military commanders.

"Seriously," someone said after we all had a good laugh. "Why all the mystery?"

We settled down and Powers regained the floor. He found out later, he said, that many missiles were fired, but it was the first one that got him. Meanwhile, the air force scrambled three MiG-19s. The Russians, believing the intruder was lower than they thought, fired more missiles, but it was actually the MiGs they were painting. One MiG was shot down, and although the pilot was able to eject, he was found dead in his parachute. This incident only fueled the fires between warring Soviet fighter and missile group commanders, but Premier Khrushchev had scored a propaganda coup like no other, and he played the Americans like a fiddle.

Of course, at this point Gary had no information about his fate, but in the outside world, much was happening. While he was being flown to Lubyanka Prison in Moscow, it was becoming apparent to the Americans that something had happened. Immediately the Agency began floating a prearranged story about a NASA weather aircraft going down somewhere in Turkey.

The next day, Khrushchev reported to the Soviet Central Committee that an aircraft had been shot down, but he said nothing about the fate of the plane or the pilot. The Americans became bolder in their dispatches of a missing weather research aircraft, hoping that the brave pilot was silent—in other words, dead!

On May 7th, Khruschev sprang his trap on the world. I can just hear what he might have said to the Central Committee to prepare them: "My comrades, I must tell you a secret. When making my report to you immediately after the spy plane of the Yankee dogs crashed on our soil, I did not mention the status of the plane or the pilot. This was deliberate; had we told everything at once, the Americans would have invented another version. But now, now I am happy to report—to you and to the press—that we have parts of the plane in our possession, and that the pilot, a young American named Gary Powers, is quite alive and kicking."

Even after Khruschev revealed his hand, the U.S. issued another press release denying the charges. Finally, on May 9th, Eisenhower took full responsibility for the U-2 program, admitting that he had authorized the overflights as a means of gaining knowledge about the Soviet military-industrial buildup.

The communists had scored a propaganda victory unequalled in modern history. It affected not only the United States, but also Pakistan, Norway, Turkey, and the British. The summit scheduled for Paris on May 16th was scuttled, and the world plunged into some of the darkest days of the Cold War.

Powers prepared himself as best he could for the possibilities of punishment. What would they do to him? A firing squad? Torture? Pulling his fingernails out one by one until he told all and then some? A good guy-bad guy interrogation, as he'd been trained for in survival school?

None of this came to pass. Instead, he was drilled relentlessly for 61 days, his interrogators hoping to trick him into saying something incriminating. His line of defense was simple: tell the truth, muck up some of the salient facts, and hope for the best. The only time he broke down, he said, was when he was quoted a news story that said his father was personally going to petition the Premier for mercy.

During his first week in captivity, he was shown the headlines from several American newspapers, including the *New York Times*. Fortunately, the facts about the U-2 program revealed in the papers told more about the aircraft and the mission than he had admitted, making his future storytelling parameters much broader. The thing he was determined not to reveal was the U-2's most important secret: how high it could fly. When he was hit, Gary claimed, he was at 68,000 feet, the maximum altitude of the plane. The Russians seemed to buy it.

"May I see a representative of the American Embassy?" he asked.

"*Nyet.*"

"May I see a representative of the Red Cross?"

"*Nyet.*"

He was assigned a lawyer, Mikhail I. Grinev. A state appointee, Grinev's claim to fame was that he'd never won a case he wasn't supposed to, although, Gary commented laughingly, he didn't learn this until much later.

Powers had no legal rights. Everything that our forefathers had written into our Constitution was null and void in the USSR. The government ran both sides of the trial process.

He was also held in solitary confinement, and if other English-speaking prisoners were in the prison, he never saw or heard them. The interrogations went on and on.

"Mr. Powers, the *New York Times* says that you took a lie detector test prior to entering the Agency, and you said earlier that you had not."

"Ah, that may be true for agents but not for pilots," Gary replied.

"The American newspapers say that you were flying at 100,000 feet, and you say that the maximum altitude of the plane was 68,000 feet. What say you?"

Gary looked at them in all seriousness. "The newspapers weren't flying the plane; I was. Could you have shot me down at 100,000 feet?" That seemed to satisfy them.

In between interrogations, he was fed, allowed to exercise, and even given mysteries to read. He figured he was safe for a while, at least until the show trial took place, and the interrogations provided a break from solitary confinement.

The Russians kept returning to two issues: Why hadn't he activated the destruct device, and why hadn't he used the poison pin? They insinuated that the destruct device was on a short fuse, designed to kill the pilot instantly, and that Powers didn't trust the Agency. None of this was true. They accused him of not using the poison pin as ordered. That also was untrue; it was optional to take along and optional to use.

The trial was to commence on August 17th, and Gary's parents and his wife Barbara were in attendance. Oliver Powers, Gary's dad, was a cobbler from hill-country Virginia. The last time he'd been any distance from home was when he went to Atlanta and Washington in 1935. Now his son was at the center of a world conflict.

The Hall of Columns was a Moscow showplace. Stalin and Lenin had lain in state here, and many celebrities had graced its stage. Now the Hall was set to host yet another show, this one perhaps its most famous yet: Francis Gary Powers versus the USSR, East versus West. For now, at least, East held all the cards.

The trial lasted for three long, grueling days. The prosecutor, Roman Rudenko, was organized, prepared, and eager to turn much of the available information into a propaganda bazaar. He used all the Soviet-speak that comedians used in their free-world acts, only with deadly purpose.[250]

Finally Grinev, Powers' defense lawyer, had his say. Had there not been so much at stake, Gary said, it would have been laughable. Grinev, too, used Soviet-speak, twisting Gary's words into statements he never made and twisting the comments he did make into anti-American propaganda.

The newspapers blared that Powers was profoundly sorry he had any part in the spy flight. "Yeah," Gary said to the group of us gathered 'round the table at Davis-Monthan. "I was sorry, all right. I was sorry that the flight was unsuccessful."

Grinev wanted him to declare that he "deeply regretted and personally repudiated the aggressive, war-making designs of the United States." He drew the line on that bit of anti-American rhetoric, although the defense

---

[250] Roman Andreyevich Rudenko (1907–1981) had been the chief Soviet prosecutor at the Nuremberg trials after the Second World War. These trials, held from November 1945 until October 1946, tried some of the most important captured leaders of Nazi Germany.

lawyer included a lot of this gibberish in his final arguments. Most observers considered the source and dismissed it.

The time for the sentencing was at hand. Gary wanted to live, yet he feared the horrors of a Russian prison. After the usual bit of propaganda flourish, the sentence was announced: three years of prison followed by seven years in a work camp. At least he wouldn't be shot.

The Powers family was given a short time together, chaperoned, of course. His dad Oliver was feisty; his mother Ida ill and worried. Barbara and Gary tried to work out the future as best they could in the short time allowed, discussing mundane things like how to ship the furniture from Turkey to the U.S. and whether or not to sell the car. Afterward, Gary was transferred to Vladimir Prison, 150 miles east of Moscow.

As he relived his days of interrogation and the trial, Gary felt he had conducted himself honorably and honestly. If he'd won any victory at all, it was selling the Russians on the fact that 68,000 feet was the maximum altitude of the U-2. Anyone with any real connection to the program would know that if he could sell that, other facts were mucked up as well.

Not long after the trial, his captors burst into his cell. According to an article in the *New York Times*, Gary's father had given a talk to the Overseas Press Club in which he stated that his son doubted a missile had shot him down. Oliver must have misunderstood the testimony during the trial. To the Soviets, the *Times* article was a huge affront to their ego. It was vital that they be given the credit for shooting down the U-2, and they wanted the facts stated correctly. Would Gary please write a letter to the *Times* and restate the event? He complied.

After his release from prison a couple years later, he read the editor's comment printed under his letter: "Military experts here said that 68,000 feet—the altitude at which Soviet reports have consistently said the plane was downed—was substantially under the maximum altitude of the aircraft, a fact that should have been known to Mr. Powers."

Aaaaaagh! Powers had built his main line of defense on protecting that information, which, unbeknown to him, had obviously been for naught. The *Times* editor had smelled a rat, but in the arena of world intrigue, nothing is as it seems.

To the Soviets with their bluster and pride, building a successful SAM that could kill at any altitude was of strategic military importance and national pride. The hint that they'd failed, and that Powers had crashed from some other event, was unacceptable.

On the other hand, the fact that the Soviets could shoot down a high-flying U.S. aircraft was devastating news to the military-industrial complex in America. This meant that our vast bomber fleet, if and when it was called upon to attack, was in grave jeopardy. Even more critical was that the XB-70, a high-flying, supersonic bomber of the future, had just been rendered obsolete.[251]

Life in a Prison Cell

Vladimir was a typical Russian prison, a place where political prisoners were segregated from each other and from the rest of the common criminals. Gary was allowed letters from Barbara and from his parents, and each month he could receive a care package with some foodstuffs and books. Occasionally he was taken to a room where he could watch a poorly done movie or exercise. The rest of the time he spent in his cell, a room 12 feet long by 8 feet wide, with a wooden floor, a window at one end, and a naked lightbulb hanging from the curved ceiling.

Before being transferred from Lubyanka, Gary said, he'd been asked if he wanted a cell by himself or one with a roommate. Knowing that loneliness could be his worst enemy, he requested a roommate. Pushing his luck, he added that he'd like one who spoke English.

The roommate he got was Zigurd Kruminsh (pronounced Zoo-gurd Crewmage), a Latvian political prisoner who'd chosen the German army as the lesser of two evils during World War II. After the war he'd been inserted back into Latvia by the British to gather information, but he'd been betrayed. Not only did Zigurd speak English, Gary said, he spoke Russian, Latvian, and German along with some Esperanto and French, and he was studying Spanish. He turned out to be an interesting guy and a good cellmate, and he told stories of war deprivation and cruelty that Powers had only read about and could barely believe.

Gary described prison as boring, cold, and endless. The food was repetitious—potato and cabbage daily—with an occasional bit of meat and a fish soup that would choke a maggot. His vision suffered from loss of nutrients; when Zigurd's parents sent some vitamins, it helped.

He had an almost limitless selection of "approved" reading materials, including socialist books and periodicals such as the *Daily Worker*, and he learned to play chess with some skill. Zigurd tried to teach him Russian and for a while Gary did well. As time went on, however, he became depressed

---

[251] The North American XB-70 Valkyrie was a nuclear-armed bomber designed for the Strategic Air Command in the 1950s. Although the program was cancelled in 1961, two prototypes were built in 1960. One crashed; the other is on display in the National Museum of the U.S. Air Force in Dayton, OH.

and was unable to concentrate. Could he survive three years in Vladimir Prison? He had grave doubts. He hoped for a pardon, a swap, or at least an early transfer to a work camp to keep his mind and body together. He wasn't harassed, and though he believed that other prisoners knew of him and his exploits, he hardly ever saw them except at a distance.

Even prior to the shoot down, Barbara and Gary's marriage had been troubled. Separation only made matters worse, and Barbara wrote less and less. However, in one very welcome letter, she said that she and his father had explored the possibility of a swap for the only eligible Soviet prisoner that America held, Colonel Rudolph Abel. There was one huge hitch in the plan, however. The Russians had never claimed Abel as one of their spies. To take it even further, they didn't even admit they used spies.[252]

President Kennedy was elected a little more than six months after Powers was shot down, and Gary said the change in administration filled him with anticipation. Maybe, he thought, he'd be released as a goodwill gesture. In reality, he was an insignificant figure by that time; all the propaganda value had been wrung out of him.

When Kennedy met with Khrushchev in January of 1961 in Austria, he did poorly, and the Bay of Pigs fiasco in April of the same year caused yet another ripple in diplomacy between the superpowers. Gary became more and more depressed. He worried about the strain on his father, who was working hard for his release; about his mother, who was ill; and about Barbara, who was having emotional problems. Letters and a monthly package from home, plus packages and books from the American Embassy, were the only things that kept his spirits alive.

Release and Reality

One morning in February of 1962, approximately 22 months after he was shot down, Powers was told to pack his few belongings. Later that day he said goodbye to his friend Zigurd and was whisked from Moscow to Berlin. The Glienicke Bridge, separating Berlin from Potsdam and East from West, was one of the few places Americans and Soviets could geographically face

---

[252] Rudolph Abel was the alias taken by William Fischer (1903–1971). (The real Rudolph Abel, who was at one time Fischer's roommate, died in 1955.) Fischer's parents were Germans who had been born in Russia but later emigrated to England. Fischer received his British citizenship in 1921, but shortly thereafter, the family returned to Russia. Fischer had a long history of espionage before he was placed in the U.S. in 1948 to reorganize the communist spy network and set up a system of radio communications with Moscow. In 1955, he was betrayed by an associate and arrested by the FBI.

each other directly, without involving one of their allies. On this bridge, on February 10, 1962, Gary Powers was exchanged for Russian spy Rudolph Abel. When the exchange was completed, Gary said, the Americans whooped with joy. The communists gave Abel an emotionless reception.

Powers had access to some news during his imprisonment, but most of it had come from Russian periodicals, so he had no idea what kind of reception to expect. After a flight back to the States in some luxury, enjoying good food and friendly faces, he was confined to a CIA safe house for a three-week debriefing. During this time, he started reading the press releases and comments from people who should have known better. Many of them cast doubt on his patriotism, courage, and integrity; and the government, who knew the true facts, did little to help.

To make matters worse, the agents who were interrogating him weren't directly associated with the overflight program. They didn't exactly accuse him of anything, but they didn't seem to believe many of his explanations, either. They asked probing questions about the poison pin. There was never a direct accusation about the fact that he hadn't taken his own life—U-2 pilots had never been advised about this one way or the other. All they'd been told was that the pin was a convenience in case the torture became unbearable. To the agents interrogating Gary, however, there seemed to be an underlying expectation that he should have used it.

They also kept coming back to the question of the destruct switch and why he didn't activate it prior to bailing out. Rumor and innuendo, mostly from uninformed reporters and politicians, posited that the switch was designed to blow up the aircraft. In reality, Gary said, the destruct device was ill-conceived at best. If he'd activated it without being able to eject within 70 seconds, he'd have been killed. After he bailed out over the side, he was unable to reach it, but even if he had, its 2½-pound charge wouldn't have been large enough to eliminate the tightly wound film and cameras. It was simply a non-issue. Accusations that his plane was being tracked by American radar were also outrageous. The technology didn't even exist.

As Gary told us this story, he appeared calm and rational. After all, he'd told it many times, to many people. When he started to talk about the time after his release, however, he became more emotional. His eyes narrowed, showing the strain. It was obvious he still felt the pain of his lukewarm reception. Although he didn't say so, I got the distinct impression from what I'd heard and read elsewhere, that he'd have been a lot more welcome if he'd arrived home in a coffin.

Many people could not forgive him, Gary said, for saying that he was "deeply repentant and profoundly sorry," but it was only half the sentence.

Anyone with brains could have filled in the unspoken sentiment: *that I did not complete the mission successfully*.

He was also asked repeatedly if he'd been drugged. He hadn't. Someone in the press—ours or theirs—insinuated that he had negotiated defection. Ridiculous! Those in the Agency knew; they were also very aware of what he didn't reveal.

One press commentator even compared Powers' trial to that of Rudolph Abel, suggesting that Powers spilled his guts and Abel didn't testify at all. The difference, of course (which only shows the ignorance of the commentator), was that Abel was tried under the American system of justice and didn't have to testify. Under Russian law, this was not the case. Should Powers have attempted to clam up, the situation would have been much worse for him and for the United States. No doubt he'd have rotted in jail or gone before the firing squad.

Later, Gary said, he met with a Senate Armed Services Select Committee. The committee was chaired by Senator Richard Russell of Georgia, and its members included Senators Prescott Bush of Connecticut and Barry Goldwater of Arizona. The senators listened quietly, questioned him, and commented on the mission. At the end of his testimony, Senator Russell thanked Gary for being a patriot and for a job well done. In unison, the committee gave him a standing ovation. Senator Goldwater handed him a pencil-written note: "You did a good job for your country. Thanks. Barry Goldwater."[253]

Allen Dulles, former head of the CIA, also thanked him for a job well done.[254]

President Kennedy ignored him.

John McCone, a wealthy businessman and newly appointed head of the CIA, snubbed him.[255]

I asked Gary if he had any recriminations or regrets.

"No," he answered thoughtfully. "I did my best." Then he paused. "It sure would have been nice, though, if Ike had invited me through the backdoor of his farm at Gettysburg and given me a pat on the back."

---

[253] Richard B. Russell (1897–1971) represented the state of Georgia in the U.S. Senate from 1933 until his death in 1971. At the time he died, he was the most senior member of the Senate. Prescott Bush (1885–1972) served in the U.S. Senate from 1952 until 1963. He was the father of George H. W. Bush, the 41st U.S. President and the grandfather of George W. Bush, the 43rd President.

[254] Allen Dulles resigned from the CIA in 1961.

[255] John McCone (1902–1991) served as the head of the CIA from 1961 until 1965 under Presidents Kennedy and Johnson. In 1987 he was awarded the Presidential Medal of Freedom by President Ronald Reagan.

Despite the fact that the CIA overflight missions may well have saved the world from accidental destruction, Powers was a tainted hero, yet his only mistake had been to survive. As I drove home that night, I hoped that someday our nation would mature enough to properly recognize the patriotism above and beyond that was demonstrated by Francis Gary Powers. He and his fellow CIA pilots risked everything to gather the information the country needed to fight the Cold War and maintain the peace. They did their jobs with valor and without question. But when it was time for the country to support one of them, we were found wanting.[256]

---

[256] CIA documents declassified in the late 1990s, plus the discovery in 2006 of the notes of Powers' interrogation in Moscow, provided irrefutable vindication of Powers' conduct as a prisoner. Although questioned for 11 hours a day, Powers said nothing proscribed by the CIA's policy for captured pilots. Francis Gary Powers died in a helicopter accident in 1977. On May 1, 2000, at an event at Beale Air Force Base in northern California, he was posthumously awarded the POW Medal, the DFC (Distinguished Flying Cross), and the CIA Director's Medal for "extreme fidelity and courage in the line of duty." Francis Gary Powers Jr. took a U-2 flight that day, taxiing up to the review stand to accept his father's medals with his mother and sister.

Chapter 80 – Night Flight

1965

Wright," paged the Operations officer, "we need you to swap out a U-2 at Barksdale." Swapping out aircraft for routine maintenance was normal procedure.

"Tomorrow," he continued, "take over the bird in the hangar and bring back the operational one. Oh, and by the way, we'll send your high-flight gear along so you can fly a night-training mission on the return trip."

The next morning I flew to Barksdale Air Force Base near Shreveport, Louisiana, in normal, low-altitude flight gear at about 37,000 feet. It was a beautiful day.

Over the years I'd been in and out of Barksdale several times. I also remember stories that my Uncle Walt, Aunt Carolyn's husband, told about when he'd been based there during the Korean War. Walt was a bombardier on a B-29 that was returning to Barksdale from a routine flight. When they prepared to land, the gear wouldn't extend, a situation made even more harrowing because there was a nuclear weapon on board. The pilots tried every trick in the book, to no avail, so as soon as the fuel was low enough, they made a long, slow final approach, feathering the props just prior to touchdown. Slithering down the foamed runway on its belly, the plane maintained perfect directional control as it came to a halt, after which the many crewmembers sprinted away from the wounded bird.

"What about the bomb?" I'd asked. Weren't you afraid of a big hole in the earth and a mushroom cloud?"

"Well," Walt had said as he puffed on his pipe, "it's true the bomb shape could have exploded, but the nuclear core was kept elsewhere in the plane." It turned out that the nuclear material was not to be loaded into the bomb until right before firing, an eventuality that thankfully never happened.

After delivering the airplane, I spent a couple of days getting checked out for my next mission. I spent the first day with the unit navigator, preparing for the night flight back to Davis-Monthan in minute detail. The following day I rested and then reported to Operations in the early afternoon. This was to be a six-hour practice session using celestial navigation. Flying high above the weather and the jet stream, I'd be using the stars instead of the sun to find my way home.

We hit the mess at Barksdale just before the flight, and it smelled as good as any mess, anywhere: steaks grilling, fried eggs popping, and large jugs of juice, milk, and coffee waiting to be tapped. This time I drank carefully; I was still learning how to balance the moisture within my body so that it came out as sweat instead of having to go through the complex bottle routine.

After the meal, it was on to the mini-physical and then to the physiological unit to get suited up. The suit fit better each time. It was still uncomfortable, but it was also familiar, like an old pair of shoes that pinched, but in a predictable way. After a thorough checkout, we shuffled off to the van and out to the Dragon Lady. I climbed over the rail, waited while the airmen connected me to the various straps, belts, and life-support systems, and stowed the green card, authentication tables, and other paperwork. I then ran my checklists, and after a final check by a master sergeant, I lowered the canopy and an airman pulled the stairs. I started the engine at the appointed time and rumbled to the takeoff position, the blue station wagon and pickup truck trailing behind me.

"Nails One, you're cleared for takeoff," said the controller.

As I did before every takeoff, I cleared my head of everything not relating to the business at hand, reviewed the initial procedures, and said a quick word to the man upstairs: a plan and a prayer. Instinct and training would take over from here, automatically dictating my course of action in both routine and emergency situations. Springtime thunderstorm activity in the area, however, made the flight questionable. The Dragon Lady was delicate and tolerated little turbulence, especially the unpredictable violence encased in thunderheads, so ground radar would inform me of the distance between storms and the path around them.

There was still plenty of space between storms as I rolled down the runway and pulled up to the 45-degree climb position, reveling in the acceleration and the feeling of flying almost straight up. I hardly had to move my head to see the ground fall away. It was almost sundown, and the sky was filled with the shadows of multiple storms. Lightning flickered within each cloud; occasionally a shaft of lightning flashed between the storms, as if the clouds were holding hands. There was barely a sound—not even thunder—only the reassuring whine of the engine as I spiraled in the troughs of clear air. I turned on the autopilot and entered the holding pattern to wait for the exact time to begin the mission.

Prior to departing, I made my final turn to the west and was treated to a sight experienced by few Earthlings. A distinct line, light and multi-hued on one side, dark and brooding on the other, moved rapidly across the sky. Dubbed by pilots "the terminator," this divider between dawn and dusk was one of the most magnificent displays I'd ever seen. As the Earth shaded the sun, it was as if a shaft of light opened to a dark space in the night. Just as quickly it was gone, replaced with a blackness punctuated by bright and unblinking stars.

Leaving the fix with the latitude and longitude set in the sextant for the appointed time, I began running the familiar checks. At the 15-minute check, the navigational star appeared close to the middle of the sextant face, bright and beaming. I centered the star, recorded the slight heading change, and turned the aircraft using the autopilot controller. This was the first check of many as I zigzagged across the country, perfecting another facet of the U-2's operation. I quickly established a routine: 10 minutes of work, 5 minutes of observation. Looking down on a blanket of billowing clouds illuminated by the flashing glow of mature, fading thunderheads was mesmerizing. Gradually the cushion of flickering lights receded to darkness. With only the occasional glow from a town or city, there were now far more stars in the sky than lights on the ground. The radios were silent, tuned to an exclusive, almost unused frequency. I was far above the Earth, navigating by the stars in the blackness of the night and more alone than I'd ever been. As I continued a slow climb to over 70,000 feet, I was at peace with the world and with myself.

The hours slipped by quickly, and soon the green card directed me to tune in St. Johns VOR and begin the long, controlled descent. Before the sun rose over Davis-Monthan I was back and listening to the welcoming words of the tower: "Cleared to land, Nails One." Were it not for the light on the aircraft, I would have been invisible. The squadron station wagon accelerated to a trailing position as I crossed the end of the runway, and the pilot inside began the familiar litany, a ritual even more critical at night when depth-perception is reduced. Ten feet, 5, 4, 3, 2, 1; 6 inches, 6 inches, HOLD IT, hold back, hold back, and then the rumble of the hard wheels at touchdown. I turned off the runway onto the high-speed taxiway and came to a stop. Almost instantly the pickup truck squealed to a stop beside me and the airmen sprang out to reinstall the pogos. Using his coned flashlight, the sergeant in charge snapped a salute and I taxied to the ramp.

The ground support folks helped me unhook, struggle down the ladder, and unfasten my helmet. Filled with subdued accomplishment and profound gratitude, I turned down the beer in favor of a glass of water. It was a flight I would treasure always.

I shed the suit, took a hot shower, dressed, and drove home. The feeling of awe went with me, but I still spent the rest of the night scratching.

Chapter 81 – Chuck Maultsby's Story

1965

The Christmas of 1956, when I was newly enlisted and stationed at Otis Air Force Base on Cape Cod, I was selected to be "airman of the day." Christmas was a day everyone wanted to be off, but since I was both new and single, it was my turn in the hopper. In later years as a young officer, still new and still single, I was again assigned Christmas duty as junior officer of the day. Even after I was promoted to captain, with a wife and three kids, I somehow continued to come up as the junior officer. Christmas 1965 was no different.

Lt. Colonel Chuck Maultsby, 1968. (*Courtesy of Jeanne Maultsby.*)

I reported to headquarters early. The senior officer of the day was Lt. Colonel Chuck Maultsby. Perhaps he was also newly promoted, thus becoming the more junior of the senior ranks. We chuckled about our respective positions and the luck of the draw that made us responsible for monitoring the worldwide intelligence network of the 4080th SRW. As luck had it, the world must have had a Christmas truce that day. Not even the phone rang.

It was a cold day for Tucson, and as we drank endless cups of coffee Chuck made some comment about the Thunderbirds. I knew he'd been a member of that vaunted demonstration team, and this seemed the perfect time for a good story. I began to ask him about his past experiences.

The Thunderbird team was made up of the most select group of pilots in the air force. To be a member took more than skill; it demanded an instinctive pilot with unusual talent, coupled with the commitment and desire to learn the complicated routines of aeronautical beauty. Chuck and I had flown together a few times in the T-33, and we always ended up in a competition of derring-do. During these times, I continued to be amazed at the smoothness and accuracy of Chuck's aero displays. And yet like many who are true experts, he was always complimentary of my skills while downplaying his own.

"When did you join the air force?" I asked.

"During the Korean War," he replied.

"What did you fly?"

"F-80s."

"Get any kills?" (I don't remember his answer, but if not, it would have been due to lack of opportunity rather than lack of skill.)

"I was shot down," he added.

"How did you get out?"

"I didn't. I spent a long time as a POW." As he said this, I could see the grimace on his face, and we didn't pursue the subject. Later I found out that he'd suffered all the hell the North Koreans could throw at him in the icy caves of the camps.

"How the heck did you go from flying shows on the deck to flying U-2s in the stratosphere?" I asked.

Chuck explained that on his last tour of shows with the Thunderbirds, they'd done a performance in Panama. As they were preparing to depart for the States, a U-2 took off ahead of them. The sinister black aircraft launched in less than 1,000 feet, climbed out at a 45-degree angle, and disappeared within moments. Chuck's time as a member of the Thunderbirds was almost up, and the U-2 looked like an interesting airplane. Besides, this wasn't long after Gary Powers had been shot down over the USSR, and Powers' salary had been well-publicized.

The departing Thunderbird pilots had their pick of assignments, and Chuck volunteered for U-2 service. At that time, the SRW was based at Laughlin Air Force Base in Del Rio, Texas. Chuck reported for duty and met with Colonel Des Portes, the wing commander. The colonel briefed him about the wing, its mission, and the generalities of the airplane. When he finished, Chuck knew that the initial briefing was complete, yet he hesitated to leave.

"Any further questions?" asked the colonel.

"Yes, Sir, I have a couple," Chuck replied. Then, with some reluctance, he inquired if the unit provided an allowance for civilian clothes and how soon it would be before he started receiving the special bonus for flying the U-2.

The colonel, first with a look of confusion and then with amusement, said, "Son, you've been reading too many newspapers. The mission you maybe thought you were volunteering for was CIA, the details of which are only divulged on a need-to-know basis. You're working for the U.S. Air Force. Here we wear uniforms and U-2 pilots draw the same pay as any other jet jockey."

Chuck leaned back and slapped his knee. I'm not sure if he'd actually fallen for that scenario, but it was his story and he loved to tell it. We both roared with laughter.

We had all day to kill, and soon I asked Chuck to describe his most memorable U-2 mission. I loved listening to war stories. Not only were they interesting, but they often provided a snippet of information that, coupled with odds and ends gleaned elsewhere, made life more convenient, solved a problem, or in extreme cases, saved a life.

It didn't take much for Chuck to settle into his tale.

"It was 1962, and at that time the unit had three main objectives for its missions: photographic, electronic, and HASP (the High-Altitude Sampling Program). The photographic part is self-explanatory. Electronically, we were supposed to gather a sampling of footprints that could be used to counter and create electronic eavesdropping. The air sampling part was multifaceted, but the most immediate need was to track the radioactivity of atomic blasts. At the time the French were blowing up hydrogen bombs in the South Pacific. We had a base in Australia to monitor the tests themselves; our job in the U-2 was to track the path and intensity of the fallout. The USSR was also conducting tests, which were being monitored from Eielson Air Force Base in Alaska. Sometimes we were able to gather information on fallout from both sites in the same mission.

On the day in question, Chuck was flying out of Eielson, collecting radioactive air samples. He flew to the North Pole, an intricate event in and of itself. At the Pole the aircraft compasses were rendered useless due to the strength of the magnetic pull, and no radio aids were available at these extreme latitudes. Chuck had to rely on a system of grid navigation, using the sextant for input, a process that complicated the entire navigational situation and introduced a much higher chance of error.[257]

The aircraft was equipped with tubes to store and record air samples, and the mission, a long flight of approximately 3,000 nautical miles, was basically a round trip to the North Pole.

"Sounds like one long, lonely mission," I commented.

---

[257] Eielson, near Fairbanks, AK, has its origins in the U.S. Army airfield Mile 26, which opened in 1943 and closed at the end of World War II. The field reopened in 1946 and in 1948 was designated Eielson Air Force Base in honor of Carl Ben Eielson (1897–1930), an Alaskan aviator who made the first flight from North America to Europe over the North Pole in 1928. As of 2008, it remains an active air force base.

"It was, but we all knew the hazards, and a support aircraft—a DC-4 with navigators and rescue personnel aboard—would be standing by. These guys were in on the mission briefing, but when I asked one of the jumpers what he would do if he had to bail out over the Arctic, he quipped, 'I wouldn't pull the ripcord.'"

Chuck allowed as how it was probably as lonely and dangerous as any mission in the unit. Navigation alone was a huge challenge. And if he ran out of things to worry about, he could always contemplate his chances of survival if he were to flame out or the aircraft fail in one of the most inhospitable places on Earth. What a combination: one sinister-looking airplane, one lonely pilot sitting on top of a single engine on top of the world, and navigation tools that had been around for centuries. The Q-bay, however, was stocked with emergency survival gear.

"I'll bet that was a comfort," I commented with a laugh.

The mission profile was typical: 15-minute cycles of activity during which the pilot was to navigate; shoot the stars and make minor corrections as needed; manage the fuel and aircraft systems; and record everything on the green card. On this mission Chuck also had to control the air-sampling units, but he would be neither rushed nor bored.

The only available radio beacon was on Barter Island, a four-mile by two-mile speck in the Beaufort Sea off the coast of Alaska. *Duck Butt*, the accompanying DC-4, would hang around this spot in case it was needed for rescue and/or advice. Soon after passing Barter Island, Chuck saw streaks of light penetrate the sky. The farther north he went, the more brilliant the display. Although intensely beautiful, the aurora borealis was masking the stars, many of them the same stars Chuck needed for navigation to maintain proper heading and timing.

Finally he reached the North Pole and reversed course, heading back to Eielson.

The next time he shot a star, he realized that it was too small and too dim to be the star it was supposed to be. Ohmagod! Suspicions confirmed! He broke out in a cold sweat as he realized he was probably lost. Since all directions from the North Pole are south, he had no clue as to where he was in this world. He could be going south in any one of 360 directions.

Chuck broke radio silence and declared an emergency.

Mayday! Mayday!! Mayday!!!

Radio contact was sporadic and weak, but Chuck could just hear *Duck Butt*. "Where is the belt of Orion located?" the DC-4 queried.

Chuck looked out and located the famous star group. "To my left," he replied.

"Turn left and continue climbing," the voice on the radio ordered with some alarm. He continued climbing as light began to break in the East.

"Keep climbing," the voice continued to encourage, and Chuck took his U-bird as high as one has probably ever flown. Later he learned the reason for *Duck Butt's* concern. In the confusion caused by the vagaries of nature, he'd accidentally flown hundreds of miles into Russian airspace, and several Russian fighters had been trying to shoot him down.

Once again he declared an emergency, this time on an international emergency channel. Were he an aggressor, he would not be declaring an emergency, so this seemed the most appropriate course of action. This may have been one the luckiest transmissions ever made, because at the time President Kennedy and Premier Khrushchev were playing chicken over the placement of Soviet missiles in Cuba. Every nuclear weapons system in the world was cocked and aimed at preplanned targets. Our B-52s and B-47s were airborne and in holding patterns worldwide, ready to attack. Aircraft had been dispatched to innumerable airstrips, tactical nuclear fighters that were ready to launch when the flag went up.

Ironically, three hours before Chuck was being talked out of Soviet territory by the men on the DC-4, U-2 pilot Major Rudolph Anderson, Chuck's close friend, was shot down over Cuba. Major Anderson was killed and subsequently awarded the Air Force Cross, the nation's second-highest award, but Mr. Murphy and his law didn't win the day. Another Irishman, this one by the name of Kennedy, eventually convinced Khruschev to back down. The Soviets removed the missiles, but the world had come closer to nuclear disaster than most people would ever know.[258]

Chuck, climbing high above the world and trying to figure out what to do next, was unaware of these events. Eventually he reached fuel starvation and shut down the engine, saving a few pounds for eventual landing. Silence. The pressure suit filled as advertised, and he established a glide. The glide ratio was as high as any aircraft flying. He shut off the battery to save it for radio use at a lower altitude and prepared for a long, quiet ride. The cockpit canopy had frozen over, so after descending to a much lower altitude, he scraped a hole in the ice. Shadowing him were two F-102s, traveling at a speed close to a stall in order to stay abreast. Chuck flipped on the battery and the radio.

"Hello there, F-102," he said.

"Follow me," said one of them. "The whole state of Alaska is undercast; we'll lead you to a safe ejection place."

One of the fighters staggered off the wing. He'd stalled due to the low

---

[258] Other U-2 pilots flying this "13 Days of October" Cuban mission received the Distinguished Flying Cross.

speed of the U-bird. "As long as I'm down here," the fighter radioed with a chuckle in his voice, "I'll check for a local army field."

The fighter soon called back excitedly. "It's unbelievable. There's a break in the undercast directly over a 2,000-foot army field. Do you want to punch out or land, Sir?" As far as Chuck was concerned, that was twice as much runway as he needed, so he spiraled down, counted off the many key altitudes, and landed on the short, icy army strip. The aircraft was unharmed, and except for being in dire need of a pee and about a gallon of hot coffee, so was Chuck.

Thus ended what was possibly the longest un-refueled mission in the colorful history of the U-2. I didn't ask, but I imagine, as he waited in the cold cockpit for assistance after landing, Chuck was having a thanksgiving that didn't need a radio to communicate. There are no atheists in foxholes.

After a very short rest, he was flown to Offutt Air Force Base in Omaha, Nebraska, for a private debrief with SAC's commanding general and head navigator, both of whom were astounded that the mission had been conducted with such antiquated equipment. However, until electronic navigation was perfected, it was the best we had.[259]

Chuck Maultsby was a skilled yet humble fighter/reconnaissance pilot, a proud American who was the point of the arrow in our nation's defense. He did his job with vigor and joy, and he was a great storyteller to boot!

---

[259] Offutt started life as Fort Cook, a U.S. Army depot commissioned by the War Department in 1890. Troops from the Army Air Corps arrived at Ft. Cook in 1918, and an airfield was built there as a refueling stop. In the 1920s, the field was named Offutt Field in honor of Jarvis Offutt, a Nebraskan killed in France during the war while flying for the Royal Air Force. The facility was renamed Offutt Air Force Base in 1948 and is still an active base in 2008.

Chapter 82 – Angst and Opportunity

1966

When it came to breakfast, Polly could compete with the best of the mess hall cooks. I was mopping up the last of my eggs and watching Tim, one of the 18-month-old twins, polish my flight boots with bacon grease. (At least it was cheaper than butter.) Five-year-old Walt, six-gun and cowboy hat in place, was trying to ride Tucson the Airedale, whose patience seemed inexhaustible.

"Andy," I heard Polly screech, as she retrieved the other twin from the living room and marched him into the kitchen by the ear. It didn't take long to discover his morning trick. He was laughing with glee, chewing on a piece of ivory he'd just peeled from Polly's piano key.

A normal morning at the homestead.

I was eager to get to work—anything they could throw at me would be easier than this—when the mailman rang the doorbell with a special delivery letter.

Polly plopped the envelope on the table and herded the troops into the padded playroom, which was almost bulletproof. After sipping the dregs of my coffee I ripped at the envelope. "Look, Polly," I yelped. "It's a letter from American Airlines with a ticket enclosed."

I picked up the letter and read aloud. "Dear Captain Wright: You have been selected from our many applicants to interview for the position of pilot. …Please report to Captain John Chenault's office at Los Angeles International Airport on Monday morning at 0800 for an interview and testing."

Polly grinned. Was she having a flashback to her carefree days as a stewardess?

Before we knew it, it was Sunday afternoon. Dressed in my Class A blue uniform, I bounded up the stairs of a gleaming American Airlines B-727, its silver fuselage emblazoned with an orange lightning bolt. I was greeted by a cheerful stewardess who seated me in first class and offered me a drink.

Within moments she was back. "The guys up front want to talk to you," she said.

I stepped into the cockpit with its familiar smells and sounds. The captain was a grizzled vet, a World War II type with eyes that had squinted through a thousand sunsets. The first officer and the engineer, now drinking coffee and trading jibes with the stews, were young guys about my age. Each of them gave me a smile.

"Going for an interview?" asked the first officer.

"Yep, does it show?"

"Not really, but these days we have recruits on almost every flight that's anywhere near a military town," he replied. "I spent eight years in the air force myself. Enjoyed most of it until I pulled a tour in Vietnam flying SPADs. That was the most screwed up operation I've ever seen. When I got back, American Airlines made me an offer I couldn't refuse, and I was promoted to first officer in less than six months. I was proud to be an air force officer, but I'm ecstatic about this airline."[260]

"How about you?" I asked the flight engineer.

"Ditto. I didn't go to Nam, but I spent many an hour on alert flying B-52s. They treated us well in SAC, but here we're treated like kings. Plus I'm a bachelor, and this is hog heaven for the likes of us."

About that time the captain piped in. "I'll guarantee this beats the heck out of flying B-17s over Germany," he added with a chuckle.

I returned to my seat feeling great. Maybe this airline gig's a good idea after all.

Monday morning found me circling the building where I was to be interviewed. I wanted to check out the exact location. In this type of business, it pays to be on time. At 0800, I popped through the door and was greeted by an attractive Asian receptionist.

"Captain Wright. I'm so pleased that you could come." She invited me to sit down and handed me a cup of coffee. "Would you like a doughnut?"

Wow, this was certainly not the perfunctory military greeting. "Sure," I replied with enthusiasm.

The receptionist was charming and inquisitive. We had a cheerful conversation as she asked about my family and where I was from.

"So what about you?" I asked. "Are you from California? How long have you worked for American? Do you like the airline?"

Her friendly answers were "yes," "five years," and "very much."

We yakked for a few more minutes before she excused herself and picked

---

[260] SPAD was the nickname given to the Douglas A-1 Skyraider, a single-seat fighter bomber designed late in World War II and used extensively in Korea and Vietnam. The original SPAD was a World War I biplane.

up the phone. "Captain Chenault, I have Air Force Captain Don Wright here in my office, and I think you'll enjoy talking with him."

"Send him in, please," was the friendly reply.

I just realized I'd been screened, and delightfully so.

The receptionist escorted me to the captain's office, introduced me, and excused herself.

Captain Chenault, the chief pilot for American Airlines at Los Angeles Airport, was an impressive man. He carried himself well and he immediately put me at ease. After offering a refill on my coffee, he joked that if his receptionist sent me in, I was as good as hired. As we started to talk, he looked through my papers, asking about various aspects of my career. When he came upon my U-2 record, his voice lit up and he wanted a thumbnail sketch of the U-bird.

"How high will it go?" he asked. Of course, this was almost always the first question from anyone, and since it was classified information, I'd gotten pretty good at dancing around the answer. My favorite was Gary Powers' famous quote: "not high enough."

After we'd talked for about a half hour, he said, "Don, as far as I'm concerned, you're hired, but we do have go through the formality of the stanine tests and the physical, so let's set you up for tomorrow. Any questions?"

"Yes, Sir," I replied. "I'd like to know more about my opportunities here."

He assumed a thoughtful stance. "American is a world pioneer in the business and is greatly respected by the public and within the airline community. I won't go into a long history, but I do want to explain what management and the pilots' union have done to make this a very desirable job.

"When I started many years ago, there was an adversarial relationship between management and flight personnel. The captain was compensated well, but the copilot and engineer were treated poorly, with frequent furloughs, low pay, and virtually no benefits. With the advent of jets in the late 1950s, the price of a ticket dropped significantly and the number of available seats tripled. We expected huge layoffs, but it didn't happen. I suppose an economist could explain it better, but once the cost of a seat went down, the traffic zoomed. Today American buys every aircraft the manufacturers can produce, and we need competent pilots to fly them.

"Once business started to increase, the pilots broke away from the national union and formed an in-house association that works fairly and honestly with the company. In fact, even though I'm the chief pilot, I'm also an association member. That's not to say we don't have our problems," he added with a chuckle, "but when we slug it out, we hold hands with one hand and hit with the other.

"Let me give you an example of how we deal with problems. When I started with the airline, it was typical for scheduling to call out a crew at 0600 to fly from New York to Boston. Then they'd have to hang around until 1800 and fly back. That was 14 hours of duty for one hour of pay. If the company does that today, there's a time-versus-pay formula that's agreeable to both parties. Many problems have been solved with negotiated settlements. It's not a perfect system, nor will it ever be, but it's one of the best in the industry, and we keep tweaking it."

He paused to see if I was taking this all in. "Please go on," I said. "It sounds good so far."

"I'm sure you're aware," the captain continued, "that you'll be taking a cut in pay for several years. However, in time you'll be very satisfied. Of course, there are no guarantees. The airlines are a prisoner of national economics and furloughs happen. Moreover, where you're assigned is dependent on the needs of the airline and your seniority, much like the military. That said, I sincerely hope you'll consider joining us."

I thanked Captain Chenault for his time and took my leave. On my way out, the charming receptionist handed me a test schedule for the next day.

After another grueling bout with the stanines—this was the second time I'd taken them, the first being when I joined the air force cadet program, I underwent a difficult physical and was on my way home. The flight back to Tucson was a repeat of the trip to L.A. I talked with the flight crew and came away with the same good feelings.

The Hero's Welcome

I burst through the front door, filled with news and excitement. The car was in the drive, but the house was empty. Obviously, there had been recent activity. The slate floor had a new patina of shoe polish and there was a perfect outline of a young boy's body in the sliding glass door, with shards of glass still stuck to the frame.

The gate to the alley was open and I could hear Polly scolding, along with what sounded like a drum and bugle corps without the bugle. All three boys had wriggled under the fence, where they'd gathered garbage can covers. Using the covers as cymbals, they were marching up and down, with Tucson trailing behind. It was Walt, I learned later, who had run through the door, miraculously escaping injury.

Polly was not happy.

As I reported my adventures, I knew she could relate. Tough as it had been, she'd loved her job as a stewardess for Pan Am. She'd look at both sides of the coin and offer suggestions, but in the end I knew it was my decision. Of course, so far there wasn't a decision to make. I hadn't formally been offered a job.

On Friday afternoon, I received a telegram from Western Union.

CONGRATULATIONS, CAPT. WRIGHT. YOU HAVE BEEN
SELECTED TO JOIN AMERICAN AIRLINES. PLS REPLY ASAP.[261]

Decision time. If the war ended tomorrow, I could be riffed. If the war continued, I'd still have to retire in nine years, start at the bottom of another ladder, and be nine years older to boot. The airline is offering me a 28-year career.

My current contract with the air force was almost up. I'd served nearly 11 years, and the decision seemed clear. I wired my acceptance.

In preparation for the transition, I drove Polly, Walt, the twins, and Tucson to Mississippi. While I was in training with American for three months, she and the boys would stay with her folks. I then returned to Davis-Monthan to close out my air force career.

It was Memorial Day, Monday, May 30, 1966, when I boarded an American Airlines jet on my way to Chicago for training. A stewardess led me to a seat in first class and offered me a drink. As I sipped it, I mused about the roads I'd taken on the way to this newest adventure. From earliest childhood, I'd been blessed with a loving mother and surrounded by a family who cared about me and each other. Living on the farm with Maude and Millard and then traveling the world had given me an ever-changing education and a range of experience that benefited me tremendously. My time in the military would always be one of the most important, happy, and beneficial periods of my life. And there is no place on Earth that affords such freedom and joy as the United States of America. Yes, it has its problems, but it is still the most equitable system of government in the world. For perfection, perhaps, we'll have to wait for the next life.

The door closed and the giant airliner began to taxi, spiriting me to a

---

[261] For more than 100 years, telegrams were a form of "instant message" sent via telegraph through the Western Union Company. Western Union opened its doors in the early 1850s in Rochester, NY, and completed the first transcontinental telegraph line in the early 1860s, an event that ultimately put the Pony Express out of business. Initially telegrams were delivered to the door of the recipient; later on, they were read over the phone. In more recent times, long-distance phone service, cell phones, email, and instant messaging nearly eliminated the demand for telegrams, and in January of 2006, Western Union discontinued the service.

new career with all of its rewards and challenges. *Toward the unknown* read the motto of the 4028th; now it was my motto as well. Just as we took off, I looked out the window. Three miles away at Davis-Monthan, a U-2 screamed into the air.

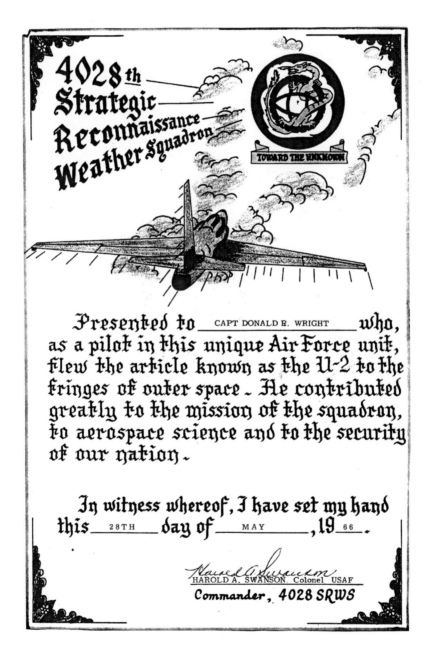

Epilogue

I remember, as I sat on the plane to Chicago in 1966, thinking about the past and the future. During my years in the air force, I'd enjoyed the travel, the opportunities, and the challenges offered to all regardless of background or race. In some ways, my time in the service had been a continuation of my early years as a wanderer and army brat. Now I'd be strictly a civilian, a prospect that left me apprehensive as well as uncomfortable.

My concerns were only temporary. That evening I checked into a hotel in Park Ridge, Illinois. "Mr. Wright," said the clerk. Huh? Then it hit me. As a civilian, I'd lost my title. I'd liked being *Captain* Wright.

"Mr. Wright," he repeated, "the gentleman next to you is going to be your roommate." I turned, stuck out my hand, and laughed. There stood Jim McManus, a longtime friend and fellow instructor from Willie. Jim was a good ole boy from the Southeast, a former sergeant who'd gone to OCS on his way to becoming a pilot. Although he had little formal education, he was one of the smartest men I knew, and he turned out to be a great help to the 20 or so guys in our American Airlines training class.

I was starting at the bottom once again, training to be an engineer on the Lockheed L-188 Electra. The Electra was another fine airplane from the design team of Kelly Johnson, and American Airlines was an even better employer than reported by my friends who'd gone before. The company expected much, but they also appreciated what we had to give. Not unlike the air force, training was ongoing, and almost all advancement was dictated by seniority. In addition, there were leadership paths available outside the seniority system.

My only sobering moment came just after I received my first assignment—Buffalo, New York. That night the 11 o'clock news reported a U-2 missing over Cuba. Based on what I knew about the program, it had to be one of two pilots, both of whom were friends. Later, Robert De De Hickman, perhaps our best friend at Davis-Monthan, was discovered dead; His plane had crashed into a mountain in Bolivia. When I left the air force

533

to join American, De De had taken my slot. The mission on which he was killed would have been mine.

Polly and I and the boys, along with the ever-faithful Tucson, moved to East Aurora. Walt was now five years old and the twins, Tim and Andy, were three. Uncle Walt and Aunt Carolyn and their kids still lived there, and it was great to be back among family. However, Vietnam was becoming a huge dividing line in America. Like many communities across the country, East Aurora was a hotbed of dissention, and it was almost impossible to be neutral. In the air force, the world was still black and white. As a civilian, I realized that murky was a much better description. Adjusting to civilian life was also difficult from a social standpoint. We were used to the camaraderie of the air force family, and civilians were just not that welcoming.

In 1968 we purchased a 50-acre farm in East Concord, just a couple of miles from Grandmother's hometown of Springville, New York. We loved living on the farm, but after a while American reduced the number of flight hours in Buffalo and I started commuting to New York City. At the time, Betty and George were deployed overseas, and they offered us the family home in Cotuit on Cape Cod. We gratefully accepted, but on this move, one of the family was missing. Tucson had been hit and killed by a car on a road near the farm. He was a great dog and we missed him a lot.

It was a hard decision to sell our magnificent farm, but economically it was a godsend. The first year with the airlines was on a probationary basis and carried with it almost starvation wages. Even though Polly taught school as a substitute teacher, we felt the pinch, and it took us years to recover.

After living in Cotuit for a year, we bought a house on Cape Cod in Centerville. We didn't feel comfortable there, either, and to make matters worse, the school system was a disaster. By 1973 we decided to seek out the perfect place for us.

By this time I was a copilot on the Boeing 727, and the captain suggested I look at some small towns in New Hampshire. We visited one he recommended, were treated like royalty, and built a home on a seven-acre lot we purchased near a small ski area. We've lived there happily ever since.

In 1979 I was promoted to captain. I liked being Captain Wright in the civilian world, too, and I was progressing up the seniority list nicely. Then in 1981, the air traffic controllers went on strike. The resulting cutback on the number of flights bumped me back to copilot, first on the McDonnell Douglas DC-10 and then on the 727.

One day in 1983 I ran into my friend Bucko Jewell at DFW (Dallas Fort Worth International Airport). Bucko was now a chief pilot for American.

"Hey, Don," he said. "You were an instructor in the air force, weren't you?"

Here I am in 1966, at the beginning
of my American Airlines career.
(*Painting by D. Coggeshall.*)

"Yep."

"Well, we just leased a fleet of Boeing MD-80s and we need instructors. You interested?"

"You bet," I replied.

As an instructor on the MD-80, the 727, and later the Airbus 300/600, I was back in the captain's seat. I held that job for the next five years. In 1988 I became the liaison between American Airlines and Airbus in Toulouse, France, responsible for coordinating the instruction of our pilots. I'd like to take credit for this but I can't. Polly's fluent French made her a wonderful facilitator during our year in France.

I spent the remaining years of my airline career as an international pilot flying the Boeing 757 and 767.

From the time they were very young, our three sons enjoyed the serenity and stability of living in one place. Tim and Andy had the additional advantage of going to a nearby private school where Polly taught French and Spanish. They all grew to be outstanding adults of whom we are very proud.

Walt graduated from Arizona State University and was commissioned as a second lieutenant in the Marine Corps, eventually flying the fearsome F-4 reconnaissance jet. He left the marines as a captain and is now a successful executive, living in the West with his wife and four wonderful children.

Tim enlisted in the U.S. Coast Guard out of high school and became a coxswain on a rescue boat, serving four years of active duty and three years in the Reserves. He graduated from Emerson College in Boston and is now a pilot for a major airline. His wife works as a pilot for another major airline and they, too, live in the West with their two fine-spirited sons.

Andy went to Lewis and Clark College in Portland, Oregon. He's enjoyed a challenging profession in the advertising business and is now an executive with a major newspaper in New York City. His wife is an executive with an international firm, and they have two fine boys.

My service with the United States Air Force was an unforgettable adventure. My years with American Airlines were less of an adventure, but they were a wonderful, fulfilling career. I retired from American in 1994, and since then, Polly and I continue to enjoy the time we spend with the

Presbyterian Church, the community, and our many hobbies. For several years after retirement, I also worked as a part-time simulator instructor for ATA Airlines. ATA, like several other airlines in these challenging economic times, went bankrupt in April 2008, so perhaps I'm ready for a new adventure once again.

Over the course of my military and civilian flying careers, I logged over 25,000 hours, and my takeoffs equaled my landings. Passengers on my watch always landed safely, and I never bent any metal.

Polly and me at home in 2007.

I played but a minor role in the operation of the U-2 and its critical mission. Soon after I departed the air force, the many government agencies that depended on information gathered through this program realized the importance of the operation. As a result, the plane that was originally envisioned to serve for a short time has undergone several improvements and is still flown today. U-2s of the 21st century are larger and more powerful than the originals, but they are still of the same sleek design created by Kelly Johnson in the Lockheed Skunk Works of the 1950s. In the 53 years since the U-2 flew its first mission, it's a safe assumption that few days have passed when one of these planes has not been monitoring something, somewhere in the world.

Some years ago, the slogan *toward the unknown* was replaced with *in*

God we trust, all others we monitor. As long as there are threats in the world, the U-2, or its equivalent, will continue to be needed. Quietly and without fanfare, the dedicated men and women who fly these planes, along with the skilled crews who support them, watch the world to help maintain the peace. As of 2008, just over 1,000 pilots have flown this spectacular airplane. As the 192nd U-2 pilot, I am proud to have been one of them.

Appendix A – Chronology

The following chronology summarizes the many moves, educational "opportunities," and significant events in my life from birth through when I joined American Airlines in 1966.

Birth – Age 7

August 14, 1934, through summer 1942 – Living in apartments with my mother Betty or at home with my grandparents, Alice and Paul McNerney, at various locations in and around Buffalo, New York; attended 11 different schools through completion of 2nd grade.

Ages 7–9

Summer 1942 through spring 1944 – Living with Maude and Millard Hudson on their farm near Wales Hollow, New York; 3rd and part of 4th grades in a one-room schoolhouse.

Ages 9–10

Spring 1944 through September 1944 – Living with Betty and my grandparents at 30 Park Place, East Aurora, New York; remainder of 4th grade at East Aurora Elementary.

Age 10

September 1944 through June 1945 – Boarding at Linsly Military Institute, Wheeling, West Virginia; 5th grade.

Ages 10–12

June 1945 through February 1947 – Living with my grandparents at 30 Park Place; 6th grade at East Aurora Elementary; part of 7th grade at East Aurora Junior High.

Ages 12–13

February 1947 through March 1948 – Living with Betty in Berlin, Germany; remainder of 7th grade and part of 8th grade in U.S. school for dependents of Allied military and government personnel.

Age 13

>March 1948 through June 1948 – Living with Grandmother at 30 Park Place; remainder of 8th grade at East Aurora Junior High.

>February 17, 1948 – Betty married George Kenna in Panama.

Ages 13–14

>Summer 1948 – Living with Betty and George in Panama.

Ages 14–16

>September 1948 through August 1950 – Living with Betty and George (joined later by Grandmother) in El Paso, Texas; 9th and 10th grades at Austin High School.

>Summers of 1949 and 1950 on Stewart ranch near Santa Elena, Mexico.

Age 16

>September 1950 through October 1950 – Living with Betty, George, and Grandmother in Ayer, Massachusetts; beginning of 11th grade at Ayer High School.

Ages 16–17

>October 1950 through January 1952 – Living with Betty and Grandmother on Nickerson Lane in Cotuit, Massachusetts (George stationed in Japan); remainder of 11th grade and part of 12th grade at Barnstable High School.

>August 1951 – Got driver's license.

Age 17

>February 1952 through June 1952 – Living with Betty and George (joined later by Grandmother) in Yokohama, Japan; graduated from Yokohama High School.

Ages 17–18

>June 1952 through June 1953 – Living with Betty, George, and Grandmother in Yokohama; working as a supervisor for the Totsuka Mail Order Department of the post office. Brother Christopher born shortly before the family returns to the States.

Age 18

>June 1953 – Return from Japan with Betty, George, Chris, and Grandmother.

Ages 18–19

>Summer 1953 – One month on the farm near Wales Hollow, New York,

with Maude and Millard Hudson; remainder of the summer with the family on Nickerson Lane in Cotuit, Massachusetts.

Ages 19–20

September 1953 through June 1955 – Living in Boston; student at Wentworth Institute of Technology. Graduated and earned Airframe and Powerplant Mechanic's license and Ground Instructor's license.

Summer 1954 – Living with Wentworth roommate Jim Miller's folks in Harwich Port, Massachusetts; working at Hyannis Airport.

Ages 20–21

June 1955 through October 14, 1955 – Living with Wentworth roommate Jim Miller in Stratford, Connecticut; working as an engine installer for Sikorsky Helicopter.

Age 21

October 15, 1955, through mid-January 1956 – Sampson Air Force Base, Geneva, New York; joined the U.S. Air Force and completed basic training.

Ages 21–23

January 1956 through October 1957 – Otis Air Force Base, Cape Cod, Massachusetts; working as an A&P mechanic on RC-121 aircraft.

November 1956 – Promoted to airman 2nd class.

Age 23

October 1957 through early January 1958 – Lackland Air Force Base, San Antonio, Texas; cadet/officer pre-flight training.

Age 23

Mid-January 1958 through July 16, 1958 – Spence Air Base, Moultrie, Georgia; cadet/officer primary flight training.

Ages 23–24

Late July 1958 through January 1959 – Greenville Air Force Base, Greenville, Mississippi; cadet/officer basic flight training.

January 28, 1959 – Received the silver wings of a jet pilot and was commissioned a second lieutenant.

Age 24

Mid-March 1959 through August 3, 1959 – Moody Air Force Base, Valdosta, Georgia; F-86 pilot training.

Age 25

August 1959 through August 13, 1960 – Greenville Air Force Base, Greenville, Mississippi; working as an instructor pilot.

October 1959 through January 1960 – Craig Air Force Base, Selma, Alabama; instructor pilot training.

July 1960 – Promoted to first lieutenant.

Ages 26–30

August 14, 1960 (26th birthday) through March 1965 – Williams Air Force Base, Arizona; working as an instructor pilot.

September 9, 1961 – Married Polly Horne in Greenwood, Mississippi.

Three months in early 1962 – Randolph Air Force Base, San Antonio, Texas; T-38 pilot training.

September 1962 – Son Walt is born.

Three months in early 1963 – Lackland Air Force Base, San Antonio, Texas; platform instructor training.

July 28, 1963 – Promoted to captain.

September 1964 – Twin sons Andy and Tim are born.

Ages 30–31

March 1965 through May 1966 – Davis-Monthan Air Force Base, Arizona; U-2 pilot training and missions.

May 1966 – Resigned from the air force. Moved with Polly, Walt, Andy, and Tim to East Aurora, New York; began working for American Airlines.

Ages 31–60

1966 through 1994 – American Airlines career as a copilot, pilot, and instructor.

Ages 60–Present

1994 through 2008 and beyond – Enjoying retirement and all its adventures.

Appendix B – Military Assignments

The chart below lists my military assignments from the time I enlisted in the air force until I left to join American Airlines in 1966.

Dates	Activity	Base	Flight	Squadron	Group/Wing
10/1955 to 01/1956	Basic Training	Sampson AFB (New York)	4734	3655th Training Squadron	3650th Military Training Wing
01/1956 to 10/1957	Maintenance RC-121	Otis AFB (Massachusetts)	None	551st Periodic Maintenance Squadron	551st Airborne Early Warning and Control Wing
10/1957 to 01/1958	Pre-flight Training	Lackland AFB (Texas)	Unknown (Class 59-E)	Unknown	3700th Military Training Wing
01/1958 to 07/1958	Primary Flight Training	Spence AB (Georgia)	Panther (Class 59-E)	3302nd Pilot Training Squadron	3302nd Pilot Training Wing
07/1958 to 02/1959	Basic Flight Training	Greenville AFB (Mississippi)	Blue Nine * (Class 59-E)	3506th Pilot Training Squadron *	3505th Pilot Training Wing
03/1959 to 08/1959	F-86 Fighter Training	Moody AFB (Georgia)	Unknown * (Class 60-A)	3553rd Fighter Training Squadron *	3550th Pilot Training Wing
08/1959 to 08/1960	Instructor Pilot	Greenville AFB (Mississippi)	Red One	3505th Pilot Training Squadron	3505th Pilot Training Wing
10/1959 to 01/1960	BIS (Basic Instructors' School)	Craig AFB (Alabama)	Unknown	3515th Pilot Training Squadron	3515th Pilot Training Wing

Dates	Activity	Base	Flight	Squadron	Group/Wing
08/1960 to 03/1965	Instructor Pilot	Williams AFB (Arizona)	Wetback * Who Dat * Others	3526th Pilot Training Squadron	3525th Pilot Training Wing
early 1962 (3 mos.)	T-38 Pilot Training	Randolph Air Force Base (Texas)	Unknown	Unknown	3510th Pilot Training Wing
early 1963 (3 mos.)	Platform Instructor Training	Lackland Air Force Base (Texas)	Unknown	Unknown	3700th Military Training Wing
03/1965 to 05/1966	U-2 Pilot (including training)	Davis-Monthan AFB (Arizona)	N/A (U-2 pilot motto: *Toward the Unknown)* *	4028th Strategic Recon. Weather Squadron	4080th Strategic Reconnaissance Wing*

*Represented by a patch pictured on the following pages.

Patches from my flight jacket. *L. to r.*: U.S. Air Force; Blue Nine
Flight–Greenville; Flight (name unknown)–Moody; 3553rd Fighter
Training Squadron–Moody.

More patches from my flight jacket: "Wetback" and "Who Dat"
are from Williams; *Toward the Unknown* was the U-2 pilot motto;
4080th SRW is from Davis-Monthan.

Appendix C – Where Are They Now?

Movies based on true stories sometimes end with a series of screens listing the present-day status of the characters portrayed. Feedback from several people who reviewed the manuscript for this book indicated that readers might want to know "the rest of the story" about the people described herein. I've been fortunate over the years to maintain close ties with most of my relatives and with many friends from childhood and from my days in the air force. Others, sadly, have slipped out of reach. Despite my attempts to locate them during research for this book, the course of their lives since the days we worked or played together remains unknown to me.

My Relatives

Grandpa Paul McNerney (1890–1976) moved to the Knights of Columbus building in Buffalo in 1947 or 1948, where he lived until suffering a stroke and partial paralysis in the late 1960s or early 1970s. He then moved to a nursing home, where he resided until he passed away. To the best of my knowledge, he and my Grandmother McNerney never saw each other again after he left 30 Park Place.

Grandmother Alice Besse McNerney (1891–1985) lived to be 94 and was as feisty as ever until almost her dying day. In her later years she owned a 1967 Volkswagen Beetle, which, in spite of her failing eyesight, she continued to drive on short jaunts near her home in Barnstable County, Massachusetts, until she was 92. She managed, as she put it, by "following the center line in the road." I have restored her Volkswagen and drive it today.

My mother, *Betty McNerney Wright Kenna* (1914–1988), died at home in Nokomis, Florida. Her life was rich and full to the end, despite a 13-year battle with aplastic anemia, and it is partly because of the many conversations we had during her last days that I've been able to recreate some of the experiences of her life and mine.

After his last visit to the farm in 1942 when I was living with Maude and Millard Hudson, I never saw my father, *Ken Wright*, again, although I did have a couple of phone conversations with him when I was in my late teens. To the best of my knowledge, he died in the mid-1970s.

My stepfather, Colonel (Ret.) *George Kenna*, is still going strong, an active and alert nonagenarian who celebrated his 90th birthday in 2008 and splits his time between Florida and Cape Cod.

My half brother, *Christopher Kenna*, is retired and lives in the South with his wife and son.

Because I spent so much time as a child living in my grandparents' home, my mother's siblings played a huge role in my childhood, and we remained close in our adult years.

Uncle Robert and *Aunt Erma Clark McNerney* had two sons. The couple remained in the Buffalo area for many years, where Uncle Robert worked as an executive for Bell Telephone. Later they moved to Cotuit on Cape Cod. They both lived into their 80s.

Uncle Dan McNerney was a career army officer whose duties took him all over the world. His wife, *Aunt Mary Hoit McNerney*, was almost always at his side, spending much of her time as a volunteer with the USO. Dan retired from the service as a lieutenant colonel and went on to serve as a civilian advisor in Vietnam, where he and Mary were in Saigon during the infamous TET offensive. Awakened in their hotel room by the sounds of rocket fire, Mary wasn't sure what to do. "Go back to sleep," Dan advised, ever the cool customer. "If the rockets don't hit us, we'll need to be alert in the morning. And if they're going to hit us, there's nothing we can do about it." After returning to the States, Dan applied the same cool head and steady hands to a term in the New Hampshire Legislature and to his lifelong hobby, photography. Dan passed away in 1994 and Mary in 2005. The couple had one son.

Uncle Walt Shed was one of the first to encourage my interest in aviation as a child. After the Second World War, Walt left the service, went to school on the GI Bill, and eventually worked as an aeronautical engineer at Cornell Labs. He and *Aunt Carolyn McNerney Shed* had four daughters. Carolyn died from cancer at the age of 49. Walt remarried and lived into his 80s.

Polly's Relatives

Polly's dad, *William (Billy) Armstrong Horne II*, passed away in 1966; her mom, *Pauline Hamer Horne*, passed away in 1995.

Polly's brother *Rut (Claude Rutledge Horne II)* and his wife live in Louisiana and raise Thoroughbred race horses. They have three sons.

People from My Childhood and School Years

During World War II, Americans supported their country in many ways. For *Maude* (1890–1974) and *Millard Hudson* (1887–1968), one of those ways was to take in an eager eight-year-old so that my mother and grandmother could work at Curtiss-Wright without leaving me unsupervised. The years I spent on the Hudsons' farm were some of the happiest of my life. As I grew up I continued to visit the Hudsons as often as I could, and when Millard died I rode in the funeral procession with Maude. "You were always Millard's boy," she said, and I always felt I was. Sadly, in her last years Maude suffered from dementia and severe arthritis and died in a nursing home, a fate she had always feared.

Nathaniel and *Bruce Darbee*, my childhood friends from days on the farm, continued to live in western New York State. Nathaniel lives there today. Bruce, a victim of type 1 diabetes, died as a young man from complications of the disease.

Dietrich, my German friend from Berlin in 1947, whose last name I can no longer recall, passed away as a young man from tuberculosis. The deprivations in Germany during and after the war were extreme, and the health of many who were youngsters at the time was significantly compromised.

Polly Frederick, my mother's lifelong friend whom she met in Berlin after World War II, continued to work for the U.S. government. After she returned from Germany, she settled in Washington, D.C., where she lived for many years. She never married and died in 2000.

The whereabouts and fate of the *State Department girls* who did so much to feed the ego of a budding teenage boy in post-war Berlin are regrettably lost to time.

Frau Steinkopf, whom I called Steiney and who was one of our servants in Berlin, had been a member of the German upper class before the war. As Germany stabilized, she regained her social status and, years later, entertained my mother in her elegant home in Berlin. I never heard what happened to our other servant, *Frau Strohm*.

The whereabouts of my friend *Harry* in Panama (another last name I've forgotten) and of my pals in Yokohama are also unknown. Military kids learn to make and leave friends easily. Some friendships last despite this, but many others suffer from time and distance.

Bob Stewart, my friend in El Paso whose dad owned the ranch in Mexico, and I wrote several times after I moved to Massachusetts at the beginning of my junior year in high school; then we let the letters drop. Over the years I have tried to locate him many times, so far unsuccessfully. We had some great summers together, and I learned a lot about myself and about how to survive from my experiences south of the border.

The Hayden family, who befriended me when we moved to Cotuit, Massachusetts, in 1950, continue to be a part of my life. *Bob and Libby Hayden* are gone now, but their children and families still gather at the Cape for family reunions, reunions to which Polly and I are always invited and which we attend whenever possible.

Bob Frazier, my best friend at Barnstable High, went on to become a music teacher at Barnstable and later the director of music for most of Cape Cod's schools. Today he is a widower, living in a grand house with a turret in Buzzard's Bay and enjoying life with his music.

Jim Miller, my roommate from the Wentworth Institute of Technology and one of my best pals from that day to this, married his sweetheart Peggy and continued to work at Sikorsky Helicopter for several years. Later he went into the metal processing business with his father-in-law, a field in which he still works part-time.

My other Wentworth buddies, *Jack Carlin* and *Ken Nylen*, are also present-day friends. Having passed the NavCad tests when Jim Miller and I failed to do so, Jack went on to a tour of duty as a navy pilot. Afterward, he worked as a salesman at various firms and later went into real estate in New York State. Ken owns a large farm in Massachusetts, along with one of every mechanical device ever built.

People from My Air Force Years and Beyond

Colonel Richard Abbey, base commander at Williams during much of the time I was there, retired from the air force as a major general. He passed away in 2001 at the age of 85.

Emil Boado, my co-pilot the day we landed our T-38 on its belly at Williams Air Force Base in Arizona when the nose wheel didn't come down, wasn't as lucky another day. In January 1969, at the age of 34, Emil was killed in Thailand, a casualty of the Vietnam War. His name appears on the Vietnam Veterans' Memorial in Washington, D.C., panel 35W, line 088.

After leaving the air force, *Charlie Clack*, one of the three students in my "best class" when I was an instructor pilot at Williams, joined American Airlines. Later he was also the mayor of a large town in Texas.

(Robert) Skip Coolidge, my fellow pilot on the trip from Williams to Miami where we nearly became alligator stew, served in Vietnam and later went on to fly for Pan Am and National Airlines. Skip passed away in 1988.

Tom Craig, my first roommate at Williams and a superb aviator, went on to become a successful combat pilot in Vietnam and a career air force officer. He retired as a major general in 1987 and now lives in his home state of Louisiana.

Tom Fincher, my co-instructor on the platform in T-38 aircraft engineering at Williams, was the ultimate warrior. He died many years ago.

Mike and *Sally Freney,* our neighbors at Williams, remained good friends over the years. Mike was a political genius. After a successful career in the air force he became a fellow at the Center for Strategic and International Studies (CSIS), a political think tank in Washington, D.C. He died far too young, while teaching at the Naval War College. Sally, who had unusual artistic talent, remained a mystical beauty until her death.

Richard Gibson (Little Gib), fighter pilot, retired colonel from the Air Force National Guard, lawyer, rancher, collector, fellow Mississippi riverboat adventurer, and still a character, remains one of my closest friends, despite the fact that he has never learned to appreciate sardine sandwiches. He and Peggy, his delightful and long-suffering wife, live in Arizona.

Life is a Piece of Cake

The whereabouts of *Captain E. C. Hall*, my superb instructor pilot at Greenville Air Force Base in Mississippi, are a mystery.

I also don't know what happened to *Don Herrell*, the base helicopter pilot at Greenville who accompanied Gibson and me on our fateful trip down the Mississippi. Hopefully he did not take up a career as a riverboat captain.

The Earl (Festus E. Heanue Jr.), my buddy at Spence Air Base in Georgia and a fellow instructor pilot at Greenville, was a master of Irish wit and entertained us all with a running stream of Pat and Mike stories. In 1980, Polly happened to be reading *The Boston Globe* as we were driving through Boston. "Don," she said as she noticed a name in the obituaries, "isn't this the Earl?" Indeed it was, and as his funeral was that very morning, just moments from where we happened to be, we stopped to attend. After a distinguished career as a full colonel in the Air Force, the Earl died from cancer much before his time, but I know he's keeping them chuckling in heaven.

On July 28, 1966, *Bob "De De" Hickman,* my handball partner and perhaps our best friend at Davis-Monthan Air Force Base, became unconscious when flying a U-2 over the Gulf of Mexico. He died when his plane crashed into the side of a mountain near Oruro, Bolivia.

Johnny Holody, my caravan partner on our trip in 1958 from Buffalo to basic flight training in Greenville, Mississippi, and a fellow explorer on our infamous camping trip with Bill Kluck when we were stationed at Williams, went on to a career as a pilot for United Airlines. Unfortunately, we have lost contact.

(Duane) Bucko Jewell, a good friend from our time together at Spence to this day, became a chief pilot for American Airlines and a successful businessman. Now retired but still an aviation enthusiast, Bucko lives in Texas.

Major Uriel Johnson, the decorated pilot from World War II and Korea who gave me my final check ride at Spence and praised me for "saving" the airplane Tom Westhafer and I nearly flew into Mt. Lemmon in Arizona, retired from the air force in the 1970s and later became a ski instructor in California. He died in 2005 at the age of 80.

John Kitchens, my instructor pilot for primary flight training at Spence and one of the best instructors I've ever encountered, died much too soon from cancer.

Despite the above-mentioned, ill-fated camping trip while we were at Williams, *Bill Kluck* continues to be one of my closest friends. After retiring from the air force as a full colonel, Bill pursued his love of art and now works as a sculptor under the professional name of Bill GirarD. He and his wife Nancy run the GirarD Fine Art Sculpture Studio and Gallery in the foothills east of Albuquerque, New Mexico.

Black Jack Matthews, my flight commander at Moody Air Force Base in Georgia and a stickler for cleanliness and the color orange, is another person from the past whose fate is unknown.

Lt. Colonel Chuck Maultsby, whose perilous U-2 flight over Soviet territory during the dark days of the Cold War is recounted in Chapter 81, had one of the most dramatic and glorious careers of any pilot I've ever known. Chuck died in 1998, but his exploits continue to be told, most recently in a 2008 book by Michael Dobbs entitled *One Minute to Midnight: Kennedy, Khrushchev, and Castro on the Brink of Nuclear War*.

Dave McCullough and I have maintained a lifelong friendship, despite my initial introduction to him as my tormentor during preflight training at Lackland Air Force Base in Texas back in 1957. Like me, Dave joined American Airlines after his stint in the air force, where the good news was that I was senior to him!

Captain John McKone, who'd been shot down by the Russians in an RB-47 over the Barents Sea and was later one of my classmates at platform engineering school at Lackland, retired from the air force as a full colonel. I do not know his whereabouts today.

Jim Mueller (Wilkinson), my partner in crime for passing a "counterfeit" $20 bill in Valdosta, Georgia, retired from the Air Force, but where he is today I do not know.

Francis Gary Powers worked for Lockheed as a test pilot for seven years after he was released from prison in Moscow and returned to the U.S. He died in Los Angeles in 1977 when a news helicopter he was piloting crashed. On May 1, 2000, 40 years after he was shot down, he was posthumously awarded the Prisoner-of-War Medal, the Distinguished Flying Cross, and the National Defense Service Medal for service to his country.

Robbie Robinson, my pal from my days as a ground mechanic with the 551st at Otis Air Force Base on Cape Cod, was discharged shortly after we worked together and went home to Pennsylvania. After that, we lost contact.

Lou Silva, my other pal from Otis, went on to make a career of the air force. We also lost contact and I am unaware of his current whereabouts.

Larry Joe (L.J.) Taylor, another of the students from my "best class" at Williams, went from the air force to a career with Delta Airlines. Now retired, Larry has the perfect life: A large farm and personal airport in Georgia, a splendid wife Joan, and two sons who are marine fighter pilots.

(Eugene) Tiger Taylor, who I first met at Lackland during preflight training and who was later my apartment mate at Moody, is another past associate with whom I've lost touch.

Dick Wade, Virginia "good ole boy," brilliant air force officer, and one-time suitor of Polly, married a Spanish flamenco dancer in Spain, became a rocket scientist, and is presently retired on a golf course in Florida.

Captain John Wall, my U-2 instructor (pull back to go up, push forward to come down), retired from the air force and still attends the 4080th SRW reunions.

Rud and Timmy Wasson, from the time I first knew them at Moody until the present, are the perfect hosts. After the air force, Rud became a medical doctor and Timmy continued to work as a nurse. Today they are retired and live in Minnesota.

Tom Westhafer, the third member of my "best class" at Williams and my fellow pilot the day we made an emergency landing at Davis-Monthan Air Force Base after the VOR failed in our T-37, remains a close friend to this day. Tom retired from American Airlines and now lives the good life in Phoenix and on his boat in California.

Bill Williams, my friend and partner in crime at Lackland when we tried to sneak into the women's quarters—the caper which resulted in each of us being given a 72-gun salute—went on to become a successful pilot in the air force followed by a career with American Airlines. Now retired, Bill lives in Florida and splits his time between his home and his boat.

Selected Bibliography

Bromley, Linda Rios. *Freedom Flight: A True Story,* edited by Nancy Ryan Keeling. Utica, KY: McDowell Publications, 2005.

Burrows, William E. *Deep Black: Space Espionage and National Security.* New York: Random House, 1987.

Dodge, Marshall and Robert Bryan. *Bert and I and Other Stories from Down East.* Ipswich, MA: Bert and I Books, 1981.

McIlmoyle, Brig. Gen. (Ret.) Gerald E. and Linda Rios Bromley. *Remembering the Dragon Lady.* Utica, KY: McDowell Publications, 2008.

Pocock, Chris. *The U-2 Spyplane: Toward the Unknown, A New History of the Early Years.* Atglen, PA: Schiffer Publishing, Ltd., 2000.

Powers, Francis Gary and Curt Gentry. *Operation Overflight: The U-2 spy pilot tells his story for the first time.* New York, Chicago, San Francisco: Holt, Rinehart and Winston, 1970.

Acknowledgments

Although the ultimate responsibility for the content of this book is mine, its pages are enriched by the encouragement and practical assistance of the many people who have helped to make it a reality. To begin with, I want to thank the members of the Kearsarge Sunapee Speakers, my fellow Toastmasters who heard many of these stories in club meetings and who provided valuable feedback that helped to make them clearer and more concise. A special vote of thanks goes to Janice MacLean, my Canadian Toastmaster friend who was the first to encourage me to put my tales on paper and also did some early editing, and to Bill Tighe, the very able leader of our local Toastmasters chapter.

Another heartfelt thank-you goes to Babe Sargent, friend, character, thespian, and artist extraordinaire, whose wit and wisdom have captured some of my more memorable experiences in the illustrations sprinkled throughout the book.

Family and friends from the times of my life related here have provided memory boosts, encouragement, and constructive criticism as they've shared their recollections of days gone by, sent photographs, helped me to track down elusive details, and/or read parts of the manuscript. For their assistance in keeping me honest and for filling in the blanks, I am most grateful. For any errors remaining, I take full blame. In particular I'd like to thank Jack Carlin; Major General (Ret.) Tom Craig; Bob Frazier; Sr. Joan Freney and Polly Rhea (Mike Freney's sisters); Colonel (Ret.) Richard Gibson; Mary Anne Haney (Aunt Carolyn and Uncle Walt Shed's daughter); Nancy Hauber Holmes (my childhood neighbor from my days on Maude and Millard Hudson's farm); Bucko Jewell; Colonel (Ret.) George Kenna; Colonel (Ret.) Bill Kluck; Jeanne Maultsby (Chuck Maultsby's widow); Jim Miller; Jayne Hayden Uyenoyama; and Rud and Timmy Wasson.

Many others who have come into my life after the events related here took the time and care to read and comment on all or portions of the manuscript in its various stages of development. In particular, the assessments, suggestions, and enthusiasm of the following individuals have been invaluable: Connie Appel, Hank Berry, Julie Boardman, Art and Enid Chandler, James Frazier,

Norm Gavin, Major General (Ret.) Bo and Sidney Grove, Jack and Michele Holton, Ron Keller, Dean LeBaron, the Reverend Bob and Ginger Merrill, Janet Paulsen, Ike Reel, Tom Rinaldi, Babe and Priscilla Sargent, Vahan Sarkisian, Victor and Bunny Stoykovich of Town and Country Press, and Bill and Lise Tighe. Thanks also to Jean Allen, historian for Wales, New York, who helped track down people and information from the years I spent on the farm and to Teena Cahill, Psy.D., speaker, educator, and author of *The Cahill Factor: Turning Adversity into Advantage*, who connected me with my editor, Susan Owens. To the many others who provided a flash of insight, an encouraging word, or a story of their own that kept me on task when the project seemed as if it would never finish, I extend my sincere appreciation.

A special thank-you is also due to the following individuals: Current U-2 pilot Lt. Colonel Jeff Olesen wrote the foreword for the book and shot the spectacular image of the Grand Canyon that appears on the back cover. Dr. Gregory Barban converted cassette tapes of my mother's voice to CDs and later took the picture of me that also appears on the back cover. And Mike Manoogian, a superb graphic designer to whom I was introduced shortly before the book went to press, worked diligently to create a memorable cover design.

Chapters 78 and 79 tell the story of the flight, shoot down, and imprisonment of U-2 pilot and Cold War hero Francis Gary Powers. I was fortunate to have met Powers in 1965 when I was stationed at Davis-Monthan Air Force Base in Arizona, and I have related his story as I remember him telling it. However, to make certain I relayed the details correctly, I also referenced *Operation Overflight*, Powers' book on the subject, and spoke at length with his son, Gary Powers Jr., founder of the Cold War Museum (http://www.coldwar.org). Gary Jr. was kind enough to review the chapters concerning his dad and to add valuable insights, for which I am particularly grateful.

For the past two years Susan Owens, my uncompromising editor, has diligently applied her wordsmanship, research skills, and attention to detail to my sometimes wandering but always enthusiastic prose. She has worked hard to keep my head out of the clouds and my feet to the fire, an anatomical combination that has unquestionably improved the readability of the finished product. Thanks, Susan! I couldn't have done it without you. Thanks also to Susan's husband and business partner, David Wilkes, for bringing out the best in so many photos, taken so long ago.

And of course, without the support of my beautiful wife Polly this book would not exist. Polly has been my partner, my best friend, and my unfailing spelling coach for more than 40 years, and though at times I'm sure she thought I was nuts to undertake this mission, she has indulged my dedication to the project each step of the way. Our three sons, Walt, Tim, and Andy, have also provided encouragement and practical support on topics ranging from grammar and business advice to Web site design and help with the vagaries of my computer. Thanks, guys; your dear old dad appreciates you more than you know.

Illustration and Photo Credits

The cartoon in Chapter 30 of me as a gun-toting track star from Texas was drawn by fellow student (now acclaimed New England artist) Brooks Kelly and given to me in 1951.

The cartoon in Chapter 31 highlighting the idiosyncrasies of my 1929 Ford was drawn by classmate Bill Childs and also given to me in 1951.

All other illustrations are by Babe Sargent, whose skills at capturing the essence of the moment are unparalleled.

Chapter 7: The photo of Carolyn McNerney Shed and Walt Shed is courtesy of Mary Anne Shed Haney.

Chapters 8 and 11: The image of Millard and Maude Hudson on their 50th wedding anniversary (extracted from a group photo taken for the occasion) and the photo of the one-room-schoolhouse classroom at Wales Hollow, New York, are courtesy of Nancy Hauber Holmes.

Chapter 30: The photos of the Hayden family and of Bob Hayden in his truck are courtesy of Jayne Hayden Uyenoyama.

Chapter 37: The photo of the barracks at Sampson Air Force Base, which is also displayed on the Sampson AFB veterans Web site (http://www.sampsonvets.com/), is courtesy of the Geneva Historical Society. Photo furnished by Gus Kilthau, Houston, Texas.

Part IV Divider Page: The watermark is from a photo of cadets walking tours at Spence Air Base, courtesy of Ray Sack of Class 60-E and the Spence Air Base history Web site (http://www.spence-air-base.com/). Photo furnished by Bruce Watson, Prescott, Arizona.

Chapter 44: The photo of the T-28A is from the National Museum of the USAF (http://www.nationalmuseum.af.mil/).

Chapter 45: The photo of the front gate of Greenville Air Force Base also appears on the Greenville AFB reunion Web site (http://members.cox.net/brsmith6/greenville.html). Photo courtesy of webmaster Billy Ray Smith.

Chapters 45, 47, and 56: The photos of the T-33A, the F-86L, and the T-37B were taken at the Pima Air and Space Museum by Ben P. Fisher Jr., Tucson, Arizona.

Chapter 54: The photo of 2nd Lieutenant Richard Gibson is courtesy of Richard Gibson.

Chapter 58: The photo of Mike Freney is courtesy of Shelley Smith.

Chapter 59: The photo of Colonel William G. Kluck is courtesy of Bill Kluck.

Chapter 61: The photo of the T-38 training Talons is from Air Force Link: The Official Web Site of the United States Air Force (http://www.af.mil/).

Chapter 77: The photo of Kelly Johnson and Gary Powers is from the National Museum of the USAF (http://www.nationalmuseum.af.mil/).

Chapter 81: The photo of Chuck Maultsby is courtesy of Jeanne Maultsby.

Back Cover: Photo of the Grand Canyon taken from the cockpit of the U-2 is by Lt. Colonel Jeff Olesen, USAF. The photo of the U-2 in flight is from USAF files. The photo of the author is by Dr. Gregory Barban.

About the Author

Captain Don Wright was born in 1934 in Buffalo, New York. His earliest years were spent surrounded by the loving ministrations of his divorced mother and his maternal grandparents, aunts, and uncles. For two years during World War II, he lived with a nearby farm family while his mother and grandmother worked in an airplane factory to support the war effort. At age 10 he spent a year in military school. At 12 he traveled unaccompanied on a Merchant Marine ship to join his mother in post-war Berlin, where she was posted with the Foreign Service.

When his mother remarried, Don joined her and his military stepfather in traveling the world, including stops in Panama and El Paso, Texas. He spent two of his high school summers on a ranch in Mexico—where meat was available only if shot and modern conveniences were nonexistent—and the second half of his senior year in post-war Japan, graduating from Yokohama High in 1952. It was the 20th school he'd attended since kindergarten.

In search of his boyhood dream of becoming a fighter pilot, Don enlisted in the U.S. Air Force in 1955. After earning his wings and working as an instructor pilot for several years, he was selected in 1965 as the 192nd man to fly America's high-altitude reconnaissance airplane, the U-2, an honor so far afforded to just over 1,000 men and women. Don resigned from the air force in 1966 to join American Airlines, from which he retired in 1994. Today he and his wife Polly enjoy a rich and varied life from their mountaintop home in New Hampshire.

If you would like Don to speak to your organization about the U-2 or other topics in this book, and/or if you have comments or questions about the material presented, please visit http://CaptainDonWright.com or send an email to info@CaptainDonWright.com.

Editor's Note

It has been a pleasure and a privilege to help Don Wright tell his story, but the tales set forth here describe more than the saga of one man's life. They also chronicle the attitudes and actions of a generation of Americans who were born in the Great Depression, came of age during World War II and Korea, and lived through many of the technological, social, and cultural changes of the 20th century.

"Those who cannot learn from history are doomed to repeat it," said oft-quoted philosopher George Santayana. Yet our history texts are often dull, fact-driven recitations that fail to spark the interest of most who read them. Personal history, or memoir, offers a different perspective, a view that engages the imagination and makes it easier for us to envision, and thus perhaps to understand, the challenges of a different era and the men and women who faced them.

Not everyone's life has resulted in memories like Don's, yet everyone's life is worthy of remembrance. Recording how we've lived, the choices we've made, and the insights we've gained is a priceless gift we leave to our families, our friends, and the world at large. If reading this book has brought to mind some of your own adventures, insights, and life lessons, I urge you to consider capturing those memories for the people you love. Remember that you don't need to write a formal book or make a professional video to preserve your experiences. Talk into an audio recorder, have a friend or relative shoot a video as you tell stories about your life, jot down your memories in a notebook, and/or write relevant names, dates, and places on the backs of those old photographs stashed in shoeboxes. If you need more help, you can find the names of many gifted interviewers, writers, editors, and videographers through the Association of Personal Historians (http://www.personalhistorians.org).

There are many ways to tell a story. Regardless of how you choose to tell yours, it will be treasured more than you can ever know, for longer than you can begin to imagine.

Susan Owens
Tales for Telling, 2008

Breinigsville, PA USA
18 August 2009
222540BV00001B/193/P